ATTENTION

MAILROOM

FROM: THE PUBLISHER

INMATE SHOPPER DOES NOT CONTAIN:

Shout Outs from Inmates
Inmate Addresses
Nudity or Sexual Acts
Descriptions of Violent Acts
Articles About Making Weapons or Hooch
Articles About Drugs, Escapes, or Smuggling Contraband

FREEBIRD PUBLISHERS

Freebird Publishers
Box 541
North Dighton, MA 02764
www.freebirdpublishers.com

Please feel free to contact us with your concerns.
Diane@FreebirdPublishers.com

ANNUAL 2019-20 CONTENTS

IN EVERY ISSUE

SPECIAL FEATURE

WHAT'S TRENDING

IN THIS ISSUE

ISSUE SEGMENTS

RESOURCES

SHOPPING

SPORTS

Distributor: Freebird Publishers Box 541 North Dighton, MA 02764
Web: FreebirdPublishers.com
E-Mail: diane@freebirdpublishers.com
Corrlinks: diane@freebirdpublishers.com
Corrlinks (alternative): corrlinks@freebirdpublishers.com
JPay: diane@freebirdpublishers.com
Toll-Free: 888-712-1987
Phone/Text: 774-406-8682

Send Letters to the Editor to the above address.

ISBN: 9781076714053

Look for our Rated 10 Emblem!

FREEBIRD
PUBLISHERS

Editor/Publisher	Freebird Publishers
Assistant Editor	Joanne McMann
Assistant Editor	Garry W. Johnson
Graphic Design	Krista Smith
Graphic Design	Freebird Publishers
Founding Editor, Retired	George Kayer
Authorized Distributors	Freebird Publishers Grant Publications
Advertising	Diane@FreebirdPublishers.com
Contributing Writer	Christopher Zoukis
Contributing Writer	A. Raby
Contributing Writer	Aubrey Dean Elwood
Contributing Writer	Anthony Tinsman
Guest Writer	Odies Murray
Guest Writer	Ronald "Double R" Rheinhart
Guest Writer	James "Stretch" Arthur
Guest Writer	Christopher L. Dixon
Guest Writer	Jamar Russell
Guest Writer	T. Michael Fox
Guest Writer	Anthony Billings
Guest Writer	Steven P. Arthur
Guest Writer	Richard Adkins (comics)
Guest Writer	Warren Henderson
Guest Writer	Cecil "Ruthless" Rotnem
Guest Writer	Melodic Matthew
Guest Writer	James Wells
Guest Writer	Joseph Devlin
Guest Writer	John Harrison
Guest Writer	Christopher Dixon
Guest Writer	William J. Patterson
Guest Writer	Tanner George Cummings
Miscellaneous Contributions	George Kayer
Miscellaneous Contributions	Patrick Bearup
Miscellaneous Contributions	Mike White

Published Annual, Split Year, June 30th to June 30th

WE NEED YOUR REVIEWS

Rate Us & Win!

We do monthly drawings for a FREE copy of one of our publications. Just have your loved one rate any Freebird Publishers book on Amazon and then send us a quick e-mail with your name, inmate number, and institution address and you could win a FREE book.

FREEBIRD PUBLISHERS
Box 541
North Dighton, MA 02764

www.freebirdpublishers.com
Diane@FreebirdPublishers.com

Thanks for your interest in Freebird Publishers!

We value our customers and would love to hear from you! Reviews are an important part in bringing you quality publications. We love hearing from our readers-rather it's good or bad (though we strive for the best)!

If you could take the time to review/rate any publication you've purchased with Freebird Publishers we would appreciate it!

If your loved one uses Amazon, have them post your review on the books you've read. This will help us tremendously, in providing future publications that are even more useful to our readers and growing our business.

Amazon works off of a 5 star rating system. When having your loved one rate us be sure to give them your chosen star number as well as a written review. Though written reviews aren't required, we truly appreciate hearing from you.

★★★★★ **Everything a prisoner needs is available in this book.**
January 30, 201 June 7, 2018
Format: Paperback

A necessary reference book for anyone in prison today. This book has everything an inmate needs to keep in touch with the outside world on their own from inside their prison cell. Inmate Shopper's business directory provides complete contact information on hundreds of resources for inmate services and rates the companies listed too! The book has even more to offer, contains numerous sections that have everything from educational, criminal justice, reentry, LGBT, entertainment, sports schedules and more. The best thing is each issue has all new content and updates to keep the inmate informed on todays changes. We recommend everybody that knows anyone in prison to send them a copy, they will thank you.

* No purchase neccessary. Reviews are not required for drawing entry. Void where prohibited.
Contest date runs July 1 - June 30, 2019.

INMATE SHOPPER
LARGEST BOOK OF RESOURCES
2019-2020 ANNUAL ISSUE

BEST 500+
NON PROFIT ORGANIZATIONS
FIND WHAT YOU NEED FAST

PEN PAL SUCCESS
THE ULTIMATE GUIDE TO GETTING & KEEPING PEN PALS

PENPALS
A PERSONAL GUIDE
PRISONERS

DIY FOR PRISONERS

Kitty Kat
ADULT ENTERTAINMENT RESOURCE BOOK
NON NUDE
MIKE ENEMIGO

CELEBRITY
STAR POWER
Josh Kruger

FREEBIRD PUBLISHERS
GIFT
LOOK BOOK
2018-19

SEXY GIRL PARADE

PILLOW TALK
NON-NUDE PHOTO BOOK

HOT GIRL SAFARI

Soft Shots

Fine Dining
PRISONER COOKBOOK

The
CELL CHEF
A COLLECTION OF RECIPES
BY TANNER GEORGE CUMMINGS

The
CELL CHEF
II
A COLLECTION OF RECIPES
BY TANNER GEORGE CUMMINGS

FREEBIRD
PUBLISHERS

Kelly Patrick Riggs
POST-CONVICTION RELIEF:
SECRETS EXPOSED

Kelly Patrick Riggs
POST-CONVICTION RELIEF:
ADVANCING YOUR CLAIM

Kelly Patrick Riggs
POST-CONVICTION RELIEF:
THE APPEAL

Kelly Patrick Riggs
POST-CONVICTION RELIEF:
WINNING CLAIMS

Kelly Patrick Riggs
POST-CONVICTION RELIEF:
C.O.A. IN THE SUPREME COURT

PRISON LEGAL GUIDE

CHAPTER 7
BANKRUPTCY
Seven Steps to Financial Freedom
DEBT

PRISON
HEALTH
HANDBOOK

LIFE WITH A
RECORD

Freebird Publishers
CELLPRENEUR
The Millionaire Prisoner's Guidebook

WRITE
& GET PAID
REVISED and EXPANDED
Anthony Tinsman

Get Money
Self-Educate, Get
Rich & Enjoy Life
Vol. 1
3 Book Series

FREEBIRD
PUBLISHERS

STOP
START THINKING
OUTSIDE PRISON

A YEAR OF
Corcoran Sun
TWELVE ISSUES IN ONE BOOK

HOBO PETE
and the
GHOST TRAIN
By Sandy Pheat

2 MUST HAVE BOOKS FOR PRISONERS

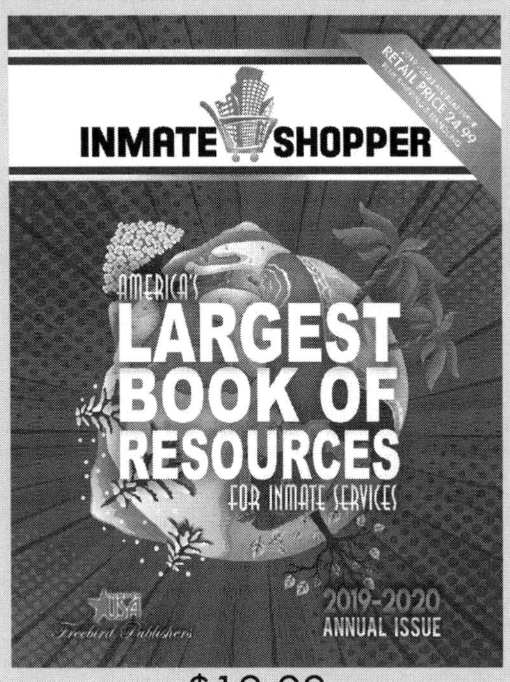

RETAIL PRICE 24.99
INMATE SHOPPER
AMERICA'S
LARGEST
BOOK OF
RESOURCES
FOR INMATE SERVICES
2019-2020
ANNUAL ISSUE
USA
Freebird Publishers

$19.99
plus $7 Shipping/Handling
with Tracking

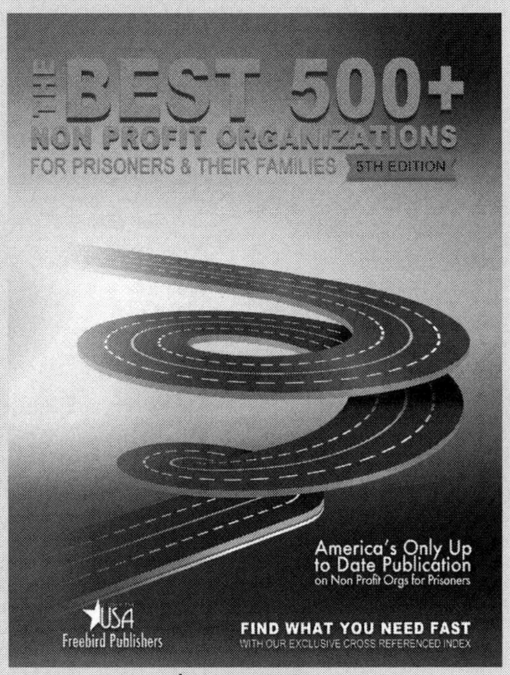

THE BEST 500+
NON PROFIT ORGANIZATIONS
FOR PRISONERS & THEIR FAMILIES
5TH EDITION
America's Only Up
to Date Publication
on Non Profit Orgs for Prisoners
USA
Freebird Publishers
FIND WHAT YOU NEED FAST
WITH OUR EXCLUSIVE CROSS REFERENCED INDEX

$16.99
plus $5 Shipping/Handling
with Tracking

NO ORDER FORM NEEDED
Clearly write on paper and send with payment.

EVERY ISSUE CONTAINS

INMATE SHOPPER

- Non-Nude Girls
- Pen Pal Resources
- Social Media
- Magazine Sellers
- Text/Phone
- Catalogs to Order
- Sexy Photo Sellers
- Typists
- Personal Assistants
- Gift Shops
- Publishing Services
- LGBTQ Resources

GET BOTH FOR JUST **$43.98** INCLUDES PRIORITY S/H WITH TRACKING

THE BEST 500+ 5TH

INCLUDES MANY RESOURCES

- Legal: Innocence, Research, Advocates, Copies
- Newsletters
- Educational
- Health & Healthcare
- Reentry & Jobs
- Family & Children
- Veterans
- Sentencing Issues
- LGBTQ Resources
- Newsletter & Books
- & Much Much More!

ALSO AVAILABLE FOR PURCHASE AT FREEBIRDPUBLISHERS.COM

NEW! 5th Edition

Federal prisoner consulting firm dedicated to assisting soon-to-be and current federal prisoners, their families and friends, and federal criminal defense attorneys with understanding of life inside the Federal Bureau of Prisons, along with governing policy and federal regulations. In addition, they published a resource book, Directory of Federal Prisons authored by Christopher Zoukis. For more info see their listing in the business directory.

THE WAY IT WORKS

Let's talk about orders not being received in the time you may think it takes. First important bits of data you must consider. Firstly, just because the prison check department takes the money off your prison books does not mean they have processed, written or mailed the check. Secondly, when the prison finally does process the order, prints the check and physically mails the check that does not guarantee it will get there. Third obstacle is United States Postal Service (USPS) is notorious for lost, misplaced and damaged mail. Letters get jammed in the automated sorting machines by the thousands, some make it out to continue the journey to the destination. Others, get so ripped up that they are no longer able to read info and are tossed into trash or sent in the wrong direction. We can tell you from many instances that even packages that have USPS tracking on them are lost, never to be found, even after completing USPS reports and filing them... you get an answer back "no future information available". We all want to know where the lost mail goes, we figure to the trash. And we have all heard on the news of mail carriers, stashing, destroying or keeping the mail so they did not have to deliver it, it is a realty nobody wants to think about.

Steps to take before writing to the company you sent the check to.

1. Look at prison for answers first.

2. Get the proof of check being received/cashed by company, this is done by requesting from the prison check department, a copy of the FRONT and BACK of check.

3. Lost checks or checks not being printed and mailed by the prison are very common. If they find this when you request copy of check in question, they can place the funds back on account and void the check. If you find the company has cashed/deposited check, and you can see what date, and are able to write them short professional letter including a copy of the check.

TALK ABOUT CONFUSING

Pennsylvania Department of Corrections (PA DOC) drama unfolded a massive investigation that lead to a drug being smuggled into the prisons by way of mail. The mail pages or magazine pages were being laced with illegal substances and being mailed to prisoners all over the state. Who in turn were getting high, some having bad experiences, some so bad, that medical attention was required?

The first reaction from PA DOC was an overreaction. They banned all publications through the entire state. Giving permission only for eBooks to be downloaded onto tablets. They had a censored list of titles and an approved vendor GTL. News spread quickly in the free world and prisoners and orgs for prisoners started complaining and pointing out this is against US constitutional rights. After, some well thought out ideas, PA DOC decided to send all mail letters, cards, photos, to Florida facility to be processed and then copied and mailed to inmate in black and white. At that time still no publication could be sent to any PA facility or the Florida mail processing facility.

As time when on, PA DOC came under a fire storm of lawyers and advocates fighting for the right to get publications. They decided to open a facility in Bellefonte PA to process all publications other than newspapers.

Due to a contraband mail issue earlier in year the state of Pennsylvania has rerouted all inmates mail. That would not be bad, but they have shipped some out of state and split up mail into two different addresses,

For letters, cards and photos

Smart Communications PA DOC
Inmate Name, Number and Facility
PO Box 33028
St. Petersburg, FL 33733

For publications except newspapers

Secure Processing Center
Inmate Name, Number and Facility
268 Bricker Road
Bellefonte, PA 16823-1667

A GOOD READ

Returning Citizens Magazine is filled with reentry resources, for veterans, men, women and more. Subscriptions available in print, online printable PDF and eMagazine on VA DOC tablets serviced by GTL. Coming to more prison tablets this year. Ask your prison to include them on your download publication list.

GONE WITH THE WIND

Snail Mail Pen Paling magazine is no longer available. The magazine is permanently Out of Print and was published by Prison Living Press. We got in touch with George Kayer and he tells us what happened, "Thanks to all our wonderful customers. The truth is the pen pal business is going to change big time. All the European countries and California have enacted tough new privacy laws. This means any business selling pen pal lists is in violation of these new privacy laws. If you're still using your criminal minds, you don't care about that. If you're running a

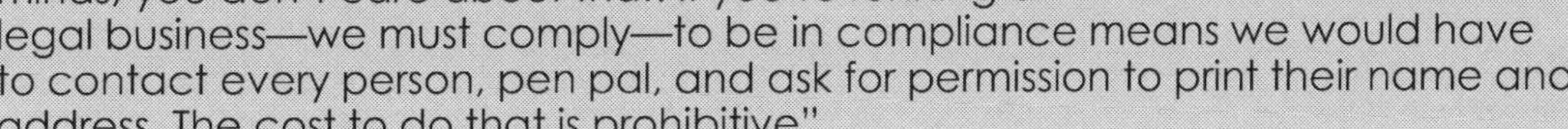

legal business—we must comply—to be in compliance means we would have to contact every person, pen pal, and ask for permission to print their name and address. The cost to do that is prohibitive".

GOT NO RESPONSE

When writing to any company always include a SASE if you expect or want any kind of reply. This professional curtesy is even more important with today's rising postal costs. Another thing vital to remember is that most businesses who service inmates are not full timers. They are part time businesses that are worked around a full-time job, life and family. They get overloaded with long lengthy letters and piles of them, some can get backed up for six months or more. Just because you do not get a response does NOT mean the company is out of business. In some cases, to relieve the mail load businesses only respond to letters that are short, to the point and includes a SASE. Or an order for a catalog that includes the correct payment required. You need to be mindful of what the listing/flyer/brochure tells you and remember to always write polite, short and simple letters and include a SASE always.

SHOUT OUT FROM OUR ADVERTISER

Hey this is G with 4 The Pack Entertainment. I hope you guys are doing great over there. I am sending this shoutout to you all because I definitely want to renew my ad in the next issue of Inmate Shopper. Advertising with you guys has been one of my best decisions yet. Thank you.

HERE THEY COME AND WHERE DID THEY GO

We can tell you that businesses in this inmate marketplace come and go faster than lightning. It all sounds easy and profitable to service inmates but…nothing could be further from the reality of it. It takes a shared connection, dedication, and heart. We have watched and seen many make it less than a year. There are some others that came along but might not be dead and gone…they are nowhere to be found. We have been beating the bushes, looking under rocks. even sending smoke signals; If you know any of businesses listed below and they ARE in business still (this means you have done business with them in the last 90 days) write us and provide us their contact information.

Distance Education
Captured Angels
Interpals
Paper Dolls
Elite Luxury Publications
Photo Services for Inmates
Prison Inmates Online
Prison Life

WHETHER OR NOT YOU PLAN TO ATTEND

"From Prison to the Stage" show at the Kennedy Center on August 31, we think you will want to look at the script. That is why Safe Streets Art Foundation have published it as a book on Amazon.com (pre-show price just $4.99 for paperback, $2.99 for digital).The book, Jailhouse Confessions, is over 100 pages and contains 61 stories written by the best and most creative prison writers across America. These are mostly humorous tall tales that hilariously demonstrate the imagination and sense of humor of incarcerated men and women. Everything you wanted to know about famous celebrities in prison, and some things you didn't want to know. Featuring stories about O.J. Simpson, Nick Nolte, Lindsay Lohan, Bill Cosby, Lorena Bobbitt and more.

PARTING WORDS

Special Miracles LLC closed their door for good. The business owner, Sandra Wallace told us this: "I've had several good years with working with the inmates but it's time for me to close...Any orders that I currently have and/or receive will be processed and shipped out." We will all miss her and the great service she extended to all.

WHAT IS IN A NAME CHANGE?

Voice Freedom Calls changed their name to Corrio Messaging. We asked but got no response to what reason is behind the name change. They are still an inmate messaging service just under a new name.

CORRIO

UNDER NEW MANAGEMENT

Street Pixs is stepping up to bat, doing better business practices and under new management. Owner cleaned house and brought in all new personnel. We love a good turnaround tale. We all know things can go bad in a blink of an eye. It is only the strong and steadfast that can pull things back together.

SIX NEW BOOKS SINCE OUR LAST ISSUE

Post-Conviction Relief: The Appeal

Post-Conviction Relief: Winning Your Claim

Cell Chef Cookbook II

Prison Health Handbook

Personal Bankruptcy

DIY For Prisoners

A PAGE TURNS

We contacted Prison Living Press and spoke with the editor George Kayer, he told us, "We had to close our magazine sales department. We spent thousands on the set up and advertising only to receive about eight orders. We apologize for any inconvenience to our customers. Prison Living Press is still in business and focusing on publishing special interest magazines for prisoners like our Prison Living Magazine: 2019 Free Stuff for Inmates".

KNOCK, KNOCK, KNOCKING ON FREEBIRD'S DOOR

Day started out as any, busy taking care of daily operation of the business. Later in the afternoon there was a knock at the door, looked out the glass front second floor office and was taken back... just a tad. We all know an unmarked police car when you see one, told the down stair offices to close the door between the loft offices to keep the dogs inside. We are dog people, so they are in our offices with us daily. We answered the door to two plain clothes officers, from Bristol County Sheriff Office in Massachusetts and walked out onto the porch to talk to them, closing the front door behind us. They were polite and professional while they explained the reason for the visit. Seems that had been having a drug problem at the local prisons and were at the end of a K2 investigation where no results on anyone being charged. Before closing the case, they decided to double check the only other local business that mails publications into prisons in the area... Freebird Publishers. All was good because we are not stupid, and we all laughed at them grasping at straws to solve the case by taking to us. Good story...true story.

BACK BY POPULAR DEMAND

F. O. S. is in full swing doing business and thriving, retirement was not to Mom's liking, too young for all that time on her hands. She is back taking orders of some of the best sexy non nude photos in the inmate marketplace. For more info see her listing in our business directory.

OOPS...SORRY

In last issue, Annual 2018-19, Books You Want ad had the wrong email address. The ad had zling13@comcast.com, it is supposed to be zling13@ comcast.net. Sorry for the misprint.

THEY HAVE COME A LONG WAY

You can't correct your mistakes you've already done, but you can face them. And that is exactly what Mail My Pix and Ring My Phone have done. They are doing much better, they answer the phone, email back and give a basic service that works. This is a big improvement from last year. We are not sure the reason for the turnaround, but it could be they worked out all the bugs with dealing with technology inside prison walls. We have taken them off the beware list but not rated yet. We need more letters to the editor from all our readers that use these companies.

INCOGNITO

Inside Out Publication, Aka Inside Out Connections, Aka Inside Out Enterprises now is on the Beware List because of numerous complaints. Seems they use their post office box as a piggy bank. They receive orders but only cash checks and never fill the orders.

JUST A REMINDER

Prison Lives, Exeter CA is bad news... they are on our Beware List. The business was started by Christian Longo on Oregon death row and his girlfriend Laci. They are both known to be less than forthcoming. Just a word to be careful not to get burned. To this day... they still sell the Prisoner Almanac and books on Amazon. If you really want to read one, we suggest having family purchase straight from Amazon, not to send any funds to Prison Lives or any of their staff directly.

CHANGE OF SCENERY

After 26 years our favorite magazine seller, Alice Grant of Grant Publications has moved... but she is still in business lucky for all of us. For more info see her listing in our directory.

AND THEN THERE WAS NONE

Weblife Services have folded in less than a year. They were new to the marketplace last year and permanently closed this year.

SHUT DOWN BY COURT ORDER

On June 29, 2018 an injunction was issued by the Orange County Superior Court effectively preventing Legal Insights from assisting any of our clients with post-conviction assistance. While Legal Insights intends to appeal this decision, we must comply with the Court Order. As such, Legal Insights ceased all operations effective June 29, 2018 except for winding down the business as required by federal and state law, returning any client files and working with our insurance carrier concerning any potential client refunds.

The California State Bar has taken possession of many client files from Legal Insights and they should be contacted directly in order to obtain your file. They can be contacted at 213-765-1000 for more information. Should Legal Insights have possession of a client file, it will be returned to the client without charge.

Legal Insights carried an insurance policy with CIMA Insurance that may provide you a refund if you are entitled to one. If you wish to submit a claim please email a detailed request along with any attachments that support your claim, to, or call 800-468-4200. You can also submit all refund requests by U.S. Mail to: CIMA, Attention: Aaron Jones, please copy all requests for refunds by U.S. Mail to: Legal Insights, Attn: Refunds, 8174 South Las Vegas Bl., #109-504, Las Vegas, NV. 89123.

Legal Insights will cooperate fully with our insurance carrier concerning all refund requests. Legal Insights remains operational only for purposes of closing the non-profit down pursuant to state and federal law, returning client files and cooperating with our insurance company concerning any refund requests. As of June 29, 2018, we cannot assist with any Evaluations, pro se pleadings or any other matter that would fall outside of these two exceptions. We apologize for any inconvenience.

TIMES THEY ARE A CHANGING

Girls and Mags have been sending out legal notices in their flyer package with their new products. There are no more pen pal lists – no more 500 Free Magazines book. They researched creating a second edition of 500 Free Magazines book and found a lot of the magazines had gone digital only or have gone out of print. Ultimately, the internet killed it.

Pen pal lists, there is no such thing as a legal pen pal list anymore. Unfortunately, the new and strict privacy laws prohibit businesses from re-printing pen pal profiles without the written authorization for each pen pal. The fine for each violation is up to $10,000. As of June 2019, Girls and Mags no longer offers pen pal addresses or profiles. For five years, we sold the freshest pen pal lists available and thank our thousands of customers.

WHAT'S IN A NAME

J Edward Services (J.E.S.) changed the name of the business to JES Elite Prisoner Solutions. For more info see their listing in our directory.

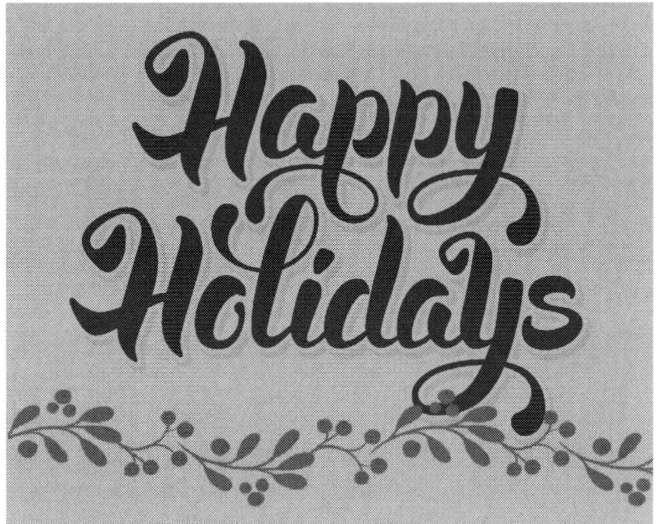

CAME TO US

Athens Books for Prisoners contacted us giving us a new address for inmates to contact them. Funny part is, they told us we had the incorrect address listed for them in our Inmate Shopper. We looked everywhere and could not find them listed inside INSH, or TB500. so, we decided to place them in both. They were very polite and thanked us for what we do, and we feel the same for what they do. For more info see their listing in our directory.

NEW DRIVER AT THE WHEEL

Help from Beyond the Walls is under new management. As of January 2019, they have been trying to straighten out all the issues that might have arisen prior to them taking over the business and the day to day operations.

ANOTHER ONE BITES THE DUST

Jail Calls from Cedar Brook New Jersey went out of business online as of August 2018.

ONE LESS GOOD ONE

Gay Prisoner USA is no longer online, the site closed down. Lee Young, owner reached out to us to say. "I was already long retired when I closed the site last year. At 72 and after 15 years of running GPUSA I was at the point that I had given all I could and was continually not looking forward to updating the site with new listings. I sincerely hope that during the long period that I have done some good in easing life behind bars and, perhaps, helping a few find their lifelong soul mate". We speak for everyone that Lee and his website will be sorely missed by many. We wish him luck on your newfound time.

CATERING TO ARTISTS

Offline Artist is a new magazine for any artist interested in snail mail resources for artists, coming soon. Articles on promoting your work, raising funds for art supplies or a project. The website every inmate artist should be on and it's free. Galleries to show inmate artists. Art buyers listed: posters, greetings cards, book publishers, magazines, contest, and art fairs. Book reviews, interviews with artists upon reentry. Underground artist news, muralists and taggers, job postings, artist glossary, art schools, and financial aid. Copyright violations. Do's and don'ts. Contact Prison Living Press, Attn: George Kayer, P.O. Box 10203, Glendale, AZ 85318

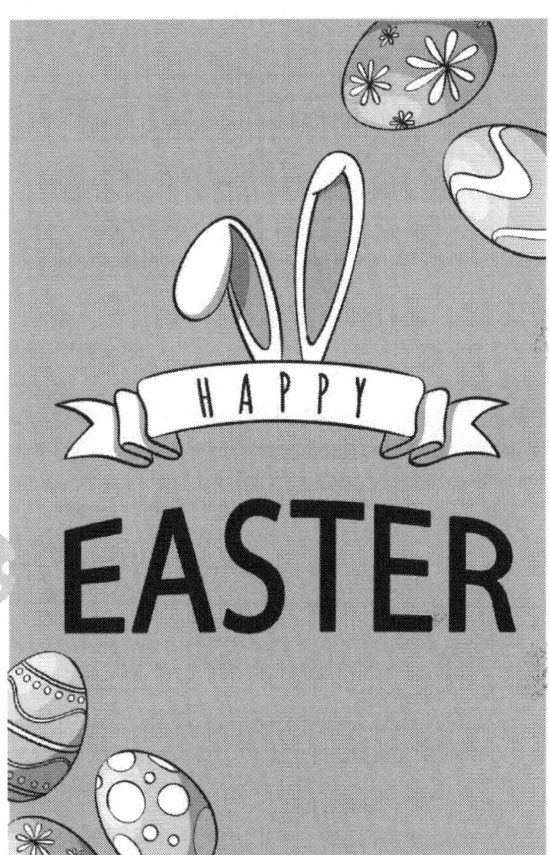

SECOND TIME AROUND

On the Beware List, Prison Legendary Services, now known as Prison L S seems to have regrouped and started again. The website has much more to offer. For more info see their new listing in our directory under Prison L S. We have reader reviews both positive and negative. We have left the old name on the Beware List.

NOT ALL EMAILS ARE CREATED EQUAL

A large percentage of the inmate service businesses are not full-time companies, they are part time, it is a second job to their full-time jobs. There are a few full timers with staff and multiple offices like us. We want to talk about an issue regarding some of the businesses listed inside the inmate shopper, those pertaining to having email addresses. Not all of them respond to inmate requests/invites through prison email websites, many do, some even advertise or list their acceptance. Every day that goes by the businesses that service inmates are realizing it is important to add emailing to their ways of contact with inmate customers.

AND THEN THERE WAS NONE

Weblife Services have folded in less than a year. They were new to the marketplace last year and permanently closed this year.

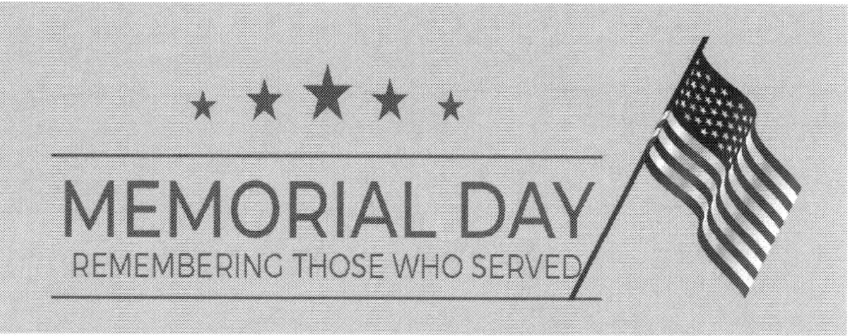

TWO TO BUZZ AROUND

We got two Buzz Photos confused. The Buzz Photos that services inmates contact information is Box 255, Webb City, MO 64870. Unfortunately, they recently have been placed on the Return to Sender list.

CHANGE OF HEART

In our 2017 issue R. Hughson emailed us, at that time he was done servicing inmates. Since he was not out of business, we placed him on Beware List with note No Inmates. Recently, we got wind he has been working with inmates over the last couple years on a much smaller scale. We have taken him off the Beware List and placed him back in the directory.

COMING TO THE RESCUE

One takes over where another ends, Art with Conviction (AwC) have not been heard from in a while and we found out they were working hard to find a way to keep their mission going. Recent developments put the future of AwC in uncertainty, but they are happy to announce that Artists Serving Humanity (ASH) is taking on the task. ASH will be continuing AwC's message to show our communities that convicted felons are people with talent and passion and a need to express themselves. ASH is an organization started in California that represent a group of artists, many incarcerated who support the mission of giving back to society through the sale and donation of their artwork. Any artists who submitted work to AwC who would like to get in contact with ASH their contact info is:

Artists Serving Humanity
PO Box 8817
Redlands, CA 92375

Artistservinghumanity@gmail.com
Artistservinghumanity.org

HOLD ON IT'S A BUMPY RIDE

The highs and lows of the inmate marketplace. Many new businesses from our last issues are now closed down and shut the doors. Last issue brought you many new businesses, all dressed to impress, sharp pencils and eagerness to make it in this harsh marketplace. Lost to the wayside are many of the newbies from last year... some were ex-offenders thinking this was a lucrative business line to get into to make fast money... they soon ran into the perils of this marketplace.

We have had a huge year of ups and downs in the inmate marketplace. Some of the old-time companies that had slid down slippery slopes to the Beware List are making come backs... we all love a good comeback story. They are under new management and trying to recoup, reorganize what was once a decent small business. Just remember to start small, and make the company earn your respect. They say, "Not all the glitters is gold". that can be easily seen over the years with businesses that service inmates.

This is not for the weak or faint of heart you need to be a stand up, straight forward businessperson and have tireless perseverance. You need a desire to help those inside no matter the long hours, short pay and never-ending mail piles of letters from all over the country. And the numerous rejections or new rules for mail in all different levels of prisons and jails.

NEW BOOKS–COMING SOON

Post-Conviction Relief: C.O.A. in the Supreme Court

Ineffective Assistance of Counsel

Fine Dining Prison Cookbook

The Pro Se Section 1983 Manual

The Habeas Corpus Manual

Stock Trading Strategies: Millionaire Prisoner's Way to Succeed

THE BOOKSTORE IS PERMANENTLY CLOSED!

Rainbow Bookstore another long-time business gone, swallowed by the giants in today's marketplaces. No need to name names, we all know who they are, even if you have been incarcerated for three decades you know the names. Rainbow Bookstore was a cooperative which had been running for over 25-years. Like every cooperative, the store was owned by a group of highly enthusiastic members of the Madison Wisconsin community. Left on the site as a reminder which had a feeling of an obituary was this: Quote Of The Day: Men do not understand books until they have a certain amount of life, or at any rate no man understands a deep book, until he has seen and lived at least part of its contents. –Ezra Pound

FISHING FOR GUPPIES

Beware of a scam being emailed and mailed from South Beach Single, or at least someone that has access to their customer contact lists. The offer is for investing in their company with a minimum investment of $5000 and promising a 50% rate of return, plus the principal paid in full, in 90 days. Nothing need more be said that screams SCAM louder than the rate of return. When something sounds too good to be true, it usually is.

FROM: Singles, Southbeach
TO: 16617074
SUBJECT: RE: HELLO
DATE: 01/29/2019 07:51:29 PM

Chad, this is the short version without the addedums to the Promissary Note but this is how it will read, let me know so we can move forward, if you need the hard copy i can send it to you but for time purposes im emailing it to you. Yes i would be interested in more, but we need to move fast on this...

PROMISSARY NOTE

On the ___ day of ______________, 20___, hereinafter known as the "Start Date", ______________ South Beach Singles a Florida Corporation Located in Miami, FL whose FEIN number is 74-3165712 , hereinafter known as the "Borrower", has received and promises to payback ________________________ to ________________________ hereinafter known as the "Lender", the principal sum of ____________________ US Dollars ($______________) with interest accruing on the unpaid balance at a rate of 50 percent (%) , hereinafter known as the "Borrowed Money", beginning as of the Start Date in the manner as follows: 1. Borrower shall pay a lump sum to be made in-full, principal and interest included, of ______________________ Dollars ($________________) on the date of______________ with the remaining balance payable on the Due Date of______________. We hereby agree to the terms as stated above and this Promissary Note is binded under the Laws of the State of Florida.

Borrower Signature

Lender Signature

NOTE TAKING ABBREVIATIONS

approx.: Approximately
b/c: Because
b/4: Before
bk.: Book
C: (*e.g.* 21C for 'twenty-first century')
c.: Approximately, roughly, about (abbreviation for the Latin *circa*)
cf.: Compared to, in comparison with
cp.: Compare
def.: Definition
diff.: Different, difference
ea.: Each
e.g.: For example
fr.: From
etc.: And so on
i.e.: That is, that means, in other words
impt.: Important
NB: Important, notice this, note well
nec.: Necessary
re.: Regarding, about
sim.: Similar
s/t: Something
T.: Theory, theoretical
tho': Though
thro': Through
w/: With
w/o: Without
viz.: Namely, that is to say
v.: Very
vv.: Extremely
vs.: Against
ppl: People
res: Research
natl: National
eqn: Equation
ed: Education
dep: Department
esp: Especially
ustand: Understand
am.: Morning
pm.: Afternoon
asap: As soon as possible
Wrt: With respect to
=ity: Equality
evryt: Everything
infl: Influence
r.: Rate (*i.e.* birth r.)
devel: Development
expl: Explanation
trad: Traditional

cult: Cultural
instit: Institution
justific: Justification
nt: Nothing
lrg: Large
soc.: Social or society
Stats: Statistics
Am't: Amount
educat'l: Educational
subj: Subject
cons: Conservative
ind: Individual
ckg: Checking
estg: Establishing
Expting: Experimenting
bkgd: Background
ppd: Prepared
prblm: Problem
C19: Nineteenth century; similarly C20 etc.
1920s: *i.e.* 1920-1929; similarly 1970s etc.
Ltd: Limited
max.: Maximum
min.: Minimum
G.B.: Great Britain
U.K: United Kingdom
Eng.: English
Brit.: British
Sts: Students

NOTE TAKING SYMBOLS

2: To, two, too
4: For
8: Anything ending in 'ate'
+: And, also, as well as, in addition to, plus
– : Minus, without
≠: Does not equal, is not the same as, does not result in
≈: Is approximately equal to, is similar to
=: Equals, is the same as, results in
>: Is greater than, is larger than
↑: Increase, rise, growth
<: Is less than, is smaller than
↑↑: Rapid increase
↓ : Decrease, fall, shrinkage
↓↓: Rapid decrease
→ : Leads on to, produces, causes
x : No, not, incorrect
xx : Definitely not, disproved
? : Uncertain, possibly, unproven, question
✓ : Yes, correct
✓✓: Definitely, certain, proven
: Number
/ : Per (e.g., £50/day instead of 'fifty pounds per day')
! : Not, isn't
@: At
Δ : Change
♀: Female or women
♂: Male or men
… : Means space in quote

2019

January

Su	Mo	Tu	We	Th	Fr	Sa
30	31	1	2	3	4	5
6	7	8	9	10	11	12
13	14	15	16	17	18	19
20	21	22	23	24	25	26
27	28	29	30	31	1	2

February

Su	Mo	Tu	We	Th	Fr	Sa
27	28	29	30	31	1	2
3	4	5	6	7	8	9
10	11	12	13	14	15	16
17	18	19	20	21	22	23
24	25	26	27	28	1	2

March

Su	Mo	Tu	We	Th	Fr	Sa
24	25	26	27	28	1	2
3	4	5	6	7	8	9
10	11	12	13	14	15	16
17	18	19	20	21	22	23
24	25	26	27	28	29	30
31	1	2	3	4	5	6

April

Su	Mo	Tu	We	Th	Fr	Sa
31	1	2	3	4	5	6
7	8	9	10	11	12	13
14	15	16	17	18	19	20
21	22	23	24	25	26	27
28	29	30	1	2	3	4

May

Su	Mo	Tu	We	Th	Fr	Sa
28	29	30	1	2	3	4
5	6	7	8	9	10	11
12	13	14	15	16	17	18
19	20	21	22	23	24	25
26	27	28	29	30	31	1

June

Su	Mo	Tu	We	Th	Fr	Sa
26	27	28	29	30	31	1
2	3	4	5	6	7	8
9	10	11	12	13	14	15
16	17	18	19	20	21	22
23	24	25	26	27	28	29
30	1	2	3	4	5	6

July

Su	Mo	Tu	We	Th	Fr	Sa
30	1	2	3	4	5	6
7	8	9	10	11	12	13
14	15	16	17	18	19	20
21	22	23	24	25	26	27
28	29	30	31	1	2	3

August

Su	Mo	Tu	We	Th	Fr	Sa
28	29	30	31	1	2	3
4	5	6	7	8	9	10
11	12	13	14	15	16	17
18	19	20	21	22	23	24
25	26	27	28	29	30	31

September

Su	Mo	Tu	We	Th	Fr	Sa
1	2	3	4	5	6	7
8	9	10	11	12	13	14
15	16	17	18	19	20	21
22	23	24	25	26	27	28
29	30	1	2	3	4	5

October

Su	Mo	Tu	We	Th	Fr	Sa
29	30	1	2	3	4	5
6	7	8	9	10	11	12
13	14	15	16	17	18	19
20	21	22	23	24	25	26
27	28	29	30	31	1	2

November

Su	Mo	Tu	We	Th	Fr	Sa
27	28	29	30	31	1	2
3	4	5	6	7	8	9
10	11	12	13	14	15	16
17	18	19	20	21	22	23
24	25	26	27	28	29	30

December

Su	Mo	Tu	We	Th	Fr	Sa
1	2	3	4	5	6	7
8	9	10	11	12	13	14
15	16	17	18	19	20	21
22	23	24	25	26	27	28
29	30	31	1	2	3	4

2020

January

Su	Mo	Tu	We	Th	Fr	Sa
29	30	31	1	2	3	4
5	6	7	8	9	10	11
12	13	14	15	16	17	18
19	20	21	22	23	24	25
26	27	28	29	30	31	1

February

Su	Mo	Tu	We	Th	Fr	Sa
26	27	28	29	30	31	1
2	3	4	5	6	7	8
9	10	11	12	13	14	15
16	17	18	19	20	21	22
23	24	25	26	27	28	29

March

Su	Mo	Tu	We	Th	Fr	Sa
1	2	3	4	5	6	7
8	9	10	11	12	13	14
15	16	17	18	19	20	21
22	23	24	25	26	27	28
29	30	31	1	2	3	4

April

Su	Mo	Tu	We	Th	Fr	Sa
29	30	31	1	2	3	4
5	6	7	8	9	10	11
12	13	14	15	16	17	18
19	20	21	22	23	24	25
26	27	28	29	30	1	2

May

Su	Mo	Tu	We	Th	Fr	Sa
26	27	28	29	30	1	2
3	4	5	6	7	8	9
10	11	12	13	14	15	16
17	18	19	20	21	22	23
24	25	26	27	28	29	30
31	1	2	3	4	5	6

June

Su	Mo	Tu	We	Th	Fr	Sa
31	1	2	3	4	5	6
7	8	9	10	11	12	13
14	15	16	17	18	19	20
21	22	23	24	25	26	27
28	29	30	1	2	3	4

July

Su	Mo	Tu	We	Th	Fr	Sa
28	29	30	1	2	3	4
5	6	7	8	9	10	11
12	13	14	15	16	17	18
19	20	21	22	23	24	25
26	27	28	29	30	31	1

August

Su	Mo	Tu	We	Th	Fr	Sa
26	27	28	29	30	31	1
2	3	4	5	6	7	8
9	10	11	12	13	14	15
16	17	18	19	20	21	22
23	24	25	26	27	28	29
30	31	1	2	3	4	5

September

Su	Mo	Tu	We	Th	Fr	Sa
30	31	1	2	3	4	5
6	7	8	9	10	11	12
13	14	15	16	17	18	19
20	21	22	23	24	25	26
27	28	29	30	1	2	3

October

Su	Mo	Tu	We	Th	Fr	Sa
27	28	29	30	1	2	3
4	5	6	7	8	9	10
11	12	13	14	15	16	17
18	19	20	21	22	23	24
25	26	27	28	29	30	31

November

Su	Mo	Tu	We	Th	Fr	Sa
1	2	3	4	5	6	7
8	9	10	11	12	13	14
15	16	17	18	19	20	21
22	23	24	25	26	27	28
29	30	1	2	3	4	5

December

Su	Mo	Tu	We	Th	Fr	Sa
29	30	1	2	3	4	5
6	7	8	9	10	11	12
13	14	15	16	17	18	19
20	21	22	23	24	25	26
27	28	29	30	31	1	2

2019-2020 HOLIDAYS AND POSTAL CLOSURES

2019

Date	Holiday
January 1	New Year's Day
January 21	Martin Luther King Jr. Day
February 18	President's Day
May 12	Mother's Day
May 27	Memorial Day*
June 16	Father's Day
July 4	Independence Day*
September 2	Labor Day*
October 14	Columbus Day
November 11	Veteran's Day*
November 28	Thanksgiving*
December 25	Christmas Day*

2020

Date	Holiday
January 1	New Year's Day
January 20	Martin Luther King Jr. Day
February 17	President's Day
May 10	Mother's Day
May 25	Memorial Day*
June 21	Father's Day
July 4	Independence Day*
September 7	Labor Day*
October 12	Columbus Day
November 11	Veteran's Day*
November 27	Thanksgiving*
December 25	Christmas Day*

* Indicates Postal Holidays.

USPS POSTAL RATES Effective Jan 2019

Quick Reference—Domestic

Shape	Size	Price

Postcards

	minimum	maximum
length	5 inches	6 inches
height	3-1/2 inches	4-1/4 inches
thickness	0.007 inch	0.016 inch

Price: $0.35

Letters

	minimum	maximum
length	5 inches	11-1/2 inches
height	3-1/2 inches	6-1/8 inches
thickness	0.007 inch	1/4 inch

Letters that meet one or more of the nonmachinable characteristics in DMM 101.1.2 are also subject to the $0.15 nonmachinable surcharge

Weight Not Over (oz.)	Stamped	Metered
1	$0.55	$0.50
2	0.70	0.65
3	0.85	0.80
3.5	1.00	0.95

Large Envelopes (Flats)

	minimum*	maximum
length	11-1/2 inches	15 inches
height	6-1/8 inches	12 inches
thickness	1/4 inch	3/4 inch

* Flats exceed at least one of these dimensions.
Pieces that are rigid, nonrectangular, or not uniformly thick pay parcel prices.

Weight Not Over (oz.)	Price
1	$1.00
2	1.15
3	1.30
4	1.45
5	1.60
6	1.75
7	1.90
8	2.05
9	2.20
10	2.35
11	2.50
12	2.65
13	2.80

Parcels

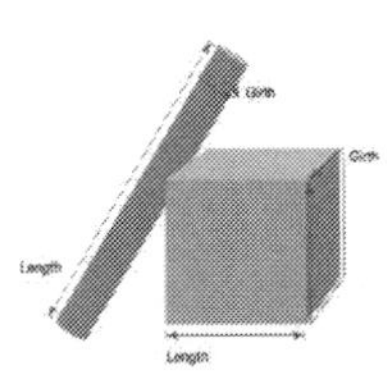

Length + girth combined cannot exceed 108 inches. (USPS Retail Ground cannot exceed 130 inches.)
length: the longest side of the parcel
girth: measurement around the thickest part (perpendicular to the length)

First-Class Package Service

Weight Not Over (oz.)	Zone							
	1 & 2	3	4	5	6	7	8	9
1	$3.66	$3.70	$3.74	$3.78	$3.82	$3.94	$4.06	$4.06
2	3.66	3.70	3.74	3.78	3.82	3.94	4.06	4.06
3	3.66	3.70	3.74	3.78	3.82	3.94	4.06	4.06
4	3.66	3.70	3.74	3.78	3.82	3.94	4.06	4.06
5	4.39	4.44	4.49	4.53	4.57	4.69	4.81	4.81
6	4.39	4.44	4.49	4.53	4.57	4.69	4.81	4.81
7	4.39	4.44	4.49	4.53	4.57	4.69	4.81	4.81
8	4.39	4.44	4.49	4.53	4.57	4.69	4.81	4.81
9	5.19	5.24	5.30	5.35	5.40	5.53	5.66	5.66
10	5.19	5.24	5.30	5.35	5.40	5.53	5.66	5.66

Flat Rate—Domestic

Retail

Priority Mail Express	Size	Price
Flat Rate Envelope	12-1/2" x 9-1/2"	$25.50
Legal Flat Rate Envelope	15" x 9-1/2"	25.70
Padded Flat Rate Envelope[1]	12-1/2" x 9-1/2"	26.20

Priority Mail	Size	Price
Flat Rate Envelope	12-1/2" x 9-1/2" or smaller	$7.35
Legal Flat Rate Envelope[1]	15" x 9-1/2"	7.65
Padded Flat Rate Envelope[1]	12-1/2" x 9-1/2"	8.00
Small Flat Rate Box	8-5/8" x 5-3/8" x 1-5/8" Inside 8-11/16" x 5-7/16" x 1-3/4" Outside	7.90
Medium Flat Rate Boxes	11" x 8-1/2" x 5-1/2" Inside 11-1/4" x 8-3/4" x 6" Outside 13-5/8" x 11-7/8" x 3-3/8" Inside 14" x 12" x 3-1/2" Outside	14.35
Large Flat Rate Boxes	12" x 12" x 5-1/2" Inside 12-1/4" x 12-1/4" x 6" Outside 23-11/16" x 11-3/4" x 3" Inside[1] 24-1/16" x 11-7/8" x 3-1/8" Outside[1]	19.95
APO/FPO/DPO Flat Rate Box	12" x 12" x 5-1/2" Inside 12-1/4" x 12-1/4" x 6" Outside	18.45

1. Packaging only available at USPS.com.

Quick Reference—International

First-Class Mail International & First-Class Package International Service—Retail

Postcards

Size:

	minimum	maximum
length	5-1/2 inches	6 inches
height	3-1/2 inches	4-1/4 inches
thickness	0.007 inch	0.016 inch

Price:

Canada	$1.15
Mexico	1.15
All other countries	1.15

Letters

Size:

	minimum	maximum
length	5-1/2 inches	11-1/2 inches
height	3-1/2 inches	6-1/8 inches
thickness	0.007 inch	1/4 inch

Letters that meet one or more of the nonmachinable characteristics in IMM 241.217 are also subject to the $0.21 nonmachinable surcharge

Price:

Weight Not Over (oz.)	Price Groups 1	2	3–5	6–9
1	$1.15	$1.15	$1.15	$1.15
2	1.15	1.72	2.13	1.98
3	1.61	2.29	3.12	2.81
3.5	2.08	2.86	4.11	3.64

Large Envelopes (Flats)

Size:

	minimum*	maximum
length	11-1/2 inches	15 inches
height	6-1/8 inches	12 inches
thickness	1/4 inch	3/4 inch

* Flats exceed at least one of these dimensions.

Pieces that are rigid, nonrectangular, or not uniformly thick pay parcel prices.

Price:

Weight Not Over (oz.)	Price Groups 1	2	3–5	6–9
1	$2.29	$2.29	$2.29	$2.29
2	2.50	2.97	3.23	3.18
3	2.71	3.64	4.16	4.06
4	2.91	4.32	5.10	4.94
5	3.12	5.00	6.04	5.83
6	3.33	5.67	6.97	6.71
7	3.54	6.35	7.91	7.60
8	3.75	7.03	8.85	8.48
12	4.79	8.48	10.72	10.31
16	5.83	9.94	12.60	12.13

Pieces that are rigid, nonrectangular, or not uniformly thick pay package prices.

Packages

Size—Other than Rolls
Maximum length = 24 inches
Maximum length + height + thickness combined = 36 inches

Size—Rolls
Minimum length = 4 inches
Minimum length + twice the diameter combined = 6-3/4 inches
Maximum length + twice the diameter combined = 42 inches

First-Class Package International Service Price Groups

Weight Not Over (oz.)	1	2	3	4	5	6	7	8	9
1–8	$10.50	$12.25	$14.25	$14.25	$14.25	$14.50	$13.75	$13.50	$14.50
9–32	17.25	21.50	23.50	24.00	24.00	24.50	23.25	22.75	24.50
33–48	26.25	33.00	35.00	36.75	37.50	38.75	37.00	34.75	38.50
49–64	39.00	47.50	52.75	59.50	61.00	63.00	59.50	55.25	62.50

SEEDS

By Odies Murray

I am a seed, that was planted inside Mother Earth.
That sprouted from the womb, like a flower from the dirt.
You grow what you plant, but don't forget the water.
The sunlight for your sons and the dirt for your daughters.
You gotta check the soil, before you plant the seeds.
You'll get a rose garden, in a field of full of weeds.
You gotta nurture all your seeds, until they all mature.
And always be faithful, seeds still grow through cow manure.
You can be the lotus that grows up from the mud.
Or maybe the palm tree that grows up to the sun.
You produce what's in you, so always keep striving.
And with that good energy, your seed will always keep thriving.
So, when I pass, bury me in fertile land.
So, when you put me in the dirt, I know my seed will grow again.
Everybody is a seed, conceived then birth.
So, my life will keep going, once my seeds in the dirt…

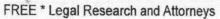

COALITION FOR PRISONER'S RIGHTS NEWSLETTERS

The Coalition for Prisoners' Rights (CPR) is based in Santa Fe, New Mexico. For 36 years (since 1981) they have been publishing their namesake newsletter.

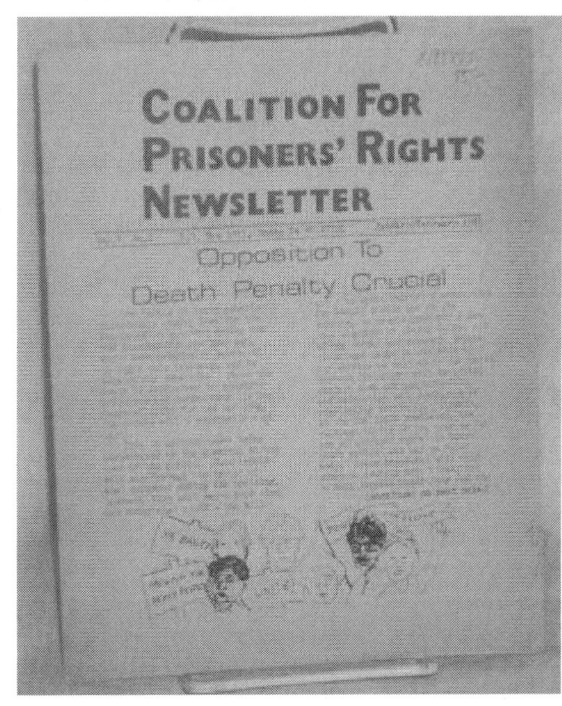

Coalition For Prisoners' Rights Newsletter

Opposition To Death Penalty Crucial

In June of 2009, they changed their eight-page bulk-mailed newsletter to a one-sheet format, front and back. They now send the previous 11 issues of their publication as part of their response to every communication they receive, along with their eight-page resource list and applicable state resource information. When requested, they supply copies of over 100 additional resource lists on a variety of topics and will continue mailing their newsletter to those who supply them with self-addressed, stamped envelopes (SASE). The amount of correspondence they receive from prisoners all over this country is overwhelming – consistently more than 300 letters a month!

In July 2009, The Real Cost of Prisons joined CPR in getting out the message. Believing in CPR's work and knowing they could no longer afford to mail their monthly eight-page newsletter to their 9,100 subscribers (including families, friends, and allies of prisoners), they began posting the *CPR Newsletters* in PDF format on their website. They hope to encourage the loved ones of prisoners to read and download the newsletter and send it to those on the inside.

To recap, if you want to receive this important source of information on your own every month, you can send CPR up to 12 self-addressed, stamped envelopes, with CPR as the return address, and they'll start your subscription right away. Or, you can read, downloaded, and print the *CPR Newsletter* online at www.realcostofprisons.org/coalition.html for free.

The coalition is a small group of volunteers, maybe a dozen at any one time. Some have been in prison, some are family members of those who still are, but all are deeply concerned about the lack of human rights in our country. They are just everyday people, no lawyers or legal workers, just people like you and me that have existed all this time, since 1972, on the thinnest of financial budgets and huge amount of focused determination and hard work.

Over the years they believe their newsletter readership exceeds the number of letters/envelopes they receive by at least a factor of ten. They have found that many prisoners keep their materials for years and then write for updates.

CPR has supported their dedicated work with individuals' donations, both in time and funds, contributions from church groups, and a few grants from progressive foundations. They recently benefited enormously from an expanding cooperative relationship with several local schools and the participation of short-term student volunteers.

The coalition's members work hard to maintain accuracy of their mailing lists. If you already send SASEs, please make sure to send them your change of address, if it occurs. Stamps as well as financial contributions are welcome and necessary.

Coalition for Prisoners' Rights
PO Box 1911
Santa Fe, NM 87504-1911
cpr1911@yahoo.com

Intuitional History

The Coalition for Prisoners' Rights is a non-profit, volunteer organization formed in Santa Fe, New Mexico, in the summer of 1976, as an outgrowth of what was then called the Women's Prison Project. It is administered by a small core group, and has an informal membership which includes ex-convicts, people who have been involved in educational and other service programs for prisoners and parolees, prisoners' family members, and legal workers. The goal of the organization is to analyze and publicize the penal system as it functions in society, and to work for prison change. Additionally, the organization produces and distributes a monthly newsletter, and assists in demonstrations, rallies and trials.

Scope and Content

Collection consists of correspondence papers, newsletters, articles, memorandums, and legislation regarding the rights of women and men incarcerated in prisons in the United States, Canada, Egypt and Israel. Additionally, this collection contains letters of prisoners regarding prison conditions, harassment, legal aid, vocational training, and conjugal visits, as well as censorship and mail regulations, and notes and literature pertaining to the Committee to Stop Executions and the National Coalition to Abolish the Death Penalty.

Mission Statement

CPR work with others, nationally and locally to gather and to disseminate information, analysis and action alternatives for those incarcerated, their family's members and allies. They work to build unity and positive opportunities for all of us affected by the US mass incarceration system. They strive to shed light on the realities of imprisonment, to improve jail and prison conditions and to reduce sentence lengths. CPR believe that the law enforcement, court and penal system is dependent on continuing the institutionalization of poverty and racism. They oppose punishment as a tool for positive social change and believe prisons as presently constituted are dangerous to community health, safety and development.

Despite what everyone envisions as the Coalition, this is the humble home, Hopeland.

Coalition For Prisoners' Rights Newsletter

Vol. 44-A, No. 1 **PO Box 1911, Santa Fe NM 87504** **January 2019**

FOLLOW THE MONEY

Years ago, people who had been working to accurately describe and change the police, court and penal system pointed out to us newcomers a most unfortunate and characteristic feature of many of our efforts based on incomplete understanding of how things really worked: every time something new was developed and adopted, instead of replacing accepted methods of dealing with the situation, everything that already existed was kept and the new ways just added on. And so it still goes. There is now imprisonment and parole and probation and intensive probation and ankle bracelets. Nothing is dropped. Only now, we have more powerful than ever before technologies that have the added benefits for those who run them of further concentrating both power and profits. Current examples follow.

As Michelle Alexander states eloquently in a November 2018 New York Times article, "Many of the current reform efforts contain the seeds of the next generation of 'e-carceration' that may prove more dangerous and more difficult to challenge."

Bail "reform" is a case in point. What's taking the place of cash bail may prove even worse. For example, in California a "presumption of detention" will effectively replace eligibility for immediate release.

And, much worse, given what appears to be a so far unshakeable confidence in The Truth Created by Computers, computer algorithms are facilitating the determination of who should be caged. In California, New Jersey and New York, for starters, "risk assessment" algorithms are used recommend to judges whether a person who's been arrested should be released.

They are based on factors that are not only highly correlated with ethnicity and socio-economic class, but are also "significantly influenced by pervasive bias" in the police, court and penal system. They are, in fact, opinions embedded in mathematics--that is, opinions masquerading as facts.

Challenging these biased algorithms may be more difficult than challenging discrimination by the police, prosecutors and judges.

Even if you're lucky enough to be released from a brick-and-mortar jail thanks to a computer algorithm, you will most likely be required to have an expensive monitoring device shackled to your ankle, which are used more and more. Such a GPS tracking device would be provided by a for-profit company that will probably charge you around $300 a month. Your permitted zones of movement may make it difficult or impossible to get or keep a job, attend school,care for your kids or visit family members. You're effectively sentenced to an "open air digital prison." One false step can bring on the cops.

And, to repeat, who benefits? For-profit corporations. Just four of them have most of the private contracts to provide electronic monitoring for people on parole in some 30 states. Their combined annual revenue is more than $200 million just for e-monitoring. One of them is GEO, also one of the largest for-profit prison companies. And so, growing numbers of people find themselves subject to perpetual criminalization, surveillance, monitoring and control.

And guess what? It turns out that what are referred to as "efforts to reduce recidivism through intensive supervision" are not working. For whom, one may ask. It is not hard to imagine that, if one really wanted to, reducing the requirements and burdens of community supervision so that people could more easily hold jobs, care for children and escape the stigma of criminality would have a more positive outcome.

If the goal were really to end mass incarceration and mass criminalization--firmly based on racism and oppression--digital prisons are not an answer. They just make a lot of money for those who already have more than their share. New systems that treat poor people and people of color as commodities to be bought,sold, evaluated and managed for profit must be labelled and judged for what they actually do. And then, stopped!

Resource:Michelle Alexander,New York Times

IN MEMORIAM -- 2018

Date	Name	State
01/18	Anthony Allen Shore	Texas
01/30	William Earl Rayford	Texas
02/01	John David Battaglia	Texas
02/22	Eric Scott Branch	Florida
03/15	Michael Wayne Eggers	Alabama
03/15	Carlton Michael Gary	Georgia
03/27	Rosendo Rodriguez III	Texas
04/19	Walter Leroy Moody, Jr.	Alabama
04/25	Erick Daniel Davila	Texas
05/04	Robert Earl Butts, Jr.	Georgia
05/16	Juan Edward Castillo	Texas
06/27	Daniel Paul "Danny" Bible	Texas
07/17	Christopher Anthony Young	Texas
07/18	Robert J. van Hook	Ohio
08/09	William Ray "Billy" Irick	Tenn.
08/14	Carey Dean Moore	Nebr.
09/26	Troy James Clark	Texas
09/27	Daniel Clate Acker	Texas
10/29	Rodney Scott Berget	S.D.
11/01	Edmund George Zagorski	Tenn.
11/14	Roberto Ramos Moreno	Texas
12/04	Joseph Christopher Garcia	Texas
12/06	David Earl Miller	Tenn.
12/11	Alvin Avon Braziel, Jr.	Texas
12/13	Jose Antonio Jimenez	Florida

There were 25 people, all men, executed in 2018. About one in seven execution sentences in 2018 came as the result of the jurisdictions that allow judges to impose execution sentences without unanimous jury recommendations.

****

To receive the CPR Newsletter by postal mail monthly, send us up to 12 self-addressed, stamped envelopes (with the CPR return address).

Keep sending us address changes and renewal requests in order for us to maintain our *only* permanent mailing list--the one for our January holiday card/new calendar, as accurately as possible.

Also, note that the correct address to be sure to reach us at is: PO Box 1911, Santa Fe NM 87504. Some resource address listings are incorrect in this regard.

And still: NONE OF US ARE LAWYERS OR LEGAL WORKERS; for our protection, please do *not* mark envelopes addressed to us as "Legal Mail."

Many, many thanks to the Real Cost of Prisons Project for posting our Newsletter on-line for free downloading and distribution. It is at: www.realcostofprisonsproject.org--this is a GREAT site! Thank you for all your support!

****

¿ Desede cuándo el gobierno de Estados Unidos comenzó su hostilidad a la revolución Cubana?

El bloqueo económico, comercial y financiero decretado oficialmente el 3 de febrero de 1962 por los Estados Unidos en contra de Cuba; habia más de seiscientos planes de atentados contra la vida de Fidel Castro y otros dirigentes; la Ley Helms Burton de 1996 internacionalizan el bloqueo y establecen el plan de recolonización de Cuba. Han sido más de cincuenta años de hostilidad por todos los medios, primero para impedire el triunfo y después para destruir a la Revolución Cubana.

The Indivisibility of Justice

The Birmingham Alabama Civil Rights Institute recently revoked its presentation of the Reverend Fred L. Shuttleworth Award to Angela Davis. The pressure to do so came from local staunchly pro-Israel groups and individuals, without the participation of all of the organization's Board members, three of who subsequently resigned. The Mayor of Birmingham also protested the action as have the City Council and the School Board among many across the country.

The award is named in honor of a early Birmingham civil rights leader whom Angela Davis, who grew up in that city, knew as a child. Her response was: "the rescinding of the award and invitation to speak was 'not primarily an attack against me, but rather against the very spirit of 'the indivisibility of justice.' In particular because of her long term support of justice for Palestine."

Davis has supported the boycott, divestment and sanctions movement ("BDS")which works to organize economic pressure on Israel to end the occupation of the West Bank, treat Palestinians equally under the, law and allow the return of Palestinian refugees. She is among a growing number who have compared the struggles of Palestinians to those of African-Americans.

"I support Palestinian political prisoners just as I support current political prisoners in the Basque Country, in Catalunya, in India, and in other parts of the world. I have indeed expressed opposition to policies and practices of the state of Israel, as I express similar opposition to U.S. support for the Israeli occupation of Palestine and to other discriminatory U.S. policies."

And, "Jails and prisons are designed to break human beings, to convert to population into specimens in a zoo."
Her books include: "Are Prisons Obsolete?, and "Freedom is a Constant Struggle"

Coalition For Prisoners' Rights Newsletter

Vol. 44-A, No. 2 **PO Box 1911, Santa Fe NM 87504** **February 2019**

ABOUT POVERTY

IN THIS PLACE

Within
the dark bowels
of this prison, the walls rise
twenty feet, blocking out the sun.
Creating a cement and steel tomb for the living,
whose life of hell is never done. No quiet or solitude,
yet always alone, trying to keep sanity in place--a hard
task for any person who has to wear a mask to cover
all emotion. Within the dark bowels of this prison,
the animal instinct needed to survive exists
in each prisoner's heart and mind,
as he continues his lone fight
to stay alive.

Robert C. Fuentes, RIP
from *Extracts from Pelican Bay*, 1995
[Thanks to Bato: In Solidarity]

Commissary Updates

December 2018, Southern New Mexico Correctional Facility, Las Cruces NM -- "In 2014 the NMCD accepted a bid given by the Keefe group to take control over the canteen (commissary). All items bought through them by NMCD inmates, mainly food and drink, and restricted the purchase of such items from any other source--which allowed the Keefe group to monopolize the NMCD and its inmates. (Since 2014), nearly every item sold has doubled in price and with no other option or source to purchase from, the Keefe group can and probably will, continue to raise prices in comparison to other vendors....I've heard, but have no proof, that the institution receives a percentage of what the Keefe group makes through these sales."

January 2019, Guadalupe County Correctional Facility (GEO Group) Santa Rosa NM -- "We were paying a little over seven dollars for a box of Banquet chicken, now we will be paying almost ten dollars that that same box. Commissary is blaming the increase on their supplier, Affiliated Foods..."

Have More, Get More

Recent academic research has,no kidding, validated all the things that we know to be true. Job growth is no panacea for impoverished urban neighborhoods. Upward economic mobility appears to hinge, at least in large part, on having a college degree, two parent households, and RACIAL EQUALITY. Since what is now often referred to as the Great Recession of ten years ago, in the lowest income 20% of zip codes, populations have dwindled and there has been almost no recovery from the recession. Places that have a lot of job growth don't tend to be places that are the most comfortable to grow up in.

Studies have found that ethnicity is pivotal to economic mobility. We call it racism. For example, upward economic mobility varies a great deal among people of different ethnic backgrounds who live in the same neighborhoods in places as widely separated as Los Angeles and Houston, among others. Upward mobility worsened in neighborhoods with a high concentration of African-Americans. Which, as we know, are not created by accident, but rather by government and business policy.

And upward economic movement was greater for those from neighborhoods with many two parent families. Also for those from neighborhoods with higher-priced housing. In other words, those who have, get. So, mobility is also generally better in neighborhoods where a high proportion of adults are working.

There is often disparity between residents of and workers in neighborhoods. Jobs appear to have gone to people who live in other, more prosperous neighborhoods or to those who commute from the surrounding suburbs.

And so the example of Los Alamos NM. New Mexico is one of the poorest states in the country. Los Alamos County is the richest *in the country*. The government bomb lab in Los Alamos employed 11,743 people in 2018. Of them 45% live in Los Alamos County, 21% in Santa Fe County and 16% in Rio Arriba County--one of the poorer counties in NM.

Tras Venezuela, EUA apunta a Cuba en esfuerzo por remodelar Latinoamérica

El periódico The Wall Street Journal (TWSJ) informa que el esfuerzo por destituir al persidente de Venezuela, Nicolás Maduro, es solo el primer paso del govierno del presidente trump para remodelar Latinoamérica, y Cuba es su siguiente objetivo. Según el informe, Estados Unidos planea anunciar nuevas medidas contra Cuba en las próximas semanas, incluyendo nuevas sanciones y el restablecimiento de la designación de Cuba como un estado defensor del terrorismo. La medida podría comprometer severamente las inversiones extranjeras el el país. Según TWSJ, Estados Unidos planea apuntar luego a Nicaragua. En noviembre, el asesor de seguridad nacional John Bolton calificó a las tres naciones de una "troika de la tiranía". La ultima semana de enero, el vicepresidente Mike Pence afirmó que a trump "no le entusiasman" las intervenciones estadounidenses en el extranjero, "excepto en este hemisferio".

The Black Alliance for Peace opposes the illegal and immoral attempts by the United States and their Organization of American States (OAS) allies to interfere in the internal affairs of Venezuela.

****

To receive the CPR Newsletter by postal mail monthly, send us up to 12 self-addressed, stamped envelopes--with the CPR return address.

Keep sending us address changes and renewal requests in order for us to maintain our *only* permanent mailing list--the one for our January holiday day/new calendar, as accurately as possible.

Also, note that the correct address to be sure to reach us at is: PO Box 1911, Santa Fe NM 87504. Some resource address listings are incorrect in this regard.

And still: NONE OF US ARE LAWYERS OR LEGAL WORKERS; for our protection, please do *not* mark envelopes addressed to us as "Legal Mail."

Many, many thanks to the Real Cost of Prisons Project for posting our Newsletter on-line for free downloading and distribution. It is at: www.realcostofprisonsproject.org--this is a GREAT site! Thank you for all your support!

****

During this month, February, next month and every month:

*** * * BLACK LIVES MATTER * * ***

MORE GRAVE INJUSTICES OF OUR TIME CONTINUED

The Birmingham Alabama Civil Rights Institute recently revoked its presentation of the Reverend Fred L. Shuttleworth Award to Angela Davis, a native of Birmingham, as we reported last month. We are pleased to report that that decision was reversed on January 25th, when Institute's Board voted to reaffirm Davis as the recipient of the Award. We do not yet know how this will be observed.

The reconsideration came after a public outcry, including a letter signed by more than 300 prominent civil rights supporters working in a variety of fields which was made public within 48 hours of the Award recall. It stated in part: "We share the view that the Israeli Occupation is wrong, and that the repressive, discriminatory and often violent policies of the Israeli government vis-á-vis the Palestinian population are wrong and indefensible." Davis herself commented in part: "The rescinding of this invitation and the cancellation of the event where I was scheduled to speak was thus not primarily an attack against me, but rather against the very spirit of the indivisibility of justice."

Michelle Alexander, the author of "The New Jim Crow," commented in her article in The New York Times: "We must condemn Israel's actions--unrelenting violations of international law, continued occupation of the West Bank, East Jerusalem, and Gaza, home demolitions and land confiscations." And Alexander also noted that: "Those who speak publicly in support of the liberation of the Palestinian people still risk condemnation and backlash....I am certain that the Rev. Dr. Martin Luther King (who was widely criticized when came out against the U.S. war in Vietnam in 1967)said on that occasion 'My conscience leaves me no other choice'-- would applaud Birmingham for its zealous defense of Angela Davis's solidarity with Palestinian people...In this new year, I aim to speak with greater courage and conviction about injustices beyond our borders, particularly those that are funded by our government."

Call Out to Florida Prisoners & Loved Ones

Julie Jones, the head of the Florida prison system from 2015 to just recently, is coming to New Mexico as the Secretary of Corrections under the new NM governor Michelle Lujan Grisham. She is being presented as a "reformer." The Florida prison system has 10 times the budget and number of prisoners as does New Mexico. We wonder why she is coming. More importantly, we wonder what she did re the prison system in Florida. Please write us!

Coalition For Prisoners' Rights Newsletter

Vol. 44-A, No. 3 | PO Box 1911, Santa Fe NM 87504 | March 2019

AND STILL WE RISE

There has been a 1,700% increase in incarceration of women since 1973. The growth of incarceration for women has grown at least twice as fast as that for men. As of 2018, there were 219,000 women incarcerated in the United States. Of them there were 99,000 held in state prisons and 89,000 in local jails. Women are much more evenly split between jails and prisons than men are. Of the women in jails, 60% have not been sentenced.

No current figures were available for those in federal facilities, which we know, due to current immigration detention policies and practices, have grown enormously in the last year. The latest figures available are that state and federal agencies pay local jails to imprison an additional 13,000 women. Drastically understating today's reality, ICE and the U.S. Marshals report contracting with local jails to hold 5,000 women.

From the available statistics, that makes a total of 102,000 women held in jails. Since incarcerated women have lower incomes than incarcerated men, they have an even harder time affording cash bail. This is despite the fact that of jailed women, 80% of women are mothers and most are the primary caregivers for their children, so are not considered to be a flight risk. Yet bail amounts are typically a full year's income.

About 25% of convicted incarcerated women are held in jails, compared to about 10% of total convicted people. And jails make it harder to stay in touch with family than prisons do. Phone calls are more expensive and other forms of communication are more restricted. In addition, jailed women are more even more likely to suffer from mental health problems than either women in prisons or imprisoned men in whatever setting.

It will come as no surprise that African American and Indigenous American women are markedly overrepresented in prisons and jails. Incarcerated women are reported as 53% "white," 29% Black, 14% Hispanic, 2.5% Indigenous, 0.9% Asian and 0.4% Native Hawaiian and Pacific Islander.

However, there is an additional form of discrimination. A third (33%) of incarcerated women identify as Lesbian or bisexual, compared to less than 10% of men. Lesbian and bisexual women generally receive longer sentences than hetero.

And then we get to the really big numbers: over a million (83%) of women are on probation and parole. Just 17% of women directly under the control of "departments of corrections" are incarcerated. But, 74% of the total--that is, three out of four--are on probation and 9% are on parole. This is in contrast to the total number of people--that is, both women and men--under correctional control, where a third (again, 33%) are imprisoned.

And again, no surprises: If you have been judged to be a "bad girl" and locked up for it, it turns out that you will be disciplined more often and more harshly than men for "low level" violations. Women, on average were given almost double the number of disciplinary violation tickets as men. And the biggest difference is the one for "insolence." Not "safety" or "security."

As we know, women in prison often have a history of trauma. And they have symptoms of post-traumatic stress disorder more than any other demographic group, including combat veterans. Often imprisoned women have a history of sexual and other physical abuse. In addition to solitary confinement, a common punishment in prisons is losing phone privileges. When that occurs, not only is the person imprisoned punished and further damaged, but so are her children.

RESOURCES:

Women's Mass Incarceration: The Whole Pie 2018, prisonpolicy.org/reports, Aleks Kajstura, November 13, 2018

Investigation in U.S. Prisons, Women Punished More Often Than Men, npr.org/2018/10/14, Jessica Pupovac

Becoming Ms. Burton, from Prison to Recovery to Leading the Fight for Incarcerated Women; Susan Burton & C. Lynn

From Her Mouth to Your Ears, A Survivors Manual by and for Women in Prison, AFSC Prison Watch,89 Market St, Newark NJ0860.

PRIMERO

Primero, ellos vinieron por los socialistas,
pero yo no hablé porque no era socialista,
Después vinieron por los sindicalistas,
pero yo no hablé porque no era sindicalista,
Luego vinieron por los judíos,
pero yo no hablé porque no era judío,
Al final vinieron por mi y, para entonces...
ya no quedaba nadie que hablara por mi.
-- por Martin Niemoeller, durante la segunda guerra mundial

UPDATE ON FLORIDA INFO REQUEST

A most heartfelt thank you to those who responded to our request for information about the then nominee for Secretary of Corrections in New Mexico under the new governor. All the letters we received were specific, detailed and in agreement. However, she, Julie Jones, previously, the head of corrections in Florida, withdrew her name from consideration. We don't know why, nor do we yet have any idea of who might be nominated next.

Clarification

We apologize for the misleading headline in our November 2018 issue regarding the current book policy in Pennsylvania prisons. It was poorly chosen, but based on the changes made to the original ones Pennsylvania came up with last fall.

If you have feedback about the current procedures for getting books in Pennsylvania prisons, we would be most interested in learning about them. We also could not find any specific information concerning exactly WHICH dictionaries all prisoners who ask for them are now supposed to get "for free."

****

To receive the CPR Newsletter by postal mail monthly, send us up to 12 self-addressed, stamped envelopes--with the CPR return address.

Keep sending us address changes and renewal requests in order for us to maintain our *only* permanent mailing list--the one for our January holiday/new calendar--as accurately as possible.

Also, note that the correct address to be sure to reach us at is: PO Box 1911, Santa Fe NM 87504. Some resource address listings are incorrect in this regard.

And still: NONE OF US ARE LAWYERS OR LEGAL WORKERS; for our protection, please do *not* mark envelopes addressed to us as "Legal Mail."

Many, many thanks to the Real Cost of Prisons Project for posting our Newsletter on-line for free downloading and distribution. It is at: www.realcostofprisonsproject.org--this is a GREAT site! Thank you for all your support!

Angela Davis says:

"Black people, especially, owe a great deal to Palestinians, who have been struggling for decades and decades and refuse to give up. They are an inspiration to people who are fighting for freedom everywhere on the planet."

No Surprise: Better Food is Better

Imprisoned people are 6.4 times more likely to be sickened from spoiled or contaminated food than others. About 44% of state and federal prisoners have experienced chronic disease, compared with 31% of the general population. Health care--$12.3 billion a year--is the public prison system's greatest expense. Changes in diet such as increasing the amount of fresh produce consumed and reducing the drinking of soda for the 2.3 million U.S. prisoners, could save more than $500 million over five years. In addition, "dietary discontent" contributed to uprising among prisoners in Michigan, North Carolina and Washington.

More nutritious food doesn't have to cost more money. There are more prison agricultural programs now that enable those imprisoned to grow some of what they eat. Such programs also improve mental health, reduce recidivism rates, and improve job skills. Of course for-profit companies are also increasingly involved in providing the typically prison provided processed meats and generally high-starch meals commonly served. The high fat, high chemical content foods provided by for-profit commissaries and vending machines also lack nutritional value, although they may provide more flavor--if you have the cash.

Of course, there are many other health risks that go along with imprisonment. They include neglect, blocked access to care, physical and sexual violence, and brutality by staff. In addition, when prisoners are sick or injured or die in custody, the circumstances are concealed.

According to a new book by Homer Venters, MD, the former chief medical officer for New York City's Correctional Health Services, which describes the conditions common at Rikers Island--and why he supports its closure--which stated: "We work in settings that are designed and operated to keep the truth hidden. Detainees are beaten and threatened to prevent them from telling the truth about how they are injured, health staff are pressured to lie or to omit details in their own documentation, and families experience systematic abuse and humiliation during the visitation process."

Coalition For Prisoners' Rights Newsletter

Vol. 44-A, No. 4 **PO Box 1911, Santa Fe NM 87504** **April 2019**

Together We Can Do What We Cannot Do Alone

On April 10,2019, the Washington State Department of Corrections (DOC) released an update to its former memo which banned free, used books for Washington prisoners. In it, the Assistant Secretary of Prisons stated: "I am now reaffirming that the Department will continue to support the receipt of donated used books."

Details of this new memo still restrict approved book providers to a narrow and incomplete list, contain ambiguities about the approval and rejection processes, and did not include a full description of how process to be used in future communication between the Washington DOC and prison book programs would be improved to avoid such a repeat of bans.

This positive change occurred because *Books to Prisoners, Seattle* (c/o Left Bank Books, 92 Pike Street, Box A, Seattle WA 98101) worked hard and skillfully to lobby effectively for it. An important part of their effort was creating a statement of support and recruiting signatory prison book program groups from around the country in support of continued prisoner receipt of donated used books. This statement of unity says in large part:

"We affirm and respect the basic human rights of every person, whether or not they are incarcerated, and we believe that intellectual freedom is in the public interest. We support an informed public and assert that all people have a right to access information....Books are vital for building new skills and for supporting educational goals....

"The American Library Association now includes in its *Prisoners' Right to Read* statement that: 'People who are incarcerated or detained should have the ability to obtain books and materials from outside the prison for their personal use.'

"In further support is Supreme Court Justice Thurgood Marshall's 1974 statement: 'When the prison gates slam behind people, they do not lose their human quality: their minds do not become closed to ideas; their intellect does not cease to feed on a free and open interchange of opinions; their yearning for self-respect does not end; nor is their quest for self-realization concluded. If anything, the needs for identity and self-respect are more compelling in the dehumanizing prison environment.'[with gender inclusivity update]

We reassert our belief in the critical and unwavering importance of prisoners' direct access to books with minimal barriers and interference."

What was crucial in recruiting the many signatory prison book programs from across the country in a matter of a few days and the success in changing the Washington State policy was the existence and timing of the *Books to Prisoners National Conference* Books Make a World of Difference"--in Boston, from April 5 to 7. There were over 100 attendees, representing at least 46 organizations engaged in a variety of books to prisons activities. The Prison Book Program (c/o Lucy Parsons Bookstore, 1306 Hancock St, Suite 100, Quincy MA 02169) played a crucial role in bringing this invaluable conference into being. Thanks so much to all who worked on it and in it!

We were fortunate to be able to attend and look forward to the next one.

EVEN MORE

There is a brand new and second edition of the invaluable resource publication *Turn It Up!*--created for and by people in prison--to find new ways to be healthy. The subtitle is: Staying Strong Inside. The contents include: Growing Gray--Staying Strong, Ramadan: Nutrition for Body and Soul, When We Dehumanize We Can Hurt Somebody Without Feeling Remorse, 5 Tips for Getting the Best Care You Can, Overcoming Barriers to Parenting, Keeping My Cool, Incarcerated People's Health Bill of Rights, Trans Health Basics, Self-Care Tips from Inside and, above all, a 10 page Resource Guide!

"To order single or bulk copies of this issue of *Turn It Up!*: The Sero Project,
PO Box 1233
Milford PA 18337
info@seroproject.com"

El Arresto de Julian Assange

El fundador de la organización WikiLeaks,Julian Assange, fue arrestado poco depués de que el Gobierno de Ecuador revocara su asilo. Ex ex presidente de Ecuador Rafael Correa criticó al actual president, Lenín Moreno, por lo que sucedió, escribiendo: "El mayor traidor en la historia de Ecuador y Lationamérica, Lenín Moreno, permitió que la policía británica ingrese a nuestra embajada en Londres para arrestar a Assange. Moreno es un hombre corrupto, pero lo que ha hecho es un crimen que la humanidad nunca olvidará.

Los abogados de Julian Assange, prometieron combatir su posible extradición a Estados Unidos tras su arresto en Londres. El jueves, la policía británica lo sacó por la fuerza de la Embajada de Ecuador en Londres, en donde había estado refugiado durante casi siete años. Poco después de su arresto,las autoriadades estadounidenses presentaron una acusación contra Assange por conspirar con la informante del Ejercito Chelsea Manning,quien filtró una gran cantidad de documentos confidenciales a WikiLeaks,incluyendo evidencia de crímenes de guerra cometidos por Estados Unidos en Irak y Afganistán. Se espera que el Departamento de Justicia de Estados Unidos prsente cargos adicionales contra Assange. La abogada de Assange en Londres advirtió que el procesamiento de Assange podría en peligro la libertad de prensa. "Esto establece un peligroso precedente para todas las organizaciones de medios y periodistas enen el resto del mundo.

****

To receive the CPR Newsletter by postal mail monthly, send up to 12 self-addressed, stamped envelopes--with the CPR return address.

Keep sending us address changes and renewal requests in order for us to maintain our *only* permanent mailing list--the one for our January holiday/new calendar--as accurately as possible.

Also, note that the correct address to be sure to reach us at is: PO Box 1911, Santa Fe NM 87504. The address listings in some lists are incorrect in this regard.

And still: NONE OF US ARE LAWYERS OR LEGAL WORKERS; for our protection, please do *not* mark envelopes addressed to us as "Legal Mail."

Many, many thanks to the Real Cost of Prisons Project for posting our Newsletter on-line for free downloading and distribution. It is at: www.realcostofprisonsproject.org--this is a GREAT site! Thank you for all your support!

****

UBIQUITOUS DATA GATHERING

First used by federal agents in 2016, this new technique depends on search warrants, sometimes called "geofence" warrants, which specify an area and a time period and require Google to gather information from an enormous Google database its employees call Sensorvault. In effect, this turns the business of tracking cellphone users' locations into a digital dragnet for law enforcement. Information thus gathered shows where you go, who your friends are, what you read, eat and watch, and when you do it. Most Android devices and some iPhones have this data available from Google.

Another example of ubiquitous data gathering is Facebook. Their new idea is to have end-to-end encrypted messaging by merging communications across Facebook, WhatsApp and Instagram.Facebook may well be moving towards being too difficult to use. So called "content moderators" are being diagnosed with post-traumatic stress disorder from sifting through numerous posted horrors.

The comparison has been made that big tech platforms like Facebook and Google are elephant poachers and our personal data is ivory tusks. Surveillance capitalism feeds on every aspect of every human's experience according to Shoshana Zuboff's new book: *The Age of surveillance Capitalism: The Fight for a Human Future at the New Frontier of Power.*

CHALLENGE TO STUDY

"I challenge you to study about your nationality and race, not for hatred but for love of self and understanding and for stronger roots. And as you study of your own self, I challenge you to take pride in the people you come from and respect the other races that have pride in themselves."

--S.M. TX

Fatal Shootings

In each of the last four years, police nation wide have shot and killed almost the same number of people: nearly 1,000. It should be noted that the U.S. does not count police killings in homicide statistics. In 2018 998 people were killed by cops. In 2017, 987. The FBI's tracking system undercounted fatal police shootings by about half. The overall demographic characteristics of those shot have remained constant over the past four years: 45% "white" men, 23% Black men, 16% Hispanic men. All women: about 5% of the total. Of those killed, about 25% were considered to be people in "mental distress."

Subscribe today to start receiving Prison Legal News every month

PLN is a 72-page monthly publication that reports on criminal justice-related issues nationwide.

PLN Subscription Rates

Sub Rates	1 year	2 years	3 years	4 years
Prisoners	$30	$60	$90	$120
Individuals	$35	$70	$105	$140
Professionals/Entities	$90	$180	$270	$360

(Lawyers, govt. & professional agencies, libraries, etc.)

Sample issue (random date) - **$5.00** each

Back issue (after publication date) - **$5.00** each

Six-month prisoner subscription for **$18.00**

PLN Subscription Options:

6 month sub (Prisoners Only)
1 year sub (12 issues)
2 year sub (24 + 2 bonus issues)
3 year sub (36 + 4 bonus issues)
4 year sub (48 + 6 bonus issues)

All purchases must be pre-paid. Prisoners can pay with new stamps (strips or books, no singles) or pre-stamped envelopes, if allowed by institutional policies.

Please send orders and payment to:

Prison Legal News
PO Box 1151
Lake Worth, FL 33460

Purchase by phone with Visa, MasterCard, Amex or Discover: 561-360-2523, or buy books and subscriptions online at www.prisonlegalnews.org

All subscriptions rates & bonuses are effective as of 1-1-18. No refunds after orders have been processed. PLN is not responsible for address changes after orders have been placed.

LIFE LESSONS

BY RONALD "DOUBLE R" RHEINHART

Sing in the shower. Treat everyone you meet as a possibility. Watch a sunset at least once a season. Leave a bathroom cleaner than when you went in (it and yourself). Never exchange a thoughtful gift. A surprise is a present you didn't know you'd want, till someone gave it to you. Strive for excellence, not perfection. Plant a tree on one of your birthdays. Learn how to tell three good jokes a year. Compliment three people every day-make sure one of them is you. Try doing something you don't think you're good at. Never waste an opportunity to tell someone you love them. By the way, I love you. Think big thoughts but relish small pleasures. Floss your teeth even if you can't brush. Asked for a raise like you deserve it. Become the most positive and enthusiastic person you know. Over tip good service. Say "thank you" a lot. Be forgiving of yourself and forgiving others will be easier. Buy whatever kids are selling on card tables or in their front yards. Wear good shoes. Celebrate all family holidays, even when not feeling it. Commit yourself to gentle improvement. Have a firm handshake. Sign your name with flare. Send lots of cards. Look people in the eye. Be first to say hello. Be last to end a hug. Smell before you taste. Eat with savoring delight. Pastries make you fat, but so what. Don't snitch to lessen your guilt. And never let others burn from your heat. Do something creative whether it pays or not. Eventually, creative works will get you paid. Answer phones cheerfully. Never value anything more than relationships or peace of mind. Feed strangers. Be dependable more than excusable. Expect life to be fair – and see that it is. Question what you don't know out loud. Stop at a mistake: admit to it and evaluate. Failure is just the universe telling you "go in another direction" or "do it in a different way." Keep in mind that anger is just one letter short of danger. We were made to be violent, to kill what we eat – most times you just don't have to be. But if you ever must fight, be a man or beast, fight hard and dirty. Pay yourself before bill collectors. Go outside sometimes at night and see the moon. Drink water often. Never withhold love to punish somebody you love. Stick to your word-to see that you do, don't give it as often. Go barefoot in the grass. Lend an ear. Especially listen to those much older than you, they do know more. Have lots of sex when you know it's right. Rekindle old friendships. Applaud even small, sincere efforts. Don't throw away love letters. Shout "fire" not "help." Take long baths. Try to work less hours, except at what you love to do. Invite lots of folks to visit. Music goes with everything. Art often trumps science. Let someone romance you. Faith is really real, prayer works. Keep most things simple. There's more to you than the worst thing you've ever done. Have a child if you can, you'll never do anything better. Be a parent to someone in your lifetime regardless. Think village, not state. Be careful of your vices. Admire character. Imitate what you admire. Big usually means some waste. Obey your moral judgment before any law. Sit in candlelight when confused. Wait to marry your best friend. Share your gifts. Recognize goodness. Exercise. Learn more than I have. Always ask your mother.

You Can't Imagine: Letter to a Past Me

By James "Stretch" Arthur

Can you imagine a world made of concrete and steel,
Where humans bet on the next to be killed?

Can you imagine the sounds of madness, and its screams,
Where no one cares, much less, intervenes?

Can you imagine being lost, and forgotten?

Where saying, "Out of sight, out of mind" is common, and heard often?
Can you imagine seeing raw hate?

Over the color of one's skin, or the complexion of one's face?

Can you imagine being truly alone,

Where no one loves you, and there's no where to call home?
Can you imagine being conditioned in a way

That you ignore others being hurt; where you're programmed to stay out of their way?

Can you imagine a place where the time stands still
Yet the clock continues to tick on, year after year?

Can you imagine a planet where kindness is perceived
As a weakness, and exploited for another's gain?

Can you imagine being so numb, and dull
That you test the limits of physical pain?

Can you imagine a place where the morals of conduct no longer apply
And most will stay there until they die?

Can you imagine being the remnant of a distant memory
Where you're left out of your family's history?

Can you imagine your stories going untold?

As your child begins to grow old.

Can you imagine being surrounded by dust and mold

While wiping your nose as it drips from your tears and the cold?

And, as you sit within the walls of your tomb
And the depression starts to loom

While that guilt continues to consume you,
And these memories inside follow you to bed,

Your imagination endorses the war that goes on inside your head...

Can you imagine a weapon made of ink and tears?

Where your pen produces sentences in an attempt to neutralize your fears?

Try to imagine that pen as an instrument of peace,
Immersed within the pressure, searching for any release.

Now, awake from that dream, and KNOW that place is REAL.
You should NEVER assume you've won at life's cheap thrills!

See, when you think you have won you've really lost.

Because, in that world, the gain is hardly ever worth the cost.

A Distant Shore

By Aubrey Elwood

This experience like all others are among those needed by me to build strength and endurance. I firmly believe, cling to as a drowning man to a branch that: We attract those experiences and conditions needed for our continual growth, a process that starts before our physical birth. The plant she sends down her roots into Mother Earth thousands of tiny fibers silently, invisibly attracted to those substances required for her vigorous growth. We also send out roots, mental roots silently, invisibly attracted to those things needed for our continual growth. The plant grows because there is a vision in the seed of what she is to become. Mr. Oak Tree had the vision of a giant oak in the tiny acorn. We too grow because we have a vision, "where there is no vision the people perish". Growth is always towards a vision, to grow translates as; To Live. To live there must be a vision by which we are drawn (attracted to) The plants vision is much more than being a plant she makes it possible for the butterfly to be and the bird to be and the fox and wolf and yes even us. As we partake of the plant, we become entwined in the vision and cannot be separated from it.

Life does not exist except in growth.

I must believe in my own philosophy. How could I write about something I myself am unwilling to explore? I must believe in the God given vision as well as the faith to step out on the water. I cannot believe this vision would come without the ways and means and power to bring it into being. Those things that are most powerful are invisible, thought is invisible, mind is invisible, wind is invisible, electricity is invisible, yet we have faith in their power and can demonstrate it by the flipping of a switch. You do it all the time taking no thought of where and how it is, because it just is. The same as I just am.

Although I am here in a frail human form, I am powerful, because I have a vision. For me a vision is like the sail on a ship. By raising the sail and setting the rudder you have faith that the invisible will come and power you to your destination. You do not provide the wind! I believe, stake my life on, with a vision comes the ways and means (Power) to get me where I am going (Vision) So with the sails set full and both hands firmly on the helm I have faith the wind will come and I will sail into those uncharted waters, I will reach the distant shores... destiny and fate, my vision.

Aubrey Elwood is a freelance writer, and blogger who enjoys sharing his love of the written word with others. You can connect with Aubrey through his website www.drawigawidercircle.com or at: drawingawidercircle@gmail.com Corrlinks accepted.

Freebird Publishers

Presents Write & Get Paid

PERFECTION IS THE ENEMY

Now you can be the envy of every writer. Take control of your career today by dipping into this book. Write & Get Paid reveals the secrets to write what sells, find the best paying jobs, and get published regularly. You'll discover easy ways to turn your way with words into wads of cash.

- Write faster and better
- Receive international recognition and payment
- Get your readers to help sell your books
- Negotiate winning contracts
- Be the master of legal issues
- Publish yourself and take the tax breaks
- Get free publicity from other bestselling authors

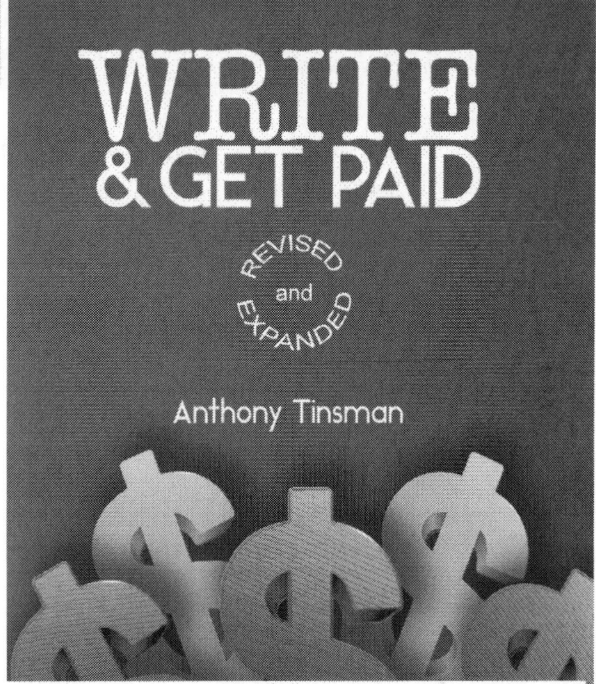

NEW REVISED & EXPANDED EDITION

A serious and easy to understand reference for writing, publishing, promotion, marketing and finding good jobs. It's perfect for writers working alone, students, or executives of publishing companies. *Write & Get Paid* will show you how to write your own ticket to happiness.

Write & Get Paid

Only **$22.99**

Plus $7 S/H with tracking

Softcover, Size 8" X 10", 175+ Pages, B&W

NO ORDER FORM NEEDED CLEARLY WRITE ON PAPER & SEND PAYMENT TO:

Freebird Publishers Box 541, North Dighton, MA 02764

Diane@FreebirdPublishers.com www.FreebirdPublishers.com

Toll Free: 888-712-1987 Text/Phone: 774-406-8682

PayPal VISA DISCOVER BANK

FORGET ME NOT

By Christopher L. Dixon

Time flies as the world turns
Well I stand alone to face the demons of my past
Karma waits in the shadows to teach lessons learned
And I pray the memory of me will last
Tomorrow is less of a struggle
Because yesterday was such a challenge
It's more comforting to forget then it is to remember
And easier for the heart to take the damage
Out of sight out of mind
Time healing the wounds of guilt
Absence completing the job of time
While life fills the gap's that have been built
Until I grace the ranks of freedom
Selfishly thinking that the world should stop
I have no right to ask such things
So I'll settle for you to forget me not.

CELEBRITY FEMALE STAR POWER

The Millionaire Prisoner's Address Book

Want to contact your favorite female celebrity? Ever wished you could write for a free photo, get an autograph, or letter back? But you didn't know how or where to send your letter? Well, now you can because this book shows you how!

Inside Celebrity Female Star Power, you learn how to:

★ Contact your favorite female celebrities and public personalities
★ Get free celebrity photos
★ Obtain autographs that you could sell
★ Use celebrity female and male birthdays (with over 2,300 birthdays!)
★ Over 4,500 female celebrity addresses including:
★ 2900 actresses (and porn stars)
★ 800+ athletes
★ 240+ models
★ 600+ musicians
★ 300+ writers
★ Real sample letters that you can use to write your letters!

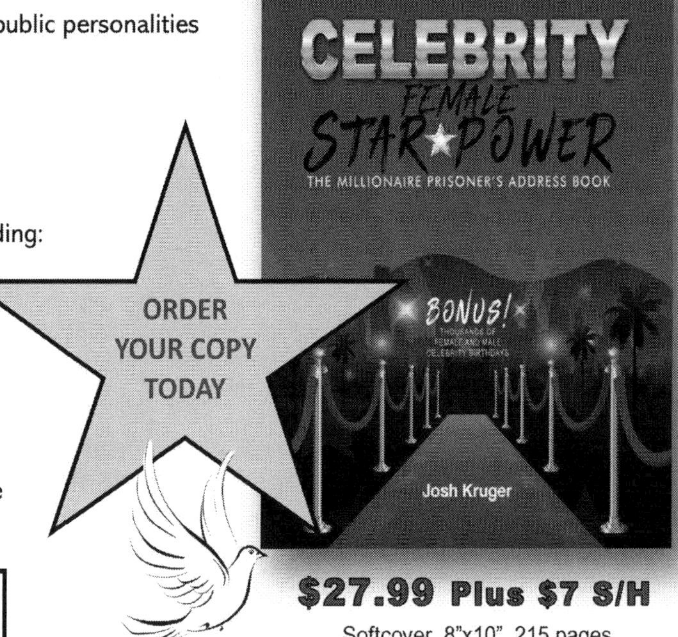

"Josh Kruger has done it again. Other companies may offer lists but nothing like the <u>thousands of addresses in this book. This book is worth hundreds of dollars!!</u> The price alone makes this book a steal. If you like celebs like I do, this book is a MUST have for you too." - A. Meyer, IL

$27.99 Plus $7 S/H

Softcover, 8"x10", 215 pages

CAUTION: **This book is only for those people who want to contact female celebrities and start getting responses today!**

<u>NO ORDER FORM NEEDED</u> Cleary Write On Paper & Send To:

FREEBIRD PUBLISHERS

Box 541, North Dighton, MA 02764 www.FreebirdPublishers.com

Diane@FreebirdPublishers.com Phone/Text 774-406-8682

We take all forms of payments. All credits cards, MoneyGram and PayPal.me/FreebirdPublishers

THE FAT BURNING SIX-PACK WORKOUT

The most effective regime is one that focuses on total-body workouts, which burn as many calories – and as much fat – in as little time as possible.

It's important that the exercises you choose work your "core" – the area from above your hips to below your pecs – so when the fat starts clearing, solid abs start appearing. It's equally important that the exercises you choose tax bigger (and therefore more calorie-guzzling) muscles at the same time.

Macaskill recommends some serious running training be incorporated into your program. "Interval sprints are a fantastic way of burning fat. Aim for short periods of rest and intense bursts of high intensity. Think how start-stop traffic burns the most fuel. Same deal here.

"To carry it further – the bigger the engine, the bigger the burn. Strength training is therefore crucial. A well designed strength program helps create a 'furnace effect' and keeps you burning calories for up to 24 hours. That's where you want to be."

TOOTHACHE?

Saline Wash

Combine half a teaspoon of salt in a cup of warm water and wash your mouth with it. Saline water has powerful cleansing qualities and can make you feel better in minutes. Using it as mouthwash can remove the harmful germs from your mouth. It also prevents your cheeks from getting swollen and makes your gums cleaner.

Hydrogen Peroxide

A hydrogen peroxide rinse may also help to relieve pain and inflammation. In addition to killing bacteria, hydrogen peroxide can reduce plaque and heal bleeding gums.

INTERMITTENT FASTING DIET METHODS

Lean Gains
- Fast for 16 Hours
- Eat within 8 hours (typically between 12-8 PM)
- Aim for largest meal post-workout
- Black coffee, tea, water and other calorie-free drinks are allowed.

Warrior
- Fast for 20 hours
- Eat within 4 hours (typically evening)
- This method is harder to adapt to

5:2
- Eat normally for 5 days
- Fast for 2 consecutive days
- Avoid overeating on normal days
- Avoid exercise on fasting days

A Dirty Fast
Most fasting methods encourage you to drink water only. A dirty fast allows you to include coffee and tea.

SIX OF THE WORST MISTAKES MEN MAKE IN BED

Not Manscaping
There are several advantages to regular manscaping. The first is that trimming the bush around the trunk generally makes the tree look bigger (if you get what we mean). The second is the other person is far likely to be more adventurous with their oral sex.

Overzealous Kisses
Kiss with passion, but don't cover the other person in saliva.

Skipping Foreplay
The more time you put into relaxing the other person and getting them in the mood, the more you will reap the rewards. Be patient and take your time: women generally need around 30 minutes to warm up in the bedroom, whereas guys take a lot less time.

Pumping Away Like A Pneumatic Drill
It's only going to make you come quickly, and who's that going to impress? For everyone's benefit, swap stabbing it around for the long game, with slow rhythmic thrust.

Coming First
You know how it's polite to let someone through the door before you? Well the same applies in the sheets – front door, back door, whichever you're dealing with. There's no bigger turn off than a selfish lover.

Porn-Star Sex
It's time we broke something to you. Porn sex, like wrestling and the tooth fairy, isn't real – and nothing good can come from thinking it is. That means not every person is going to want your ... stuff ... all over their face. We're humans, not actors.

CRAZY FACTS

If a part of your body falls asleep you can almost always wake it by shaking your head.

Putting dry tea bags in gym bags or smelly shoes will absorb the unpleasant odour.

Sleeping without a pillow reduces back pain and keeps your spine stronger.

There are at least 6 people in the world who look exactly like you. There's a 9% chance you'll meet one of them in your lifetime.

If you sit for more than 11 hours a day, there's a 50% chance you'll die within the next 3 years.

The smell of oranges and act of eating an orange can help reduce stress up to 70%.

DID YOU KNOW

There's a song that has been proven to reduce anxiety by 65%. It's called "Weightless" by Macaroni Union, and it was specifically designed to slow your heart rate, reduce blood pressure, and lower cortisol levels. It's so effective that it is dangerous to drive while listening to it, because it can make you drowsy.

The smell of chocolate increases theta brain waves, which triggers relaxation.

Anxiety affects your balance. When you experience severe levels of anxiety you can also have frequent balance problems or dizziness.

TOP TRENDING HAIRSTYLES

Waves + Low Fade

Waves + Low Fade

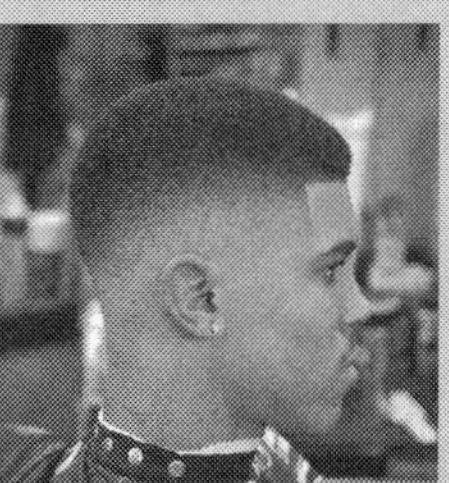

Short + Low Taper

Fade + Surgical Line

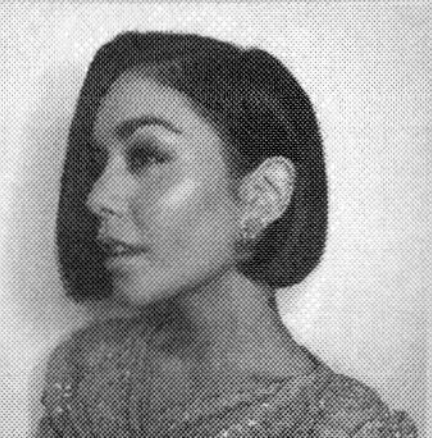

Rounded Bob

No-Fuss Lob

Textured Curls

STAY HEALTHY

» Drink plenty of water
» Be happy
» Sleep 8 hours
» Do cardio
» Don't drink fizzy drinks
» Brush your teeth
» Cut back on sugar
» Laugh
» Read
» Listen to music
» Walk
» Wash your hands
» Eat less salt
» Moisturize
» Stretch
» Eat nuts

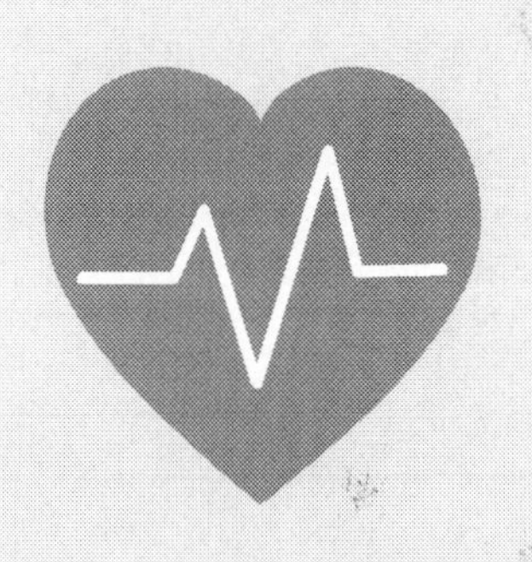

ROOT BEER FLOAT (Lactose Free)

By Goeorge Kayer

Ingredients:

1 Root Beer Soda
4 Coffee Creamers (Keefe now offers a variety of flavored creamers. Irish cream and Hazelnut are good choices for root beer.)

Directions:

(On Ice):

1. Pour 4 or more (to taste) creamers over ice in a cup.
2. Pour in root beer
3. Pour one creamer on top.

(In the Bottle)

1. Remove 3 to 4 ounces of root beer
2. Add 4 creamers of your choice
3. Do not shake; gently roll the bottle on a flat surface (table) until creamers are mixed in.

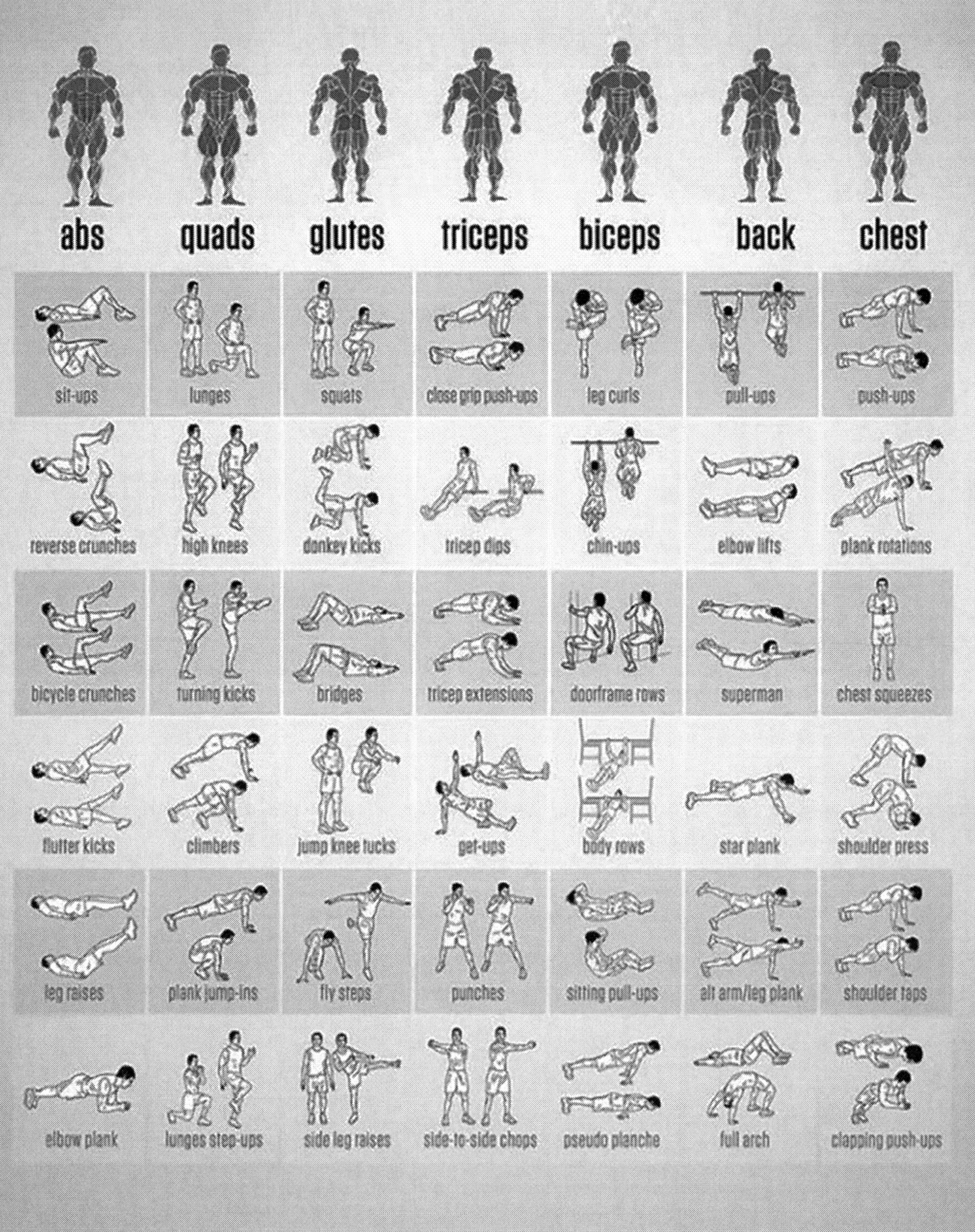
Bodyweight Exercises
abs
quads
glutes
triceps
biceps
back
chest
sit-ups
lunges
squats
close grip push-ups
leg curls
pull-ups
push-ups
reverse crunches
high knees
donkey kicks
tricep dips
chin-ups
elbow lifts
plank rotations
bicycle crunches
turning kicks
bridges
tricep extensions
doorframe rows
superman
chest squeezes
flutter kicks
climbers
jump knee tucks
get-ups
body rows
star plank
shoulder press
leg raises
plank jump-ins
fly steps
punches
sitting pull-ups
alt arm/leg plank
shoulder taps
elbow plank
lunges step-ups
side leg raises
side-to-side chops
pseudo planche
full arch
clapping push-ups

CHUNKY AND SPICY ONION SOUP (Serves 5)
By Patrick Bearup

Ingredients:
2 whole onions OR 2 1/2 bottles of dehydrated chopped onions
1/4 cup instant milk OR poultry gravy
1/4 cup chopped jalapeños
1 cup chopped celery
1 bag instant rice
1 instant soup
1 ranch dressing mix
2 cheder squeeze cheese
3 tsp butter
2 tsp garlic
4 tsp jalapeño salsa

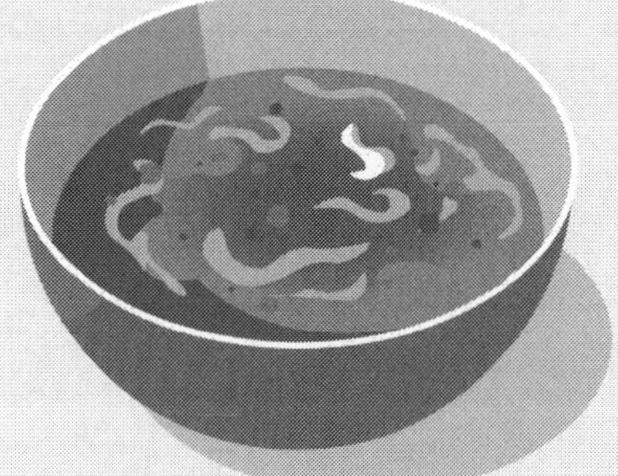

Directions:
1. Wash and chop all veggies; place in large bowl
2. Mix in salsa, cheese, ranch mix, and garlic
3. Add 4 cups of water
4. Boil until onions are clear and veggies are tender
5. Add 1/4 cup powdered milk
6. Mix in rice and noodles
7. Add butter and let sit for 10 minutes in covered bowl
8. Serve it up with your favorite sprinkles, croutons, or crackers on top.

WORKOUT CHILI (106 grams protein)
By George Kayer

Ingredients:	Grams of protein:
2 Chili with Beans (11.25 oz size)	38
1 Beef Crumbles - Spicy (6 oz size)	37
1 Jerk Pork (5 oz size)	27
1 Squeeze Cheese	4
	Total – 106 grams

Note: You may substitute one pack of Vienna sausages for the jerk pork, for a less-spicy version

Directions:
1. Heat up all ingredients in individual packages or in a 1 1/2 qt. pot.
2. Stir well.
3. Serve it up in two bowls
4. Top with favorite crackers and squeeze a few lines of cheese over the top.

SCUM

Scum is a card game based on the ideals of cutthroat American Capitalism: to wit, the rich get richer, and the poor ... well, don't be poor.

Scum works best for four players, but it is possible to play with more. For reasons that will become clear later, you will need at least four to play.

Scum can be played with pretty much any deck of cards that has a definite hierarchy (*i.e.*, Ace is highest, then King, then Queen, and so on down to Two) and two wild cards. For example, I learned to play with a Rook© deck. For the purposes of this presentation, I will assume you're using a standard deck (the kind used to play poker) with two jokers. You can adjust for other decks as necessary. If for some reason you find that you're not playing with a full deck, well, I can't help you.

There are four positions that the players will fill while playing Scum. They are, in descending order of importance and desirability: President, Manager, Worker, and Scum. The object of the game is to rise above your fellow players to become President. Once you have reached that position, your object is to stay there.

A word is in order now about the poor schmuck ... that is, the player who is Scum. This player is responsible for all the dirty work in the game. Scum has to shuffle and deal the cards between games, and also has to pick up the cards between tricks. In addition, Scum is most likely going to be the target of a lot of abuse during the course of play. So why play? Because, to rephrase the Law of Conservation of Angular Momentum, "What goes around comes around." The player who is Scum this game may be President next time around, and vice versa.

The object of each round is to be the first player to get rid of all their cards. This player then becomes President for the next round. The next player to get rid of all their cards is Manager, and the next is Worker. The last one still holding cards – you guessed it – is Scum.

Before the game starts, it will be necessary to determine who will fill what positions for the first trick. How you do this is entirely your prerogative. We usually draw cards at random from the deck, with the highest being President and the lowest being Scum. You can also determine the opening positions alphabetically, by height, by arm wrestling, by Rock-Paper-Scissors, or by any other method you choose. Once the opening roles are determined, the players should sit in a circle – preferably around a table of some sort – in descending order. This will place Scum and President next to each other, by the way. (If possible, try to enhance the mood by having chairs appropriate to each position, such as a La-Z-Boy recliner for the Prez, one of those intolerable metal folding chairs for Scum, and that sort of thing.)

The round begins when all players are seated and all the cards are dealt. In dealing the cards, Scum first deals to Worker, then to himself, then to President, then to Manager, and so on, until all the cards are dealt. The observant reader will note that this means Worker and Scum already have one more card to get rid of than President and Manager. But wait, there's more.

The hierarchy of cards is as follows: Joker is highest, followed by Ace, King, Queen, Jack, 10, 9, 8, 7, 6, 5, 4, 3, with 2 as the lowest. I thought I'd mention this now, because after the cards are dealt, Worker has to give the highest card in his hand to Manager. That's right, the highest card, no questions asked. Manager then gives one card she doesn't want (not necessarily the lowest, mind you) to Worker. Now, Scum, before you laugh, you should know that you have to do the same with President, except you have to give him your two highest cards, and you'll get back two cards the President doesn't want.

Now game play begins. The President leads on the first trick; after that, the last player to play on the previous trick leads. The leader will play one or more cards. The next player in line must then beat that play. This is done by playing a higher card or combination of cards. Matching is not enough; a player must play something higher. That is to say, you can't play a 5 if the player before you played a 5. You must play a 6 or higher. The same applies with pairs, triples, and four-of-a-kinds. If that player cannot beat the play, they pass to the next player. They may also pass if they feel it is to their strategic advantage to do so. When all four players have had a chance to play, the trick is over, and Scum clears the table. The last player to lay down a card (or cards) leads the next trick.

It is important to note that a player must always play the same number of cards as the player before him. For example, if one player lays down a 6, the next player must lay down a 7 or higher. If the player lays down three 4's, the next player must lay down three 5's or higher. A single must be beaten with a higher single, a pair with a higher pair, and so on. The only exception is that a single Joker will beat any other play. A Joker will, for instance, beat four Aces. Consequently, when a Joker is played, the trick is over. Players must stick to 'sets'; that is to say, a player can never lay down more than one card with different values. For instance, a player cannot lay down a 5 and a 7 to try to beat a pair of 4's. Any player who attempts to do this should be treated like Scum.

Here is a description of a couple of tricks, just to help you get the concepts down:

1. President opens the game by playing a 6. Manager follows by playing an 8. Worker plays a 9, and Scum plays a Jack. Scum then cleans up the cards before the others start taunting him.
2. Scum leads off the next trick with three 6's. President passes, having no triples. Manager has three Jacks but wants to save them for later in the game; she also passes. Worker plays three 9's. Scum is a little slow getting the trick cleared, and Manager says, "Pick it up, Scum!"
3. Worker plays a pair or 8's. Scum follows with a pair of Queens. President, who has a hand full of singles and is sick of all the multiples being played, throws down a Joker. Manager silently laments the pair of Kings she can't play this trick. Scum cleans up the cards, and President will lead the next trick.

BASIC ONION SOUP

By Mike White

Ingredients:

2 beef bullion cubes or 3 tsp brown gravy mix
1 1/2 tsp onion powder
1/2 tsp garlic powder
1/4 tsp Ms. Dash (original blend)
1 or 2 onion(s), minced, (fresh onion)

Directions:

1. In a pan or microwavable bowl add 6 cups of water and rest of ingredients above.
2. Bring to a boil then simmer for 30 minutes.
3. Stir every 5 to 8 minutes

Serving Tips:

The onions will sink to the bottom, so be sure to scoop equal amounts into each bowl. Top with croutons and favorite cheese.

LIFE HACKS

- Get a stuck zipper unstuck by rubbing some crayon on both sides of the zipper.
- You can un-shrink a sweater by soaking it in warm water and hair conditioner for a few minutes.
- Use a razor and "shave" sweatshirts to get rid of pills.
- To quickly remove wrinkles from a shirt place the garment on a clean surface and place a damp towel flat on top of the garment. Using your hands press down on the towel and smooth out wrinkled areas with your hands.
- Baby powder works wonders at getting oil stains out of your clothes. For optimal results, brush or shake on powder, sweep off excess and then let the powder sit for several minutes.
- Stop smelly shoes by placing dry tea bags inside them.
- OR use dryer sheets to remove the odor and give them a fresh smell.

DO YOU KNOW THESE SURPRISING HEALTH FACTS?

With new studies and reports being released daily, it can be hard to keep track of what's new in health and wellness. To help you stay on top of your health knowledge we've put together 10 health-related facts that just might surprise you.

10. Drink something hot to cool down
Conventional wisdom may tell you that if you are hot, drinking something cold will cool down your body. However, research has shown that on a hot day, drinking a hot beverage may help your body stay cool. The reason being that when you drink a hot drink, your body produces sweat to cool down your body temperature. Initially you may be adding heat by drinking the hot liquid, but the amount of sweat that your body produces to cool down more than makes up for the added heat from the liquid. The increased perspiration is key; when the sweat evaporates from your skin, it is able to cool down your body temperature.

9. Your sweat is mostly made up of water
Speaking of sweat, our sweat is composed mostly of water – about 99 percent! How much we sweat is unique to each individual; factors like gender and/or age can contribute to a person sweating more or less.

8. The strongest muscle in your body is ...
Our muscle strength can be measured in different ways. If you are referring to the muscle that can exert the most force, then your calf muscle, the soleus, would be the winner. However, if you want to find the muscle that can exert the most pressure, then the jaw muscle, or the masseter, would be the strongest. The human jaw can close teeth with a force as great as 200 pounds, or 890 newtons!

7. More than half your bones are located in your hands and feet
We are born with approximately 300 bones and cartilage, which eventually fuse together by the time we reach adulthood. The adult human body consists of 206 bones. Of these bones, 106 of them are located in our hands and feet. Bones in the arms are among the most commonly broken bones and account for almost half of all adults' bone injuries.

6. You can physically see high cholesterol
It is possible to see signs on your body that you may have high cholesterol. Xanthelasmata, or xanthelasma, are cholesterol-filled bumps that form under your skin. It can be an indicator of possible heart disease. The lesions can be found all over the body and tend to appear on the skin of older people with diabetes or other heart ailments.

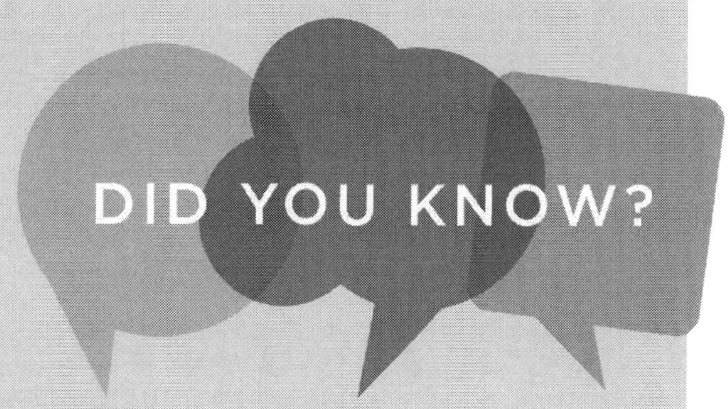

5. Cholesterol-free can be bad for your cholesterol
Food labels may say that it is cholesterol-free, however, that does not mean that the food is good for your cholesterol levels. Trans fats, which are cholesterol-raising, naturally have no cholesterol but can be detrimental to your cholesterol levels. Trans fats can be found in many fried foods and baked goods. Trans fat, such as partially hydrogenated vegetable oils, and saturated fats are not good for your cholesterol levels and should be avoided as much as possible.

4. If you are tired, exercise will help
If you are physically tired, the best thing to do is exercise as it will give you more energy than sitting. Studies have found that the blood and oxygen flow through the body will give you more energy and improve your mood. The increase in endorphin levels can contribute to a feeling of well-being.

3. Cold temperature can be good for your health
If you live in Canada, you know all about cold weather. But did you know that colder temperatures can benefit your health? Colder temperatures may help reduce allergies and inflammation and research has shown that it can help you think more clearly and perform daily tasks better. The cold can also help lower the risk of disease; mosquitoes that carry diseases such as Zika, West Nile virus and malaria are not around during the winter season.

2. **Bananas can help improve your mood**

A banana has approximately 30% of your daily recommended intake of vitamin B6. Vitamin B6 helps the brain produce serotonin, which is considered a mood stabilizer. Serotonin impacts your motor skills and emotions. It is also the chemical that helps you sleep and digest food. Eating a banana can help relieve depression and anxiety by stimulating the serotonin levels in your body.

1. **Optimism may help you live longer**

Can seeing the glass half full help you live longer? Studies have found that there is a correlation between increasing levels of optimism with decreasing levels of death from cancer, disease, infection and stroke. This is particularly true for cases of cardiovascular disease. Those who had the highest levels of optimism had an almost 40% lower risk of heart disease.

HOW TO: FIND THE BEST BEARD STYLE FOR YOUR FACE SHAPE

Distinct face shapes call for different beard styles. These rules will help you achieve what we like to call the "optimal beard."

When it comes to facial hair styles, here is the guiding principal to keep in mind: Your beard and your jaw should work in tandem to achieve a nicely graduated, oval shape. If you have a square or round jaw, you'll want to grow your beard fuller on the bottom to elongate your face. If you have an oblong or rectangular face, you'll want more hair on the sides while avoiding more length beneath the chin.

Square Face
Keep hair fuller on the chin, shorter on the sides.

Round Face
Grow hair longer on the bottom, shorter on the sides.

Oblong or Rectangular Face
Keep the sides fuller, and the bottom shorter.

Oval Face
Oval faces are a middle ground between the other shapes, so most styles will work well.

THE BEST TATTOO IDEAS FOR MEN, ACCORDING TO A CELEBRITY TATTOO ARTIST

Animals
Animals that have presence or represent admirable traits, like lions, eagles, bears, or leopards. These are often the animals that the wearer might identify his "spirit animal."

Portraits
Tattoos of loved ones and icons (like rock stars, actors, and athletes) are especially common with male clients. Similar to a spirit animal, the wearer of a portrait tattoo wants to honor the legacy of the person he preserves in ink.

Lettering
Lettering always has been popular, and always will be. You can work with your artist to find the font and lettering style that suits your taste. And the tattoo itself can be as simple as a significant date, a quote, a loved one's name, or a significant word.

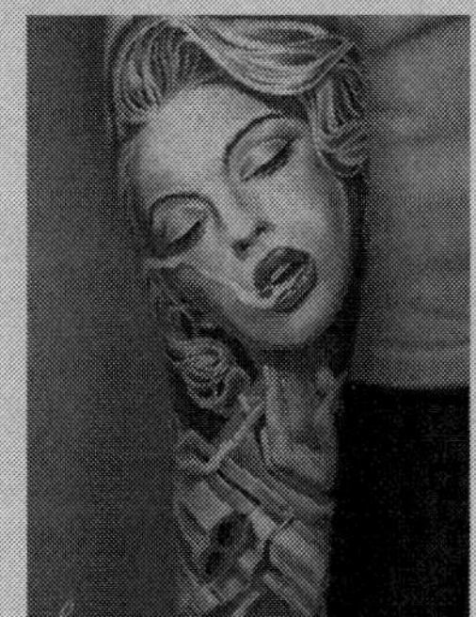

APPEARANCE HACKS FOR THE MODERN MAN

Hair
Tailor your haircut to your face shape. If you have a rounder face, get a haircut that's tighter on the sides. If you have a longer face, ask for longer hair on the sides and around your temples. Wash your hair three times a week.

Shaving
The basicity of liquid and bar soap dries your skin out and leaves it rough. Use a non-soap cleanser before shaving.

Shirts
Roll your sleeves correctly. Flip the cuff back and pull it to just below your elbow. Then take the bottom (inside out portion) and fold it up so it traps and covers the bottom cuff.

Suit Jackets
The top should sometimes be buttoned, the middle should always be buttoned and the last should never be buttoned. Always use cedar wood hangers to avoid moths and absorb moisture.

Shoes
After washing shoes, tuck shoelaces into the dryer door before drying. This will keep them from tumbling and avoid damage.

EASY ENOUGH UP-DOS FOR WOMEN

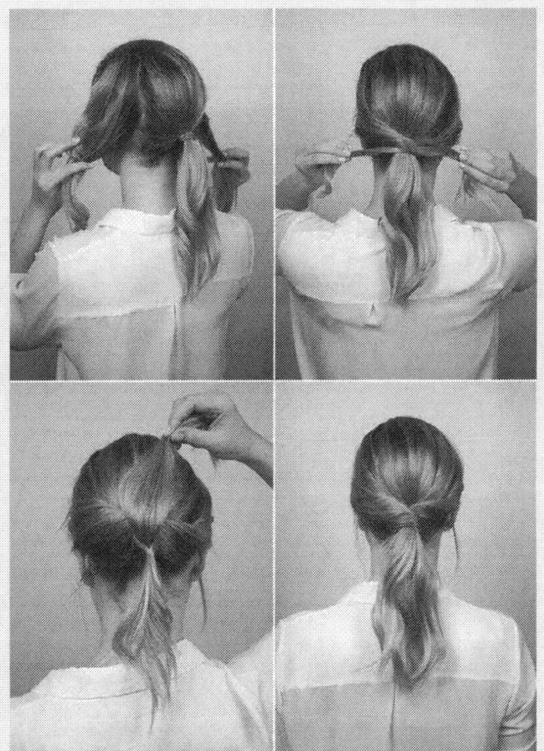

TATTOO FACTS

- According to a survey, more women than men in the U.S. have tattoos.
- Your skin is Pierced 50 to 300 times per minute by the tattoo machine when you get a tattoo.
- American's spend a staggering $1.65 billion on tattoos per year.
- The most popular tattoo images are angels and hearts.
- A tattoo is etched in the second layer of the skin called the dermis. The cells of the dermmis are more stable than those of the epidermis.
- 'Tattoo' is one of the most misspelled words in the English language.
- Laser surgery is the most effective tattoo removal technique. Black is the easiest color to remove while green and yellow are the most difficult.

TO WASH OR NOT TO WASH

According to Who What Wear, you should be washing jeans every four or five wears, because anything else will fade the dye. They should also be washed in cold water instead of chucked in with a normal wash.

The CEO of Levi's, Chip Bergh, caused controversy when he claimed people should never wash their jeans.

PRISON LEGAL GUIDE

The Facts You Need To Succeed In The Judicial Arena

THIS BOOK IS A "MUST HAVE" SURVIVAL TOOL THAT EVERY INMATE NEEDS! KNOW YOUR CIVIL RIGHTS AND THE PROCEDURES THAT CAN BRING YOU THE WIN!

U.S. law is complex, complicated, and always growing and changing, and many prisoners spend days on end digging through its intricacies. Pile on top of the legal code the rules and regulations of a correctional facility, and you can see how well the deck is being stacked against you. Information is the key to your survival when you have run afoul of the system (or it is running afoul of you). Whether you are an accomplished jailhouse lawyer helping newbies learn the ropes, an old head fighting bare-knuckle for your rights in the courts, or an inmate just looking to beat the latest write-up – this book has something for you. Freebird Publishers has drawn from the best legal offerings of the Lewisburg Prison Project, to put together this comprehensive guide to your legal rights. With this information in hand, you are well equipped to beat the charge or fight back against the persecution.

There are many of us out here on your side. Never give up the fight.

LEARN ABOUT

- Litigation
- First Amendment
- Status
- Due Process In Prison
- Cruel and Unusual Punishment
- Medical Care
- Post Conviction

Civil Action in Federal Court, Legal Research, Access Records, Federal Tort Claims Act, Injunctive Relief, Religious Rights in Prison, Speech, Visitations, Association, Rights of Pretrial Detainees, Disciplinary Hearings, Urinalysis Drug Testing, Assault and Beatings, Conditions of Confinement, Medical Rights, Psychiatric and Disability Rights, AIDS in Prison, Post-Conviction Remedies, Detainers (Choices and Strategies), PA Megan Law, DNA Collection and Testing and more.

<u>NO ORDER FORM NEEDED</u>

On paper clearly write your full contact information and product info.

PRISON LEGAL GUIDE

Only $24.99

plus $7 s/h with tracking

Softcover, 8" x 10" 210+ pages

FREEBIRD PUBLISHERS

PO Box 541,
North Dighton, MA 02764
www.FreebirdPublishers.com
or Amazon.com
Diane@FreebirdPublishers.com
We accept all forms of payment

amazon.com

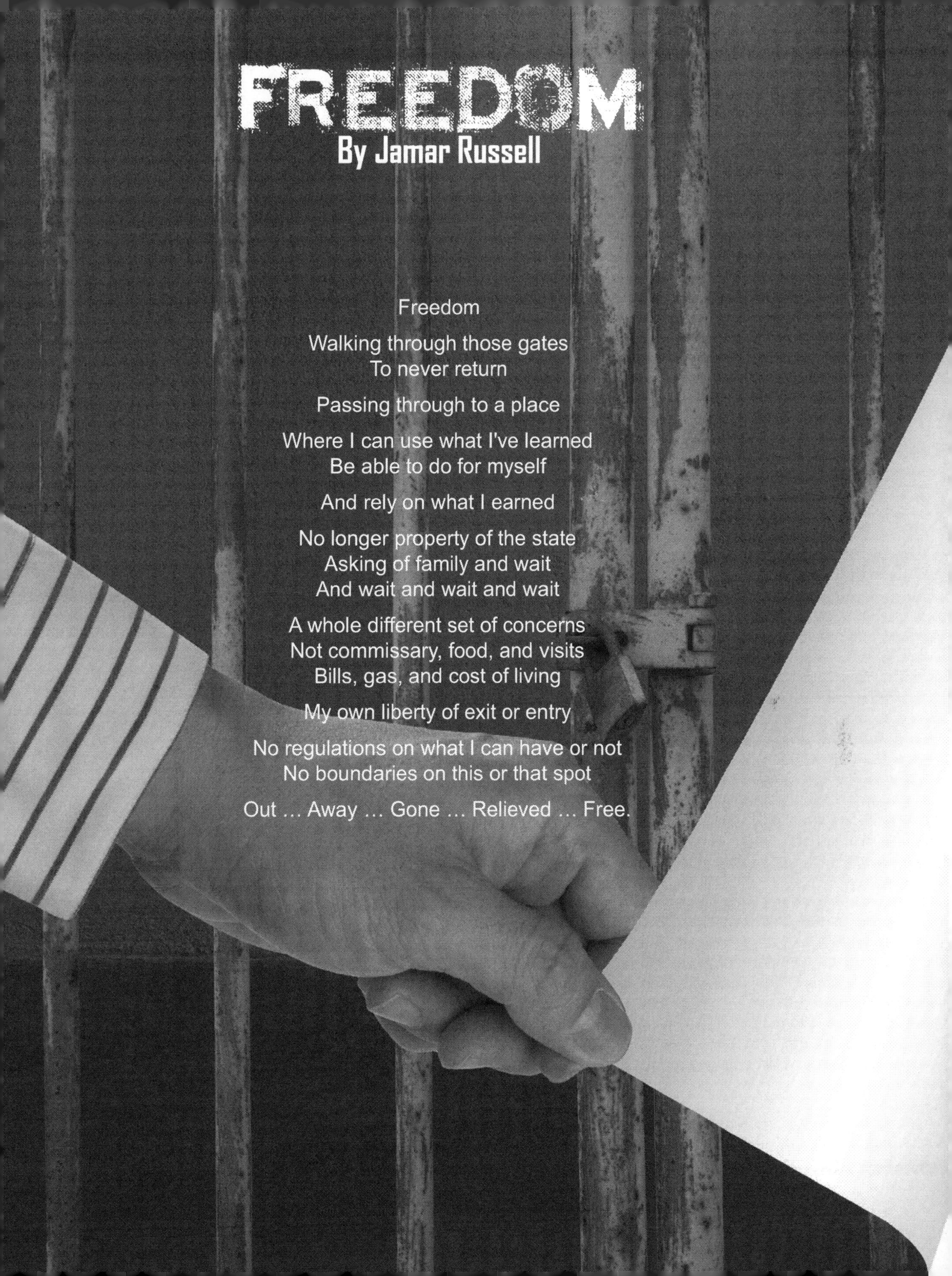

FREEDOM

By Jamar Russell

Freedom

Walking through those gates
To never return

Passing through to a place

Where I can use what I've learned
Be able to do for myself

And rely on what I earned

No longer property of the state
Asking of family and wait
And wait and wait and wait

A whole different set of concerns
Not commissary, food, and visits
Bills, gas, and cost of living

My own liberty of exit or entry

No regulations on what I can have or not
No boundaries on this or that spot

Out … Away … Gone … Relieved … Free.

THE DAY I FOUND OUT I WAS WHITE

By T. Michael Fox

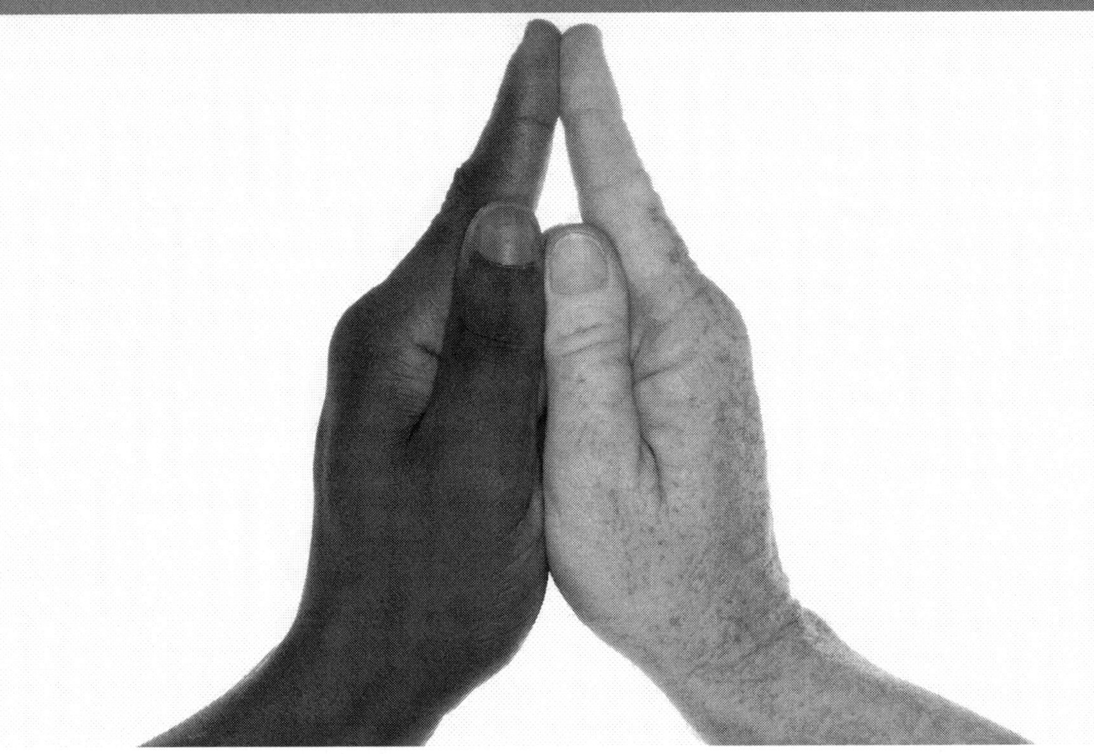

Tommy Fox was a young boy raised on a farm in up-state Illinois, about 45 minutes northwest of Chicago on the Wisconsin border. He was outgoing and friendly, small for his age with bright blue eyes and wispy white hair, cut short. Tommy spent the first eight years of his life doing what most young children do: he explored his world in an ever-widening circle of mischief and amusement. These years on the farm were both isolating and insulating.

Born in 1958, Tommy only left the farm to go into the small farming town of Woodstock, Illinois, it's population in those days less than three thousand people. Woodstock was nothing more than a town-center square, with a handful of other small streets surrounded by small rolling hills, forests, and farmland. There was only one other town up the train tracks from Woodstock – Harvard, Illinois, and that is where the trains were parked at night.

Tommy loved the wide-open spaces, all the animals, and even the chores, most of which consisted of gathering eggs, milking the cow, and feeding the other animals.

Tommy's grandparents, Anna and George Fox, lived in Chicago. To Tommy, Chicago was like a whole other planet: noisy, dirty, filled with cement and streets going in every direction, for as far as the eye could see.

One day in the summer of 1963, just after Tommy's fifth birthday, his father had to go to the hospital for some tests. Tommy's mother decided it was time for him to visit his grandparents in Chicago. Tommy's mother, Pat, was a big woman who worked hard all day to tend to the house and the farm. Pat had already asked the conductor on the commuter train in advance to look after Tommy, who was going to be traveling alone.

The conductor was an older man with a big toothy grin and lots of stories about trains. He dressed in a classic train conductor's uniform, all spit and polished, with a fancy over-sized pocket watch hanging from a bob in his vest pocket. He sat with Tommy all the way to Chicago, telling him stories about all the places and things going by outside the train's window. The conductor handed Tommy off to Tommy's Grandma Fox, who was waiting for them with a taxi at the train platform.

Grandma Fox was 75 years old and very frail looking. She looked like a strong Chicago wind could carry her away, but she was energetic and spry. Grandma Fox would live to be a hundred years old. The last twenty of those years would be spent alone in her own apartment. But in 1963, she still had her husband, George.

Grandpa George Fox was a fourth generation Chicago resident, a retired bookkeeper for an import/export company called National Tea. The opposite of Grandma, he never got out much and spent most of his time in his favorite chair in their second-floor flat. From his chair he could watch the street below, look through the kitchen out the back door, quietly read, listen to the radio, or just sit and smoke his pipe.

That first night in Chicago, Grandma fixed a nice dinner of corned beef and cabbage. Then Tommy sat and listened to Grandma play the piano, and they all sang old folk songs.

The next morning Grandma had to go to the church two blocks away, called St. Sabina's. The church and the neighborhood looked like they had been there for as long as Grandma had been alive, maybe even longer. South Throop Street and 78th Place was a tree-lined, brick and brown stone, Victorian-style neighborhood. It was quiet and well kept, but in steady decline.

Grandma asked Tommy to walk her to the church so she could talk to someone there about coming over regularly to bring communion to Grandpa. When they got there, Grandma told Tommy to play in the playground just outside the back door to the church, and she went inside. Grandma was not inside long, and when she came out, she found Tommy playing on the swings. A look of melancholy came over her. "Are you sad, Grandma?" Tommy said. "No, little one. It is just that your father used to pick that very same swing when he went to school here. He was a little older than you are now, back then," Grandma said.

While walking back to Grandma's house, Tommy had trouble keeping up. As little as Grandma was, she was a fast walker, and Tommy's had to put his little legs into overdrive to keep pace.

Playing by himself in front of one of the old brick, three-story buildings, two doors from Grandma's house was another little boy. When he looked up and saw grandma coming he looked really happy to see her and waved saying, "Hi, Misses Fox." Grandma motioned him over and said, "Amos I want you to meet my grandson, Tommy." Amos Moses was maybe a year or two older than Tommy, but not much bigger. He was dressed in cutoff jeans and a well-played-in, old faded green T-shirt, bare footed with a crew cut style haircut. He came running up to Grandma Fox and Tommy, with a big grin on his face. He was very friendly and polite.

Grandma introduced Tommy and Amos to each other, and asked Amos if he had eaten his lunch yet. Amos said, "No ma'am, sure haven't." "Well the two of you go up to the house, and I'll go tell your mother where you are at." Grandma went around the back of Amos' house and up the back steps to the second floor. She reached for the screen door that lead to the kitchen. "Yoo whoo, Dorothy, it's me."

Dorothy Moses, Amos' mom, was standing inside her kitchen wearing a sun dress adorned with yellow flowers and green leaves. The dress was long past her knees, covered in front by a grey and black apron, and she wore a yellow scarf over her hair. She was nice looking, in her 30s, and was pulling something out of the oven. "Oh, hi Anna, I was just baking a little bread for tonight. Nice to see you, how have you been?" she said. "Oh, as good as it gets for me, I suppose. I wanted to tell you that I have Amos for lunch. If you need him just call," Grandma said. "Oh, is that boy bothering you again," Dorothy asked. "Oh no, heavens to betsy, he is never a bother. Pa'pa and I enjoy his company. It's just that my grandson Tommy is going to be with us for a while, and I invited Amos to spend some time with us, you know, to see if the boys may keep each other company," Grandma said. "Oh, your grandson, you must send him over sometime so I can meet him. Don't let Amos be a pest now. I will call if I need him," Dorothy said.

Amos and Tommy became fast friends. Amos was an only child just like Tommy, and while Grandma got lunch ready the boys went down into the basement to explore. The unfinished basement smelled of damp dirt, dust and moist stale air. In the corner, gathering dust, rust, and cobwebs was a long wooden box that looked as though it had been there since the house above it was built, filled with toys and other junk from some by-gone era. Next to the box was an old peddle car hanging from a hook, an army trunk with a lock on it, and all sorts of old things gathering dust. On top of the pile of stuff in the box was an old metal model airplane. Well played with, and now forgotten it was the first thing to come out of the box, along with a small model car, also made of metal. Tommy, and Amos brought the toys up into the light, and the back yard of grandma's house. Grandma came out on the porch and looked down at the kids playing with the toys rescued from oblivion, and once again a strange sort of sadness took root on her face. "Where did you boys find those things?" She asked. Amos pointed at the door that led down to the basement. Grandma said, "Oh my, you boys shouldn't go down there… might be creatures down there. Little boys could get eaten up."

Grandma came down to hang some laundry on the clothesline, and told the boys that lunch was on the table up-stairs. Grandpa George was sitting in the living room, in his chair smoking his pipe when the boys came running in from outside. Grandpa sat up on the edge of the chair, and said, "Aye looky 'ere now w'at tis it that the cat 'as drugen, 'ow ya laddies a doin'?" Amos went into the living room with Tommy right behind, and said, "Hi, Mr. Fox, got any chores for me to do today?" "No, mee boy, not ta-day. Still saven up for that t'ing-a-ma-bod is ya?" "Yes sir, I almost got enough for that yo-yo, just a few more chores, and my dad will let me buy one. "He said if I wanted one, I would have to earn the money myself." Amos boasted. Grandpa stood up, and said, "I 'eard ta: two of yahs wit' ta misses, be getten along alright are" yas, getten inta a bit of the mischief is it?" Tommy said, "No, Grandpa, just playing with some of the toys from the box in the basement." Grandpa smiled, and said, "o' t'at ol' stuff tis it, I t'out Ida gotten rid of t'ose t'ings years ago. Amos mee lad 'ow's that ma'ma of yours?" "She is just fine, sir." Amos said. "Shore, an be gorra now, ya boys need ta wash the cobwebs off 'for ya eats, run along now." Grandpa said as he got up from his chair, he sat down his pipe, and added, "Let us now see 'ere w'at tis it the misses 'as got for us men ta eat. Leftovers tis it now. Cabbage soup, corned beef on homemade pumpernickel bread. A good ol' fashion supper of kings tis it." They all sat down, and Grandma joined them. After saying grace, all ate their fill. The meal took a bit longer because Grandpa had to tell the boys at least one story, this one was about the toys they had been playing with.

“Tommy, mee lad, t'ose toys belonged ta ye father. We give 'im t'ose one every Christmas, till 'ee no longer a played wit' 'em. Now ta misses hides 'em aways in the dark. Tis a pleasure ta see 'em 'ave a bit o' life again, doun't cha know." Suddenly the phone rang. Grandma hurried to answer it as the boys cleared the plates and went to go back outside. "Ok, sure he is right here, Dorothy, I'll send him on his way, oh you're welcome, Amos is always a bright spot in our day, and he, and Tommy seem to be getting along just great. Ok, bye now." Grandma hung up the phone and said, "Amos, your mom needs you to come home, and finish your chores before your father gets home."

"Shore now were tis ta fire?" Grandpa said. "I got to run Mr. Fox; my ma'ma needs me. Thank you for the soup, and sandwich, ma'am." And with that Amos, and Tommy went to run out the door.
"Hey where do you think you are going, mister?" Grandma said to Tommy. "Amos has chores to do for his mom, and you need to put those things back where you found them. You can play later." "See you, Amos." Tommy said.

Tommy was happy to have a new friend, any friend. Life for Tommy back in Woodstock, on the farm was a bit lonesome, with no other kids to play with. It would still be a few months before he would meet others at pre-school, or kindergarten, and maybe a year, or two before other kids moved onto the road where the farm was. So, Tommy was missing his friend Amos almost as soon as he was gone. After supper Grandpa told stories till Tommy fell asleep.

Tommy being a farm boy was up before dawn, but so was grandma, they helped each other fix something for breakfast. While they were making toast on the fire there came a knock on the back door. Grandma said, "Who I wonder could that be?” And she winked at Tommy. Tommy opened the door, and there stood Amos, still wearing the same clothes he had on the day before, "I could smell the bacon as soon as I got to the street. Can you come out, and play?” Amos said.

"Aye, w'at tis all the shenanigans so early in the day it tis? Oh, sure it be thee wee lads, I felt fa shore it twas leprechauns. Ya know? How ye be Amos ma boy?" Grandpa said, as he came around the corner from the bedroom. "It appears we have yet another for breakfast, Pa'pa." Grandma said. "Tommy invite your friend in for breakfast." She added with a wink to Amos. Tommy looked at Amos and asked if he was hungry. "Oh yes." He said, adding shyly, "Mrs. Fox do you have any of those biscuits, you always have!" "Oh no, not today Amos, but we do have fresh baked bread, and Tommy has been making toast on the fire. You can help him if you like." Grandma said.

Both boys spent the morning together. Then about noon the hot summer sun began to make the asphalt soft, and sticky. The breeze from Lake Michigan was not so cooling as most days. The boys discovered the comfort of a garden sprinkler, and Amos asked Tommy if he would like to come over to his house. Tommy looked over at Grandma, and she said yes. Then they were gone. Grandpa looked up from his paper, and said, "Sure tis a good feelin' ta have the sound of wee ones around again, tis it not ma'ma?" Grandma reached over and squeezed the old man's hand.

Down the back alley, over two houses, and up the back stairs of Amos' house the boys ran. There just inside the back door was Dorothy Moses; Amos' mom. She had on a bright yellow dress with white trim, and a red, and black checked apron. She had her head wrapped in a green, and yellow scarf, and she was taking cookies out of the oven. The kitchen smelled wonderful. Mrs. Moses looked up and was very surprised to see Tommy. "Oh, I bet I know who this is." She said. "You must be Anna's grandson, Tommy, aren't you child?" She added. "Yes ma'am." Tommy said a bit shyly. "You know I bet your daddy's name is George, isn't it?" She said. Tommy brightened up and said yes. Mrs. Moses explained how she had known his father when he was just a teenager. And how she had even been to his father's wedding when she was only 16, in 1947. "My ma'ma worked for your grandma, and grandpa." Mrs. Moses said, adding "My ma'ma took care of your daddy when he was a baby. When my ma'ma died, she left me this house. All of us, your grandparents, and the Morriseys next door have been neighbors fifty years or more. Not many people left around here from back then."

"You know my Uncle Tom, and Aunt Florence too?" Tommy asked. "Oh yes child, but they are not really your aunt and uncle, are they?" Then she added, "Tommy Morrisey was your father's best friend growing up, and Florence is his mom." "Uncle Tom is my godfather, I was named Tommy because of him, and I do not know why I call Aunt Florence my aunt," "Oh I can guess at that one Tommy" Mrs. Moses said. "Your grandma and Florence grew up together, they were best friends, like sisters, before either of them grew up, and got married,"

"Here are some cookies, and lemonade; just made them. You boys take them cookie outside, so you don't make a mess on my clean floor. Go now, I have dinner to worry about," Tommy and Amos went outside, and sat down on the front steps of the house, a bit sooty from coal fired boilers in the neighborhood.

When they were done with their snack Tommy started to go back inside with his glass, but Amos stopped him. "My pops is home now so we can't go inside." Tommy asked why, and Amos told him it was because he was white, and his pops didn't like white folks much. The boys sat the empty glasses down on the steps and started to walk back down to Tommy's grandparent's house. "What do you mean, I'm white?" Tommy asked, Amos grabbed Tommy's arm, and held it next to his own, and said, "Look see here, you're white, I'm black." Tommy was confused, and said, "You are not black, that soot there on the sidewalk is black. You are brown." "Oh yeah, but you are still white." Amos quipped. Tommy was about to say something when Mrs. Moses called Amos in for dinner. A feeling of uneasiness, dread came over Tommy, confused, and a bit hurt Tommy went up the steps, and into grandma's house. Slowly he walked through the kitchen, thinking hard on what had just happened. "Child what is wrong? It looks like you have swallowed a lemon. You're not sick, are you?" Grandma said. "Grandma" Tommy said sadly, "Am I white?" Grandpa piped in, and said, "Auck, child you is Irish, and we Irish tend ta be a bit oh pink doun't cha know, and the Scottish they be pale blue." "Oh, stop teasing the boy, Pa'pa, can't you see he is troubled. Child, tell grandma where is it that you heard you were white."

"Amos' daddy got home, and Amos said he didn't like white folks, and we had to go play someplace else." Tommy spit out these words almost crying. Grandpa said something under his breath, and then said plainly, "Gone tis the child now ma'ma, now he becomes a man." Grandma stepped over to Tommy, and put her arms around him saying, "There are all sorts of people in the world child, black, brown, white ... " Tommy cut her off, and pushed away looking up into Grandma's face, and said, "And blue and pink, Grandma?" "Yes, child blue and pink ones as well." The mood eased a bit, and Tommy was smiling again.

The next day Tommy looked at the world a bit differently. Now, he was looking at people's skin, and wondering about differences, and whether or not anyone else would not like him because he was white. What did it mean? Why would someone not like him because he was white? What difference did it make? After all, back on the farm Tommy had dozens of chickens, all sorts of different colors, sizes, they even had different colored eggs. He didn't like any of them any less or more than the others. After all they were all just chickens.

The next day Amos and Tommy walked down the street to the church. There they met up with another boy and his mom. In a very short period of time there were other kids there also. They had all planned to go to the YMCA to go swimming in the outdoor pool. Tommy's grandma had already talked about this with Dorothy and reassured her that Tommy had learned how to swim while still in diapers. Tommy had also taken lessons at the Woodstock City Pool.

When they all piled out of the station wagon at the "Y" Tommy was amazed. He had never seen so many kids at one place, at the same time. Not at church, the park, or anyplace else including the Woodstock pool. Tommy also for the first time realized that he really was different, for he was the only white kid there. Nobody paid him any mind, and he just stayed in the water, and watched all the others. He noticed other things like their hair, the bottoms of their feet, and the palms of their hands. He thought to himself that they were not all black, or brown. Then he saw this really tall skinny kid who was actually dark purplish and thought maybe this was one of those Scottish persons he had heard about from Grandpa. Then there was this other kid who had yellow hair, reddish skin, and lots of brown spots on him, everywhere. Wow!", he thought, there really were other colors, shapes, and sizes. Just like chickens. Why had he never noticed this before?

Tommy and Amos had many great adventures together, fireworks on the Fourth of July, a bus ride to Lake Michigan, they even snuck into a Cubs game, but got thrown out about a half hour later. The adults were worried about something going on in the news. But Amos and Tommy didn't pay it any mind, until just before the end of the summer. It was almost time for Tommy to go home, kindergarten would be starting soon. And the boys were invited to the Morrisey's for dinner. Uncle Tom and Aunt Florence were watching the news when the boys came in. Big crowds led by a man named Dr. King were marching on someplace called Washington. Tommy realized that these crowds were made up of both black, and white people. They were unhappy about how the blacks were being treated by the police, and others. Tommy and Amos didn't understand, but they also could feel the worry in the room from the adults. The news guy talked about how there was a march for Civil Rights at the beginning of the summer, they showed pictures of people getting beaten by police officers in a riot because of something about schools, and now the boys were listening intently; then right about the time Tommy was to come to Chicago something else had happened to a man named Evers. Everybody was fighting, and lots of people were angry at each other. The boys were scared, and worried. Their lives would never be the same. But they would always be friends, they hoped.

Then a few days later Tommy's mom and dad showed up to bring him home, Tommy was quiet all the way home. His father asked him, "Well son, what have you been doing all summer?" Tommy came back from thinking about Chicago, and the news, and said, "I met a friend, his name is Amos Moses, and he lives ... “Oh, you met Amos did you?" Tommy's father broke in, and added, "I knew his mom when I was growing up, and his grandma too. Really nice people. Did you and Amos get along alright?" "Oh yes Daddy, he is my best friend, he makes me want a little brother." "What about a sister?" Mom asked. "Sister?! No. Can Amos come to visit sometime?" Tommy asked. Tommy's mom looked over at his father and asked who Amos was. "You know dear, Dorothy's kid." "You mean Dorothy's little baby?" Tommy's mother asked. Her husband looked over at her and said, "That little baby is two years older than Tommy. He must be in regular school this year." "Really has it been that long, we must go visit sometime. That new husband of her's can't be all that bad. How long they been married now?" Tommy's mom said. “Seven years, honey." Dad said. "We must really make an effort to reach out more often to our friends, George. We have been gone to the farm way too long.” Mom said. Then suddenly Tommy spoke up and asked, “ma'ma, are you black?” Very surprised by this question, Tommy's mother answered, “oh my goodness no, why would you ask me that?" "Look," and Tommy leaned over the car seat, and he held his arm next to his mom's, just like Amos had done with his own arm.

Tommy's mom worked hard outside and loved to sun-bathe in the yard. "See, you are just as dark as Amos, and Amos said he is black, even though he is brown, and look so are you." Tommy's mother looked surprised, and then a little sad as she reached over her shoulder and kissed her boy. She looked at her husband, and said, "George, it sounds like your son did a bit of growing up these past couple of months. He has been taught about the world of adults." Turning to his son dad said, "And what else did you learn in Chicago son?" Tommy answered quite matter of factly, "That Irish people are pink, and Scottish people are pale blue. "Tommy's dad laughed, and said, "Not to worry ma'ma, there is a bit of the child still in there." "Oh, I think that sounds more like your father, George." Tommy's mom said. They all laughed.

A week or two later Tommy entered Kindergarten. He was really excited about school and meeting other kids. He fit right in and made many new friends. But he did notice one thing, there were not any black kids, or brown kids. There was one kid however that had a little babies arm coming right out of his shoulder, and a metal hook on the other arm. His name was Walter. No one paid too much attention to Walter, and when everyone went outside to play, everyone ignored Walter, and he sat by himself off to the side of the playground. Tommy felt sorry for him and went over to make friends. He stuck out his hand, like he had seen adults do, and Walter looked up, shyly, and sad. Tommy pushed his hand into Walter's face and said, "My name is Tommy, what's yours?" Walter reached out with his shoulder and shook Tommy's hand with his little stubby baby's arm sticking out of his shoulder. Neither boy made any mention of Walter's handicap. However, Tommy wanted to see the hook hand. Walter explained how it was attached, and how he made it work. Tommy was fascinated, and him, and Walter became friends. They played by themselves and were ignored by all.

A Halloween party was planned at the local chapter of the VFW in Woodstock. Tommy's father went just about every week to the VFW to visit with other veterans of foreign wars, play cards, and plan stuff to raise money for their cause. Everyone's family members were invited, and dad bought tickets for him, mom, and Tommy. Tommy was going to meet some of his dad's friends. He had already met Roger Nolan, Tommy called him Uncle Roger. Tommy got all dressed up, just like going to church, and was looking forward to the party. All the kids were told to bring a bag, or pillowcase, to put candy in, because there would be some door to door trick or treating after it got dark. Costumes were ok, but not needed. Tommy's mom got an old sheet and cut two holes in it for his eyes. Tommy was going to be a ghost. Tommy was surprised when all the other kids there were already in their costumes.

Tommy had been a bit obnoxious ever since coming home from his summer in Chicago, asking people where they were from and whether or not they were black. The City of Woodstock, Illinois was very diverse. On the city square; the center of everyday activity in town There were all sorts of examples of the different influences. These different influences all built a picture of the people that settled this area of up-state Illinois over the years. There was a Jewish Deli, a Swedish bakery, a Greek restaurant, an Italian tailor, a German leather and craft store. On the way to the VFW hall, they had to wait for the train to leave the station. Tommy saw his friend the conductor, and realized the man was black. He had not remembered that.

What Tommy had noticed is that no one disliked him for the way he looked. Everybody liked the old conductor. Tommy himself hadn't had any problems except at kindergarten whenever he got around this one girl, she would say something mean, or just make a face, and run away.

There were all kinds of people at the VFW Hall that afternoon. Dad, and his buddies pulled some tables together for themselves and their families. Tommy's dad started to introduce him around the table. There was Buddy, his family had left Spain when he was just a twinkle in his father's eye. Buddy's dad had come to America to escape the hatred of his people, they raised sheep.

Buddy's family were call Basques. Then there was a man named Aragon. He would become Uncle Rico. He raised and trained horses, just as his family had done in Mexico, some hundred years ago. Uncle Roger was there. He was to become the town drunk. He smoked big cigars and smelled like grandpa. Then there was

Uncle Boom-Boom. Boom-boom was his nickname. He worked with explosives in the war. Him and my dad got together every now, and then to blow stumps on the farm or anything else. This drove Tommy's mother crazy, and some of the chickens would not lay eggs for a while. Then there was Uncle Cree. A giant of a man who had been a cook in the army. He made things out of metal. Mailboxes, wind vanes, latches, fire pokers, and even horseshoes. But he didn't like to be called a blacksmith, or even smithy. He considered himself a craftsman, an artist. His family had been brought from Africa by white men who sold them as slaves to other white men. Uncle Cree even made house calls. What Tommy noticed the most about him were his hands. They were huge. Cree was always getting challenged to arm wrestles. Tommy never saw him lose.

Tommy grew up a bit more that night and learned the most important lesson; people are just people, and they come in different shapes, sizes, and colors.

Tommy and Amos became as brothers. Amos and his mother came to the farm to visit. But not Amos' father. Tommy never did meet him.

Amos came to the farm once or twice by himself on the train, as did Tommy to Chicago. They spent every chance they could together for over three years.

One day, Tommy was now eight years old, he was on his back looking up at the clouds, and a jet going over. Tommy's dad came over and laid down next to him. "What you doing, son? " He asked. "Just watching the planes go by, and the shapes in the clouds. "Son, how would you like to take a ride on one of them planes someday?" Dad asked. "Really, can we?" Tommy said, all excited. "How about we all go to California, and see that Mickey Mouse place, what's it called again'!" Dad said. "Disneyland! REALLY?" Tommy exclaimed. "Yes, your mom, and I are going this weekend, and you are coming with us." Dad said. Tommy jumped up, and yelled he was very happy, an airplane ride, and Disneyland wow! He couldn't wait.

There was so much happening around the country in 1966, riots, over race, the war, people getting hurt, police on the news every night. It was bad, and Amos and Tommy couldn't understand why white people would treat others that way. It all had to do with the slavery thing. But it was so much more than that. Sometimes the boys would wonder if they would ever hate each other one day. So, they made a pact no matter what they would always be brothers.

Tommy was having a blast in California. The family was staying in a Hotel, in Orange County called the Saddle-back Inn. He not only got to go to Disneyland, but to some movie studio, the ocean, and a berry farm that was kind of like Disneyland. Then one day Tommy's mom took him to get a uniform for some school. That day they went and looked at their new apartment. There were all their things from Woodstock, even the car. Are we not going home? Tommy thought. He asked his dad about it. "You are home son; we are staying here in California." His dad said. "But what about the animals, the farm, his friends at school, what about Amos, his brother in Chicago, or Grandma and Grandpa." Tommy cried.

Tommy never had a chance to say good-bye to any of it. He was mad, madder than he had ever been with his dad. A rift opened up between them, a rift that only got bigger over the years.

Uncle Tom, Aunt Florence, Grandma, and Grandpa Fox, and even Grandma Berg Tommy's other grandma all joined Tommy, and his mom and dad in California. But Tommy never saw his friend Amos again. It was like he had died. He never forgot him. He even went looking for him when he was 16 years old taking a bus to Chicago. But his family was long gone.

He never had another friend as close to him as Amos was. Tommy never would forget that first summer in Chicago, Amos or the day he found out he was white, ever.

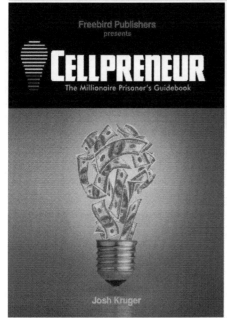

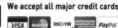

Get Inmate Shopper

By Anthony Billings

G ot Inmate Shoppers newest edition in September 2018
E nclosed I found information, that was very helpful to me
T hese eight years I've been down, there's been really rough times
I nmate Shopper pages I found, a literary escape of mine
N ew editions out every year, I already can't wait for the next
M ade a fan of me and my peers, we all vote it's the best
A resource book like no other, even offers tips to improve health
T ips from sisters and brothers, who are in the same shoes as yourself
E ven if you're looking for pen-pals, there's a section just devoted to that
S everal pictures of beautiful gals, and ball game schedules in the back
H ope in a book believe it or not, and editors who knows just what we want
O rder your own it helped me a lot, second to none and I'm just being blunt
P uzzles inside to take away stress, quotes and other empowering words
P ublished by one of the best, and they go by the name of Freebird Publishers
E veryone should order one fast, while supplies last before it's too late
R ecommended by me and now I ask, have you gotten your own copy today.

BUSINESS LISTINGS BY CATEGORY

INMATE SHOPPER INDEX

BUSINESS LISTINGS BY CATEGORY

INMATE SHOPPER INDEX

BUSINESS LISTINGS BY CATEGORY

INMATE SHOPPER INDEX

BUSINESS LISTINGS BY CATEGORY

PACKAGES
KINGHTS OF MONEY CRISTO PASS
REENTRY ESSENTIALS, INC.

RELIGIOUS SUPPLIES
ALEPH INSTITUTE, THE
AMERICAN BIBLE ACADEMY
AZURE GREEN
BIBLE TRUTH PUBLISHERS
CHUANG YEN MONASTERY
CRAZY COW TRADING POST
GOLD STAR
HALALCO BOOKS & SUPERMARKET
JEWISH SUPPLY
KABBALAH RESEARCH INSTITUTE
NALJOR LIST
NOC BAY TRADING CO
PENN HERB CO. LTD
PRISON YOGA PROJECT
SHAKTICOM
TIBETAN SPIRIT

SOCIAL MEDIA SERVICES
ALSO, SEE: PERSONAL ASSISTANTS
A LASTING EXPRESSION
INCARCERATE US
INMATE SCRIBE
WEBLIFE SERVICES

SPORTS
ESPN
INMATE SERVICE CORP
OUTSIDE TOUCH
PAC TELEPHONE SERVICES
SPORTS ILLUSTRATED
SPORTS WEEKLY

STAMP BUYERS
GREAT GOODS
FRIENDS BEYOND THE WALL
MOONLITE PRODUCTIONS
PRISON STAMP EXCHANGE

TEXTING & MESSAGING
FASTER LINKS
INMATE E CONNECT
PAC TELEPHONE SERVICES
RINGMYPHONE
TEXTINMATE.COM
TEXT TO WRITE

TV GUIDES
CHANNEL GUIDE MAGAZINE
SATELLITE DIRECT MAGAZINE

TYPEWRITER REPAIR
PACKERLAND BUSINESS EQP.

TYPING
AMBLER DOCUMENT
ELITE PARALEGAL
FULL HOUSE TYPING AND EDITING
HAWKEYE EDITING
INMATE SCRIBES
LET MY FINGERS DO YOUR
MIDNIGHT EXPRESS BOOKS
MILLER PARALEGAL TYPING

VETERANS
ALSO, SEE: COMPLETE VETERAN SECTION
MILITARY RECORDS
VETERANS ADVOCATE
VETERANS AFFAIRS, DEPT. OF

WEBSITE SERVICES
CYBER HUT DESIGNS
EHELP4PRISONERS
FREEBIRD PUBLISHERS
HELP FROM OUTSIDE
WOW ME WEB DESIGNS

WRITERS RESOURCES
HAWKEYE EDITING
INSTITUTE OF CHILDREN'S LITERATURE

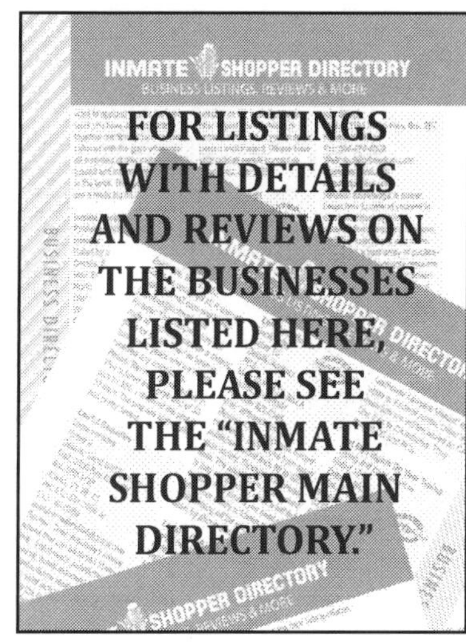

PEN AMERICA
PENN FOSTER
POETS AND WRITERS MAGAZINE
WE WUV POETRY
WRITER'S DIGEST MAGAZINE
WRITERS MARKET

WRITERS WANTED
CUSTOM BOOK PUBLICATIONS
GOGI PROJECT
HASTINGS WOMEN'S LAW
INMATE SHOPPER: SUBMISSIONS
OATMEAL STUDIOS
PRISONERS' FAMILY AND FRIENDS UNITED
SAFE STREETS ART FOUNDATION
VORTEX PUBLISHING
WE WUV POETRY

Comics

By
Richard Adkins

BITCH, SEND ME THE MONEY!
ARE YOU STUPID? THAT WOMAN'S OUT THERE WHERE "JODY" CAN GET HER AND YOU TREAT HER LIKE THAT?
THAT AIN'T MY GIRL, THAT'S MY MAMMA.
©R 9.9.17
I'M SORRY BABY, I NEVER HAD THIS PROBLEM IN PRISON, I TOOK A SHOWER EVERY DAY AND THAT'S WHERE I TOOK CARE OF MY "NEEDS". THAT'S IT!
SHHHHHH
SOAP
SHHHHH
OH, RICKY!
©R 9.9.17
SOAP

WHAT'S WRONG, SON?
I'VE BEEN IN PRISON FOR 30 STRAIGHT YEARS, NOW THAT I'M OUT I CAN'T SLEEP.

I KNOW WHAT'S WRONG. ROLL CALL COUNT, LINE UP AND SOUND OFF!
DISMISSED!
ADKINS, #123456!

LET MAMA TUCK HER SWEET BOY IN.
© 9.9.17

WHERE'D RICKY GO?
I DON'T KNOW, HIS MATTRESS IS GONE TOO. IT'S HIS FIRST NIGHT OUT OF PRISON IN 30 YEARS.

HEY, I HEAR SNORING COMING FROM THE BATHROOM.
ME TOO.

9.9.17 ©
ZZZZZZZZ

PRISON ETIQUETTE,

THE DO'S AND DON'TS OF LIFE INSIDE.

ALWAYS, ALWAYS, KEEP THE T.P. IN YOUR HANDS.
© R
5.26.17

ALLWAYS, ALWAYS, LEAVE ONE LEG OUT OF PANTS, JUST IN CASE.
© R
5.26.17

ALWAYS CHECK THE FLUSH BEFORE YOU GO.
BA-WOOSH!
© R
5.26.17

NEVER ASSUME ANYTHING.

WELL, I'm GONNA DIE IN PRISON, BUT AT LEAST I'LL GET SOME PRIVACY AND PERSONAL SPACE WHEN THEY BURY ME.
INFIRMERY
I.C.U.
ADKINS

WE DON'T HAVE ENOUGH ROOM TO DIG THAT LAST GRAVE.
THROW THE LAST TWO IN THE SAME HOLE TOGETHER, IT DON'T MATTER.
BAKER
ADKINS
D.O.C.
D.O.C.
© R
8.8.17

SPORTS + GAMES ARE ROUGHER IN PRISON, BEWARE.
HORSESHOES
BONK
RINGER!
GOLF
FORE.
HIDE + SEEK
HE OWES ME 200 BUCKS, WHERE IS HE?
SIMON SAYS
SIMON SAYS RUB MY FEET, BITCH!
SIMON
THE GAME OF LIFE
SENTENCE: LIFE
YEARS TILL PAROLE: 1,000, 000,000, 000, 000,000,000, 000,000,000, 000,000,000+1/2
NOSE-HAIR POKER
I GOT 4!
PLUCK
I GOT 7!
I GOT 15, I WIN!
©R 5·26·17

PRISON TALENT SHOW ENTRY
THE SPICE BOYS:
KILLER SPICE
ROBBER SPICE
CHESTER SPICE
PUPPIES, KITTENS, TOYS, CANDY, ...
JOLLY FARMER
SHIFTY SPICE
ARSON SPICE
METH SPICE
©
9.9.17

Fine Dining Prison Cookbook

150 Secrets from "The Inside"

There are many people on the inside, as well as those of you on the outside, that love to cook a delicious tasty meal, with ordinary low-cost ingredients. This cookbook is designed to meet the needs and desires to do just that.

Many of the recipes have been developed by prisoners, for prisoners, however these recipes can also be enjoyed by college students, foodies, and thrifty cooks. These recipes have been compiled and shared from all over the U.S.A. Everyone, everywhere, can enjoy fine dining, no matter what their budget. No matter who you are or where you come from there is something for everyone, that will leave you craving for more.

Making good food is a pleasure but sharing it with those around you makes it even better. The Fine Dining Prison Cookbook has all you need to prepare easy recipes, new taste sensations and a little encouragement along the way.

Fine Dining Prison Cookbook is filled with hundreds of great recipes. The recipes are divided into five sections.

- ★ Tasty Drinks
- ★ Condiments, Dips & Creamy Spreads
- ★ Side Dishes & Quick Snacks
- ★ Gumbos & Chowders
- ★ Meals for Every Craving
- ★ A Few Delicious Pizzas
- ★ Cakes & Pies of All Kinds
- ★ A Few Cheesecakes
- ★ Sweets & Treats of All Kinds

150 SECRETS FROM "THE INSIDE"
Fine Dining
PRISON COOKBOOK

Only $15.99

plus $5 S/H with tracking

SOFTCOVER, 6" x 9", 255 pages

What makes Fine Dining Prison Cookbook better than others?

Bonus Content included inside Fine Dining Prison Cookbook: inspiring quotes, tidbits of knowledge, food history, monthly foodie holidays and national food days.

No Order Form Needed: Clearly write on paper & send with payment of **$20.99** to:

Freebird Publishers **Box 541, North Dighton, MA 02764**

Diane@FreebirdPublishers.com www.FreebirdPublishers.com

A Dozen Roses

BY WARREN HENDERSON

I met a girl,
She had no idea who I was,
I gave her something,
It made her very high,
It made her shake,
It scared her,
She had never experienced the feeling before,
She was hooked on it,
She cried,
She loved it,
I only gave her true love,
From my heart.

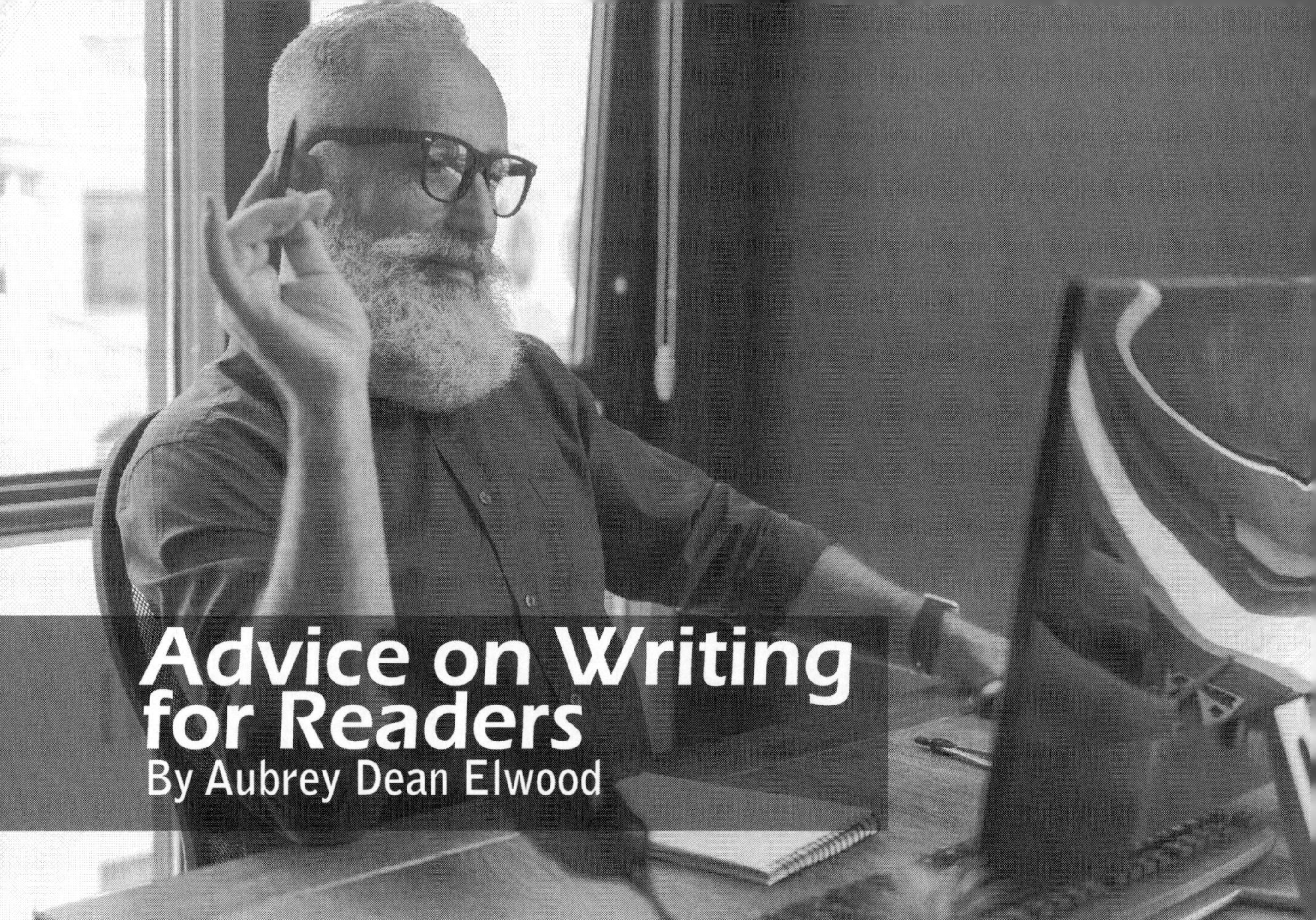

Advice on Writing for Readers

By Aubrey Dean Elwood

Captivating Your Readers

We've all read stories that keep us enthralled the whole way through. The plot captivates us, and the characters tug at our hearts. Then there are the stories that we can easily put down after a few pages or a couple of chapters. We don't relate to or care about the characters, and the plot doesn't hold our interest.

So, how do you write a story that keeps readers invested?

The key to mesmerizing your readers is portraying emotion in your characters. What creates emotion? Desire and fear. Each of us experiences a deep range of emotions, motivated by our individual desires and fears, so reading about characters with the same nuances has the power to draw us in and make us *feel*. Readers should never doubt what a character wants and what characters fear. If you show these two aspects in each scene, then in every turn of events, your readers will continue to read.

Identify Desires and Fears

Often, desire and fear go hand-in-hand. A character wants something – a victory, a love interest, a promotion, a change – and fears it won't happen or the character will lose the very thing they wants. When pinpointing desires and fears, it's crucial to dig deep. Start with a general desire – love, security, peace, acceptance – and note the many ways that desire manifests itself in your character's life. Then look at a general fear – death, rejection, failure – and consider the instances in which your character could encounter that fear.

Keep that primary desire and fear consistent, and don't be afraid to put your character at risk. Force the character to make difficult choices. Allow them to fail. A story is most interesting when a character will risk anything for what they want – and when they must face their greatest fear in the process.

Express Strong Emotions

To make emotions authentic, recall and tap into your own feelings in various situations. Show (don't tell!) a whole range of emotions within a character. But remember, in fiction, you have the freedom to raise the stakes and intensify emotion. Sometimes, it's even necessary to take a fictional story beyond realistic parameters in order to make it interesting. After all, we often read to "escape" real life, right? But whatever you do, please don't leave your character alone in a room, crying and wallowing. Readers want to experience emotion through action and dialogue. Limit introspection to when it's absolutely necessary. Experiment with writing a single-character scene and see what happens. As the story progresses, heighten the tension (it's called rising action for a reason!). Nearing the climax create a scenario in which it seems impossible for your character to get what he or she wants or to avoid their greatest fear. A satisfying ending happens when a character fulfills their desire, but it can certainly be unpredictable or in a different way than the character (or your readers) may have expected. Consider what kind of emotion you want to end with, what you want your readers to feel as they finish your truly captivating story.

What emotions are present in your writing? What does your character desire and fear the most? Practice! Practice! Practice!

Aubrey Elwood is a freelance writer and blogger who enjoys sharing his love of the written word with others. You can connect with Aubrey through his website www.drawigawidercircle.com or at: drawingawidercircle@gmail.com Corrlinks accepted.

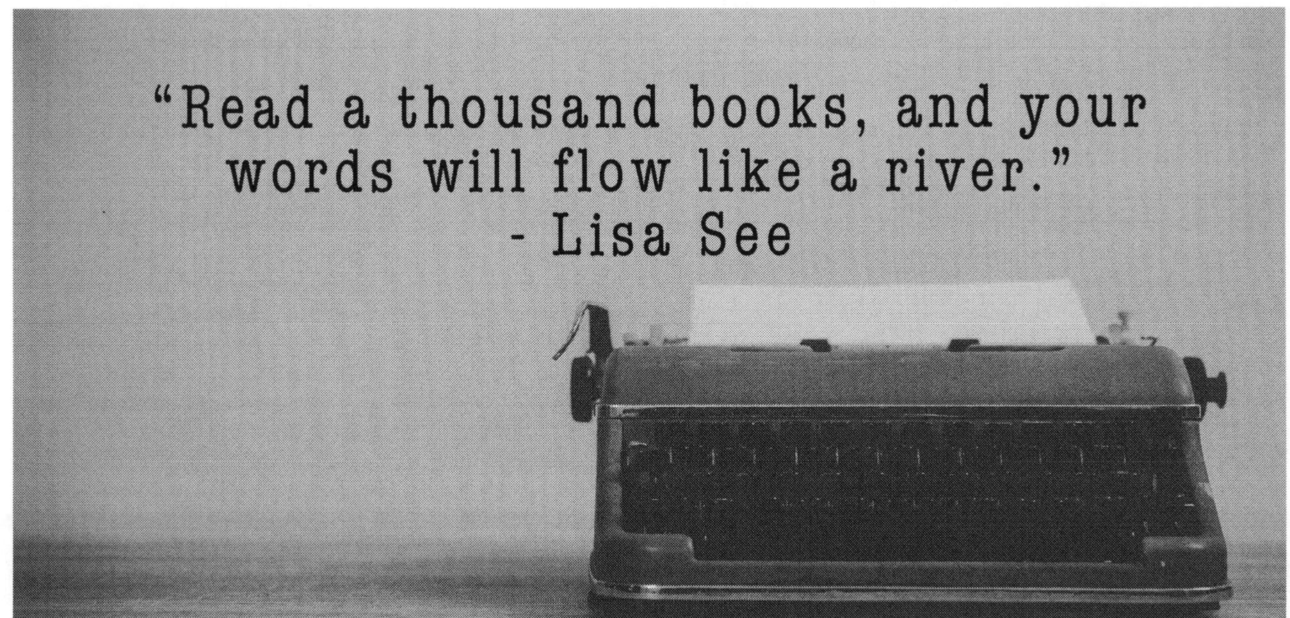

"Read a thousand books, and your words will flow like a river."
- Lisa See

Pathfinder 50% OFF FOR ALL PRISONERS

Pathfinder
pathfinderpress.com

50% OFF
FOR ALL PRISONERS

Write today for your free catalog in English, Spanish, or French, which includes several hundred more titles by revolutionary, working-class leaders.

PATHFINDER PRESS RATED 10!

"It is really exciting to see different and profound in one catalog and Pathfinder Press is both. Books for the free-thinker and revolutionary."

—*The Inmate Shopper*

Malcolm X, Black Liberation, and the Road to Workers Power
JACK BARNES
Also in Spanish, French, Farsi, Arabic, and Greek.
~~List price $20~~; inmate price $10

Thomas Sankara Speaks
THOMAS SANKARA
Also in French. ~~List price $24~~; inmate price $12

Tribunes of the People and the Trade Unions
KARL MARX, V.I. LENIN, LEON TROTSKY, FARRELL DOBBS, JACK BARNES
Also in Spanish. ~~List price $12~~; inmate price $6

In defense of the US working class
MARY-ALICE WATERS

In Defense of the US Working Class
MARY-ALICE WATERS
Also in Spanish. ~~List price $7~~; inmate price $3.50

Women in Cuba: The Making of a Revolution Within the Revolution
VILMA ESPÍN, ASELA DE LOS SANTOS, YOLANDA FERRER
Also in Spanish, Greek and Farsi. ~~List price $20~~; inmate price $10

"It's the Poor Who Face the Savagery of the US 'Justice' System"
The Cuban Five talk about their lives within the US working class
Also in Spanish, Farsi and Greek. ~~List price $15~~; inmate price $7.50

Is Socialist Revolution in the US Possible?
MARY-ALICE WATERS
Also in Spanish, French and Farsi. ~~List price $10~~; inmate price $5

Are They Rich Because They're Smart?
JACK BARNES
Also in Spanish, French and Farsi. ~~List price $10~~; inmate price $5

Malcolm X Talks to Young People
MALCOLM X
Also in Spanish, French, Farsi & Greek. ~~List price $15~~; inmate price $7.50

The Jewish Question
ABRAM LEON
Also in Greek. ~~List price $25~~; inmate price $12.50

The Changing Face of U.S. Politics
JACK BARNES
Also in French, Greek, Spanish and Farsi. ~~List price $24~~; inmate price $12

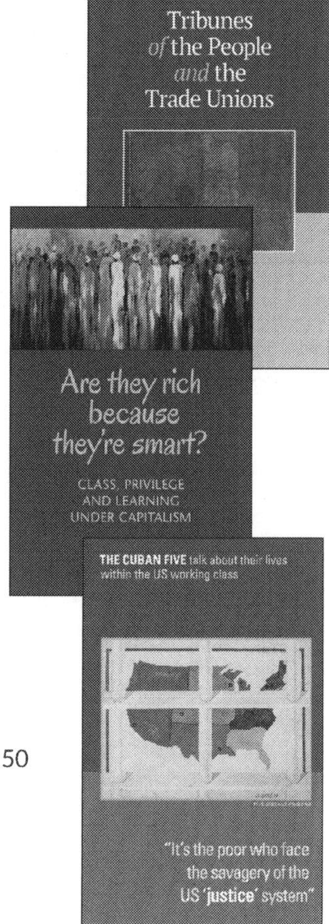

Mention this *Inmate Shopper* ad with your order and get FREE shipping and handling, normally $2.75. All orders must be pre-paid.
A friend or relative may purchase books for you and you will still qualify for the discount.
Write today for your free catalog in English, Spanish, or French:

Pathfinder Press, P.O. Box 162767, Atlanta, GA 30321-2767 | orders@pathfinderpress.com

DO YOU KNOW

By Cecil "Ruthless" Rotnem

Do you know what its like
to forget how to cry,
Do you know what its like
to be completely desensitized
Do you know what its like,
to have your freedom taken away.
Do you know what its like,
to have to listen and obey
Do you know what its like,
to always live in fear,
Do you know what its like,
to have your life as your worst nightmare.
Do you know what its like,
to live in anxiety and pain,
Do you know what its like,
to wonder if you're going insane
Do you know what its like,
to feel completely alone,
to you know what its like,
to dream of a place called home.
Do you know what its like,
to lose all of your ambition,
Do you know what its like,
to live your life in prison. ...

Freebird Publishers

Presents A New Self-Help Reentry Book

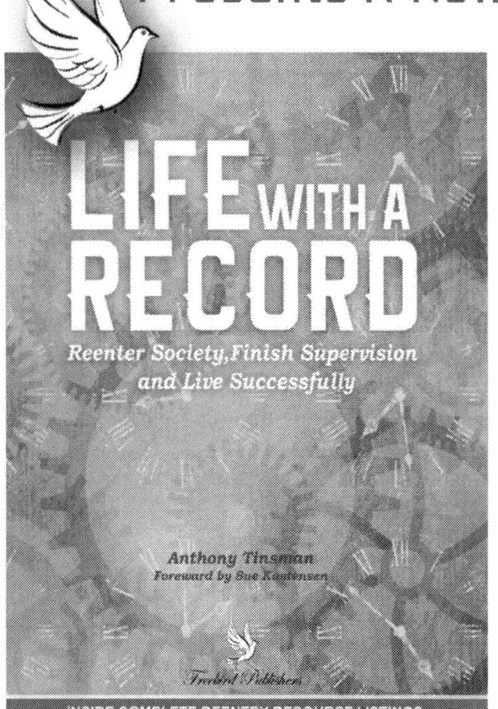

INSIDE COMPLETE REENTRY RESOURCE LISTINGS

Hundreds of complete, up-to-date entries at your fingertips.

Life With A Record

Only $25.99

Plus $7 S/H with tracking

Softcover, 8" x 10", B&W, 360 pages

NEW RULES FOR A NEW YOU

Things don't magically change after you get kicked out of prison. Life starts all over again but there's a catch, having a record impacts almost every part of your life. With this book you'll find out how to prepare for life as an ex-offender. Filled with insights, advice, contacts, and exercises the information strikes legal, personal and professional levels. A real world guide for minimizing disruptions and maximizing success.

Life With A Record helps make sense of the major challenges facing ex-offenders today. Ten hard hitting chapters outline the purpose of making a Strategic Reentry Plan and making peace with supervisors, family, your community and your future. Written by well-known reentry technician Anthony Tinsman, it packs an amazing amount of material into its pages and gives you a quick, easy to follow, full spectrum of instruction.

Inside You Will Find:

- ☑ How to rebuild your credit and begin financial recovery
- ☑ Halfway house rules and supervision terms
- ☑ Special grants and loans to finance education, job training, or starting a business
- ☑ Legal tips for dealing with discrimination in employment, housing and collegiate settings
- ☑ Discussion of success stories, best practices, reuniting families, plus much more
- ☑ Directory with hundreds of reentry contacts
- ☑ Sample forms and documents that cut through red tape
- ☑ How to regain your civil and political rights

Life With a Record explores the most commonly confronted issues and attitudes that sabotage reentry. It provides tools that cut across functions of discrimination, in corporations, political life and throughout society. It opens the door to empowerment, reminding ex-offenders that change and long term freedom begins with a commitment to daily growth. Addressing the whole reentry process, Life With a Record is "must" reading for anyone preparing to leave prison and face the world. It's an ideal book for ex-offenders with decades of experience as well as first time prisoners who need help jump starting their new life.

NO ORDER FORM NEEDED CLEARLY WRITE ON PAPER & SEND PAYMENT TO:

Freebird Publishers Box 541, North Dighton, MA 02764

Diane@FreebirdPublishers.com www.FreebirdPublishers.com

Toll Free: 888-712-1987 Text/Phone: 774-406-8682

amazon.com

PayPal VISA DISCOVER BANK

By A. Raby

THE RIGHT MAN FOR THE JOB

There is a new director of the Federal Bureau of Prisons (BOP), but not much is known about retired General Mark Inch. However, a look at his words from his time at the United States Disciplinary Barracks (USDB), from 2006 to 2008, can do much to shed light on his leadership style. In August 2017, Attorney General Jeff Sessions appointed General Inch as the Director of the BOP and notified the media through a press release. Sessions stated, "General Inch is uniquely qualified to lead our prison system." After this press release, prison reform advocates, as well as law enforcement officials, speculated about his plans and leadership in the role, but both sides admitted to not knowing much about the career of the military policeman. "He is kind of a mystery man way out of the blue," said Ed Chung, vice president for criminal justice reform at the center for American Progress. Anthony Gangi, a contributor for Corrections One, a website devoted to the law enforcement community, stated, "In my opinion, we'll see a shift in priority. For the last few years, rehabilitation has superseded punishment. I believe General Inch will find the needed balance between punishment and rehabilitation." Others seemed to celebrate the military man, as they assume he is going to be a strict disciplinarian, coming from his military background. Prison reform advocates worried about the militarization of our prison system, citing abuses at Abu Gharif.

During all of this, it seems Inch has kept quiet in the job, getting to know the lay of the land. This strategy is indicative of his military leadership training: know the terrain of the battlefield. This should encourage everyone, as it shows a methodical man who will not make decisions without having all of the facts.

Still, what does the corrections community know of him and his leadership style? Not much. Being Incarcerated at the USDB, I had the ability to look through old files of the prisoner-produced newspaper, *The Passing Times*. In nearly every issue, there is a "Commandant's Corner," a column in which the military commander of the prison shares his or her thoughts with the general population. Reading through several of these Corners gave me a glimpse into his command philosophies.

First, he values transparency. In the August 2007 of *Passing Time*, the forebear of the current newspaper, he wrote about the tours he personally guided around the USDB. He wrote, "I allow tours to ensure there is transparency in our operation. Every tour, in essence, is a mini-inspection." Transparency also means accountability, which can hopefully reduce abuses by staff members of prisoners under their care.

Second, he cares about rehabilitation. In the same column, he wrote "I believe we … (focus) on corrections, and not merely warehousing. I show off our programs to protect (our) annual resources … And to remind those not familiar with our mission that the vast majority of (prisoners) will return to society and become our neighbors." The motto for the USDB is "Our mission is your future." This appears to be the sentiment he truly takes to heart.

Third, he has empathy with those who suffer from mental health issues. To put it bluntly, the man has seen some things. He served in Somalia at the time the events of the movie *Black Hawk Down* occurred. He suffered from post-traumatic stress disorder after his return from Somalia. Long before he shares these experiences with a military blog in March 2017, he shared these experiences with the men of the USDB.

"I experienced a period of loss of patience and some general disorientation," he wrote. "I often jump at loud, unexpected sounds, and would feel agitated in large crowds, and claustrophobic in tight places. I had difficulty talking about my experiences and when I did, my heart (would) race, and I would perspire. Quite honestly, I returned to Somalia almost every night in my dream life … There is no need for you to wrestle alone with … Stress, the way I did 14 years ago." With this, he encouraged the prisoners of the USDB to seek help. I believe this bodes well for the thousands of men and women within the BOP who suffer from mental health issues. Not to mention, Inch's candor should be a breath of fresh air for those who constantly try to pierce the obscurity the BOP works within.

Lastly, he believes the mentorship. In the February 2008 issue of *Passing Time*, he wrote about the Japanese word *sensei*. "The deeper meaning of the word within the Japanese culture is 'one that has gone before me.' The meaning conveys an appreciation and respect for one's elder, recognizing that the elder's life experiences are of value." Not only does this undoubtedly shape how he leads the staff under him, but he also encourages prisoners to follow this example and calls for leaders within the population to stand up and guide men in positive ways, such as towards racial equality and understanding.

These are wonderful sentiments, filled with pretty words, but what about actions? Does he back up what he says? I believe he does. One of his actions left a significant impact on the USDB: he allowed the prisoner-produced newspaper to form. As Walter Lippman, the renowned journalist once said, "Without criticism and reliable and intelligent reporting, the government cannot govern." This holds true within the prison system. While a prison newspaper can face as much censorship as a Chinese state-run paper, it still provides prisoners with a voice. Inch allowed the prisoners under him to have a voice, and that action alone speaks volumes. Personally, I have a debt of gratitude to the man, as I currently work as the editor for *The Passing Times*. If it were not for this program, I am not sure I would be achieving my dream as a professional writer.

I was not incarcerated at the USDB during General Inch's tenure as commandant, but in light of these writings, I believe Sessions truly chose the right man for the job. He appears to be more than equal to the task of leading the nation's prison system. He may be much more amenable for the prison reform advocates to work with, and he will do much that law enforcement will agree with. Military prisoners hope he remembers us, and all of the veterans currently incarcerated throughout the system.

Update as of May 2018: There was no immediate reason provided for the departure of General Inch, who had just assumed leadership of the country's largest detention system in September. As director, Inch oversaw 122 detention facilities, 39,000 staffers, and 186,000 inmates.

Prison Education Guide — $49.95

Christopher Zoukis

ISBN: 978-0-9819385-3-0 • Paperback, 269 pages

Prison Education Guide is the most comprehensive guide to correspondence programs for prisoners available today. This exceptional book provides the reader with step by step instructions to find the right educational program, enroll in courses, and complete classes to meet their academic goals. This book is an invaluable reentry tool for prisoners who seek to further their education while incarcerated and to help them prepare for life and work following their release.

The Habeas Citebook: Ineffective Assistance of Counsel, Second Edition — $49.95

Brandon Sample & Alissa Hull

ISBN: 978-0-9819385-4-7 • Paperback, 275 pages

The Habeas Citebook: Ineffective Assistance of Counsel is the first in a series of books by Prison Legal News Publishing designed to help pro-se prisoner litigants identify and raise viable claims for potential habeas corpus relief. This book is an invaluable resource that identifies hundreds of cases where the federal courts have granted habeas relief to prisoners whose attorneys provided ineffective assistance of counsel.

Disciplinary Self-Help Litigation Manual, Second Edition — $49.95

Dan Manville

ISBN: 978-0-9819385-2-3 • Paperback, 355 pages

The *Disciplinary Self-Help Litigation Manual, Second Edition,* by Dan Manville, is the third in a series of books by Prison Legal News Publishing. It is designed to inform prisoners of their rights when faced with the consequences of a disciplinary hearing. This authoritative and comprehensive work educates prisoners about their rights throughout this process and helps guide them at all stages, from administrative hearing through litigation. The Manual is an invaluable how-to guide that offers step-by-step information for both state and federal prisoners, and includes a 50-state analysis of relevant case law and an extensive case law citation index.

Prisoners' Self-Help Litigation Manual, 4th Edition — $45.95

John Boston & Dan Manville

ISBN: 978-0-1953744-0-7 • Paperback, 928 pages

The *Prisoners' Self-Help Litigation Manual,* in its much-anticipated fourth edition, is an indispensable guide for prisoner litigants and prisoner advocates seeking to understand the rights guaranteed to prisoners by law and how to protect those rights. Clear, comprehensive, practical advice provides prisoners with everything they need to know about conditions of confinement, civil liberties in prison, procedural due process, the legal system, how to actually litigate, conducting effective legal research and writing legal documents. It is a roadmap on how to win lawsuits.

The Day I Met Me

BY MELODIC MATTHEW

A life worth living is full of emotion,
Like hope and love, it's poetry in motion.
But there's also sadness and shame, and more than a little guilt,
Threatening to tear down all that we've built.
So, stay true to you and reach for the stars,
In this war called life, Rock your Battle Scars!
Claim them as Badges of Honor for all you've been through,
Hold your head up high, for there's nothing you can't do!
We are not our labels, our last worst act,
We are not our past, that's a cold hard fact.
I am the sum of my heart, all that's important to me,
No small part of which is my AVP family.
The question I now ask for all like me,
Afraid to look inside for what they might see.
Can't you imagine all that you could do?
Wouldn't it be great, to meet the real you?
My life is Brighter now, more Harmonious too,
There is a great strength here, between me and my crew.
Most important of all is that my heart's been set free,
I'll never forget the day I met me!

REBECCA
FEMALE ESCORT COLLECTION
WHITE

Madam Photo
A FREEBIRD PUBLISHERS COMPANY

PRESENTS

BYRON
MALE ESCORT
COLLECTION
BEAR

ELENA
FEMALE ESCORT COLLECTION
LATIN

BRANDY
FEMALE ESCORT
COLLECTION
WHITE

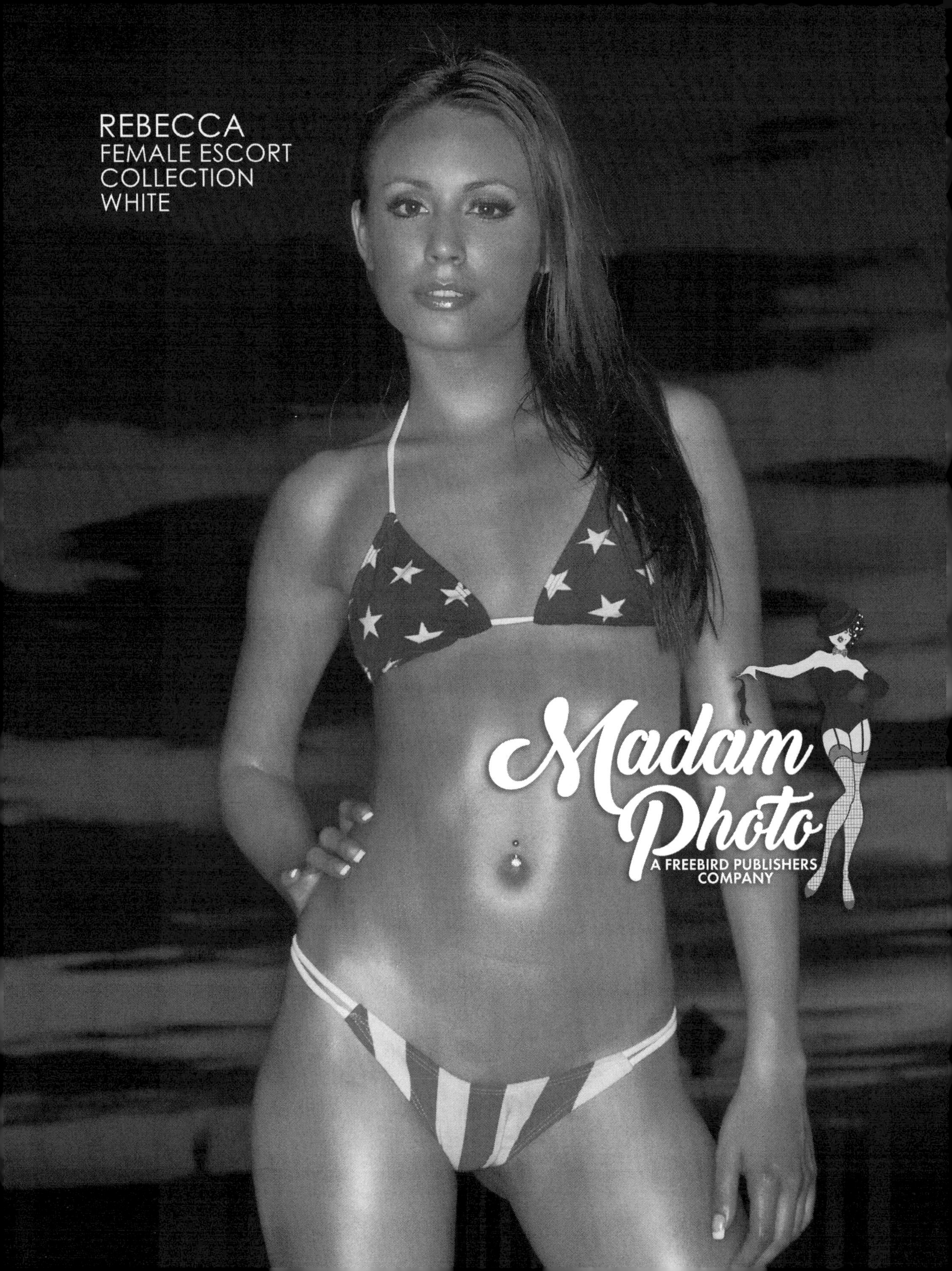

REBECCA
FEMALE ESCORT
COLLECTION
WHITE

Madam
Photo
A FREEBIRD PUBLISHERS
COMPANY

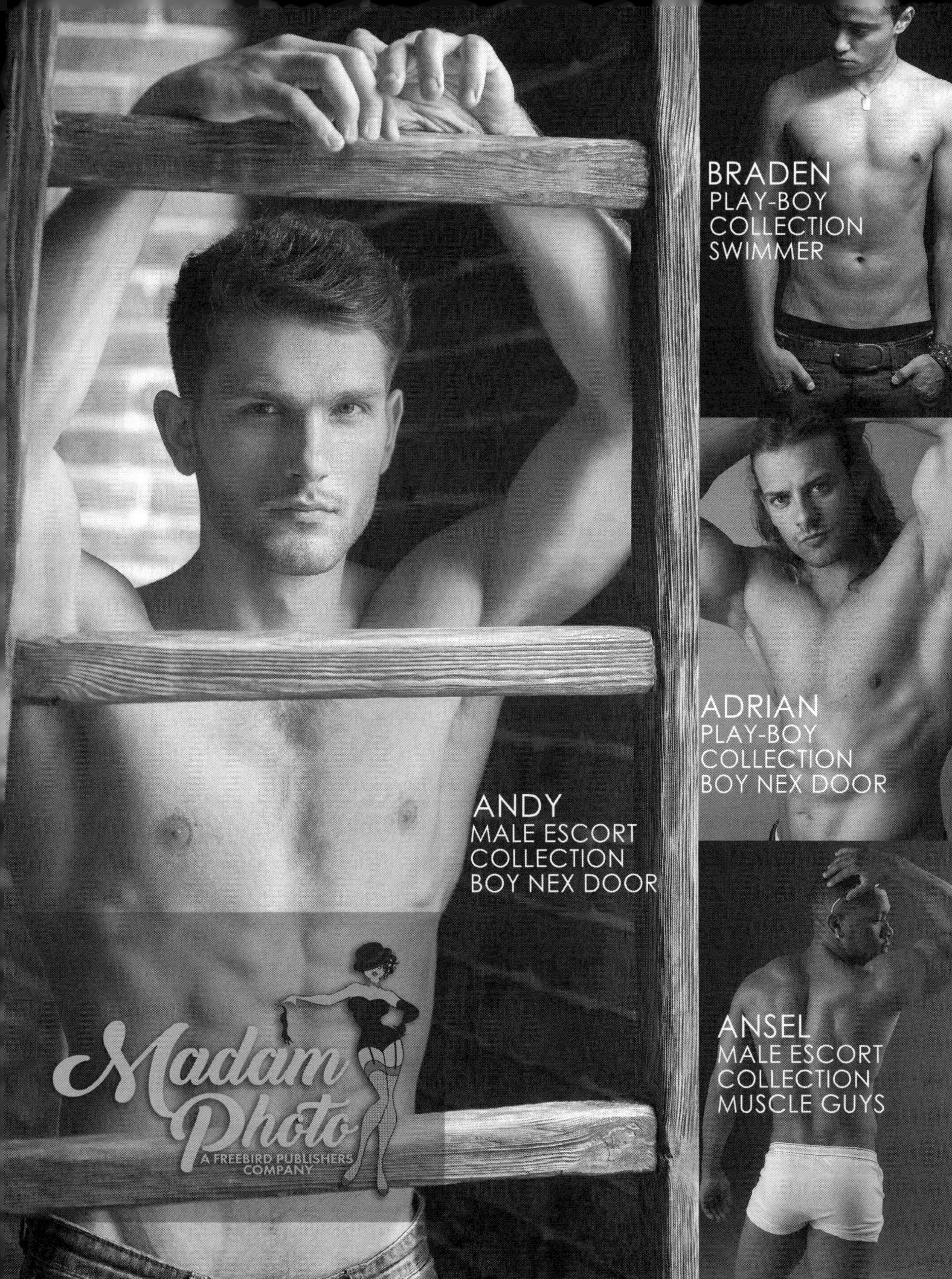
BRADEN
PLAY-BOY
COLLECTION
SWIMMER
ADRIAN
PLAY-BOY
COLLECTION
BOY NEX DOOR
ANDY
MALE ESCORT
COLLECTION
BOY NEX DOOR
ANSEL
MALE ESCORT
COLLECTION
MUSCLE GUYS
Madam Photo
A FREEBIRD PUBLISHERS
COMPANY

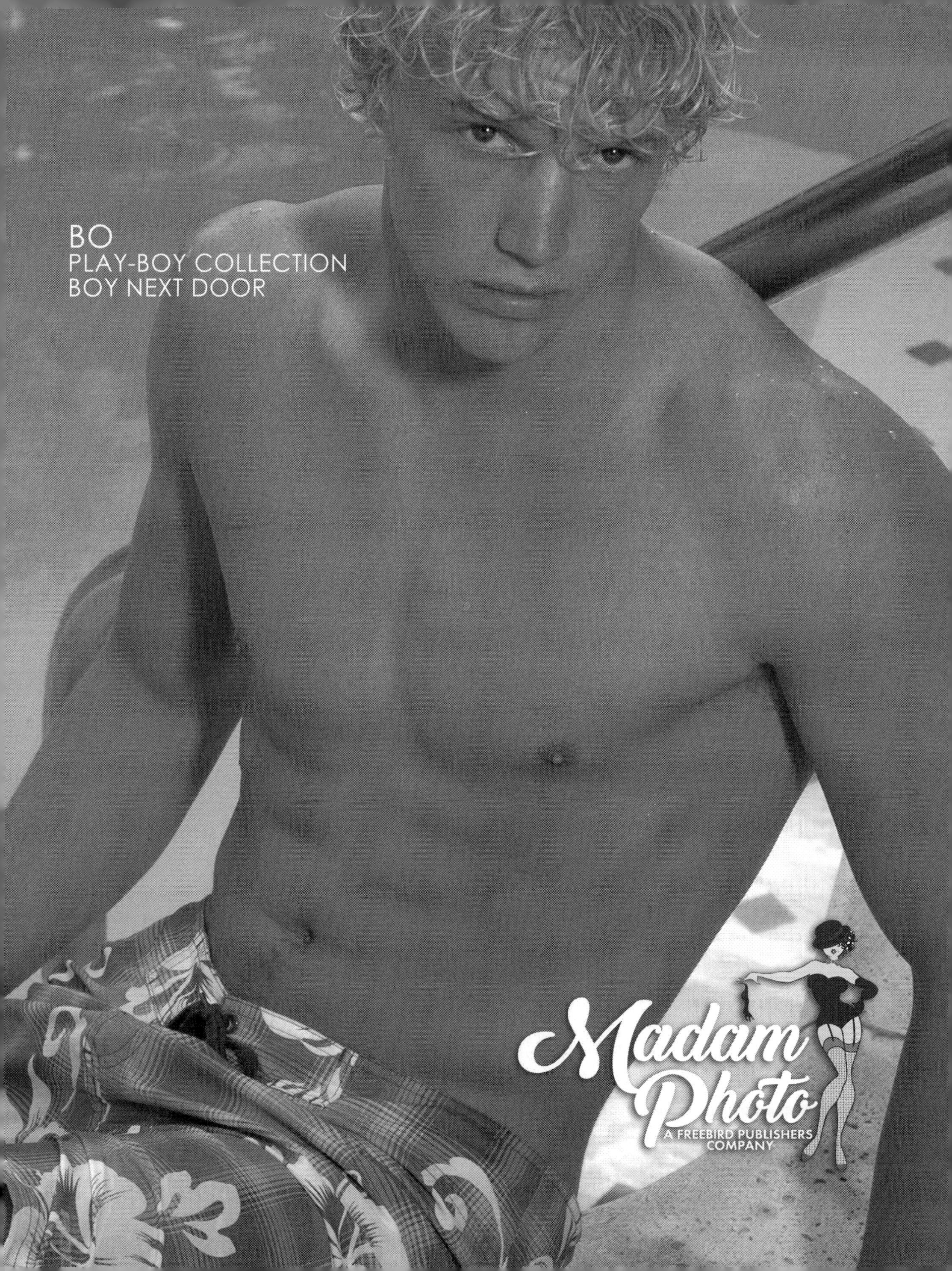

BO
PLAY-BOY COLLECTION
BOY NEXT DOOR

VONDA
PLAY-GIRL COLLECTION
BLACK
Madam Photo
A FREEBIRD PUBLISHERS COMPANY

TONY
FEMALE ESCORT COLLECTION
WHITE

Madam Photo
A FREEBIRD PUBLISHERS COMPANY

To all our readers: We have edited our directory to include the most up-to-date information in all our listings. We research and contact each and every business that is listed in our directory. We have updated, edited and corrected all the reputable businesses in our business directory of resources. We have updated our three lists to assist our readers: "Return to Sender (RTS)," "Out of Business" and "Beware." As we all know, this is a never-ending project. We will continue to maintain our publication to be comprehensive and accurate, for better quality that you can count on.

We at Freebird Publishers greatly appreciate the assistance of our readers. Your efforts truly matter in helping us maintain accurate updates in our publications. In order for us to confirm that a company is a Return to Sender (RTS), we need to see the original front or a copy of the RTS envelope. When you send in a review of a company, please remember to be direct, short and to the point. When sending in new companies from which you have recently ordered, please include all the information you have on them and a couple of sentences on what they offer. If you have any extra materials, please send them as well.

Thank you for your interest in our publications and for your support. As always, be strong, stay safe and know you are not forgotten.

Respectfully,

Freebird Publishers

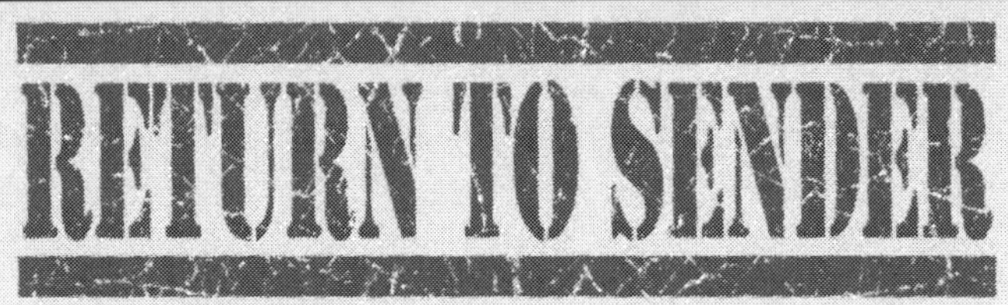

Ace Services Organization
Alexander Byrd Optics
American Magazine Service
Andrew Schatkin, Esq.
Angels Kites
Assistants Online
Bare Expressions
Beckland and Associates
Beneficial Enterprises
Blackwood Productions
Bludaman Entertainment
Bookrak
Brothers Behind Bars
Butler Legal Group
Buzz Photo (MO address)
Caged Bird Publishing
Caged Services
Camel Toe Photos
Capon Bargain Shop
Carbone, Charles
Church and School of Wicca
Clean Slate News
Computers 4 Convictz
Cutie Connection
DFL Research Services
Disc World Depot
DT Enterprises
Eagle Paralegal Service
Exclusive Prisoner
Eloxite
Fabulous Gift Box Creations
Fi Inc.
Food For Thought Books
For Your Eyes Only
Forever Connected
Free World Services
FreedomLine
Frogs R Us
Gillin's Typing Service
Ghost Photos
Heavenly Letters
Hoe Squad
Honey Bear Books
ICC Line
Inmate Phone Service
Inmate Solutions Services
Inmates Matter Too
Innocent.org
Innovative Sentencing Solutions
Inmate Concierge Services
InmateMags.com
Inmate Support Project
Intelligent Solutions Advisory
Intimate Love
Jail Calls
Jaguar Books
Jenn Dur Services
Junk Zine
Justice Matters Newsletter
Kink Magazine
Lapidany Journal
Lifetime Liberty Group
Lighthouse Resource Center
Locked Out
Lone Wolf
Loompanics Unlimited
Loving A Convict
L.W.P.P.
Massive Dynamics
Millennial Masterpieces
Miller Fant Photos
Native American Indian
Oceana Press
Omega-17, LLC
On Demand Inmate Services
P. P. D. C.
PPS of PA LLC
Pen Pal Connection
Perfect Score
Perspectives
Pictures211.com
Pictures Entertainment
Prison Art
Prison Living Magazine
Prison News Network
Prisoner Assistant
Prisoner Solidarity
Q. B. S.
Rainbow Book Cooperative
Remember Me Photo
Roni Raye Fan Club
Seek His Holy Face
SGDiproducts
Slammer Books
Slumber Party
Southland Prison News
Spanky's Quality Photos
Speed Limit 55 Entertainment
Sun Subscriptions
Sure Pleasurez
T.I.P. Journal
T. C. E. Online
T.F.L. Services
T. G. I.
The Simple Business
Three Squares Greetings
UIU-MAO

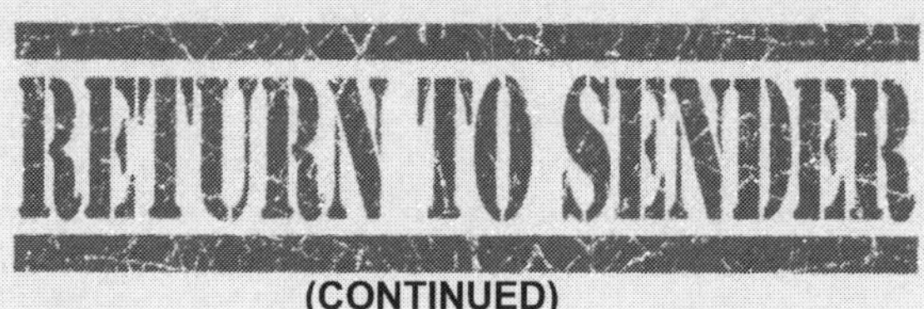

(CONTINUED)

Ultimate Inmate Services
United Inventors Asso.
VI Prisoners
Voices For Inmates
Wet Sticky Flix
Whirling Rainbow
Writers Resources
Wordstation
XS Services

Beware - This list is compiled of companies that are still in business and were once listed in our INSH Business Directory or sent in by readers. We do not recommend using these businesses for many different reasons.

3G Company
A Creative Touch (ACT)
Atlantis Saunders
American Magazine Service
ATS Henderson
Bad Girl Erotic Inc.
Cold Crib
Con Communications
Cosign Pro
Crystal Clear Express Images
Devine Books
Direct Prison Connection
ELI Solutions
Flex Flick
Feelings of the Heart (No inmates)
Free photo Club
Freedom Empowerment
Global Tel Link
Hamden Consulting
ICC Line
Image Fusion
Imagination Magazine
Inmate Photo Service
Inside Out Publications
Inside Out Enterprises
Inside Out Connections
Inventor Mento
J. M. E. C. Ent.
Kill Shot King
Lenoir Publications
Lifetime Liberty Group
Lockdown Bookstore, The
M. R. S. Photos
Mary Hall
Mail My Pixs
My Photo Flirt
NY Express
Outside Access
Patent Search Int'l (No Inmates)
Prison Legendary Services
Prison Lives
Prison Official
Prisoner Assistant
Prison Inmate Family Services
Ring My Phone
Senza
SFO Optical
Shots That Rock
Simmons Company, The
Simple Business
Soiled Doves
Southern Comforts
Spear and Shield Publications
T. J. E.
Tiff Services, LLC
Tru Talk Nation
U.S. Mint Green/Ryan MacConnell
UVP

OUT OF BUSINESS

Ace Services Organization
Assistants Online
Bare Expressions
Beckland and Associates
Beneficial Enterprises
Blackwood Productions
Bludaman Entertainment
Bookrak
Brothers Behind Bars
Butler Legal Group
Bust The Move
Buzzow
Caged Bird Publishing
Caged Services
Cameltoe Photos
Capon Bargain Shop
Cash 4 UR Stamps
Chi-Ey
Chuck Edwards
Computers 4 Convictz
Corcoran Sun Newsletters
Cosmic Cupid
DFL Research Services
DT Enterprises
Fabulous Gift Box Creations
Fi Inc.
Fredas Things Just For You
FreedomLine
Friendly Connections
Frogs R Us
FTW Mags
Gillin's Typing Service
Glamour Girl Photo
Ghost Photos
Heavenly Letters
Hoe Squad
Honey Bear Books
ICC Line
Imagination Magazine
Infinity Publishing (no inmates)
Inmate Book Service
InmateMags.com
Inmate Concierge Services
Inmate Solutions Services
Intelligent Solutions
Intimate Love
Inventor Mentor (no inmates)
Jail Calls
J&J Holdings
Junk Zine
Justice Matters Newsletter
Kink Magazine
Legal Insight
Lifetime Liberty Group
Lighthouse Resource Center
Lone Wolf
Loompanics Unlimited
Loving A Convict
Meshall Baldwin Photo
Millennial Masterpieces
National Institute of Corrections (no service)
Northwest School of Business
Oceana Press
Omega-17, LLC
Our Lady of Enchantment
Pen Friends and Services
Perfect Score
Photo Tryst
PPS of PA, LLC
Premier Gifts
Prisonworld (out of print)
Prison Art
Prison Living Magazine
Prison News Network
Prisoner Assistant
Prisoner Inmate Family Services
Q. B. S. Disc World Depot
Rainbow Book Cooperative
Remember Me Photo
Roni Raye Fan Club
Seek His Holy Face
Simple Business
Slumber Party
Southland Prison News
Special Miracles
Subscription Services
Three Squares Greetings
TFL Serivces
Tools for Freedom
Tradewinds Magazines aka Island Publications
UFO Magazine
Uncle Pokey
United Inventors Association
VI Prisoners
VIP Prisoner Services
Voice Freedom Calls
Vorttex Publishing
Weblife Services
Wet Sticky Flix
Whirling Rainbow
Wordstation, The
WCK

39DollarGlasses.com
Sells eye wear and metal-free frames
▶ **RATED 10!**
Catalog: Free
Mail: 60 Plant Ave. Ste. 4
Hauppauge, NY 11788
Phone: 800-672-6304
Web: 39DollarGlasses.com
Review: Offers unisex, semi-rimless, rimless, plastic, and metal. Prices range from $39 to $198. Upgrades include: polarized, tinted, transitions, and no-line bifocals.

4Ever Connected, LLC
Prisoner services
Rated 7
Details: Send SASE
Mail: Box 471898
Tulsa, OK 74147
Phone: 918-524-9722
Web: 4everconnected.net or 4everconnectedllc.net
4everconnectedllc@gmail.com
Review: They offer services to keep their customers connected to the outside world, such as messaging, email, social media, pen pal, calling plans, photos, financial news, penny stock quotes, and sports feed with predictions and wagers. Easy payments to your account by friends and family online, by MoneyGram or checks. May 2018

4 The Pack Entertainment
Photo services
▶ **RATED 10!**
Details: $3 for pack flyers
Mail: Box 4057
Windsor Locks, CT 06096
Web: 4thepackentertainment.com
4thepackentertainment@gmail.com
Review: New to the marketplace but know your needs while inside. Provide a vast array of services most aimed at making inmate's days a little better. Offer package of flyers for $3. Non nude photos $0.50 each, no minimum, shipped in envelopes of no more than 25 per, shipping is $1 per envelope. In addition, they have Private Stock Photos, Internet Models, Celebrity Photos and Professional Photo Shoots. Mar. 2018
Reader Review: Mark S. in MD-They're the real deal, very professional, high quality photos, the price is worth it.
Reader Review: Martin D in IA-Excellent customer service. In my place of confinement they tend to deny most flyers when I let them know what was allowed they took the time to edit the flyers so they would be accepted. June 2019
—SEE OUR AD—

60 Minute News Show
National media news
▶ **RATED 10!**
Mail: Story Editor
60 Minutes
CBS News
524 West 57th St.
New York, NY 10019
60m@cbsnews.com
Review: To suggest a story or to bring a matter to the attention of 60 Minutes, write via postal mail. They request that all story suggestions be submitted in concise, written form. Please do not send any original documents or additional materials that would need to be returned. CBS receive a large number of story suggestions each week and cannot guarantee response or return of materials. Alternately, you may send your request via email. If a 60 Minutes producer does not contact you directly within 4 to 5 weeks, you many assume CBS News is not going to report your story.

7 Star Photos
Photo seller
Rated None
Details: Send SASE
Mail: 602 N. Main St. #7
Lansing, KS 66043
Phone: 816-343-4201
7starphotos@gmail.com
Review: They have three different flyers that each come with two photos for $5 each. Categories: PG, RR and XXX. Photos are $1 each. Each order must have $2 shipping included. They require an outside address so the prison can return any rejected photo to that address and not the company. Payment by checks and money orders only and every order or letter must include an SASE. May 2019
Reader Review: Harry D in NJ-The quality of PG photos were blurry, non glossy and appeared to be printed on post card stock. And do not forget to include SASE, that will hold everything up. I do not recommend this company to anyone. Apr. 2019
Reader Review: Donald U. in AZ-Sent for info and received in three weeks. Two sample catalogs were included, offers three levels of sexy PG, RR and XXX. Great quality, Quick reply. May 2019

Abolitionist Newsletter
Prison advocate publication
Rated 8
Details: $15 One Year (3 issues)
Published by: Critical Resistance
Mail: 1904 Franklin St. #504
Oakland, CA 94612
Phone: 510-444-0484
Web: criticalresistance.org

crnational@criticalresistance.org
Review: CR's bilingual paper is called The Abolitionist, written mostly by prisoners, former prisoners, and community advocates. The Abolitionist is a medium for prisoners and community members to grapple with the present-day reality of the prison industrial complex, to understand its relationship to what's happening in our various communities, and to figure out what it will take for us to realize a world without cages. This newspaper is dedicated to looking at issues primarily through an abolitionist lens. June 2019

A Book You Want
Books, CDs, gifts
► **RATED 10!**
Details: Send SASE for info
New Mail: Box 16141
Rumford, RI 02916
zling13@comcast.net
Review: A Book You Want has been in business since 2008. They order books, print out lyrics, send gifts and more. They provide ordering and shopping services to assist you with all of your outside needs with a personal touch. They include a cool newsletter with each reply. Accepts Stamps, CC, and MO. They are sister companies with Third Eye Tie Dye, see listing.
Reader Review: Prentiss in TX – I have dealt with this company now on several occasions, and I have been extremely satisfied with their services. Mar. 2018
Reader Review: Brandon L in VA – This company is second to none. I have used them over a year and have bought many books, catalogs, magazine and items from the gift selection. Great smooth transactions every time. Mar. 2018
Reader Review: Johnson G. in WI – I have being doing business with this company for a number of years now, and have never had one single problem in getting requested books or information. They respond in a timely manner. I look forward to doing future business with this company. Apr. 2018
Reader Review: Shannon A. in IN-Quick service and good amount of services offered, more than just books. Only negative thing is they are a little pricey. Apr. 2019

Affordable Inmate Calling Service
Phone services
Rated None
Mail: 10880 Lin Page Place
St. Louis, MO 63132
Mail: Keefe Commissary Network
Box 17490
St. Louis, MO 63178-7490
Phone: 866-755-8108
Web: aicsllc.net
billsupp89@gmail.com
Review: 100% digital telephone service, ten plus years experience. Inmate calling, messaging, offering local vanity numbers, texting, pictures, voice mail. Services start as low as $5-$25 per month and they have bundles to save you money. Mar. 2018

Affordable Inmate Services (AIS)
Parole service for Texas inmates
Rated 8
Details: Send SASE or $1
Mail: Box 635145
Nacogdoches, TX 75963-5145
Phone: 936-564-3403
Web: aicinmate.com
Info@aisinmate.com
Review: Company dedicated to assisting inmates and their families prepare for parole hearings. They are the primary provider of parole related and information services. Helps inmates and loved ones be better informed and present themselves in the best possible way the to the BPP. Send for product and service catalog which includes letter writing, hardship transfer requests, legal research, general and photo services, religious items and gifts. Feb. 2019

Ahrony, Graham and Zucker, LLP
Legal service
Rated 8
Details: CA cases only Send SASE
Mail: 401 Wilshire Blvd., 12th FL
Santa Monica, CA 90401
Phone: 310-979-6400
Web: ahronygraham.com
Info@legalinsight.org
Review: California cases only. A post-conviction law firm. Appeals, habeas corpus, writs, parole hearings, SB 260/261 hearings, MDO hearings, re-sentencing, probation violations, rap sheet corrections, proposition 47, prisoner rights, expungement, parole suitability hearing prison and parole issues, 115 discipline issues. Service CA and Federal Courts. Unsolicited documents will not be returned. June 2019

A Lasting Expression
Prisoner services
Rated 7
Details: Send SASE
Mail: Box 222704
Hollywood, FL 33022
Alastingexpression@gmail.com
Review: They offer email, internet research, social media photo printing, gifts for your loved ones and more.
Reader Review: T. Edgington–I've

been doing business with them since October 2013 and couldn't be happier with their services. They are excellent at what they do and are reasonably priced.

Access Catalog Co.
Music and clear prison products.
Rated 9
Mail: 10880 Lin Page Place
St Louis, MO 63132
Mail: Keefe Commissary Network
Box 17490
St. Louis, MO 63178-7490
Phone: 866-754-2812
Web: keefegroup.com
(All four companies can be reached at the above one website)
Review: Access is an affiliate of Keefe Group, who operates Keefe Supply Co., Keefe Commissary Network and Crawford Supply Co. The Access SecurePak is from Access and KCN.

ACE Lanfranco Publications
Ad sheets and publications
Rated 8
Details: Send SASE for info
Mail: 5447 Van Fleet Ave.
Richmond, CA 94804-5929
Review: They offer Ad sheets and other publications, such as The Golden Gate, The Bay Area Advertiser and more, ten in all.
Offers great prices for running ads too. Send SASE for ordering info and tell them you saw them inside Inmate Shopper.

Acme Publications
Female celebrity photos
► **RATED 10!**
Details: Send SASE
Mail: Box 131300
St. Paul, MN 55113
Review: They offer photos of over 300 celebrities in color, in easy to read and clear catalogs with thumbnail photos. They sent us a 6" x 9" sample photo, good quality, on thick photo stock but has white border. This flyer is not their non nude catalog. Their prices are very low and offer specials: 4" x 6" are $0.35 cents each, 8" x 10" are $1.50 each. Order 20 photos or more and get 3 free. Order 38 and get 8 free. Order 200 or more and get 52 free. June 2019
Reader Review: Harry D. in NJ-I disagree with some of the reader reviews, such as not getting the big catalog. I received it with my first order, about 70 pages. Photos are of good quality mostly, some are from films and video so not as clear. Order took 2 to 3 weeks. I ordered from them 7 times, I am satisfied. Jul. 2018
Reader Review: Donald U. in AZ-Sent for info came back in about three weeks. Must order $10 or more to receive full Celebrity catalog. Not my thing but great for those who love celebs. May 2019

Adams State University
College courses
► **RATED 10!**
Details: Catalog – free
Price: $550 for a 3-credit course
Mail: Correspondence Education Program
208 Edgemont Blvd.
Alamosa, CO 81102
Phone: 719-587-7671
exstudies@adams.edu (corrlinks accepted)
Offers: They offer prisoner college program with a very broad range of individual courses and complete degrees, all of which are available in a correspondence format accessible to prisoners. Print-based correspondence. They also offer the only regionally accredited MBA correspondence program available to prisoners. ASU is a top rated college correspondence provider in the Prison Education Guide by Christopher Zoukis (Prison Legal News Publishing 2016). Online have many forms, lists, applications in PDF that can be printed off easily. Jan. 2018

Ajemm Brothers
Customized greeting cards for prisoners
► **RATED 10!**
Details: Send SASE for catalog
Price: $3.50
Mail: Box 10354
Albany, NY 12201
Review: This business values each customer and takes care of them. They have greeting cards that are the best we've seen for prisoners; top-shelf graphics.

AK Press
Anarchist books, T-shirts, caps, CDs, DVDs, posters, pins, and more
► **RATED 10!**
Details: Send SASE for small brochure
Mail: 370 Rynn Ave. #1000
Chino, CA 95973
Phone: 510-208-1700
Web: akpress.org
Info@akpress.org
Orders@akpress.org
Review: Founded in 1990. AK Press no longer produces a full print catalog. Printing and mailing costs became prohibitive. They offer a printable catalog online. Currently they only produce a small brochure twice a year that features only a

few new releases and is basically designed to drive customers to their website, where their entire line is available. Accepts VISA, MasterCard and prison checks. AK Press is a publisher and book distributor that specializes in radical left and anarchist literature. June 2019

Aleph Institute, The
Jewish religious services
► **RATED 10!**
Details: Send SASE for application
Mail: 9540 Collins Ave
Surfside, FL 33154
Phone: 305-864-5553
Web: aleph-institute.org
Receptionist@aleph-institute.org
Review: Helps Jewish inmates get in touch with their heritage. Aleph ships thousands of Jewish publications, videos and religious books to inmates around the country. You can also request and receive religious articles such as prayer books, Torah volumes, prayer shawls and Tefillin. All Jewish inmates on their mailing list receive four issues of the "Week in Review" on a monthly basis. The Week in Review is a publication that helps one understand the deeper meaning of that portion of the week. They will only put you on their mailing list and send you books if you fill out their application form in its entirety. Mar. 2019

Alternative Ad's, Contacts and Opinion Newsletter
Free sample
► **RATED 10!**
Detail: Send SASE for sample
Mail: Box 963, 1921 1st St.
Cheney, WA 99004
aaco58@gmail.com
Review: There are 4 to 8, 8.5"x11" inch pages. Circulation is 500 to 1,000 subscriptions. Locally distributed in WA. Their ad rate is $2 for 60 words. Typical alternative newsletter: Underground culture, ads and anti-government libertarian resistance content.

Ambler Document
Type, design, layout pages (No legal docs)
Rated 8
Details: Free
Price: From $2 per DS page
Mail: Box 938
Norwalk, CT 06852
Phone: 203-849-0708
Jane@protypeexpress.com
Review: Great customer service. Accepts your hand written pages.
Reader Review: David V. in TX – I wrote them on 2-10 and they replied 3-14 with a one page list of discounted rates for prisoners for typing manuscripts. No legal documents, no stamps.

American Correctional Association
Professional org. for guards
Rated None
Review: Occasionally we find this ACA listed on prisoner resource lists and think, what's this? This association has NO services for prisoners. Experiences with the ACA members have been mostly positive.

American Bible Academy
Bibles, religious books and studies
Rated 8
Details: Send SASE
Mail: Box 1627
Joplin, MO 64802-1627
Phone: 417-781-9100
Web: abarc.org
Info@arm.org
Review: They offer to United States inmates free bibles in English and Spanish. Also offer to prisoners and their legally recognized spouse free enrollment in the American Bible Academy. To get info your spouse must fill out form online and they will mail paperwork for you. In addition they provide prison chaplain resources. Mar. 2019

Art Schools
Free directory of art schools
► **RATED 10!**
Details: Online
Web: artschools.com
Review: Covers all art schools on the planet. Searchable database of schools plus info on financial aid. We don't know if any of the schools offer classes by snail mail, but it's possible.

Artists Serving Humanity
Sells and displays prisoners art
Rated 9
Details: Send SASE and letter
Mail: Box 8817
Redland, CA 92375
Web: artistsservinghumanity.org
artistsservinghumanity@gamil.com
Review: They took over the mission of Art with Conviction late 2019. They are not an "inmate business" but rather a opportunity for artists to use their talents to make positive contributions to society. They sell artwork to assist artists in replenishing art supples and pay towards restitution. A charitable donation is made with every sale. To get in touch have family member leave message on the website or email. You can write them a professional short letter introducing yourself, kind of art, how

long, median you use, and asking how you and your art can become part of their organization. The org is limited to good art. June 2019

Athens Books to Prisoners
Books to Ohio Inmates
► **RATED 10!**
Details: Send request
Mail: Box 45
Rutland, OH 45775
Web: athensbookstoprisoners.weebly.com
athensbooks2prisoners@gmail.com
Review: Send free books to prisoners in Ohio upon request. They accept donations of books, and volunteers in Ohio area for book-packing sessions. Feb. 2019

Asian Classics Institute
Correspondence course
Rated 7
Details: Send SASE for info
Mail: 7055 Juniper Dr.
Colorado Springs, CO 80908
Review: Offers a free Buddhist-based course to prisoners using books and CDs. Others can enroll and pay a small fee for the course. The course is extensive and takes years to complete.

Autoweek Magazine
Car racing magazine
► **RATED 10!**
Details: $29.95 per year
Mail: Autoweek Media Group
1155 Gratiot Ave.
Detroit, MI 48207-2997
Review: is a biweekly automotive enthusiast magazine. The magazine publishes information on upcoming models, test drives of recently released models, articles about professional racing and past models that have shaped automotive history. Magazine is known well by anyone who is interested in automobiles, whether they watch racing on the weekends or work with cars professionally. Mar. 2018

Azure Green
Religious and spiritual products
► **RATED 10!**
Details: $5 for catalog, 150 pages
Mail: 16 Bell Rd., Box 48
Middlefield, MA 02143
Web: AzureGreen.net
Phone: 413-623-2155
azuregreen@azuregreen.net
Review: In business for 33 years in Wiccan, Pagan and Magical Communities. Supply products for all paths to the divine, as well as gift items for personal enjoyment. You will discover items for: Wicca, Witchcraft, Shamanism, Santeria, Norse, Asatru, Druidism, Mysticism, Occult, Buddhism, personal spirituality, and many other divine and religious traditions. Catalog is online, in printable format for free. The catalog is 205 pages, so might want to tell loved one what section or items you are looking for. Mar. 2019
Reader review by: Ian D. – Great customer service. They offer spiritual items, books, tarot cards, jewelry for WICCA, Druidism, Astra, Voodoo, Hindu, and Buddhist. In business since 1986 and approved for most CA prisons.

Babe's Emporium
Photo seller
Rate 7
Details: Send SASE
Mail: Box 769941
San Antonio, TX 78245
Review: New to the marketplace, sells sexy photos. Send SASE to get flyer. Mar. 2019
Reader Review: Donald U. in AZ- Sent for info and have not received anything not even a RTS notice. May 2019

Back So Soon Blog
Reintegration Blog
Rate None
Details: Twice weekly
Web: backsosoonblog.com
backsosoonblg@gmail.com
Review: Blog dedicated to the success of reintegration of sex offenders back into society. Part of the name "sosoon" is an acronym for "Sex Offenders Strategies, Opportunities and Occupational Network." Accepted by Corrlinks and other email website systems. Posts on Tuesday and Fridays. Follows legal cases and legislation dealing with sex offenders, provides articles and reentry tips to help upon release. Mar. 2019

Baker Bay Bead Co.
Beading, findings, supplies
► **RATED 10!**
Details: Send SASE
In biz since: 1994
Mail: 35655 Shoreview Dr.
Dorena, OR 97434
Phone: 541-942-3941
Web: bakerbay.com
Beads@bakerbay.com
Review: Thousands of beads for hundreds of projects. Feature beads made of glass, bone, metal, stone and shell in many sizes and styles. Specializing in supplies for Native American Regalia. Have an extensive selection of Delicas, Charlotte Cuts, Seed Beads, Hex Cuts, Bugles, Faceted, Rounds and Crow Beads. They

have online catalogs. Wholesale Mail Order Catalog, 66 pages color can be ordered for $2 by mail. Mar. 2019
Reader Review: by S. Quigg in WA – Huge selection of beads, pendants, findings and books.

Barkan Research
Colossal book of criminal citations, three-book set
▶ **RATED 10!**
Details: $99.95 free S/H
Mail: Box 352
Rapid River, MI 49878
Phone: 906-420-1380
Web: barkanresearch.com
Review: They offer a comprehensive law book that comes in a three-book set. 8.5" x 11" soft cover, 783 plus pages, 4750 plus citations for supreme, district and state courts. Over 125 topic covered, prosecution strategies revealed, dire questions, district court and innocence project addresses, over 450 legal definitions and more. Book also available electronic PDF. Three-book set in paperback is $99.95. They offer a Colossal Book of Civil Citations 2019, 300 plus pages, softcover, 8.5" x 11" price $49.95. June 2019
Reader Review: Alexander O. in AZ – I saw their ad inside INSH and ordered their books and received great service. Feb. 2018
Reader Review: Oscar R. in AZ – I ordered a copy of their book after seeing the ad inside Inmate Shopper. I got delivery in about two weeks after the check was mailed. The book is possibly the best resource I ever bought. The cases are organized by topic, about 120 topics covered. I give them a 10 and you get what you paid for with Barkan, great book and fast professional service. Mar. 2018
Reader Review: Rex W. in AZ – I have ordered legal cases from directly from them. They are quick to deliver, lol, faster than my own friends and family. I am very happy with them and would happily tell others about their business and services. Mar. 2018

B. B. P. D.
Bookseller to prisoners
▶ **RATED 10!**
Details: Free book/mag list
Mail: Box 248
Compton, MD 20627
Web: BooksToInmates.com
Info@bookstoinmates.com
Review: Offers same-day shipping on most orders and flat rate $7.95 shipping for entire order. We received their catalog in about 10 days. The catalog is text only, contains hundreds of titles in over 20 categories including: Used – Out of Print, Libros En Español, Prison Life, Street Life, Law, Classical , Business, Civil Rights and more. They also offer about 20 men's mags, single issue from $6 to $15. They offer prepaid accounts and gift certificates. June 2019
Reader Review: Ryan D. in WI-They have a huge listing of books. Modest to pricey book list. Aug. 2019

Best 500+ Non Profit Orgs for Prisoners
Resource directory of orgs for prisoners and more
Rated by our readers
Price: Prisoners $16.99 plus $5 S/H with tracking
Free to Prison Libraries
Review: 5th Edition Available
Mail: Freebird Publishers
Box 541
North Dighton, MA 02764
Web: FreebirdPublishers.com
Diane@freebirdpublishers.com
Review: book has hundreds more added, way over 500 listings. New sections, Registry of Motor Vehicles by state, Social Security by state, Internal Revenue Service by state and region, Immigration by state and US Congress by state and district. The book lists orgs with descriptions of what each one offers. The best part is the book is cross indexed by states, names of orgs and subjects so you can find what you want fast. The full title is: The Best 500+ Non Profit Orgs for Prisoners and Their Families. Available from Freebird Publishers, Amazon, and Prison Legal News. 5th Edition available. We mail free to prison libraries when the "staff" email a request to us.

Between the Bars
Free blog service
▶ **RATED 10!**
Details: Send SASE
Mail: Box 425103
Cambridge, MA 02412
Review: This service has asked us to notify our readers that they are no longer accepting new bloggers.

Bible Truth Publishers
Bibles and religious books
Rated 8
Details: See below
Mail: Bible Truth Publisher-Bible
59 Industrial Rd.
Addison, IL 60101 OR
Bible Truth Publisher-Catalog
Box 649
Addison, IL 60101
Phone: 630-543-1441
Web: bibletruthpublishers.com
freebible@bibletruthpublishers.com

Review: They offer free bibles in English and Spanish to prisoners in United States. For Bible: email or mail to the street address your name, number, prison address, and your choice of language. Write to the above P.O. Box address to request a catalog. Mar. 2019

Black Lyfe Publications
Urban and street-life book
Rated None
Details: $10 plus $5 S/H
Mail: 2065 Fulton St.
Brooklyn, NY 11233
Web: ishaqmumin.wix com/183rddevolutionofag
Review: The book is titled "Evolution of A G." If you are from Harlem or 183rd, if you are from the ghetto, if you are about the life then you want to read this book. This book will get your game up, get your game back on track.

Black Media Family
Urban and street mags, books,
► **RATED 10!**
Details: Free
Mail: Box 27514
Lansing, MI 48909-7514
Phone: 313-757-0263
Web: blackmediafamily.mybigcommerce.com
Blackmediafamily@gmail.com
Review: Been in business since 2011. We received their info in about 30 days after writing. They carry Indore, sweets, F.E.D.S., Straight Stuntin, BGM riders, Lowriders, erotic books, calendars and more. They have a $10 book section online, $10 DVD's and even a scratch and dent sale area. We see no sign of them closing, maybe what they might be considering is only taking orders online? But that is our speculation only. The prepaid account section online is not available. June 2019
Reader Review: Ryan D in WI-Decent selection of urban books and plenty of mags. But they are not taking in new stock and plan on closing the business in 2019, Sept. 2018

Black Star Music and Video
Rated None
Mail: 352 Lenox Ave.
New York, NY 10027
Phone: 888-252-2595
Web: gorillalawfair.com
Review: Their ad offers legal info, motion writing and a law book called "Gorilla Law Fair" for $37.50. Excellent spot to purchase single copy magazines and books. Must go online to get catalog.

Blackstone Career Institute
Paralegal correspondence courses
Rated 9
Mail: 1011 Brookside Rd. Ste. 300
Box 3717
Allentown, PA 18106-0717
Phone: 610-871-0031
Web: Blackstone.edu
Info@blackston.edu
Review: This school is accredited nationally and regionally offering inmate paralegal training program and specialized paralegal courses. Enrollment can start for just $59 down and payment plans as low as $30 monthly. You can have loved ones' sponsors and track online, shipments, progress, grades, payments etc. The entire program including soft-covered books, study guides, exam evaluation services, and a certificate upon graduation. Also include all shipping and handling, M-W Law dictionary and Writing to Win. You can write for info or have your loved one request online to have materials sent to you. All materials shipped are soft-covered and approved by most facilities. June 2019

Boagie Report, The
Business opportunity newsletter
Rated 8
Details: Sample $1, and SASE
Mail: Box 1335
Stanton, CA 90680
Web: TheBoagieReport.moonfruit.com
Review: This business also runs ads under various names: Webber Addus, LIST, J. Cha, FSBO – all the same box number. They are quick on replying to requests. They offer all the popular "Get Rich" offers, keys to success, big mails, wanted contacts, a directory of publishers of ad sheets and newsletters etc. for $8. Accepts stamps. We recommend you send for a sample first.

Books N Things Warehouse
Book seller
► **RATED 10!**
Details: $2 Catalog
Mail: Box 7330
Attn: Catalog Request Team
Shrewsbury, NJ 07702-7330
Phone: 800-681-2740
Web: mybntw.com or booksnthinswarehouse.com
Review: Catalog contains a list of several thousand books in all genres. Also sell magazines, books, calendars, games, journals, toys and more. 2019 Master Catalog now available online or by mail. Order forms available to print online. Feb. 2019
Reader Review: Russ H. in AK-Awesome catalog, excellent cus-

tomer service. When some books got rejected I was able to get new re-shipped with shipping payment. Fast responses, overall good company. Reader Review: Shannon A in IN – This company is a little pricier than a lot of other places but they are reliable and fast. Apr. 2019

Bottle Thoughts
Gift sellers
▶ **RATED 10!**
Details: Free Catalog
Mail: Box 596
Wills Point, TX 75169
Phone: 877-705-0425
Web: bottlethoughts.com
Sales@bottlethoughts.com
Phone: 877-705-0425
Review: Established 2005, family-run business providing unique gifts to express your love for that special someone. Message in a bottle, fresh cut flowers, glass and stone art, beautiful solid sterling silver jewelry, scrumptious and delicious desserts, plush bears, kids toys, and much more! Orders shipped same day with free shipping. Open 7 days a week. Tell them you saw their listing in the INSH and receive free catalog. Offers prepaid accounts. June 2019

Branlettes Beauties
Photo seller
▶ **RATED 10!**
Details: Send SASE for flyers
Mail: PO Box 5765
Baltimore, MD 21282
Review: Offer non nude and nude sexy photos. They have White, Black, Asian and Latino catalogs (60 volumes). Photo styles – provocative poses or nude. Send 2 First Class Forever stamps and an SASE and they will send to you one nude or BOP-friendly sample catalog (1 per customer) with 84 gorgeous girls in full color. Act now as this offer will not be around long. Branlettes Breathless Beauties Bag: A random selection of 50 of the rare and exotic. Plus 2 color catalogs (you pick the volumes), only $19.99. (Please specify nude or BOP-friendly.) Their regular shipping/handling policies apply and all sales final. June 2019
Reader Review: Donald U. in AZ-Sent them a letter and got response back within two weeks. Their reply included a sample flyer with deals and ordering info. Multiple packages at varying rates. May 2019

Brown's Legal Research Books
Self-help legal books
▶ **RATED 10!**
Details: Send SASE for info
Books by Michael H. Brown
Mail: Box 723
St. Charles, MO 63302
Web: BrownsLegalResearch.com
Brownslegalreseach@gmail.com
Browns Lawsuit Cookbook: How to Sue and Win – $27 plus $3 S/H
The Bill of Rights Handbook – $6 plus $1.50 S/H
Why You Have No Civil Rights – $6 plus $1.50 S/H
Defending A Drug Case $59 plus $3 S/H, an encyclopedia of info attorneys will never tell you.
Review: They offer a "Talk to Mike" service for inmates and families. Make sure you have legal facts and know the best way to proceed in all stages of your case. Appointments are made on their website or send an SASE for a printout of the website page. Mike is an ex-felon that has been educating and assisting inmates with legal problems for 40 years. He has experience in federal and state law, with both civil and criminal law. No personal checks. Money orders made payable to Betty Coleman.

Bud Plant Art Catalogs
Sells artist books, prints
▶ **RATED 10!**
Details: $5 for catalog
Mail: Box 1689
Grass Valley, CA 95945
Web: budplant.com
Review: This incredible catalog contains illustrations, graphic novels, comics, photography, etc. In the other catalog, they carry all nude art. Aka "Bud's Art Books"

Butterwater, LLC
Photo Seller
▶ **RATED 10!**
Details: Send SASE
Mail: Box 669
Matthews, NC 28106
Web: Butterwater.com
Webmaster@butterwater.com
Review: They sell high-quality photos at great prices. Free catalog of over 300 photos. Specials, Photo Packets: 10 – 4" x 6" photos for $5.50 free S/H.
Reader Review: Carlos C in FL – I bought some of their photos, good quality.

California Lifer Newsletter CLN
Legal and lifer issues in CA
▶ **RATED 10!**
Details: See below
Price: $30 for 6 issues,
Sample $6
Mail: Box 277
Rancho Cordova, CA 95741
Phone: 916-402-3750

Web: lifeSupportAlliance.org
Review: CLN no longer provides copy services of legal cases, articles, and news or internet materials. Write clearly, they do not buy stamps, sell products, no pen pal service. They don't have or send out brochures. No free copies of CLN. Please do not send 10 pgs. rants, they have no attorneys and no way to help. Do not send them your transcript or legal papers. Here is some of what they do: There are three unpaid volunteers who attend parole board hearings, put on Lifer Family Seminars, attend BPH executive board meetings, and make weekly visits to CA state capital for your issues. They publish CLN and Lifer-Line monthly, ask your people to get on their email list for free copies of Lifer-Line monthly. CLN contains Federal cases that apply to BOP and the rest of the USA. Many issues are raised in CA years before the rest of the country catches on so, if your into legal stuff send them $30 for 6 issues, one year. 50 pgs. Write on the envelope: Subscription so it may be quickly processed.

California Prison Focus
Magazine on inmate issues
► **RATED 10!**
Details: Sample copy $2.
Price: $10 per year
Mail: 1904 Franklin St. Ste 507
Oakland, CA 94612
Phone: 510-836-7222
Web: prisons.org
Review: B&W, 8"x10", 30 pgs. per issue. Price is free to CA SHU prisoners. All other prisoners $5 yr. all other people $20 yr. Sample copy $2 or 5 FCS. Responds in 3-5 weeks. Prison Focus is a newsprint magazine published on behalf of prisoners in CA Max Units. They do welcome articles, opinions, news reports, poetry, cartoons and artwork. Inmate Shopper supports their battle for prisoners' rights.

Carbone, Charles Esq.
Attorney at law, prisoner rights
Rated 8
Details: Free
Mail: Box 2809
San Francisco, CA 94126-2809
Phone: 415-981-9773 or text 415-531-1980
Web: charlescarbone.com
Charles@charlescarbone.com
Review: Charles is a former Board Member of the respected human rights group California Prison Focus which has defended and advanced the rights of prisoners in California for nearly 20 years. CPF can be found at www.prisons.org. He is also cohost and coproducer on 89.5FM KPOO every week in the longest running radio program in the nation dedicated to prisoner issues. Listen every Thursday from 11 a.m. to noon at 89.5FM in San Francisco or at www.kpoo.com. Plus, he is a founding member of PASS (Prisoner Assistance Scholastic Service) which is the only nationwide school of rehabilitation for prisoners. PASS can be found at www.passprogram.org. June 2019

CCBC
Sponsor and scholarship programs
Rated None
Details: Free
Mail: 17955 Arlington Court
Anderson, CA 96007
Web: christchurchbiblecollege.org
Phone: 530-710-2210

Cell Block, The
Prisoner resource with over 1400 resources
► **RATED 10!**
Title: The Best Resource Directory for Prisoners
Author: Mike Enemigo
Details: 8.5" x 11" Softcover, 130 pgs.
Price: $19.99 plus $5 S/H
Mail: The Cell Block
Box 1025
Rancho Cordova, CA 95741
Web: TheCellBlock.net
Facebook/thecellblock.net
Review: The book has over 1400 resources. The Best Resource Directory for Prisoner has been corrected to remove the outdated information. Their goal is to make the directory more like 'an experience'. The resource directory is only one aspect of their business. The bigger part of the business is the books written by inmates. Apr. 2019
—SEE OUR ADS—

Cell Block Supplies and Services
Photo seller and inmate services
Rated 8
Details: Send SASE
Mail: 6650 W. State St.
Unit D, Box 279
Wauwatosa, WI 53213
Review: Offer catalogs $2 and up, nude in a few categories. All photos $1 each, every 10 photos ordered get two free, no shipping cost. Print photos or JPay electronic. Not responsible for rejected lost or stolen photos, no refunds, no substitutions. Services offered: celeb addresses, photo reproduction, document copy, song/rap lyrics, pen pal ad set-up, ordering service, sports logos, people search and more. May 2019
Reader Review: Harry D in NJ-I

have ordered photos from them and referred them to others. Couple of them used them for People Search. As for the photos, they are matte finish not glossy but very clear. They have pretty good selection not found anywhere else. Mar. 2019

Cell Door Magazine
Genre prisoner publication
▶ **RATED 10!**
Began publishing: 2000
Publisher: Laird Carlson
Seasonal addresses!
Sept. 16th – June 30th
Mail: 12200 Rd. 41.9
Mancos, CO 81328
July 1st – Sept. 15th
Mail: 6 Tolman Rd.
Peaks Island, ME 04108
Web: celldoor.com
Publisher@celldoor.com
Review: Digital color, 6 x 8.5, print 1,500 copies per issue, 20 pages. They have a wide variety of writing and art by prisoners. This is a non-profit project so please donate generously.

Cell Shop Gifts
Gift Seller
▶ **RATED 10!**
Catalog: Free
Mail: Box 1487
Bloomfield, NJ 07003
Phone: 973-770-8100 (voice mail)
Web: cellshopgiftshop.com
Review: Have been in the marketplace for a long time. Carry a wide variety of gifts for all ages and every occasion. Flowers, toys, stuffed animals and more. Prices are affordable. New selections are always available. Checks and money orders accepted, payable to Cell Shop Gifts. They ship to all US states, No international shipping available. Expect 3-4 weeks for your gift to arrive from the date they receive the order. June 2019

Cellmate and Convict Services
Photo seller
▶ **RATED 10!**
Details: Send SASE for info
Mail: Box 653
Venus, TX 76084
Web: cellmates2015.com
cellmates2015@yahoo.com
Review: They offer photos, catalogs, futoshiki and sudoku puzzle pages, mazes and song lyrics. They have used books and a book trade program. To order catalogs must send an SASE and two separate stamps per B&W catalog or $1.50; color catalogs are $4. They have many categories of catalogs to pick from. Photo sizes, 4" x 6", 5" x 7", 8" x 10". Photo prices range from $0.50 cents to $2 plus S/H. They offer inmate credit accounts, accept PayPal, Moneygram. Other payments options: money orders, checks, credit cards, and e-check. Pre-paid accounts also available. All payments must clear before orders are shipped. They offer Privacy Ordering, which means your family can order for you but they will not see the photos. Send SASE for more info. June 2019
Reader Review: Robert W. in TX – This is a good company. I do a lot of business with them. Mar. 2018.
Reader Review: Mark S. in MD-This company is very nice, catalogs have a lot of photos to choose from, they are fast and have great deals. Apr. 2018
Reader Review: Mark B. in TX – This company should be an 11. They put out on hell of a collection of photos and fast, dependable and have quality photos. Been dealing with them since 2015 and never had a problem. Feb. 2019
Reader Review: Paul K. in WA – While it took better part of 8 months to complete their end of a very large transaction, not only did they do it, they did it better than I've ever seen in my 25 years inside. They invested time and listened to get the precise images wanted. I felt everyone should know! Feb. 2019
Reader Review: Harry D in NJ – They offer good deals as far as prices. They use specific color coded order forms for different deals, so might take you a couple letter with SASE enclosed to get the best form for you. Jul. 2018
Reader Review: Shannon A. in IN – Best picture selection of any company I have used. Over 30 orders and always received what I asked for. Willing to work with you for special shipping instructions. My only gripe is the quality of their B&W catalogs can vary from poor to good but you will always get your order. Apr. 2019
Reader Review: Ryan D. in WI – I think the catalogs are kind of pricey but they have many to pick from. Their photo selection is huge and diverse. Aug. 2018
—SEE OUR AD—

Center for Children of Incarcerated Parents
Printed guides on parenting
▶ **RATED 10!**
Catalog: Send 3 FCS
Mail: Box 41-286
Eagle Rock, CA 90041
Phone: 626-449-2470
Web: e-ccip.org
Review: They have been doing this a

long time, have lots of helpful ideas and resources for becoming a better parent. Supported by donations.

Center for Health Justice
Hotline for prisoners with HEP & HIV
► **RATED 10!**
Phone: 323-822-3838
or 800-260-8787
Web: hivla.org
Collect Calls Accepted
Review: Collect calls accepted. Services available: inmate hotline, advocacy for health care, transitional case management, HIV prevention needs and job training.

Channel Guide Magazine
Monthly TV guide
► **RATED 10!**
Editor's Choice
Details: See Review
Price: $35 for 12 issues, $65 for 24 issues
Mail for Subscriptions:
Box 8501, Code: AADPJSA
Big Sandy, TX 75755
Phone: 866-323-9385 (orders)
Review: With over 200 pages and over 3,000 movie listings in every issue, Channel Guide Magazine is your guide to great T.V. If you're not already a Channel Guide reader, subscribe today at a 70% savings and see for yourself when ordering a yearly subscription. Want to try one issue? Send order and funds for a single issue of Channel Guide Magazine at the cover price of $7.99. No Free Issue or samples.
Reader Review: Phillip B. in OR – I have been subscribing for years and have noticed my guide being 1-8 days late. I have written but did not get a response. I have written to the USPS in may area as well as prison mailroom, no real answers to as why. June 2019
—SEE OUR AD—

Cherry Hill Seminary
Courses on pagan
Rated 6
Details: Send SASE for info
Mail: Box 212804
Columbia, SC 29221
Phone: 888-503-4131
Web: cherryhillseminary.org
Review: They offer education by mail on the teachings of leadership, ministry and personal growth. Provider of education and practical training in leadership, ministry and personal growth in Pagan and Nature-Based spiritualities. Certificates, Master's Degrees, Insights Course and print lessons for incarcerated Pagans. Jun. 2019

Cleis Press
Gay erotic books
► **RATED 10!**
Details: Send SASE
Mail: 101 Hudson St., 37th FL
Ste. 3705
Jersey City, NJ 07302
Phone: 212-431-5455
Web: cleispress.com
Cleis@cleispress.com
Review: Publishers of gay books founded 1980. Publishes 45 books a year, gay and lesbian, sexual politics, feminism, gender studies, self-help, human rights. Cleis Press is the largest independent sexuality publishing company in the United States. With a focus on LGBTQ, BDSM, romance, and erotic writing for all sexual preferences, Cleis Press books are consistently changing the way people read and think about sexual behavior, culture, and education. If you wish to submit a book proposal, please follow the following guidelines: Digital proposals should be emailed to acquisitions@cleispress.com. Please attach a CV, a list of previous publications, and the full manuscript in either MS Word or PDF format. Please also paste the first chapter of the book in the body of the email. Print proposals can be mailed to their mailing address and add Attn: Publisher, c/o Start Publishing. June 2019

Choice Eyewear
Eyeglasses for inmates
Rating: 8
Details: Send 2 stamp SASE
Mail: 745 Portola Drive
San Francisco, CA 94127
Phone: 415-753-8801Web:
choiceeyewear.com
Info@choiceeyewear.com
Review: They sell prescription glasses by mail to inmates. Incredibly low prices, outstanding quality and vast choices of styles and colors. To order a catalog, send them an SASE with 2 stamps and short letter asking for catalog. They carry all the new technology on lenses. Frames start at $7 to $80. They also give you a tip for choosing frames from a catalog and how to measure your current eyeglass frame – the frame width can be measured from the inside of one temple to the other in millimeters. (frame width = FW). Compare the frame widths. On the inside of the temple or arm of the frame there are usually a set of three numbers. For example, "51-18-140": 51 is the lens width, 18 is the nose bridge, 140 is the temple length. These tips will be very helpful when purchasing from catalog. June 2019

INMATE SHOPPER DIRECTORY

BUSINESS LISTINGS, REVIEWS & MORE

BUSINESS DIRECTORY

Chuang Yen Monastery
Buddhist books
Rating: 8
Details: Send SASE for info
Mail: Attn.: Rev. Richard Baksa
Prison Program
2020 Route 301
Carmel, NY 10512
Web: baus.org
rbaksa@mac.com
Review: They offer a Buddhist book program and correspondence course program to prisoners. The course is about mediation, mindfulness, anger management by way of Metta mediation and free to prisoners. They send Buddhist books to prisoners, prison libraries and help you to establish Sanghas in your prison. Mar. 2019

CNA Entertainment, Casey Nall
Photo seller
► **RATED 10!**
Details: SASE for sample and info
Mail: Box 185
Hitchcock, TX 77563
Cnatexas@live.com
Review: Best catalogs with a few in each categories, white, black, Asian, assorted, young, older, retro and assorted guys. They have 1.4 MILLION photos of hot models for your entertainment and enjoyment: non nude and nude. Now offer photos as low as $0.45 cents in a New Release Grab Bag. Catalog photos you pick, only $0.70 cents for a 4" x 6" . All orders shipped the next day. SPECIAL – Order 100 or more 4" x 6" photos, write Inmate Shopper on the order and pay only $0.55 per photo (regular price $0.70) June 2019
Reader Review: Corey G. in MN – They are exactly like they advertise! They really ship the next day which is deal maker. Best selection by far for non nude photos. Apr. 2019
Reader Review: Richard A in SC – All I can say is EXCELLENT – 10!!. Feb. 2018.
Reader Review: Harry D in NJ-You list and have positive reviews about this company and I agree. I ordered from them and found the quickest reply of any company i have ordered from, 8 days. Great timing NJ to TX. Jul. 2018
Reader Review: Ryan D. in WI – CNA is my go to place for my sexy photos. Huge selection in the business and the catalogs are reasonable. You can not go wrong with them. The order comes fast too! Sept. 2018
Reader Review: Donald U. in AZ – Sent for info and was received immediately. Great spreads, plenty of options. I sent 3 FCS in Feb. for flyers. Placed a second order and noted that the flyers never came. They sent them anyway with my second order. Good service! May 2019.
Reader Review: Martin D in IA-Fast service, it only took 12 days from the check leaving until receiving photos. June 2019
—SEE OUR ADS—

Coalition for Prisoners' Rights (CPR)
Newsletter of prisoners' issues
► **RATED 10!**
Details: 2 pages, 8.5" x 11"
Price: Donation of $5 per year
Mail: Box 1911
Santa Fe, NM 87504-1911
cpr1911@yahoo.com
Review: We loved their old 8-page newsletter because it contained a snapshot of issues on each yard across America. We have contacted CPR about helping to restore their 8-page publication, keeping alive CPR's valuable network of voices exposing various forms of oppression of prisoners by both corporations and governments. All funds are used to publish the newsletter; they donate their time to keep us informed. Monthly newsletters are free to currently and formally incarcerated individuals and family members. Stamps and donations needed.

College For Convicts
Book on higher education
► **RATED 10!**
Details: Online Only
Web: macfarlandpub.com
Web: freebirdpublishers.com
Review: Book examines a wealth of studies by researchers and correctional professionals and the experience of educators, show the drop in recidivism rates drops dramatically with each additional level of education attained. Soft cover, 6" x 9", ISBN 978-0-7864-9533

College For Divine Metaphysics
Education courses
Rate 8
Details: Send SASE-discounts available for prisoners
Mail: Box 910
Moab, UT 84532
Web: divinemetaphysics.org
Ann@gordoncomputer.com
Review: They offer education courses on metaphysics.
Earn certificate or three different degree programs Ms.D.- Doctor of Metaphysics, D.D.-Doctor of Divinity and Ph.M.-Philosopher of Metaphysics. Course catalogs are available in print or PDF by email. Definition: Metaphysics is the systematic study or science of the first principles

of being and of knowledge, the reasoned doctrine of the essential nature and fundamental relations of all that is real. It was first applied to Aristotle's writings by Andronicus of Rhodes, the editor of Aristotle's works. Aristotle wrote of the essence of being and the categories of cause and of the existence of God. As we understand the word and use it in our educational work, Metaphysical means "that which is beyond the material or physical" and deals with the study of the laws of being, the Universal Laws, and their practical application to life and affairs. History shows that mankind has made advancement along material lines exactly in proportion as he has made mental progress. No one is larger in any way than the action of his or her mind. Mind action has everything to do with a person's health, finances, environment, and affairs.
May 2019

Complete Administrative Services
Legal and educational books and kits
► **RATED 10!**
Details: Send SASE for info
Mail: Box 140905
Staten Island, NY 10314
Phone: 518-870-2165 or
347-268-8899
Completeservices1000@gmail.com
Review: Has been advocating or inmates and their families for over 10 years now. They are a class-action settlement administration. They are prisoner and public people advocates' organization with strong roots that believe knowledge is power. They are a division of Sovereign Education Ministry. They carry the largest compilation of material compared to other publishers in this area of study. The list has over 250 plus titles, 50 New Addition books, kits and more. All directed to assist you in your desire for wisdom, knowledge, understanding, freedom, education, God-given, unalienable constitutional/contract, common law rights and remedies through redemption. Prices/Donations start at low as $10 and postage is included. June 2019
Reader Review: Hans A in NY – I recently read the review above on this company that I feel is unfair and unfounded. For this reason I must counter this review. CAS are a group of American advocates for justice. They are very professional and have assisted me in resolving a $40K child support case. They give you all the tools you need to succeed and their documents are of premium grade. I recommend their educational materials and document preparation service. The customer service is great too. Mar. 2018

ConArt Consignment LLC
Inmate art and craft sales
Rated 8
Details: Send SASE
Mail: 2300 East Fry Blvd.
Box 909
Sierra Vista, AZ 85635
Phone: 520-452-0536
Web: conartconsignment.com
Web: cafepress.com/conartconsignment.com
franksipple@conartconsignment.com
Reviews: They are new and have a website where they place art and crafts of inmates to sell on a consignment basis. Consignment means you do not get paid until your piece has been sold and paid for. For this they keep a fee of the sale. For more info on the costs send them a letter with an SASE. They sell original art but also offer the design on different products, like cards etc. to help promote more sales, they call this digital art. And they sell printed art which is original art that has been printed on different stock papers. For the printed art and digital art items they have them listed on different website www.cafepress.com/conartconsignment. They also have crafts of all types, from wooden toys, beaded jewelry to superhero statutes. This new company seems dedicated to work within the system to increase clients from all over the United States. May 2018

Conscious County Courier
Newsletter for prisoners
► **RATED 10!**
Details: Send
SASE for sample
Published by: Tony Klabunde
Mail: Box 502461
Indianapolis, IN 46250
Review: The newsletter is ten pages, 8.5" x 11", three or four issues per year with a circulation of 1,000. Published by one of us who have been touched by the system. This is a feel-good newsletter. Tony includes a little about his personal struggles as an ex-offender, prints prisoner poetry and happenings in their CCC family. Thanks, Tony for sharing your struggles, dreams, failures and freedom with us through your newsletter CCC.

Convicts Education Group
Book
► **RATED 10!**
Details: SASE
Title: The Convict's Guides
Mail: 19141 Stone Oak Pkwy.,

Ste. 104
San Antonio, TX 78258
Review: The Convict's Guides publishes prison publications on advance strategies on how to thrive behind bars and out. Their latest book is, How-to Get Girls from Prison No Matter How Long Your Sentence. If you want to get ahead and stop wasting time, then write for their free report of this latest book

Corrio Messaging
Phone Messaging Service
Rated None
Details: Send SASE for info
Mail: Online only
Web: corriospc.org
Reviews: Previously Voice Freedom Calls. New service allows you to receive and leave messages at any time. You will be given a new personal phone number. When you your phone number they can: Listen to voice messages that have been left for them. Listen to text messages that have been left for them
Leave a voice message for anyone that has left them a message. Place a return phone call to anyone that has left them a message. If you leave message for loved ones they received text. Your loved one can then reply to the text just as you would any other text message. They can listen to the voice message by tapping the text message. They can call the inmate's phone number to listen to messages and leave voice messages. $5.95 per month per number, $0.25 cents per voice or text message, less than $0.11 per minute to make calls. Feb. 2019

Crazy Cow Trading Post
Smudging, beads and medicine supplies.
► **RATED 10!**
Details: Send SASE for info
Mail: Box 847
Pottsboro, TX 75076
Phone: 800-786-6210
Web: crazycow.com
Review: Since 1970, they provide the best quality products at fair and competitive prices. Crazy Crow Trading Post offers the biggest line of Native American Indian and Mountain Man arts, crafts, craft supply and kits available anywhere. Your Indian Powwow or Mountain Man Rendezvous, camp and shooter craft supply source.

Crime Magazine
Crime stories
Rated None
Details: Internet Only
Mail: Crime Magazine LLC
Box 10085
Naples, FL 34101
Phone: 360-464-1909
Web: crimemagazine.com
Review: Crime Magazine is an Internet only publication and is not mailed to subscribers. New address since the Holiday 2014 issue. This company offers a thrilling magazine filled with true crime stories about murder, celebrities, forensics, heists, justice issues, organized crime, books/films, sex and more. Stories can be printed off the website. Cost range from $2.99 for a month to $29.99 for year. There are thousands of stories in hundreds of categories of true crime to choose from.

Criminal Legal News
Legal news magazine
► **RATED 10!**
Details: Send SASE
Mail: Box 1151
Lake Worth, FL 33460
Phone: 561-360-2523
Web: prisonlegalnews.org
info@prisonlegalnews.org
Review: CLN is published by Prison Legal News, a non-profit Human Rights Defense Center. A monthly magazine full that reports on the criminal justice-related issues and civil litigation topics nationwide. CLN covers criminal case law, policing, prosecutorial misconduct and related issues. CLN focuses on individuals' constitutional rights as they relate to interactions with the criminal justice system and the persistent expansion of the police state in America. In addition, CLN provides case summaries of the latest state and federal appellate court decisions of importance for anyone with an interest in the most recent developments in substantive criminal law and criminal procedure. Specifically, CLN's coverage of criminal justice issues includes, but is not limited to, police brutality, prosecutorial misconduct, abuse of power, habeas corpus relief, ineffective assistance of counsel, sentencing errors, militarization of police, surveillance state, junk science, wrongful convictions, false confessions, witness misidentification,paid/incentivized informants, search and seizure, Miranda warning, and due process rights. 6 month Subscription (Incarcerated Only) $28, 1 Year Print Subscription for Incarcerated Individuals 12 issues $48.00, Non-Incarcerated Individuals $96. Sample $5. Back Issue $5 Allow 6 weeks for delivery.
—SEE OUR AD—

CurbFeelers
Photos by mail
Rated 8
Details: Send SASE
Mail: Box 421175 or 42295
Houston, TX 77242-1175
Reviews: They sell mail order photos in various categories. They are old fashion, orders by mail and checks. They have no email, website, phones, take no credit cards, Paypal etc. Write them for info include an SASE. Mar. 2018

Custom Book Publications
Publishing
Rated 8
Details: By email
Web: customBookPublications.com
Jamie.Lau@customBookPublications.com
Reviews: They are seeking fiction, thrillers, adult romance and selected books for teens. No poetry or short stories. The main office is in Hong Kong so this is the first time we've seen a publisher from China solicit manuscripts in America.

Cyber Hut Designs
Graphic and web design
► **RATED 10!**
Prices: $35 per half hour
Mail: Box 541
North Dighton, MA 02764
Editor's Review: Cyber Hut Designs does graphic design work scheduled by queue appointments with Freebird Publishers. Excellent service and quick turnaround. Websites start at $500.00, basic four page. Provides flyers, brochures, book covers, websites and much more. Cyber Hut Designs is an affiliate company of Freebird Publishers.

Defense Investigation Group
Private investigator in LA and Orange County, CA
Rated None
Details: Free
Mail: Box 86923
Los Angeles, CA 90086
Web: crimepi.com
Review: Their private investigators license number is PI24807. Before you send any money hire a person to verify the business is a business and get your bid in writing, in detail.

Deviant Art
Sell and post art for artists
► **RATED 10!**
Web: deviantart.com
Review: Deviant Art is the largest online social website for artists. At 14 million members, it attracts all kinds of businesses looking for cover art, CD art, clip art and fine art, with over 2,000 categories. Free for artists to sort their art, photos, personal profile page and a blog. Does not yet have a free message service. Members must sign up for a pro plan to access that feature. One membership level is $30 year. At this level, it opens up a feature that lets artists offer for sale, prints of artwork and pays royalties based upon the selling price you set. USERS BEWARE!! Most people don't read those "user agreements" that all online sites make you agree to before you are allowed to join a site. Many, if not all online portfolios (including those like Facebook and Myspace) have as part of their End License or User Agreement a clause that gives FULL, UNRESTRICTED USE, to the site, of any photos, artwork, etc. that you upload to your port. Unrestricted means they can use a piece of YOUR artwork or YOUR photo, for anything; such as their own Advertising purposes. And because you clicked on "I Agree" when you signed up, the site is not obligated to compensate or pay you in any way ... also part of that User Agreement. A good rule of thumb when uploading photos or artwork to an online port is to get the person that scans in your images to "watermark" your images so the site won't want to take them and use them for their own uses. A simple © (Copyright) mark at the bottom of an image simply isn't enough. Those can easily be cropped out or erased with a graphic design program. When you sign up with an online site and click on the "I AGREE" button, you are basically giving the site your permission to use your work for free! Take the time to READ the User Agreement for each site, before uploading artwork and images!

Diamma Ak Hewel
Halal and Islamic products
Rated None
Details: Free catalog
Mail: 934 NE 21st. St.
Oklahoma City, OK 73105
Phone: 405-521-8817
Web: diammaAKHewel.com
Review: This company sells all uncut, natural and designer oils. They have a wide variety of other products, imported incenses, soaps, shea butters, healing ointments, and gift bags. Diamma Ak Hewel is proud to offer their customers quality products at a great price. Their product line is created to assist with enhancing the body, mind, and spirit.

Dick Blick Art Supplies
Supplier of art supplies

► **RATED 10!**
Prices: Catalogs,
$25 each, Flyers
$5 S/H included both
Mail: Box 1267
Galesburg, IL 61402-1267
Web: dickblick.com
Review: They have been in business for over 20 year. Their catalogs are offered on the website for free, your loved ones can print easily. You can request by mail. They offer two catalogs and two flyers, Blick School Catalog, Blick Studio Catalog, Blick School Flyer, and Blick Studio Flyer.

Directory of Federal Prisons
Information about every federal prison, including cultural data
► **RATED 10!**
Details: 6" x 9", 500 pages
Price: $49.95
Website: PrisonerResource.com
Review: The Directory of Federal Prisons profiles every prison within the Federal Bureau of Prisons. The Directory profiles basic information about every federal prison (e.g., address, phone number, email address, security level, inmate housing structure, etc.), programs offered (e.g., psychology services, health services, drug treatment, recreation, etc.), cultural information (e.g., level of politics and violence, if vulnerable populations can walk each yard, and what inmates like and dislike about the facility), and recent news items (e.g., guard and inmate arrests, prison disturbances, etc.). If you are in a federal prison or have a loved one confined therein, you need this book. Learn all of the hard-to-obtain information you need about every federal prison. "Directory of Federal Prisons is a resource that people in fed prisons and their loved ones need. As we know, the BOP transfers people to over 100 prisons throughout the country. This Directory will give you the 'heads up' info to know yourself before transfer as well as to share with your family and friends. Charles Sullivan, President, International CURE, Washington, DC. June 2019

Directory of Programs
Programs for prisoner loved ones
► **RATED 10!**
Details: Send SASE
Mail: NRCCFI at Rutgers–Camden
405-7 Cooper St. Room 103
Camden, NJ 08102
Phone: 856-225-2718
Web: nrccfi@camden.rutgers.edu
Review: The Directory of Programs Serving Children and Families of the Incarcerated is an update of the Directory of Programs Serving Families of Adult Offenders, dated October 2001. This revised directory lists programs in the United States and around the world that offer services specifically for children and families of the incarcerated. Online information. June 2018

Discount Magazine
Discount magazine subscriptions
► **RATED 10!**
Details: Send SASE
Mail: Box 60114
Fort Myers, FL 33906
Phone: 239-274-6868
Web: discountmagazineweb.com
Info@discountmagazineweb.com
Review: They offer magazine subscriptions at 50% off retail prices. The current catalog/list contains about 600 magazines. They have around 70 titles for teens and children. No porn. But if you are seeking something else they have access to over 60,000 magazines. They also offer a price guarantee if a publisher authorized agency offers a lower current price on any magazine, they will match or refund the difference upon notification. Accept CC, CK, and MO. Mar. 2018
Reader Review: Charles H. in MA – I sent an SASE for a catalog so I could order and never received anything, it has now been three months. Mar. 2018

Distance Education Accrediting Commission (DEAC)
List for courses
Rated 8
Details: Send SASE for info
Mail: Attn: Distance Education Association
1101 17th St. NW Ste. 808
Washington, DC 20036
Phone: 202-234-5100
Web: deac.org
Info@deac.org
Review: This is the real government directory list for accredited correspondence courses and programs in high school, full diploma programs, not GED, Post-secondary programs and degree granting schools. Once get the list you have to directly contact those on the list. Mar. 2019

Diversified Press
Sells unique gifts
Rated 7
Details: Send SASE, accepts FCS
Mail: Box 135005
Clermont, FL 34713-5005
Review: These folks have been serving prisoners at least six years. They offer your photo and message on greeting cards and puzzles, $7

Personal pg., $10 photo mask and backgrounds. New lower shipping fees. Give them a look.
Reader Review: Paul K. in WA – Did not respond to my letter of specific inquiry and kept my SASE. Apr. 2018

Dubuque Mats
Art supply: mats only
► **RATED 10!**
Details: free
1605 Pressmans
Home Rd.
Rogersville, TN 37857
Phone: 423-272-5967
Web: customcutmats.com
Dubuque@wildblue.net
Review: Wholesale mats, bevel cut, ovals, rectangles all at the same competitive prices. Supply and cut wholesome mats for over twenty years. Wide selection of colors from major mat board manufacturers.

DYME Magazine
Fashion modeling beauty magazine
Rated 8
Details: Single $5/6 Issues $20
Phone: 617-906-1062 or
857-269-9536
dymemagpr@yahoo.com
Web: dymemag.com
Review: Dyme is the number one women's fashion modeling and beauty magazine on the market. If you are interested in sexy models in today's hottest fashion you are sure to love this publication. See models such as Bubbles, Toccara Lanett, Ashley Letizia, Isabelle Du, Anastasia Malandrenia, Kurage, La Mode and more. Articles on the current scenes, up to date issues and celebs, such as Pretty Boy Lude, Riva Williams, and more. Prices $5 for single issue, $20 for 6 issue subscription. Bimonthly circulation. Apr. 2018

Eden Press
Publisher
► **RATED 10!**
Catalog: $2 or 4 FCS
Mail: Box 8410
Fountain Valley, CA 92728
Phone: 800-338-8484
Web: edenpress.com
Edenpressinc@hotmail.com
Review: New privacy catalog available online to print for free. Offers business plans for independence and financial success. Eden Press has been supplying "How-to" books for over 20 years. Every prisoner should have their catalog.

Ed Lee Music
Song writing agent
Rated None
Mail: Box 23878-WP
Ft. Lauderdale, FL 33307-3878
Review: Poems/Lyrics Needed By Hit American Songwriters. Offers professional guidance to poets and lyricists.

Edward R. Hamilton Book Seller
Discounted and current books
► **RATED 10!**
Details: Free catalogs
Mail: Box 15
Falls Village, CT 06031-0015
Web: hamiltonbooks.com
Review: They offer fiction and non fiction books, CD's, DVD's and Blue-rays. Catalog available online to print for free or there is a Catalog Order Form that can be printed and mailed to you to fill out and mail to them. Their service and prices are impeccable. They update catalogs a few times a year. Catalogs come in many different categories, cookbooks, bargain music, arts/entertainment, military, science/nature, fiction, healthy living, biography and more. June 2019
Reader Review: Richard A. in SC – I have only one thing to say EXCELLENT. Feb. 2018
Reader Review: Shannon A in IN-I have been using them for 15 years. Good prices, free catalogs and they ship within 24 hours. If there is a problem they resolve it, this is my number one place for books. Apr. 2019
Reader Review: Donald U. in AZ-Got my catalog in couple weeks. Great selection of books! Worth checking out. May 2019

eHelp4Prisoners
Prisoner Services
Rated None
Details: Send SASE
Mail: 539 W. Commerce St. Ste. 118
Dallas, TX 75208
Text Order: 469-290-2260
Web: ehelp4prisoners.com
Review: They are new to the marketplace. They offer internet searches, remove all white space and ads to give you more results. Website builds of blog sites, ecommerce and presentation sites. Facebook business pages and other social media. Payments by check or accept stamps in full books. Send SASE for more info. Mar. 2019

Elite Luxury Publishing
Magazine luxury lifestyle
► **RATED 10!**
Details: 10" x 13", 150 pages
Price: $155 6 issues
Mail: 80 State St.
Albany, NY 12207-2543
Phone: 847-559-7576

Web: elitetraveler.com
elitetraveler@omeda.com
Review: Multiple award-winning folio offering stunning photography of items of luxury and high fashion from Bentleys, Executive Jets, Glashütte, Louis Glick, Harrods, Ferrari, Dolce and Gabbana, Gucci and many more. The magazine has great sections like, top watches, 50 great adventures, top 100 hotels, drink of the week, best hotel suites in the world, top 100 restaurants in the world and more. Prices are steep, 1-year, 6 print issues $155 or 2-year 12 issues $265., Order online. Mar. 2019

Elite Paralegal and Prisoner Services (EPS)
Legal and web searches
► **RATED 10!**
Details: Send SASE, accepts FCS
Mail: Box 1717
Appleton, WI 54912-1717
Phone: 920-749-1060
Web: eliteparalegalservices.us
Eliteparalegalsvs@yahoo.com
Review: EPS has been in business since December 2009. Currently, they provide services for prisoners in every state and internationally. Important thing to understand when dealing with paralegal services orders take time.
Reader Review: Gregory L. in TX: I sent for a catalog, it took only a month. I wrote letter asking about particular services couple months later got a reply and told to start an account. I sent the funds and two pages of info to locate my son. Two months later I got letter telling me they were unsuccessful. I asked for refund, they did a second search even though I did not ask, trying hard to find him for me. Once again came up empty, they sent be balance of my account less the fees. Nov. 2018
Reader Review: Ryan D. in WI- Offer a wide variety of services, were very helpful, flexible and knowledgeable . Responses took a couple weeks, depending on the nature of my request. July 2018
Reader Review: Donald U. in AZ- Sent for info with SASE, came in two weeks time but the facility considered it contraband. Reason is not their fault but strict rules of mailroom here. it contained B&W flyers on non nude, sample photos. I am trying their search service to find some people, we will see how that goes and update. May 2019

Empire Music
Song writer and agent
Rated None
Details: Send SASE for info
Mail: Box 2145
Newburgh, NY 12550
Phone: 846-565-2900

ESPN
Sports news
► **RATED 10!**
Publish: ESPN the Magazine and ESPN Insider Magazine
Mail: 935 Middle St.
Bristol, CT 06010
Web: espn.com
Phone: 860-766-2000
Review: This site is huge and offers so much online. They offer the ESPN Insider as a bonus if you order ESPN the Magazine subscription. We found no way to order this special by mail. Only offered online. Ask a loved one to assist you.

Executive Clemency
Sentence convicted assistance
Rated 8
Details: Send SASE for info
Mail: 3324 W. University Ave. #237
Gainesville, FL 32607
Phone: 954-271-2304
Web: nationalclemencyprojectinc.com
nationalclemencyprojectinc@gmail.com
Review: They offer information on sentence reduction through executive clemency. Over 35 years' experience of clemency, parole assistance and transfers under the International Prisoner Treaty. Preparing application packets to be submitted on behalf of State and Federal inmates alike. Feb. 2019

Executive Services
Prisoner services and more
Rated 9
Details: By Corrlinks Only
executivserv@gmail.com
Review: They offer sexy non nude photos, stories and local numbers. They handle book orders and research. Only handle customers that have access to Corrlinks emailing. Apr. 2019.
—SEE OUR AD—

Exoneration Project, The
Wrongfully convicted assistance
Rated 7
Details: Send SASE for info
Mail: 312 North May St., Ste. 100
Chicago, IL 60607
Phone: 312-789-4955
Web: exonerationproject.org
Review: Helps inmates with DNA, coerced confessions, police misconduct, junk science, use of faulty evidence. IAC, etc.

Exotic Fragrances, Inc.
Oils and sensual stuff
▶ **RATED 10!**
Details: Free catalog
Mail: 1645 Lexington Ave.
New York, NY 10029
Phone: 877-787-3645
Web: exoticfragrances.com
Review: Family owned business for twenty-five years. Company has over 1000 of top quality grade – A pure fragrance oils. Catalog available online to print for free. They carry a full selection of essential oils, aroma diffusers, bath products, and aromatherapy products.

Exotic Magazine
Covers adult entertainment
▶ **RATED 10!**
Detail: Send SASE for information
Mail: X Publishing Inc.
818 SW 3rd Ave. Ste 1324
Portland, OR 97204
Phone: 503-241-4317
Web: Xmag.com
Info@xmag.com
Reviews: In business since 1993 with 75,000 circulations at 200 plus sites. Archived issues available. Issues available to download from online.

Fair Shake
Reentry Resources
▶ **RATED 10!**
Details: Send SASE
Mail: Box 63
Westby, WI 54667
Web: fairshake.net
Information@fairshake.net
Phone: 608-634-6363
Review: Fair Shake is dedicated to supporting the successful reintegration of formerly incarcerated people into society. Free ready to print reentry packet on the website.

FAMM
Families Against Mandatory Minimums Org.
▶ **RATED 10!**
Mail: 1100 H St. NW, Ste. 1000
Washington, DC 20005
Phone: 202-822-6700 (No collect calls)
Web: famm.org
Famm@famm.org
Review: FAMM (Families Against Mandatory Minimums) includes info about injustices resulting from Mandatory Minimum Sentencing laws. FAMM works with the American Legislative Exchange Council (ALEC) working on reforms in federal, Massachusetts and Florida that are saving taxpayer money without endangering the public. If you're incarcerated in federal prison and want to receive updates from FAMM, please add famm@famm.org to your Corrlinks account. They no longer offer FAMM magazine. All updates are online only. If you are not in BOP have your loved ones go on the website and print latest info on reforms. Reader Review: Kenneth W in IL – I seen you had Fair Shake in there and wanted to pass on some feed back. I have used it many times with great findings. There are something's it can't find like people, but as for companies it has worked great. It is the best resource an inmate can have in here while trying to look up places without outside help of family. They also has their research email at info@rzero.org and their straight email address to the woman who runs it so well it is outreach@fairshake.net. Again it is one of the best resources that we can have in here.

Fast Law Publishing
Law books for prisoners
▶ **RATED 10!**
Title: "Winning Habeas Corpus" Revised 7th edition
Details: 7" x 10", soft cover 640 plus pgs.
Price: $59.50 includes S/H (no personal checks)(prisoner price)Title: "Post-Conviction Relief for Washington State – the Personal Restraint Petition"
Details: 8.5" x 11" soft cover 300 plus pgs.
Price: $45.50 includes S/H (no personal checks)
Mail: Box 2315
Port Orchard, WA 98366
Web: fastlaw.org
fastlawpa@gmail.com
Review: We have confirmed they have two law books for sale which we have reviewed. One is strictly for prisoners in WA. They have a complete study guide for how, when and where to file a personal restraint petition. The other is for people who seek info on the post-conviction process in federal and state courts. We have listed the two books they have published and know these books to have a wealth of information. The WHC 8th edition is available. Both books can be purchased at address above or Amazon, and FreebirdPublishers.com. Apr. 2019
—SEE OUR AD—

Fast Law Research
Legal research
▶ **RATED 10!**
Details: Send SASE for info
Mail: Box 2315
Port Orchard, WA 98366
Reviews: New services to an outstanding established company.

Fast Law has added a new department to the offices, they now do legal research. Priced by the page. Mar. 2019

Faster Links
E-Correspondence
Rated 8
Details: email or call only
Mail: No mailing address
Info@fasterlinks.com
Maria1984fl@gmail.com
Phone: 855-671-LINK
Reviews: choose your own personal number and use for texting and receiving pics. If have Corrlinks, your emails can get straight through text. They text your personal number you get a Corrlinks email back. Starting at $20 per month.

Federal Prison Handbook
Federal prison survival book
► **RATED 10!**
Details: 6" x 9", 350 pages
Price: $29.95 ($49.95 from Amazon)
ISBN # 978-0-6927997-3-4
Mail: Prison Legal News
Box 1151
Lake Worth, FL 33460
Website: PrisonLegalNews.org, PrisonerResource.com
Phone: 561-360-2523
Review: Federal Prison Handbook by Christopher Zoukis is the definitive guide to surviving incarceration in a federal prison. This guide teaches individuals facing incarceration, prisoners who are already inside, and their friends and family everything they need to know to protect themselves and their rights. Both prison life and the governing policy and federal regulations thereof are covered. The thorough information has been compiled by an advocate currently serving time at a federal prison. Importantly, this text provides detailed instructions on how prisoners can protect their rights. According to Mark Varca, Chairman of Fed-CURE, "This is the most informative prison handbook that we've ever seen." June 2019

Fire Inside, The
Newsletter for women prisoners
► **RATED 10!**
Began publishing: 2000
Published by: CA Coalition for Women Prisoners
Copies Printed: 3,000
Issues: 4 per year
Pages: 16-20, Size: 8.5" x 11"
Print Type: Digital B&W
Mail: CCWP
1540 Market St., Ste. 490
San Francisco, CA 94102
Phone: 415-255-7036
Web: womenprisoners.org
Info@womenprisoners.org
Review: See their ad under "Free 44 word Ad" in this edition. Review: All of the issues are available for free on the CCWP website. Your loved ones can easily print them for you. They do not offer an order by mail for the newsletter, available only online.

FIYA Girls
Non nude and nude photo seller
► **RATED 10!**
Details: Send 25 FCS or $6 for each catalog.
Mail: Box 192
Dequincy, LA 70633
Email: fiyagirls@yahoo.com
Review: All photos in all catalogs are now $0.50 cents each. New Non Nude Pop Shots Vol. 1, 2, 3, 4, 5 catalogs. Each catalog has tons of photos to choose from and comes with 10 free photos, see above for details on how to order. They have everything from camel toe, G-strings, thongs, bikinis, hot faces! Plus "super big bottoms", black girls, and Spanish girls in bikinis, G-strings, thongs, and very hot poses! All of you apple bottom lovers will love it.
Reader Review: Shannon A. in IN- Decent selection but highest shipping cost I have come across. I have put in three orders, they changed their rules and asked for more money all three times. I got my photos but they were so creepy about it, I won't use them again. Apr. 2019
—SEE OUR AD—

Flix 4 You
Photo seller
Rate 9
Details: Send SASE for info
Mail: Box 290249
Columbia, SC 29229
Review: They offer sexy good quality photos and fast service. They have over hundred catalogs to pick from in many different categories. Offer great deals. June 2019
Reader Review: Donald U. in Az- Sent for info and got my reply from them in little over two weeks, came with sample flyer. Overstock sale 20 photos for $7.50, choice of race and front or back shots. Full list of catalogs came in the info. Good options over 180 catalogs. I made an order but it was blocked by my facility (they are super strict DOC-AZ). May 2019

Forbes Magazine
Financial information magazine
► **RATED 10!**
Mail: Box 5471
Harlan, IA 51593
Mail: Forbes Media LLC

60 Fifth Ave.
New York, NY 10011
Web: ForbesMagazine.com
Review: Forbes is published 24 times a year except for two issues combined periodically into one and occasional extra or premium issues. Combined, expanded, and premium issues count as two subscription issues. Your first issue will arrive in 4 to 6 weeks. Offering special $20 for one year, we saw this special online. We recommend if you have no one to assist you order online then send them an SASE first to get the correct ordering instructions

Fortune News
Prisoner publication
► **RATED 10!**
Published by: The Fortune Society
Pages: 24, Size: 8" x 10"
Price: $5 donation
Mail: 29-76 Northern Blvd.
Long Island City, NY 11101
Phone: 212-691-7554
Web: fortunesociety.org
info@fortunesociety.org
Review: Description: Provides post-release services and programs for prisoners in the New York City area and publishes Fortune News. Been in business since 2001, four Issues per year, 8" x 10", 24 pages.
Review: A subscription is available on website and printing for the issues. Paper copies are still available and can only be ordered by subscribing by email according to the website.

F. O. S.
Photo seller
► **RATED 10!**
Details: Send SASE for free catalog and photo.
Mail: Box 42922
Phoenix, AZ 85080
Phone: 212-691-7554
Review: Back by popular demand! In business for eight years with excellent customer service. 50 photos at $0.50 cents each. Orders over $5.00 are $0.75 per photo, orders under $5.00 are $1.00 per photo. Sorry, no stamps. May 2019

Foundation For Innocence
Legal referral
Rated None
Details: SASE
Mail: Box 1033
Kula HI 96790
Phone: 808-269-0452
innocencehawaii2002@yahoo.com
Fox Broadcasting
Fox television
Rated None
Mail: Box 900
Beverly Hills, CA 90213

Freebird Publishers
Publishing and various services
Rated by our customers
Details: $2 or 6 FCS for catalog (52 pgs, full color, ship first class USPS)
Mail: Box 541
North Dighton, MA 02764
Web: FreebirdPublishers.com
Diane@freebirdpublishers.com
Review: offer self-publishing services, specialize in prisoner publications and is the publisher and distributors of Inmate Shopper New Annual Split Overlapping Year Issues, due out Mid-year but current until the end of the year. We publish many prisoner books in categories as Resource books, Pen Pal Books and services, Law-Legal books, Self-Help books, Cookbooks, Photo books (non nude), Photo sets (non nude), Entertainment book, gift books, gifts for all holidays and occasions. Accepts Corrlinks and JPay. Accepts all forms of payments and FCS with prior correspondence. We recommend sending $2 or 6 FCS to receive 52 page full color catalog. They have a huge line of quality gift baskets for every occasion and theme. Touchstone jewelry made of all pure metals and Swarovski crystals. Fast turn-around and processes orders within 24 hours of receiving.
Reader Review: Rev. Warren P. in MI – This note was written into a greeting card with photo of him and his son :)...Thank you all so much for your great work and service, helping us who are on lock down. I have made some special people in my life happy because of you. Jan. 2018
Reader Review: Timothy M. in PA – I received my Kitty Kat non nude photo resource book. It's awesome and was delivered so fast. Thank you. Feb. 2018
Reader Review: Richard A. in SC – Good people, great service says it all. Feb. 2018
Reader Review: Ryan D. in WI-Very friendly, responsive and carry a great selection of publications and services. Sept. 2018
Reader Review: Forrest M. in TX-I have recently started doing business with them. I have many of their prisoner publication titles. The books give me a feeling of freedom while I am reading them. I just wanted to say thank Freebird! It's the little things we forget or take for granted. I am a customer from here on out. Yall are awesome. Mar. 2019
—SEE OUR ADS—

Freerksen Publications
Newsletter
Rated 7
Details: Send SASE
Mail: Box 105
Kasson, MN 55944-0105
Phone: 507-634-3656
Review: Independent Business Marketer newsletter. They offer a newsletter filled with ads for various things. In addition, you can place an ad for a small fee. Newsletter offers a sample issue for the price of $2 first class stamps. For more info write and send SASE. June 2017

Freedom of Information Act
Provides print-outs of unclassified government documents.
► **RATED 10!**
Web: fbi.gov/foia
Review: Everything from your FBI file to White House emails by the President and UFO sightings.
How to Make a Request: Anyone may submit a FOIA request. There is no central FOIA office in the District government. Each public body responds to requests for its own records. To submit a request, you should determine which public body is likely to maintain the records you are seeking and submit a request to the FOIA Officer of that public body. Please refer to the FOIA Officer list for contact information. A FOIA request may be submitted orally or in writing and may be mail, fax or email. Oral requests may be honored, but the agency has the right to request that it be submitted in writing. When submitting your request, please mark the outside of the envelope or the subject line of the fax "Freedom of Information Act Request" or "FOIA Request."Please include a daytime telephone number, email address or mailing address in your request letter so that the FOIA Officer may contact you if necessary. Describe the record(s) you are seeking as clearly and precisely as possible. In your description, please be as specific as possible with regard to names, dates, places, events, subjects, and other pertinent details that will help the public body to identify the records. The more specific you are about the records you are seeking, the more likely the public body will be able to locate those records. If your request is vague or too broad, they may ask you to be more specific, and this may delay processing your request. Since there are so many areas and different types of public bodies to search for. And there is not just one mailing address to write to. If you need to search for a record, we suggest you hire a personal assistant to do this for you.

Friends Beyond The Wall, Inc.
Stamp buyer
► **RATED 10!**
Details: Send SASE
Mail: Attn: Stamps for Cash
36 Cottage St., Ste. 202
Poughkeepsie, NY 12601
Review: Buy new Forever stamps at 70% face value. Covert your stamps to cash. Minimum of 200 stamps, only accept books or strips. No single or loose stamps. Payment sent to by company check to your address or outside people.
Reader Review: Shannon A. in IN-Sent them an SASE, they did respond been 60 days, maybe they are backed up in mail? Apr. 2019

Fresh Start Life Styles
Recruit on demand training program
Turn Key Business Prototypes
Rated 7
Details: Investment $15
Mail: Box 1092
Attn: C. Todd
Pocahontas, AR 72455
Phone: 870-202-2042
camtoddmwr@@gmail.com
Review: This is a training program that will prepare you for their turn key business model. The program gives you the know-how, connection, support and investment that you need to be your own entrepreneurial person. For the price of $15 you will get everything you need to learn and start this business opportunity to make money. For more information, you can request a brochure by sending an SASE. Or jump right in and mail your $15 check today! Aug. 2017

Full House Typing and Editing
Typing and editing.
► **RATED 10!**
Details: Send SASE,
Reply in 12 days
Mail: Box 361402
Decatur, GA 30036
Review: Offers only manuscript and document typing and editing. NO book formatting or publishing services. In addition, have a formal copyright service. This is an old-school manuscript typing service. This means they type your project to basic publisher's guidelines. The standard guidelines are: 1" margins all around. Double spaced. Courier New, 12 pt. type, 8.5" x 11" white bond paper, and black ink. Priced at $1.50 per pg. That is average to low pricing for this service. No content containing Satanism, vampires or

witchcraft themes. Pornographic descriptions are okay if in line with the context of the story but not the entire theme of the story.

Gain Peace
Religious information
Rated None
Mail: 215270 Summit Ave. Ste. 100
Oakbrook Terrace, IL 60181
Phone: 800-662-ISLAM
Web: gainpeace.com
Watch: peacetv.tv
Sabeel@GainPeace.com
Salman@icnachicago.org
Review: They teach about Islam, the way of Noah, Abraham, Moses, Jesus and Mohammed. Mar. 2018

Gay and Lesbian Review World-wide
Reviews LGBTQ books and literature
► **RATED 10!**
Price: $23 yr., $39 for 2 yrs.
Mail: Box 180300
Boston, MA 02118
Phone: 617-421-0082
Web: glreview.org
Review: Bimonthly magazine of history, culture and politics with a print run of 11,000. Accept credit cards and PayPal for online payment. Free issue for first time subscribers and free and instant online access.

Genealogical.com
Books about ancestry and genealogy
► **RATED 10!**
Catalog: Send SASE
Mail: 3600 Clipper Mill Rd. Ste. 260
Baltimore, MD 21211
Phone: 410-837-8271
Web: Genealogical.com
Sales@genealogical.com
Review: They publish genealogy books and CDs. Whether you are just beginning to explore your family tree or are an experienced researcher looking for in-depth genealogy data. They offer over 2,000 genealogy books and compact discs featuring colonial genealogy, Irish genealogy, immigration, royal ancestry, family history, and genealogy methods and sources. The best way to order is over the Internet at www.genealogical.com (for print books) or library.genealogical.com (for ebooks); email orders: orders@genealogical.com
June 2019

Genealogical Research
Family history
► **RATED 10!**
Details: Free 20 pg. booklet
Mail: Reference Service Branch
National Archives and Records Administration
8th and Pennsylvania Ave. Rm. 205
Washington, DC 20408
Phone: 202-523-3218
Review: Are you interested in learning who you are related to and where your bloodline began, then this is the business for you.
Reader Review: J. Newell in NC: They responded in two weeks.

Get Connected
Discount call service
Rated 6
Mail: 2127 Olympic Parkway
Ste. 1006-248
Chula Vista, CA 91915
Phone: 866-514-9972
Web: getconnectedus.com
Review: We have verified this business is real. Costs: One-time $6 fee, $5 per month, $2 per call for 30 mins, $20 deposit. Total set-up $31.

Get Grandpas FBI File
Online FBI file service
Rated None
Details: Online
Web: getgrandpasfbifile.com
Web: getmyfbifile.com

Gifts From Within
Gifts
Rated None
Details: SASE
Mail: Box 5636
Peoria, IL 61601
giftsfromwithin2@yahoo.com
Reader review: Jason H. – Says they have a nice catalog.

Girls and Mags (GAM)
Porn and TV Star Fan Photos, Celebrity Addresses
► **RATED 10!**
Details: Send SASE flyers
Prices: $1 and up for StarLISTS, Fan photos free, only pay printing, handling and shipping.
Mail: Box 319
Rehoboth, MA 02769
Review: They have been in business five years and have launched a new product line specializing in fan photos of your favorite TV stars and porn stars. Fan photos, Top 20 Female Porn Stars, Top 20 Male Porn Stars each catalog with photos and bio/ad. Each list full color, letter size paper and 10 sides. $2 each and comes with order form for fan photos. In addition, StarLISTS in four categories Network TV Female Stars, Network TV Male Stars, Network Cable Stars and Network Telenovela Stars, each list of names with order forms for fan photos, $1 for one or $3 for all four lists of network stars. Fan Photos are free, you only pay for printing, handling and shipping, sets of 10 photos.

Only $9.99. Special offer is the new, VIP Custom Star which allows you to pick your favorites star name(s) and order fan photos in sets of 10 photos for free, you only pay printing, handling and shipping of $14.99. We still have the largest selection of Celebrity addresses. June 2019
—SEE OUR ADS—

Global Nomad Distributors
Photo Seller
Rated None
Details: $5 for catalog/info
Mail: 1827 Alfresco Place
Louisville, KY 40205
Review: New photo seller, offers non nude sexy photos in print and digital start at $0.70. Vids by email start at $3 available by catalog order. Send $5 to get catalog and ordering info. Feb. 2019

GOGI Project
Self-help books, making tools
▶ **RATED 10!**
Details: Free
Mail: Box 88969
Los Angeles, CA 90009
Review: Getting Out by Going In (GOGI) was designed by – and for – prisoners and has emerged as a leader in providing donor-subsidized certificate programs to the incarcerated. If you want to earn certificates and want to learn new things but maybe there are no courses where you are or there is a long waiting list, GOGI is a great option. Or maybe you just don't like that classroom setting. That's cool because GOGI in self-study. No matter what, it's likely that GOGI Self Study programs will work for you. Write the volunteers (mostly formerly incarcerated) in the GOGI mail room and ask for free information on the GOGI TOOLS FOR POSITIVE DECISION MAKING, which were created by prisoners for prisoners. You can also ask for information on their donor-subsidized CERTIFICATE PROGRAMS, which are acknowledged by many boards, for many courts, as part of re-sentencing, clemency and alternatives to sentencing. GOGI's Anger Management Course is their latest release and only $50.00 for the 6-week certificate program. GOGI relies on donor support so if you have stamps that you are not using they can be put to good use as GOGI responds to hundreds of prisoner letters each week from across the USA. GOGI is proud that they have more prisoner donors than any other type of donor. Aug. 2017

Golden State Care Packages
Music, shoes, food, clothing
Rated 9
Details: Free catalog – See review
Mail: 212 E. Rowland St. #424
Covina, CA 91723
Phone: 866-387-9830
Web: goldenstatecp.com
Csr@goldenstatecp.com
Review: They offer a printable online catalog. Offer secure packages to CA prisoners. They have a wide selection of food, personal hygiene, clothing and special purchase products and are constantly working to procure new products at competitive prices.

Gold Star Fragrances
Sells men, women and unisex Fragrances
▶ **RATED 10!**
Details: Free catalog
Mail: 4 West 37th St.
New York, NY 10018
Phone: 212-279-4474
Web: goldstarfragrances.com
gstarfragances@gmail.com
Review: They carry 1000 of the finest perfume oils and have been in business since 1976. We have updated the new address number, please note. In addition to the line of high quality scented oils, they sell soaps, incenses, shea butter, shower gels, prayer rugs, Kuffies and more. We recommend sending for this catalog, good prices and there is always a new listing of products and great sales. Good people, quality products and professional fast service. Mar. 2018.
—SEE OUR AD—

Granite Shore Financial Group
Financial services for inmates
Rated None
Details: Send SASE
Mail: Box 111104
Clevland, OH 4111-7104
graniteshoregroup@gmail.com
Review: New to the marketplace started January 1, 2019. Catering to inmates financial needs. They offer inmate bank accounts, investing, shopping services, sending funds by Western Union, Green Dot cards and more. For more informaton write. Always remember to be careful when dealing with new companies especially ones in the financial fields. May 2019

Grant Publications
Discount magazines
▶ **RATED 10!**
Catalog: Send SASE
Mail: Box 28812
Greenfield, WI 53228-0812
Review: Fast friendly service, free

mail corrections when you move. Their catalog carries 500 to 600 titles and points out any super bargains. Carries Beckett, Avengers, Blue Ribbon, Dell, DuPont Registry, Kiplinger, Military Mags, Transworld, Ultimate Comics, USA Today and many titles you won't find elsewhere. Tell them you saw us in Inmate Shopper; order Reader Review: Paul K. in WA –Stellar service, integrity and responsiveness. Apr. 2018
Reader Review: Ryan D. in WI-The best magazine subscription service. I have come across so far. Huge selection, best prices and unmatched customer service. Don't pass them up! Sept. 2018
—SEE OUR AD—

Great Courses, The
College courses on CD
▶ RATED 10!
Details: Free
Mail: 4840 Westfield Blvd., Ste. 500
Chantilly, VA 20151
Phone: 800-832-2412
Web: TheGreatCourses.com
Reader Review: Zachary S – I bought Building Great Sentences for $35. They have courses on everything and reasonable prices.

Gravity Records
Music: cassettes and CDs
▶ RATED 10!
Details: Send SASE
Price: Catalog $2
Mail: Box 512
Mentone, IN 46539
GravityRecords@qualityservice.com
Review: They offer many album/cassettes from $3.99 and up. Plus $5 shipping per order. No screws, prison friendly. Custom cassettes (15 songs) $9.99 plus shipping. Their catalogs contain hundreds of current titles at $11.99 each and over 300 titles at $3.99 each. Available on cassette or CD.

Great Goods
Stamp buyer
▶ RATED 10!
Under New Management
Details: Send SASE
Mail: Box 888
Lake Worth, FL 33460
Web: Greatgoods.org
Greatgoods888@gmail.com
Review: They offer great service and good rates of exchange. Stamps for cash, 70% to 60% face value. Payment sent within 24 hours of receipt. They also offer your stamp payment to be sent to Approved Package Vendors and no extra charge. Minimum money order $20.

GSM Advocacy
LGBQ support network
Rated 8
Details: Send SASE
Mail: 1111 Highway 73
Moose Lake, MN 55767
Review: Started late 2017 they combine members of the LGBTQ community, their families, friends and allies together to advocate for promote for referrals to one another as members of community. Membership is free. June 2019

Halalco Books and Supermarket
Muslim religious items and oils
▶ RATED 10!
Details: Free Catalog
Mail: 5918-B Leesburg Pike
Falls Church, VA 22041
Phone: 703-532-3202 or 703-542-3212
Web: halalco.com
Review: Offers large selection of Muslim items. Books, CDs, incense, religious items, soaps, foods and more. Their body oils are for everyone, inexpensive and mostly based on designer scents. June 2019

Haney Family Chronicles
Quarterly newsletter
Rated 8
Details: See below or
Send SASE for info
Mail: 5111 Hillrose Dr.
Baxter, TN 38544-5348
Review: From the creators of Cosmic Cupid and Pulp Fiction. A newsletter filled with interesting stories, ads, tips and more. Issued 4 times a year. 8.5" x 11" B&W, 10 pages. $2 or 4 stamps for a sample issue. Annual subscription $7 or 14 stamps. Back issues available #1-6, $2 each or all five for $8. Accept cash, stamps and all checks payable to GW Brown. Jan. 2017

Harlem World
Music and video
Rated 8
Details: Send SASE for info
Mail: 21700 Greenfield Rd. Ste. 104
Oak Park, MI 48237
Phone: 248-968-0987
harlemworldvideos@comcast.net
Review: Specializes in rare and diverse black classic films from the early 70s to the current feature and independent films. They also carry many urban documentaries from crime, music, and life lessons. They carry over 500 urban book titles from Independent authors local and abroad Have a large music selection from Jazz, Blues, Hip Hop, Reggae, RandB, Soca, Salsa and Reggaeton Tour Urban Magazine selection

are Don Diva Magazine, F.E.D.S., A.S.I.S., Street Elements, Fame, Straight Stuntin, Skin Tones, Crave, F.E.D.S. Sweets, A.S.I.S. Assets, and many more. Ship to all prisons on every level.
Reader Review: Nevin G. in MI – I can't say enough great things about this company. They sell great products and even faster service. If they do not have it they will get it for you at no extra fee.

Harvey R. Cox.
Prisoner consultant
Prison: Transfers, parole, grievances
Rated None
Mail: Box 1551
Weatherford, TX 76086
Phone: 817-596-8457
Web: prisonerconsultant.com
hrcox@yahoo.com
Review: Offers reasonable rates for help in pre-sentencing services, prison designation, prison transfers, parole, grievances and expert witness. We've been told that he responds quickly.

Hastings Law Journal
Seeks female writers
Rated None
Mail: 100 McAllister. Ste. 2207
San Francisco, CA 94102
hwlsubmissions@gmail.com
Review: Since 1989, the Hastings Women's Law Journal has been committed to giving voice to people outside the traditional legal community. They offer and maintain an inclusive space for feminism, race theory, multiculturalism, animal rights, disability rights, language rights, international human rights, criminal defendants' right and prisoners' rights, among others. HWLJ seeks submissions from women in prison about your experiences. They would like to publish a collection of these pieces. One possible topic is your experiences with lawyers – How do they touch your life? How could they have done more? Write whatever you like; a letter, a real-life story, a letter to a make-believe person, a poem or a song. Please refrain from saying anything possibly defamatory. They may change names to protect identities.

Hawkeye Editing
Proofreading, editing and typing
Rated 8
Details: SASE for info
Mail: Box 16406
St. Paul, MN 55116
Phone: 651-222-2742
Review: They offer a wide variety of services needed to assist you in creating a professional finished document. They offer services on legal papers, a manuscript, book or just some short stories or poetry. They offer estimates on each project and will not start a project until you send back confirmation. There is no charge for evaluating a manuscript of any length, if you enclose postage for return of your documents. They will give you an honest critique and a brief summary with their comments. This is a very important step that you should take BEFORE you order a transcription of any book that you have authored. Their experience has been that NO ONE's book is ready to be published, until it has been thoroughly proofread. Regardless of the type of material submitted, to get a quote on specific jobs it is necessary to submit a good sample of your work. This can be anything from a single page to a chapter, and the cost will depend on three factors: 1– The length. 2– The number of errors of all types. 3– The legibility of the handwritten work. Sept. 2017

Help From Beyond the Walls
Inmate services
► **RATED 10!**
Details: Send SASE new info
Mail: Box 318
Palmyra, ME 04965
helpfrombeyondthewalls@gmail.com
Review: As of January 2019 under new management. Offer publications their list is complied of books to help prisoners, processed within week. Letter forwarding, to any address of your choice, letter will be sent from business within 3 days, cost of $1 or 3 FCS. Buy your books of first-class postage stamps in perfect, unused condition for 75% of face value. ($8.25 per book of stamps). Accept a minimum of 100 stamps. (5 books) Funds will be sent in the form of a money order to whomever you name on the form within ten business days. Large quantities of stamps – 10 books or more – will receive $8.40 per book. Please write to inquire if they are currently buying stamps before sending your postage. Huge selection of high-quality erotic photos. We have over 100 catalogs to choose from with over 25,000 photos in our collection. Write to get order form for photos catalogs. Also offer erotic stories and novels. June 2019

Help From Outside
Professional services
► **RATED 10!**
Details: Send SASE
Mail: 2620 Bellevue Way NE, #200
Bellevue, WA 98004

Phone: 206-486-6042
Web: HelpFromOutside.com
info@helpfromOutside.com
Review: HFO offer an array of professional services in different categories. The Business Services offer administrative, research/Information and paralegal. They also have Personal and Social Services which include shopping, website design and maintenance, as well as social media. The Creative Services offer book/manuscript publishing and editing and many other listings. The prices are billed hourly. The rates start $30 per hour. HFO requires an application and a minimum deposit of $200 to open an account.
—SEE OUR AD—

Hip Hop Weekly
Magazine on Hip Hop Culture
▶ RATED 10!
Details: Free catalog
Mail: 9663 Santa Monica Blvd.
Ste. 526
Los Angeles, CA 90210
Phone: 800-361-3903
Web: hiphopweekly.com
Review: Weekly magazine based on Hip Hop society filled with news, music, videos, indie artists and more. They are experienced in shipping to facilities. One year subscription, 69.99 can be ordered online or by mail. Available in print or digital. Please allow 4-6 weeks for the first issue to be delivered for new subscription. June 2019

Hit Pointe, The
RPG items, binding, graphic novels
▶ RATED 10!
Details: Free catalog
Mail: 540 N Lapeer Rd. #255
Orion Township, MI 48362
Phone: 248-845-8229
Web: HitPointe.com
services@hitpointe.com
Review: They sell all kinds of RPG Books like D&D, Pathfinder, Starwars, just to name a few. Also, some board games, trading card games like 'Magic the Gathering' and of course dice for your RPGs. They also sell a few old RPG Magazines. They sell novels, a lot of fantasy listed in their catalog and some other popular authors. Lots of Sci-Fi too. It's a geek's one stop shop.
Reader Review: Richard A. in SC – Sent for catalog, came in good time and it has a large selection. Feb. 2018
Reader Review: Shannon A in IN- Decent selection of fantasy novels and games. Quick shipping but high prices. I only use them when I can not find the book elsewhere. Apr. 2019
Reader Review: Russell H. in AK- These guys deserve Rated 10! They are the fastest book seller I've dealt with by far, and were very understanding when my facility rejected some items. They printed me bunch of items to help me decide what to order. They are awesome! And you guys rock too! Apr. 2019

Hot Dreams
Photo seller
▶ RATED 10!
Details: Send SASE with $2 or 5 FCS for each catalog
Mail: Box 192
Dequincy, LA 70633
Review: They carry two catalogs. Each catalog has over 450 to choose from and comes with a free photo, see above for details on how to order. Catalog #19 – contains white and Spanish girls. You will love it. It has everything from camel toe, G-strings, thongs, bikinis, hot faces! Catalog #18 – has "super big bottoms", black girls, Spanish girls in bikinis, G-strings, thongs, and very hot poses! All of you apple bottom lovers will love it.

HotFlixx
Photo Seller
Rated 9
Details: $5 per catalog (170 photos)
Mail: Box 137481
Fort Worth, TX 76136
Review: Sell non nude photos sets of many categories. June 2019

Hustle University
Books on business education
Rated 7
Details: Send SASE for info.
Mail: Box 831731
Stone Mountain, GA 30083
Phone: 404-294-7165
Web: HustleUniversity.org
Web: MakeAWayNow.com
hustleuinc@gmail.com
Review: They provide books for entrepreneurs. Offer two books, The Hustler's Bible, it consists of three books in one and is the ultimate success guide of today's urban entrepreneur. Their second book is The Hustler's Mind-Set had six books in one, and is higher learning for the hard-core entrepreneur. Prices start at $35 to $97 and includes shipping.

ICARE Packages
Inmate and family packages
Rated: 9
Details: Online only
Service Area: check online
Web: Icaregifts.com
Review: provides care packages for

both inmates and their families. They market by introducing a wider variety of products for you to choose from. Every month they will be adding Special Event and Holiday theme care packages, seasonal greeting cards, wide variety of magazines, top selling books, clothing and much more! These items are shipped directly from their distribution center to your facility with speed, efficiency and accuracy. Have family check online to see if they service your facility. Free shipping for all orders over $100. June 2019

IMailToPrison.com
Books
► **RATED 10!**
Details: Send SASE
1115 FM 517 Rd. East
Dickinson, TX 77539-8644
Phone: 281-534-3370
Web: IMailToPrison.com
Review: Been online serving inmates since 2007. adamneve.com Offer books, magazines in many titles. New books, used books, paperbacks, hardcovers, calendars, puzzle magazines, back issue magazines and a Spanish selection. Send SASE or $0.75 cents for a listing. Also you have to know your facility mailroom rules in regards to receiving publication. June 2019
Reader Review: David R. in TX – Nice people and were recently impacted by Hurricane Harvey. The prices are very high. Not recommended. Apr. 2018

Immigrant Advertiser
Ad sheet
Rated 5
Details: Sample $2 or 6 FCS
Mail: 5447 Van Fleet Ave. #30127
Richmond, CA 94804-4929
Review: We sent for this and received 4 or 5 pages of ad sheets and flyers consisting of mostly ads.

Immigration Service
Services for illegal aliens
Rated None
Mail: 105 East Grant Rd.
Tucson, AZ 85705
Phone: 520-620-9950

Incarcerate Us
Social Media Prison Platform
Rated 8
Details: Email for info
Web: incarcerateus.com
incarcerateus@aol.com
Review: They provide a free multi purpose social media profile page. Online only, need to email them for info or have outside assistance go to website and sign up for free to get a profile/member page. Can upload unlimited audio, images, word that will be shared to all major social media sites. Page can be used for networking, display essays, articles, poetry, artwork, social media and entrepreneur marketing and to seek friends. June 2019

Indian Life Magazine
American Indian resources
► **RATED 10!**
Details: Sample send $1.50 or 4 FCS
Mail: Box 32
Pembina, ND 58271
Phone: 204-661-9333
Web: indianlife.org
ilm@indianlife.org
Review: Their real office in is Canada: Box 3765 – Redwood Post Office Winnipeg, MBR2W 3R6 CANADA

InfoLincs
Inmate services
► **RATED 10!**
Details: Send SASE for Info
Mail: Box 165
Eagle Point, OR 97524
Phone: 541-878-2600
Web: Infolincs.com
Review: They help the incarcerated stay in touch with the "free-world". Services offered are sport services, photo forwarding, unlimited texting and offer a text and photo special. Prices are monthly, quarterly, yearly for services that start at $20 and up. Pricing on the photo forwarding start at $10 and up for 20 credits. June 2019

Ink From The Pen
Inmate Art Magazine
Rated 8
Details: Send SASE for info
Mail: 1440 Beaumont Ave.
Ste. A2-226
Beaumont, CA 92223
Web: inkfromthepen.com
inkfromthepen@yahoo.com
Review: New company that accepts prison art work to be considered for publication. Need to follow and use "How to Submit Artwork" form, can be printed online or sent for with self-addressed stamp envelope. Do NOT send artwork without. Art can be sent by email with an attached JPG file. They publish magazine filled with prison art, $19.95 plus $5.95 S/H per issue. Will mail to all prisons except Kern Valley in Delano CA. In addition, they create clothing, blankets and pillows from artwork. Feb. 2019

Inmate E Connect
Messaging services

Rated 9
Details: $25 per month
Phone: 347-464-1432
inmateeconnect@gmail.com
Review: New to the marketplace and provide services with features. message single or groups, send question and get Google answers, send URL and get page info, follow unlimited number of twitter channels and can even get the weather for any area. Offer monthly pay plan $25 flat fee that will be processed once a month. Mar. 2019
—SEE OUR AD—

Inmate Call Savings
Discount calls
Rated None
Details: Must call or go to Web
Phone: 305-900-3093
Web: inmatecallsavings.com
Support@inmatecallsavings.com

Inmates' Little Helpers
Inmate services
► RATED 10!
Details: Send SASE
Mail: Box 4234
Oakland, CA 94614
Phone: 5875-9437
Web: inmateslittlehelper.com
inmates123456@gmail.com
Review: Offer a huge list of services. Everything from long distance and local toll calls, to assisting in paying your child support payments. They claim to be a jack of all trades with a list of services that is over 20 items. Accept institutional checks, BP-199, MoneyGram and PayPal. For more info send SASE. They also run Nothing Butt Pictures. June 2019
—SEE OUR AD—

Inmate Magazine Service
Discount magazine sales
Rated 7
Details: Send SASE
Mail: Box 2063
Fort Walton Beach, FL 32549
Phone: 855-936-4674
Web:inmatemagazineservice.com
customerservice@inmatemagazine-service.com
Review: They offer magazines by mail. You can order by mail or online. They require an SASE when writing them. They send out a confirmation/receipt of your order. Offer specials 3 for $20, 6 for $25 and 10 for $35. Order by mail or online. Send SASE for listings and order form. On the website there is customer service email fill in form, that is the best way to get an answer any issues. There is also a Change of Address fill in form, again best to have someone on the outside use these forms to get results. Mar. 2019
Reader Review: James M. in TX-Just a heads up...I ordered their 10 mags for $41.99, money was sent out July 2018, since then I have only received 5 out of the 10 magazines. I have written twice, my wife has gotten in touch with them online, still same. It ticks me off how they do and get away with this, just wanted you to know.
Reader Review: Ryan D. in WI-They have great selection at good prices, the specials are the bread and butter which can't be beat price wise anywhere. Customer service is responsive. But, they take several weeks. Feb. 2018

Inmate Photo Pro
Photo reproduction and editing
Rated 8
Details: Send SASE
Mail: Box 2451
Forrest City, AR 72336
inmatephotoproinfo@yahoo.com
Review: They offer a variety of services including photo reproduction services texted/emailed from family members; a variety of gift items such as flowers, calendars, etc. as well as social media services as well as magazine subscriptions. They take photos that family and friends send to them via email and text and then mail it to the inmate. They will open an account with a $10 deposit and if BOP inmates use the Money Gram they will take $2.50 off all orders. They also will do ebook pages and other social media. Aug. 2017

Inmate Photo Service
Greeting cards, stationary, photos
Rated 6
Details: paparazzi style photos
Mail: Box 245895
Sacramento, CA 95824
Review: For $3 you receive 8 color pgs. 2 pgs. of CA girls. In fact, these girls get around a bit so these photos aren't sold in CA. Black, white and Asian girls, very nice. Also included are some greeting cards. Limited selection mostly Asian but they're looking for artists and will buy your art or trade. Stationary cost from $2.50 to $25. A family run business that answers their mail.
Reader Review: Louis J. in PA- I sent them an check for $3 plus an SASE over three months ago. Their email address is no good anymore. Buyer Beware. June 2019

Inmate Scribes
Email and social media
Rated 6

Details: Send SASE
Mail: Box 818
Appleton, WI 54912
Info@inmatescribe.com
Review: They offer set up services for social networks and dating sites. They have one cent billing. This simplifies how to charge for email, social network services, typing and messages etc. It's a penny a word. They do not have any email or social media for themselves. We have heard many complaints about the speed, or rather lack of it. Another, problem with this company, is customer service, they do not have any. We have been told numerous times, the inmate set-up an account and paid their money … and then nothing for months.
Reader Review: F. Stephen in WA – I have been working with them for a few months now, they are slow but seem to be getting their act together.

Inmate Services
Photo Seller
► **RATED 10!**
Details: B&W catalog with SASE
Mail: Box 535547
Grand Prairie, TX 75053
Phone: 214-298-2603
Web: InmateServices.biz
J161jones@yahoo.com
Review: Been in business since 2010. Offers sexy non nude photos, calendars, art patterns, magazine subscriptions and gift service Free B&W catalogs: Send SASE with one stamp will ship one catalog, SASE with two stamps will ship three catalogs. They sell 4" x 6" non nude photos of women for $0.45 cents, art patterns for $0.35, gifts to loved ones for $12. (Includes S/H), full size calendars for $5, pocket calendars for $2. They also offer a color catalogs in the form of a book for $2 each. Accept stamps face value, checks, and money orders. They swap out denied photos with photos of their choice. They offer fast and reliable services and have good communication skills. Apr. 2019
Reader Review: Shannon A. in IN-Good prices, selection and quick response to small orders. But as soon as you in a big order, you have a problem. They spent three months denying they received my money, after I did a track and showed they got it , they spent another three months saying it was already been sent. Then spent another piecemealing my books and photos to me, each time saying we were square, took me 10 months of letters, emails and calls to get the complete order. Buyer beware. Apr. 2019
—SEE OUR ADS—

Inmate Service Corp.
Sports and gifts
Rated 8
Details: Send SASE info
Mail: Michelle McDonald
2155 Aunia Rd.
Kehel, HI 96753
fiolines1@gmail.com
baseballinfoonly1@gmail.com
Review: they offer sports information for your gaming needs. There email service is free to keep informed, sign up today Corrlinks email package for full year football lines only $105. In addition they offer gift services. June 2019

Inmate Shopper
America's largest book of resources for inmate services
Rated: Loved by prisoners, 5 stars on Amazon!
Began publishing: 2010
Published by: Freebird Publishers
Published through: KDP (An Amazon Co.)
Founding editor: George Kayer, RETIRED as of Sept. 2013 (AZ State Prisoner)
Issued: New ANNUALLY Split Year (2019-20, 2020-21 etc.) Releases Mid-year, every year.
Print Quality: HD Digital, In-Print, B&W with Full color cover and ebook
Size: 8" x 10", soft cover, 360+ pgs.
Issues: Regular or Censored (censored contains no pen pal or sexy photos/sellers)
Price $19.99 plus $7 S/H tracking
Mail: Box 541
North Dighton, MA 02764
Web: freebirdpublishers.com
Diane@freebirdpublishers.com
Review: We have given the INSH a fresh new look, with up-to-date formats, new content, sections and special features. Every issue will have new content in the issues sections layouts. Criminal Justice News, Entertainment, Special Features Sports Schedules, What's Trending, LGBTQ, Reentry and many more. You will find some of your original favorite sections too!
Reader Review: Christopher K in OR-I recently borrowed an your books from someone and could not believe all the resources. I love your book. Keep doing what you all oar doing, this is an amazing resource for any inmate/convict. Thank you. Apr. 2019
Reader Review: Alexander O. in AZ – Nice resource book and a great book to share but I like my own copy because I refer to the book so much. Feb. 2018

Reader Review: Phillip B. in OR –I recently had the opportunity to review this book and was impressed with its contents. I will certainly be ordering the next issue. Feb. 2018
Reader Review: Richard A. -SC – Rate 10 in my book, a excellent recourse book, can not believe I survived this long without one. Feb. 2018
Reader Review: Erik L. in OR-I recently purchased current issue thru amazon and i do appreciate all the work that goes into keeping up with all our issues and concerns as inmates. I would like to say thank you. Mar. 2019
Reader Review: Marcus S. in TN-My family sent me copy of Inmate Shopper. On behalf of myself and other inmates that are lucky enough to have access to this book... We thank you for your service you provide. The resources you provide are helpful and entertaining. Thankful to all your staff and look forward to doing more business with you all. Sept. 2018
Reader Review: Anthony B. in CA-My people recently purchased me a copy of your current issue. Let me say, this book has it all! I found it incredibly helpful. Thank you so much for making this publication for people like me. Matter of fact I was so satisfied with the book that I have written a poem about it and mailed to your submissions department. Oct. 2018
Reader Review: Kyle I in CA-I am incarcerated at the Navel Consolidated Brig Miramar and I recently purchased a 2018-19 Inmate Shopper and fell in love with your company. Thank you so much for what you all are doing and all the help you provide. Mar. 2019
Reader Review: Juan M. in PA-I want to start by saying I love your book. I have been viewing your book since 2010. Very helpful. June 2019
—SEE OUR AD—

Inmate Shopper: Submissions
Publishes writings by inmates
Rated by our Readers Enjoyment
Details: See Below
Mail: Box 541
North Dighton, MA 02764
Diane@freebirdpublishers.com
Web: freebirdpublishers.com
Compensation: A free issue of the INSH your piece is printed in and the pride and recognition of your talents. Submission Guidelines: We accept bios written in third party, on all art categories (writers, poetry, artwork, music etc.). Tell us about yourself and your skill, past, present and future, include photos, drawings, promotions tag line for any published books, websites, blogs, etc. Submission Guidelines: We accept writings, poetry, and artwork, music by mail or email. Do not send complete manuscripts. We accept articles about prison life, book reviews, how-to, fictions, prison hustle for a buck, commissary products, jokes, cartoons and more. No political-prison policy, religious, no heavy sexual content or vulgar language. NOTE: We no longer sell art or hobbies on our website. Thank you.

Innocence Project
Legal help for the innocent
► RATED 10!
Details: Send SASE for
Mail: Intake Department
40 Worth St., Ste. 701
New York, NY 10013
Phone: 212-364-5340
Web: innocenceproject.org
Info@innocenceproject.org
Reviews: They handle only DNA evidence cases. To submit a case to them you need their Intake Form, can mail in for it, they will mail 10 page questionnaire. This intake form is available on the website for free in PDF format. The Innocence Project is not equipped to handle case applications or inquiries by email or over the phone. All case submissions and follow-up correspondence will be handled by mail or overnight delivery services only. If you are seeking legal assistance, please read the following guidelines for submitting your case. The Innocence Project ONLY considers cases that are: Post conviction—the trial and direct appeal are over and final. There is physical evidence that, if subjected to DNA testing, will prove that the defendant is actually innocent. This means that physical evidence was collected – for example blood, bodily fluids, clothing, hair – and if that evidence can be found and tested, the test will prove that the defendant could not have committed the crime. Examples of crimes where biological evidence can prove innocence include sexual assaults, homicides, assaults with close physical contact or a struggle and some robberies—where physical evidence was collected that was worn by or in contact with the actual perpetrator. The defendant must have been convicted of a crime. They do not review claims where the defendant was wrongfully suspected, arrested or charged, but not actually convicted. The crime occurred in the United States, but not: Arizona, California, Illinois, Michigan, Ohio, Washington, Wisconsin, or Puerto Rico. The intake is currently closed

to these states. Available online a list of innocence organizations in those states. The Innocence Project does NOT review claims where DNA testing cannot prove innocence. We do not handle the following types of cases. Consent/Transaction: The defendant claims that there was no crime because the victim consented to the events (e.g. agreed to sex) and/or received some form of payment in exchange for the activity. (e.g. Prostitution, drug transaction) Self Defense/Justification: The defendant admits to causing the injury/ death but believes the acts were justified because he/she acted in self defense or to protect other people. Sustained Abuse – The defendant is accused of crimes against the victim(s) that happened more than once and over a period of time (e.g.,allegations of long term sexual abuse of a family member). Illegal Possession/Distribution of any controlled substance: The defendant is only challenging a possession or distribution charge, RICO: The defendant has been charged under RICO, DWI or DUI: The defendant was convicted of driving while intoxicated (DWI) or driving under the influence (DUI), Fraud/Identity Theft/Forgery: The defendant was only convicted of one or more of these crimes. Stalking/Harassment – The primary charges against the defendant involve stalking and/or harassment. Sentencing reduction/overcharged – The defendant wants to challenge the charge or length of sentence but does not claim innocence. Feb. 2017

Inside-Out Bars
Pre & Probiotic Protein Bars
► RATED 10!
Details: Send SASE
Mail: 1859 Powell St. #102
SanFrancisco, CA 94133
Phone: 415-723-0675
Web:insideoutbar.com
Seth@insideoutbar.com
Review: First, let us say, these bars are good and good for you. Yes, we know you being in prison can not order them to support this great cause, but your loved ones can. Other than raising awareness of our mass incarceration issues, this is also an employment opportunity for anyone, just released or your loved ones. Prices are good and bars are a huge part of today's market. Two flavors, Peanut Butter Choco Chip and Cranberry Almond. Cost $1.80/ bar May 2019
—SEE OUR AD—

Institute of Children's Literature
Writing school
► RATED 10!
Details: Free catalog
Mail: 93 Long Ridge Rd.
West Reddington, CT 06896
Phone: 800-243-9645
Web:theinstituteofchildrensliterature.com
Review: They take you all the way with a personal writing coach, even to help you choose a publisher, send in your MS, etc. If you are serious about children's books, this would be a good place to start.

Intelligent Solutions Advisory
Tools for Freedom National Catalog
► RATED 10!
Details: Send for Free color catalog, 88 pgs.
Mail: 4-1104 Kuhio Hwy.
Ste. 101 #143
Kapaa, HI 96746
Phone: 800-770-8802 ext. 1
Web: toolsforfreedom.com
Customerservice@freedomprivacy.com
Review: Knowledge is power. Learn how to defend yourself in court, successfully omit unlawful fines, fees and citations, and stop foreclosure and more. They have a vast array of publications in their sovereignty resource section, establishing your sovereignty, learn how to win in court, becoming a secure party creditor, healthcare and more. In addition, they carry hundreds of other publications in a wide variety of subject matter, there is something for everyone. Tools for Freedom,catalog with featured articles are published quarterly, the editors and researchers never hesitate to tackle subjects that conventional news sources suppress. Feb. 2019

International Christian College
Correspondence course
Rated 8
Details: Send SASE for info
Mail: Box 530212
Debary, FL 32753-0212
Web: ICCSCampus.org
Review: Offers degrees from Associates to Doctorates via correspondence courses in Christian counseling. Ordination services are available. Inexpensive. Offer a free evaluation. Feb. 2019

Jaden Moore of New York
Gift service
► RATED 10!
Details: Catalog, 5 FCS
Mail: 309 Main St., Suite 1
Poughkeepsie, NY 12601
Web: jadenmooreofnewyork.com
Gifts@jadenmooreofnewyork.com

Review: We could write several pages about the people at Jaden Moore. They're wonderful professional people that care about quality and customer service because the system has touched their lives too. When you need that special gift for your loved one, you can count on JMNY to provide the best quality and personal service.
Reader Review: Shannon A. in IN-A place for gifts, especially if you need to ask for specifics that other companies will not do, they will work with you. Nice selection and quick response. Apr. 2019

Jailhouse Lawyers Manual
Legal resource guide
► **RATED 10!**
Details: Publications in English or Espanol
Price: $30 includes S/H, Supplements $15 each
Mail: Columbia Human Rights Law Review
Attn.: JLM Order
435 West 116th St.
New York, NY 10027
Phone: 212-854-1601
Web: jlm.law.columbia.edu
jlm.board.mail@gmail.com\
Review: The 11th edition has been completely revised and updated. Been in circulation since 1978. 10th edition was dated 2014. Offer printed order forms online. For a limited time you can order up to three chapters of 10th edition of JLM for free.
The JML is produced to assist prisoners and others in negotiating the U.S. legal system. With chapters on legal rights and procedures including the appellate process, federal habeas corpus relief, the Prison Litigation Reform Act, religious freedom in prison, the rights of prisoners with disabilities, and many more, the JLM is a major legal reference for prisoners and libraries across the country. Publish a Spanish version of the JLM. Finally, the JLM offers an Immigration and Consular Access Supplement, Texas State Supplement in both English and Spanish language versions. Feb. 2019

Jailmate Cards
Greeting Cards
► **RATED 10!**
Details: Cards with mailing services
Web: jailmatecards.com
jailmatecards@hotmail.com
Review: They come from the UK but are professional and friendly people. Their service is #1, really wonderful cards and they are quick too. Online but can do business by email with them. Make sure to give your family and loved ones their website info so they can use too!.Corrlinks and JPay but we know if you have another email provider they will accept your invite. They personalize every card, upload photos onto front/inside, offer unique poetry, rap cards, that relate to incarcerated. Write own letter and messages. Cards of support, daddy, miss you, humor, over 18's, birthdays, valentines, halloween, criminal bear collection, court, parole, release and everything in-between. All with the jailmate theme. Spread the word. June 2019
—SEE OUR ADS—

J.E.S. Elite Prisoner Solutions
Prisoner assistant
► **RATED 10!**
Details: Send SASE
Mail: Box 304
Lovejoy, GA 30250
Web:jaclynelise.com
jeliselegal@gmail.com
Review: The are under new name and management. They are not affiliated former company. They are solely dedicated to assisting the incarcerated. They offers document prep, legal research, social media management, internet search, photos and printing, website design, graphic design and more. Payment plans are available, no minimums or account fees. They accept email from all prison email/messaging systems (Corrlinks, JPay, Getting Out etc.) Apr. 2019
Reader Review: Christopher K. in OR-Jackie has typed, edited, and formatted my manuscript for me, and she's been awesome. Writing a book is hard, and takes longer than a lot of people expect. Jackie is first class and full of integrity, and I can't say enough good things about her. If you're trying to publish a manuscript, I would certainly recommend her. Thanks to her work, I'm going to be published soon.
—SEE OUR AD—

Jessi Kyann
Ads, reports, info by mail
Rated 7
Details: See Below
Mail: Box 1148
Newport, OR 97365
Review: A small one person business by mail only. They offer different kinds of printed materials. Some of their products are Packets of Ads priced at 4 stamps for 4 months, Grab Bag Reports, $1 each to get a list of reports need to send them $1 plus one stamp, How To Sell Information By Mail, 15 page booklet price $4, Reports: 99 Businesses for

Retirees $1, Business for Students $1, 54 Ways to Fight Grocery Prices $2, 200 Helpful Household Hints $2, Make Money Selling Recipes $2, Fat Burning Soup $2, 21 Envelope Tricks $2, 45 Tips to Reduce Cost of Living $2, 18 Ways of Free Advertising $2, 44 Ways to Cut Cost of Gasoline $2. As you can see these reports are considered by some to be scam mail, but others like this kind of reading and information. Order at your own discretion. Feb. 2017.

Jewish Supply
Jewish items
Rated 7
Details: Verified Jewish Inmates Only
Mail: 9540 Collins Ave.
Surfside, FL, 33154-7127
Phone: 305-866-5875
Web: jewishsupply.com
Sales@jewishsupply.com
Review: FREE bimonthly magazine for verified Jewish Prisoners. Prisoners given discount prices on all things Jewish – Daily Prayer/Ritual Items (Siddur, Tallit, Tefillin, Tzitzit, Yarmulke, etc.), Sabbath Ritual Items (must be ordered with prior approval of institution), many books: on prayer, Jewish History, Hebrew Language study, keeping Kosher, Torah Study and Educational Materials (Chumash and Tanach in Hebrew/English, Tanya, Chassidic Series, Talmud Travelers Edition, Midrash etc.). Also many learning DVDs and a few CDs (if allowed by institution). Accepts orders directly from inmates, from family for inmates, and by institutional staff for inmates. Aug.

JND Ads and Contacts
Zine
Rated 8
Details: Free zine send SASE
Mail: Box 950
Spokane, WA 99210
Review: Issue No. 11, Nov., 2014, 12 pages. Zines, Buy, Sell, Network, Trade, Pen Pals. Price: $2, Free to Prisoners, stamps or SASE appreciated.

Julie's Gifts
Gift service
► **RATED 10!**
Details: Free catalog, 4 pgs., Color.
Mail: Box 1941
Buford, GA 30515
Review: Business is owned by Wad Magazine. Gift selections are priced from $20-$80, plus shipping. Each gift is sent with your personal letter or card, wrapped, a 13" red, scented silk rose, greeting card and a bonus gift of a free, 1 year magazine subscription. Check them out! You may find just what you've been looking for. June 2017
Reader Review: David R. in TX – this company is very responsive and thoughtful. The gift I ordered for my wife was very nicely wrapped and included a handwritten note. They also wrote me a note on my receipt. Highly recommended. Apr. 2018

Justice Denied
Books on prisoner issues; Online coverage of 3,000 wrongly convicted
► **RATED 10!**
Online Only: 2010
Published by: Hans Sherrer
Editor: Natalie Smith-Parra
Mail: Box 68911
Seattle, WA 98166
Phone: 206-335-4254
Web: justicedenied.org
hsherrer@justicedenied.org
Review: One of the best at covering this area; following the people and stories from beginning to release.. Anyone may submit a case account of a wrongful conviction for consideration by JD However your account should be no more than 3,000 words in length. Short accounts are more likely to attract people to your story. A typed account is best, but not necessary. If you hand write your account, make sure it is legible and that there are at least ½" margins to the edge of the paper. First impressions are important, so it is to your advantage to pay attention to the following guidelines when you write the account that you submit to JD.

Justice Now
Seeks women's true stories
► **RATED 10!**
Details: Free
Mail: 1322 Webster St. #210
Oakland, CA 94612
Phone: 510-839-7654
Web: jnow.org
Cynthia@jnow.org
Review: Justice Now is the first teaching law clinic in the country solely focused on the needs of women prisoners. Interns and staff provide legal services in areas of need identified by women prisoners, including: compassionate release, healthcare access, defense of parental rights, sentencing mitigation, placement in community-based programs.

Justice Solutions of America
Prison consultants
Rated None
Details: Send SASE
Mail: Box 3830293
Ocala, FL 34483-0293
Phone: 888-577-4766

Web: federalprisonconsultants.com
Web: stateprisoneconsultants.com
Review: They have two divisions, federal and state. Each provide prison advocacy and prison consulting services, with documented results, on behalf of criminal defendants and their criminal defence attorneys, as well as prison inmates incarcerated within all prison facilities. They offer pre-sentence consulting services, Incarcerated consulting services such as Residential Substance Abuse Treatment Placement (RDAP), Non Residential Substance Abuse Treatment (NRDAP), sex offender treatment, medical transfers, institutional transfers between federal prisons, redesignation, compassionate release from federal prison, elderly offender release from federal prison, administrative remedy program filing in federal prison, federal prison furlough, good time credits. In addition, they offer post sentence and commutation of sentence services such as commutation of sentence and pardon petitions. Mar. 2018

Kabbalah Research Institute
Free correspondence course
▶ **RATED 10!**
Details: Free
Mail: 2009 85th St. Ste. 51
Brooklyn, NY 11214
Phone: 800-540-3234
Review: The Kabbala is one of the best for purity of message. Facts change, eternal truths remain the same throughout time.

Kenneth Passaro
Photos via JPay
Rated 8
Details: $1 per pic, 20 photo min.
Mail: Box 18 Belmont Ave. #2
Haledon, NJ 07509-1799
aorganization3@aol.com
Review: He is former prisoner and a Christian who did nearly ten years in the New Jersey state prison system. He offers non nude photos, no kids, don't ask. Nothing obscene in photos, only one person per. $1 per photo with a 20 photo minimum order. He is here to help and won't do anything illegal or immoral. Accepts stamps, facility check and Paypal for payments. Send payments to Kenneth Passaro. For more info send invite on JPay. May 2018

Knights of Monte Cristo
Parole and reentry services
Rated 9
Details: Send SASE
Mail: 60644
Houston, TX 77025
Phone: 346-302-8932
Web: knightsofmontecristo.com
Info@knightsofmontecristo.com
Review: They are a fraternal style membership based organization that assists inmates and their families through the incarceration and reentry process. They have reentry services, parole packets, support letters, ID acquisition and resumes. General Services, product/magazine/book ordering. B&W copies, internet searches and more. Memberships are yearly $100 which gives you discounts off all the services and some free of charge. Their most popular service is the Parole Packet, which costs $300 for non-members and $250 for members. June 2019

Krasnya, LLC
Photo seller
Rated 8
Details: See review
Buys stamps: $6 per book.
Mail: Box 32082
Baltimore, MD 21282
Corrlinks accepted at: KrasnyaStuds@hotmail.com and KrasnyaBabes@hotmail.com
Review: Offer female and male sexy photos. The company has 120 nude or non nude photos on a catalog page for $4.50. They've been in business two years and we've received one complaint (last review, below).
Reader Review: G. Hernandez in TN – I ordered their grab bag of 50 photos for $25. I received the photos in 32 days. The photos are high quality and pretty decent.
Reader Review: Donald U. in AZ- Very similar to Branlettes Beauties, sent to them, got my reply within two weeks with sample flyer, even the deals were similar. May 2019

KSR Wear and Food Catalog
Inmate clothing and foods
▶ **RATED 10!**
Details: NY – Online Catalog
Mail: Box 7644
Hicksville, NY 11801
Phone: 516-350-8751 or 516-459-9520
Web: ksrwear.com
ksrwear@yahoo.com
Review: KSRwear (Keepin' Style Real) is a family business based in New York. Their goal is to provide excellent service to those incarcerated and their family members. They provide quality merchandise at competitive prices. They also offer free shipping on orders $150 dollars or more. Browse through the online (only) catalog of apparel for sports, everyday wear, food snacks, shades, dictionaries, cosmetics, food storage and more. June 2019

Lawful Remedies
Legal services
► **RATED 10!**
Details: Send SASE for Info
Mail: 3300 Bee Cave Rd.
Ste. 650-1185
Austin, TX 78746
Phone: 512-551-3606 or
512-789-6864
lawfulremedies594@gmail.com Review: Their specialities involve issues that can be raised at any time: indictments, jurisdiction, due process, actual innocence, and quo warranto. Some research shows that no valid indictment has been issued in the last 20 years. Even in the Oklahoma City bombing, the government admitted that a key witness had committed perjury before the court, which was reversible error. We have certain procedures in order to help you. We have been involved in over 90 wins.

Law Office of Matthew S. Pinix
Appellate attorneys
Rated 8
Details: WI and IL Send SASE
Mail: 1200 East Capital Dr., Ste. 360
Milwaukee, WI 53211
Phone: 414-963-6164
Web: pinixlawoffice.com
Info@pinixsoukup.com
Review: Special in criminal appeal cases and Civil rights. They handle direct appeal, post-conviction and habeas cases in the states of Wisconsin and Illinois Only. Attorneys with over 15 years combined experience. June 2019

Left Bank Books
Book seller
► **RATED 10!**
Details: Accepts FCS
Mail: 92 Pike St. Box A
Seattle, WA 98101
Phone: 206-622-0195
Web: leftbankbooks.com
Review: A rare, employee owned book store. Sells books from small publishers priced from $8 to $25 a wide variety. Thousands to choose from. The problem we experienced is they run about six months behind on mail. This means you need to have your family or friends to print their catalog off the website, then order by phone or online.

Legal Services For Prisoner With Children
Legal services, info and referrals
► **RATED 10!**
Details: Send SASE
Mail: 1540 Market St., Ste. 490
San Francisco, CA 94102
Phone: 415-255-7036
Web: prisonerswithchildren.org
Review: They offer copies of the "Jailhouse Lawyers Manual" to any state or Federal prison. Other legal materials are written based on CA law; free to CA inmates. They accept CC and FCS.

Legit Styles
Self-publishing services
Rated 9
Details: Send SASE for info
Mail: 16501 Shady Grove Rd.
Ste. 7562
Phone: 301-605-4382
Gaithersburg, MD 20898
Phone: 888-572-8845
Web: legitstylespublishing.com
info@legitstylespublishing.com
Review: Offering self-publishing services, to the bring exposure to the artistic literature. Services are typing, typesetting, book covers, ebook formatting, interior book layout, editing, ghost writing and online book distribution. June 2019

Let Me Write It For You
Writing services
► **RATED 10!**
Details: Send SASE for info
Mail: Box 156
Clarksville, TN 37041
Phone: 931-269-9718
Web: jobwinningresumes.net
letmewriteitforyou@gmail.com
Review: Professional writing services. Can't Say it? Can't get the interview? Can't get your resume into the hands of your ideal company? Can't produce a job-winning resume? Don't know what's wrong with your resume? They will write it for you. They offer a free newsletter/welcome kit. They offer many packages at many price levels. June 2019

Let My Fingers Do Your Typing
Typing and copy services
► **RATED 10!**
Details: SASE
Mail: Box 4178
Winter Park, FL 32793
Phone: 407-579-5563
Review: Two years in the typing business, medium priced. They do not partnership or barter or do manuscripts.

Lewisburg Prison Project
Legal how-to bulletins
► **RATED 10!**
Details: Send SASE
Mail: Box 128
Lewisburg, PA 17837
Phone: 570-523-1104
Reviews: They counsel and assist prisoners who write to them when they encounter treatment they perceive as illegal or unfair. Their

geographic coverage area includes four federal institutions (Allenwood, Lewisburg, McKean, and Schuylkill), 11 Pennsylvania state prisons, and 34 county jails in the middle district of Pennsylvania. They write to and visit inmates and assist them by talking to prison authorities, furnishing inmates with appropriate legal materials, and evaluating individual cases to determine if wish to represent inmates in civil litigation.

Liberty News Program
Business opportunity newsletter
Rated 8
Details: Send SASE for info
Mail: Box 1110
Rogue River, OR 97537
Review: The company offers how to make money advertisement newsletters. Offers like $10 on time fee for 60 top quality network marketing leads that could earn you up to $5550. Send for brochure with SASE for ordering details. March 2017

Love In A Gift Box
Gift service
► **RATED 10!**
Details: Send SASE for info
Mail: 206A, S. Loop 336 W #239
Conroe, TX 77304
loveinagiftbox@yahoo.com
Review: Beautiful heirloom gift. Handmade baby bonnet traditionally worn home from the hospital or Christening or Dedication day then on their wedding day the bonnet transforms into a handkerchief (something old). One of the most thoughtful gift ideas for babies. Price is $19.95 plus $7.95 S/H and you may include a card or letter to be sent with the bonnet. Carry a complete line of Christian jewelry featuring horseshoe crosses. Will ship your order gift wrapped at no additional charge with your personal message attached. Catalog not yet available. Send a brief note with SASE and they will respond with suggestions, photos and pricing.

Lower Cost Calls
Federal inmate calling service
Rated 8
Details: Send SASE for info
Mail: 1890 Star Shoot Pkwy.
Ste. 170-153
Lexington, KY 40509
Phone: 502-603-9130
Web: lowercostcalls.com
Client@lowercostcalls.com
Review: The company been in business since 2015, they service federal prisoners. They provide local numbers that are linked to a cell or land line phone number of each person you wish to call, the person's phone number does not change. BOP inmates can save $1.50 per 15-minute call in US and $2.15-$15.85 on 15-minute international calls using this service. They offer a special $15 Sign Up bonus online. May 2019

Lulu-Guide to Earning Law and Law Related
Degrees Non-Traditionally
Education book
Rated 8
Details: Send SASE for info
Mail: Lulu Customer Care
3101 Hillsborough St.
Raleigh, NC 27607-5436
Phone: 919-459-5858
Web: lulu.com
Review: The book covers schools that offer paralegal programs, law degrees (bar or non bar) and law related (legal secretary, forensics, PI, criminal justice etc.) programs. Over 400 schools most offering correspondence learning. This book is available in print or ebook. $24.95 plus $7 S/H, 302 pgs. Author K. Seneca.

Magazine City
Discount magazine subscriptions
Rated 7
Details: Online or phone
Phone: 800-787-1414
Web: magazinecity.com
Review: Sell and ships to prisoners. Online and phone orders only! No printed catalog.

Madam Photo
Photo seller and more
► **RATED 10!**
Details: Send SASE info
Mail: Box 552
North Dighton, MA 02764
Phone: 774-406-8682 (text)
Madamphoto@freebirdpublishers.com
Review: A sister company of Freebird Publishers that has been being created for the last couple years. Seller of non nude photo sets, female and male models, all which share their first name with you. The photo collections are Female Escort, Male Escort, Play-Girl, Play-Boy, Call Girl and Gigolo. Female collection models are separated into nationality and hair color. Male collection models are divided into bears, boys next door, muscle guys and swimmers. Photos sets have 5-8 and/or 9-12 photos per set. The choices do not stop there, difference photo finishes and sizes are offered for each too. Each photo set comes with an added Bonus. In addition you can order Designer Collage Posters available in any photo set and Designer

Single Photo Posters available in any single photo from any photo set, posters come in different paper finishes and sizes. Madam Photo will also be offering speciality items personalized with a photo, to be send to you (if prison mail rooms allow) or for sending as a gift to someone on the outside, items like playing cards, puzzles, mugs, etc. Color Gloss catalog has over 500+ photos (more being added every month), one from each photo set for your ordering selections send $9.99 plus $4 for tracking. June 2019
—SEE OUR ADS—

Magazine Price Search
Discount subscriptions
► **RATED 10!**
Details: Online
Web: magazinepricesearch.com
Review: Monitors subscription prices of 2,593 magazines and offers the lowest prices anywhere

MailMyPix
Photo and Text Service
Rated None
Details: Online only
Phone: 870-494-9590
Web: mailmypix.com
Support@mailmypix.com
Review: Sister company with Ring-MyPhone.com. This service allows you to send and receive messages through corrlinks.com to any USA based cell phone. Unlimited monthly messages $10 not including corrlinks fees. You receive instructions on how to create a message and dedicated SMS phone number for their loved ones to send and receive messages. Your loved one can send photos with purchase of photo credits, all photos are printed and mailed to you within 72 hours. Feb. 2019

Majestic Records
Agent for song writers
Rated None
Details: Send SASE
Mail: Box 1140
Linden, TX 75563

Malefic Productions
Music and book publishing
Rated 7
Details: Send SASE for flyer
Mail: c/o Mike Fulkerson
501 Lake Ave. Ste. 26
Gothenburg, NE 69138
maleficproductions88@yahoo.com
Reviews: Offers music and book publishing services. They do not offer inmate services, they are music producers and book publisher. They do not offer anything else, no photos, no cover designs. Feb. 2017

Michael R. Levine, Esq.
Legal newsletter and book
Rated 7
Mail: 1001 SW Fifth Ave., Ste. 1414
Portland, OR 97204
Web: services-commerce.com
Review: Mr. Levine is the author of "138 Mitigating Factors" and offers a newsletter and legal updates; $100 year.

Mickey Gardener's Gift Shop
Gifts
Rated 7
Details: Send 2 stamps for info
Mail: Box 2445
Stone Mountain, GA 30086
Phone: 770-695-3935
Review: They sell all kinds of items and gifts. From flowers to Teddy bears. Jewelry to lingerie and more. Aug. 2017

Middle Ground
Legal referrals and fee based service
Rated 8
Details: Serves only AZ
Mail: 139 E. Encanto Dr.
Tempe, AZ 85281
Phone: 602-650-1376
Web: MiddleGroundPrisonReform.org
Reviews: Legal referrals for civil and constitutional rights issues; advocacy on issues affecting all prisoners; fee based help for individuals and prisoners.
Reader Review: Alexander O. in AZ – I have had bad experience with them. They fail to answer letter unless you have mailed in money. They do not seem to really do anything for the average inmate and prisoner issues. Feb. 2018

Midnight Express Books
Publishing services
► **RATED 10!**
Details: Send SASE
Mail: Box 69
Berryville, AR 72616
Phone: 870-210-3772
mebooks1@yahoo.com
Review: We've reviewed over 300 business serving prisoners with their publishing needs. Of those 300, Victor and Linda's Midnight Express is certainly in our top 10. You may not like what they tell you about your project but they speak the truth. They know from experience how to get your project in print.
Reader Review: T. Wayne in SC – MEB published two novels, one magazine, and several essays for me since we began working with each other in 2012. MEB also created and expertly designed my website StraightFromthePen.com), which has

a link to WordPress for me to post my blogs on with their assistance. Visitors may purchase my books from the website. I compared prices with other companies that offer similar services and none can touch what Victor and Linda Huddleston charged me at MEB. I give them a "Ten" and a standing ovation.

Midwest Pages to Prisoners
Reading materials
Rated 9
Price: Free
Mail: c/o Boxcar Books
408 East 6th St.
Bloomington, IN 47408
Phone: 812-339-8710
Web: boxcarbooks.org
Boxcar@boxcarbooks.org
Review: an all-volunteer effort that strives to encourage self-education among prisoners in the United States. By providing free reading materials upon request. They exist because prisoners are not strangers: they are brothers, sisters, friends, cousins, mothers and children.

Military Records
Copies of your service records
Rated None
Price: Free
Mail: One Archives Dr.
St. Louis, MO 63132
Review: Military national personal records center.
Reader Review: Karl M. in WI – Ask for paper copy or DVD copy. Send your request with your last duty station and military ID number. Also see: Veterans Affairs Entry.

Miller Paralegal
Legal research, copies
▶ RATED 10!
Details: SASE
Mail: Box 687
Walnut, CA 91788
Phone: 626-839-0900
law@docmail.com
Review: Your place for serious legal research, legal copies, decisions, statutes and regulations. Specializing in parole hearings and litigation.

Money Mart
Money services
▶ RATED 10!
Details: Online
Mail: 200 locations Nationwide
Web: momeymart.com
Review: Send you money in jail or prison, check cashing, pre-paid Visa cards, Western Union and Money orders.

Moonlite Productions
Photo seller and more
▶ RATED 10!
Details: Send SASE
Mail: Box 1304
Miami, FL 33265
Review: Offers girls from bikini photos to XXX. Excellent customer service. In business since 1998. Also offers calendars, gifts and more. Tell Lexi you saw her review in Inmate Shopper. Response time is 2 to 3 weeks.
Reader Review: Ian D. in IL – I know from personal experience their photos are the bomb, fast response and great customer service.
Reader Review: Donald U. in AZ- Sent for info, received in about three weeks, they have many options for membership, free shipping for VIP for example. They offer photos and letters of their models, will accept stamps as payment (not loose). Also have social media services and more. A full catalog is only $1.50 or 5 stamps. May 2019

Movie Market, The
Celebrity photos seller
Rated None
Details: Send SASE, see below
Mail: Box 699
San Juan Capistrano, CA 92693
Phone: 949-488-8444
Web: moviemarket.com
Inquires@moviemarket.com
Review: No longer prints catalogs but if you write, send SASE and ask they will send you a list of available photos, along with tiny photo of the celeb you requested. Photos are 4" x 6" and 8" x 10." High quality.

Music by Mail
Music Seller
▶ RATED 10!
Details: Catalog $2
Mail: Box 329066
Bush Terminal
Brooklyn, NY 11232
Phone:718-369-6982
Web: musicbymail.net
customerservice@musicbymail.net
Review: They mail a one-sheet list with about 150 current CD's. Offer Hip-Hop, Rock, Top 10, Country, Christian Rock, Comedy, Gospel, New Age, Latin, Blues, Soundtracks and many more. They carry some clear electronics, books, art and office supplies. The website says they are no longer talking orders online. June 2019
Reader Review: Ryan D. in WI-Tons of CD's for sale, some clear electronics for states that allow them. Also one of he best current book selections including cheap puzzle books. Jul. 2018

My Freedom Services
Parole assistance
Rated None
Details: SASE
Mail: 4287 Katonah Ave.
Bronx, NY 10470
Phone: 800-218-5419 or
925-218-0158
Web: MyFreedomSerivces.com
Info@myfreedomservices.com
Review: They offer services to assist inmates prepare a parole board package for hearing appearance. Offer initial family consultation, initial inmate prison visit, parole board package preparation, monitoring submissions to prisons to meet deadlines. They bridge the gab between courtroom sentencing and parole board hearing. They are administrative parole board specialists not attorneys. Brochure available in Spanish. Mar. 2018

NAL JOR List
Largest list of orgs
► **RATED 10!**
Price: List is Free Online
Web: naljor.us
Review: They offer a list of non-profit organizations; what each of them offer and the best list of free services. They update their resources year after year that you have the best lists available.

Nasco Arts and Crafts
Sells arts and crafts supplies
Rated 9
Details: Catalog Free
Mail: Box 901
Fort Atkinson, WI 53538
Phone 800-372-1236
Web: enasco.com
Custserv@eNasco.com
Review: They have what you're looking for – school supplies, farm and ranch products, art materials, health care trainers, educational and teacher resources, senior care items, and more! They have an extensive listing of catalogs, Agricultural Sciences, Arts and Crafts, Dissection Materials, Early Learning, Elementary Education, Family and Consumer Sciences, Farm and Ranch, Geometry/Algebra, Hands – On Health, Health Care Educational Materials, Laboratory Sampling Products, Math, Nutrition Teaching Aids, Reading Resources Science, Senior Activities, Showing and Grooming, SIMLAB (Previously titled: Anatomical and Nursing), Special Education, Team Sports-Physical Education-Health.

Nation University
Biblical studies
Rated 8
Details: SASE for info
Mail: Box 3342
Brentwood, TN 37024
Web: NationU.org
prison.serivces@nationu.org
Review: Free tuition at an accredited for prisoners education with one time $25 enrollment. Founded in 1995 provides undergraduate (certificate and bachelor's degrees) and graduate (masters degrees) in biblical studies for inmates. Just pay for your textbooks and extended readings, requires a proctor from your education or chaplain department and GED or high school diploma. One of the nation's most active prison outreach programs through higher education. Open to Christians and Non-Christians.

National Clemency Project, Inc.
Sentence reduction and transfers
► **RATED 10!**
Details: SASE
Mail: 3907 N. Federal Hwy., Ste. 151
Pompano Beach FL 33064
Phone: 954-271-2304
Web: nationalclemencyprojectinc.com
Nationalclemencyprojectinc@gmail.com
Review: Founded in 1983. They handle petitions for clemency and commutations in all 50 states in the country. Their director has over 30 years in preparing clemency applications packets on behalf of federal and state inmates. They fill the inmates need for professional assistants that he or she can afford. Does not provide legal representation but rather offers professional assistance in the preparation of the submission package to obtain a serious review of the clemency request. Are not a non-profit, however, the fees are less than private law firms.

National Criminal Justice
Reference service
► **RATED 10!**
Details: Free
Mail: Box 6000
Rockville, MD 20849
Phone: 800-851-3420
Web: ncjrs.org
Review: Provides all kinds of stats and research on crimes and prisons.

National Directory of Catalogs
Listings of catalogs
► **RATED 10!**
Details: info@nmoa.org
Web: nmoa.org/catalogmailorder
Phone: 612-788-4197
Review: They list 12, 230 catalogs.

Print version is no longer available. They offer a searchable database online only.

National Geographic
Magazine
Details: See review
► **RATED 10!**
Mail: Box 62130
Tampa, FL 33663-2130
Web: NationalGeographic.com
ngsline@customersvc.com
Review: One Year (10 issues) for $19 for printed edition. They have expanded their line of mags, NG Kids Magazine, 10 issues for $19, NG Little Kids Magazine, 6 issue for $19 and NG Traveller Magazine 8 issues for $19. The offer all the mags in digital editions too. June 2019

National Lawyers Guild
Assist jailhouse lawyers
► **RATED 10!**
Mail: Prison Law Project
132 Nassau St. Rm. 922
New York, NY 10038
Phone: 212-679-5100
Web: nlg.org
Review: NLG offer free legal self-help books. The NLG is dedicated to the need for basic change in the structure of our political and economic system. They seek to unite the lawyers, law students, legal workers and jailhouse lawyers to function as an effective force in the service of the people, to the end that human rights shall be regarded as more sacred than property interests.
Native American Prisoners' Rehabilitation research project
Rated None
Details: Free
Mail: 2848 Paddock Ln.
Villa Hills, KY 41017
Review: Offers legal, spiritual and cultural programs assistance.

Native American Rights Fund
Legal aid
Rated None
Details: SASE
Mail: 1506 Broadway
Boulder, CO 80302

Natural Health Prison Project
Free health info.
Rated None
Details: Send SASE for info
Mail: 32 Greenwood Ave. #4
Quincy, MA 02170-2620
Review: Provides answers to personal questions about diet, exercise and maintaining a healthy body.

Nevada Jurisprudence and Prison News
Reports on current legal issues of criminal law and prison policies that effect prison life.
Rated 8
Details: Send SASE for info
Web: nvjurisprudenceandprisonnews.webs.com
nvjurisprudence@gmail.com
Review: Offers a discount if done through the internet. Email rates are $3 for 6 mos., $5 for 12 mos. By snail mail, the rates are $8 for 6 mos., $15 for 12 mos.

Nickels and Dimez
Non nude adult photos
► **RATED 10!**
Details: Send SASE for info
Mail: 14173 Northwest Fwy. 154
Houston, TX 77040
Phone: 832-756-3377
Web: NickelsandDimez.com
nickelsanddimez1@gmail.com
Review: They are new to the marketplace. They offer color catalogs for $2 and B&W for $0.50 cents, 144 photos. Due to mail volume limit your letters to orders or checking order status. Always send a complete SASE or they will not respond. Stamps accepted on purchases. May 2018.
Reader Review: Donald U. in AZ-Sent for info, received in three weeks. They sent me one large sheet with a long explanation about services, charges and prices in big paragraph. Offer limited flyers, prices are good and worth checking out. Sent for $7 order will be here any day now. May 2018

Nina's Discount Oldies
Music CDs and books
Rated 8
Details: Free Catalog
Mail: Box 77
Narberth, PA 19072-0077
Phone: 800-336-4627
610-649-7565
Web: Oldies.com
Orders@oldies.com
Review: Been in business since 1980, has over 30,000 classic albums, current music, 3,300 collectible records all on CDs. Carry thousands more of music related items, books etc. When ordering tell them to include your inmate number in your mailing address.

Noble Knight Games
Books, comic books, video games
► **RATED 10!**
Catalog: Free
Mail: 2835 Commerce Park Dr.
Fitchburg, WI 53719
Phone: 608-758-9901
Web: nobleknight.com

nobleknight@nobleknight.com
Review: They sell new, used and out-of-print books, comics, fantasy and more. Mail order experts in new and out-of-print Role Playing Games, War Games, Board Games and Miniatures! Since 1997, they have helped thousands of gammers from around the world save money, and find exactly what they need. They have ebay rating of over 167,000 reviews and over 99.8% positive feedback, that is impressive. May 2019
Reader Review: Shannon A in IN-Good selection of fantasy novels and games. Decent prices and easy to work with, only down side is catalog setup. I still continue to use them. Apr. 2019

NOC Bay Trading, Co.
Smudging and other supplies
► **RATED 10!**
Details: Catalog $3
Mail: Box 295
Escanaba, MI 49829
Phone: 800-652-7192
Web: nocbay.com
Sales@nocbay.com
Review: Features Native American Crafts and Art Supplies.

Notes and Novels
Sell books
► **RATED 10!**
Details: Info send SASE
Price: Catalog for $9 or 30 FCS
Mail: 12436 FM 1960 W.
Box 177-IMS
Houston, TX 77065
Phone: 2818908911
Web: notesandnovels.com
Sales@notesandnovels.com
Review: They have been in business since 1983. Caters to Inmates, Catalog is over 95 pages with thousands of books to choose from. Calendars, date books, journals, dictionaries, Bibles, magazines, greeting and note cards, envelopes, notebooks, paper and coloring books. Hours of business Mon.-Fri. 9am-6pm CT. Sat. 9am-5pm CT. Sun. 10am-4pm CT. June 2019

Nothing Butt Pictures
Photo Seller
Rated 9
Details: Send SASE plus 5 stamps for catalog
Mail: Inmate Little Helpers
Box 4234
Oakland, CA 94614
Web: InmatesLittleHelpers.com
nothingbuttpictures@gmail.com
Review: This photo company is run and owned by Inmates' Little Helpers. Offer many different categories of photos. To request catalog send SASE plus five First class stamps to cover printing costs. Offer Special 10 photo deal $6.75 in-house photos June 2019

Nubian Princess Entertainment
Photo Seller
► **RATED 10!**
Details: SASE with 3 stamps
Mail: Box 37
Timmonsville, SC 29161
writesomeone@aol.com
Review: Been in business 8 plus years; over 7,000 photos. They offer partial info or complete info packages. If you want partial info (without catalog) you MUST send an SASE with $1 (3 forever stamps) worth of stamps affixed. Or if want all their complete info (with catalog) send $10. In addition offer DVDs. June 2019

Nuclear Resister Newspaper
Global resistance to nuclear power
► **RATED 10!**
Published by: The Nuclear Resister
Editors: Jack and Felice Cohen-Joppa
Detail: Free Sample issue upon request (send postal address)
Price: Prisoners $15; all others $25; $50 Contributing
Mail: Box 43383
Tucson, AZ 85733
Phone: 520-323-8697
Web: nukeregister.org
nukeResister@igc.org
Review: Now 34 years in print. Information about and support for imprisoned anti-nuclear and anti-war activists. They produce 2000 copies of 11" x 17", 12 to 16 pgs. Four issues per year. Each issue provides the names and jail addresses of currently imprisoned anti-nuclear and anti-war activists. Readers are encouraged to provide active support by writing letters to those behind bars and in other ways requested by the prisoners. About the Nuclear Resister: Since 1980, the Nuclear Resister has provided comprehensive reporting on arrests for anti-nuclear civil resistance in the United States, with an emphasis on providing support for the women and men jailed for these actions. In 1990, the Nuclear Resister also began reporting on anti-war arrests in North America, plus overseas anti-nuclear and anti-war resistance with the same emphasis on prisoner support. Published about every two months.

NY Campaign for Telephone Justice
Fights high cost of calls in NY
Rated None

Details: Free, SASE is faster
Mail: Center for Constitutional Rights
666 Broadway Ave. 7th Floor
New York, NY 10012
Phone: 212-614-6481
Web: CCRJustice.org

Oatmeal Studios
Buys art
▶ **RATED 10!**
Details: SASE for writer's guidelines
Mail: Box 138 Town Rd. 35
Rochester, VT 05767
Web: oatmealstudios.com
Review: Accepts submissions from prisoners. Pays $75 per card idea. Send an SASE and ask for their writer's guidelines and samples of what they want to buy.

OCSLocal.com
Discount calls
Rated None
Details: Online
Price: $18.50 mo.
Mail: Box 782154
Orlando, FL 32878
Phone: 888-813-0000
Review: The price listed is their basic plan, other plans available.

Office of Correctional Education
Money for school
Rated None
Details: Free
Mail: US Dept. of Education
400 Maryland Ave. SW
Washington, DC 20202

Omega Bible Institute
Correspondence course
Rated 8
Details: Send SASE
Mail: 2149 Hwy. 139
Monroe, LA 71203
Phone: 888-837-4951
Web: omega.edu
admin@omega.edu
Review: Nationally accredited, offers Bachelor, Master and Doctorate degrees. You can test out all of the courses, all available without leaving your cell. Inexpensive, Free catalog and evaluation.

Open, Inc.
Books
Rated None
Mail: Box 472223
Garland, TX 75047
Web: openinc.org
Review: Includes titles like "99 Days" and "Man, I Need A Job!" Prisoner priced at $4.95 and up.

One Stop Service Center
Professional service
▶ **RATED 10!**
Details: Send SASE for info
Mail: 1271 Washington Ave., Ste. 313
San Leandro, CA 96577
Phone: 800-777-4662
nerds800@gmail.com
justourservices@gmail.com
one1stopservices@gmail.com
Review: They are sister companies to Inmates' Little Helpers, Nothing Butt Pictures. Offer professional services preparing and filing legal documents like contracts, credit report, divorce and more. They accept BP-199 and all other facility issued payments. June 2019
—SEE OUR AD—

Outside Inmate Package Program
Inmate care packages
▶ **RATED 10!**
Details: Service NY, NJ, CT, OH, MD
Mail: Box 130344
Brooklyn, NY 11213
Phone: 347-461-9970
Web: outsideinmatepkg.com
Service@outsideinmatepkg.com
Review: They have an huge selection and tons of brand names items. Packages are available via inmate catalog, online and for pick up. Family coming to visit? Save time and delivery charge, by placing the online order and arranging for pick up at their store. Family running short of time? Place the online order, and for an additional $20.00, it can be delivered to your family at the bus pick up. They sell, clothing, footwear, electronics, beverages, foods in a pouch, canned goods, cooked meats, west Indian market, puzzles/games, snacks. Coming soon, music, books and magazines. Just some of the brand names they carry Hanes, Jerzeeys, Etonic, Gilden, US Polo, Norelco, Hillsboro Farms, Hebrew National, Pepsi, Coca Cola, Hormel, Ocean Spray, Tyson, Big Bambo, Linstead Market, Jamaican Choice, Hostess, Keebler, Pepperidge Farm and many more. June 2019

Outside Touch
Sport and internet services
Rated 8
Details: Corrlinks Email Users Only
Mail: 500 Westover Dr. #13938
Sandford, NC 27330
outsidetouch123@gmail.com
Review: New to the marketplace they offer daily opening and current lines sports lines, odds, scores and injury info. College and national sports. $20 a month, get NBA, NCAAB, NFL, NCAAF and the MLB as one package. UFC, Boxing and other sports as a different package. With MLB get daily probable pitchers with stats With NFL get important players with stats. In addition, they offer internet

topic searches. You give them the subject matter and they email you the info they find from internet within legal regulations. Prices start at $10 for 20 queries. Add their email address to you contact list and get started today. May 2019
—SEE OUR AD—

Pack Central Music
Sells CD's and cassettes
Rated None
Details: Catalog 600 titles
Price: $2
Mail: 6745 Denny Ave
N. Hollywood, CA 91606-2206
Phone: 816-760-2828
Info@packcentral.com
Review: In business since 1980, Pack Central has offered thousands of cassettes and CD's in clear cases, with or without screws. Prices start at $3 and up. Approved vendor and a great choice of all varieties of music. WARNING: Most of their cassette prices are now $75 to $100 per tape.

Packages R Us
Food packages
Rated 7
Details: Online
Web: packagesrus.com
Phone: 866-303-7787
Review: This is the same company as Golden State Package (see listing for more details).

Packerland Business Equip.
Repair typewriters
► RATED 10!
Details: Send SASE for info
Mail: 1006 Shadow Lane
Green Bay, WI 54304
Phone: 920-435-5241
Review: They offer many business machines and supplies, but we have them listed because they repair typewriters of all models. Good turnaround times and low prices. They have high ratings online but no website or email. Write to them first. 2018
Reader Review: Everett G. in NY-I have had a positive experience with this company. I honestly feel the Swintec Corp. (brand of typewriter) could not have done better. I found this repair service company inside the Inmate Shopper. June 2019

Pantee Publishing
Photo seller
Rated 8
Details: SASE for info
Mail: Box 233
Hawthorne, NJ 07507
Review: They offer non nude and nude, so you must specify when ordering. Their catalogs are $1.50 with photo order each. If you need a catalog without photo order (only 1st time) send 4 stamps. Catalogs come in many categories (i.e. ebony, white, Latino and more). Min. order 10 photos is $11.50 (with free catalog of choice). Offer other hot deal and specials on photo orders of 25, 50, 60, 85 and 120. Jul. 2018

Paralegal Institute of Brighton College, The
Paralegal school
Rated 8
Details: Free
Mail: 8777 E. Via de Ventura
Ste. 300
Scottsdale, AZ 85258
Phone: 800-354-1254 or
602-2112-0502
Web: theparalegalinstitute.edu
Admissions@theparalegalinstitute.edu
Info@brightoncollege.edu
Review: Their diploma program meets the requirements for National Association of Legal Assistants; is DETC accredited. Associate degree program available. Both programs are available with monthly payments.

PAC Telephone Services
Phone, message, text and sports
► RATED 10!
Details: SASE or email for info
Mail: Box 36488
Cincinnati, OH 45236
Phone: 760-561-9300
Web: pactelephone.com
Support@pactelephone.com
Review: They offer services by Corrlinks. Local phone services, messaging to mobile phones, email to outside emails, photo printing and voice mail services. Pay-as-you-Go Calling Plan. Calls to US homes $0.05 cents/minute, ask about international rates too. Flat rate mobile plan 325 minutes mobile phones $4.50 per month. There are two kinds of messaging services, to a mobile phone or to another emails address (family does not need Corrlinks). Texting messages only $15 per month. The photo services depend on who is paying for the pictures that determines the cost and number that your loved ones must send the picture to, so for best results, contact them for complete information on services. Sport reports daily by corrlinks, subscribe and get sports scores, player stats, team updates for all major sports. They offer 9 Sport Channels, NFL, NFL Fantasy, NCAAFB, NBA, MLB, NHL, Soccer and Gold Sheet. Pricing starts at $30 per year per channel, Gold Sheet/ Hotpicks $10 per year

when added to any Sports Channel purchase. Packages, Pick any 3 Sports Channels $80 per year, pick any 4 Sport Channels $100 per year and get ALL Sports (as many as you want) $195 per year or $20 per month. June 2019

PASS
Prisoner rehabilitation course
Rated 8
Details: Free
Mail: Box 2009
San Francisco, CA 94126
Phone: 888-670-7277
passprogram@passprogram.org
Review: It looks like a pretty good correspondence program.

Pastel Journal
For pastel artists of all skill levels
▶ RATED 10!
Details: Subscription 6 issues/yr
Price: $32 per year
Web: pasteljournal.com
Review: Magazine is packed with gorgeous pastel artwork, insights on technique and inspiration.

Pathfinder Press
Book seller
▶ RATED 10!
Details: Free Catalog
Mail: Box 162767
Atlanta, GA 30321-2767
Web: pathfinderpress.com
orders@pathfinderpress.com
Review: It is really exciting to see hundreds of different and profound books in one catalog. Books for the free-thinker, revolutionary and working class leaders. Titles are available in Spanish, French and English. Priced from $5 and up. Half-price for prisoners. Order online or mail. Look for their full page ad, they have a special offer for you. Apr. 2019
—SEE OUR AD—

Pelipost
Photo sending services
▶ RATED 10!
Details: Online Only
Web: Pelipost.com
Support@pelipost.com
Review: They send photos to inmates by having your loved ones use their website. How it works for your loved ones is they upload photos from their phones, Facebook or Instagram to their website. They print the photos and ship them to your facility. They ship to all state and federal correctional facilities in the country. Shipping is free by USPS and delivery time is about 3-5 days. They also have a photo editor that your family can use to personalize their photos with add captions, stickers, color filters etc. All photos are printed in their office for privacy protection. Prices start at 5 photos for $2.99, 10 photos for $5.99 and 20 photos for $8.99 Offer prepaid inmate accounts. Feb. 2019
Reader Review: Ryan D. in WI-This service is easy to use by family and has decent prices. 4" x 6" photos come with white borders, because they do not resize mobile phone photos. May 2018
—SEE OUR AD & BACK COVER—

Pen America Center
Publishes the journal Pen America.
▶ RATED 10!
Details: SASE
Mail: 588 Broadway
New York, NY 10012
Web: pen.org
Review: They sponsor many writing contests and writing education information, too numerous to list here. Most is free for prisoners, so check them out.

Penn Foster
Education by mail
▶ RATED 10!
Details: Free catalog
Mail: 14300 N. Northwest Blvd. Ste. 111
Scottsdale, AZ 85260
Phone: 800-572-1685, ext. 5993
Web: pennfoster.edu
Review: They offer 22, AA Degree programs and also 60 diploma programs. Penn Foster is accredited by DETC and CSS, MSA and licensed in and by Arizona State Board for Private Post-Secondary Education. Courses are available in print. No computer needed! Monthly payments available.

Penn Herb Co. Ltd
Herb products
Rated 8
Details: Free catalog
Mail: 10601 Decatur Rd., Ste. 2
Philadelphia, PA 19154-3293
Phone: 800-523-9971
Web: wwwPennHerb.com
Order@pennherb.com
Review: They offer large selection of herbs, vitamins and oils. Herbs sealed in reusable packages. An AZ Approved Vendor.

Pennsylvania Prison Society
Prison newsletters
▶ RATED 10!
Graterfriends and Correctional Forum
Details: For sample, send SASE and 2 FCS
Price: Prisoners $3 per year
Mail: 245 N. Board St.

Philadelphia, PA 19130
Web: prisonsociety.org
Review: The mission of the Pennsylvania Prison Society is to advocate for a humane, just and restorative correctional system, and to promote a rational approach to criminal justice issues. A long and uphill battle in this country. Over the years this once small org has grown into a pillar of strength and hope for many inmates with their Prison Reentry Network.
Review: As a fellow advocate, We are members and strong supporter of this organization. In addition, I have had my writings printed in their newsletter a few times over the years.

Penthouse Magazine Co.
Sophisticated pornography
▶ **RATED 10!**
Mail: Orders by Mail
Box 420235
Palm Coast, FL 32142-0235
Phone: 800-455-2392 24/7
Web: Penthouse.com
Review: In print since 1969 with a monthly magazine. Contact for current prices. As of Feb. 2018 39.95 for one year mailed in the USA. Writer's guidelines send a #10 SASE.

People Magazine
Celebrity gossip mag
▶ **RATED 10!**
Mail: 245 N. Board St. Ste. 300
Philadelphia, PA 19107
Phone: 866-769-0199
Web: People.com
Review: 54 issues per year. Available in print and digital edition. Yearly subscription, $134.46 print version, only $2.49 per issue.

Phone Donkey
Inmate long distance telephone service
▶ **RATED 10!**
Details: No payment needed, just an email address.
Phone: 855-420-0880
Web: phonedonkey.com
Support@phonedonkey.com
Review: No credit check. Have your loved ones contact this company online ONLY for a free trial on long distance phone service with your Inmate ID number. They service the federal BOP inmate long distance. You can save $33 a month which is over $395 per year if you talk 300 minutes a month. Also see TextInmate.com for their other Corrlinks Texting Service

Photo Service for Inmates
Photo service
Rated 7
Details: Send Int'l SASE for brochure
Mail: Anna Sperber
Sturmstrasse 10, 90478
Nuernberg Germany
servicephoto@rocketmail.com
Review: They can embellish photos taken in prison. They change backgrounds, clothes, add persons etc. You will be surprised by the results! Be sure to place enough postage to cover postage fees equalling $1.15 or an international stamp on your SASE. No longer have a website. May 2018
Reader Review: Ludwig E in TX-I was surprised to see this company still in business. A few years back they did not give me my order and kept my money. Well, maybe they are better now it has been a few years.

Photoworld
Celebrity photo seller
Rated 7
Details: Send SASE
Mail: Box 401016
Las Vegas, NV 89140
Review: Offer photos of the stars. Photos are magazine type non nude. Send SASE for information. Free shipping on orders $20 or more Oct. 2017
Reader Review: Donald U. in AZ- Sent and never got a reply, not even a RTS notice. May 2019

Picture Donkey
Photo services
▶ **RATED 10!**
Details: Online
Phone: 855-499-0880
Web: PictureDonkey.com and InmatePic.com
Support@inmatepic.com
Review: They send pictures from your loved ones computer, phone, or tablet, through a web browser, print them out and mail to anywhere. Photos are 4" x 6". Photos have new simpler billing packages, 5 photos $3.50, 10 photos $6.50, 20 photos $10, 40 photos, $18, 60 photos $24, 80 photos $32 and 100 photos $40. With InmatePic.com you can even add captions to ANY/ALL of the pictures FREE! You can include a message or tell them who is in the picture. June 2019

Pigeonly Products
Inmate technology services
▶ **RATED 10!**
Details: Send SASE
Mail: 701 Bridger St., Ste. 690A
Las Vegas, NV 89101
Phone: 800-323-9895 or 702-514-4291

Web: Pigeonly.com
Support@pigeonly.com
Review: They have an inmate database that anyone can find an inmate anywhere. Plus they have many communication services to help inmates and their loved ones keep in contact and save money doing it. They offer Voice: prison phone calls at low rates. Photos: send printed photos right from any electronic device and printed ones mailed to inmate. Print: share online articles and websites from loved ones to inmate. Letter: send quick notes between loved ones from any electronic device. Greetings: send a greeting for any occasion. Pay for a single month or take advantage of their discounted subscription plans. Apr. 2019

Pineapple Pictures
Photo sellers
Rated 7
Details: Send SASE
Mail: Box 7732
Round Rock, TX 78683
Review: They sell photos in many categories specialize in photos for LGBTQ. Write for info. Now carrying erotic stories. Feb. 2019
Reader Review: Ken B. in IL-I give them a 12 on a scale from 1 to 10! Besides being speedy, provide great quality and wide assortment of photos. Gay special interests, like twinks, bears or even feet. Even celebs! They have stories for every fetish. I highly recommend.

Platinum Publications
Self-publishing services
Rated None
Details: Send SASE
Mail: Box 4234
Oakland, CA 94614
Review: They are sister companies, to Inmates's Little Helper, Nothing Butt Picture. They offer everything you need for self-publishing or in house publishing. They offer promoting, Marketing, Instagram, Twitter, Facebook, Platinum Publications advertising, Google Plus, Inmates' Little Helpers Facebook and Website, Quarterly Promotional flyers mailed out with each new release advertised, online book store, 3 local bookstore contract for paperback revenue, we will mail paperback novels directly to facilities for lower overhead, monthly contest for free books and free Kindles advertisements with all social media. June 2019

Poets and Writers Magazine
Writer's resource
► **RATED 10!**
Price $15.95 yr.
(6 issues), $25.95 two yrs. (12 issues)
Mail: Box 422460
Palm Coast, FL 32142
Phone: 386-346-0106
Web: pw.org/magazine
Poets@pw.org
Review: Are you a serious writer? Want to sell your poems or win a contest? Then you need to subscribe to Poets and Writers. Every issue is packed with hundreds of ads for contests, grants and awards, call for submissions, buyers of poems and articles, editing services and lots more.

Prism Optical
Sells glasses and frames
Rated 8
Details: Send SASE for catalog
Mail: Box 680030
10954 NW 7th Ave.
North Miami, FL 33168
Phone: 800-637-4104
Web: PrismOptical.com
Contact@prisonoptical.com
Review: They has been serving prisoners a long while; 7 plus years. Quality prescription eye wear by mail.

Prisonartware
Sell prisoner art
Rated None
Details: $10. Licensing Package Info
Mail: c/o Intern Mandy
304 S. Jones Blvd. Ste. 1683
Las Vegas, NV 89107
Phone: 702-570-9219
Web: PrisonArtWare.com
gallerysupport@prisonartware.com
Review: Prison Art Wanted
They are a new for-profit online gallery offering artist services at the non-profit level. Offer a Lifetime Prison Art Listing and Archival Service. $129.95 They list your name, 300 word bio, and direct link to your portfolio on their website. In addition just some of the benefits are social media posting. Create video of your art to post on YouTube channel and others. They will also build and maintain social media accounts for your art business. For more details send SASE. June 2019

PrisonConnect
Phone services
► **RATED 10!**
Details: Send SASE
Mail: 2711 Centerville Rd., Ste. 400
Wilmington, DE 19808
Phone: 855-971-1121
Web: prisonconnect.us
Support@prisonconnect.us
Review: They offer lower phone costs so you can talk for less. Plans

for federal or state inmates. They have lower rates than GTL, Securus, ICSolutions, Paytel etc. They offer one simple plan – only $4.99 per month with the first month Free. The plan includes an individual number that is local to the facility that allows you to speak with a minimum ("local") rate. NO per minute charges, NO activation fees. NO connection or disconnection fees. NO cancellation fees – you can cancel your account whenever you like. Need to have loved ones' sign-up online. All the information and details are easy to understand online on the steps to setup, manage and receive calls with them. One thing we see about this phone company is they offer a toll-free number for your loved ones to use if they need assistance or are not computer savvy. June 2019

Prison Creative Arts Project
Michigan prisoners ONLY
► **RATED 10!**
Details: Free
Mail: Prison Creative Arts Project
University of Michigan (No Box or Street address needed)
Ann Arbor, MI 48109
Review: This is an Art Exhibit. Contact them for more info.

Prison Legal News
Legal news magazine
► **RATED 10!**
Details: Send SASE
Mail: Box 1151
Lake Worth, FL 33460
Web: prisonlegalnews.org
Phone: 561-360-2523
Info@prisonlegalnews.org
Review: PLN a project of the non-profit Human Rights Defense Center, is a 64 page monthly magazine full of criminal justice issues and prison and jail-related civil litigation, with an emphasis on prisoners' rights. PLN has published continuously since 1990 and covers a wide range of topics that include prison labor, rape and sexual abuse, misconduct by prison and jail staff, prisoners' constitutional rights, racial and socioeconomic disparities in our criminal justice system, medical and mental health care for prisoners, disenfranchisement, rehabilitation and recidivism, prison privatization, prison and jail phone rates, women prisoners, the Prison Litigation Reform Act (PLRA), prison censorship, the death penalty, HIV and Hep C, solitary confinement and control units, and much more. 1 Year Print Subscription for Incarcerated Individuals 12 issues $30.00, Non-Incarcerated Individuals $35. Sample $5. Allow 6 weeks for delivery.
—SEE OUR ADS—

Prison Life Magazine
Newsletter/newsprint publication
Rated None
Details: Send SASE
Mail: Box 4845
Frankfort, KY 40604
Phone: 502-353-4138
Web:davidnharding.com
Contact@prisonlifemagazine.com
Review: Published by Good Acres Sanctuary with the commonwealth of KY content restrictions. A quarterly publication for America's incarcerated, parolees, ex-felons and their families. Priced at for $25 a printed subscription (4 issues per year), digital online $6. Publication size 7x11, 20 pages. In addition, they donate free magazines to 1719 state and 102 federal prison libraries. At present, they publish the magazine quarterly, but are considering going monthly. They accept submissions, short article/essays should be fewer than 750 words. Longer articles/essays should be fewer than 1600 words. Longer pieces considered. They are part of The ReCenter Foundation that assists improve the mental, emotional, physical, and spiritual health and well-being of that struggling with addictions, homelessness, and post-incarceration issues through Christ-centered rehabilitation, counseling, education, recovery support, and advocacy. June 2019

Prison Living Press
Magazine seller and publisher
► **RATED 10!**
Details: Send SASE
Mail: Box 10302
Glendale, AZ 85318
Phone: 602-384-7591
Web:prisonlivingmagazine.com
George@prisonlivingmagazine.com
Review: They publish Prison Living Magazine. The first edition is the popular, 2019 Free Stuff for Inmates. Contains over 150 resources that have totally free stuff for prisoners. Your loved one can view it free on their website and download the e-zine for $7.98 or purchase the color magazine for $14.98 with free shipping.
Update: Prison Living Press has had a rough first two years. They got into subscription magazine sales and got only eight orders so had to close that. Then they published a Snail Mail Pen Paling magazine and the UK and California enacted tough new privacy laws about publishing peoples names and addresses – so they had to cease publishing this sold out pen pal magazine. We wish

them all the best. May 2019
—SEE OUR AD—

Prison L S
Photo Seller
Rated None
Details: Send SASE
Mail: Box 686
Eustace, TX 75124
Phone: 430-808-3228
Web: prisonls.com
Help@prisonls.com
Review: They are new on the marketplace under this name, the site seems to have knowledge so that leads us to believe they might have done business under different name. Just our opinion. They offer non nude photos sets and specific catalog photos picks. Have monthly photosets, female named sets, and photos that can be purchased from catalogs. Photo set prices range from $40-$200. Catalogs have 800 photos on four pages front and back prices from $4-$10. In addition, they offer Add Money To Inmate Account from $50-$300 and a Parole Package for $400 marked down from $500. May 2019
Reader Review: Despite this company prior being on the Beware List under Prison Legendary Services, I have never had an issue with them. They are a little slow, but always fill my orders. I would rate them as average. Apr. 2019
Reader Review: John B in CO-I sent a check for $18 on 2/22/18 and have proof (copy front & back endorsed check) being cashed. I never received anything. I wrote, I was ignored. Wrote again with copy of proof, I was ignored again. Do not order from them they are rip off. And the check which was made out business name, Prison L S was signed and cashed by Kathryn Boyle at Prosperity Bank in Texas. Buyer Beware. June 2019

Prison Mirror
Prisoner newsletter
Rated 9
Details: Send SASE
Mail: 970 Pickett St. N.
Bayport, MN 55003
Phone: 651-779-2700
Web: doc.state.mn.us
Review: This newsletter is published by Minnesota Correctional Facility–Stillwater. Published monthly by the men of this facility. They accept and welcome submissions, keep letters and poems to 250 words or less, commentaries, articles and stories to 750 words or less. May 2017

Prison Project
Yoga newsletter
Rated 8
Details: Free yoga newsletter
Mail: Box 99140
Emeryville, CA 94662
Phone: 510-893-4648
Web: siddhayoga.org/SYDA-foundations/prison-project
prisonproject@siddhayoga.org
Review: The Prison Project is dedicated to disseminating the Siddha Yoga teachings and practices to incarcerated individuals. Sends free monthly newsletter and Home Study Course to prisoners. Siddha Yoga teaches that within each of us, behind the mind, body, and ego, is a divine power called the Self. We meditate to harmonize our actions, thoughts and words with this power. Over 5,000 students in 1500 prisons are currently enrolled. Also available in Spanish. April 2017

Prison Publications Inc.
Books
▶ RATED 10!
Details: Send SASE
Mail: Box 174
Thompson, CT 06277
Info@prisonpublications.com
Review: In business since 2008. They offer direct sales of books to prison inmates. They offer gently used books, and magazine subscriptions at prices that are hard to beat.
Reader Review: John M. in CT–I never received my order, so I wrote and included SASE several time and still heard nothing. I would say beware of this company. Maybe write them before ordering to see if you get a response. Jan. 2017

Prison Stamp Exchange
Stamp buyer
Rated None
Details: SASE for order form
Mail: 536 Woodworth Ave
Clovis, CA 93612
Support@prsionstampexchange.com Web:prisonstampexchange.com
Review: New to the marketplace they used to be Sell Unused Stamps. They offer 70% face value on all new condition, Forever stamps. They also offer 50% face value on usable condition Forever stamps. Get check, JPay, Access SecurePak, PayPal or a bank wire. They do not pay by money order, cash, transfers services like Wal-Mart or Western Union. For more information on details of acceptance of stamps condition and order form send SASE. June 2018

Prison Wizard Magazines
Discount magazine subscriptions
▶ RATED 10!

Mail: Box 1846
Bloomington, IN 47402-1846
Web: magwiz.com
Wizard@magwiz.com
Review: Been in business for seven years. Medium priced and good selection.

Prison Yoga Project
Yoga book
Rated 8
Details: Free yoga book
Mail: Box 415
Bolinas, CA 94924-0415
Web: prisonyoga.com
Review: "Yoga: A Path for Healing and Recovery" by James Fox. The book covers basic of yoga postures, starting a prison yoga program and the history of the CA Prison Yoga Program.

Prisoners' Family and Friends United (PFFU)
Prison Inspired Book
▶ RATED 10!
Title: The Unvarnished Truth About The Prison Family Journal
Authors: Carolyn Esparza, LPC; and Phillip Don Yow, Sr.
Details: 9 x 6, SC, 326 pgs.
Price: $24.99 includes S/H
Mail: 2200 N Yarbrough, B-245
El Paso, TX 79925
Web: ppfunited.org
Info@ppfunited.org
Order through ppfunited.org, amazon.com, inmateshopper.com, or freebirdpublishers.com
Review: One frantic call from the local jail catapults an entire family on a frightening journey that no family would wish to travel. Their traumatic journey encounters endless frustration and infuriating madness from which there is no escape. Millions of Americans are traumatized by the mass incarceration in this country. The Unvarnished Truth about the Prison Family Journey is an exceptional resource for prison families, as well as those serving them in the fields of criminal justice, education, ministry and mental health care. The authors have over fifty years combined personal and professional experience with the criminal justice system.

Prisoner's Family Conference
Art, crafts, and creative writing Submission
▶ RATED 10!
Details: Send SASE for guidelines
Mail: Creative Arts Competition
Prisoner's Family Conference
Box 343
Vancouver, WA 98666
Web: prisonersfamilyconference.org
info@prisonersfamilyconference.org
Review: Prisoners yearly competition for creative writing, art/drawing and crafts: woodworking, leather work and jewelry. You must send an SASE to get the guidelines mailed to you prior to submitting anything. Please do not send anything without first getting necessary paperwork and permission to submit. They also offer a newsletter by email, just email a request to them. They do not offer a printed option. They have a conference in October yearly in Dallas TX, called Inter National Prisoner's Family Conference where visitors can find helpful information and resource. June 2019

Prisoners Self-Help Litigation Manual
Legal "how-to" book
▶ RATED 10!
Details: SASE
ISBN # 978 0195374407
Price: $45.95 includes postage
Mail: Oxford University Press
Attn: Order Department
2001 Evans Rd.
Cary, NC 27513
Phone: 866-445-8685
Web: oup.com/us
Review: Recommended by Prison Legal News Magazine and they know a lot more about legal stuff than most of us, so let's go with them on this one.

PrisonEducation.com
Educational reference website
▶ RATED 10!
Details: Website
Website: PrisonEducation.com
Review: PrisonEducation.com is the leading source for news and information on prison education programs in the United States and abroad. The website features an online correspondence program guide, the latest news on prison education programs in American prisons, and detailed research concerning the public safety benefits of education and rehabilitation in our nation's prisons. June 2019

Prison Education Guide
Educational Reference Book
▶ RATED 10!
Details: 8 x 10, 280 pgs.
Price: $49.95
ISBN # 978-0-9819385-3-0
Mail: Prison Legal News
Box 1151
Lake Worth, FL 33460
Website: PrisonLegalNews.org
Phone: 561-360-2523
Review: Prison Education Guide by Christopher Zoukis is the most com-

prehensive guide to correspondence programs for prisoners available today. This exceptional book provides the reader with step-by-step instructions to find the right educational program, enroll in courses, and complete classes to meet their academic goals. This book is an invaluable reentry tool for prisoners who seek to further their education while incarcerated and to help them prepare for life and work following their release. Correspondence programs at the graduate, undergraduate, career, high school, personal enrichment, and Bible study levels are profiled. June 2019

Prisons Foundation
Publishes books by prisoners and art
► **RATED 10!**
Details: Send SASE for complete guidelines
Mail: 2512 Virginia Ave. NW #58043
Washington DC 20037
Staff@prisonsfoundation.org
Review: Any prisoner who has written a book, or would like to write a book, they want to publish it. All books on any subject are welcome. All books must be minimum of 100 pages and they do not sensor or edit your book, so you are free to write anything you wish. There is no charge to you to publish your book and no charge to anyone who wishes to read it. Plus you retain full rights to your book if you later wish to place it with a literary agent or commercial publisher. Placing your book on their website is in fact a good way to bring it to the attention of agents and larger publishers (and protect it under common copyright law). When they receive your book, it will be scanned in its entirety, just as you submitted. Do not send only a portion of your book! They will publish only what you initially send and will not add to the book later. You may send more than one book to be published. Any language is acceptable. Whether handwritten or typed, your book will be scanned and published exactly as they receive it. It can even contain drawings and photos if you wish to include them (at beginning or end only–the same thing applies to color). Art donations are posted on SafeStreetsArts.org
Reader Review: Donald U. in AZ- Got my info back in couple weeks, included info pack of what they offer for services, criteria for publishing on their site, submission form etc. May 2019

Pulp Fandom Magazine
Sci-fi newsletter
Rated None
Details: SASE or 3 FCS for 1st issue
Mail: Pulp Fandom
Box 383
Cookeville, TN 38503
Review: Old style, photocopy, 8.5" x 11" newsletter.

Ramsey Kearney
Agent songwriters
Rated 8
Details: See review
Mail: 602 Inverness Ave.
Nashville, TN 37204
Phone: 615-297-8029
Web: ramseykearney.com
Ramsey1030@comcast.net
Review: He provides a melody as well as tighten up your lyrics on a 50/50 basis, personalized co-writing on select song material, demo etc. How to submit your lyrics for evaluation. Write or type your lyrics legibly and mail them to address above. Or if you would like to use a submission form go online. Or submit your lyrics by email directly to Ramsey Kearney at email listed above.

Razor Wire Newsletter
Topics: Drug-war issues
► **RATED 10!**
Details: SASE
Prices: Prisoners $10, all others $30
Mail: 282 West Astor
Colville, WA 99114
Phone: 509-684-1550
Web: november.org
moreinfo@november.org
Review: November Coalition began publishing the newsletter in 1997 which reports on drug related issues and restoring civil rights. Two issues per year.

Reaching Out
Narcotics Anonymous newsletter
► **RATED 10!**
Details: Send SASE for Free Issue
Mail: Reaching Out – NAWS
Box 9999
Van Nuys, CA 91409
Phone: 818-773-9999
Web: NA.org
handi@na.org
Review: They publish Reaching Out newsletter. Reaching Out in its design helps incarcerated addicts connect to the NA program of recovery, enhances HandI efforts and offers experience from members who successfully transition from the 'inside' to be productive members of society. They have current and back issues in PDF printable format on their website. Paper copies (English only) are free for addicts who will be incarcerated for more than 6 months.

Redbat Books
Law books for prisoners
▶ **RATED 10!**
Details: Send orders with payment
Author: Zachary Smith
Price: $36.95 each plus $7 S/H
(CA Residents add $2.18 tax)
Mail: Sold on Amazon.com, inmateshopper.com and freebirdpublisher.com
Title: Smith's Guide to Habeas Corpus Relief,
Title: Smith's Guide to Executive Clemency,
Title: Smith's Guide to Chapter 7 Bankruptcy
Review: Smith's Guide to Habeas Corpus Relief, is specifically for state prisoners under 28 U.S.C. 2254. Complete with sample pleadings from beginning petition to final writ of certiorari. This book is designed to be used by prisoners working on their own behalf, it also serves as a guide.
Review: Smith's Guide to Executive Clemency, is specifically for state and federal prisoners who have exhausted all legal remedies or have sentences that are too long to serve. The book is an invaluable resource for any prisoner fighting for his or her freedom. Smith lays out every aspect of the clemency process, step by step.
Review: Smith's Guide to Chapter 7 Bankruptcy, shows you have to get immediately freedom form liens against offender account (including from incarceration reimbursements, halfway house, probation and parole costs, and other debt) by filing Chapter 7. A fundamental goal of the federal bankruptcy laws enacted by Congress is to give debtors a financial "fresh start" from burdensome debts.

Reentry Essentials, Inc
Reentry services
▶ **RATED 10!**
Details: Send SASE brochure
Mail: 98 4th St., Ste. 414
Brooklyn, NY 11231
Phone: 347-973-0004
WEB: reentryessentials.org
Info@reenryesstenials.org
Review: This organization strive to engage in reentry for any person and family that has been directly impacted by the criminal justice system. They currently have supporting projects and developing more designed to address four specific areas of need. Innovative Reentry Resources, Opportunities to Engage Families and Communities in successful returning citizens. Strategies to reduce the youth involved in justice system and solutions to strengthen the family member impacted by the system. They offer many tools and resources from program materials for free or low-cost to publications in a wide variety of subjects. Some of the resources they have are reentry, personal ID, employment development, legal, transportation, family development, government assistant, housing, grooming/clothing/housewares, education, health, business, LGBTQ, mentoring, faith based, videos/webinars and state resources. June 2019
—SEE OUR AD—

Returning Citizens Magazine
Inmate Magazine
▶ **RATED 10!**
Details: Quarterly issue (4)
Price: $29.99 year
Mail: 15000 Potomac Town Place Ste. 813
Woodbridge, VA 22191
Phone: 877-871-4172
WEB: returningcitizensmag.com
Info@returningcitizensmag.com
Review: This new magazine provides information on topics like expungement, second chance housing, second chance jobs, and other needed reentry programs. Additionally we look forward to sharing upcoming national reentry job fairs, and let you know which second chance employers are willing to give you a second chance. Subscriptions are available in print and digital. Can be ordered online or by mail. Checks accepted by mail payable to Scalable Consulting LLC. Oct. 2018

ReMind Magazine
Entertainment mag
▶ **RATED 10!**
Details: See full page ad
Price: $23.88 for 12 issues, $42.76 for 24 issues and $5.97 for 3 issues
Mail: 213 Park Dr.
Troy, MI 48083
Phone: 877-871-4172
WEB: remindmagazine.com
Review: This magazine offers a fresh take on TV, movie, sports and movie personalities of days gone by. Each issue is jammed packed with puzzles, trivia, quizzes, classic comics and features for hours of fun. Enjoy monthly themes and content like Sudoku, movie stars, word sleuth, retro ads, and articles. This is a must have magazine for any inmate. The 3 issue for $5.97 special is great for those on a tight budget. June 2019

R. Hughson
Photo seller

Rated 9
Details: Send SASE
Mail: Box 1033
Neenah, WI 54957
Review: They offer a variety of services other than photos, we suggest send them an SASE for updated information.
Reader Review: C. Chapman in TX-I can't say enough good things about this company. High quality photos, super-fast shipping. He will sub pictures if they are not in stock, but as cheap as his prices are, who cares?
Reader Review: Shannon A. in IN-The info in the last couple INSH was incorrect, he was still doing business with inmates. I used them for 5 years, bought photos, sold stamps and never a problem. His services are specifically for inmates, the only complaint would be photo selection cannot compete against some of the other photo sellers. Apr. 2019
Reader Review: Donald U. in AZ-I ordered the end of February and the order came in April. A couple of the guys here have great business with him. Great flyers, offers deals of bulk orders. May 2019

Richard Linn, Esq.
Attorney for WA state cases
Rated 8
Details: Send brief letter
Mail: 12501 Bel Reed Rd. Ste. 209
Bellevue, WA 98005
Phone: 425-646-6028
Reviews: Been in practice for 32 years. Law office has two attorneys Services for CCB and ISRB hearings; personal restraint petitions and consultations on civil and criminal cases. Law services include constitutional law and federal appellate practice. Mar. 2019

RingMyPhone
Phone, text and photo services
Rated None
Details: Online Only
Phone: 870-494-9590
Web: ringmyphone.com
Review: Sister company with MailMyPix.com. They provide phone calls for as low prices, $10 a month, can have up to three local numbers and 300 minutes per month. Calls on domestic and international. All your loved one needs to know to sign you up is your name and prison identification number. Feb. 2019

Robert Angres, Esq.
CA parole, writs
Rated None
Details: Free. Only CA cases.
Mail: 4781 E. Gettysburg Ave. Ste.14
Fresno, CA 93726
Phone: 599-348-1918
Web:robertangresattorneyatlaw.com
Review: They have litigated several hundred criminal appeals in the California Courts of Appeal and the California Supreme Court. A prisoner at a suitability hearing has a statutory right to the assistance of counsel. Their firm can provide effective representation by reviewing the prisoner's central file, assisting with the formation of parole plans, presenting letters of support, conducting a direct examination of the prisoner at the hearing (if appropriate), and arguing at the hearing for the prisoner's release on parole.

Robert Young, Esq.
Attorney at law, CA
Rated 7
Details: Send SASE
Mail: 7127 Hollister Ave.
Ste. 25A-332
Santa Barbara CA 93117-2317
Phone: 805-968-1814
lawofficesrey@gmail.com
Review: Locations are in San Diego, Los Angeles, and Santa Barbara. They offer 27 different services and prices.

Ruby Red Entertainment
Magazine Urban Life
Rated None
Details: Single $10/1-Year $35
Mail: Box 155
Covington, VA 24426
Phone: 571-255-5119
Web: rubyredentertainment.com
admin@rubyredentertainment.com
Review: New to the market. Started by ex-inmate. The self-published Tru Royalty Magazine is about street life in VA, NY and more. 100 pages, color, 8.5" x 11". Due to the content and this not being a prisoner magazine, be careful of mailroom rejection. Start with the single issue just in case. Single issues are $10 and a yearly subscription which is four issues is $35, printed quarterly. Apr. 2018

Safe Streets Art Foundation
Publishes written plays and art
▶ **RATED 10!**
Details: See Review
Mail: Box 58043
Washington DC 20037
Phone: 202-393-1511
Web: safestreetsArts.org
Staff@safeStreetsarts.org
Review: The Safe Streets Arts Foundation reviews prisoner-written plays for consideration in their annual "From Prison to the Stage" show at the Kennedy Center. Calling all prisoners or ex-prisoners, we want

you to know about this opportunity to showcase your writing at the Kennedy Center. Not only do they pay for all accepted submissions but they publish every play they receive, whether accepted for their Kennedy Center show or not. (See submission guidelines at www.PrisonsFoundation.org or write to Prisons Foundation, 2512 Virginia Ave. NW, Washington, DC 20037. Web. prisonsfoundation.org

San Quentin News
Prisoner publication
► **RATED 10!**
Details: Receive mailed copy, send $1.61 in FCS
(Repeat every month for current newsletter)
Mail: San Quentin News
1 Main St.
San Quentin, CA 94964
Web: sanquentinnews.com
Review: The San Quentin News encourages inmates, free staff, custody staff, volunteers and others outside the Institution to submit articles. All submissions become property of the San Quentin News. Please use the following criteria when submitting:
• Limit your articles to no more than 350 words.
• Know that articles will be edited for content and length.
• The newspaper is not a medium to file grievances. (For that, use the prison appeals process.) We encourage submitting articles that are newsworthy and encompass issues that will have an impact on the prison populace.
• Please do not use offensive language in your submissions.
• Poems and art work (cartoons and drawings) are welcomed.
• Letters to the editor should be short and to the point.
Send Submissions to:
CSP-San Quentin
Education Dept-S.Q. News
1 Main St.
San Quentin, CA 94964
Review: San Quentin News is also available online. Ask your loved ones to print the free PDF for you or use the updated info on mail copies and submissions listed above. They offer current issue, bonus content and back issues.

Satchidananda Prison Project
Yoga products and newsletter
► **RATED 10!**
Details: Send SASE, free catalog
Mail: 108 Yogaville Way
Buckingham, VA 23921
Phone: 800-476-1347
Web: Shakticom.org
Review: This group had been online only and is now offering a prison outreach project with newsletter. Their store offers yoga books, DVD's, mats, CD's charts, etc.

Satellite Direct Magazine
Direct TV guide
Rated 8
Details: See Review
Mail: 2180 Maiden Lane
Saint Joseph, MI 49085-9801
Web: satellitedirectmagazine.com
Review: Monthly guide covers all major channels, local and premium, 24 hr schedule. Two options by mail at $49.95 per yr. (12) or Download Online at $20 per yr. Also offer print online on a monthly basis, $2/month.

Save On Prison Calls
Phone, message and more
Rated 9
Details: Online
Web: saveonprisoncalls.com
Review: This service is cool because it gives your people a local phone to call you. If you pay $20 for an out-of-state call, with this service, you pay $2-$3 to the provider, plus $14.95 per month for service. A computer is required. Easy to follow directions are on their website. They also offer to send magazines, books, photos, and greeting cards. Handle federal and state prisons, as well as service USA and Canada. June 2019

Scott Handleman. Esq.
Attorney at law
Rated None
Mail: 115 1/2 Bartlett St.
San Francisco, CA 94110
Phone: 415-285-6004
Review: Has seven years of experience. Specializes in CA parole, misdemeanor trial defense, federal appeals, and prisoner thirty year hearings.

Second Chance Book
Newsletter and prisoner books
Rated 8
Details: Send SASE for info
Mail: Box 4149
Philadelphia, PA 19144
Phone: 716-969-8120
Review: They offer Second Chance Newsletter, The Ill Effects of Prison, Poetry from Behind the Walls, The Art of Hustling and more. They offer a huge selection of books to choose from, fiction, non-fiction, bios, dictionaries, adult, and other subjects. All book prices vary. Offer only $5 for shipping.

Second Chance Group LLC
Sell books to BOP inmates

Rated 9
Details: Send SASE for info
Mail: 14 Weaver St.
Buffalo, NY 14206
Phone: 716-969-8120
Web: SecondChanceCatalog.com
SecondChanceBooks@outlook.com
Review: Offer many genres, fiction, mystery, horror, fantasy, romance, western, urban, classic, historical and many more. Average books cost $5.99-$7.99 and up. Can ship up to 5 per order for $5 flat shipping fee. SCG no longer sells or supplies NYC DOC inmates. SSCG sells books to BOP inmates across the country. Now offer prepaid accounts for your loved ones by going to their website. May 2019
Reader Review: Bryan B. in IL – I have written this company twice in the past three months attempting to get an updated category listing, with no reply. Apr. 2018 (note from editor – notice they sell books to BOP inmates, which are Federal inmates. This is no excuse for a company not to reply but...)
—SEE OUR AD—

Secure Electronics
Sells clear products to inmates
► RATED 10!
Details: Send SASE for info
Mail: 56 Gardinertown Rd.
Newburgh, NY 12550
Phone: 845-232-0618
Web: secureelectronics.biz
jewellzm@secureelectronics.com
Review: They sell clear electronics to inmates across this country. Supplying clear radios, watches, and pocket prison radio units to inmates nationwide Authorize deal of Crane. June 2019

Select Legal Topics
Law book
Rated None
Details: Send SASE
Price: $74.95, 638 pgs.
Mail: University Press of America
Box 191
Blue Ridge Summit, PA 17214-0191
Phone: 800-462-640
Web: rowmanlittlefield.com
ISBN # 0-7618-4644-1
Review: Written by one of New York's best attorneys, Andrew J. Schatkin. The focus is on key decisions and crucial elements of legal practice you need to know to win. Topics: Civil, Criminal, Federal, Evidentiary, Procedural, and Labor.

Sentel
Local number provider
► RATED 10!
Details: Send SASE for info
Mail: 9550 S. Eastern Ave. #253
Las Vegas, NV 89123
Phone: 702-430-9445
Web: sentelinmatecall.com
Sentel.nv@gmail.com
Review: Provides services to federal inmates who want cheaper phone calls at 6 cents a minute. Domestic or International. Plans start as low as $1 pay as you go. Does not serve state prisons or county jails. Apr. 2019
Reader Review: Cole M. in FL – I have used Sentel for years. They provide fast and affordable service. Even switched my numbers for me to my new institution at no cost. Their customer service is the best in the industry. I have never had any problems with them."

Sentencing Project
Stats and facts about prisoners
► RATED 10!
Detail: Send SASE for brochure
Mail: 1705 DeSales St. NW 8th FL.
Washington DC, 20036
Web: sentencingproject.org
Staff@SentencingProject.org
Review: Established in 1986, The Sentencing Project works for a fair and effective U.S. criminal justice system by promoting reforms in sentencing policy, addressing unjust racial disparities and practices, and advocating for alternatives to incarceration. They offer printable newsletters on the website called Sentencing Times.

Sentencing and Justice Reform Advocacy (SJRA)
Advocate newsletter
► RATED 10!
Details: Send SASE
Mail: Box 71
Olivehurst, CA 95961
Phone: 530-329-8566
Web: sjra1.com
yeswecanchange3x@aol.com
Review: This great newsletter is only available online as a printable file. The site has all of the issues listed to print for free. Ask your loved ones to print some of them for you.

Shakticom
Yoga products
► RATED 10!
Details: Phone or online orders only
Mail: No Paper Catalogs or Snail mail
Phone: 800-476-1347
Web: shakti.com
shop@shakticom.org
Review: Offers yoga books, DVD's, CD's, mats, charts etc.

Review: We have contacted the company and they only offer online ordering. They are rated a 10 because they are a good company and have great customer service. Unfortunately, like others trimming budgets they have gone with the sole means to sell their products.

Shasto Baskets and Gifts
Amazing pop up greeting cards
► **RATED 10!**
Details: Free catalog
Mail: 304 Main Avenue
Ste 292
Norwalk, CT 06851
Phone: 203-899-0373
shastogifts@yahoo.com
Review: Been in business since 2011 but was gone for a while on hiatus. The now have mazing and affordable 3D pop up cards. The cards are hand assembled are available for any occasion. New designs are being added to the catalog all the time. For a color catalog send them an SASE. May 2018.
Reader Review: Shannon A. in IN- Sent them an SASE took 4 mouths to get the brochure. They must be buried in mail? Apr. 2019

SJE Photos
Photo seller
Rated 8
Details: See Below
Mail: Box 50
Alvarado, TX 76009
Review: New to the marketplace, sister company of Cellmates & Convict Service. They sell non nude photos. Catalogs prices, two stamps per catalog and one SASE per four catalogs. Catalogs, are one page, two sided with 70 images per catalog. Catalogs available in color or B&W. Six catalogs released every 30 days. Photos are priced $0.70 each 4" x 6", $2 each 5" x 7", $5 per 8" x 10" with free S/H. They offer exchanges with return of denied photos and SASE. They offer inmate house accounts. They only offer photos nothing else. June 2019
—SEE OUR AD—

Smithsonian Magazine
Inspires and fascinates
► **RATED 10!**
Price: Current issue $5.99
Mail: 420 Lexington Ave. Ste. 2335
New York, NY 10170
Attn.: Current or Back issue
Phone: 800-766-2149
Web: SmithsonianMag.com
Smithsonian@customersvc.com
Editor: This magazine is a winner and is sure to entertain. The array of topics are vast, such as, smart news, history, science, innovation, arts and culture, travel, at the Smithsonian and more. We have updated the entire listing with current information. Your first issue will arrive in 6-8 weeks. Other prices include back issues for $7 (many are out of print) and full year (12 Issues) for $11.

Sneakers By Mail
Footwear seller
Rated None
Details: SASE for catalog
Mail: 6050 South Country Club Rd.
Ste, 180
Tucson, AZ 85706
Phone: 520-547-0922 x1002
Review: In business since 2014. They sell to inmates that facilities will allow. Male and female affordable stylish footwear. They have a wide selection of sneakers in name brands, many categories and great color choices. Yeezy, Adidas, Omemix in styles like classic runners, high and low tops, fashion athletic, joggers, running and more. They even offer women's Australia Classic tall boots in two colors, sizes 4-10 only $65. Sneaker prices start at $30 and up, flat fee for shipping is $6. Sizes seem to a little limited to the smaller end of the scale. Men's 8 -11, Women's 5-9, some half sizes are available. Accept checks, money orders, facility checks. Order by mail or phone. They also sell copies of Bars Behind Bars $10. June 2019

Socialist Viewpoint
Magazine for working people
► **RATED 10!**
Details: One year
(6 issues)
Prices: New Readers Special $20 for one year.
Mail: 60 29th St., Ste. 429
San Francisco, CA 94110
Web: socialistviewpoint.org
Info@socialistviewpoint.org
Review: The Socialist Viewpoint Publishing Association publishes Socialist Viewpoint in the interests of the working class. SV reprints articles circulated on the internet when they deem them of interest to their readers. Such articles are reprinted exactly as they appeared in the original source, without any editorial or stylistic changes by them. Signed articles do not necessarily represent the views of SV. These views are expressed in editorials. The magazine is thick and packed with interesting reading. They offer a two year subscription for $35.

Soiled Doves
Photo Service

Rated 7
Details: SASE for free brochure
Mail: Box 12536
Reno, NV 89510
Review: They are a high resolution photos in categories of non nude to non nude and penetration photos. And for those who can get them nude soft porn scene photos. Color catalogs, Vol. 1-5 available now, photos start $0.80 cents minium of 10 photos per order plus $1 S/H. They offer a special photos, prices start at $1.50 per photo and $1 S/H per envelope. Accept all forms of payment except personal checks and case. Feb. 2019
Reader Review: Paul K. in WA-I wrote a letter telling INSH that I was ripped off by this company. I had done business with them in the past. It has been over 6 month and nothing. And don't you know, no sooner did I mail the letter about them taking my money and running...I received my order. Yes, 257 days from date I sent and for some reason it was the best order fulfillment I had ever from them. May 2018

South Beach Singles
Photo Seller
▶ **RATED 10!**
Details: Send SASE for brochure
Mail: Box 1656
Miami, FL 33238
Web: southbeachsingles.ning.com
rd@southbeachsingles.org
Review: Web page services $38, calendar $15, photos $1 each, 20 photos $24, $1 puts you on their mailing list.
Reader Review: Shannon A. in IN-Something not right! I placed an order which I never received. When I asked about it, they did not respond to my inquiry, but offered to "allow me to invest $10K in their company" with guarantees of 50% profit in three months. Need I say more? Apr. 2019
Reader Review: Donald U. in AZ-Fast reply, great spreads, flyers are high quality. Prices are my only deterrent to purchasing more. I will try buying something else later on. May 2019

Southern Poverty Law Center
Legal resource books, info, etc.
▶ **RATED 10!**
Details: Free
Mail: 400 Washington Ave.
Montgomery, AL 36104
Web: SPLCenter.org
Review: Specializes in hate crimes. Teaches tolerance programs and offers legal resources.

Sovereign Newspaper, The
The newspaper of the resistance
▶ **RATED 10!**
Detail: Sample Issue $4
Price: $35 yr. NO free samples
Mail: Box 1601
Old Chelsea Station
New York, NY 10113
Web: thesovnews.com
Letters@thesovnews.com
Review: This is the newspaper of the resistance. Whatever you want to resist you may find it in here. Anti-Obama and every other issue on the hot list. Great entertainment for the price. WARNING! Ask your mail room before you order. This paper has something to tick off nearly everyone.

Spain Telecom
Discount calling
▶ **RATED 10!**
Details: Call, write or email for more info (Espanol)
Mail: 1220 Broadway #803
New York, NY 10001
Phone: 845-326-5300
Web: inmatefone.com
Clients@inmatefone.com
Review: Their ad states "Save up to 90% on out-of-state and international calls from county jails, Federal and State prisons." Verify, before you buy.
Reader Review: J. Snyder – My mom pays $24.99 at home and I get six local numbers, cutting my phone costs drastically. I pay $.05 cents a minute in here which is roughly $18 for 300 minutes instead of $70. However, I seem to get 400 minutes for that price. I was able to add them to Corrlinks and set up the numbers I wanted. I can change them as often as needed. They are extremely responsive when I send a change request...usually within hours. I rate them a 10!

Special Needs X-Press
Books and magazines
▶ **RATED 10!**
Details: online seller
Mail: 927 Old Nepperhan Ave.
Yonkers, NY 10703
Phone: 914-623-7007
Web: shopsnx.com
Info@specialneedsxpress.com
Review: Ship books and magazines to inmates, hospital patients and customers in USA. Over 1,000 magazines and 1,000,000 printed books available to be special ordered from their data base. Books, novels, upcoming magazines, discounted titles, Spanish featured titles and more. Also carry planners, calenders and dictionaries. They offer prepaid accounts for inmates loved ones to add funds to online. They accept all

inmate email providers corrlinks.com, JPay, ConnectNetwork/GLT, Getting-Out etc. June 2019
—SEE OUR AD—

Sports Illustrated
Sports news
► **RATED 10!**
Details: Order online
Price: $39 yr., 56 issues
Mail: Box 61290
Tampa, FL 33661-1290
Phone: 800-806-4833
Web: si.com
Review: We could not verify this address or find a mailing address at all for them online. These days everything is order online, read online. We know the magazine is Rated 10 but we recommend ordering your subscription with Grant Publications May 2019

Sports Weekly (USA Today)
Sports stats magazine
► **RATED 10!**
Details: Mail-in
Order form is available online
Price: $13 for 13 wks.,
$25 for 26 wks.,
$45 for 52 wks.
Mail: Box 682669
Franklin, TN 37068-2669
Phone: 800-USA-1415 (872)
Web: service.ustoday.com
Review: The only sports magazine to print stats on NFL and MLB. Arrives weekly.
Editor: USA Today handles this magazine. You can write in for a mail-In order form or have a loved one print one for you.

Stable Entertainment
Photo Seller
Rated 6
Details: Catalog, 2 FCS or $1
Mail: Box 1352
Lancaster, TX 75146
69stable@gmail.com
Review: Been in business since 2011. SE is a premiere source for high quality non nude photos. Their quality is unparalleled and unsurpassed by no one in the sexy photo selling business in our marketplace today. They offer full color catalogs, photo membership club for bulk purchases and super-fast, flat-rate shipping with a ten day guarantee! They even offer a monthly photo subscription service. If you want catalogs send 2 stamps or $1 for each.

Steve DeFilippia, Esq.
Attorney at law for serious felonies and parole
Rated None
Details: Free, CA state and Federal
Mail: 625 N. First St.
San Jose, CA 95112
Phone: 408-292-0441
Review: For serious felonies and parole.

Stratford Career Inst.
Education by mail
Rating: 6
Details: Free
Mail: Box 1560
St. Albans, VT 05478
Phone: 612-788-4197
Web: scitraining.com
Review: They offer education in 52 career fields.

Streamline, LLC
Discount calls
Rated None
Details: Send SASE
Mail: Box 77981
Charlotte, NC 28271
Phone: 866-912-2492
Web: streamlinellc.org
Sales@streamlinellc.org
Review: They offer discount, rollover monthly plans for federal and state prisons and county jails. Plans start at $15 month depending on how many minutes you purchase.

Street Pixs
Photo Seller
Rated None
Details: Send SASE for catalog/info
Mail: Box 302-IS
Humble, TX 77347-0302
Review: They offer sexy photos, stories and books. Nude and non nude catalogs available. New catalogs every three months. Recently, a member of family took over management of the business and will be straightening customer service issue out, be patient and polite for any mess was not the fault of the person in charge now. Feb. 2019
Reader Review: Michael A in CA- I have placed three orders of 100 photos each over the time, and only received half of the photos. I have written letters and no response. May 2019
Reader Review: Shannon A. in IN- Put in an order four months ago, still no photos, no response to inquires. Buyer beware. (Remember they have been recently under new management) Apr. 2019
Reader Review: Donald U. in AZ-
—SEE OUR AD—

Street Seen Magazine
Local car shows and girls
► **RATED 10!**
Sample: $4 or 14 FCS
Mail: 14173 NW Fwy. Ste. 203
Houston, TX 77040

Web: streetseen.com
Review: Covers car show culture. Low riders, mini trucks and car girls. They have beautiful cover to cover (non nude) issues. They also have an entire magazine of car show girls for $10.
—SEE OUR AD—

Sub 0 Entertainment
Phat Puffs Magazine
▶ RATED 10!
Details: Online order only
Web: sub0world.com
Review: Sub 0 has a high glossy professional magazine filled with girls gone wild. Models, strippers, housewives, MILF, and porn stars. All non nude photos. Order the latest issue today. It's a must have for entertainment collection. Online orders only. May 2018
—SEE OUR AD—

Sunshine Artist Magazine
Art genre magazine
▶ RATED 10!
Price: $34.95 yr.
12 issues
Mail: 4075 L B McLeod Rd. Ste. E
Orlando, FL 32811
Phone: 407-648-7479 or
800-597-2573
Web: sunshineartist.com
Review: Sunshine Artist lists over 2000 art craft shows and events in each issue for the subsequent 11 months. This is not a directory of art contests or art suppliers. If you are going to be released soon and would like to sell your art or crafts in your state or across the country, this is your best "in print" source.

SureShot Books
Book seller
▶ RATED 10!
Details: Catalog $12.95
Mail: 15 North Mill St.
Nyack, NY 10960
Phone: 845-675-7505
Web: sureshotbooks.com
customer.service@sureshotbooks.com
Sales@sureshotbooks.com
Tracking@sureshotbooks.com
customer.service@sureshotbooks.com
Review: They sell books in a wide variety of categories, such as Christian book, puzzle books, men's interests, women's interests, urban market, video gaming, what's hot and more. They also sell newspapers from all states and offer a wide range of magazine subscriptions. Also, have pre funded accounts. Order their most current catalog, send $12.95 with all your mailing information. June 2019
Reader Review: Ryan D. in WI-The catalog is pricey but they have a good selection, that is also pricey, but i guess the prices of everything in society has gone up including books. They now offer a few single issue mens mags. May 2018

Surrogate Sisters
Various products
▶ RATED 10!
Details: Send SASE
Mail: Box 95043
Las Vegas, NV 89193
service@surrogatesisters.com
Review: They offer sexy photos, non nude/nude,and female/male. Have a variety of gifts and erotic stories. Send an SASE for info.
Reader Review: Paul K in WA – I always type and clearly place my orders, the wrong photos sent and/or the photo quality was lousy. Recently, they have not replaced wrong photos that were their mistake and have kept several SASE's. Apr. 2018
Reader Review: Donald U. in AZ-Sent to them and got response about a week. Ordered flyers from their list and was okay quality. They allowed me membership deals/rates without being a member. I will be purchasing the membership ASAP!. Good deal, especially for those with a long sentence. 10 free photos and 1 flyer with membership sign up. May 2019

TCM Professional Subscription Services
Magazine seller
Rating: 9
Details: Send SASE
Mail: Box 62120
Tampa, FL 33662-2120
Review: TCM (Time Consumer Marketing) Is part of Time Inc. They offer a large variety of magazine subscription at low prices.
Reader Review: Mark K. in DE – I subscribe to a lot of magazines and have tried many vendors. TCM has the fastest turnaround time I have ever seen.

Texas Prison Bookstore
Books, magazines, stationary.
Rated 9
Details: Send SASE for catalog
Mail: 1301 DuPont Cir.
Orange, TX 77630
Web: TexasPrisonBookstore.com
TexasPrisonBookstore@yahoo.com
Reader Comments: Fast and good customer service.
Review: We received their 32 page, 8.5 x 11 catalog in 12 days. They offer writing supplies, coloring books and puzzle books for $2.99 each.

Reference, recovery, educational, and spiritual titles in addition to hundreds of fiction and nonfiction titles, many at $3.99 each. Single copies of magazines, comics, and graphic novels.

TextInmate.com
Inmate texting service
► **RATED 10!**
Details: Corrlinks
Phone: 855-420-0880
Web: textinmate.com
Support@textinmate.com
Review: is offering a new Corrlinks to text message service for your loved ones on the outside. The service allow you to text your friends and family USA based cell phone on the outside with your own dedicated phone number using Corrlinks. Tell your friends and family on the outside to sign you up today at for free at www.textinmate.com.

TextToWrite.com
E-Correspondence
Rated 8
Details: Send SASE
Mail: 37 N. Orange Ave. #500
Orlando, FL 32801
Phone: 818-500-5275
Web: TextToWrite.com
Support@textotwrite.com
Review: offers unlimited letters and pictures to be sent to inmates by loved ones. They can text message or email as many letters and pictures as they want and TextToWrite will create a time line (similar to a time line one would see on their favorite social media websites) of the letters and pictures and send it to inmate every week. Many plans to pick from. Send for info or have someone go to the website.

Third Eye Tie Dye
Custom gifts
Rated None
Details: Send SASE
Mail: ABYW/Third Eye
Box 16141
Rumford, RI 02916
Review: They are sister company of A Book You Want. Offering custom handmade Tapestries, Bandanas and T-shirts gifts for your loved ones.

Thomas D. Kenny, Esquire
Attorney at law
► **RATED 10!**
Details: Write or call for info
Mail: 1500 J. F. Kennedy Blvd.
Ste. 520
Philadelphia, PA 19102
Phone: 215-423-5500
Web: KennyBurnsMcGill.com
Review: Offers legal and business services to inmates and their families during and after incarceration. Complete criminal defense, appeals, PCRA, Habeas hearings, parole, pardons, wills, living wills, trusts, power of attorney, business information and administrative services.
—SEE OUR AD—

Tibetan Spirit
Buddhist items
Rated 8
Details: Free catalog
Mail: Box 57
Boonsboro, MD 21713-0057
Phone: 888-327-2890
301-416-2712
Web: tibetanspirit.com
Shop@tibetanspirit.com
Review: They offer quality Buddhist religious items at lower prices than others.

Tightwad Magazines
Discount mag subscriptions
► **RATED 10!**
Details: For a mini-catalog, send SASE
Mail: Box 1941
Buford, GA 30515
Review: The owners of Julie's Gifts, Tightwad has been in business since 1999. Their customer service has improved greatly, they work hard to get magazines delivered behind the walls. When an inmate is moved and their mail was not forwarded to them, Tightwad works with the publishers to update the mailing address and try to get the subscriptions extended to make up for lost issues. They offer a special promo, if you send them an SASE to request a catalog. They will send a coupon for you to select a free magazine. If you cannot send an SASE you can request a coupon.
Reader Review: Prentiss in TX – is another very excellent company that I have had great service from. Mar. 2018

Time Magazine
News magazine
► **RATED 10!**
Price: $30 for 52 Issues
Mail: Time and Life Building
Rockefeller Center
New York, NY 10020-1393
Phone: 800-843-8463
Web: time.com

Time Served, LLC
Inmate services
Rated 9
Details: Send 2 Stamps for Info
Mail: 7 Saint Clair Ave. Ste. 315
Cleveland, OH 44144
Web: timeservedllc.com
timeservedllc@gmail.com

Phone: 276-299-1199
Review: Provides a list of services for inmates by mail and email. Some of the services are Facebook, friend finder (people search), gift packages, photo forwarding. June 2019

Time Zone Gifts
Gifts services
► **RATED 10!**
Details: Free Catalog
Mail: Box 41093
Houston, TX 77241
Phone: 800-731-6726 or 832-416-2651
Web: timezonegifts.com
Shop@timezonegifts.com
Review: They have been in business since 2010. They provide a free glossy, full color, 44 page catalog. There is over 150 gifts to choose from, prices ranging from $2 through $24.95 most include free S/H. There is a large variety of gift like greeting cards, stuffed animals, jewelry, gift baskets, colognes, perfumes, T-shirts, toys, bath and beauty supplies and more. All orders are packaged with care and shipped USPS with tracking. Some of the gifts such as watches and wedding bands can be ordered by inmates and sent directly to them in prison. Feb. 2019
Reader Review: Everett G in NY- I bought a watch when I saw INSH Rated 10, watch came in but within days noticed the watch was not keeping time correctly, immediately contacted TZG. When they finally responded back die to having family helping track them down. They told me they do not fix watched, did not know anywhere to get fixed and since was over the 30 day guarantee return policy nothing could be done. I was told it was my responsibility to have returned the watch immediately for replacement.

Treasure Hunter Newsletter
Monthly newsletter
Rated 8
Detail: Sample issue, $3
Price: $15 for 6 mos., $24 one yr.
Mail: Box 66
Atlanta, IL 61723
Review: A twenty-page, 5" x 8", B&W newsletter with a lot of interesting content, if you like entering sweepstakes and reading classified ads. This is like a mini-Craigslist in print. You'll find ads for free cash, personals, cash for gold, collector's classified, and say no to aliens, gold and diamond mines for sale and that's just one page. Beware of the "get rich quick" ads but beyond those, this little newsletter is worth the price. The response time is 2 to 3 weeks.

Triarco Art Supplies
Art supplies
► **RATED 10!**
Detail: Free catalog
Mail: 9909 S. Shore Dr. Ste. 1015
Plymouth, MN 55441-5037
Phone: 763-559-5590
Web: triarcoarts.com
Reader review: M. Ludden – It's a good biz but didn't tell us how much the catalog is.
Review: We contacted the company and they send catalogs for free.

Turning the Tide
Newsletter
► **RATED 10!**
Details: Sample $3
Price: $16 for one year
Editor: Michael Novick
Pay to: Anti-Racist Action
Box 1055
Culver City, CA 90232
Web: tideturning.org
Review: The newspaper has been in print 25 years. It is 11" x 17" and covers the fight against austerity, inequality and racism. Well written, covers California and national issues. Publishes writings by prisoners.

UnCommon Law
Prisoner rights services
Rated None
Details: Send SASE
Mail: 220 4th St. Ste. 201
Oakland, CA 94607
Phone: 510-271-0310
Web: theuncommonlaw.org
Review: They work with prisoners for months or years in advance of their parole board hearings, and they represent them in those hearings and in court petitions challenging the parole board and the governor. They offer a guide to Lifer Support Letters, Insight to CA Life Sentences, and Overview of California's Parole Consideration Process.

Under Lock and Key (ULK)
Prisoner magazine
► **RATED 10!**
Details: Free to prisoners
Published by: Maoist International Ministry (MIM)
Accepts inmate submissions
Mail: MIM (prisons)
Box 40799
San Francisco, CA 94140
Web: PrisonCensorship.info
mim@prisoncensorship.Info
Review: This magazine is 8.5" x 11" with 16 pages. There are six issues per year. They accept inmate submissions. Are you a thinking man or woman? Whether or not you agree with their political views, ULK offers

news from inside on protest, riots, hunger strikes and oppression written by prisoners on the yard. We are all aware how local press publishers are whatever the prison press release states – never interviewing prisoners about the event so it's nice to see a publisher that is hands on. MIM (Prisons) is a revolutionary anti-imperialist group fighting criminal injustice, and helping prisoners to organize and educate themselves. Sends free political books and dictionaries, offers a free subscription to their newspaper Under Lock and Key, and runs correspondence study courses. Write for a free subscription.

Union Supply Co. Inc.
Clear products and music
Rated 8
Details: Write for free music or merchandise catalog
(They do not send catalogs to AZ)
Mail: Box 9018 Dept. 200
Rancho Dominguez, CA 90220
Phone: 866-404-8989
Web: unionsupply.com
Customerservice@unionsupply.com
Review: Since it's founding in 1991, has been a supplier of commissary goods and services. Union Supply provides food, apparel, footwear, electronics, and personal-care products to State, Federal and County correctional institutions nationwide. Check with your facility to see if they accept USC, if yes, to order catalog for your state write to the address above.

University of Arizona
Education
► **RATED 10!**
Details: Free
Mail: Box 210158
Tucson, AZ 85721-0158
Phone: 520-621-2211
Web: arizona.edu/correspondence
Review: We received a list of 120 courses in 30 different subject areas. Most courses can be completed without a computer. Priced at $252 per credit hour. You don't have to live in AZ to take these classes.

Up North Services
Inmate care packages
Rated None
Catalog: Printable Online
Mail: Box 370688
Brooklyn, NY 11237
Web: upnorthservices.com
Phone: 718-715-1419
Review: UNS offer a catalog of products that are all pre-approved for shipment to NYS correctional facilities. Up North Services Incorporated was founded in Brooklyn during the spring of 2002. They offer a large variety of categories, appliances, clothes, cosmetics, electronics, foods, housewares, music, publications and more.

Urban Fiction Editor
Publishing services – editing
Rated 7
Details: Send SASE
Mail: 500 Westover Dr. #2358
Sanford, NC 27330
Phone: 704-286-6142
Web: urbanfictioneditor.com
Info@urbanfictioneditor.com
Review: Offers free marketing tips and free three page edit of your writing. Average to low price range. We sent them an SASE July 24, 2013 and received their info in two weeks. If you're a new writer you should be aware of the importance of hiring the correct specialist for your project. Hiring any old editor for your Urban Fiction book is a potential train wreck. May 2017

USA Song Writing Contest
Contest
Rated 6
Details: See review
Mail: 2881 E. Oakland Park Blvd. Ste. 414
Ft. Lauderdale, FL 33306
Web: songwriting.net
info@songwriting.net
Review: Since 1995, sponsored international song writing events, has been honoring songwriters, composers, bands, and recording artists everywhere. This is open to all, regardless of nationality or country origin. 25th Annual USA Song writing Competition. If you enter by mail, each entry must include: (A) Completed entry form (or photocopy). All signatures must be original. (B) CD or Audio Cassette(s) containing one song only, five minutes or less in length. Lyrics Only category do not require audio CD or cassette. (C) Lyric sheet (please include English translation if applicable). Lyrics are not required for instrumental category. (D) Check or money order for $35. (US currency only). You may total all entries on one check (example: 6 entries = $210.). If paying by credit card, $35. Per song entry will be charged to your account. All entries must be entered by May 29, 2020 or earlier. June 2019

USA Today Newspaper
Newspaper
► **RATED 10!**
Mail: 7950 Jones Branch Dr.
McLean, VA 22108
Mail for subscription payments

Mail: USA Today, Subscription Processing
Box 677454
Dallas, TX 75267-7454
Mail for back issues:
Box 682669
Franklin, TN 37068-2669
Phone: 866-602-0746
Review: Subscription cost: Subject to change. 1 Month $25, 12 months $300. Most special offer sale prices you see advertised will not work, for mailed newspapers. The reason is, most newspapers do not handle their own mailing subscriptions, and they are called courier services. Allow about 30 days until your first copy. June 2018

US Dept. of Justice
Civil rights
Rated 9
Details: Free
Mail: 10th St./Pennsylvania Ave. NW
Washington, DC 20503
Review: They will investigate valid claims by you, against jails and prisons and their staff. Send your letter several times as letters to the DOJ tend to get lost by mail rooms.
Ventura Mail Order Books
Offers erotica and other genres
Rated 9
Details: SASE for catalog
Mail: 7928 Oak St.
Los Molinos, CA 96055
Vmobooks@gmail.com
Review: Under new management and fully staffed with a new and improved catalog. Small book company offers personal service, may publish your erotica? Accepts all forms of payment.

Veterans Advocate
Vets law and advocacy issues
► **RATED 10!**
Published by: Vet Legal Services
Mail: Box 65762
Washington, DC 20035
Web: NVLSP.org
Review: This is a quarterly online journal covering veteran's issues at the state and federal levels. $80 per year, two yrs. $120.

Veterans Affairs, Dept. of
Resources for veterans
Rated 8
Details: Free
Mail: 3225 North Central Ave.
Phoenix, AZ 85012
Phone: 800-352-0451
Review: Provides assistance to Vets; financial employment counseling and referral. Also see: Military Records.

Villa Entertainment Co., Inc.
Magazine publisher and photo seller
StreetSeen, Car Show Hotties and American Hotties- plus now photos!
► **RATED 10!**
Details: Send SASE for info
Mail: Villa Entertainment Co. Inc.
Dept. ISFI-0915
14173 NW Freeway, Ste. 203
Houston, TX 77040
Phone: 713-465-9599
Web: StreetSeen.com
Streetseen@ymail.com
Review: Based in the Lone Star State, their magazines cover custom car show culture and gorgeous car show models (non nude). Lowriders, Minitrucks, Dubstyle, Swangas, 4x4's and more! Special offer for Inmate Shopper readers, see ad. In addition to StreetSeen mag they also offer American Hotties, Car Show Hotties. Special offer StreetSeen Photos of glossy 4" x 6" non nude photos of the hottest ladies to grace the pages of the magazine. Order a sample of 10 comes with free catalog. June. 2019
Reader Review: Ryan D. in WI-They have various car show model mags and photos too. Great looking women, really hot... Love the vehicles too, some sick rides. Aug. 2018
—SEE OUR AD—

Voices.Con Newsletter
Long-term incarceration issues
► **RATED 10!**
Details: SASE for free resource directory
Price: $11 for 12 issues
Mail: Box 361
King City, CA 93930
Web: voicesdotcon.org
Editor: Dave@Voicesdotcon.org
Review: They started publishing in 2003. Voicesdotcon.org publishes 400 copies of their eight page, digital B&W, 8.5 x 11 newsletter monthly. Ask a loved one to print it off their website and mail to you. Submission Guidelines: We have only one agenda: advocating on behalf of the term-to-life prisoner and distributing information that will further this cause, enabling the term-to-life prisoner to effectively advocate on his or her own behalf. You may write an essay, article on any related subject or issue of concern to the term-to-life prisoner population.

Vortex Publishing
Publishes only true stories
Rated 8
Details: Send SASE

Mail: Box 352
Osceola, IA 50213
Review: The company's authors are looking for true stories of crimes where the person "got away with it." If they include your story in their book, they will pay you cash. True stories ONLY. Inmates welcome. Identity not published. Write for full details.

Walkenhorst's
Sell inmate approved products
► **RATED 10!**
Details: SASE for catalog
Mail: 540 Technology Way
Napa, CA 94558
Phone: 800-660-9255
Web: walkenhorsts.com
Info@walkenhorsts.com
Review: For over 25 years, Walkenhorst's has made it possible to send packages to inmates incarcerated in correctional facilities. Their response time is two to five weeks. They are a Securepak approved vendor. Sells everything; clear plastic items, food, clothing, music, etc. They offer the catalog online or by mail.

Wall Periodicals Online
Urban magazine sellers
Rated 9
Details: SASE for info
Mail: Box 2584
Plainfield, NJ 07060-0584
Phone: 718-285-0421 or 718-819-1693
Web: wallperiodicalsonline.com
Info@ wallperiodicalsonline.com
Review: In business since 1986. They are the largest Urban wholesalers in US. Large inventory of urban and speciality titles. They sell singles, current issues and have a printable catalog online. They now offer along with magazine, books, calendars, DVDs and Christmas cards. June 2019

Walter Reaves, Esq.
Specialities: criminal defense and federal crime
► **RATED 10!**
Details: Free ebook on their Web "Hiring a Criminal Lawyer" and more
Mail: 100 N. 6th St., Ste. 902
Waco, TX 76701
Phone: 254-781-3588
Web: waco-criminal-attorney.com
Review: Criminal Defense Attorney Walter Reaves has been practicing law in Waco, Texas for 37 years. During that time he has represented hundreds of people charged with all types of offenses in both State and Federal Courts – from minor misdemeanors all the way to capital murder. In addition to his membership in the State Bar of Texas, Mr. Reaves is also a member of the Texas Criminal Defense Lawyers Association. Office offers work on post-conviction, appeals, case evaluation and motions, criminal defense, expunctions and disclosures. The website offers 10 free ebooks online titles from, Don't Hire the Wrong Lawyer, You're Been Arrests-What So You Do Know?, Learn What You Need to Know Bout Texas Marijuana Cases, Freedom through Science, Don't Become Another Victim of the Criminal Justice System in Texas, An Inmates Guide to Habeas Corpus and more. We received our free download of Hiring a Criminal Lawyer and found the 10 pages filled with interesting content. Have your loved ones request the ebooks and print you copies. May 2019

Watercolor Artist
How-to master water media
► **RATED 10!**
Details: Order mags online
Price: $7.99 to $8.99 each issue
Mail: F and W Media Inc.
10151 Carver Rd., Ste. #200
Blue Ash, OH 45242
Web: artistsnetwork.com
Review: They publish 6 issues per year of print magazines. Also accepts freelance writer's artist techniques, send SASE ask for writers guidelines. Magazines can be ordered online. They also publish Artists Magazine, Pastel Paint Water, and Southwest Art Magazines. June 2019

Waterfront Gifts and Art
Personalized gifts
► **RATED 10!**
Details: Send $5 for catalog
Mail: 135 Fisherman's Cove
Miramar Beach, FL 32550
Phone: 850-225-8827
Review: They sell personalized gifts for you to help you keep in touch with your loved ones. Jewelry, stuffed animals and more. Each gift is wrapped, shipped and includes a hand-written card with your personal message. They now have art and do henna tattoos. This place looks likes its name, really beach, sun, wind and life vibe. Color Catalog $5 Good things come in small packages. June 2019

Ways to Wealth
Photo Seller and reports
Rated 9

Details: SASE or $4 or 9 FCS
Mail: Box 751352
Memphis, TN 38175
Phone: 731-671-5531
Waystowealthpublications@gmail.com
Facebook.com/ways2wealthPublications
Review: is a mail order business that covers topics on economical empowerment, business ideas, business start-up, loans, grants, scholarships, economical literacy, business management, ways to wealth, money making opportunities, housing programs, job resources, HUD programs, wholesale jewelry, non nude erotic models photo program sale, stocks, bonds, probates, mutual funds, consumer resource information, marketing strategies, advertisement strategies, how to start a mail-order business, how to profit from various auctions, home-base business information, how to create a superb credit history, how to build a $500,000 line of credit, how to create a totally new credit file, information on the entertainment and music industry, government benefits and programs, legal resources, religious and spiritual resources, correspondence resources to college – vocational – technical courses, various advocacy organizations pertaining to many needs and much more. Send 20 First Class stamps or $10 and receive 7 publication catalogs loaded with info mentioned above. They offer classified ad placement, info is inside the above catalogs or contact them. They have two non nude erotic models photo program catalogs in female or male. Photos costs are $0.50 cents each, to order photo catalog each are 20 First Class stamps or $10, tell female or male. They do NOT accept self-addressed stamped envelopes. June 2019

We Wuv Poetry
Poetry newsletter
▶ RATED 10!
Details: SASE for info
Mail: Box 4725
Pittsburgh, PA 15206
Phone: 866-234-0297
Review: This is a B&W newsletter filled with poetry. For those who like to read or submit poetry send for info. Aug. 18

Whoa Books
Urban book sellers
Rated 9
Details: Send SASE for info
Mail: Box 226
Bloomfield, NJ 07003
Web: whoabooks.com
whoabooks1@gmail.com
Review: They carry top selling urban titles and popular brands. They carry books, magazines, DVDs, calendars and now adding digital magazines to the list. They offer prepaid accounts. June 2019
—SEE OUR AD—

William Schmidt, Esq.
Attorney at law
▶ RATED 10!
Details: Free
Mail: Box 25001
Fresno, CA 93729
Phone: 559-261-2222
911civilrights@gmail.com
legal.schmidt@gmail.com
Review: legal service for California Inmates. Appeals, writs of habeas corpus, civil rights litigations, catastrophic injury/excessive force, gang issues, transfers and more. Please submit a sing le page summary of your case. Due to the volume they cannot return documents or respond to all inquires. They are not a low cost or pro bono firm but is you want results, write them. June 2019

Winning Brief, 3rd Ed., The
Legal writing book
Rated 7
Details: See review
Mail: Oxford University Press
2001 Evans Rd.
Cary, NC 27513
Web: oup.com
Review: Authored by Bryan A. Garner, the editor of Black's Law Dictionary, is a must have for anyone writing briefs. Shows you how to trim the fat, phrase the issue and present a winning argument. Cost average of $60 plus S/H. Aug. 2018

Winning Habeas Corpus and Post-Conviction Relief
Law book for prisoners
▶ RATED 10!
8th Edition Available
Details: 7" x 10" SC over 640 pgs.
Price: $58.50 includes S/H (no personal checks)
Mail: Fast Law Publishing
Mail: Box 2315
Port Orchard, WA 98366
Web: fastlaw.org
fastlawpa@gmail.com
Review: the book contains case cites through 638 F. 3d Covers habeas procedures for 2254, 2255 and Rule 60(b). Sixth Amendment and IAC, pre-trial duty to investigate, plea bargain process, Jury instructions, sentencing, time bar, and tolling. Over 1800 Cases cited. Prisoner Price $59.50 includes

S/H.(a prisoner purchase with above address only) This publisher has two law books, see their listing under Fast Law Publishing for more info. Both books can be purchased by address above or Amazon and FreebirdPublishers.com.

Witches and Pagans
Magazine about the pagan community
▶ **RATED 10!**
Details: 4 issue $23
Mail: Box 687
Forest Grove, OR 97116-0687
Phone: 503-430-8817
Web: witchesandpagens.com
editor2@bbimedia.com
Review: Magazine is quarterly for more info on ordering send SASE or stamp. All about Pagan life filled with wonderful stories and more. The magazine subscription or renewal can be completed by PDF download or printed and mailed to US, Canada or Overseas. Witches & Pagans or Sage Woman available in 4, 8, 12 issues subscriptions, prices $24, $44, $62. They also odder both mags in a bundle to save money.
They also do book reviews. Accept pristine first class stamps for payment, facility checks, money orders and credit cards. June 2019
Reader Review: Matthew K. in ND – Fast and loving service. They have great replies and shipping. Although they do not take credit cards in the mail any longer. Would recommend if your are learning or into Wicca and Paganism! Mar. 2019

Word Out Books
Publishes inmate authors
Rated 8
Details: Send SASE
Mail: Box 2689
Eugene, OR 97503
Review: This is a pilot program launched by parent company Winding Halls Publishing, created late 2017. They are publishers that will publish inmate authors under the Word Out Books imprint, paperback and ebooks. They set prices, sell books and more. Write for more information on publishing fees and how it works. Do NOT send them any manuscript without prior permission. May 2019
—SEE OUR ADS—

Wow Me Web Designs
Web/graphic design
▶ **RATED 10!**
Mail: 6659 Scheafer Rd. Suite 1089, #1098
Flint, MI 48507
Phone: 520-477-7923
jamika@wowmewebdesigns.com
Contact@wowmewebdesigns.com
Review: They offer a three-page website for as low as $299.99. The site consists of Home, Contact and a third page of your choice. Monthly updates starting at $35 and up. No update, no fee. Mar. 2019

Writer's Digest Magazine
Info for writers and contests
▶ **RATED 10!**
Details: Online orders only
Phone 800-333-0133
Web: writersdigest.com
Review: If you are or want to be a writer and are in prison, you must have this magazine. It's that simple. Their charter publication, Writer's Digest, literally "wrote the book" on writing and getting published. For more than 90 years, the experts at Writer's Digest have been publishing books, magazines, competitions, conferences and distance education materials for writers who want to polish their skills and hone their craft.

Writers Market
Lists buyers of writing and art
▶ **RATED 10!**
Price: $29 95
Discount booksellers list $19.95
Mail: F and W Publications
4700 E. Gallbraith Rd.
Cincinnati, OH 45236
Phone: 800-333-0133
Web: writersmarket.com
Review: Includes 3500 listings for book publishers, greeting cards, consumer magazines, trade journals, literary agents and more

Wynword Press
Law books for prisoners
▶ **RATED 10!**
Title: Battling the Administration
Author: David J. Meister
Details: 11" x 8.5", SC, 566 pgs.
Mail: Box 557
Bonners Ferry, ID 83805
Phone: 208-267-0817
Web: wynwordpress.com
Review: An inmate guide to a successful lawsuit, know your civil rights and how to defend them in court. This self-help manual guides readers through the complex civil court systems, teaches them how to pursue a lawsuit in the face of the constraints imposed by incarceration, and enables a successful outcome for the prisoners' civil rights lawsuit. Includes extensive

case-law citations and advice on organizing, investigating and prosecuting a case. Aug. 2018

Zoukis Consulting Group
Federal prisoner consulting firm
► **RATED 10!**
Details: email or online
Web: PrisonerResource.com
Info@PrisonerResource.com
Phone: 843-732-1740
Review: Zoukis Consulting Group (PrisonerResource.com) is dedicated to assisting soon-to-be and current federal prisoners, their families and friends, and federal criminal defense attorneys with understanding life inside the Federal Bureau of Prisons, along with governing policy and federal regulations. On the site, we discuss every facet of life in federal prison and offer a large number of resources, to include discussions of prison life, profiles of every federal prison in the country, a national inmate locator tool, and much more. We offer assistance with in-prison matters (e.g., health care, disciplinary defense, administrative remedies, transfers, emails and phone calls to BOP officials, etc.) for between $500 and $1,000 per issue. Halfway house and home confinement maximization is billed between $1,000 to $1,500. Reentry planning packages are available from $1,500 to $2,500. And supervised release preparation and consultation packages are available from $1,500 to $2,500. June 2019

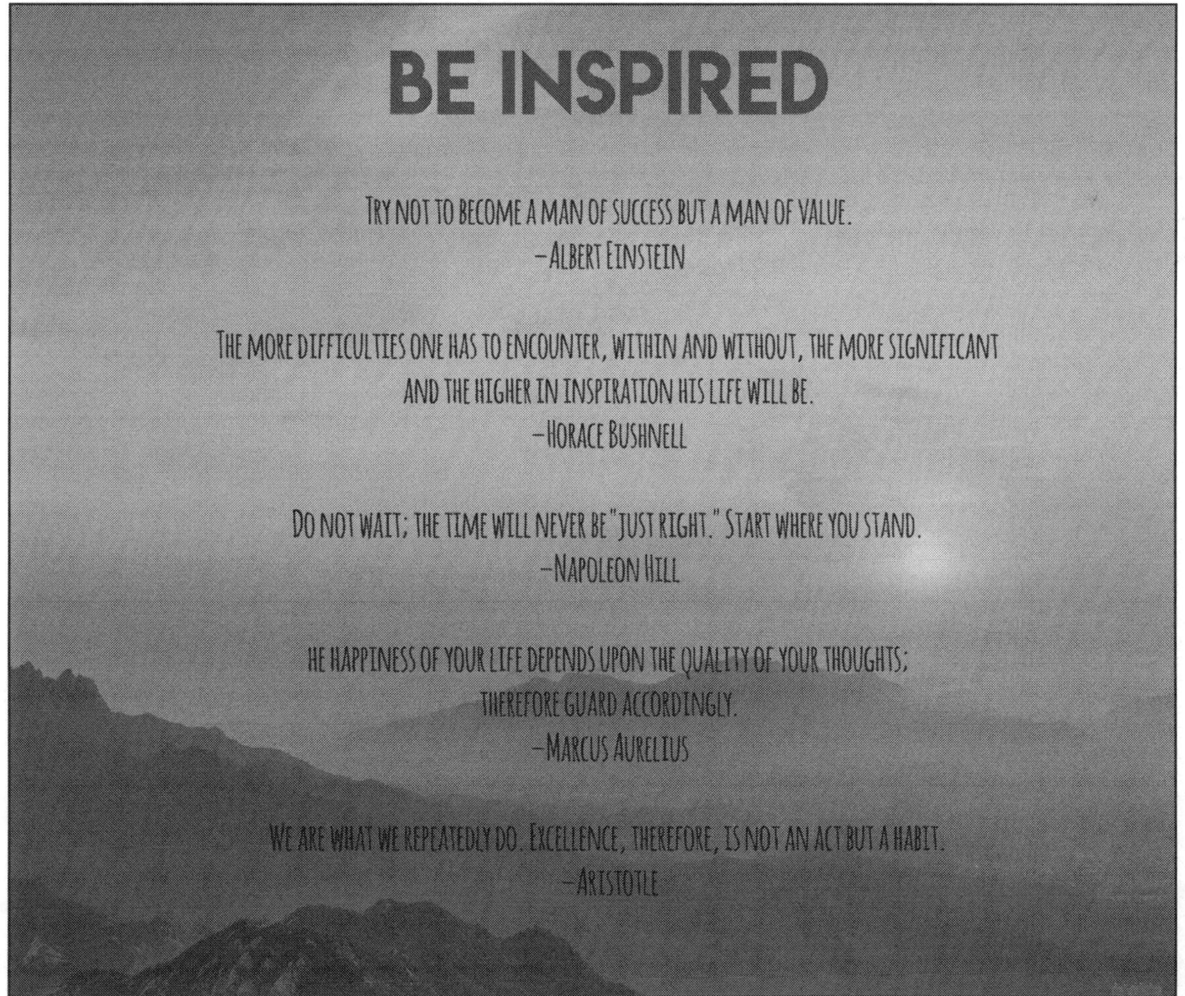

BE INSPIRED
TRY NOT TO BECOME A MAN OF SUCCESS BUT A MAN OF VALUE.
–ALBERT EINSTEIN
THE MORE DIFFICULTIES ONE HAS TO ENCOUNTER, WITHIN AND WITHOUT, THE MORE SIGNIFICANT
AND THE HIGHER IN INSPIRATION HIS LIFE WILL BE.
–HORACE BUSHNELL
DO NOT WAIT; THE TIME WILL NEVER BE "JUST RIGHT." START WHERE YOU STAND.
–NAPOLEON HILL
HE HAPPINESS OF YOUR LIFE DEPENDS UPON THE QUALITY OF YOUR THOUGHTS;
THEREFORE GUARD ACCORDINGLY.
–MARCUS AURELIUS
WE ARE WHAT WE REPEATEDLY DO. EXCELLENCE, THEREFORE, IS NOT AN ACT BUT A HABIT.
–ARISTOTLE

CNA Entertainment LLC

PO Box 185
Hitchcock, Texas 77563
www.CNAEntertainment.com
CNATexas@live.com

We are a visual media entertainment mail order LLC that distributes photos of a wide variety of models to the prison population across the country. We currently have over 50,000 photos with a variety of different themes. We also offer custom printing of bookmarks, small calendars, proof sheets and personal photo reproduction. For more information about this service and others of our pictures, please drop us a line. Hope to hear from you soon and have a great day.

No minimum order
No membership required

All 4x6 photos are only 70¢ each. Order 1 or 1000, shipping is only $2 if shipped in 1 envelope. Mention this ad with photo order and get 1 free picture. Most orders shipped the next business day!

Send orders to:
CNA Entertainment
PO Box 185
Hitchcock, TX 77563

Email us at:
CNATexas@Live.com

Hannah & Tai Ling
Catalog Prefix: AMHT

Sunee
Catalog Prefix: AMS

Black Beauty Model Variety 1
Cat Prefix: BBMV1

Mariska
Catalog Prefix: EBYM

Bath Time 2
Catalog Prefix: BT2

Vanessa
Catalog Prefix: NMV

Fresh Faces 2
Cat Prefix: FF2

Hot Panties 3
Catalog Prefix: HP3

Flat To Little Bosoms 2
Catalog Prefix: FC2

Latina Lovers 3
Catalog Prefix: LL3

Pornstars Latinas
Cat Prefix: PSLA

Alexis Texas
Catalog Prefix: PSA

Extreme Shots 2
Catalog Prefix: ES2

G-Strings 3
Catalog Prefix: GS3

Just Feet Emily
Cat Prefix: JFE

Selfies 1
Catalog Prefix: SLF1

Selfies 2
Catalog Prefix: SLF2

Black Amazing Amateurs
Catalog Prefix: BAA

Chunku Monkeys 4
Cat Prefix: CM4

Extreme RedHeads 2
Catalog Prefix: ERH2

So here's the situation….. We are out of space to add new catalogs right now till we find a larger packaging facility so we are going to try something different that will allow us to release photos and be able to give them to you at a lower price. We have 1.4 million photos of which we can not use about 80% of them for various reasons (too close to the same pose as before, little blurry, too explicit, penetration and the like). That leaves quite a few individual photos that we can use but do not have the room for. What we are doing is offering "New Release Grab Bags" that contain 100 @ 4x6 photos for $45 each set. That means each photo is 45¢. These are photos that are not in any current catalogs but will be in future catalogs as space permits. At that time, you can buy individual photos at the normal price. We are starting out with 14 different grab bags that are non nude sets. Each individual set has 100 different photos and they will be the exact same today as 6 months from now and so on. So if you want different photos then order different sets (for example "White Girls 1", "White Girls 2" and "White Girls 3" will yield 300 different photos whereas 3 @ "White Girls 1" will yield 3 identical sets of 100 photos). We can offer them to you at this price because the photos will never be put into individual sleeves for individual packaging but will be put in master packs of 100 the day they arrive here which saves lots and lots of time and space. So, our lack of space is your gain and we will add more sets as we see a need for them and maybe different genres also - all depends and what I find in the new sets. You can order TODAY! The different sets are listed below and the shipping is the same as described on the fourth page of this ad. Just write what you want on a piece of paper, add it all together and send in your order with complete payment and the order ships the day after it is received. There are no returns, refunds or exchanges on any photos in these sets.

$45 per set of 100 photos

White Girls 1, White Girls 2, White Girls 3
Black Girls 1, Black Girls 2
Asian Girls 1
Assorted Girls 1
Young (18+) Ladies 1, Young (18+) Ladies 2, Young (18+) Ladies 3
Older Women
Retro (80's & 90's) Girls
Assorted Guys 1, Assorted Guys 2

New Release Grab Bags

Bambi
Catalog Prefix: EBYB

Victoria
Catalog Prefix: EBYV

Marie Luv
Catalog Prefix: PSML

Faye Reagan
Catalog Prefix: PSFR

Christy
Catalog Prefix: EBYC

Tatyana
Catalog Prefix: EBYT

Just Feet 2
Catalog Prefix: JF2

Sativa Rose
Catalog Prefix: LMSR

Aleksandra
Catalog Prefix: EBYA

Sasha
Catalog Prefix: EBYS

Chloe Knox
Catalog Prefix: FFMC

Hot Mommas Courtney
Catalog Prefix: HMC

Top Heavy Model Louisa
Catalog Prefix: THML

Larisa
Catalog Prefix: BYAL

Thigh Highs & Fishnets
Catalog Prefix: TF

Gia Steel
Catalog Prefix: PSGS

Aaliyah Love
Catalog Prefix: PSAL

Sydnee Capri
Catalog Prefix: PSSC

18 U.S.C. § 2257 Compliance Notice
All models, actors, actresses and other persons that appear in any visual depiction of actual or simulated sexual conduct appearing or otherwise contained in or at were over the age of eighteen (18) years at the time of the creation of such depictions. We are a secondary producer.

Order pictures by number and specify the size and quantity. These pictures are printed on lab quality paper utilizing lab quality ink. Our pictures are sometimes borderline but all regular photos should make it through but I am in no way guaranteeing that they will. You may get someone who feels differently and if that happens, return the picture and we will replace it once with one like it but more reserved. Unfortunately, we only accept returns on MAILROOM DENIED 4x6 photos except for the "E" series which are none at all (all special sizes are printed specially for you). You may order by money order or check from the unit or have a family member make the order for you. Pictures come in the 4"x6" (most popular) size only now. Add all pictures together then add $2.00 for shipping & handling and that's your total. No refunds.
SHIPPING NOTE: You may now insure your package for $3 extra for the first envelope only to make sure it arrives to your unit or get it replaced. This is USPS insurance and not ours so it is a Federal crime that will be investigated if someone intercepts it or makes false claim (mail fraud). Another choice is to put $2 Delivery Confirmation on it to only prove that it has arrived. This is not insurance but just proof that it has arrived at your mailroom/mail box or not. No refunds
ADDITIONAL SHIPPING NOTE: States that have limits on photos/inserts per envelope will have to pay a higher shipping for additional envelopes used to mail your stuff. So, figure this up before you do the shipping. Lets say your state only allows 3 items per envelope and you order 15 photos. That will require 5 separate envelopes with 5 separate postages and 5 separate labels and so forth.... It is only 50¢ per extra envelope times the number of envelopes you need. You already know if you live in a state like this so please figure your shipping accordingly. ONLY order extra envelopes if you NEED them mailed in different envelopes. Please give instructions on how to divide your order if you do order them. Also, ALL envelopes are mailed out on the same day but may not arrive to you on the same day. BOP orders over 25 photos are normally delayed by 2 days so the whole order does not arrive on the same day. So if you see like "1 of 15", then 15 envelopes have been mailed out. You may make your own order form, use this one or request one.
ORDERING CATALOGS: Due to many requests for multiple catalogs, we offer multiple catalogs for 50¢ each plus $1 for shipping. For example, if you want 20 catalogs, it will be $10 plus $1 for a total of $11. Send a list with the ones you want from our current list and send the appropriate payment. We DO NOT replace lost, denied, unwanted or stolen catalogs.

Photo Size & Price:
Extra Large (X)
4"x6"
$0.70 each

SPECIAL!!!!
Order 100 or more 4x6 photos, write Inmate Shopper in the notes and get them for only 55 cents each!!!

If you make your order CORRECTLY AND ACTUALLY PAY FOR IT, there is no problem and it will be mailed out the next business day after it was received.

I HIGHLY recommend Delivery Confirmation!!!!!!!!
Prove it has shipped & arrived at your unit!!!!!!!

ALL that I do is easy and plainly spelled out.
Don't over complicate things and everything will go smoothly.

Fill out your order completely, legibly & correctly. If not, we will try to fill it as close as possible and that is what you get so do it right. You can use your own paper and make the order form if you wish. Double check your order!!!

Item Letters / #'s		Size	Qt'y	Item Letters / #'s		Size	Qt'y	Item Letters / #'s		Size	Qt'y
For example: To order DU105, separate it as seen below.....											
DU	105	X	1								

Total in pictures $____.___

Shipping (1st envelope) + $ 2.00
Additional mailed envelopes are 50¢ each. So if you require 4 envelopes it will be an extra $1.50 total for the additional 3 envelopes (3 x 50¢=$1.50).

# of extra envelopes x 50¢ = $______.____

$3 Insurance (Optional)
-OR- + $_____.00
$2 Delivery Confirmation (Optional)
RECOMMENDED!!!! + $_____.00

Only available on the first envelope

========

Grand Total $_____.___

Make payment to and mail to:

CNA Entertainment
PO Box 185
Hitchcock, TX 77563

Our partial non-nude catalog titles are currently:

PREFIX TITLE	DESCRIPTION
AA-Amazing Amateurs 1 & 2	(Various amateur female photos)
AMHT-Asian Model Set Hannah & Tai Ling	(Two Asian models in a variety of shots)
AML-Asian Model Set Lin	(Asian model Lin in a variety of shots)
AMNM-Asian Model Set Nyomi & Mika	(Two Asian models in a variety of shots)
AMS-Asian Model Set Sunee	(Asian model Sunee in a variety of shots)
BAA-Black Amazing Amateurs 1	(Black female amateur model photos)
BBMV-Black Beauties Model Variety 1 & 2	(All Black female model sets in a variety of shots)
BMA-Blonde Model Sets - Angel	(19 year old blonde Angel in various scenes)
BMA-Blonde Model Sets - Suzie Q	(19 year old blonde Suzie Q in various scenes)
BMV-Blond Model Variety 1	(Several Different Blond Models)
BT-Bath Time 1 & 2	(Various models in tub or shower pics)
FC-Flat To Little Bosoms 1 & 2	(Small to no boobed females)
FCME-Flat Chested Model Erin Nicole	(20 years old small chested model)
FCML-Flat Chested Model Lydia	(19 years old small chested model)
FF-Fresh Faces 1 & 2	(Younger females - 18+ y/o)
FFMC-Fresh Faces Model Chloe Knox 1, 2 & 3	(18 years old sexy little honey)
HM-Hot Mommas 1 & 2	(Assorted MILF's/older ladies in a variety of shots)
HMC-Hot Momma Model Sets - Courtney	(Hot MILF Courtney in various scenes)
HP-Hot Panties 1 & 2	(Assorted females in hot & cute lil panties)
JF-Just Feet 1 & 2	(Assorted females showing their feet)
JFB-Just Feet Model Set - Beth	(Model Beth in a variety of shots showing feet)
JFE-Just Feet Model Set - Emily	(Model Emily in a variety of shots showing feet)
M-Male 1, 2, 3, 4, 5, 6, 7, 8, 9, 10, 11 &12	(Assorted males posing in a variety of shots)
MYB-Young Men Model Set - Benji - MALES	(18 y/o Male)
MYH-Young Men Model Set - Hunter- MALES	(18 y/o Male)
P-Pigtail Princesses 2	(Assorted females with pigtails)
PRG-Pregnant Chicks	(All pregnant females in a variety of shots)
RH-Redheads 1 & 2	(Assort redheaded females in a variety of shots)
RCC-Rednecks, Country & Cowgirls	(Assorted hot country girls)
SLF- 1, 2, 3, 4 & 5 * Selfies	(Self shots of various hotties)
TF-Thigh Highs & Fishnets	(This replaces Pantyhose catalog)

Pornstars: - PSA-Alexis Texas, PSAL-Aaliyah Love, PSAG-Aria Giovani, PSAB-Audrey Bitoni, PSFR-Faye Reagan 1 & 2, PSGS-Gia Steel 1, 2 & 3, PSJF-Jada Fire, PSLA-Latina Assortment 1, PSL-Luscious Lopez, PSML-Marie Luv, PSP-Pinky 1, 2 & 3, PSPC-Pinky & Cherokee, PSSC-Sydnee Capri

Model Sets - FMB-Berlin, FMD-Destiny, FME-Eesha, FMG-Geri, FMH-Hilary, FMK-Katrina, FS-Katie Jordan 1 & 2 , FMN-Nadya, FMV-Veronica, FMY-Yasmine,

PREFIX TITLE	DESCRIPTION
LMSR-Latina Model Sets - Sativa Rose	(Caliente Sativa Rose in various scenes)
NML-Nubian Model Sets - LaShelle	(19 year old Nubian Princess LaShelle)
NMV-Nubian Model Sets - Vanessa	(19 year old Nubian youngster Vanessa)
RMC-Redhead Model Sets - Charisma	(19 year old redheaded Charisma)
RMD-Redhead Model Sets - Dana	(19 year old redheaded Dana)
RMLRedhead Model Sets - Laura	(24 year old redheaded Laura)
THML-Top Heavy Model Set Louisa	(19 year old Louisa with large breast)

Variety Of Sexy Safe Flix 1, 2, 3,4 ,5 ,6 7, 8, 9, 10 & 11: (Catalogs full of photos that SHOULD be completely safe in 99% of all units. Sexy shots with no bare butts , no cupped breast, no see-through, no girl girl, no inappropriate touching, no guys, no simulated sex or masturbation.)

Below is the newest series to be released is an "E" series set. E Series catalogs are a very risqué set of catalogs for the most part. If you order them you may not get them. Also, any photos ordered in the E series are non-returnable and are order at your own risk.

"E" Series Blossoming Young ladies (you can see them on the third page of the ad) are models that are very fresh. They are as follows:

EBYA-Aleksandra (18 y/o) EBYB-Bambi (18 y/o) EBYC-Christy (18 y/o) EBYH-Hailey (18 y/o)
EBYK-Katya (18 y/o) EBYL-Larisa (18 y/o) EBYM-Mariska (18 y/o)
EBYP-Polliana (18 y/o) EBYS-Sasha (18 y/o) EBYT-Tatyana (18 y/o) EBYV-Victoria (18 y/o)

All models in all of our sets are at least 18 years old and older at the time the photographs were taken.

Chunky Monkey Malibu Candi
Catalog Prefix: CMC

Topless/Nude catalogs are available upon special request for units/states that allow them. If your unit/state does not allow this, PLEASE DO NOT REQUEST IT CAUSE YOU WILL NOT GET IT!

Due to many requests for multiple catalogs, we are now offering multiple catalogs for 50¢ each plus $1 for shipping. For example, if you want 20 catalogs, it will be $10 plus $1 for a total of $11. Easy enough? Send a list with the ones you want from our current list and send the appropriate payment. We DO NOT replace lost, denied, unwanted or stolen catalogs. Send requests/orders to:

CNA Entertainment, LLC
PO Box 185
Hitchcock, TX 77563

CNATexas@live.com

www.CNAEntertainment.com

We accept checks, money orders & credit cards via PayPal

Black Amazing Amateurs
Catalog Prefix: BAA

Cell Chef Cookbook I & II...

Each Book All Brand-New Recipes

Are you eating the same thing day in and day out? Tired of the same boring, bland tasting food? Are your meals lacking flavor and originality? Then our Cell Chef Cookbook II will hit the spot!

The Cell Chef Cookbooks are filled with hundreds of fantastic recipes, that can be simply made with everyday, commonly sold commissary/store foods. Every recipe has been tried and thoroughly tested. Loved by everyone.

In the Cell Chef Cookbooks the recipes are divided into four sections:

√ **Meals and Spreads**

√ **Sandwiches, Sauces and Dips**

√ **Drinks**

√ **Sweet Desserts**

The Cell Chef Cookbooks have extensive Glossary and Indexes, created to assist you in the process of your preparations and leading to the pleasure of enjoying these wonderful, tasty dishes.

The Cell Chef Cookbooks' recipes have each been organized with a list of all the needed ingredients, and easy-to-follow directions on how to make them to perfection.

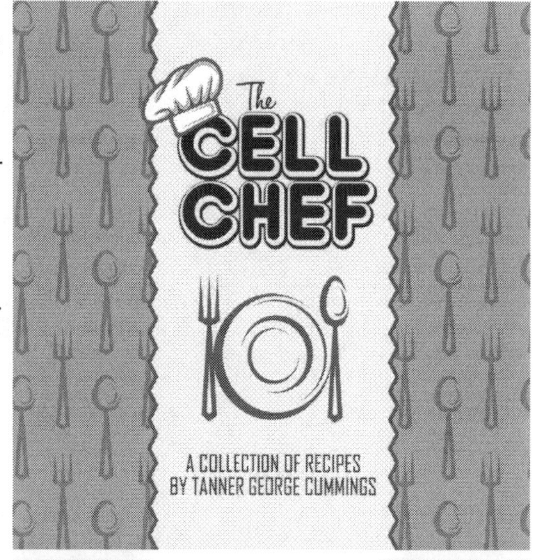

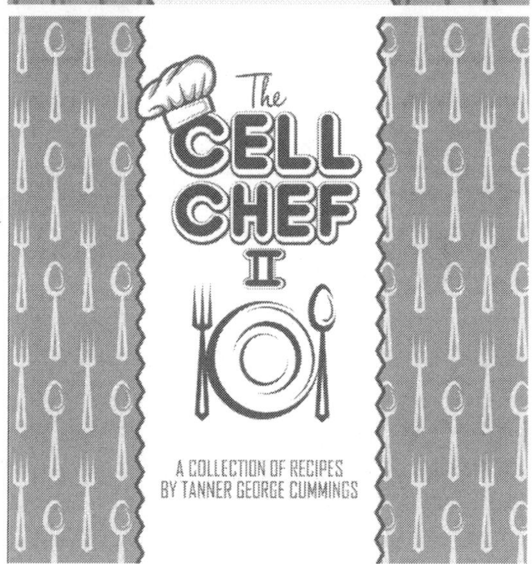

Food is essential to life; therefore, make it great.

Softcover, Square 8.25" x 8.25",
B&W, 180+ Pages Each Book

The CELL CHEF Cookbook I... $13.99 plus $5 s/h w/tracking
The CELL CHEF Cookbook I I... $13.99 plus $5 s/h w/tracking
Get BOTH Books SAVE Combo... ONLY $34.98 w/tracking

NO ORDER FORM NEEDED CLEARLY WRITE ON PAPER & SEND PAYMENT TO:

Freebird Publishers Box 541, North Dighton, MA 02764
Diane@FreebirdPublishers.com www.FreebirdPublishers.com
Toll Free: 888-712-1987 Text/Phone: 774-406-8682

The Cell Block

Folks, I'm putting together a book titled "Lessons of The Game." It's going to contain short stories, essays, letters, maybe a rap/poem or two.

The stories, etc., should be geared towards young thugs in the game – like troubled youth – revealing to them the TRUTH of The Game – that it's all a scam, a trap. But I don't want the stories and letters to be "preachy." Ain't no young thug tryna read that crap. They need to be RAW, AUTHENTIC, and HONEST. I want REAL game – REAL jewels. No wack crap.

Let me give you an example of a raw story with a REAL message. The folks, GURU, his mom made him watch the movie Carlito's Way when he was young. Gangsta movie, right? Good movie. But the point was to teach GURU the lesson that his friends will be his downfall. He learned that lesson and remembers it to this day. Why? Because it was a dope movie. It wasn't preachy. It kept his attention, and in the end, provided him a very important jewel.

This is the type of stuff we need. Things a young thug will actually read. What lessons have YOU learned, the HARD way, that you can pass in the form of a jewel to someone else? For example: Maybe your homie got into a beef of some sort, then ran to you for backup. You went back to handle things, with and for your folks, but end up smokin 01' boy. Then, when you guys get caught, your friend turns on you and testifies for a deal. There's a major jewel there. Your friends are not loyal like you think they are. Or, maybe you kill somebody on behalf of your gang, got life in prison or whatever, but once there, you never hear from your "friends" again. They don't do nothin for you, your mama, nothin. In fact, they just start messin with your BM and tell her you was a bitch anyway.

These examples are how The Game REALLY goes. It's a scam. It's a con. The Game don't give a crap if you come or go. To The Game, you ain't important, and it will NEVER love you back. You can write about any element of The Game – sex, drugs, money, murder, loyalty, betrayal, gangs, whatever. Just make sure there's a clear lesson at the end of it. We want authentic stuff, too – nonfiction. Each submission should be between 1,000-4,000 words, but you can submit as many as you want. Title each story, letter, etc. that you submit.

Anybody is welcome to submit, but I don't want no wack crap. You gotta be able to write halfway decent. Don't slide me your first draft. Write what you want, then go over it several times and tighten it up to make it better. Once it's the BEST you can do, then slide it, written nicely. I will make small edits where needed and hold the right to do so.

Those who participate with SUBSTANCE, I'll compensate you with a copy of the book when it's finished. You'll be a published author, on Amazon, etc. For those of us who need to appear before the board, I think it would be good if we can show them we've taken our own initiative to guide young thugs away from making some of the decisions we've made, which have ruined our lives and the lives of others. Being in our situation is NOT the bidness, and whoever thinks it is, is a wanksta ...

Whoever participates, make sure you give me your real name and number (if I don't already have it), but send it on a separate piece of paper. On your actual submission, if I don't already have it, just write your real name and your state. If you write your prison address, etc., I won't get the submission. My people will keep records of that. I don't personally need it. Also, at the end of your submission, give me a half-page bio – your aka, the gang you are/were from, the city you're from, what you were charged with, what you were sentenced to, etc. Keep the charge/sentence part vague, I'll know what you mean and tighten it up for you. We don't want customs rejecting your crap.

Send submissions to

The Cell Block

RE: Lessons of The Game
PO Box 1025
Rancho Cordova, CA 95741

PS: Pass the word around!

LOL  LOL  LOL

- Just changed my name to "no one" on facebook. That way when I see stupid posts I can click like and it will say "no one likes this".

- I am nobody. Nobody is perfect. Therefore I am perfect.

- Got approached by a prostitute today who said she would do anything for $10. Guess who just got their car washed?

- My clever friend said onions are the only food that can make you cry. So I threw a coconut in his face.

- I asked my wife to let me know the next time she has an orgasm. She told me she doesn't like to call me when I'm at work.

The Vowels

BY JAMES WELLS

A Amazed by the depths of your curves
I speak passionately love you through these words

E Eligible for Love with a beauty so rare
I promise purity that's fresh as air

I Identical thoughts of prominent lust
Ensues the essence of our dust

O One plus one equals two
Simple problem but no one equals you

U United in love our hearts remain true
And out of the vowels I was drawn to U

BOOK REVIEW

By Tanner George Cummings

On October 30, 2018 I finally finished reading the Inmate Shopper 2018-2019 Annual Issue and have come to realize just how inadequate my resource guide collection is compared to Freebird Publishers Inmate Shopper is. There is so much content that there is always something for everyone. With its constantly up-to-dated information, and double-checked source of information, Freebird Publishers has out done themselves. They not only include our voices in our reviews about a company's handling of us incarcerated, but they even go beyond and check for themselves to attest to the accuracy of the complaint and even at times try to assist us inmates across the U.S. They have list of business names that tell you if a business out of business, return to sender and these you should be aware of. They even have some games, funnies, facts, and many other things that are much too important not to read. If you're looking for a resource guide that will give you more than just the basics then Inmate Shopper is your best bet. I most definitely recommend this book to everyone. Inmate Shopper is a must have for all inmates. Heck, I am the author of The Cell Chef I & II, and I need this book to continue my research.

I give this book a Rated 10 for sure.

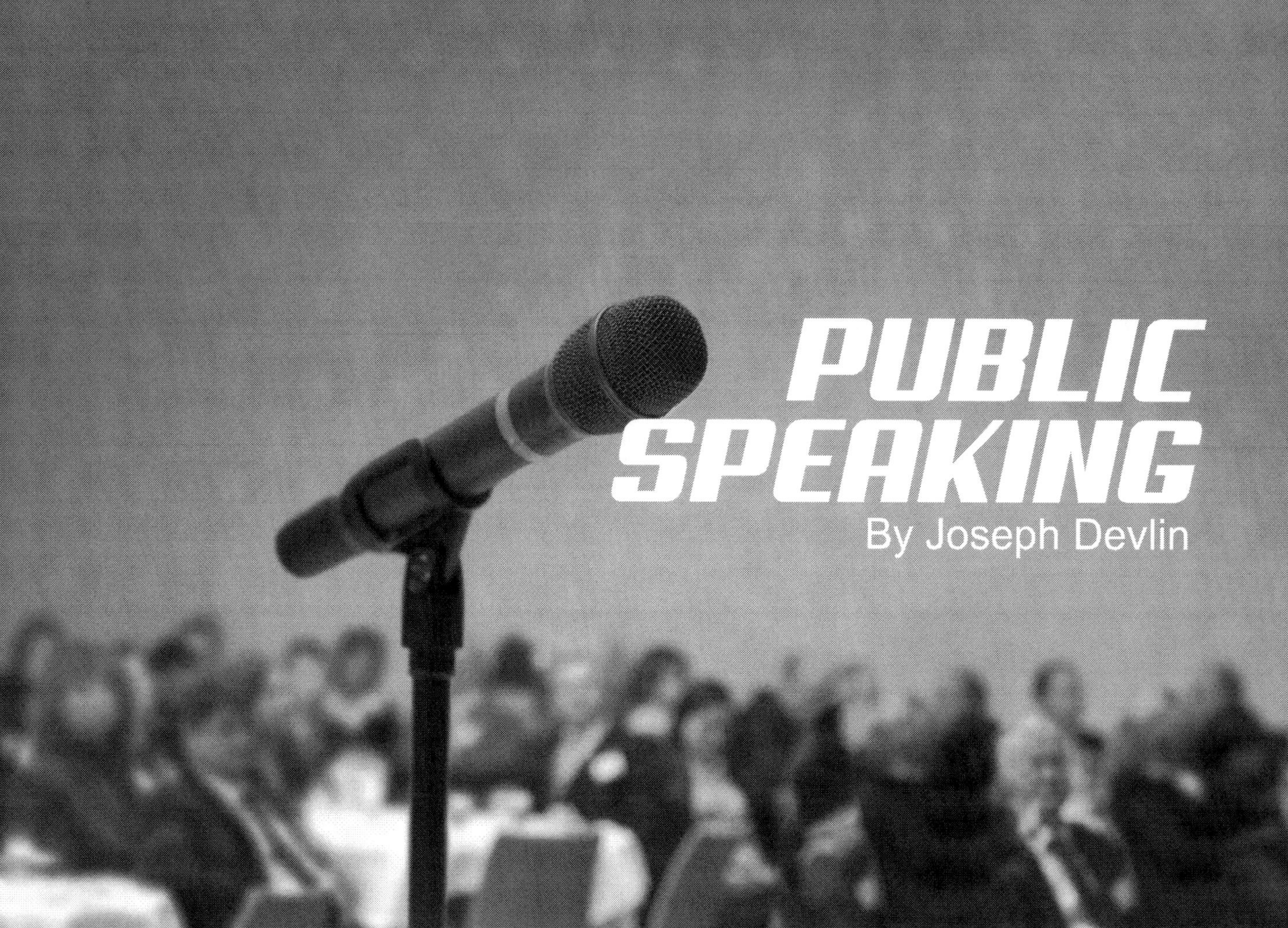

Overcoming Fears

As a former professional comedian and radio talkshow host, I can tell you public speaking is a skill you can and should master. The good news is you're halfway there. Every time you're with friends and family you succeed in public speaking. The fear most of us have is the idea of speaking to a group of strangers.

This fear is natural. I still get nervous before stepping on stage to perform even after 30 years. These fears can be overcome and I'm going to share those techniques with you.

It took a long time to finally realize my friends were the most difficult audience I'd ever face. The reason is, they have no problem interrupting, hackling, or giving me a hard time about whatever I had to say. I never gave it a second thought because I was comfortable around them. Truth be told, this is trial by fire.

Strangers are more polite and want to hear what you have to say. They rarely interrupt and in general accept what you have to say more graciously. Why? Because strangers have no pre-imposed expectations or impressions about you or your topic.

The real fear is thus self-imposed and only in your head. Andrii Sedniev, author of "Magic of Impromptu Speaking" sums up this mental block best. I am paraphrasing here.

The two hemispheres of the brain are divided into the creative side and the logic side. The creative side works one million times faster than the logic side. If you've ever had to come up with an excuse in an instant, then you know this to be true. The logic side takes all thoughts and mulls them over and over and over and… This allows doubt and fear to creep in.

We get past this by refocusing our thoughts on two specific beliefs. They are:

1. Yes, we still stand and speak.
2. It may not always be perfect.

When we commit ourselves to these beliefs, we remove the logic log jam. By believing “we will do it” all arguments to the contrary are shut down. By meeting that it “may not be perfect“ we release the stress associated with being “perfect.“ Though, I don't know who coined the phrase, “while we strive for the intangible perfection we may become excellent along the way.“ The thought is profound.

I was hired to do stand up at a convention in Washington DC in 2006. I had not done comedy on stage in several years, so I was nervous. In fact, I was stressed out about it so much I had no idea what I was going to do as I was stepping onto the stage. At that moment I decided, “I will do this. “(a little late to back out, I was on stage.) I also decided that no matter what, I was going to have fun. It turned out to be the best show I've done in 20 years. The audience was in tears laughing so hard and I walked off the stage feeling like a rockstar.

By allowing my creative brain to take over, the results without my thoughts had a speed and clarity I didn't know was possible.

The next step is this; the audience wants you to succeed also. Like you, their time is valuable, so, if they are there, they already presume you are worth their time. If they believe it, you should too.

Along the same line of thought, never apologize to the audience. If you forgot a point or have a brain fart skip it and move on. They don't know you forgot, so don't tell them. Keep going.

Lastly, speak slowly and clearly. Yes, people can understand what it is said at 300 words per minute but the optimal rate for a listener to understand is 100 to 150 words per minute. Take your time. Speak at a normal pace and clearly and enjoy being in the spotlight. You'll be just fine.

I'll discuss preparing your speech in the third article, I discuss how to connect with your audience.

How to Prepare

In the first part we discussed overcoming your fears. Now we will build on that by discussing how to prepare for a speech or presentation. These steps work regardless of the length of your speech, one minute or one hour. These are the steps to prepare yourself:

1. Determine exactly what points you want (or need) to make. Take the time to write them down in an outline format. Now this doesn't mean it has to be a report at college level standards for an outline it simply means to put them in a list with major points and some points listed so you know what they are.
2. Organize this list in such a way that it it tells a story from beginning to end. For example, you don't give a presentation about building an engine by starting with turning the carburetor. You skipped a bunch of steps that will leave your audience confused. By mapping out a step-by-step process of one, two, three this helps the audience follow along and grasp the concept you are presenting.
3. Then make notes about each point you want to make during your presentation. These notes should begin to shape your story from start to finish.
4. Now, take your notes and write a first draft of your speech. Write it out word for word. Rewrite it and edit out anything that is confusing or unnecessary. Get it in a second draft format.
5. Take the second draft and stand in a room and read the speech out loud by yourself. Listen to how it sounds. Adjust phrasing from written to conversational tones. For example: “I would not want to be where you are at, without help.” This reads very clean but it's clunky for *spoken* word it's better to write “I wouldn't want to be where you're at without help.” Once you have identified all the clunky and awkward verbiage, repeat step four. Re-write your speech again, then repeat step five. As soon as you're happy with the final draft go on to step six.
6. Take your final draft and by hand, not with a typewriter or computer, rewrite your final draft word for word. This commits the speech to memory faster than memorizing it. Take this version and highlight or

underline the keywords or phrases for each point you plan to make. These keywords should be limited to no more than three words. For example, I wrote a chunk (multiple jokes run together) about taking my family on vacation and how it reminded me about my parents taking us on vacation as a kid. I broke the whole chunk down to one word, "vacation."

7. Take your keyword list, which just looks similar to your original outline. By now you have the speech totally written. Take your keyword list and find a quiet place to lay down and relax. Close your eyes and imagine yourself as part of the audience and watch yourself give the speech. See yourself giving the speech without the written version in hand. Mentally go down your keyword list, point by point. Ask yourself, are you enjoying the presentation? What could you do better? Do you look confident and comfortable?

8. Go through it several times. Then when you are comfortable with where you are, begin reducing the keyword list to a smaller version. Rather than 1A, 1B, 1C, it should simply be 1 and so on. Then put the version on a 3 x 5 card or a single sheet of paper.

9. Now you're familiar with your speech. You have imagined yourself in the audience several times. You're ready. Print a copy of your word for word speech. Put it in an envelope and put it in your pocket. When you stand up to give you speech use only the 3 x 5 card as a reference. If you need the complete hardcopy, you have it in your pocket. But let your creative brain tell your story from the 3 x 5 cards. You'll find you're more relaxed and speak more fluently and with ease. Hopefully, you will also find that you are enjoying giving your speech.

Connecting with the Audience

There are so many details that are part of this I could write a book. So, we'll discuss some basics from which you can build on should you choose. We've all endured the endless droning of a monotone speaker who reads off a sheet of paper and never looks up or engages with those suffering through such a boring speech or lecture. It makes you want to pull your hair out by the roots just to break up the boredom. Don't be that person!

An audience wants to know you care as much about the subject matter as you want them to. Monotone speakers never touch their audience. Therefore, our time in front of an audience should be dynamic and exciting for the audience and for us. Yes, this involves a little theater, but we can entertain without being a clown.

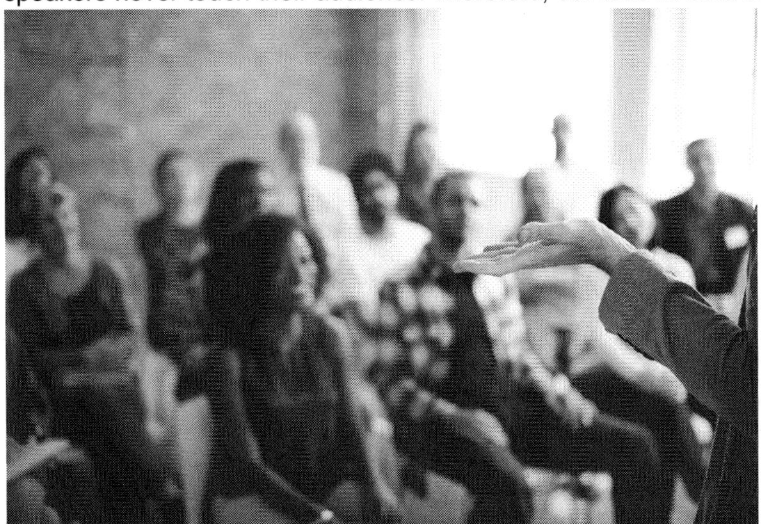

There are five ways to connect with your audience: eye contact, facial expressions, verbal cues, body language, and hand gestures.

For nervous speakers, the fastest way to get past your nerves is to make eye contact with someone and *talk* your speech to them. As you relax, find a different person to make eye contact with and talk to them and so on until you made eye contact with everyone in your audience. Eye contact makes your audience feel as though you generally care about their reception to what you have to say.

Eye contact is by far the most important and I suggested you close your eyes and sit in the audience and watch yourself give your speech, not to memorize it but free you from the page so that you're able to make eye contact without losing your train of thought.

Facial expressions convey emotions. Smile, frown, grimace, frustration, joy, and so on. As you make your speech use those facial expressions to exaggerate those emotions to your audience. You don't need to go over the top rather you need to only be conscious that "this is part of my speech should make people smile," so smile. "This part should disturb them" so look disturbed or upset. Let the emotions you want to elicit from your audience play out on your face.

The beauty of this is that if you are relaxed and enjoying yourself this facial expression will mirror their verbal counterparts in the speech. You only have to let them happen and maybe ham it up a bit.

Verbal cues will help with facial expressions. These are the bold, italicize, or all capital words in your speech. The exclamation point at the end of your sentence. As a former professional comedian, I learned more about verbal cues from Chris Rock than any other entertainer alive. His ability to take a simple, mundane, every day, run-of-the-mill life experience and make it hilarious is all because of his inflections.

Inflection is like hitting the high notes in a song or a change in tempo. We emphasize words that are important to the speech's continuity. Sunday morning preachers on TV are experts at this. Read the following conversation in a monotone voice.

"Hey, I just hit *$500 in <u>a lottery ticket</u>*. "

"That's *<u>great</u>*. Where are you taking *<u>me</u>* to dinner? "

"Yeah, <u>I</u> said I hit for 500 not *<u>we</u>* hit. "

"Gee thanks, *<u>butthead</u>*. "

Now, reread it and emphasize the underlined words. You can see how much more interesting the conversation is with inflection on some keywords.

Body language is similar to facial expressions but using your whole body. Step toward the audience to bring them into a secret or step back to convey distance from them. Turn your body away to feint shyness or hide something. Let your body language add inflection to your facial expressions. Where the head goes the body will follow. As it were. Spread your arms to welcome people into your inner circle of thoughts. It's the subtle and not-so-subtle cues that again add context and meaning to what you want to express in your speech or presentation.

Lastly, are the hand gestures. This is the most difficult for people. We typically have no idea what to do with our hands when we speak, keep them in our pockets, at our sides, scratching something. We all start off very self-conscious about our hands. In American sign language, they create a three-dimensional box that goes from waist to top of head in 6 inches on either side of your shoulders and about 18 inches from your chest. Within this box your hands tell the story of your written words. You don't need to know sign language to know how to make a fist, wave and hold your hand to signal stop or come on or wait or any of 100 other gestures.

Again, this is where some theater comes into play as you take some time to exaggerate the points you want to make emphasized with simple hand gestures. The good news is, if you let go and allow yourself to have fun with your speech or presentation, these will come to you unconsciously. As you can guess, none of these tips are new to you. It's just a matter of incorporating them into your speech. Go back and imagine yourself in the audience and watch yourself incorporate the five elements to connect with the audience. Then stop, back up, change, or adjust a movement or inflection and see if it doesn't make your point even more clear.

When you have it nailed down in your mind, the real thing should be as easy as pressing play on a video. You will give your speech or presentation with little to no fear and few if any flaws. Much to the entertainment of the audience and more importantly to yourself.

Now, go get 'em!

INMATE E CONNECT

Affordable Inmate Messaging

We at Inmate E Connect provide the best possible services for the inmates with super features which includes;

- ☑ Email to single recipient or to many recipients at once,
- ☑ We provide a phone number for unlimited SMS to US and Canada
- ☑ The user can setup groups and send messages to groups by using the group name
- ☑ The user can send questions and we google it and send back to the user
- ☑ The user can submit a URL and we send back the page info
- ☑ The user has the ability to follow unlimited number of twitter channels
- ☑ The user can check a 5 day weather forecast for any location.

Contact Info:
Email: inmateeconnect@gmail.com
Phone: 347-464-1432

All with a simple path to follow, for a flat fee of $25 per month, we can setup monthly charges which will be processed once a month.

We have the Sexiest, Freakiest Pixs, & Stories for all our incarcerated friends!

- ⇒ We have off the chain Specials!
- ⇒ We offer Nude and Non Nude!
- ⇒ We have New Catalogs!
- ⇒ We also offer gifts for you loved ones including children!

SPECIAL 100 PIXS FOR $25.00 YOU PICK THEM

STREET PIXS

PO Box 302-IS
Humble, TX 77347-0302
832-286-8857

HOT OFFER– Get 2 Starter Catalogs Send 2 Forever Stamps and a SASE

Let's get these sexy ass ladies to you...

STREET PIXS

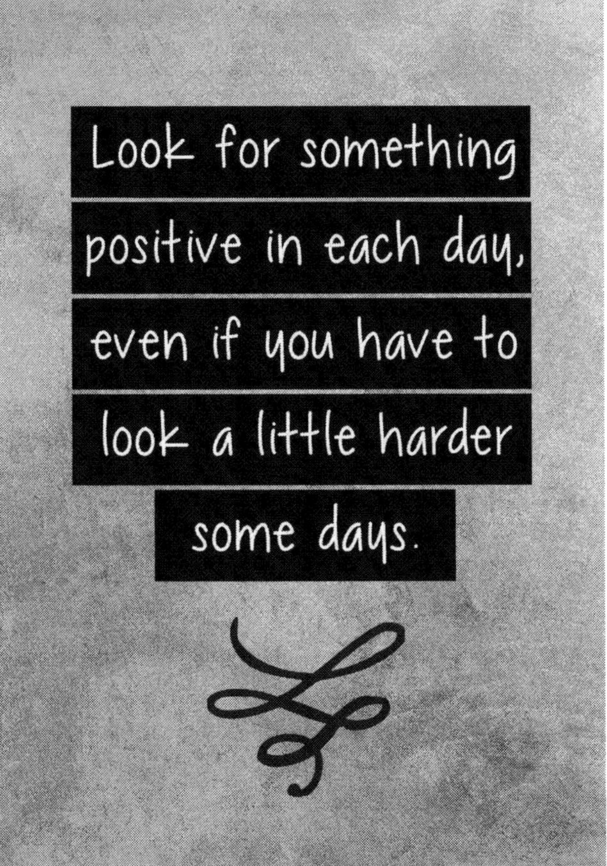
Look for something
positive in each day,
even if you have to
look a little harder
some days.

We Listen To Our READERS

ALMOST Everything in Inmate Shopper Is Because You Asked For It.

Thank You For Making Us Better.

The Year is 3014

By John Harrison

The Eternal Champion of the Alpha Imperial Empire is Jeremy Magnus. He rules the quadrant of the dark abyss with an iron fist. As the guardian of the Beta Stronghold outpost, word of his stellar protection of the colonies in the dark abyss caught the attention of the Lord Blitzkrieg, a conqueror of planets.

Blitzkrieg, Lord of the Universe, is a megalomaniac. Throughout his reign of terror, he has left in his wake an untold amount of death, burning villages and cities. Lord Blitzkrieg engages cosmic defenders in battle and overpowers them with a Crimson Ion Impulse Sword, and he has decided to challenge Jeremy Magnus. The outcome of the deadly dual will determine the fate of the inhabitants of the dark abyss.

Jeremy Magnus was given a Sovereign Star Sword by Queen Tee Tee. A custom in the Alpha Imperial Empire requires that the Eternal Champion of each outpost wear a Sky Dragon gauntlet on each wrist. A magician performs a ritual and sprinkles star dust, which activates a force field.

A spy has informed Lord Blitzkrieg that Beta Stronghold's Eternal Champion Jeremy Magnus has assured Queen Tee Tee that he will defend the outpost to his last breath. Unknown to the Eternal Champion Jeremy Magnus, Lord Blitzkrieg has a secret weapon that is engineered into his body. The transplant device is a Maelstrom Regulator, which generates a sonic energy ray that incinerates most objects made of matter. This awesome power has allowed Blitzkrieg to conquer the neighboring star system and to overtake planetary defense worlds without end.

At the Presidential Palace on planet Hydra Five, Lord Blitzkrieg teleports up to his battle cruiser, Shadow Phoenix. On the bridge, he summons his acolytes to program the trajectory distance to the Hellion Asteroid. Through an open channel, Jeremy Magnus refuses to bow down to the Lord of the Universe, the new God.

Immediately, Lord Blitzkrieg teleports down to the surface of the planet Bellum, which is in the orbit of the Hellion Asteroid. To Lord Blitzkrieg's surprise, he sees the Eternal Champion with his sword drawn. Without uttering a single word, Lord Blitzkrieg pulls his sword from his sheath and ignites the powerful weapon, slashing against the Sky Dragon force field. Jeremy Magnus repels the attack. The sparks and fire from the impact of the weapons cause tiny fragments of matter to set fire to the surrounding villages. Suddenly, Jeremy presses a hidden gem in the hilt of his sword to increase its power, but when he tries to slice Lord Blitzkrieg across the midsection, the swords clash.

Both weapons are rendered useless.

Lord Blitzkrieg knows that the only protection Jeremy Magnus has left in his arsenal is the Sky Dragon Gauntlet force field. Without delay, Lord Blitzkrieg activates his Maelstrom regulator and presses against the magnetic force field. The screaming impact hurls Jeremy into the mountains. The two energy forces push back and forth, one weakening, and the other strengthening the opponent.

At the depletion of Jeremy's energy reserves, Lord Blitzkrieg foresees the conquest is at hand and strikes viciously with the death blow. Jeremy closes his eyes and wills an unknown gene in his body, which endows him with the extraordinary ability of kinetic fusion. It reverses the polarity of the Maelstrom regulator and obliterates Lord Blitzkrieg.

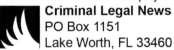

Freebird Publishers

Show Your Loved Ones You Appreciate Their Support

Best of Whitman Gift Basket

From melt-in-your-mouth Peanut Butter Cups to Pecan Crowns, Dark Chocolate Coconut to our signature Assorted Chocolates — this wonderful gift contains a selection of our most popular sweets. Handsome wicker basket comes packed with all-time favorites, including: Whitman's Sampler® Nut, Chewy & Crisp, 12 oz., Whitman's Sampler® Assorted Chocolates, 1.75 oz., Whitman's Sampler® Assorted Chocolates, 12 oz., Whitman's Sampler®, 5 oz., Whitman's Assorted Chocolates, 20.5 oz.

Item # WM152206 Price $55.99 *FREE S/H*

Best of Stover Collection

From melt-in-your-mouth Dairy Cream Caramels to Pecan Delights, Mint Dream to our signature Assorted Chocolates- this wonderful gift contains a selection of our most popular sweets. Handsome white oval tin comes packed with all-time favorites, including: Dairy Cream Caramels, 10 oz. Maple Fudge Pecan Roll, 1.75 oz., Assorted Chocolates, 12 oz. Nut, Chewy & Crisp Assortment, 12 oz. Peanut Butter Delights, 3.9 oz., Milk Chocolate Mint Dream bar, 1.125 oz. (2) Dark Chocolate Mint Dream bar, 1.125 oz. (2) Pecan Delights, 11 oz.

Item #RS16124 Price $ 55.99 FREE S/H

Sugar Free Delights Gift Basket

This Sugar Free Chocolate Gift Basket. The oval tin comes loaded with: 8.25 oz. Sugar Free Chocolate Candy Assortment, 7 oz. Sugar Free Jelly Beans, 6 oz. Sugar Free Solid Dark Chocolate Miniatures, 10 oz. Sugar Free Multi-Flavor Candies, 1.2 oz. Sugar Free Peanut Butter Cups, 10 oz. Sugar Free Pecan Delights

Item # RS151875 $55.99 *FREE S/H*

Russell Stover Boxed Chocolates

Delicious assorted boxed chocolates with your favorite fillings. It's a pleasure to all when you give these boxes of our most popular chocolates. Assortments: you'll receive creams, caramels, crisps and crunches, all drenched in rich milk chocolate or smooth dark chocolate. The 5lb box has over 20 varieties. Dark: 18 varieties dark chocolates from coconut to caramels, truffles to nougats, creams to nuts. Nut Chewy Crisp: 11 varieties from Fruit & Nut Caramels to Cashew Clusters, Molasses Chews to Coconut Clusters. Each piece is covered in rich milk or dark chocolate.

- Assorted 5 lb. Box #0005 $74.99 FREE S/H
- Assorted 3 lb. Box #0003 $48.99 FREE S/H
- Assorted 2 lb. Box #0002 $36.99 FREE S/H
- Dark 2 lb. Box #0172 $35.99 FREE S/H
- Nut, Chewy, Crisp 2 lb. #0022 $35.99 FREE S/H

Boxed chocolates can be wrapped for FREE in holiday papers (seasonal).

FREE S/H CHOCOLATE GIFTS ABOVE

HOW TO ORDER Marketplace Gifts:

NO ORDER FORM NEEDED On blank paper, clearly write each order separately that is be sent to a different address. Be sure to include all needed info for each 'send to' address, provide their phone & email to insure delivery. If there is any special delivery instructions, please state. Include your complete contact info with payment to: Freebird Publishers for the full amount of the sale, sales tax (7% of sale amount) plus S/H (listed on each item).

We accept all checks, money orders, credit/debit cards, PayPal, MoneyGram & Cash.

Hot Weather Shipping 5/1-10/15 2nd Day only shipping (write for prices avg. $30)

NOTE: Shipping & Handling to Hawaii and Alaska extra on all gifts

We offer a COMPLIMENTARY Gift Message on all of our gifts. You may include a FREE message up to 75 characters.

Post Office Box 541
North Dighton, MA 02764
www.FreebirdPublishers.com
Diane@FreebirdPublishers.com
TEXT/PHONE 774-406-8682

31 DAYS OF KIND NOTES FOR LOVE

Make someone close to your heart smile all month long with this incredibly romantic gift. Inside a keepsake glass jar finished with a lovely red ribbons, they'll discover 31 Kind Notes®. Each one specially individually packaged message of love and devotion enclosed in linen cardstock envelopes to make them feel truly adored. 31 Days of Kind Notes for Love: **Item #139935 $49.99**

Love Note Message Samples:
Always and forever you will be in my heart. Every day I am thankful you are mine. I love you just the way you are. I love you more every day. I love you with all my heart. The thought of you makes me smile. Thank you for being there when I needed you. You are the love of my life. You're my happiness. You're the reason I look forward to waking up each day. Have I told you today how much I love you?
I can't imagine life without you.
P.S. I love you. You inspire me to do great things.

31 DAYS OF KIND NOTES FOR INSPIRATION

Inspire someone special all month long with a gift that picks them up and tells them to follow their dreams. A keepsake glass jar arrives filled with 31 individually packaged Kind Notes®, all finished with turquoise ribbons and featuring inspirational quotes and sayings that express your support. 31 Days of Kind Notes for Inspiration: **Item #97804 $49.99 plus $14.95 s/h**

Inspiration Note Message Samples:
And in the end, it's not the years in your life that count. It's the life in your years." – Abraham Lincoln, "Be kind, for everyone you meet is fighting a hard battle." – Plato, "Be who you are and say what you feel, because those who mind don't matter and those who matter don't mind." – Dr. Seuss, "Change your thoughts and you change your world." – Norman Vincent Peale and many more...

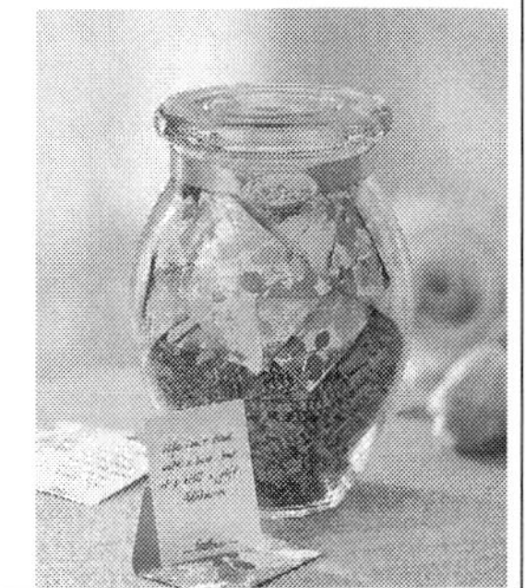

31 DAYS OF KIND NOTES FOR BIRTHDAY

Make their birthday celebration last all month long with our cheerful keepsake gift. Inside a charming glass jar finished with a lovely turquoise ribbon, they'll discover 31 festive mini envelopes, each containing a special Kind Note of friendship. Make their big day truly unforgettable by adding delicious chocolate chip cookies from Cheryl's, one of our gourmet food brands!

31 messages of friendship for their birthday, each individually enclosed in cardstock envelopes featuring a festive "Happy Birthday" message with balloon and confetti

31 Days of Kind Notes for Birthday : Item #139841 $49.99 plus $14.95 s/h,
Add cookies $55.99 plus $14.95

TAILGATE GRILLING GIFT W/WEBER SMOKEY

Your favorite griller will love this classic Weber Smoky Joe® Grill complete with a sturdy metal tongs, oven mitt, hickory wood chips, and these Stubbs® treasures: Hickory Bourbon Bar-B-Q Sauce, Pork Marinade Rub, Chicken Spice Rub, BBQ Spice Rub, Steak Spice Rub, and BBQ Hickory Liquid Smoke. Stubb's® Bar-B-Q Sauces and rubs are a Texas institution. Measures 10.75"L x 6.75"W x 15.375"H

Tailgate Grilling Gift Set with Weber Smokey Joe Grill: Item #164235 $109.99 plus $16.95 s/h

PERSONALIZED GLASS MUGS

Give something personalized with this stylish 18 oz. glass mug. Gift boxed, Personalize with two lines up to 10 characters per line.

► **Glass Mug 18 oz.** Item #165677 $25.99 plus $12.95 s/h

Give your Dad his own personalized mug, High-Quality American Arc Glass Holds up to 25 ounces Hand Wash with Care Features a Heavy, Starburst Base with Strong Handle. Gift boxes. Personalize with one line up to 20 characters.

► **Best Dad Ever Glass Mug 25 oz.** Item #168597 $25.99 plus $12.95 s/h

PERSONALIZED DELUXE CAMOUFLAGE COOLER SEAT GIFT

Cooler can hold a standard 12 pack, folds up and has a padded carrying strap. Cooler has handy pockets and net compartments for storage. Cooler can be removed from metal seat frame for versatility.

Measures 11 1/2" x 12" x 10 1/4", Weighs 3 lb. 10 oz. Embroidered with up to 7 characters in one of our 20 signature thread colors.

Note: longer names will be size adjusted to fit within embroidery space.

► **Personalized Camo Cooler**
Item #165670 $54.99 plus $16.95 s/h

PERSONALIZED TOMMY TEDDY BIRTHDAY

Our large, plush Tommy Teddy™ arrives festively dressed in a cotton T-shirt with a cheerful confetti & balloons graphic. Best of all, his shirt can be customized with your own personalized message. Whether you're sending Tommy alone, or with our birthday candy & balloon gift - this lovable keepsake companion is sure to make the celebration memorable. 24"H from head to toe; sitting height is 16.5"H,

▶ **Personalized Bear: Item #155045 $49.99 plus $16.95 s/h**

▶ **Personalized Bear <u>with balloon & candy</u>: Item #155045C $59.99 plus $16.95 s/h**

Sample Personalized Messages 10 Letters up to 3 Lines

Happy Birthday Cindy — Sending Birthday Love

Big Birthday Hug — Daddy Loves Trisha

PERSONALIZED TOMMY TEDDY XOXO

Touch the heart of someone special with a personalized gift they can hold close to theirs! Our oversized cuddly plush Tommy Teddy arrives wearing a soft white cotton T-shirt featuring a cute heart graphic with X's and O's, and can be customized on three lines with your own loving message. Whether you're sending him alone—or with our sweet heart-shaped lollipop —this adorable keepsake companion is sure to delight them for years to come! 24"H from head to toe; sitting height is 16.5"H,

▶ **Personalized Bear: Item #15d034$49.99 plus $16.95 s/h**

▶ **Personalized Bear <u>with heart shape candle lollipop</u>: Item #155034C $59.99 plus $16.95 s/h**

Messages 10 Letters up to 3 Lines

William Loves Kate — I Adore You

Daddy Loves Sophia — Yours Forever More

BIRTHSTONE BRACELET CHARM BEADS

Birthstone Color, Rhinestone Crystal, Metal Beads, One Size Fits All, 7" Chain with extra ring fit up to 8", It's a ideal piece for gift, bridal, prom, anniversary ceremony, Mother's Day, Valentine's Day or other celebration holidays. Mailed in gift box.

#A02-OB07234 $24.99 FREE s/h

January=Garnet (Dark Red), February=Amethyst (Purple), March=Aquamarine (Aqua), April=Diamond (Clear), May=Emerald (Green), June=Lavender (Light Purple), July=Ruby (Red), August=Peridot (Light Green), September=Sapphire (Sapphire), October=Pink Tourmaline (Pink), November=Citrine (Topaz), December=Blue Zircon Light Blue)

I LOVE YOU TO THE MOON AND BACK

Drinkware with the saying I LOVE YOU TO THE MOON AND BACK. Give your loved ones a special gift to remember you by each time they use it to have their favorite beverage. All drinkware is microwave and dishwasher safe. Holds up to 11 oz. of hot or cold liquids.

Made of 100% Ceramic - White exterior with black lettering, yellow stars/moon and a cute red heart over the letter "I". Interior you have choice of black, white or pink.

Designed and Created in the USA. Includes a Gift Box.

I Love You To The Moon and Back Coffee Mug with FREE Gift Box - Great Gift for Birthdays, Valentines Day, and Christmas Gift.

#A1301-MOONBACK $24.99 FREE s/h

MALA BEADS WRAP BRACELET/NECKLACE NATURAL GEMSTONE FOR WOMEN & MEN

Mala beads wrap bracelet or necklace, 35 inches long. They symbolize auspiciousness, peace, safe, health and good luck. This necklace/bracelet have special meaning when given as gift. All beads are made from natural gemstone such as amazonite, agate, topaz, jade and coral stone and so on.

#GVUSMIL $28.99 FREE s/h

<u>Pick From</u>

- Amazonite (pastels)
- Green King stone (bright green)
- Hematite (mirror black)
- Lava Rock (black)
- Amethyst (purple)
- Pink Cat Eye stone (light pink)
- White Cat Eye stone (all white)
- Sky Blue Cat Eye stone (sky blue)
- Off White Turquoise (off white)

SINGING LUFFIE LAMB WITH BIBLE

Help guide a young child in their faith with our beautiful gift set from Precious Moments®. Luffie Lamb is a huggable musical plush that plays "Jesus Loves Me" when you wind it up. Complete this special gift by adding our International Children's Bible in pink or blue, which makes a wonderful keepsake for Christenings, Communions or baby showers. Lamb made of polyester. Measures 10"H. Safe for ages 0 and up. Bible pink or blue, 20 pgs. full color graphics, a presentation section to record family information and a children's dictionary to explain difficult words and phrases Measures 9"H x 5.9"W

▶ **<u>Luffie Lamb Only</u> Item #155586 $35.99 plus $12.95 s/h**

▶ **<u>Luffie Lamb with Bible</u> (pick pink or blue) Item #155586B $49.99 plus $16.95 s/h**

SONOMA LAVENDER HAND & FOOT SET

Pamper them from head to toe with luxurious spa set from Sonoma Lavender Collection. A plush neck pillow is filled with aromatic lavender and flax seed can be warmed or cooled and used to melt their tension and troubles away. Plus slippers and mitten set with coordinating lotions.

♥Hand & Foot Set **#155226 $179.99 Free s/h**

Porcelain bone china tea cup and saucer set features elegant lavender field design; tin teas, gift boxed.

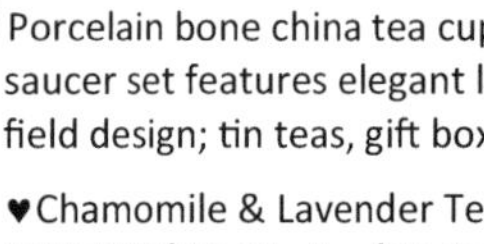

♥Chamomile & Lavender Tea Set **#155230 $49.99 plus $12.95 s/h**

PERSONALIZED AFGHAN

This gift will last forever and it should be displayed and enjoyed in every home to can be admired every day with this Personalized Afghan. A way of displaying your love. This is a constant reminder of how special the person means to you. Perfect gift for any occasion. 100% natural cotton, off white, two layers, 36" x 48", honeycomb heart woven pattern, Up to 40 Characters on one line includes embroidered double hearts.

#GFYN83123453 $75.00 FREE s/h,

Fancy Gift Box Add $7

SONOMA LAVENDER BATH GIFT SET

Pamper, soothe and delight her with an elegant lavender bath set "Love Lavender" collection. Includes a fragrant lavender heart-shaped sachet, lavender bath salt, butterfly-shaped lavender scented soap and fragrant lavender candle, in gold gift box. For a indulgent experience, add to her gift a luxurious ultra-plush lavender colored robe that will help her relax and unwind!

♥Sonoma Lavender Bath Set in a gold gift box. **#F155227 $68.00 FREE s/h**

♥Add Luxurious ultra-plush lavender robe is cozy and comfortable; one size fits most. **#F155227R add $99.00**

BIG BEARS GIVE BIG LOVE

Tons of fun, tons of smiles. Great big, super-cuddly plush bear delivers every time! Perfect gift for that special someone. Plush Big Bear (31") and Beary Big Bear (6') has golden brown fur with cream fur on his muzzle, belly and feet; off-white satin ribbon around his neck. Henry Bear (48")brown fur with cream fur on his muzzle, belly and feet; Red satin ribbon around his neck.

Safe for ages 3 and up.

♥Lotsa Love Bear 31" **#F95690 $75.99 plus $14.95 s/h** 3rd photo

♥Handsome Henry Giant Bear 48" **#F89760 $129.99 plus $16.95 s/h** 2nd photo

♥Bearly Big Bear 6 Feet Tall **#F139335 $219.99 plus $19.95 s/h** 1st photo

WATERFORD CRYSTAL ROSE

Avail: Glass-Lavender-Pink-Red

Imagine the look of joy on her face when she receives this beautiful rose, crafted from the finest crystal. Available in clear, pink, red, or lavender, the exquisite bloom is etched in stunning detail by the skilled artisans at Waterford® to create a keepsake gift of timeless elegance. **#97712 $99.99 plus $16.95 s/h**

PERSONALIZED ROSE

Our elegant personalized rose is a unique and lasting expression of love. " It comes with a metal hangtag, you can choose to have engraved with custom name/message, creating a beautiful keepsake. Silver-plated rose is non-tarnish with red or pink bloom; measures 12.75" L Personalize name or message, up to 10 characters. **#139093 $39.99 plus $9.95 s/h**

24K GOLD DIPPED ROSE

Available in Red or Pink

A brilliant bloom, in your choice of red or pink, is delicately preserved to maintain its natural features and carefully dipped by hand in shimmering 24k gold. Arriving in a gift box, it's a luxurious gift that will be cherished for years to come. Available Red or Pink. **#155097$85.99 plus $14.95 s/h**

SUNSHINE MARKET GARDEN

This garden is reminiscent of the brightly colored flowering planters that decorate the front windows and entryways of quaint homes throughout Europe. We've paired bright oranges and yellow to brighten up any living space. Plant varieties may vary. Quantity of blooms will vary. Includes our exclusively designed Faith Love Hope wooden container.

Market Garden $79.95 plus $16.95 s/h #PF30215459

Add-on: small box of chocolates $15

PRAYING ANGEL DISH GARDEN

Let the serenity and graceful beauty of our ceramic praying angel planter provide a moment of peace during times of sorrow or as a guardian. Paired with a lovely dish garden of vibrant green plants, it expresses your feelings beautifully while serving as an elegant remembrance for family and friends. Fresh, easy-to-care-for dish garden of assorted green plants Keepsake white ceramic planter with praying angel in front; measures 4"H.

Appropriate to send to the home of friends and family members as an expression of sympathy or just as a guardian angel

Angel Dish Garden $49.99 plus $16.95 s/h #101507

Add-on: remembrance angel figurine 5" gift boxed $20

LOVE YOU PLANT GIFT SET

Get romance blooming with a radiant red rose plant in a sleek silver planter. Keep the "awws" coming with our exclusive Lotsa Love plush teddy bear that's too cute to resist. Then we finish it off with a fun heart-shaped balloon. Red rose plant arrives budding and ready to bloom into full beauty. Set in a round silver tin planter with scallop trim and cut-out design. Plant in container measures 10-12"H. Paired with a white teddy bear in red satin bow from our exclusive Lotsa Love plush collection; 9"H; air-filled "Love You!" Mylar balloon; 4"D

Love you plant gift: #101191 $42.99 plus $16.95 s/h

MRS. FIELDS CLASSICS

Give them their favorites from Mrs. Fields. Each cookie, brownie and muffin in this gift is baked fresh and packaged with care, down to the hand-tied bow. Cookies, Assortment may include: Milk Chocolate Chip, Semi-Sweet Chocolate Chip, Semi-Sweet Chocolate Chip with Nuts, Triple Chocolate, Cinnamon Sugar, Oatmeal Raisin with Nuts, Peanut Butter, White Chocolate Macadamia Nut, 18 Brownie Bites, Assortment may include: Double Fudge, Toffee Fudge, Blondie, 6 Mini Muffins, Assortment may include: Blueberry, Chocolate Chip, Butterscotch

30 Nibbler Basket $49.95 plus $16.95 s/h #PF30122657 / 60 Nibbler Basket $69.95 plus $16.95 s/h F30129888

STARBUCKS RECHARGE GIFT

For the passionate coffee drinker, we have created this signature gift box of classic Starbucks® delights - all designed to enhance those thoughtful moments throughout the day. **#PF30034375 $59.99 plus $14.95 s/h**

YANKEE CANDLE with SCARF

Classic scent meets modern style in this one-of-a-kind gift. Garden orchids tumbler candle. Warm up with a lovely purple pashmina scarf. Styled with trendy twisted fringe, worn in a variety of ways to keep you feeling cozy & looking chic. **#139503 $39.99 plus $9.95 s/h 24"W x 71"L**

BEARINGTON BIRTHDAY BEAR w/ CHERYL'S COOKIES

Always dressed and ready to party, this cuddly birthday cub comes bearing gifts! With soft features and a distinct design that lets you know, Bearington, arrives ready to party with a festive hat and bow around his neck, and paired with Cheryl's signature "Sending Sweet Smiles" flower-shaped sugar cookies. **#89857 $29.99 plus $12.95 s/h**

Freebird Publishers MARKETPLACE

100 BLOOMS OF CHEER

This abundant bouquet of alstroemeria, known as Peruvian lilies, will add vibrant color to any room. This colorful bouquet contains 100 blooms of 4-6 blooms per stem. To allow these beautiful flowers to last much longer, they are shipped fresh, budding, and ready to bloom. At least 17 stems. In glass vase. 20" tall.

Bouquet (described above) $39.99 plus $16.95 s/h #PF960

Double the Blooms $59.99 plus $16.95 s/h #PF960X2

Add-on: small box of chocolates $15, small teddy bear $10 , New Indulge Spa Set $15 or I Love You or Happy Birthday pick/sign $5

SPRING SPECTACULAR

Pink Asiatic lilies and fresh cut blue iris will burst open and bloom right before your eyes. The combination of colors in this bouquet make it a wonderful gift for romance, new babies, or as a pick me up. Truly spectacular. 4 large lilies, 10 blue iris 20" tall.

Bouquet $39.95 plus $16.95 s/h #PF5543

Deluxe (shown) $59.95 plus $16.95 s/h #PF5543X2

Add-on: small box of chocolates $15, small teddy bear $10 , New Indulge Spa Set $15 or I Love You or Happy Birthday pick/sign $5

BIRTHDAY FRILLS WITH PETITE CAKE

It's the perfect gift for someone who deserves all the frills surprise them this year with our Flowers and mini birthday cake, covered in rainbow confetti sprinkles, candle and a hidden confetti surprise inside. Assorted flowers and roses with glass vase 16" tall. Cake 4" wide. Both gifts will arrive together in gift box.

Birthday Party $89.99 plus $16.95 s/h #PF30213488

Add-on: small box of chocolates $15, small teddy bear $10 , New Indulge Spa Set $15 or I Love You or Happy Birthday pick/sign $5

BOUQUET OF FRILLS WITH 6 BERRIES

All the Frills™ is feminine and full of color. This sophisticated combination of multi-hued pink roses and pink alstroemeria are contrasted with green Fuji mums. 20" tall, fresh cut, in glass vase. To make this the perfect gift, also included 6 delicious dipped strawberries. Each one is dipped then topped with festive decorations.

Flower Berry Combo (6) $59.95 plus $16.95 s/h #PF30192547

Add-on: small box of chocolates $15, small teddy bear $10 , New Indulge Spa Set $15 or I Love You or Happy Birthday pick/sign $5

BUY A 20" BEAR & 18 oz GIFT CHOCOLATES - GET FREE S/H on BOTH

LIMITED TIME

BEAR & GIFT BOX COMBO

$50. Free S/H

BIRTHDAY SURPRISE

No need to monkey around when it comes to their birthday or anytime gift! Send sure-fire smiles with our cheerful mini pink rose plant, arriving in a festive planter shaped like a present. Pair it with our cuddly, smiling plush monkey or Happy Birthday Yankee Candle® (it smells just like a cupcake!) for a little extra fun. **#101249** $45.99 plus $14.95

20" PLUSH TEDDY BEAR

People love to receive Teddy bears because they're a warm and cuddly way to show you care. 20" plush brown bear is the perfect gift when paired with delicious Russell Stover chocolates or alone.

#RS402265-White OR Brown

24.99 plus $8.95 s/h

18 oz GIFT BOX CHOCOLATES

10 flavors of our creams, three varieties of our most popular caramels and chews, and four types of nuts. A perennial favorite for generations of chocolate lovers.

#RS4041 $24.99 plus $5.95 s/h

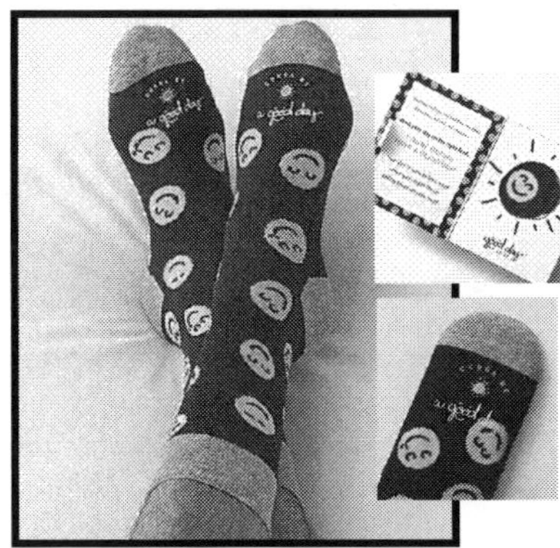

GOOD DAY SMILEY SOCKS

"Gonna Be a Good Day™", on each toe, bringing an extra hint of happiness and positivity every time they put them on. This fun and colorful pair features a happy face motif and comes in a coordinating gift box to start someone's day off on the right foot! **#139663 $19.99 FREE s/h** Size men 10-13, women 9-11

GOOD DAY PATRIOTIC SOCKS

Our Good Day socks with the uplifting message, "Gonna Be a Good Day™", on each toe. These fun and festive socks feature an American flag motif and come in a coordinating gift box, gift for patriotic holidays, birthdays or simply to start someone's day off on the right foot! **#139640 $19.99 FREE s/h** men's size 10-13

GOOD DAY BEER SOCKS

When his socks are loaded with mugs of beer, his day is sure to be full of good cheer! Message, "Gonna Be a Good Day™", on each toe. Socks with playful beer motif and comes gift box, making them a truly original gift for birthdays, get well or simply to start someone's day off on the right foot! **#139670 $19.99 FREE**

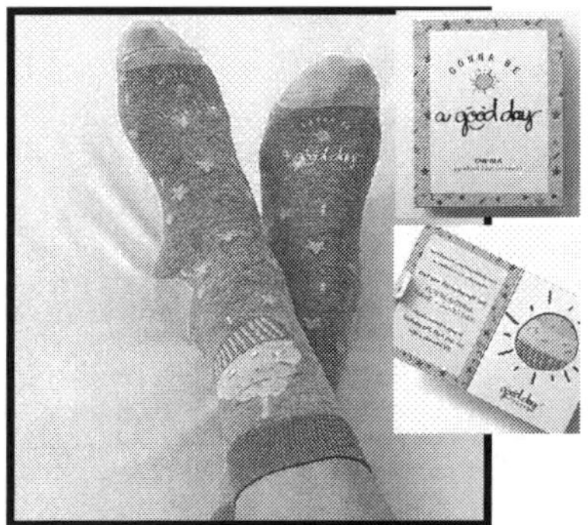

GOOD DAY BIRTHDAY STOCKS

Need a unique gift for the birthday girl? Our Good Day socks were thoughtfully designed with the uplifting message, "Gonna Be a Good Day", on each toe. fun and colorful graphic of sprinkles and a cupcake with a candle, and arriving in a coordinating gift box. **#139639 $19.99 FREE s/h** women's size 9-11

GOOD DAY STRIPED SOCKS

If you want to make sure her day really rocks, give her these fun polka dot socks! Our Good Day socks were thoughtfully designed with the uplifting message, "Gonna Be a Good Day™", on each toe, bringing an extra hint of happiness and positivity every time they put them on. **#139662 $19.99 FREE s/h** woman's size 9-11

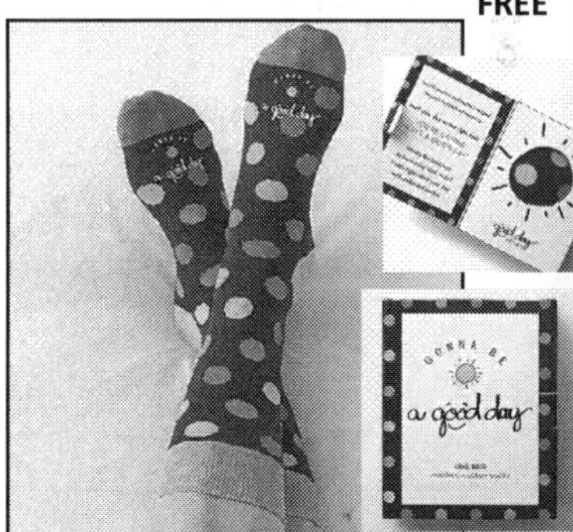

GOOD DAY POLKA DOT SOCKS

If you want to make sure her day really rocks, give her these fun polka dot socks! Our Good Day socks were thoughtfully designed with the uplifting message, "Gonna Be a Good Day™", on each toe, bringing an extra hint of happiness and positivity every time they put them on. **#139637 $19.99 FREE s/h** woman's size 9-11

RED ROSE BOUQUETS

True love. Sweet love. Beautiful love. Celebrate all flavors of love with this elegant arrangement of Long Stem Red Roses in a glass vase. It's a wonderful choice for letting that special someone know how much you care. 20" tall. Fresh cut.

One Dozen (12) $49.95 plus $16.95 s/h #PFRED012

Two Dozen (24) (shown) $69.95 plus $16.95 s/h #PFRED024

Add-on: small box of chocolates $15, small teddy bear $10 , New Indulge Spa Set $15 or I Love You or Happy Birthday pick/sign $5

RAINBOW ROSES

Imagine the overwhelming sense of abundance when your loved ones receives this splash of color. No lovelier statement can be made and these superb Rainbow Long Stem Roses in a glass vase. Colors will vary, includes at least 4 colors. 20" tall. Fresh cut.

One Dozen (12) (shown) $49.95 plus $16.95 s/h #PFRNW012

Two Dozen (24)$69.95 plus $16.95 s/h #PFRNW024

Add-on: small box of chocolates $15, small teddy bear $10 , New Indulge Spa Set $15 or I Love You or Happy Birthday pick/sign $5

SEND YOUR LOVED ONE A NEW PERFUME TO WEAR FOR YOU ON VISITS AND TO SCENT THEIR LETTERS AND CARDS.

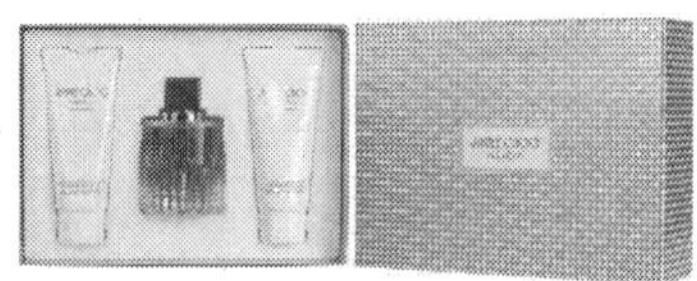

JIMMY CHOO ILLICIT SET

Eau De Parfum Spray 3.3 oz. and Body Lotion 3.3 oz. and Shower Gel 3.3 oz. by Jimmy Choo **#285035 $78.99 plus 8.95 s/h**

Jimmy Choo Body Lotion 5 oz. $41.99

Jimmy Choo Shower Gel 5 oz. $32.99

Jimmy Choo Perfum Spray 3.3 oz. $53.99

Each complete order add $8.95 s/h

VERSACE BRIGHT CRYSTAL

Eau De Parfum Spray 3 oz and Shower Gel 5 oz and Eau De Parfum Rollerball 0.3 oz Mini by Versace **#310985 $96.99 plus 8.95 s/h**

Versace Shower Gel 5 oz. $25.99

Versace Parfum Spray 3.0 oz. $69.99

Each complete order add $8.95 s/h

GUCCI GUILTY GIFT SET

Eau De Toilette Spray 1.6 oz and Body Lotion 1.6 oz. and Shower Gel 1.6 oz. by Gucci **#246808$99.99 plus 8.95 s/h**

Gucci Parfum Spray 2.5 oz. $69.99

Gucci Shimmering Body Powder 5 oz. $41.99

Each complete order add $8.95 s/h

ANGEL GIFT SET

Eau De Parfum Spray Refillable 1.7 oz. and Free Body Lotion 3.5 oz. **#279575 $94.99 plus 8.95 s/h**

Angel Shower Gel $47.99

Angel Body Powder $35.99

Angel Deodorant 1.8 oz roll-on $28.99

Angel Deodorant 3.4 oz spray $28.99

Angel Body Lotion 7 oz. $52.99

Each complete order add $8.95 s/h

MARC JACOBS DAISY GIFT SET

Eau De Toilette Spray 3.4 oz and Luminous Body Lotion 2.5 oz **#257689 $95.99 plus 8.95 s/h**

Eau De Toilette Spray 3.4 oz and Luminous Body Lotion 5 oz and Eau De Toilette 0.13 oz Mini **#165247 $118.99 plus 8.95 s/h (not shown)**

Marc Jacobs Parfum Spray 1.7 oz. $61.99

Marc Jacobs Body Lotion 5 oz. $36.99

Each complete order add $8.95 s/h

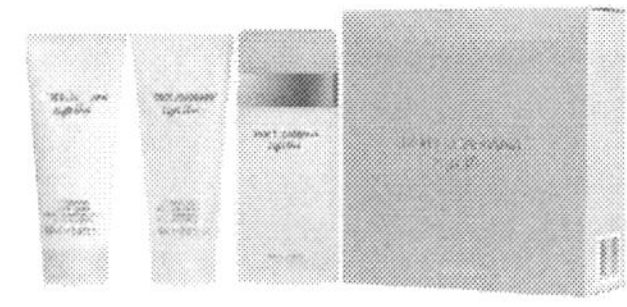

D&G LIGHT BLUE GIFT SET

Eau De Toilette Spray 3.3 oz. and Body Cream 3.3 oz. and Shower Gel 3.3 oz. by Dolce & Gabbana **#140928 $107.99 plus 8.95 s/h**

D&G Shower Gel 6.7 oz. $51.99

D&G Body Cream 6.7 oz. $64.99

D&G Parfum Spray 3.3 oz $82.99

Each complete order add $8.95 s/h

For the man in you life

VERSACE SIGNATURE

Eau De Toilette Spray 1.7 oz and Hair & Body Shampoo 1.7 oz and Aftershave Balm 1.7 oz **#192576 $57.99 plus 8.95 s/h**

Signature Deodorant spray 3.4 oz $52.99

Signature Shower Gel 5 oz $29.99

Signature Hair & Body Shampoo 8.4 oz $51.99

Signature Aftershave 3.4oz $58.99

Each complete order add $8.95 s/h

CALVIN KLEIN OBSESSED

Eau De Toilette Spray 4 oz and Hair and Body Wash 3.4 oz and Deodorant Stick Alcohol Free 2.6 oz by Calvin Klein **#311313 $63.99 plus 8.95 s/h**

Obsessed Aftershave Balm 6.7 oz $24.99

Obsessed Deodorant Stick 2.6 oz $16.99

Obsessed Eau de toilette spray 4 oz. $48.99

Each complete order add $8.95 s/h

BVLGARI MAN IN BLACK

Eau De Parfum Spray 3.4 oz and Aftershave Balm 2.5 oz and Shampoo and Shower Gel 2.5 oz and Pouch by Bvlgari **#272079 $92.99 plus 8.95 s/h**

Man in Blk Aftershave 2.5 oz. $11.99

Man in Blk Shampoo/Shower Gel 2.5 oz. $8.99

Man in Blk Soap 3.5 oz $21.99

Each complete order add $8.95 s/h

SEND YOUR LOVED ONE A NEW PERFUME TO WEAR FOR YOU ON VISITS AND TO SCENT THEIR LETTERS AND CARDS.

TIFFANY & Co. SET

Eau De Parfum Spray 2.5 oz and Body Lotion 3.4 oz and Eau De Parfum 0.17 oz Mini by Tiffany **#316085 $139.99 plus 8.95 s/h**

Tiffany Eau De Parfum Spray 1.7 oz. $101.99

Tiffany Eau De Parfum Spray 2.5 oz. $125.99

Each complete order add $8.95 s/h

BVLGARI OMNIA CRYTALLINE

Eau De Toilette Spray 2.2 oz and Body Lotion 2.5 oz and Soap 2.6 oz & Pouch by Bvlgari **#3283767 $84.99 plus 8.95 s/h**

Bvlgari Shower Gel 3.4 oz. $24.99

Bvlgari Shower Oil 3.4 oz. $24.99

Bvlgari Eau De toilette Spray 1.3 oz. $34.99

Each complete order add $8.95 s/h

WHITE DIAMOND

Eau De Toilette Spray 3.3 oz and Body Lotion 3.3 oz and Body Wash 3.3 oz and Eau De Toilette Spray 0.33 oz Mini by Elizabeth Taylor **#227035 $43.99 plus 8.95 s/h**

White Diamond Body Cream 3.3 oz. $11.99

White Diamond Body Wash 6.8 oz. $13.99

White Diamond Soap .87 oz. $3.99

White Diamond Eau de toilette spray 3.3 oz. $30.99

Each complete order add $8.95 s/h

VERSACE YELLOW DIAMONDS

Eau De Toilette Spray 1.7 oz and Body Lotion 1.7 oz and Shower Gel 1.7 oz. by Gianni Versace **#268597 $64.99 plus 8.95 s/h**

Eau De Toilette Spray 3 oz & Eau De Toilette Spray 0.34 oz Mini & Pouch **#320453 $75.99 plus 8.95 s/h (not shown)**

Versace Eau de toilette spray 1 oz. $39.99

Versace Shower Gel 5 oz. $39.99

Versace Deodorant 1.7 oz spray $45.99

GUCCI BAMBOO

Eau De Parfum Spray 2.5 oz and Body Lotion 3.3 oz and Eau De Parfum Rollerball 0.25 oz Mini by Gucci **#288795 $124.99 plus 8.95 s/h**

Eau De Parfum Spray 1.6 oz and Body Lotion 1.6 oz and Shower Gel 1.6 oz (Travel Offer) **#290450 $86.99 plus 8.95 s/h (not shown)**

Gucci Bamboo Parfum Spray 1.6 oz. $68.99

Each complete order add $8.95 s/h

ARMANI SI

Eau De Parfum Spray 3.4 oz and Body Lotion 2.5 oz by Giorgio Armani **#278514 $126.99 plus 8.95 s/h**

Armani Si Body Lotion 2.5 oz. $17.99

Armani Si Eau de toilette spray 1.7 oz. $80.99

Each complete order add $8.95 s/h

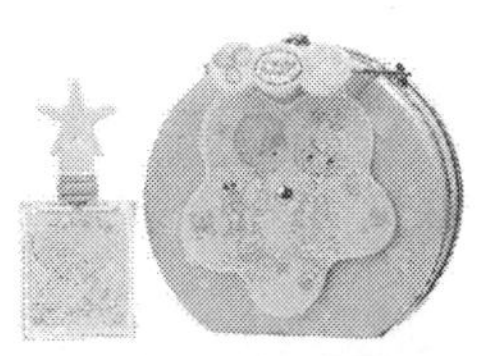

For the little girl in you life

PRECIOUS MOMENTS

Eau De Toilette Spray 1.7 oz and Metallic Lunch Box by Air Val International **#156453 14.99 plus 8.95 s/h**

DISNEY PRINCESS SET

Eau de toilette spray 3.4 oz and metal lunch box by Disney **#267771 $19.99 plus 8.95 s/h**

Disney Princess Body Spray 6.8 oz. $10.99

Each complete order add $8.95 s/h

HELLO KITTY GIFT SET

Eau De Toilette Spray 3.4 oz. and Lunch Box by Sanrio Co **#260512 $19.99 plus 8.95 s/h**

Hello Kitty Body Spray 6.7 oz. $21.99

Hello Kitty Parfum Spray 1.7 ox. $13.99

Each complete order add $8.95 s/h

SEND YOUR LOVED ONE A NEW PERFUME TO WEAR FOR YOU ON VISITS AND TO SCENT THEIR LETTERS AND CARDS.

TOWER OF SWEETS

Tower of sweets and treats! We've included buttercream frosted flower cut-outs, key lime white chocolate, lemon burst and strawberry sugar cookies along with our delightful buttercream frosted ladybug cut-out cookies. We've also included a snack size cookie assortment of gourmet flavors, deluxe drizzled pretzels 24 pc. **#CC207021 $45.99 plus 13.95 s/h.**

SUNNY DAY COOKIE GIT

Delicious assortment of cookies delivered in cheerful gift boxes! We've included classics like chocolate chip, salty caramel and chocolate chocolate chip along with buttercream frosted butter pecan and flower cut-out cookies Gift Boxed 12 pc. **#CC178251 $39.99 plus $13.95 s/h**

BIRTHDAY PARTY IN BOX

Enjoy buttercream frosted birthday cake cookies and our frosted strawberry sugar cookies, our snack size chocolate chip crunchy cookies and buttercream frosted chocolate cookies, a mini birthday cake, gummy stars, sweet and salty pretzel clusters and a hand decorated crunchy sugar cookie shaped like a cupcake Gift Boxed 24 pc. **#CC172851 $35.99 plus $13.95 s/h**

PRINCESS BIRTHDAY PARTY

Buttercream frosted heart shaped cut-out cookies, our snack size chocolate chip crunchy cookies and buttercream frosted chocolate cookies, a mini birthday cake, foil wrapped chocolate hearts, sweet and salty pretzel clusters and a hand decorated crunchy sugar cookie shaped like a crown. 24 pc. **#CC172821 $39.99 plus $13.95 s/h**

SUGAR FREE SAMPLER BOX

unique bear arrangement! Handcrafted from fresh white blooms, our adorable cub arrives in a charming basket filled with a vibrant mix of flowers. Holding his own little bouquet of yellow daisy's, and finished off with a purple satin bow, 24 pc. **#CC193741 $35.99 plus $13.95 s/h**

PICK A HOLIDAY GIFT

Send love and support to a friend, or family member near or far with our dessert gift bundle. We've included a delicious selection of individually wrapped snack size cookies and our sweet and salty cluster pretzels 24 pc. Gift Boxed **#CCHOLIDAY $39.99 plus $13.95 s/h** (tell us what holiday or occasion)

POPCORN SMILEY SAMPLER

The cheery gift box is filled with Dry-roasted Peanuts, Chocolate Chip Cookies, a Smiley Face Cookie, Gummy Bears, Smarties® and 3 flavors of gourmet popcorn: Cheese, Caramel and Chocolate. Serves 2–4. **#PFC02765 $39.99 plus $13.95 s/h**

HANG IN THERE DELUXE SAMPLER

Sweet plush frog accompanied by a delightful combination of goodies. The sampler sends good wishes with a White Gourmet Rainbow Pretzel, Cocoa Gems, Gummi Bears, Honey-roasted Peanuts, and 3 flavors of popcorn: Cheese, White Cheddar and Drizzled Caramel Corn. Serves 1–2. **#PFC7466 $39.99 plus 13.95 s/h**

POPCORN TINS

3-flavor classics: Butter, Cheese and Caramel. 2-Gallon tins hold 32 cups of popcorn, 3.5 Gallon tins hold 56 cups, and the 6.5 Gallon tin goes "all-in" with 104 cups. **2-Gallon $39.99 plus $13.95 s/h, 3.5-Gallon $45.99 plus $13.95 s/h, 6.5-Gallon $59.99 plus $13.95 s/h** Tell us the holiday or occasion we might be able to get upgraded tin)

WEEKEND GARDENER TOTE

What a lovely out-doors treat you'll give with the Weekend Gardener Tote gift basket. With 3 assorted sunflower packs and a lovely inspirational book entitled Wisdom from the Garden, she can take time out from her gardening to enjoy the garden fresh flavors of lemon, dill, mint, and more with the treats inside this tote! #8412152 $68.99 plus $14.95 s/h

GREEN THUMB GARDENER The Green Thumb Gardening Tote includes: solid wood tote box, 3 assorted seed packets, The curious Gardener - Book of gardening tips, hints and antidotes, floral drawer sachet, cherry bon bons candies, water spritzer bottle, spade, foam knee pad, garden stepping stone, Pretzel Sticks, Moisturizing hand cream, gardening gloves, 2-herbal teas. This gift is completed with cellophane and topped with a handmade floral bow. #8413402 $58.99 plus $14.95 s/h

USEFUL GARDENER GIFT Have a wonderful gardener in your life? Send them this adorable garden planter filled with gardening treats and tools. We've included garden seeds, a mini wind chime, a gardening knee pad, nourishing hand cream to sooth those hard working hands when they are done in the garden. A truly thoughtful gift. #8413772 $59.99 plus $14.95 s/h

CUCUMBER MELON The all Natural Cucumber & Melon offers wonderful treatments for body, mind and soul. We've included Jasmine green tea to calm their mind, a revitalizing face mask, nourishing hand cream and more. It's the total spa package in a rich keepsake bamboo caddy. These are full size 8 oz. bath products, not Trial sizes. They are of high quality aromatic scents, not something found at a general store or any of our competitors. #8413702 $58.99 plus $15.95 s/h

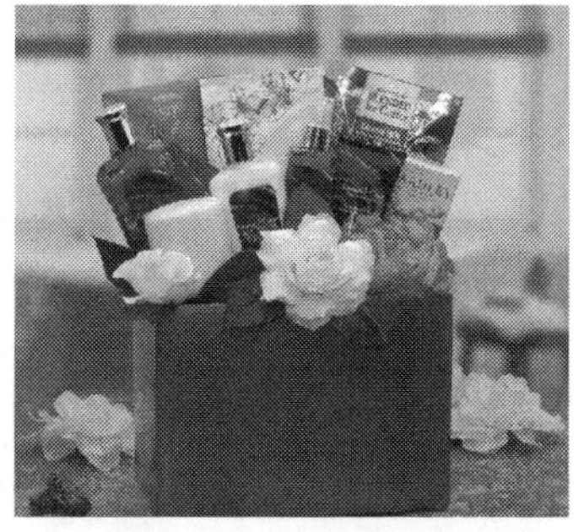

CARAMEL INSPIRATIONS SPA

Caramel Indulgence Spa Basket surrounds the body in an intoxicating essence delicate and thoroughly romantic. Creamy caramel and soothing cream infuse an invigorating shower gel, luxurious body lotion, hydrating hand cream and other gifts included in this comforting Spa collection. full size 8 oz. bath products, not Trial sizes. high quality aromatic scents, not something found at a general store. #8413572 $48.99 plus $14.95 s/h

VANILLA ESSENCE CANDLE GIFT

Classic and traditional the warm scent of Vanilla soothes your senses while it's aroma fills the air with its relaxing properties. Filled to overflowing with the sweet scent of vanilla this exclusive gift is sure to be a big hit and is perfect for almost any occasion. #8413432 $58.99 plus $14.95 s/h

TEA LOVER'S LITTLE TEAPOT

They'll love the delicate rose stoneware teapot and matching cup with two varieties of rich, tea to savor. Includes: White gloss basket, Stoneware rose teapot, rose tea cup with saucer, Chocolate truffle cookies, Raspberry chocolate cake, green tea, breakfast tea, butter toffee caramel corn, Chambery truffles, chocolate covered pretzels, completed with floral enhancements and a butterfly. #8413132 $68.99 plus $14.95 s/h

LOTUS BOTANICALS The Lotus Blossom symbolizes the purity of heart, mind, represents long life, health and luck. Made in the U.S.A. Gift Box includes: Floral garden gift box, aromatherapy poured glass candle, fingernail bristle brush, exfoliating bath mitt, back washing strap, pedicure gift set, aromatherapy drawer potpourri sachet, hot or cold gel eye mask, 8 oz. Lotus blossom body lotion, 8 oz. Lotus Blossom bath gel, 8 oz. Lotus Blossom body spray, 6 oz. Lotus Blossom hand cream. #8413832 $59.99 plus $14.95 s/h

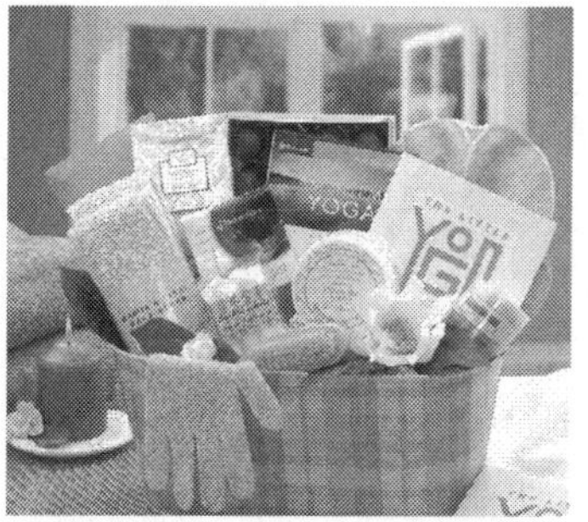

YOGA & GREEN TEA GIFT

A little Yoga anyone? We've included a fully illustrated Yoga book as well as an instructional DVD great for beginners or advanced Yoga enthusiasts. The soothing combination of green tea bath and body enhancements along with the aromatherapy candles complete this bath and body sensation collection. #8412431 $79.99 plus $15.95 s/h

MASTER GRILLER

Set your favorite griller up this barbecue season with a gift set featuring Classic BBQ Sauce, barbecue kettle chips, beer cheese dip, flammin hot Smokey beef steak jerky and other gourmet goodies. They'll be ready to roll on the grill right now and straight on through the summer! Pack cooler bag, mini barbecue grill mates for grilling vegetables or smaller meats. Hand towels are assorted designs. #810831 $89.99 plus $19.95 s/h

MOVIE MADNESS Movie Night Mania Blockbuster Gift Box. You'll find old-time movie going goodness in the Movie Madness gift basket. There's movie theatre popcorn, cookies, Cracker Jacks, peanuts, and candy plus Classic Root Beer in this popcorn gift box. Get for family fun or your favorite movie buff. #820112 $39.99 plus $14.95 s/h

BACONATOR Do you smell bacon? A most unique gift for any bacon lover in your life. Real bacon jerky made from thick slab bacon, Snackle Mouth bacon maple clusters, BLT dip to eat with the Maple bacon kettle chips and more....You won't believe how much bacon is jam packed into this all wood pine crate with lid and rope handles. A truly one of a kind gift! #810851 $94.99 plus $19.95 s/h

SWEET SAVORY

Sweet and savory munchies are ideal for movie night, family gatherings, holidays or anytime. This lovely wicker serving tray has pounds of snacks ready to eat. This gift feeds a lot of people, good for a party or household that loves snacking. #8820312 $46.99 plus $13.95 s/h

CUT ABOVE

Filled with our delicious Heart of Wisconsin cheeses, mustards, sausages, and crackers. Includes wooden handled mini cleaver.

#7114 $29.99 plus $13.95 s/h

SWEET FRUIT

A sampling of sweet rich tastes! Perfect for both small business or lighter appetites, this is over 1.5 lbs. of perfectly presented fresh, huge nuts and rich, delicious dried fruits. Wonderful for those that love healthy snacking and plenty of it! #8820132 $44.99 plus $13.95 s/h

CUP OF JOE

Wake up your favorite sleepy head! Get'em up and out of bed with this Java Joe basket packed with treats to perk them up and brighten their day. Lovely gift for those that enjoy coffees and a tasty treats to go with it.

#810592 $58.99 plus $15.95 s/h

TEA ENLIGHTENMENTS Perk up your favorite tea fan with this sweet Tea Enlightenments gift chest. This stained gift chest with handle and latch features 2 gourmet flavored teas, honey, old fashioned vanilla caramels, chocolate cream puff tea cookies and more. A great gift for almost any occasion including get well, birthdays or just because! #820572 $54.99 plus $15.95 s/h

BOOK LOVERS Send your book lover the Book Lovers gift basket. This gift comes in a book end chest filled with sweet treats and coffee to enjoy during reading time. Barnes and Noble gift cards can be added in $15 or $25 denominations. Give gift basket to your favorite book worm! Reading and snacking what could be better. #810203 $64.99 plus $15.95 s/h (ADD extra for gift cards in amount of $15 OR $25)

LITTLE DISNEY PRINCESS
Send her the magic of a Disney Princess today. This gift comes wrapped in cellophane and topped with a handmade bow. Large gift measures 14" long by 8" wide and 14" tall and weighs 5.5 pounds.
#890432 $59.99 plus $12.95 s/h

FAMILY GAME NIGHT PACKAGE
Send them a care package to create memories with. One night a week of family fun, filled with games and treats. Every family should be afforded the luxury of time together filled with fun and sweet treats to eat.
#819531 $49.99 plus $12.95 s/h

DISNEY FUN & GAMES
Deliver the Magic of Disney today with our Cars themed Disney Fun & Games gift basket. Perfect for any occasion. Large gift measures 14" long by 8" wide and 14" tall and weighs 5.5 pounds.
#890591 $59.99 plus $12.95 s/h

BIRTHDAY CELEBRATION PACKAGE
Care Package features 8" birthday bear. The bear will greet your loved one with the birthday smile while they discover all the treats and gifts inside. Make someone's birthday special!
#818013 $54.99 plus $11.95 s/h

HERE'S TO YOU! HAPPY BIRTHDAY
Make their birthday wishes come true when you send this festive celebration birthday hat accompanied by tasty treats in this Happy Birthday celebration
#819652 $54.99 plus $12.95 s/h

BIRTHDAY SURPRISE PACKAGE
Make their birthday the biggest celebration of the year with our fabulous package. Just for your birthday star we've included Jelly Belly Jelly beans 20 flavor, Fudge brownies, Birthday candles and more.
#819491 $34.99 plus $12.95 s/h

WE BELIEVE IN SANTA Santa's bag is always filled with delicious treats and an assortment of classic scrumptious goodies to satisfy their sweet tooth. Actual bag measures 11" wide and 19" tall. Completed gift weighs 3 pounds.
#8161852 $54.99 plus $12.95 s/h

NIGHT BEFORE CHRISTMAS
Be good (for goodness sake!) when you send someone special this Care Package-it's sure to put an end to both pouting and crying for all the little Elves on your list.
#8161852 $54.99 plus $12.95 s/h

FROSTY'S WINTER WONDER
Little Frosty snowman 6", Foil wrapped chocolate marshmallow snowman, 2 holiday cocoas, fun dough with stamper, 2 snowman pops, fruity bubbles, 20 flavor jelly bellies and a holiday cookie
#816403 $34.99 plus $11.95 s/h

HOLIDAY GREETINGS GIFT
Holidays celebration sensation when you send our wooden Trellis Gift Basket. It's an elegant, crowd-pleasing collection of sweet and delicious delicacies complete with Nutcracker chocolates filled with vanilla caramel and old fashioned fudge.
#816312 $46.99 plus $12.95

WINTER WONDERLAND GIFT BOX
Delicious treats to share this year. No matter how far or near everyone eon your list is sure to love the tasty chocolate chip cookies, milk chocolate truffles, peppermint drops an more that has been included in this festive holiday gift pack.
#8161702 $44.99 plus $12.95

FALL SPLENDOR scrumptious assortment of delectable treats are encompassed by a hunter green fall basket. Created with an upscale fall presentation this delicious gift will leave them remembering how thoughtful you were.
#91529 $44.99 plus

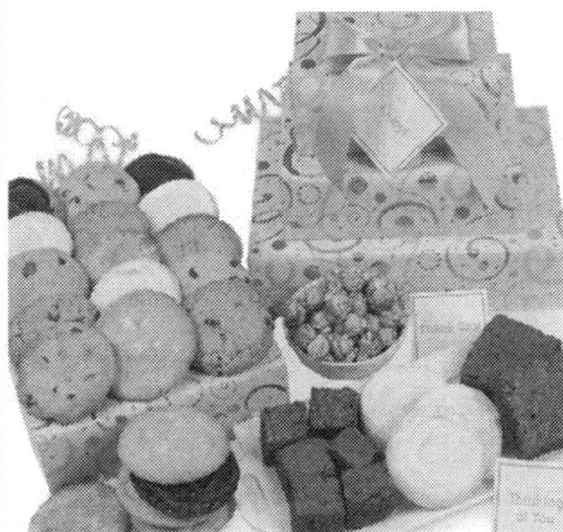

DAZZLING DELUXE SWIRLS trio of decorative boxes layered with eighteen assorted gourmet cookies, six buttercream iced cutouts, two decadent chocolate chunk brownies, six brownie bites and a bag of caramel corn is a delicious way to celebrate.
#CB-TWR-ALL $64.99 plus $12.95 s/h

SHADES OF FALL SNACK BASKET
autumn leaves fall from the trees, surround those you care about in the comfort of delicious snacks and treats. Overflowing with delicious treats, decorated with blazing fall leaves this beautiful basket makes a grand impression
#91612 $49.99 plus $12.95

HOLIDAY SWEETS & TREATS GIFT
red gift boxes bring gifts of great taste when you send the Holiday Sweets and Treats Gift Boxes. Filled to the brim with holiday favorites for young and old, this gift is sure to please the most discriminating holiday snacker.
#815159 $49.99 plus $12.95

SEASONS GREETINGS SLEIGH
Filled this beautiful brass decorative holiday sleigh, not with toys, but with plenty of goodies, and he's on his way to all your friends and family with your good wishes for a happy holiday season!
#815313 $44.99 plus $12.95

28 pc shown

TRUFFLE TOWERS GIFT 28 Pc
truffles will delight the receiver, so whether you are saying thank you, job well done, I love you or I'm sorry, this is the perfect gift for you. The Truffles gift basket is available in two sizes. #81121(28pc) $36.99 or #81122 (13pc) $28.99 plus $11.95 s/h

HOLIDAY CELEBRATIONS BASKET
Fill any gift-giving need this holiday season. This year-round favorite is all dressed up in its holiday best and can handle any event from a family get-together to the company party.
#81543 $49.99 plus $12.95

TOP OF THE CLASS MAX

10" Dances and sings to the song "Best Day of My Life" Comes with boxed candy and a balloon.

#156502 $55.99 plus 12.95 s/h

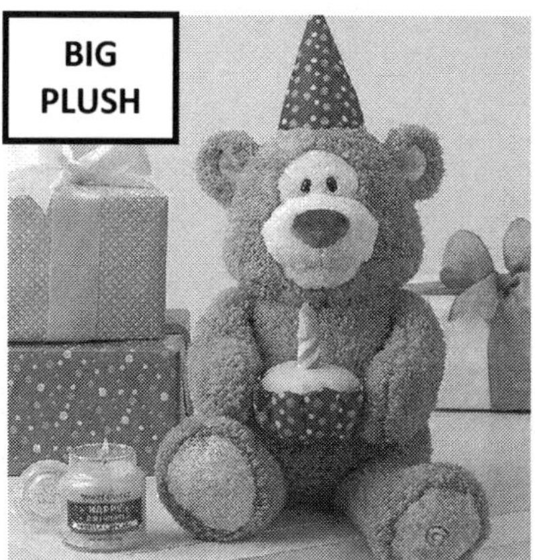

HAPPY BIRTHDAY BEAR

16" Gund® bear wears a party hat, holds a cupcake with a candle that lights up; head and mouth moves sing "Happy Birthday"

#155066 $49.99 plus 12.95 s/h

Add-on: 3.7 oz Cupcake scent candle $10

GET WELL FEVER FROGGY

11" plush frog features rosy cheeks, an ice pack on his head and a thermometer in his mouth; moves his head and body while singing "Fever"

#139563 $49.99 plus 12.95 s/h

Add-on: Chicken Noodle soup mix $10

BANABA BOAT BRUNO

11" Plays "(Day O) The Banana Boat Song," sways and spins his feet. Comes with banana fruit flavor candies.

#155918 $55.99 plus 12.95 s/h

MOTHER GOOSE STORYTELLER

Animated plush Mother Goose wears blue bonnet, matching cape and ribbon; stands 14". Beak opens and body moves as she recites 7 classic nursery rhymes.

#139840 $49.99 plus 12.95 s/h

Add-on: Story Book $10

ABC PUNKY LEARNING PUP

14" Animated GUND® plush dog moving mouth and paws; sings several songs and repeats various phrases. Press letters and numbers on his paws, wipe clean fur.

#1551360 $49.99 plus 12.95 s/h

Add-on: ABC Puzzle w/Light & Sound $20

YOU'RE MAGICAL UNICORN

15" Plush unicorn with silver horn, fluffy pink mane, and metallic red heart displaying the sentiment, "You're Magical"

#156381 $45.99 plus 12.95 s/h

FISHIN FLYNN BEAR

13" Bounces and moves his mouth to the song "Sittin' On the Dock of the Bay"

#155044 $49.99 plus 12.95 s/h

ANIMATE BIRTHDAY PARTY

12" "Flappy Birthday" plush dog Flaps his ears and dances to "Birthday" song from the Beatles. All-in-one birthday gift bundle include all shown.

#156211 99.99 plus 12.95 s/h

MR. BEAN DELUXE MACHINE A push of Mr. Jelly Belly's handle turns the real working gears and dispenses Jelly Belly beans through the chute. Machine come with a 1oz sample bag of beans. Machine holds approx. 23 oz. of beans 9.25" **#86110 $29.99 plus 15.95 s/h**

BIG PLUSH

HUGS & KISSES BEAR w/ Chocolates
12" bear, 19 pcs. cream centers, cherry, coconut, mint, peanut butter & mocha

#816023 $39.99 plus 15.95 s/h

BIG PLUSH

BUNNY & COOKIES
Fully jointed with moveable head, arms and legs; measures 14"H comes with Fresh Baked Cookies **#155768 $29.99 plus 12.95 s/h**

BIG PLUSH

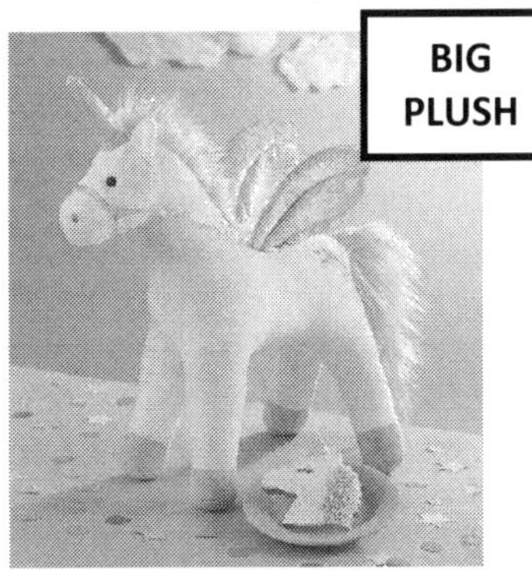

LIGHT UP UNICORN 17" plush features a brilliant rainbow mane and tail, sparkling wings and accents. Pet its mane to produce a twinkling sound effect and watch its wings light up in dazzling display **#156408 $59.99 plus 13.95 s/h**

PERSONALIZED MESSAGE IN A BOTTLE

'You & Me' keepsake glass bottle is filled with red and gold rose petals and message scroll of your choice. Measures 12"H. Choose one of three messages: true love; new love; or someone special. Personalized up to 4 lines, 22 characters per line. Arrives in a red gift box.
#155780 $49.99 plus 14.95 s/h

♥ "Couples/New Relationship" scroll reads: You & Me, The way you look at me, the way you hold my hand. The way you make me feel like there's no one else around. I never expected to find someone who made me feel like this. When I'm with you it is true bliss.

♥ "True Love" scroll reads: You & Me, Over time our love has grown more than words can say. It is in the little ways we show it each and every day. It's these everyday moments that we share together that promises you have my heart forever.

♥ "Someone Special" scroll reads: You & Me, It's the kindness you show to everyone around you. The way you always go above & beyond. The warmth behind your smile and welcoming nature. For these reasons and more, I am so fortunate to have such a special person like you in my life.

BEAR ANGEL & ANGEL PIN
10" heavenly plush "Peace" angel Bear, created by Bearington. Teddy bear has a soft, cream-colored coat and sweet angel wings. Paired with a gold-and-silver Guardian Angel pin **#156243 $44.99 plus 12.95 s/h**

YANKEE CANDLE LILAC GIFT SET
Relaxing retreat right in their own home. Our Yankee Candle® gift set comes complete with a radiant votive holder, votive candles and tea lights in a variety of alluring and heady aromas to create the perfect peaceful ambiance. **#155859 $44.99 plus 14.95 s/h**

SIP SIP HOORAY ROSE WINE & GLASS SET brilliant, hot pink California Rosé that draws you in, a Sip Sip Hooray Stemless Wine Glass. Project 7 Party Mix Gummies and Chocolate Cliche Dark Chocolate Strawberry Bubbly Bar **#174858-Set $75.99 plus 16.95 s/h**

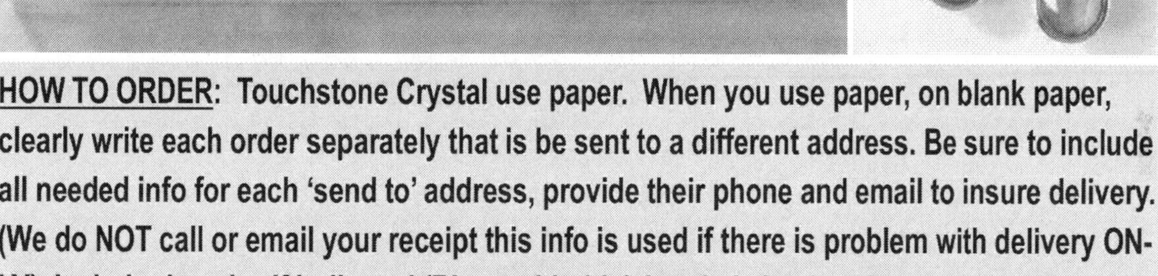

<u>HOW TO ORDER</u>: Touchstone Crystal use paper. When you use paper, on blank paper, clearly write each order separately that is be sent to a different address. Be sure to include all needed info for each 'send to' address, provide their phone and email to insure delivery. (We do NOT call or email your receipt this info is used if there is problem with delivery ONLY) Include ring size if indicated (Rings with thick bands in back order one size larger). Include your complete contact info with payment to: Freebird Publishers for the full amount of the sale, sales tax (7% of sale amount) plus $6.95 s/h for orders up to $120 or 5% of order amount over $120 for <u>each</u> address you are shipping to. We accept all checks, money orders and credit/debit cards.

INDEPENDENT CONSULTANT
TOUCHSTONE
CRYSTAL BY SWAROVSKI

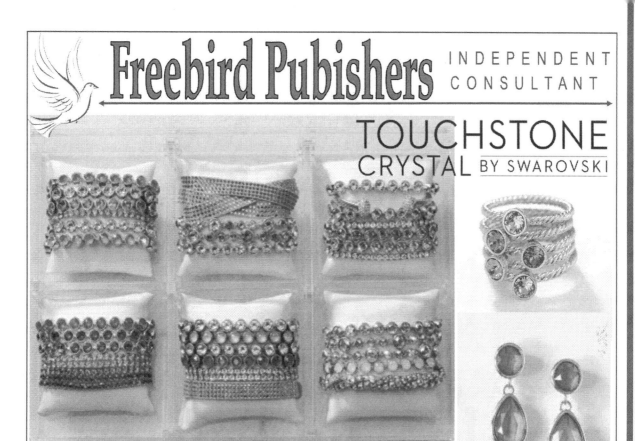

Post Office Box 541, North Dighton, MA 02764
www.TouchstoneCrystal.com/Freebird & www.FreebirdPublishers.com
E-mail: Diane@FreebirdPublishers.com

LITTLE
BLACK
DRESS
TOUCHSTONE
CRYSTAL BY SWAROVSKI
WANT TO SEE IN COLOR
ORDER-FULL COLOR CATALOG
LAST PAGE OF JEWELRY SECTION

WANT TO SEE IN COLOR
ORDER-FULL COLOR CATALOG
LAST PAGE OF JEWELRY SECTION

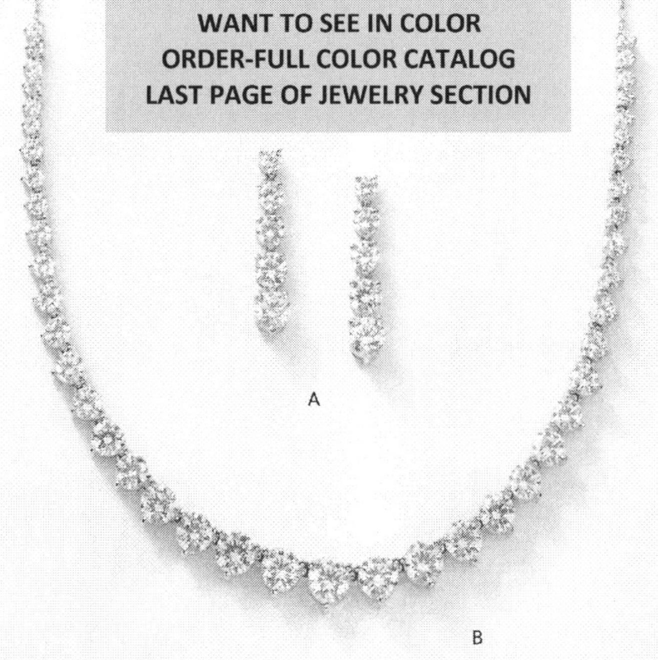

A

B

Our **Little Black Dress** Collection is made with Swarovski® Pure Brilliance Zirconia, set in Sterling Silver, and plated in rhodium for extra shine and tarnish protection.

ZIRCONIA — FROM — SWAROVSKI SINCE 1895

Each piece is marked with a microscopic quality seal assuring the utmost precision and brilliance, a result of cutting standards equal to those of the world's highest-quality diamonds.

TOUCHSTONE CRYSTAL BY SWAROVSKI

C

D

A. **Everlasting Earrings** 9015E / $99
B. **Everlasting Necklace** 9014N / $299; 16" to 18".
C. **Society Bracelet** 9019B / $139; 9" adjustable.
D. **Everlasting Cuff** 9018B / $169; 2½" inside diameter.

LITTLE BLACK DRESS

WANT TO SEE IN COLOR
ORDER-FULL COLOR CATALOG
LAST PAGE OF JEWELRY SECTION

C

D

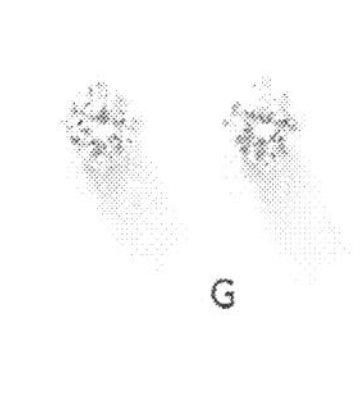

A

B

E

F

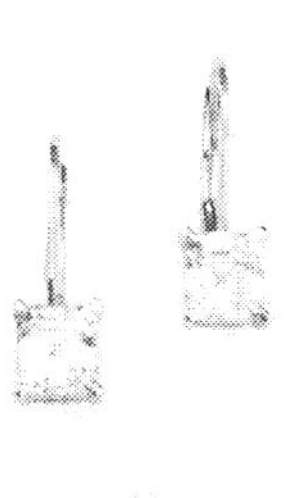

TOUCHSTONE CRYSTAL BY SWAROVSKI

High-end styles without the diamond price tag.

ZIRCONIA FROM SWAROVSKI SINCE 1895

G

H

I

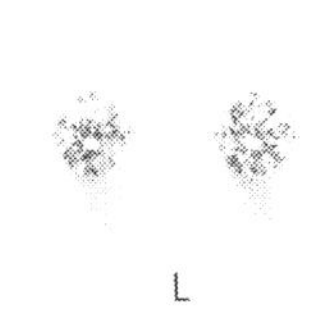

M

J

K

L

A. Brilliant Pendant 9013N / $49; 15" to 18".
B. Brilliant Earrings, Large 9012E / $59
C. Faith Cross Necklace 5754NF / $59; 15" to 18".
D. Ever After Necklace 5760NF / $89; 15" to 18".
E. Ever After Earrings 5761EF / $89
F. Divine Necklace 9017N / $89; 16" to 18".
G. Golden Monte Carlo Earrings 5748EF / $42; gold vermeil.
H. Golden Millionaire's Club Earrings 5749EF / $49; gold vermeil.
I. Urban Climber Earrings 9004E / $39
J. Legacy Earrings 5705EF / $55
K. Millionaire's Club Earrings 5548EF / $45
L. Monte Carlo Earrings 5678EF / $40
M. Astoria Earrings 9008E / $69

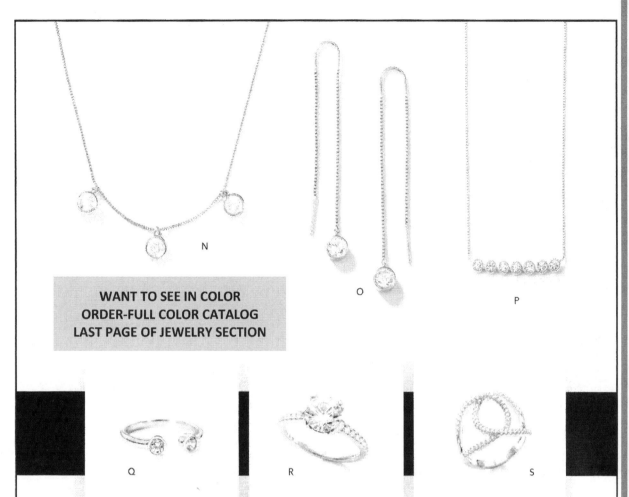

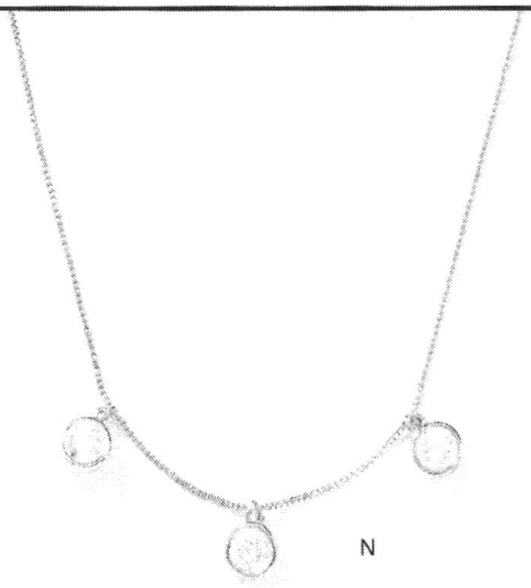

N

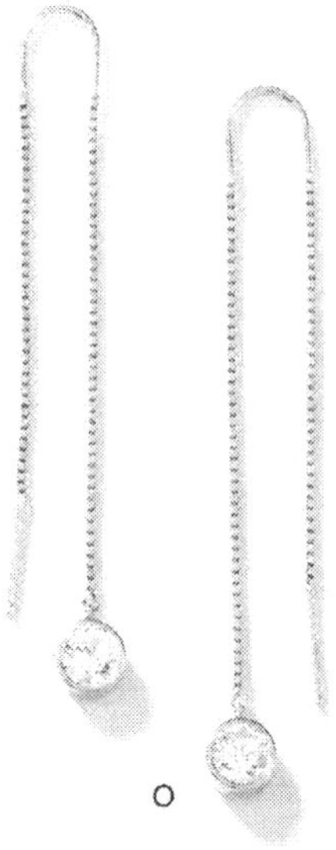

O

P

WANT TO SEE IN COLOR
ORDER-FULL COLOR CATALOG
LAST PAGE OF JEWELRY SECTION

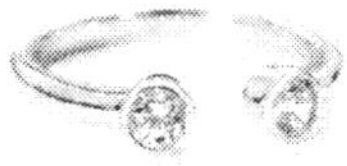

Q

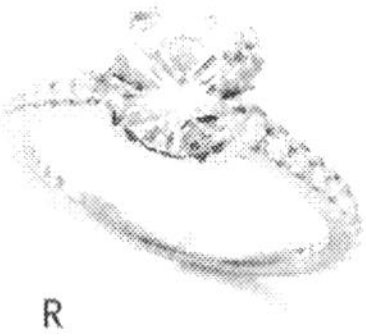

R

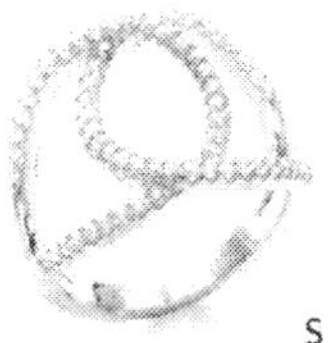

S

TOUCHSTONE
CRYSTAL BY SWAROVSKI

T

DARE TO
dazzle

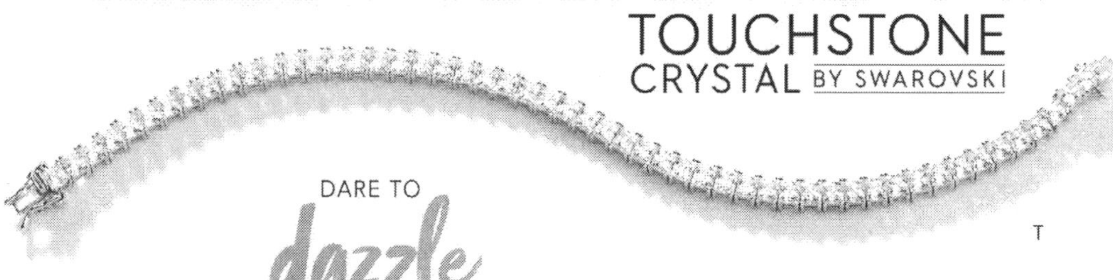

N. Darling Necklace 9016N / $99; 15" to 18".
O. On Trend Earrings 9003E / $49
P. Society Bar Necklace 9010N / $89; 15" to 18".

Q. Open Mind Ring R3199 / $49; sizes 6 – 10.
R. Bright Future Ring R3207 / $89; sizes 6-10.
S. Alliance Ring R3206 / $89; sizes 6-10.

T. Beautifully Brilliant Bracelet
Small 5767BF / $199; 7".
Large 5751BF / $199; 7½".

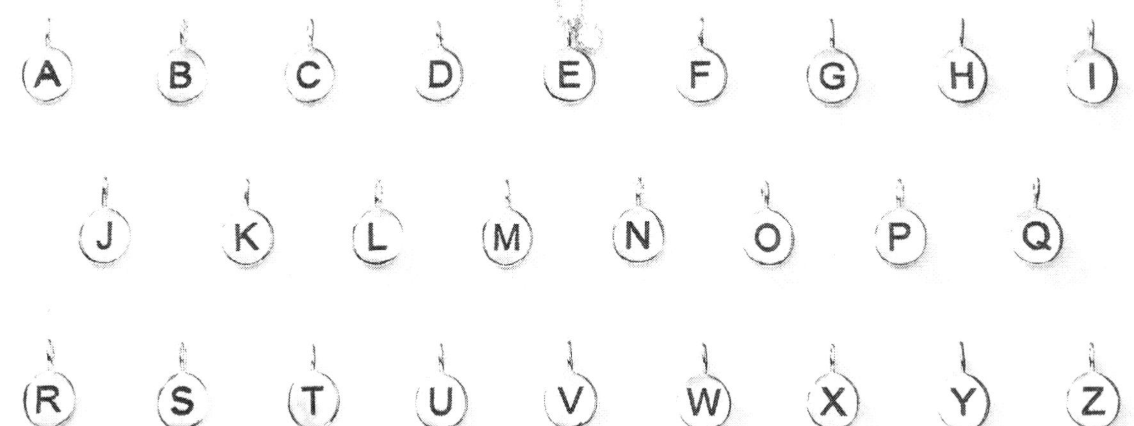

INITIAL NECKLACES

With mini chanelle accent. Great for gift giving.

1000N / $30 Crystal; rhodium plating; 15" to 18"

WANT TO SEE IN COLOR
ORDER-FULL COLOR CATALOG
LAST PAGE OF JEWELRY SECTION

A

VERSATILE

Wear it long, or wear it short

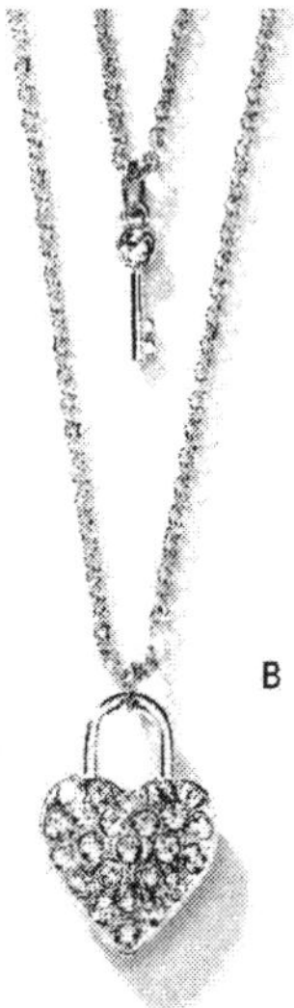

B

C

D

TOUCHSTONE CRYSTAL BY SWAROVSKI

E

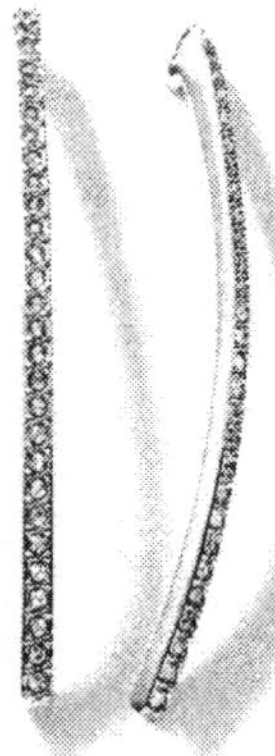

F

G

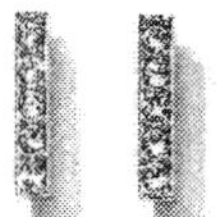

H

I

J

K

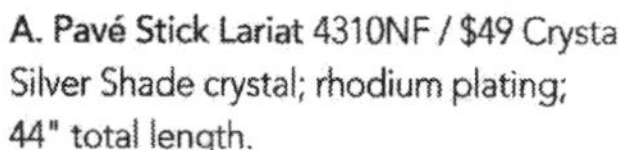

A. Pavé Stick Lariat 4310NF / $49 Crystal Silver Shade crystal; rhodium plating; 44" total length.
B. Key and Heart Necklace 4404NF / $49 Crystal; rhodium plating; 16" to 19".
C. Trinity Necklace 3475NF / $49 Crystal; rhodium plating; 15" to 18".
D. Petite Cross Necklace, Crystal 1183N / $39 Rhodium plating; 15" to 18".

E. Chain Drop Earrings 1094E / $49 Crystal; rhodium plating.
F. Curved Bar Earrings 1095E / $49 Crystal Silver Shade crystal; rhodium plating.
G. Pavé Bar Necklace, Rhodium 4046NF / $39 Crystal; 15" to 18".
H. Pavé Bar Earrings, Rhodium 4054EF / $24 Crystal.

I. Over the Moon Necklace 1287N / $39 Crystal Moonlight crystal; rhodium plating; 15" to 18".
J. Luck of the Irish Necklace 1286N / $39 Crystal; rhodium plating; 15" to 18".
K. Petite Circle Necklace, Rhodium 4331NF / $39 Crystal; 15" to 18".

SUICIDE NOTE

BY STEVEN P. ARTHUR

Detective Larson held out the plastic evidence bag containing a single sheet of blood-smeared paper. My wife Elizabeth had been missing for forty-seven hours and counting; this was the first I had heard about a suicide note. To think Liz would or could hurt herself was laughable, insane. She's a beautiful, energetic and joyful mother of three jewels from her womb. I hardly remember a time in my life before her. We'd been together since high school and have only had one serious blowout.

I took the bag with an unsteady hand, which I'm sure Detective Larson noted, neither of them seemed to believe a word I said, but he seemed to like me the least. He and his cohort, Detective Barrows, had begun the interview cordially enough. By the tenth hour our meeting had regressed into a full-blown interrogation, and I was not only under suspicion but the only suspect. Somehow, in their feeble minds I had single-handedly left my office on 34th street, walked through a sea of paralegals and interns that know me by first, middle and last name, took the A train 30 minutes to our home and murdered my wife of two decades. Not to mention, I had forcefully convinced her to write a suicide note clearing me and any would-be suspects of nefarious deeds. They had not located any physical evidence as far as I knew, but the fact there was a smear of blood on the note and a very large and fast-moving river near our home, did not bode well for me to begin with.

Now, after they had two days to confirm my alibi, the detectives wanted my cooperation. I'm supposed to read the note and point out any abnormalities, which I thought was obvious: the blood smear. I had been awake for almost three days, but I would have recognized her tight back-slanted handwriting under any circumstances.

When we had met in school, honors English, we had started exchanging notes. In a very short time these notes had become more and more intimate, so with this in mind we devised what we thought was a brilliant form of subterfuge. To foil an eye that might have happened upon our letters, especially old Mr. Nelson with his cheap hair piece, we created a method of messages by leaving key letters out of words. To everyone else they would merely look like letters with poor spelling or grammar. The letters themselves would be innocuous, letters on a subject or event about school. But when combined, these "missing letters" would spell out the true message or intent, which were typically "I miss you," or "meet me for lunch." Which I admit was childish, but we were in love, and love fogs the senses of even the most mature beings. We did this for several years, even spilling over into college for awhile. So, it must have been a real shock to the detectives to watch my sleep-deprived and haggard express transform into a shit-eating grin as I read my wife's suicide note. The letter in my hand was only half a page, describing how she didn't want to live anymore and not to look for her, but there were clearly and exactly ten letters missing. Easy to decipher. I looked up at the detectives and read her message aloud: "Still Alive."

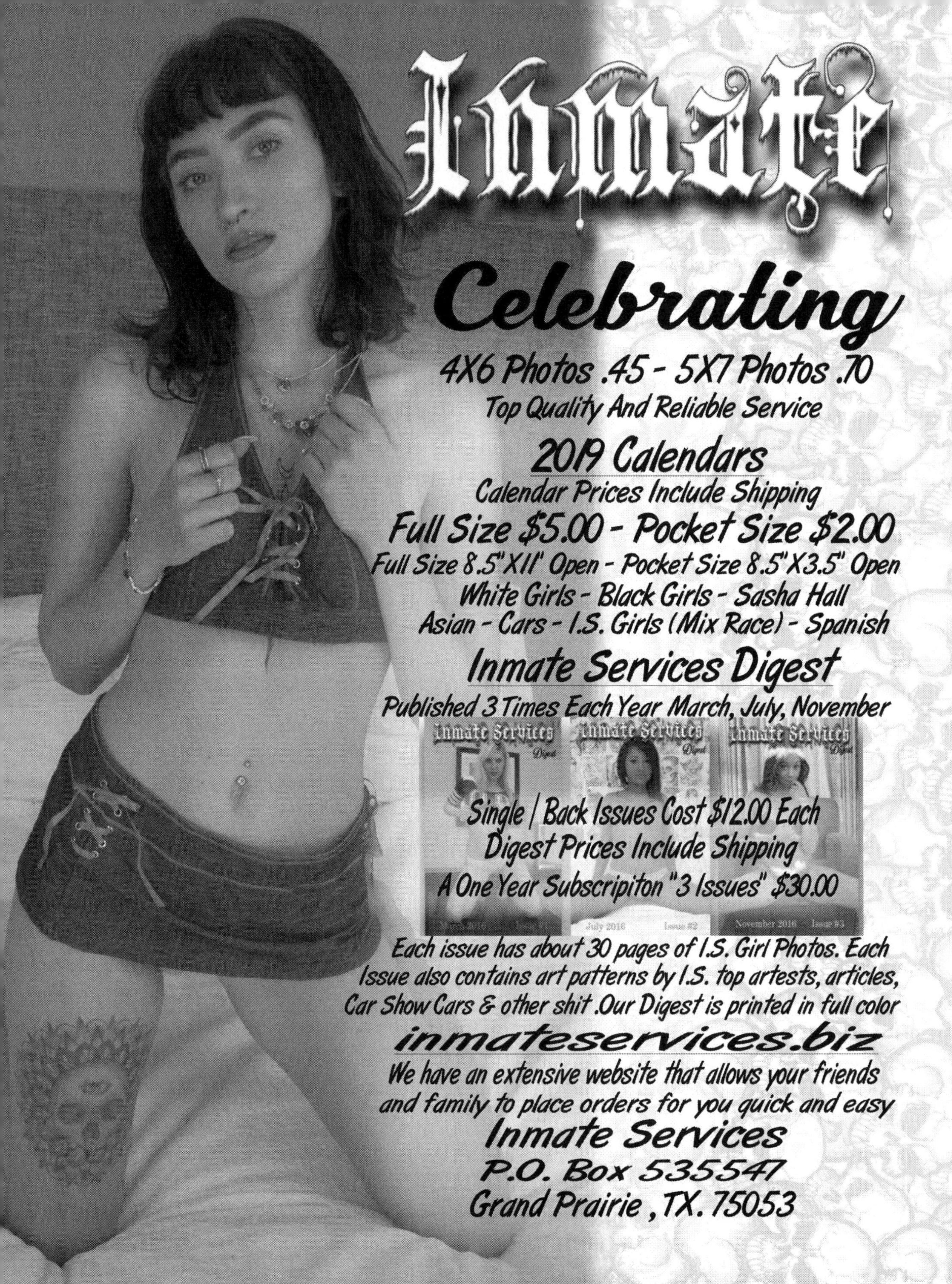
Inmate
Celebrating
4X6 Photos .45 - 5X7 Photos .70
Top Quality And Reliable Service
2019 Calendars
Calendar Prices Include Shipping
Full Size $5.00 - Pocket Size $2.00
Full Size 8.5"X11" Open - Pocket Size 8.5"X3.5" Open
White Girls - Black Girls - Sasha Hall
Asian - Cars - I.S. Girls (Mix Race) - Spanish
Inmate Services Digest
Published 3 Times Each Year March, July, November
Inmate Services Digest
Inmate Services Digest
Inmate Services Digest
Single / Back Issues Cost $12.00 Each
Digest Prices Include Shipping
A One Year Subscripiton "3 Issues" $30.00
March 2016 Issue #1
July 2016 Issue #2
November 2016 Issue #3
Each issue has about 30 pages of I.S. Girl Photos. Each
Issue also contains art patterns by I.S. top artests, articles,
Car Show Cars & other shit .Our Digest is printed in full color
inmateservices.biz
We have an extensive website that allows your friends
and family to place orders for you quick and easy
Inmate Services
P.O. Box 535547
Grand Prairie ,TX. 75053

Services
Our 10th Year
Art Patterns .30 Each
Art Patterns are printed on standard size paper
8.5" X 11" and printed in black and white
Color Catalogs Now $2.00
These catalogs are in the form of a book
and the price includes shipping.
Black And White Catalogs
New catalogs come out 3 times each year January, May, and September. Catalogs are still in print back to January 2011. Black and white catalogs are free. You must send a self addressed stamped envelope to cover shipping, 1 stamp ships 1 catalog 2 stamps covers the shipping of 3 catalogs
DO NOT have people call us to request catalogs.
Other Useful Info
No Inmate Email : The best way to contact us is U.S. Postal Mail. If you have a house account with us you will have to send your orders in the mail. We do not do business with county jails. Hit us up when you make it to the Feds or State Prisons. We ship only using white envelopes. We do not charge extra to split orders up per mailroom rules or for shipping on different days. We swap out our rejected photos with denial paperwork. As far as we know we are the only company still doing swaps. We take stamps at face value for purchase of our products. We want flat books or strips of at least two stamps.
Photo/Pattern Shipping
1-8= .50 9-16=$1.00 17-25=$1.50 26-34=$2.00
35-43=$2.50 44-52=$3.00 53-62=$3.50 63-71=$4.00
72-80=$4.50 81-89=$5.00 90-98=$5.50 99 and up = Free

Chapter 7 Bankruptcy:
Seven Steps to Financial Freedom

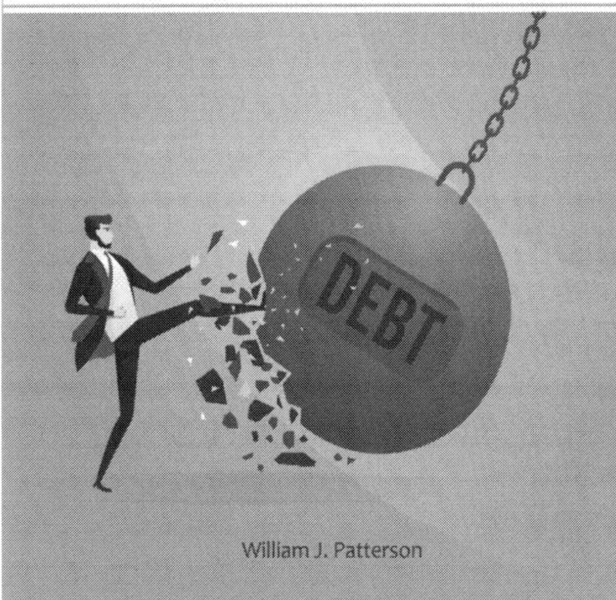

Only $22.99
plus $7 S/H with tracking
SOFTCOVER, 8" x 10", 240+ pages

Much of bankruptcy procedure is technical and very straight forward. More often than not, there is only one way to complete a required form and only one set of rules that apply to that form. Being familiar with the legal system, prisoners understand that one misstep can cost you your freedom. With Chapter 7 Bankruptcy, your financial freedom is at stake.

This book is designed to be an all-inclusive resource guide with step-by-step instructions for prisoners filing their own Chapter 7. It details the basic information on different aspects of federal bankruptcy laws, as well as the author's own personal experience in filing a successful Chapter 7 claim.

Here are sample forms, schedules, and instructions you need to obtain your financial freedom! In these pages you will learn a wealth of information and have the technical points explained in easy to follow language. Also featured is a basic explanation of the different chapters under which a bankruptcy case may be filed and answers to some of the most commonly asked questions about the bankruptcy process.

The goal of this work is to help you through all of the steps, to point out obstacles along the way and resources both inside and outside of prison, and finally, to provide you with inspiration and encouragement that you too can do this on your own. With preparation, patience, and perseverance, you can accomplish anything – including the successful discharge of your own Chapter 7 Bankruptcy. If you follow these 7 basic steps to completing a Chapter 7 Bankruptcy, you too can enjoy the freedoms that a fresh start will provide.

No Order Form Needed: Clearly write on paper & send with payment of **$29.99** to:

Freebird Publishers **Box 541, North Dighton, MA 02764**
Diane@FreebirdPublishers.com www.FreebirdPublishers.com

CRIMINAL AND ADDICTIVE THINKING PATTERNS

Criminal and addictive thinking patterns are linked. Each criminal thinking pattern is closely related to an addictive thinking pattern. They are defined as follows:

Criminal Thinking Patterns	Addictive Thinking Patterns
• victim stance	• self-pity stance
• "good person" stance	• "good person" stance
• "unique person" stance	• "unique person" stance
• fear of exposure	• fear of exposure
• lack-of-time perspective	• lack-of-time perspective
• selective effort	• selective effort
• use of power to control	• use of deceit to control
• seek excitement first	• seek pleasure first
• ownership stance	• ownership stance

Now we'll take a closer look at those patterns.

1. Victim Stance This criminal thinking pattern allows you to blame others for situations you usually created for yourself. You make excuses and point your finger at others, claiming you were the one who was really wronged. You try to justify your behavior.

2. Self-Pity Stance This addictive thinking pattern makes you believe the world is just out to get you. You claim that since your life is so miserable and screwed up, you have a good reason to drink or use drugs.

3. "Good Person" Stance When you adopt this criminal thinking pattern, you consider yourself to be a good person, no matter what. You work hard to present that image to others. In fact, you may not only consider yourself a good person, but may think you're better than others! As a "good person" stance addictive thinker, you focus on the good things you've done and ignore the harm.

4. "Unique Person" Stance This criminal thinking pattern allows you to believe no one in the whole world is like you or has experienced what you have. Rules don't apply to you. You commit crimes because you never think you'll get caught. You believe that if you think it, then it must be that way. You also use "unique person" stance to feed your addiction. Maybe you think your alcohol or other drug use makes you especially cool.

5. Fear of Exposure You act like you are fearless, yet you're full of fear. You fear that you're nobody and that you'll be found out; you're afraid that you'll be exposed as being full of fear. One of your biggest fears is the fear of fear! Fear of exposure addictive thinking is fear of self-knowledge, excessive or inappropriate trust, addict pride, and zero state*. Zero state is a fear that you cannot change.

6. Lack-of-Time Perspective When you use this criminal thinking pattern, you do not learn from past experiences or plan for the future. You see behaviors as isolated events. Your philosophy is "I want it, and I want it now." You expect to be a big success with little or no effort. You make choices based on what you want to be true, rather than what is true. When you adopt this addictive thinking pattern, getting high is the most important thing in your life; you live only in the present when you are high and only in the near future ("How can I get more soon?") when you are not high. Lack-of-time perspective addictive thinking helps you do that.

*The zero state consists of these beliefs:

- You are nothing.
- Everyone else also believes you are worthless.
- Your "worthlessness" will last forever and can never be changed.

Reprinted from Hazelden Foundation

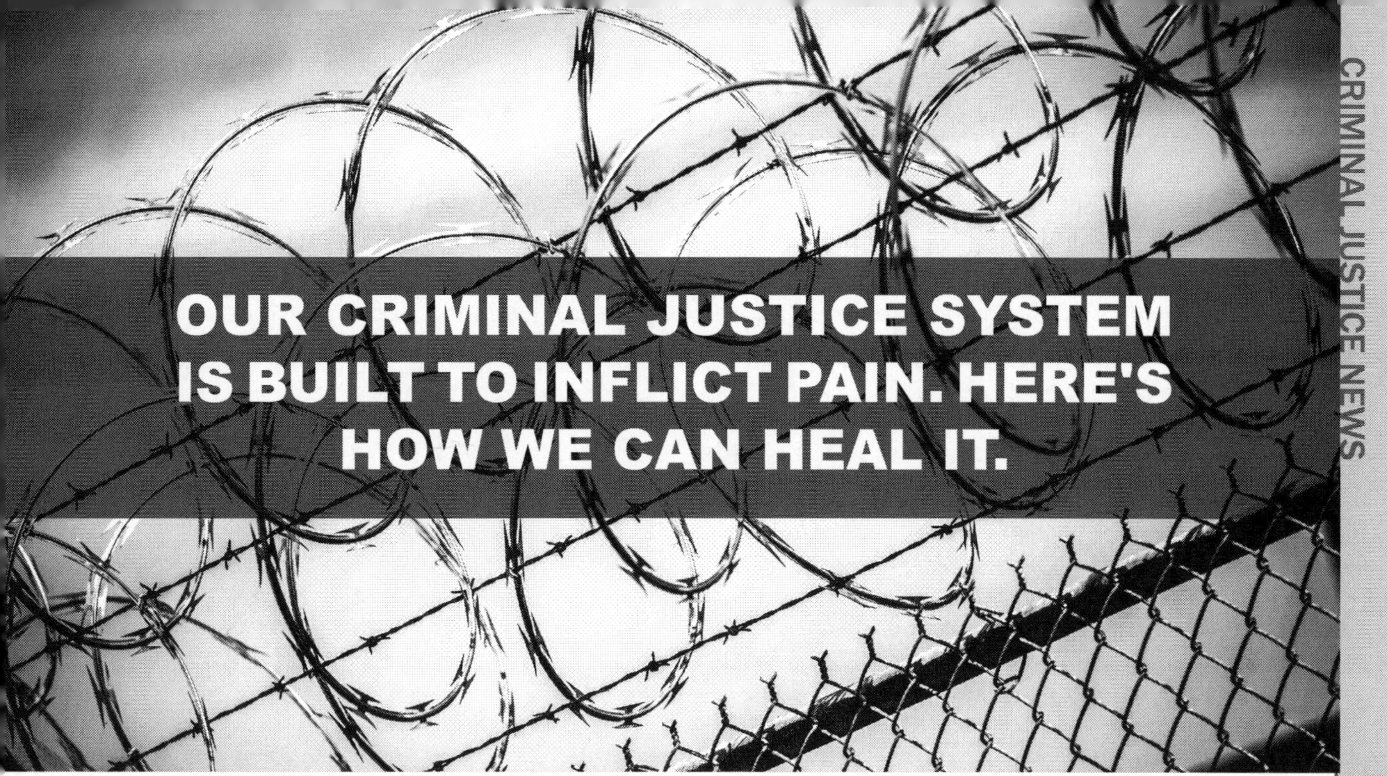

OUR CRIMINAL JUSTICE SYSTEM IS BUILT TO INFLICT PAIN. HERE'S HOW WE CAN HEAL IT.

California's San Quentin is one of the oldest prisons in the country. Located on a parcel of land jutting out into the San Francisco Bay, the mammoth 167-year-old facility has a lonely and intimidating look from the outside – and on the inside, it's just as forlorn.

None of this should be surprising; that's how our criminal justice system has designed these facilities. American prisons are built on the idea of retributive justice, where the primary goal is to punish and seek vengeance. It's a model that aims to incapacitate people who commit crimes and create powerful, painful incentives for them to act right in the future. The bottom line: You harm someone, and we harm you. You hurt others, and you will hurt.

This approach makes some intuitive sense. The problem is that adding harm to harm inevitably produces more harm. Too often, people come out of prison bitter – not better. While they're locked away, their children suffer and may be led astray. And rather than derailing the cycle of violence and trauma, our system's retributive approach may often support and even accelerate that destructive cycle: According to the Bureau of Justice Statistics, 68% of state prisoners are arrested again within three years.

This system also isn't good for victims of crime. Retribution intentionally damages the offender, but it can also accidentally leave victims with new injuries by neglecting their needs and silencing their voices. In the present system, victims and their loved ones are barely involved in the process of meting out justice. As soon as the crime is committed, a huge professional apparatus kicks in, and a massive, inhuman bureaucracy takes over. The police, lawyers, investigators, jurors, and judges all start doing whatever they think is right. Neither the crime victims nor their family members get to ask their own questions, determine the punishment, or seek an apology.

During a trial, practically everyone talks except the people actually impacted. After a trial, those convicted of a crime are sometimes legally forbidden to contact the people they hurt, even to offer an apology. The system attempts to shield survivors from unwanted contact with the wrongdoer, but that also robs victims of the opportunity to ask the questions that haunt them: "Why?" "What were you thinking?" "What were my son's last words?"

As a result, the amount of communication between the two parties is practically nonexistent – except for an impact statement from the victims, delivered right before the guilty party is sentenced.

We know that this system isn't working. To help cure what ails our justice system, reform advocates say, we need to think differently. We need to think about restoration.

Restorative justice shifts our understanding of crime and punishment and asks us to use a completely different logic. The goal is not to create more damage, but to create more healing – often through a dialogue between a crime survivor and the person who hurt them. The goal is not to add more pain, but to ameliorate as much pain as possible. At the end of the day, the goal is for all parties – and the community itself – to be restored to whatever degree of wellness and wholeness is possible. It seeks accountability from the trespasser, but ultimately healing for everyone involved.

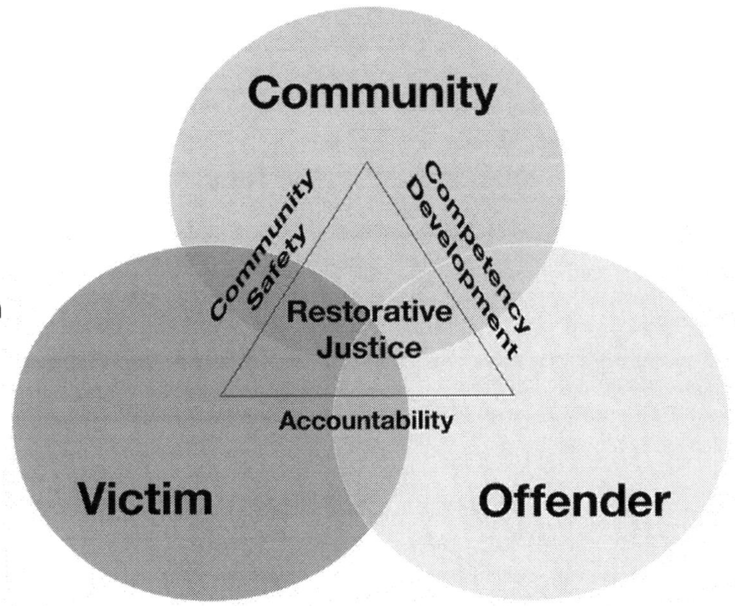

That's why in these conversations between those who harmed and those who were harmed, there usually isn't a big audience or large army of professionals – just a facilitator and some support people, maybe five people total. The process involves tremendous emotional and logistical preparation, including trading questions in advance.

These exchanges come out of older, wiser traditions that recognize the many dimensions of harm, and that many threads of connection are severed when someone commits a crime. In these traditions, villagers would sit in circles, discuss the issue and find a just way forward – to restore the dignity and sense of belonging for both the victim and the perpetrator.

We are rediscovering that spiritual wisdom today, and it is changing lives. I recently visited San Quentin for an episode of "The Redemption Project" to meet a young man named Chris Smith. When Chris was 16, after a rough upbringing that led him into gang life, he says he followed orders to shoot at a car parked outside a high school. He did not realize that one of his former classmates – LoEshé Lacy – who was only 16 herself, was in the car. LoEshé was killed and Smith had to face the consequences.

Through restorative justice, he began a process of rehabilitation and self-reflection that led to a remarkable dialogue with Donald Lacy, LoEshé Lacy's father. And Donald finally got more insight into what led Chris into gang culture and to the terrible decisions that took his daughter's life. I was lucky enough to witness the encounter – and to film it for CNN viewers – as a part of "The Redemption Project."

The really good news is that something new is brewing, not just in San Quentin, but across the criminal justice system. In fact, it has even reached Washington. With massive bipartisan majorities, both houses of Congress last year passed The First Step Act, the most significant piece of criminal justice reform legislation in decades.

The First Step Act began with a recognition that prisons can't just be places of punishment. They must also create opportunities for rehabilitation and transformation. The law expands programming throughout the federal prison system and adds incentives that encourage men and women to pursue classes that will help them successfully return to their families and communities. It also scaled back some of the harshest criminal penalties, like mandatory life sentences for third-strike drug offenses, and retroactively applies other reforms to give thousands of people an opportunity to petition a judge for their freedom. It also added important protections for incarcerated women, banned solitary confinement for juveniles, and much more.

But we will still need second, third, and fourth steps – fully implementing the act quickly and effectively, rolling back other lengthy prison sentences (and continuing to do so retroactively to bring home as many people as we safely can), investing in alternatives to incarceration, scaling back systems of mass supervision like probation and parole, reducing barriers for people with criminal records, and so much more.

The First Step Act at least opens the door to begin that wholesale rethinking of our criminal justice system. No longer are retribution and incapacitation the sole aims of our public safety policies. Now, rehabilitation officially matters, too. And for some, nothing is more powerfully rehabilitative than sitting face-to-face with people you have harmed, in an effort to heal.

Reprinted from cnn.com

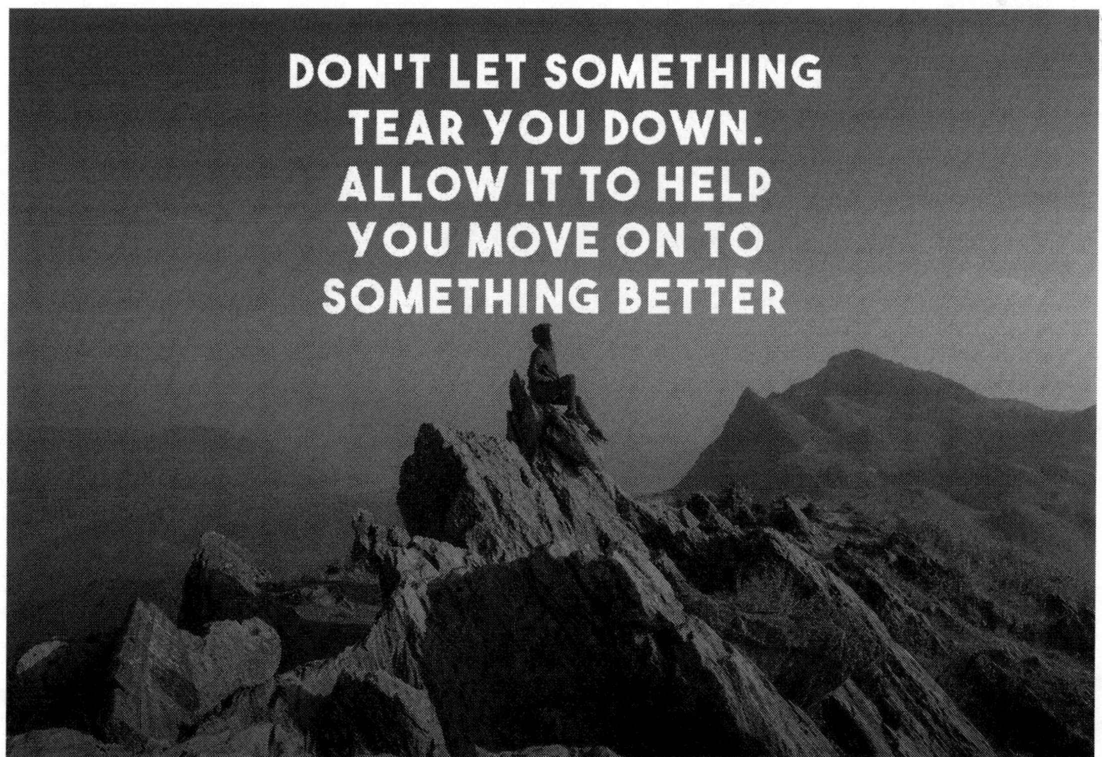
DON'T LET SOMETHING
TEAR YOU DOWN.
ALLOW IT TO HELP
YOU MOVE ON TO
SOMETHING BETTER

LET FREEDOM RING

By Aubrey Dean Elwood

TODAY, I am not homeless and live in a and state of perpetual gratefulness for this act of kindness. Although my current home is by no means sustainable at this point. I am under a cloud of uncertainty. Several things must happen before I am totally free. Freedom is not being out of prison, but is being able to provide for yourself the basic essentials of existence. It is wonderful to have others that are willing to help support me and my endeavors. However, the sooner I can actually put into practice those long hours, days, and years of study, the sooner I will be free. As the great Holocaust survivor Viktor Frankl concluded, the reason for life is meaning. Should one's life have no meaning, there is no sustainable existence for him.

To return from prison to homelessness is to continue to live without freedom. Being homeless is not just about being deprived of a roof over your head; it is about being deprived of a sense of belonging, a sense of community, full participation with a voice in society. There can be no doubt that a life defined by three bleak words: "no fixed address," is a life deprived of the most basic entitlements that most people take for granted. Whether homelessness takes the form of being forced to sleep on the streets or being placed in emergency shelters with all the uncertainty that entails ... homelessness removes so many of the acts of discretion that define FREEDOM.

Homelessness and the Justice System

Homelessness and the justice system are inextricably linked. People experiencing homelessness are 11 times more likely to face incarceration when compared to the general population, and formerly incarcerated individuals are almost 10 times more likely to become homeless than the general public. In fact, four-to-six times the annual rate of homelessness than in the general population.

I did not want to become another statistic of one returning to Nowhere. I have already spent my life living in Nowhere, U.S.A. When you are reading what I write please keep in mind that my experiences gave me the impetus to ask for help. Not just for me but for those that come after me in this struggle – for those of us that have been left behind for so many years.

Every community should get involved in the reentry of those returning from prison, from addiction, and from mental illness. This is the only way out of mass incarceration, which is costing YOU, the taxpayer, billions of dollars a year. Money that could be better spent on the future of our country, on crime prevention, drug programs and better healthcare! Let us all stand up and declare that "It takes a village to raise a child." This goes just as well for all those who suffer from mental illness and who are coming from prison or drug rehabilitation.

Freedom is gained through contributing to community, service to others; it's drawing a wider circle.

Let FREEDOM RING!

Peace and light,

Aubrey Dean Elwood
Oklahoma City, Oklahoma

LGBTQ PRISON LIVING

ACLU GLBT RIGHTS / AIDS PROJECT
Mail: 125 Broad St, 18th Floor
New York, NY 10004
Review: Experts in constitutional law and civil rights, specializing in sexual orientation, gender identity and HIV/AIDS.

ANTI-VIOLENCE PROJECT
240 West 35th Street Ste 200
New York, NY 10001
212.714.1141

BLACK AND PINK
Mail: 614 Columbia Rd.
Dorchester, MA 02125-9918
Web: BlackAndPink.Org
Review: Free monthly newspaper for LGBT prisoners. They print stories of prisoners who get harassed by staff and other short stories.

BROKEN YOKE MINISTRIES, INC
Contact: Bob and Cathie Van Domelen
Mail: Box 361
Waukesha, WI 53187
Review: Ministry for inmates struggling with sexual abuse or homosexuality and seek healing in Christ. Produces the newsletter: Wellspring

BROTHERS BEHIND BARS, RADICAL FAERIE DIGEST
Mail: Box 68
Liberty, TN 37095
Review: Quarterly list of BGT male prisoners produced and

distributed upon request. Donation of $3-$10 is requested for the list.

GAY AMERICAN INDIAN AIDS PROJECT
Mail: 1347 Divisadero St, #312
San Francisco, CA 94115
Mail 2: 333 Valencia St., #207
San Francisco, CA 94103
Review: An AIDS awareness and prevention program.

GAY AND LESBIAN RIGHTS PROJECT OF THE ACLU
Mail: 132 West 43rd St
New York, NY 10036
Review: Handles issues involving gays and lesbians, including discrimination, HIV/AIDS, must make initial contact through ACLU state affiliate

JENN DUR SERVICES
Mail: N9494 Haltur Lane
Eagle, WI 53119
Review: Publishes the magazine "Tran Spirituality for TIGV prisoners and allies, and offers the TransAction Program, a post-release program specifically for transsexual ex-prisoners. Magazine free to prisoners.

THE KEY MINISTRY
Contact: Rodel Eberle
Mail: Box 97
Wykoff, MN 55990
Review: Support and help for anyone who wants to overcome the homosexual lifestyle.

LAMBDA LEGAL DEFENSE AND EDUCATIONAL FUND
Mail: 120 Wall Street, #1500
New York, NY 10005
PH: 212-809-8585
Review: Focuses on defense of persons with gay, lesbian, and HIV/AIDS issues.

LGBT BOOKS TO PRISONERS
Mail: Outreach LGBT Community Center
600 Williamson St.
Madison, WI 53703
Review: Send books and other educational materials free of charge to LGBT-identified prisoners. They also offer a Newsletter available for print off of their website.

LIVING HOPE MINISTRIES
Mail: Box 2239
Arlington, TX 76004
Review: A special ministry for homosexuals who desire change through Jesus Christ.

NATIONAL GAY & LESBIAN TASK FORCE
Mail: 1824 14th Street NW
Washington, D.C. 20009
PH: 202-332-6482
Review: Education and lobbying on same-sex relationships. Seeks to combat all sexual orientation-based discrimination. Information clearinghouse for 3,000 nationwide organizations. No legal services.

POWER INSIDE
Mail: Box 4796
Baltimore, MD 21211
Review: Provides women-centered services to women including trans women and trans men. Offers support and advocacy for those who are incarcerated, homeless, addicted or in the sex trade.

PRISON CORRESPONDENCE PROJECT
Mail: C/O QPIRG Concordia
1455 De Maisonneuve W.
Montreal, QC H3G 1 MB
Canada
Review: Send letter of request for Bi-Annual Newspaper with great info and resources especially on health and erotic and gay celeb gossip.

RAINBOW BOOKSTORE
Mail:426 W. Gilman St.
Madison, WI 53703
Review: They offer free books to the LGBT prisoners. Write and include your complete mailing address, regulations on receiving books, area of interests and whether you can receive new or used books. July 2015

T.I.P. JOURNAL
Mail: 3895 Upham St., Ste 40
Wheat Ridge, CO 80033
Comment: Newsletter for transgender prisoners "Gender Identity Center of Colorado, Inc" Write for details.

SYLVIA RIVERA LAW PROJECT
147 West 24th Street 5th Floor
New York, NY 10011
SRLP.org

TRANSGENDER, GENDER VARIANT AND INTERSEX JUSTICE ACT
Mail:
342 9th St. Ste. 202B
San Francisco, CA 94103
Review:TGI Justice Project is a group of transgender people inside and outside of prison seeking survival and freedom through unity.

TRANZMISSION PRISON BOOKS
Area Served:
Mail: Box 1874
Asheville, NC 28802
Comment: Offers free books and resources.

ULTRA VIOLET NEWSLETTER -- QUEER INSURRECTION
LAGAI
3543 18th Street #26
San Francisco, CA 94110
info@lagai.org

LGBTQ Music

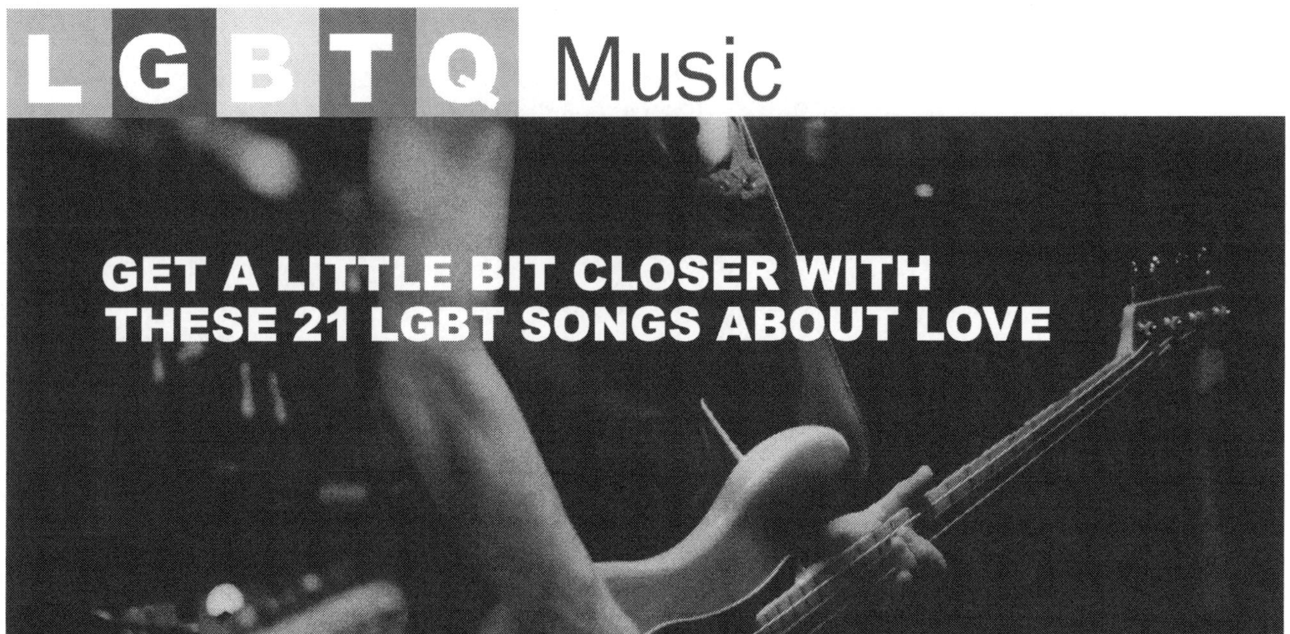
GET A LITTLE BIT CLOSER WITH
THESE 21 LGBT SONGS ABOUT LOVE

There's nothing like a great love song to inspire you to reach for your own romantic heights. It's even more powerful when you can really relate to the lyrics. Yet, in the hetero-heavy world of romantic music, great gay love songs and fantastic lesbian love songs can be hard to find. So, we've created a playlist of LGBT songs about love that can help change all that.

Boy Meets Boy: 7 Gay Love Songs

1. Hold Each Other – A Great Big World
Best love lyric: Something happens when I hold him/He keeps my heart from getting broken

Chad King sang love songs with female pronouns bcause, as he told Billboard, "it's just what people do". Hold Each Other shows King getting real. When bandmate Ian Axel sings about the woman he loves, King joins in–singing about the man who belongs in his arms. It's wonderful.

2. Capers – Kele Okereke
Best love lyric: No, I'm not in love, I don't claim to be/But are you free on Sunday?

Best known as the front man of Bloc Party, Kele Okereke's solo projects show a whole new side of the gay indie icon. Capers, for instance, is a sweetly jaunty love song about a man who insists he's not in love...but his skipping heart and delight in the date revel the truth.

3. Forrest Gump – Frank Ocean
Best love lyric: Forrest Gump you run my mind boy/Running on my mind

Even in 2019, when openly out artists sing love songs, it's more common to hear 'you' rather than 'him'. Frank Ocean is different. *Forrest Gump* is that rare gay love song that doesn't shy away from male pronouns–in this case the teenaged dream who a younger Ocen once loved from afar. Anyone whose high school crush was unrequited can sympathize.

4. My My My! – Troye Sivan
Best love lyric: No, I'm not in love, I don't claim to be/But are you free on Sunday?

Best known as the front man of Bloc Party, Kele Okereke's solo projects show a whole new side of the gay indie icon. Capers, for instance, is a sweetly jaunty love song about a man who insists he's not in love...but his skipping heart and delight in the date revel the truth.

5. Just Some Guy – Anthony Rapp
Best love lyric: And I've said these things to other boys, but right now the old words feel so new

Seen *Rent*? Then chances are you know Anthony Rapp, aka the definitive Mark Cohen. He's also responsible for *Just Some Guy*, possibly the worlds sweetest gay love song. Nothing else quite captures that gleeful disbelief you feel when the man of your dreams loves you back.

6. Love is Love – Trey Pearson
Best love lyric: Don't wanna leave can't get enough / I know that LOVE is LOVE

Trey Pearson found fame as a married, straight, Christian rock singer. Then in 2016, he made the decision to come out publically, quickly becoming an advoate for gay Christians who crave a more accepting kind of faith. Even if you don't share his religion, you can believe in 2017's *Love is Love*, a magical song about finally allowing yourself to embrace true love and desire.

7. What A Beautiful Day – Brett Every ft. Belinda Crawford
Best love lyric: Your father said, while giving his toast/That, "Of all my beliefs, I believe in love most.

A gay love song sure to strike a chord with marriage-minded singles, Brett Every's tale of two men getting hitched is simple and beautiful (and hard to listen to without a few happy tears!). Written in 2012 to support same-sex marriage rights, the song is just as poignant today–it's no wonder it won 'Best Love Song of the Year' at the Out Music Awards in 2012.

Girl Meets Girl: 7 Lesbian Love Songs

1. All I Want is To Be Your Girl – Holly Miranda
Best love lyric: I wasn't looking for love but she found me

Since The Jealous Girlfriends went on hiatus, lead vocalist Holly Miranda has been busy with solo projects, like this oh-so-catchy song about new love. If you're crushing on a lady, this is the ideal tune to play while dancing around your bedroom – hairbrush mic optional.

2. She – Jen Foster
Best love lyric: It's simple as can be/I love her, she loves me

Over the last 15 years, Jen Foster's *She* has become a lesbian love anthem. It's easy to see why: *She* is both a beautiful love song about an inspiring romance and a demand for tolerance (with lyrics like 'Just try and stop me, just try and stop us/Good luck to you,' this is no mere plea).

Music

3. Girl – The Internet ft. KAYTRANDA
Best love lyric: Would you let me call you my girl, my girlfriend, my girlfriend?

The Internet's Syd is not without controversy, but here she's simply smitten and ready to give her girl to the world. The dreamy, electro-soul of this track is the perfect accompaniment to her vocals, creating the musical equivalent of ecstatic, late-night, whispered sweet nothings.

4. Constant Craving – K.D. Lang
Best love lyric: Maybe a great magnet pulls/All souls to what's true

Is it even legal to create a playist of lesbian love songs and not include the iconic K.D. Lang? *Constant Craving* turns an astonishing 26 years old in 2018 (it was released in 1992, the year K.D. Lang came out as gay), and yet is still fresh and fantastic. In fact, it's possibly the definitive tune about lesbian longing, desire and love.

5. Come to My Window – Melissa Etheridge
Best love lyric: Come to my window/I'll be home soon

The first single Melissa Etheridge released after coming out in 1993, this song struck a chord with lesbians and queer identifying folk everywhere. So much so that they changed the meaning - the line 'what do they know about this love anyway' originally referred to gossipy friends, but Etheridge says the gay community has helped it mean much, much more.

6. Better Than Love – Hayley Kiyoko
Best love lyric: Somebody tell me what's better than love?/Better than love

Hayley Kiyoko made a huge impact with 2015's *Girls Like Girls.* Since then, the former Disney star has been experimenting with different takes on the lesbian love song-here, she switches out the tough gay anthem for pure, bubbling joy. As romatic songs go, this is pretty special.

7. She Keeps Me Warm – Mary Lambert
Best love lyric: Do you like kissing girls?/Can I call you 'Baby"?

She Keeps Me Warm started life as the hook of Macklemore's mega hit *Same Love.* Soon, however, people were clamoring to hear a full length version from singer Mary Lambert - and oh boy did she deliver. This gorgeous lesbian love song is so heartfelt and happy, we even had to include it on our list ove the 100 best love songs of all time.

Reprinted from Elite Singles

LGBTQ Magazines

Out Magazine
$19.95/year
10 Issues

A gay and lesbian perspective on style, entertainment, fashion, the arts, politics, and culture.

Mail: Out Magazine
c/o Here Media
10990 Wilshire Blvd, PH
Los Angeles, CA 90024

Metrosource
$19.95 6 Issues
$34.95/year

Choose between NY, LA or NAT Editions.

Mail: Metrosource
137 West 19th Street, 2nd Floor
New York, NY 10011
www.metrosource.com
info@metrosource.com

The Advocate
$19.95/year
6 Issues

The U.S. based national gay and lesbian news magazine.

Mail: The Advocate
c/o Here Media
10990 Wilshire Blvd, PH
Los Angeles, CA 90024

She
$30/year
12 Issues

Monthly publication for the women of the GLBT community.

Mail: She Magazine
6511 Nova Drive, #173
Davie, FL 33317

Passport
$19.99/yr
9 Issues

America's only Gay and Lesbian Travel Magazine. Passport Magazine

Mail: Passport Magazine
PO Box 16585
North Hollywood, CA 91615-6585

Gay Parent
$22/year
6 Issues

A Leader in Gay Parenting Resources since 1998. Family stories and resources.

Mail: Gay Parent magazine
PO Box 750852
Forest Hills, NY 11375-0852

Instinct
Instinct Magazine has a notice on their website that they have recently ceased printing.

www.instinctmagazine.com

Curve
$48/year

The best-selling magazine for Lesbian and Bisexual Women. Delivered Bi-Monthly.

Mail: Curve Magazine
PO Box 17138
North Hollywood, CA 91615

LGBTQ Slang Expressions

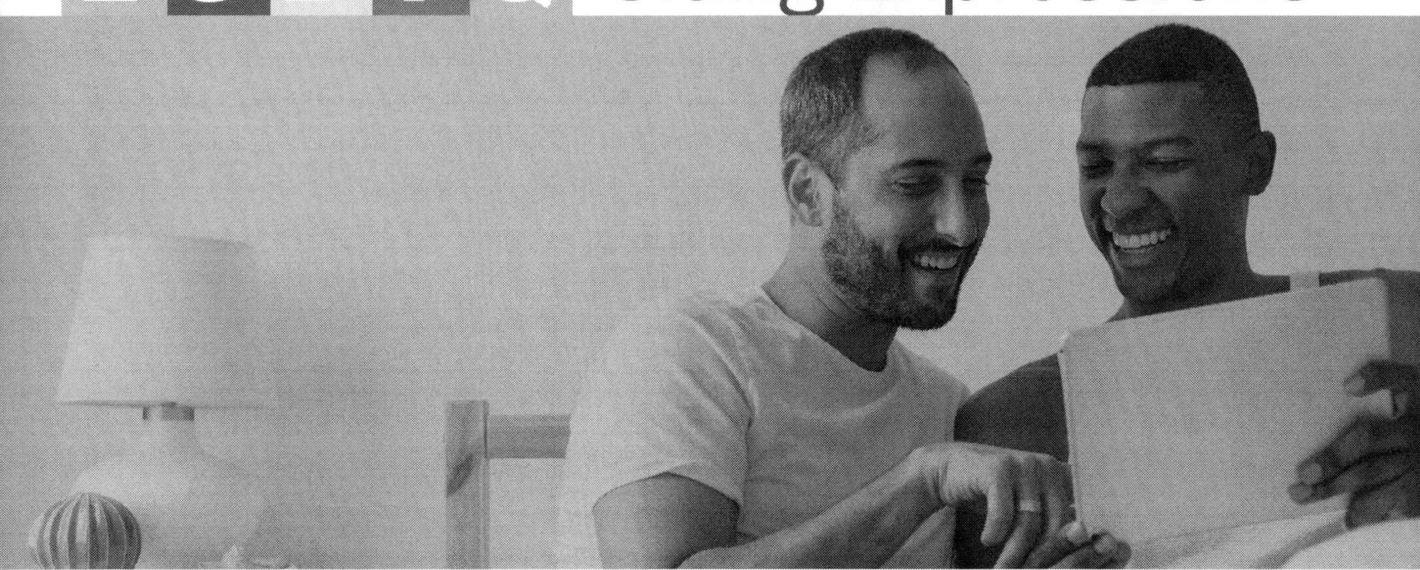

1. **Angel food (n.)** – homosexual male pilot currently serving in the Air Force.
2. **Basket shopping (v.)** – when cruising or checking someone out, British term refers to examining the object of your affection's private areas through their clothing.
3. **Beat (adj.)** – extremely wonderful or great, "fabulous." *Example*: "Did you see her at the club tonight? That look was beat."
4. **Bulldagger (n.)** – a masculine woman, closely related to "butch lesbian." Also see: "Diesel lesbian," term referring to queer women who look like truck drivers.
5. **Chapstick lesbian (n.)** – queer identified woman who is sporty and athletic. The word denotes that she's the not the type to wear makeup (ala a "lipstick lesbian") and goes for a more natural look.
6. **Chicken (n.)** – a young homosexual male seeking older men; see also: Chicken hawk, referring to an older gay male looking for younger partners.
7. **Cottaging (v.)** – British slang for hooking up in public restrooms.
8. **Donald Duck (n.)** – a homosexual male who is dishonorably discharged from the Navy for their sexuality; see also: "Dishonorable Discharge," or masturbating solo after trying to pick someone up and failing.
9. **Doris Day (n.)** – 90s South African slang for Gay Pride. *Example*: "The gays will march on Doris Day."
10. **Eyeball queen (n.)** – person who derives pleasure from watching others engage in intercourse.
11. **Fanny bellhop (n.)** – gay male employed by the hospitality industry, such as a concierge or a bellhop at a hotel.
12. **Fish and chips (n.)** – pejorative 90s British slang for the spouse and children of a married "heterosexual" lover.
13. **Full house (n.)** – term used to denote having more than one Sexually Transmitted Infection at once.
14. **Girl scout (n.)** – military man on leave, currently seeking sex.
15. **Grimm's fairy (n.)** – often used to describe an aging gay male, similar to "auntie"
16. **Hetty (n.)** – shortened version of the word "heterosexual," similar to "hetero" or "het."
17. **Horatian (n.)** – from the late 19th century, term used at Oxford amongst Lord Byron and his compatriots to refer to a bisexual person; see also: "Gillette blade," referring to a bisexual female.

18. **Hoyden (n.)** – slang from Britain in the 16th century to refer to an untameable, wild woman or a tomboy.
19. **Ice cream (n.)** – someone so sweet that you have the desire to lick them.
20. **In sisters (n.)** – two effeminate gay men who have an intimate but non-sexual relationship, usually best friends.
22. **Iron closet (n.)** – individual in deep denial about their own sexuality, one who might never come out.
24. **Lacy (adj.)** – used to refer to an very effeminate homosexual male.
25. **Lounge lizard (n.**) – someone who frequents bars, trying to pick up other peoples' mates.
26. **Lucky Pierre (n.)** – the middleman in an Eiffel Tower.
27. **Miss Congeniality (n.)** – extremely negative term referring to an unlikable or "bitchy" homosexual male.
28. **Mother Superior (n.)** – older and wiser gay male who has been around the block a few times; similar to "auntie," but more favorable.
29. **Nine-dollar bill (n.)** – extremely outward homosexual, one three-times more flaming than someone who is "queerer than a three-dollar bill."
30. **On the make (adj.)** – single person eligible for dating or casual sex. See also: "In circulation."
31. **Orphan (n.)** – someone who has recently been broken up with.
32. **Over the bridge to Pimpleton (n.)** – cumbersome term for homosexual sex.
33. **Passion fruit (n.)** – old Hollywood term referring to an extremely straight-acting and traditionally masculine male.
34. **Ring snatcher (n.)** – during sex, the person who performs the bottom role. Also see: "Pratt."
35. **Rumpy-Rumpy (n.)** – homosexual intercourse; see also: "Bumper to Bumper," referring to lesbian vaginal sex.
36. **Sappho Daddy-o (n.)** – gay male who enjoys the company of lesbians, similar to "Fruit Fly" for straight women.
37. **Saturday Night Lesbian (n.)** – term for lesbians who present themselves as heterosexual on their normal weekdays and may be in the closet to friends and co-workers.
38. **Slacks (n.)** – no-longer-in-use term to refer to a lesbian; see also: "Muffer" or "Kissing Fish."
39. **Smurf (n.)** – another term for twink, usually more pejorative, as it implies a "bitchy" demeanor.
40. **Tinkerbelle (n.)** – queer man who enjoys being urinated upon.
41. **Ursula (n.)** – queer woman who hangs out with "bears;" also called a "Goldilocks."
42. **Vampire (n.)** – gay men who go out looking for hookups late at night.
43. **Vegetarian (n.)** – homosexual male who will not give oral.
44. **Warm bruder (n.)** – German phrase used to identify a gay male; "warm" is German slang for "homosexual."
Note: If you live in Germany, you've definitely heard this one. English and American German-speakers have a bad habit of saying "Ich bin warm" on hot days, not knowing what they are actually saying.
45. **Wendy (n.)** – a Caucasian person.
46. **Wolf (n.)** – gay male who is neither a twink nor a bear, but falls somewhere in between the two poles; similar to a cub.
47. **Wrinkle room (n.)** – pejorative term for a bar whose clientele primarily consists of older gays.
48. **Yard boy (n.)** – gay male who enjoys having sex in public, particularly in outdoor venues.
49. **Yestergay (n.)** – former homosexual who now identifies as straight, also referred to as "ex-gays."
50. **Zipper club (n.)** – a sex party or orgy that takes place in a public area, like a bathhouse or a bar.

Reprinted from ThoughtCatalog.com

KNOW YOUR RIGHTS

Laws, Court Decisions and Advocacy Tips to Protect Transgender Prisoners

The ACLU put together a guide which identifies laws, court decisions, advocacy tips and other resouces that can be helpful for adult transgender prisoners. The full guide can be found on ACLU.org.

SEARCHES & PRIVACY

Know Your Rights: Laws, Court Decisions, and Advocacy Tips to Protect Transgender Prisoners

Transgender prisoners are frequently targeted for excessive, harassing, or public strip searches. Courts have recognized, however, that prisoners have a right to privacy during full body searches.[53] Therefore, staff must have a good reason to do strip searches and cannot use them to harass or intimidate prisoners.[54]

Courts have also held that staff must do strip searches professionally and respectfully even when those searches are legally justified. For example, a strip search conducted in full view of other prisoners and prison staff may violate a prisoner's privacy rights.[55] If there is no emergency, courts have also held that male staff should not strip-search women (including transgender women) and that female staff should not strip-search men.[56] Additionally, some jails have -policies stating that transgender prisoners are allowed to choose the gender of the staff who will search them.[57]

The PREA Standards also state that cross-gender strip and pat-down searches should not happen unless there is an emergency (or when performed by a medical practitioner)[58] and that staff cannot search or physically examine transgender prisoners solely to determine their genital status.[59] Prisons and jails must train staff to perform respectful searches of transgender prisoners.[60] Finally, the PREA Standards require that transgender prisoners be given access to private showers if requested.[61]

Transgender prisoners have a right to privacy and confidentiality regarding their transgender status or sexual orientation. Therefore, prison staff are not generally allowed to publicize or disclose the fact that a prisoner is transgender or gay.[62]

Here are some general tips regarding searches and privacy:

- If you are asked to strip down in front of other prisoners, politely ask to be moved to a separate area.
- If you cannot use a private shower, ask to be able to shower at a different time than other prisoners or in a private area (as the PREA Standards require).[63]
- If you do not want to be searched by a staff member of a particular sex, politely ask for a different staff member to search you. You should inform staff that you do not feel safe being searched by staff members of that sex. In some prisons or jails, you may also be able to get a general order or piece of paper (sometimes called a "chrono") that says you should only be searched by women (if you are a transgender woman).
- Ask for your facility's official policy regarding searches. If not provided, it may be available in the law library or can be requested through a public records request.

HOUSING & ADMINISTRATIVE SEGREGATION

Know Your Rights: Laws, Court Decisions, and Advocacy Tips to Protect Transgender Prisoners

> "Soltary confinement is...cruel and unusual punishment that benefits no one, and nothing about it rehabilitates anyone."[45]
>
> —Dee Dee Webber, transgender woman in NY men's prison on her four years in solitary confinement

Prisons and jails generally separate prisoners by sex, which they decide based on a prisoner's external genital characteristics or assigned sex at birth, regardless of their gender identity or presentation. However, the PREA Standards require prisons and jails to make individualized housing and program placements for all transgender and intersex prisoners, including when assigning them to male or female facilities.[46] Staff also have to consider housing and program assignments at least twice a year to review any threats to safety experienced by the prisoner and must take into account a prisoner's own view of his/her safety.[47] The PREA Standards also make clear that staff cannot make housing or program placements based solely on a prisoner's LGBT status.[48]

Many correctional facilities house transgender prisoners in long-term segregation, claiming they are doing so to protect the prisoners from violence. Prisoners who are placed in administrative segregation are often kept in their cells for nearly 24 hours a day and cannot participate in education, jobs, and other programming. Although staff have a lot of power over the decision to put prisoners in administrative segregation, there are some protections for prisoners. The PREA Standards do not allow staff to place you in administrative segregation against your will unless they have found—within the first 24 hours of involuntary segregation—that there is no other way to keep you safe.[49] The PREA Standards also state that you cannot be segregated against your will for more than 30 days, and that prisoners placed in protective custody must be given access to programs, privileges, education, and work opportunities to the extent possible.[50]

Whether you can be segregated for safety concerns depends on the exact purpose of segregation, the existence of alternatives, the harshness of the conditions, the duration of segregation, and whether the placement in segregation is regularly reviewed.[51] Prisons are not supposed to put LGBT prisoners in segregation for long periods of time without regularly and meaningfully considering other, less restrictive places where they can be housed.[52]

Here are a few things you can do if you do not feel safe in your housing situation:

- If you are placed in segregation and do not want to be there, file an appeal about your placement. You should also appeal anything that seems unfair about your placement, such as not being able to participate in a hearing, not being told why you were moved to segregation, not being able to participate in programming, or not being told when you can get out.
- If your placement is based on so-called safety concerns and you would feel safer in a women's facility (as a transgender woman), request such a transfer and file appeals if you do not get one.
- As always, appeal all denials as soon as you can and within the time frames required by the grievance process.

Reprinted from aclu.org
https://www.aclu.org/sites/default/files/assets/121414-aclu-prea-kyrs-1_copy.pdf

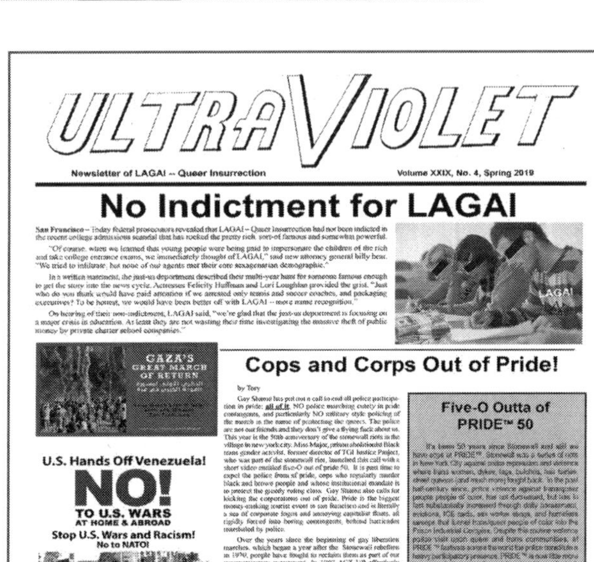

ULTRA VIOLET

Newsletter of LAGAI -- Queer Insurrection

Volume XXIX, No. 4, Spring 2019

No Indictment for LAGAI

San Francisco – Today federal prosecutors revealed that LAGAI – Queer Insurrection had not been indicted in the recent college admissions scandal that has rocked the pretty rich, sort-of famous and somewhat powerful.

"Of course, when we learned that young people were being paid to impersonate the children of the rich and take college entrance exams, we immediately thought of LAGAI," said new attorney general billy bear. "We tried to infiltrate, but none of our agents met their core sexagenarian demographic."

In a written statement, the just-us department described their multi-year hunt for someone famous enough to get the story into the news cycle. Actresses Felicity Huffman and Lori Loughlan provided the grist. "Just who do you think would have paid attention if we arrested only tennis and soccer coaches, and packaging executives? To be honest, we would have been better off with LAGAI -- more name recognition."

On hearing of their non-indictment, LAGAI said, "we're glad that the just-us department is focusing on a major crisis in education. At least they are not wasting their time investigating the massive theft of public money by private charter school companies."

GAZA'S GREAT MARCH OF RETURN

Cops and Corps Out of Pride!

by Tory

Five-O Outta of PRIDE™ 50

U.S. Hands Off Venezuela!

NO! TO U.S. WARS AT HOME & ABROAD

Stop U.S. Wars and Racism!

No to NATO!

Sunday, March 31, 2019

Oakland Federal Building

13th Street and Clay, Oakland, 1:00 PM

LAGAI
3543 18th Street #26
San Francisco, CA 94110
info@lagai.org

Ultra Violet is a newsletter which is FREE to prisoners.

LAGAI is a grassroots organization doing direct action and education for radical social change from a queer perspective which produces the bimonthly newspaper "ULTRAVIOLET."

Website:
http://www.lagai.org

Phone Number:
510-434-1304

Email Address:
info@lagia.org

Mailing Address:
3543 18th St #26
San Francisco, CA 94110
United States

So...Which one of you is the fork?

LGBTQ Magazines

Out Magazine

$19.95/year
10 Issues

A gay and lesbian perspective on style, entertainment, fashion, the arts, politics, and culture.

Mail: Out Magazine
c/o Here Media
10990 Wilshire Blvd, PH
Los Angeles, CA 90024

Metrosource

$19.95 6 Issues
$34.95/year

Choose between NY, LA or NAT Editions.

Mail: Metrosource
137 West 19th Street, 2nd Floor
New York, NY 10011
www.metrosource.com
info@metrosource.com

The Advocate

$19.95/year
6 Issues

The U.S. based national gay and lesbian news magazine.

Mail: The Advocate
c/o Here Media
10990 Wilshire Blvd, PH
Los Angeles, CA 90024

She

$30/year
12 Issues

Monthly publication for the women of the GLBT community.

Mail: She Magazine
6511 Nova Drive, #173
Davie, FL 33317

Passport

$19.99/yr
9 Issues

America's only Gay and Lesbian Travel Magazine. Passport Magazine

Mail: Passport Magazine
PO Box 16585
North Hollywood, CA 91615-6585

Gay Parent

$22/year
6 Issues

A Leader in Gay Parenting Resources since 1998. Family stories and resources.

Mail: Gay Parent magazine
PO Box 750852
Forest Hills, NY 11375-0852

Instinct

Instinct Magazine has a notice on their website that they have recently ceased printing.

www.instinctmagazine.com

Curve

$48/year

The best-selling magazine for Lesbian and Bisexual Women. Delivered Bi-Monthly.

Mail: Curve Magazine
PO Box 17138
North Hollywood, CA 91615

Newly Revised and Expanded!
350+ Pages!

REENTRY SOURCEBOOK, 3RD EDITION

An extraordinarily comprehensive and insightful resource, the Reentry Sourcebook is ideally suited to help those in need:

- Successfully reintegrate back into communities
- Obtain and retain legitimate and productive employment
- Advance educational goals
- Move from social dependence to self-sufficiency

With 14 hard-hitting chapters covering such topics as mental health, substance abuse, housing and homelessness, consumer education, financial assistance, education and employment, identification, family and relationships, and entrepreneurship, the Reentry Sourcebook is an ideal solution to the challenges faced by those reentering society.

$19.95 + $6.50 Shipping

LIFE SKILLS SERIES: BASIC SKILLS FOR LIFELONG SUCCESS

HOW TO MANAGE STRESS

SUCCESSFUL MONEY MANAGEMENT

Free Certificate Included!

$6.00 Each
+ **$2.50** Shipping

Transforming words into deeds, knowledge into action... that's what our interactive workbooks are all about.

Workbooks help apply key facts to your own situation, and are ideal for ongoing reference. They combine detailed, ready-to-use information with hands-on worksheets, quizzes, and other exercises to help you develop positive life-management skills.

DEMONSTRATE REHABILITATION

This series of interactive workbooks will provide you with the skills necessary to successfully reenter society. Each workbook includes a transcript and certificate upon completion. Ideal for demonstrating rehabilitation to a parole board, case manager, probation officer, judge, potential employer or even your family and friends.

- Anger Management and You
- Being a Successful Employee
- Better Self-Esteem
- How to Manage Stress
- Managing Anger and Conflict
- Managing Credit Wisely
- Managing Family Conflict
- Relaxation for Your Health
- You and Your Health
- Your Resume and You
- Community Reentry: Tools for Success
- Active Parenting During and After Prison
- Parenting and Anger Management
- Successful Money Management

STATE REENTRY RESOURCE DIRECTORIES

Order one of our comprehensive State Reentry Resource Directories today! Each resource directory contains detailed descriptions, contact information and much more for local state and national reentry service providers in your state. Independently verified by our team of professionals, each listing is accurate and up-to-date.

$12.00 + $1.50 Shipping

Subscribe to our Newsletter. TRULINCS, JPay and GTL Friendly!
newsletter@ReentryEssentials.org

Reentry Essentials, Inc.
98 4th Street, Suite 414, Brooklyn, NY 11231

Contact Us! **347.973.0004**

info@ReentryEssentials.org **www.ReentryEssentials.org**

Reentry Essentials is designated as a tax-exempt organization under section 501(c)(3) of the Internal Revenue Code and is a publically supported charity. All proceeds support projects and initiatives of Reentry Essentials, Inc.

HOW INSIDE-OUT BAR BEGAN

My name is Seth Sundberg, and I'm the CEO and Founder of The Inside-Out Bar.

From playing professional basketball in Europe and in the NBA with the LA Lakers, then working as a branch manager for a mortgage company and founder of an investment firm, my journey to Inside-Out Bars has been an interesting one.

In 2009 I was engaged, had a beautiful daughter, and was living in California. Then I made some terrible personal decisions. In the blink of an eye, I found myself incarcerated for tax fraud, and my world was turned completely upside down.

While incarcerated, I faced incredible feelings of worthlessness. The prison system is designed to make you feel like you screwed up. It can be tremendously difficult to hold on to anything positive you can offer other people. This message of worthlessness even carried through to the food that we ate.

I spent several years working in the kitchen while incarcerated – I remember handling a box of chicken marked 'not for human consumption,' and this sparked a realization for me: even our food was telling us that we had lost our basic human dignity.

It was this humbling, horrific realization that led me to realize that I had to take control of what I could and create some positive change.

Nutrition has always been my passion and a big part of my life. When you're making a living as a professional athlete, the food you eat and how you treat your body are pretty important.

After deciding to make a positive change through food, I got some guys together and we purchased the healthiest items we could from the commissary. These items were the ingredients for the earliest version of The Inside-Out Bar. At that point, I found my first market for my protein bars – behind the very bars that were housing me. I started selling bars to inmates as a healthier meal supplement for the usual food available to them in the chow hall.

Once released, I was reunited with my family and my daughter. I began digesting the process that I had just lived through, and started rebuilding life. I enrolled in school full time studying economics, took a job at a laundromat, and started looking for ways to give back.

Knowing that there was a market for Inside-Out Bars inside – and seeing the huge market for healthy, nutritious, probiotic filled nutrition bars across the country – I decided to bring my Inside-Out Bars to the outside world. I signed up for a program called Defy Ventures through a Craigslist Ad. Shortly thereafter, I found myself competing as an Entrepreneur In Training.

I'm very grateful – I've had tremendous support from Defy, other partners, mentors, and investors during this process. I'm confident that together we are building something truly special.

I want Inside-Out Bars to be a company that demonstrates redemption, second chances, hard work, good choices, and giving back. I want this to be a company that embraces basic human dignity.

And I want all of these values inside each of our wholesome and criminally delicious, functionally nutritious protein bars. I'm committed to making our bars without hydrogenated oils and with whole, gluten-free, non-GMO ingredients. The food in prison destroyed my healthy gut bacteria, and I'm on a mission to rebuild it and offer the millions of other Americans who have low levels of good microbiota a delicious option to do so as well.

I'm committed to making our bars in the USA with pride, hope, and determination to create pathways for second chances and redemption.

As we grow Inside-Out Bar, our goal is to hire the best and the brightest into our workforce, regardless of their criminal record, and use our influence to have open-hire policies permeate our entire supply chain and vendor relationships.

Thank you for joining us in this journey. I hope you enjoy your Inside-Out Bars, and I am so grateful to have you with us.

– Seth

Reprinted from https://insideoutbar.com

On Federal Student Financial Aid

REENTRY MYTH BUSTER!

A Product of the Federal Interagency Reentry Council

MYTH: A person with a criminal record is not eligible to receive federal student financial aid.

FACT: Individuals who are currently incarcerated in a federal, state, or local correctional institution have some limited eligibility for federal student aid. In general, restrictions on federal student aid eligibility are removed for formerly incarcerated individuals, including those on probation, on parole, or residing in a halfway house.

- Through the Department of Education's Second Chance Pell pilot program, an estimated 12,000 eligible incarcerated individuals can now receive Pell Grants to pursue postsecondary education.
- Although an individual incarcerated in a federal or state prison is eligible to receive a Federal Supplemental Educational Opportunity Grant (FSEOG) and Federal Work-Study (FWS), he or she is unlikely to receive either FSEOG or FWS due to the FSEOG award priority, which is that the grant must be given to those students who also will receive a Federal Pell Grant, and due to the logistical difficulties of performing an FWS job while incarcerated.
- Those incarcerated in correctional institutions other than federal or state institutions are eligible for a Federal Pell Grant, FSEOG, and FWS but not for federal student loans. Also, it is unlikely that incarcerated individuals in correctional institutions other than federal or state institutions will receive FSEOG or FWS due to school funding limitations and to the logistical difficulties of performing an FWS job while incarcerated.
- Incarcerated individuals may not receive federal consolidation loans.
- Upon release, most eligibility limitations (other than those noted below) will be removed. In addition, you may apply for aid in anticipation of being released so that your aid is processed in time for you to start school.
- You may be able to have your federal student loans deferred while you are incarcerated, but you must apply for a deferment and meet its eligibility requirements. To apply for deferment, contact the servicer of your loan(s). To find out what kind(s) of loan(s) you have, and/or to find contact information for your loan servicer, call 1-800-4-FED-AID (1-800-433-3243) or visit www.nslds.ed.gov.
- If your incarceration was for a drug-related offense or if you are subject to an involuntary civil commitment for a sexual offense, your eligibility may be limited as indicated in the two bullets below.
- A student convicted for the possession or sale of illegal drugs may have eligibility suspended if the offense occurred while the student was receiving federal student aid (grants, loans, or work-study). When you complete the *Free Application for Federal Student Aid* (FAFSA[SM]), you will be asked whether you had a drug conviction for an offense that occurred while you were receiving federal student aid. If the answer is yes, you will be provided a special worksheet to help you determine whether your conviction affects your eligibility for federal student aid. You may preview the worksheet in the FAFSA Information section at www.studentaid.ed.gov/pubs.
- If you have been convicted of a forcible or nonforcible sexual offense, and you are subject to an involuntary civil commitment upon completion of a period of incarceration for that offense, you are ineligible to receive a Federal Pell Grant.

For More Information:

Guide to Federal Student Aid for Students with Criminal Convictions:
https://studentaid.ed.gov/sa/eligibility/criminal-convictions

How Do Drug-Related Convictions Affect My Student Loan Eligibility?:
https://www.whitehouse.gov/sites/default/files/ondcp/recovery/fafsa.pdf

Federal Student Aid Eligibility for Students Confined in Adult Correctional or Juvenile Justice Facilities:
https://studentaid.ed.gov/sa/sites/default/files/aid-info-for-incarcerated-individuals.pdf

What is a REENTRY MYTH BUSTER? This Myth Buster is one in a series of fact sheets intended to clarify existing federal policies that affect formerly incarcerated individuals and their families. Each year, more than 600,000 individuals are released from state and federal prisons. Another 11.4 million cycle through local jails. When reentry fails, the social and economic costs are high -- more crime, more victims, more family distress, and more pressure on already-strained state and municipal budgets.

Because reentry intersects with health and housing, education and employment, family, faith, and community well-being, many federal agencies are focusing on initiatives for the reentry population. Under the auspices of the Cabinet-level interagency Reentry Council, federal agencies are working together to enhance community safety and well-being, assist those returning from prison and jail in becoming productive citizens, and save taxpayer dollars by lowering the direct and collateral costs of incarceration.

For more information about the Reentry Council, go to: https://csgjusticecenter.org/nrrc/projects/firc/

Reprinted from http://csgjusticecenter.org

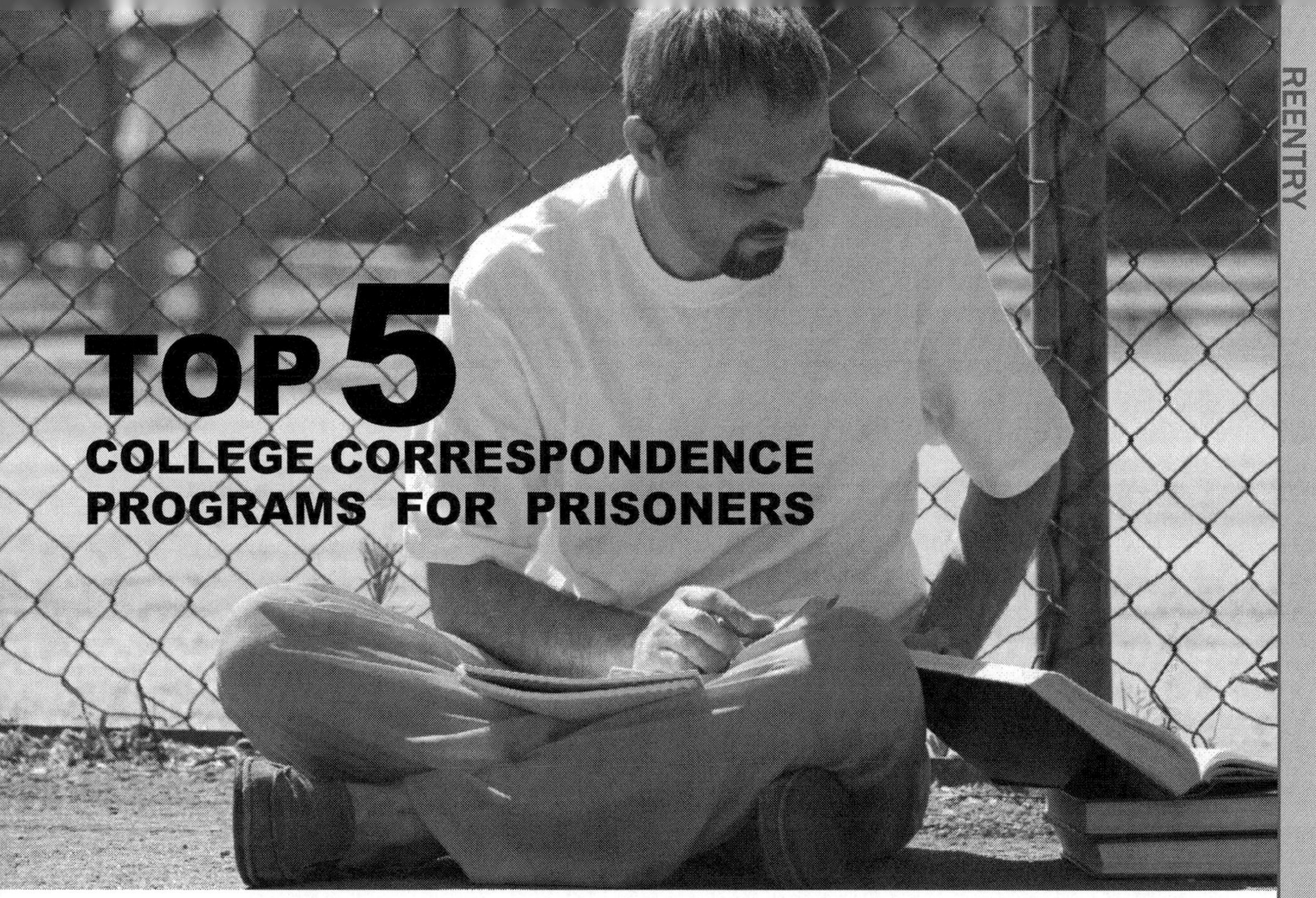

TOP 5 COLLEGE CORRESPONDENCE PROGRAMS FOR PRISONERS

In the realm of higher education, behind bars correspondence studies reign supreme. While traditional college students attend school in-person, and some even via internet technologies such as Blackboard, prisoners largely participate in higher education the very old fashioned way: through correspondence courses, where all communication between school and student is accomplished through the U.S. Mail.

A large problem for prisoners desiring to further their education is a lack of viable information on what correspondence programs are available to them. After all, American prisoners almost categorically lack access to the internet. As such, they often ask their loved ones and friends to search online for suitable educational offerings. That is where this article comes in.

Below you will find the top five college correspondence programs for prisoners. As a long-time incarcerated student and holder of a bachelor's degree (earned entirely through correspondence education while in prison) I have taken courses from many of these educational providers. These are the college correspondence course providers that I recommend for incarcerated students:

1. Adams State University

Adams State University's Prison College Program is my top pick by far. Regionally accredited by the North Central Association of Colleges and Schools, ASU offers a plethora of certificates, associates and bachelors degrees, all of which are available entirely through correspondence education. Each course costs around $500 and incarcerated students have 12 months to complete each. Currently certificates are available in paralegal studies, and associates and bachelors degrees are offered in business, business administration, English/liberal arts, history, interdisciplinary studies, political science, and sociology. [Full Disclosure: I received my bachelor's degree from ASU.]

2. Upper Iowa University

Upper Iowa University's Self-Paced Degree Program is a newer player in higher education for prisoners, but they make a bold statement. Regionally accredited by the North Central Association of Colleges and Schools, they offer a large number of certificates, associates, and bachelor degrees. Many of their courses can be completed entirely through the mail. The only drawback is that their courses run just shy of $1,000 each. Incarcerated students have six months to complete each course, but can request a free six-month extension if needed. Certificates are offered in management and psychology, while associates and bachelors degrees are available in business, liberal arts, psychology, business administration, management, public administration, and social sciences.

3. Colorado State University at Pueblo

Colorado State University's Distance Education Program is another great option for incarcerated students, though their degree offerings are somewhat limited. Regionally accredited by the North Central Association of Colleges and Schools, they offer bachelors degrees in social sciences and sociology. Each course runs around $500 and students have six months to complete each. While the offerings aren't as extensive as Adams State University's, Colorado State University is a very well-respected institution of higher education for prisoners.

4. Ohio University

Ohio University's Correctional Education Program is also a great provider of correspondence courses for prisoners. Back in the 1990s, Ohio University was the hottest thing in prison education, but in the past several years they have slimmed down their course offerings. Regionally accredited by the North Central Association of Colleges and Schools, Ohio University offers several associates and bachelors degrees, though more limited than ASU and CSU. Courses run around $1,000 each and students have eight months to complete each.

5. California Coast University

California Coast University is the wildcard of the batch. Not regionally accredited, which means that their courses might not transfer to other colleges and universities, CCU offers a surprisingly wide range of certificates, associates, bachelors, masters, and doctorate degrees through the mail. Courses run around $500 each. While any non-regionally accredited school that offers so many options immediately raises red flags in my mind, California Coast University does appear to be a legitimate university, albeit one with special distance learning focus.

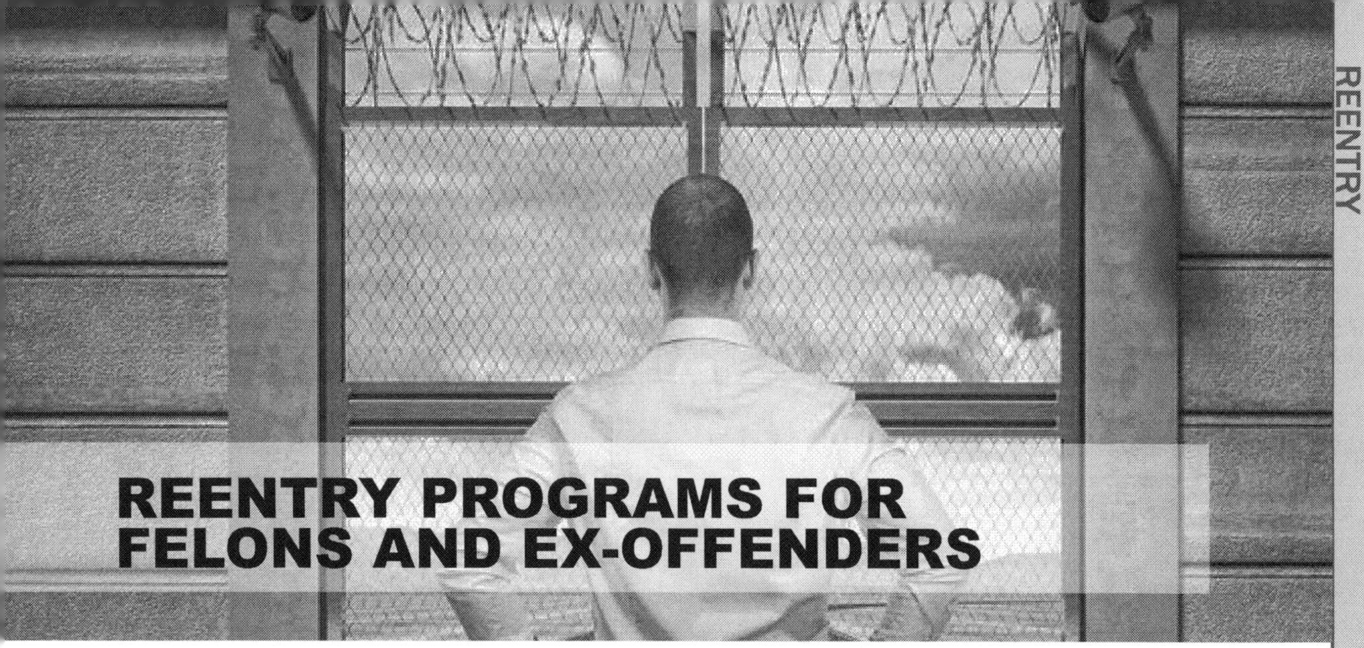

REENTRY PROGRAMS FOR FELONS AND EX-OFFENDERS

The process of leaving prison can be very difficult, especially for ex-offenders and felons that have had to serve lengthy sentences. Reentry programs for ex-offenders can be very helpful for those that need a helping hand once outside prison. Below we have a comprehensive, by state list of reentry programs for ex-offenders who need the help.

ALABAMA

The Lovelady Center
7916 2nd Avenue South
Birmingham, AL 35206
Phone: (205) 833-7410
A very powerful organization for women who are released from prison. Love Lady is a very reputable center that provides support and help for ex-offenders.

Renascence
215 Clayton Street
Montgomery, Alabama 36104
Phone: (334) 832-1402
Very nice "halfway house" that provides an excellent reentry program for ex-offenders.

ALASKA

Alaska Native Justice Center
3600 San Jeronimo Dr.
Anchorage, AK 99508
Phone: (907) 793-3550
Adult reentry services for ex-offenders.

Partners for Progress
419 Barrow Street
Anchorage, AK 99501
Phone: (907) 258-1192
They provide comprehensive reentry support including employment services, transitional housing assistance, counseling and mentoring.

ARIZONA

Old Pueblo Community Services
4501 E. 5th Street
Tuscon, AZ 85711
(520) 546-0122
Welcomes men, women and families reentering the community from incarceration, military service, hospitalization treatment - people with a strong desire to change the course of their lives. This is a wonderful organization for ex-offenders.

CASS
230 S. 12th Avenue
Phoenix, AZ 85007
Phone: (602) 256-6945, x1100
Emergency shelter and job placement services.

ARKANSAS

Arkansas Community Correction
Two Union National Plaza
105 W. Capitol Avenue
Little Rock, AR 72201
Offers a wide variety of help and programs for those reentering society.

Our House
Box 34155
Little Rock, AR 72203
Phone: (501) 374-7383
Three housing programs that are designed to encourage sustainability. All residents must be willing and able to find and maintain a full time job.

CALIFORNIA

A Brighter Day
264 S. La Cienega Blvd Suite 151 Beverly Hills, CA 90211
Free housing, new start program.

Clean 360
4107 Broadway
Oakland, CA 94611
Phone: (510) 451-0570
Help with employment and employment skills.

COLORADO

Colorado Gives
Community First Foundation
5855 Wadsworth Bypass, Unit A
Avada, CO 80003
Reentry help and anti-recidivism programs.

FOCUS Reentry

4705 Baseline Rd.
Boulder, CO 80303
Mentoring program whose mission is to reduce recidivism and enhance community safety.

CONNECTICUT
EMERGE Connecticut
830 Grand Avenue
New Haven, CATA 06511
Phone: (203-562-0171
Transitional Workforce Development Program with the goal of providing recently released ex-offenders in the New Haven area with the opportunity to end the pattern of recidivism.

Family Reentry
75 Washington Avenue
Bridgeport, CT 06604
Phone: (203) 576-6924
Appears to be one of the best reentry organizations in Connecticut.

DELAWARE
VOA: Delaware Valley
531 Market Street
Camden, NJ 08102
Phone: (856) 854-4660
Volunteers of America Delaware Valley's Re-Entry Services Division has a proven record of commitment, experience, versaitilty and competence in operating community reintegration programs.

FLORIDA
Project 180
Box 25684
Sarasota, FL 34277-2684
(941) 677-2281
Reentry help and support

Reentry Alliance Pensacola, Inc.
2615 West DeSoto Street
Pensacola, FL 32505
Services provided for Reentry, includes basic needs.

GEORGIA
NewLife-Second Chace Outreach
4519 Woodruff Rd. Unit 4 #344
c/o The Mail Room
Columbus, GA 31904
Local jobs and job related services such as training and development.

HAWAII
Hope Services Reentry Services
296 Kilauea Avenue
Hilo, HI 96720
Phone: (808) 935-3050
Helps ex-offenders and felons with housing, jobs and job skills.

IDAHO
Wellbriety for Prisons
912 12 Ave S. Suite 204
Nampa, ID 83686
(208) 461-3764
Reentry Information

ILLINOIS
Safer Foundation
571 W. Jackson Blvd.
Chicago, IL 60661
Help with GED exams, housing, jobs and career skills for ex-offenders.
Re-Entry Employment Service
33 South State Street
Chicago, IL 60603

INDIANA
New Leaf
1010 S. Walnut St.
Bloomington, IN 47401
Phone: (812) 355-6842
Programs for people both during and after incarceration that will reduce recidivism and build their capabilities and life skills.

Brothers Keeper
P.O. Box 6164
Evansville, IN 47719
Addressing the needs of men as they return from prison to society with job search/employment, self help skills, conseling, transportation and healthcare.

IOWA
Reentry Aftercare
Altoona, IA 50009
Phone: (515) 230-8815
Educational and career support

Hope Ministries - Door of Faith
6701 SW 9th
Des Moines, IA 50315
Phone: (515) 974-0545
Recovery program called Journey of Hope.

KANSAS
Oxford House for men
Brian Holms
1739 N. Harvard
Wichita, KS 67208
Great reentry program with housing.

Oxford House for Women
Stephanie King
704 S. Barlow Street
Wichita, KS 67207

KENTUCKY
Kentucky Reentry
Phone: (502) 782-9547
Helping returning citizens and justice-involved individuals on their journey to reentry.

Goodwill Industries of Kentucky
909 E. Broadway
Louisville, KY 40204
Phone: (502) 585-5221
Program to help individuals by providing classes and job leads while helping maintain motivation during job search.

LOUISIANA
Reentry Solutions for Louisiana
1617 Branch St. Suite 500
Alexandria, LA 71301
318-443-0189
Employment and housing help.

Batron Rouge DRC
2751 Woodale Blvd.
Baton Rouge, LA 70805
Phone: (225) 218-4636
Dedicated reentry facilities with full service programs.

MAINE
Restorative Justice
Box 141
Belfast, ME 04915
Phone: (207) 338-2742
This reentry program offers a wide variety of services and help.

MASSACHUSETTS
Dismas House
Box 30125
Worcester, MA 01603
A supportive community that provides transitional housing and services to former prisoners.

MICHIGAN
Michigan Prisoner Reentry Program
1333 Brewery Park Blvd #300
Detroit, MI 48207
Phone: (517) 372-3653
Helping prisoners return to the

community prepared for success.

Michigan Works
2500 Kerry Street, Ste. 210
Lansing, MI 48912
Associate established in 1987 to support Michigan's workforce development.

MINNESOTA

Second Chance Ranch Group Home
25167 Highway 248
Minnesota City, MN 55959
Phone: (507) 450-1045

Freedom Works
3559 Penn Ave. N
Minneapolis, MN 55412
Phone: (612) 522-9007
A Christian community providing housing and a pathway to meaningful employment.

MISSISSIPPI

New Way Mississippi
916 Inge St, Jackson, MS 39203
Phone: (601) 500-5670
Transitional and permanent housing acquisition; ongoing recover supportive services; trasitional employment and economic develeopment opportunities.

Crossroads Outreach Ministries
P.O. Box 3075
Ridgeland, MS 39158
Phone: (601) 855-2332
Reentry program for Women.

MISSOURI

Power House
263 W. Morgan
Marshall, MO 65340
Phone: (660) 886-8860
Providing housing, transportation and substance abuse recovery for offenders being released from prison.

Start Here
Box 220721
St. Louis, MO 63122
Phone: (314) 726-2092
An overall resource directory for reentry.

MONTANA

Great Falls Rescue Mission
408 2nd Ave South
Great Falls, MT 59405
(406) 761-2653
Recovery programs, shelters for both men and women, meals, medical help and more within a Christian environment.

NEBRASKA

Released and Restored
Box 22962
Lincoln, NB 68542
Phone: (402) 806-0565
Provides inmates and ex-offenders in Nebraska with the tools and support systems needed for learning how live moral, ethical and legal lives in our communities.

Reentry Alliance of Nebraska
http://re-entrynebraska.org
Helping men and women make successful transitions back into the community by providing job training, life skills, transitional living, clothing and more. Unfortunately the only contact information is a contact form on their website.

NEVADA

Hope for Prisoners
3430 E Flamingo Rd, Ste 350 Las Vegas, NV 89121
(702) 586-1371
Helping men, women and young adults reenter society successfully.

Ridge House
900 West 1st Street Suite 200
Reno, NV 89503
Phone: (775) 322-8941
Counseling, job training, job placement, self help support groups, mentoring services and more.

NEW HAMPSHIRE

Alternative Solutions Associates, Inc.
Phone: (413) 626-7597
E-mail: Email: kevin@alternativesolutionsassociates.com
Provides a range of services including reentry program design, linkage to employment training and job development, casework and community linkage staff training and more.

NEW JERSEY

Reentry Coalition of NJ
986 Broad St.
Trenton, NJ 08611
Phone: (609) 706-2684
An organization committed to offender rehabilitation.

NJ Reentry Corporation
398 Martin Luther King Jr. Drive
Jersey City, NJ 0730
Phone: (551.) 222-4323
Reentry information for people living in or around Newark, NJ

NEW MEXICO

A Peaceful Habitation
P.O. Box 53516
Albuquerque, NM 87153
Phone: (505) 440-5937
A Christian ministry that provides transitional housing, support and services to women reintegrating into society.

NEW YORK

Rising Hope, Inc.
Box 906
Cronton Falls, NY 10519
Phone: (914) 276-7848
Rising Hope, Inc. provides one year of college-level courses to people incarcerated in New York state prisons.

Second Chance Reenty
244 Fifth Ave., 2nd Fl.
New York, NY 10001
Phone: (212) 726-2637
Our mission is to advocate for humane treatment and care to the proportionate segment of our society disabled and disenfranchised.

NORTH CAROLINA

CSI Resource Center Without Walls
Box 61114
Raleigh, NC 27661
Phone: (919) 715-0111, Ext. 239
Work with men and women in prison, former prisoners, people in transition, and their families by providing small group trainings and individual mentoring in general life skills, leadership, entrepreneurship, financial literacy, and areas related to transitioning back into family and community life.

Going Home Initiative
Dept. of Correction–Research & Planning, 2020 Yonkers Rd., 4221 MSC, Raleigh, NC 27699
Phone: (919) 716- 3089
Creating a systemic pre-release, community transition and reentry infrastructure. Creating the

seamless system is a theme of the Going Home Initiative.

NORTH DAKOTA

Bismarck Transition Center
2001 Lee Ave.
Bismarck, ND 58504
Phone: (701) 222-3440, Ext. 101
A comprehensive community-based correctional program designed to help eligible, non-violent offenders transition back into the community.Provides essentials such as employment and housing once they are released into society.

Northlands Rescue Mission
420 Division Ave.
Grand Forks, North Dakota 58201
Phone: (701) 772-6600
A place of rescue, relief and restoration for all– no matter their needs or challenges.

OHIO

Ohio Ex-Offender Reentry Coalition
OH Dept of Rehabilitation and Correction-Court and Community
770 W. Broad St
Columbus, OH 43222
Phone: (614) 752-0627
To ensure successful offender reentry, reduce recidivism and enhance public safety.

New Home Islamic Re-Entry Society
2302 Putnam Ave.
Toledo, OH 43620
Phone: (419) 283-2290
Providing a faith based home for men who are homeless and/or who have recently been released from prison.

OKLAHOMA

The Oklahoma Partnership for Successful Reentry
Box 60433
Oklahoma City, OK 73146
Phone: (405) 615-6648
A statewide coalition of organizations working in the field of reentry, which is helping ex-felons reintegrate into society, especially after prison, but also including those reentering from jail, probation, or moving here from out-of-state.

Turning Point
Community Action Agency of Oklahoma City,
319 SW 25th Street
Oklahoma City, OK 73109
Phone: (405) 232-0199
Job Readiness Resume preparation, interview preparedness and clothing & transportation allowance.

ORGEGON

ROAR (Reentry Organizations and Resources) Alliance
Mercy Corps Northwest
Skidmore Fountain Bldng.,43 SW Naito Pkwy.,
Portland, OR 97204
Phone: (503) 896-5073
A collaboration of over 40 non-profit, faith-based and government agencies working to promote successful reentry from incarceration to the community.

Better People
4310 NE Martin Luther King Jr. Blvd.,
Portland, OR 97211
Phone: (503) 281-2663
An established employment and counseling program solely dedicated to helping individuals who have legal histories find, keep and excel in well paying jobs with fair, decent employers.

PENNSYLVANIA

Safe Haven Re-Entry Program (SHaRP)
P.O. Box 3477
Philadelphia, PA 19122
PHONE: (215) 763-3079
A faith-based ministry committed to reaching-out and empowering incarcerated men, women and their family members through re-entry & life action skills to help reduce the recidivism pattern.

Stephen's Place, Inc.
729 Ridge St.
Bethlehem, PA 18015
Phone: (610) 861-7677
Halfway House Halfway house for non-violent adult males with a history of substance abuse who are coming out of prison and need a safe environment where they can re-integrate into society.

SOUTH CAROLINA

South Carolina STRONG
2510 N. Hobson Ave.
North Charleston, SC 29405
Phone: (843) 554-5179
To rehabilitate criminals and substance abusers and move people into economic self-sufficiency.

New Life Deliverance Worship Center
Prison Ministry
361 Whitney Rd.
Spartanburg, SC 29303
Phone: (864) 285-1745
Helps men and women getting out of prison with clothing, food, job referrals and transitional housing.

SOUTH DAKOTA

Center of Hope
225 E 11th St., Ste. 101
Sioux Falls, SD 57104
Phone: (605) 334-9789
Providing for those who struggle including family concerns, relationship strains, addictions, financial concerns, joblessness, incarceration, hospitalization, spirituality questions, or feelings of hopelessness.

TENNESSEE

Dismas House-Nashville
1513 16th Ave., S.
Nashville, TN 37212
Phone: (615) 297-4511
A housing and intensive case management program that serves men who have recently been released.

Men-Of-Valor Aftercare & Re-Entry
1410 Donelson Pke., Ste. B-1
Nashville, TN 37217
Phone: (615) 399-9111
Prisoners participating in Men of Valor are released into a yearlong Aftercare/ Re-Entry program aimed at giving them the support, skills and accountability they need to succeed in the community.

TEXAS

SEARCH Homeless Services
2505 Fanin St.
Houston, TX 77002
Phone: (713) 739-7752
To engage, stabilize, educate, employ and house individuals and families who are homeless.

Texas Offenders Reentry Initiative
Box 4386
Dallas, TX 75208
Phone: (214) 941-1325, Ext. 300
Committed to helping and improving the

lives of people who've made mistakes in their pasts which make their acceptance back into society a very difficult task. With T.O.R.I. you will find people who are ready to assist ex-offenders in making better decisions in order to avoid repeating an often dangerous and destructive life-cycle.

UTAH
MentorWorks
Foundation for Family Life
1733 W. 12600 St., S., Ste. 230 Riverton, UT 84065
Phone: (801) 679-3921
The MentorWorks program has been developed to serve the needs of men and women as they are released from county or state correctional facilities and are now transitioning back into society.

VERMONT
Dismas of House Vermont
103 E. Allen St.
Winooski, VT 05404
Phone: (603) 795-2770
A supportive community for former prisoners transitioning from incarceration and university/college students who are also in transition with their lives. Living in community accomplishes the Dismas mission of reconciliation. Community is fundamentally about relationship and it is precisely the relationship between the offender and their community that is broken, first by the crime committed and subsequently by the resulting incarceration. In reconciliation, wholeness is restored to the former prisoner and to society.

Lamoille Restorative Center
Reentry Program
Box 148
Hyde Park, VT 05655
Phone: (802) 888-0657
Males and females returning to the community from incarceration receive support services from a program coordinator and a team of volunteers. Offenders work with coordinators to develop a plan to reintegrate back into their community successfully.

VIRGINA
Step Up, Inc.
5900 East Va. Beach Blvd., Ste. 102
Norfolk, VA 23502
Phone: (757) 588-3151
The purpose of STEP UP, Inc. is to help re-integrate offenders into society by providing them the knowledge, skills and training they will need in order to make a successful transition from a correctional facility to the rest of their lives.

Total Action for Progress (TAP)
T302 2nd St., S.W.
Roanoke, VA 24011
(540) 283-4903
Helps individuals and families achieve economic and personal independence through education, employment, affordable housing, and safe and healthy environments.

WASHINGTON
The STAR Project
321 Wellington Ave.
Walla Walla, WA, 99362
(509) 525-3612
STAR's mission is: to provide persons being released from incarceration with the essential tools to successfully re-integrate into the community as productive, contributing members of society.

Conviction Careers
Box 432
Lynnwood, WA 98046
Phone: (866) 436-1960
To fill a gap between employers and job seekers with criminal backgrounds. We know from Department of Corrections studies that our program cuts the recidivism rate by 50%.

WEST VIRGINIA
Covenant House
600 Shrewbury St.
Charleston, WV 25301
Phone: (304) 344-8053
To help people with the fewest resources meet their basic needs: food, clothing, and shelter. After 30 years, our core mission remains the same.

WISCONSIN
Project 180
Phone: (414) 270-2957
728 N. James Lovell St.
Milwaukee, WI 53233
A Center for Self-Sufficiency (CFSS) program designed to improve employment outcomes for those who have been incarcerated and to lower their likelihood of re-incarceration. Project 180 participants are offered individualized services to help them in a successful return home to Milwaukee.

Fair Shake
Box 63
Westby, WI 54667
Phone: (608) 634-6363
Dedicated to reducing the recidivism rate through personal and community focused ownership and engagement opportunities for inmates and former felons in connection with families, employers, property managers, corrections and communities.

WYOMING
Second Chance Ministries
201 W. Lakeway Rd.
Gillette, WY 82718
Phone: (307) 682-3148
To help men and women released from incarceration into Campbell County by providing re-entry assistance, during the first 4 months after release, to our clients and to help rebuild their lives through a transformation of hearts and minds through Jesus Christ, as demonstrated by our actions and kindness.

Transitional Housing & Self-Sufficiency Program CALC
211 W. 19th St.
Cheyenne, WY 82001
Phone: (307) 635-9291
Offers a variety of tools to help families and individuals recover from economic, medical and other setbacks. Provides transitional housing to homeless individuals and families, as well as, affordable housing to low-to-moderate income families.

COMMON JOBS FOR NEWLY RELEASED

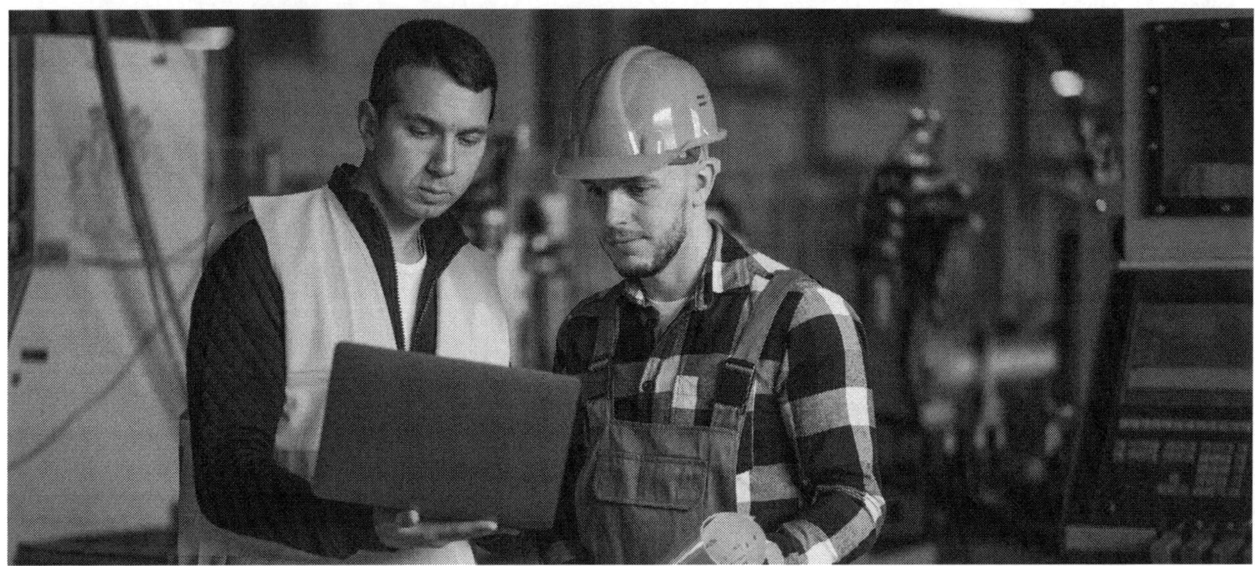

Finding a job is an important part of transition after incarceration. Ideally, you will find a job that matches your skills and interests. The reality is that the first jobs many newly released ex-offenders find do not match their desired careers.

Transition Jobs

Think of your first few jobs after release as "transition jobs" that help you become financially stable and move up into a career that you enjoy.

These jobs might have low pay or not relate to your long-term career goals. That's OK.

In addition to a paycheck, there are benefits to working in a transition job:

- A chance to prove you are dependable and self-reliant
- An employment history that can help you find better jobs later
- Time to learn about different ways of thinking and doing things
- A feeling of pride and accomplishment
- Employment could be a condition of your supervised prison release, so taking any job is better than not working. This does not mean that you have to keep working in a job you don't like.

Starting a Career

When you are ready to Explore Careers, and find work that fits you better, use the chart on the next page to think about how a transition job or other entry-level position can lead to a higher-paying and long-term career.

	Entry Level	1st Step Ahead	Next Step Ahead
Restaurant & Food Service	Food Preparation Worker	Short Order Cook	Chef and Head Cook
Warehouse Operations	Freight and Stock Laborer	Transportation Attendant	Transportation, Storage, and Distribution Manager
Information Support	Customer Service Representative	Computer User Support Specialist	Network and Computer Systems Administrator
Construction	Construction Laborer	Roofer	Carpenter
Mobile Maintenance	Tire Repairer and Changer	Automotive Body Repairer	Automotive Service Technician and Mechanic
Production	Team Assembler	Computer-Controlled Machine Tool Operator	Industrial Production Manager

If you see a position that interests you, you can find a link at careerwise.minnstate.edu/offenders/find-job/common-jobs.html to read more. Be sure you read about that job's Work Activities. That section describes the "essential functions" of the job. To be qualified for that job, you must be able to perform the essential functions.

People with disabilities may be qualified for a job if you can do the essential functions with "reasonable accommodations," like using special software, equipment, or a different workspace. An employer is required to provide reasonable accommodations if you disclose or tell them about your disability.

A job coach can help a person with disabilities and other job seekers to understand the essential functions and the reasonable accommodations for many jobs.

The careers listed on this page are just a few of your options. If you work hard, make good choices, build your network and get additional training, you will have even more options.

Before you apply for these or other positions, check with your Supervised Release Officer or Parole Officer (PO) to find out if there are any restrictions to the type of work you can do or where you can work.

Also, talk to a job coach to help you make a career plan. Then let your PO know your goals.

Next Steps:

- Know how to job search after release.
- Understand how to keep your job and succeed at work.
- Revisit your career goals and plan your next move.

Reprinted from careerwise.minnstate.edu/offenders/find-job/common-jobs.html

By Anthony Tinsman

RECIDIVISM ZERO

"Let me be very objective for y'all on the way out there: Prepare for your reentry! Don't get out THEN try to figure it out." – Branon Carter, released 04/14/2019

Thirty miles south you'll find gators, pelicans, and offshore oil rigs, but inside the Bayou of Concrete different wildlife roams under constant surveillance. It was about to be home to my next franchise. The pitch for the Reentry Resource Center had gone well. I delivered the entire thing – standing – in a 15-minute presentation, including graphs and FAQ's. RRCs have helped a lot of inmates and made a few guards look good. The counselor was still skeptical, though, until I showed him my centerpiece, a letter of referral signed by a staff member.

For the finale' I displayed my book, *Life With A Record*. It weighs about 10 pounds. "It's got 98% of what I use. Addresses, directions, all that. We'll just need a few forms printed off the internet to help specific cases." For the hundredth time I eyeballed the Marine's emblem (an eagle clutching an anchor and trident) painted on the Counselor's office wall. It suggested we shared some values. His meshed fingers rested atop his stomach "Okay. You've given me enough to think about."

The first day I boldly planted a chair in the staff corridor, put up a sign, and 14 inmates lined up to speak with me. Jose needed a copy of his high school diploma from Puerto Rico so he could enroll in Beaumont's college-partnership with Lamar university. Balancing LWAR in my lap, I copied down the address on page 269. Then someone stepped up with a driver's license suspension and surcharges. On it went for an hour.

Staff bitched about the commotion in their area. The Marine conceded, "You need your own office." It was a good sign for common sense. When a small operation is run right, it can impact a lot of lives. I'd developed institutional versions called Reentry Opportunity Centers and the success stories were measured in numbers with commas. We cleared out a broom closet, added a seat and desk, and the head orderly stenciled 'RRC' on the wall, my office hours below it.

On a roll, the Marine made copies of the documents I had (annual credit report, child support change order, many others). "Essential step," I assured. "Once inmates get results from the RRC we'll see a spike in participation. After that it'll run steady, couple people a day." We installed a dangling document holder on the wall. I was in my element. It felt right. A week into the job he asked, "Can you make a list of what else you need?" The full website addresses and document names took about 5 minutes to copy down from LWAR.

Form DOJ-361, Certificate of Identity (bop.gov/foia/DOJ361.pdf)

FASFA student aid School Code Book

Indigency/Incentive Application for Reduction of Surcharges

and a dozen other inmates were waiting for....

Upon review he said "I'll do a few each week. How's the inmate response to this?" I showed him the log sheets. Two dozen signatures, dates, and comments scarred the paper. Each entry had notes about the topic and nature of assistance. It all matched the documents I'd requested.

Everyone saw that all I carried to work was a big blue book (LWAR) and log sheets. "What's that book?" many asked. After they'd flipped through it, seeing it's a warehouse of information, most asked "Where can I get one?" "It's on Amazon." I'd say, thumb through chapters, then start solving their reentry crisis.

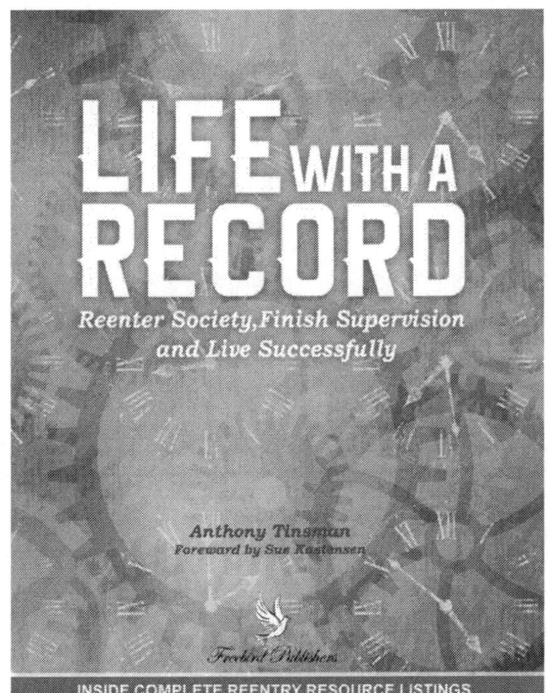

Week by week the work fell into a rhythm. A to-do list was created, letters and resumes needed drafting, it was time to prod an application for temporary housing through approval. The one-man operation forced me to marshal years of expertise. To-do list scratch outs grew more sophisticated. (X) Draft requests for apprenticeship pre-screening. (X) Connect entrepreneur with Richard Harris - SCORE counselor in Houston. (X) Critique Mr. Green's GED essay.

"Tinsman come here, something for you in my office," the Marine announced. He'd printed hundreds of pages of USPS weight and postage charts. Instead of delivering what we'd agreed on, he tasked me with a pile of unfolded red-white-and-blue Priority Mailboxes. "Manage this for me." It felt like something was off. Maybe I expected too much. The nature of favors often comes at the expense of setting boundaries. But I agreed to take them off his hands – from a heap on the table – quid pro quo. "Patience." I told myself.

"These people (staff) ain't about their job," Deshawne said. He pointed towards the case manager's door, blinds down, a sign announced, "Do Not Disturb." He continued, "I showed her my parole paperwork from state (prison) but she won't update my status, and that's keeping me from going to a halfway house." I leaned back in my dumpster-salvaged chair. "Take your documents and explain everything to the unit manager, then the CMC." I framed exactly what the process was, step-by-step. Deshawne was so excited he almost left without signing the log. "What do I put?" he asked, pen hovering over the 'Purpose of Visit' section. To provide us both some deniability I suggested, "How about 'General Information'?"

Jailers' keys rattled one morning, as the Marine came down the long isle banked by rows of barracks style cubicles. He stopped at mine. "The Warden is inspecting, go stand in your office. Look sharp." I still had faith that if we made each other look good we could achieve our separate goals. I put the mail-room half of my office on display, then jammed a piece of wood behind the document holder to keep the reentry half straight. The warden, captain, lieutenant, and some suits peered in, made blank faces. "Warden." I nodded, at attention. They went on.

When I followed up about the documents for the RRC the Marine deflected, "I'll do that next week." But next week never seemed to come. Three months passed without a single one. He looked at me, "Make a report. Something I can show the boss. Maybe after that we could do a small class in the unit?"

My irritation made for short language. "There's almost 100 inmates on these log sheets." I flipped pages.

He shook his head. "Make it more detailed."

When reciprocation fails, negotiation turns into ransom. Expected to load toilet paper boxes on Tuesdays and pass out Priority Mailboxes during office hours, it was clear that my role was unclear to the Marine. I wrestled with what to do about my job without an easy solution.

Having taken a similar franchise to a regional level, I'd been exploited by staff before. It follows a pattern. Staff, aware of the political perks or promotion, prioritize whatever sped that along, while never committing to the actual operation. I yearned for simplicity. My RRC's mission was to reduce recidivism through technical assistance. That's why I'd written *Life With A Record*. I damn sure wasn't going to kiss ass now. If that pissed-off the Marine, then I'd still help as many inmates as circumstance allowed.

I introduced Mr. Benedez to a new service called Recidivism Zero. "Their slogan is 'one request – one email – one line,' done right you get an address and phone number like the yellow pages, in 24 hours." It was obvious he was overwhelmed, but I continued. "The first line must be FIND, JOBS, GET, or HELP (all caps), then your request, followed by IN (all caps) and the city, and state or zip code."

Like this:

FIND attorney X SMITH IN Harris, TX

Not like this:

Please help me find the address for attorney X Smith in Harris, TX.

It wasn't breaking through. "You want me to type it for you?" I offered. He chuckled in relief, "Yeah. Thank you." RZero was handy for locating addresses not in *Life With a Record*, mostly county and federal courthouses. When combined, that helped Mr. Benedez. He filed a "180-day Writ" that got his charges dismissed at the Jim Hogg Municipal Court, lifting the warrant for driving without insurance, which removed the detainer that was blocking him from going to a halfway house. It would also help get his license back.

Five months in, and the clock was still ticking. It struck high noon during 'Team,' a ritual twice a year where inmates stand in line all day to see their case manager. It was a raggedy bunch, men in flip flops and torn shorts – none expected to accomplish anything, it was just a mandatory conduct review: sign some papers, maybe get a question answered. I walked along the line, LWAR and clipboard in hand, spotting RRC clientele.

"Any progress on your Child Support change order?" Me and a young Latino man spoke about it. "Have staff print out your inmate account as well to speed up the process?"

I hit the line passing them information.

"You still need the middle initials fixed on your GED? Have staff call this number, here."

Exhaustion melted from widening eyes as I hailed every other man.

Deshawne popped in from the barracks and horse played with one of his "homeys." I approached, "Did your state parole issue get settled?" I asked. He said it had, but they were only putting him in for 3 months in the halfway house. It was just too late to push for the full 6. "Well, it's 90 days out of the Bayou!" "Yeah. I'll take whatever they give me," he said. I stayed around to ask how 'Team' went. Obscenities and outrage caved in as they all reported, "He said bring it to him next week." I nodded, hefted LWAR, "Follow up. Stay on them."

High noon drug on to 3:45, and staff were getting ready to leave for the day. I waited in the corridor, back to the wall, until the Marine left his office. Silence is the grandest machismo. A grunt escaped him as soon as he noticed me. "I know you're busy," I said. "And that a lot of these requests aren't what you're used to, but these are real-world solutions in line with the objectives of Bureau of Prisons policy towards reentry." His attempts at a corkscrew comeback full of distractions and anomalies went in one ear and out the other. He stopped talking, saw it wasn't getting him anywhere and said, "I'm working on it."

This is how 8 months of patience ends: Summoned by the Marine, he escorted us on a raid of another unit's supply closet. We stole jugs of wax. There and back in the blistering sub-tropic heat of summer he asked the head orderly, "Did we get enough? Do you need more?" In a good mood he smiled in my direction, "How's that report coming?" All I could think about was that in no way were shiny floors for the Warden's next visit more important than keeping an agreement. "I'm working on it," I said.

The Report

Record of Assistance – Reentry Resource Center UA/UB 2/13/18 to 10/2/18 – Credit Report 19, VA 9, Birth Certificate 8, Driver's License 16, Child Support 15, Education 16, Job Training 10, Resume 3, Detainer/Warrant 7, Immigration 7, Health/Disability 5, Halfway House 8, General Info 32, TWIC 2

Total 152 – This serves as notice of permanent vacation.

One month later, it was a 10-minute movement. The guard unlocked the door, threw up her hands and yelled, "Go on! Get out!" Inmates poured through to their destinations. As part of the crowd I entered the winding corridor that led to the exit. I had information to deliver, another address from LWAR, the Good Will Reentry Program might be able to help find this guy a car. That's when the door to the left opened and the Marine merged into roaring traffic. He halted, face pail and waxen. "Tinsman," he said. I excused myself. The franchise works. Some other prison, some other counselor.

At a bulletin board near the exit, creating a pocket of traffic, I attached a couple flyers. One read "Top rated reentry services – outreach@fairshake.net – info@rzero.org – Tap into the community of ex-offenders and free world advocates who champion reentry success." I pressed the tape on the next flyer and felt the nerves of hope. It was for *Life With A Record*, THE number one easy reference.

"ACHIEVING SUCCESS DURING AND AFTER PRISON"

By William J. Patterson

I recently attended and participated in a class titled "Countdown to Freedom." I couldn't help but wonder how many inmates in attendance were prepared for their release? Have you taken a close look at yourself to see how you can improve your life as it relates to success both during and after prison? My experience has taught me that many inmates allow negative attitudes to dictate their lives while incarcerated. Rather than making the best of each day by keeping a positive outlook and upbeat attitude, they walk around with resentment and anger surrounded by negativity. Life in prison does not have to be this way. You can set yourself free from the chains of hostility and find freedom within yourself. Change must start with you. You can expect to experience some painful moments during your self-transformation. However, in order for you to allow growth and to achieve success you must know that it involves some type of pain. Let's look at the different aspects of what is needed for you to achieve success both while incarcerated and after your release.

Have you given any thought about what direction you want your life to take or how you plan to pursue becoming successful? It's easy to fall into the trap of becoming part of the status quo crowd. In other words, you can find yourself waking up each day and doing what everyone else around you choose to do. This is where your own ambition, goals, desires and dreams have to take charge in your life. You must separate your goals from others and determine exactly what it is you wish to achieve in your life. First, set attainable and realistic goals for yourself. Then, take the initiative and begin to do the work necessary to achieve them. Create a vision not only for today but for your future of unlimited possibilities. If you are waiting on the success bus to arrive without putting forth your efforts, you'll be waiting for a bus that never comes.

Take a look inside yourself and find the courage necessary to move forward and make the needed changes in your life. Courage is not being cocky or taking stupid risks. Rather, it's the fortitude that allows you to overcome obstacles encountered along the way in order to get where you want to go. Expect to face fears from time to time. Some will be warranted and others not. Many of your fears are based on things that will never come to pass. Others are based on your past experiences. However, very few turn out to be legitimate fears. Whatever your circumstances, don't allow your fears to stop you from moving ahead in life, getting to your desired destination, or becoming the person you desire to be. Failure is inevitable from time to time. Don't let your fear of failure, or failure itself stop you from achieving success. Instead, use any failures you may experience along the way as a teaching moment and consider it a gift from wisdom itself. In other words, each time you fail, you learn something new. Perhaps, one of these newly learned skills will be your increased adaptability.

The ability to adapt and change is key if you want to be successful in your endeavors. You must maintain the attitude that there is always something to learn in life. Your ability to show humility in everyday life is critical to your success. You are human and cannot be expected to be perfect, nor can you expect that of others. Believe in yourself but realize that you are not the center of the universe. Be confident, but at the same time be humble and have respect for others. Always hold yourself accountable and accept responsibility for your past actions and behaviors. Finally, stop blaming everyone and everything for the circumstances of your life. Your power, freedom, and success rely on you taking 100% percent responsibility for your feelings, thoughts and actions.

Patience and perseverance are required in order to live a successful life. Events and circumstances may not always occur when or in the order that you want them to be. Success and change never happens overnight. It's a process that requires your commitment, effort, and time. You will experience problems along the way, but remember, only some of your problems allow you to do something about them. The problems that you cannot resolve are just a fact of life. In those situations, see your problems as potential opportunities. Keep a positive attitude and look for ways to work around apparent problems that you have no control over. Practice discipline in your actions and sacrifice quick returns for the long-term worthwhile results. Allow those results to help you focus on your greater purpose in life.

Our purpose in life is our reason for existence. Have you given any thought regarding what your contribution could be in life? Most people want to live a meaningful and fulfilled life. Unfortunately, sometimes it takes something devastating like incarceration or other tragic events to wake people up. Since my arrest and during my incarceration, I for one, most certainly have discovered my purpose and what matters most to me in life. Have you discovered what matters most to you? During my incarceration a number of things became apparent to me. I became aware of my mortality and realized that time is my most precious asset. I can never create more time. I've learned that this moment, now, is all I have; therefore, I must make the most of it. I realize that my children, family members and friends mean more to me than anything else in this world. They come first, and I come second. I have a strong desire to be of service to others going forward in my life. This is where I've discovered my greatest joy. I encourage you to see past your past identities and create a new beginning. Your past does not have to define you today or tomorrow. Once you begin to be a more authentic human being, more natural and confident with yourself and others, you will develop the resilience required to make your dreams come true.

Resilience is our ability to survive and bounce back after failure. It's our ability to learn from a dreadful experience and take the knowledge learned to use in preparation for our futures. Contrary to what some may believe, I believe our futures are not pre-determined. Our futures are what we make them. They are ours to alter or change for better or worse. Our words, thoughts and actions affect the outcome of our future. I heard a teacher recently say, "If you want to see what your future looks like, just look in a mirror." I don't know about you but that gives me pause and requires me to look more closely at how I am living my life every moment of each day. Remember, the only time we really have is now, this very moment. Use yours wisely.

William J. Patterson is author of *Chapter 7 Bankruptcy: Seven Steps to Financial Freedom* currently available for purchase at Freebird Publishers. Mr. Patterson is currently writing a second book about incarcerated fathers and how they bridge the separation they may be experiencing with their children.

Freebird Publishers

Post-Conviction Relief: Winning Claims

POST-CONVICTION RELIEF:
WINNING CLAIMS

SEEKING EARLY RELEASE? GET EXAMPLES OF WINNING CASES THAT HAVE RAISED CLAIMS IN EVERY STEP OF THE CRIMINAL PROCESS.

A homerun starts with a strong swing at a good pitch. In the post conviction relief process a homerun requires a constitutional error and your second claim. This book is provided to give beginners and new practitioners a head start. This book contains hundreds of claims and cases of those who have won.

Between these covers you will find:

- **The best place to start claim development**
- **Only winning cases**
- **The claims they raised**
- **Issues for every stage in a criminal proceeding**
- **Legal claims the court will not hear**
- **In the back of the book, you will find an exercise based on a case that was ruled on in a federal court. You will see what a district judge is willing to do to deny relief even to the innocent and why. Above all, you will learn how to counteract their efforts.**

4th BOOK IN SERIES OF 7

Watch For More COMING SOON!

Only $19.99

plus s/h $7

This book will save you hundreds of hours in research by showing you upfront what works and what does not work. You will see how far you must go to win.

Softcover, 8" x 10", B&W, 218 pages $26.99 (19.99 plus $7. s/h)

Written in simple terms for everyone to understand, it's not just for lawyers anymore.

NO ORDER FORM NEEDED CLEARLY WRITE ON PAPER & SEND PAYMENT TO:

Freebird Publishers

Box 541, North Dighton, MA 02764

Diane@FreebirdPublishers.com www.FreebirdPublishers.com

Toll Free: 888-712-1987 Text/Phone: 774-406-8682

amazon.com

INCARCERATED VETERANS BENEFITS

Incarcerated Veterans
Veterans can sometimes run into issues with law enforcement and the criminal justice system resulting in incarceration. It is important justice-involved Veterans are familiar with VA benefits, including what VA benefits they may still be eligible to receive, what happens to the VA benefits they are already receiving if they become incarcerated, and what programs are available to assist them with reintegrating back into the community once released from incarceration.

VA Benefits
Despite the circumstances, some justice-involved Veterans may be eligible for VA benefits. Disability compensation, pension, education and training, health care, home loans, insurance, vocational rehabilitation and employment, and burial. Please be aware many VA benefits can be affected by incarceration. The following sections provide information on programs for justice-involved Veterans.

Health Care for Re-entry Veterans (HCRV) Program
The HCRV Program is designed to help incarcerated Veterans successfully reintegrate back into the community after their release. A critical part of HCRV is providing information to Veterans while they are incarcerated, so they can plan for re-entry themselves. A primary goal of the HCRV program is to prevent Veterans from becoming homeless once they are reintegrated back into the community.

Veteran Justice Outreach (VJO) Initiative
The VJO initiative is designed to help Veterans avoid unnecessary criminalization of mental illness and extended incarceration by ensuring eligible justice-involved Veterans receive timely access to VA health care, specifically mental health and substance use services (if clinically indicated) and other VA services and benefits as appropriate.

How Incarceration Affects Eligibility for VA Benefits
VA can pay certain benefits to Veterans who are incarcerated in a Federal, State, or local penal institution; however, the amount depends on the type of benefit and reason for incarceration.

Disability Compensation
VA disability compensation payments are reduced if a Veteran is convicted of a felony and imprisoned for more than 60 days. Veterans rated 20 percent or more are limited to the 10 percent disability rate. For a Veteran whose disability rating is 10 percent, the payment is reduced by one-half. Once a Veteran is released from prison, compensation payments may be reinstated based upon the severity of the service connected disability(ies) at that time. Payments are not reduced for recipients participating in work release programs, residing in halfway houses (also

known as “residential re-entry centers”), or under community control. The amount of any increased compensation awarded to an incarcerated Veteran that results from other than a statutory rate increase may be subject to reduction due to incarceration.

Pension
Veterans in receipt of VA pension will have payments terminated effective the 61st day after imprisonment in a Federal, State, or local penal institution for conviction of a felony or misdemeanor. Payments may be resumed upon release from prison if the Veteran meets VA eligibility requirements. Failure to notify VA of a Veteran’s incarceration could result in the loss of all financial benefits until the overpayment is recovered.

Apportionment to Spouse or Children
All or part of the compensation not paid to an incarcerated Veteran may be apportioned to the Veteran’s spouse, child or children, and dependent parents on the basis of individual need. In determining individual need, consideration shall be given to such factors as the claimant’s income and living expenses, the amount of compensation available to be apportioned, the needs and living expenses of other claimants as well as any special needs, if any, of all claimants.

Additional Information:

- VA will inform a Veteran whose benefits are subject to reduction of the right of the Veteran’s dependents to an apportionment while the Veteran is incarcerated, and the conditions under which payments to the Veteran may be resumed upon release from incarceration.
- VA will also notify the dependents of their right to an apportionment if the VA is aware of their existence and can obtain their addresses.
- No apportionment may be made to or on behalf of any person who is incarcerated in a Federal, State, or local penal institution for conviction of a felony.
- An apportionment of an incarcerated Veteran’s VA benefits is not granted automatically to the Veteran’s dependents. The dependent(s) must file a claim for an apportionment.

Education Benefits
Beneficiaries incarcerated for other than a felony can receive full monthly benefits, if otherwise entitled. Convicted felons residing in halfway houses (also known as “residential re-entry centers”), or participating in work-release programs also can receive full monthly benefits.

Claimants incarcerated for a felony conviction can be paid only the costs of tuition, fees, and necessary books, equipment, and supplies. VA cannot make payments for tuition, fees, books, equipment, or supplies if another Federal State or local program pays these costs in full.

If another government program pays only a part of the cost of tuition, fees, books, equipment, or supplies, VA can authorize the incarcerated claimant payment for the remaining part of the costs.

Additional Information
Each VA Regional Office has a Homeless Veterans Outreach Coordinator who assists justice-involved Veterans. They are a direct point of contact for you to learn more about what benefits you qualify for, assist you with applying for those benefits, and refer you to other organizations and resources that will help you with your specific needs. To find your local Homeless Veterans Outreach Coordinator, please call VA’s National Call Center for Homeless Veterans at 1-877-4AID-VET (1-877-424-3838).

Reprinted from benefits.va.gov

VETERANS RESOURCES

THE AMERICAN LEGION
Mail: 1608 K. St., NW
Washington, D.C. 20006
Web: Legion.org
PH: (202) 861-2700
(800) 433-3318
Comments: Assists veterans in obtaining benefits, including health care and compensation from the Department of Veterans Affairs and provides information on employment and homeless veterans.

FAMILY ALLIANCE FOR VETERANS OF AMERICA
Area Served: USA
Contact: Rhonda Jordal
Mail: 100 N Clark
Forest City, IA 50436
Web: fava@westcare.com
Comments: Assists vets with resources for family-related issues and seeks to create a paradigm where elected officials and American society have a clear understanding of the issues confronted by the federal inmate population.

FedCURE
Mail: Box 15667
Plantation, Florida 33318-5667
Web: FedCURE.org
Comments: Advocacy on behalf of the federal inmate population is the central focus of Federal CURE, Inc.

NATIONAL COALITION FOR THE HOMELESS VET
Mail: 333½ Pennsylvania Ave, SE
Washington, D.C. 20003
Email: nchv@nchv.org
Web: nchv.org
PH: (800) VET-HELP

STARS AND STRIPES
Mail: Stars and Stripes
529 14th Street NW, Suite 350
Washington, D.C. 20045-1301
PH: 312-763-0900
Web:Stripes.com
Stars and Stripes exists to provide independent news and information to the U.S. military community, comprised of active-duty servicemembers, DoD civilians, contractors, and their families.

US VETERANS MAGAZINE
Mail: 18 Technology Drive, Ste. 170
Irvine, CA 92618
Web: usveteransmagazine.com
Comments: Provides the latest, most important veteran news, covering virtually every industry helping veterans to find work & business opportunities. 1 Year Subscription (4 issues) - $18

VA HEALTH CARE
Area Served: USA
Web: med.va.gov
PH: (877) 222-8387

VETERANS ADVOCATE
Area Served: USA
Contact: Vet Legal Services
Mail: Box 65762
Washington, D.C. 20035
Web: NVLSP.org

VIETNAM VETERANS OF AMERICA
Veterans Incarcerated Liaison
Mail: 8605 Cameron St. Ste 400
Silver Springs, MD 20910
Web: vva.org
PH: (800) 882-1316
Comments: Publishes “From Felon to Freedom, A pre-released guide for Imprisoned veterans”

On Veterans Benefits

BUSTER!

A Product of the Federal Interagency Reentry Council

MYTH: Veterans cannot request to have their VA benefits resumed until they are officially released from incarceration.

FACT: Veterans may inform VA to have their benefits resumed within 30 days or less of their anticipated release date based on evidence from a parole board or other official prison source showing the Veteran's scheduled release date.

The Veterans Administration (VA) is proactive with ensuring Veterans are receiving their full entitlement of benefits once released from incarceration.

If the evidence is dated no more than 30 days before the anticipated release from incarceration, VA may resume disability benefits prospectively from the anticipated date of release based on evidence received from a parole board or other official prison source showing the Veteran's scheduled release date.

If the release does not occur on the scheduled date, VA will inform the Veteran that benefits will be discontinued or reduced effective from the date of increase without advance notice.

VA staff conduct outreach in correctional facilities across the nation to share this information with Veterans and prison staff in preparation for release.

For More Information:

VA website
www.va.gov

eBenefits
www.ebenefits.va.gov

VA Benefits
1-800-827-1000

Homeless Hotline
1-877-4AID-VET

What is a REENTRY MYTH BUSTER?

This Myth Buster is one in a series of fact sheets intended to clarify existing federal policies that affect formerly incarcerated individuals and their families. Each year, more than 700,000 individuals are released from state and federal prisons. Another 9 million cycle through local jails. When reentry fails, the social and economic costs are high -- more crime, more victims, more family distress, and more pressure on already-strained federal, state, and municipal budgets.

Because reentry intersects with health and housing, education and employment, family, faith, and community well-being, many federal agencies are focusing on initiatives for the reentry population. Under the auspices of the Cabinet-level interagency Reentry Council, federal agencies are working together to enhance community safety and well-being, assist those returning from prison and jail in becoming productive citizens, and save taxpayer dollars by lowering the direct and collateral costs of incarceration.

For more information about the Reentry Council, go to:
www.nationalreentryresourcecenter.org/reentry-council

Reprinted from http://csgjusticecenter.org

INMATE-RUN PROGRAM HELPS VETS BEHIND BARS NAVIGATE VA MAZE

Inmate and Vietnam veteran Ed Munis works on his computer at the Veteran Service Office, which he helped start more than a decade ago, in California's Soledad Correctional Training Facility.

~

Veterans serving time behind bars are still entitled to some – but not all – of the benefits earned through military service. Inmates struggle in trying to inform the Dept. of Veterans Affairs about their incarceration. Today, we look at a one-of-a kind inmate-run program trying to help other incarcerated veterans work and communicate with the VA to get benefits.

~

Jerry Lytle never collected the benefits he earned from service in the Army, and once he was behind bars, he didn't realize he still could.

"In 2004, I met up with another veteran who was getting benefits, and he said, 'You know, you should get your benefits. You're entitled to them,'" Lytle says.

He's serving 32 years to life for murder. Even so, he's still entitled to disability benefits from the Department of Veterans Affairs, because he suffers from PTSD and exposure to Agent Orange in Vietnam.

But he's not eligible for the amount he would have received on the outside. At most, Lytle can get just over $100 a month. If he wasn't incarcerated, his monthly payment would be more than $1,000.

When he filed for disability, he says he got the runaround.

"I think because I was in prison, I couldn't deal directly with them. I was dealing with them through the mail, the only process I had," he says. "I really believe that they were really trying to discourage me."

He didn't give up, but it wasn't persistence that finally worked. It was a transfer to the Soledad Correctional Training Facility in California's Salinas Valley, which is home to a unique inmate-run program.

Inside the prison is a Veteran Service Office, where incarcerated vets can get help filing – and fighting for – VA benefits, including disability, educational, and burial benefits, for those who die behind bars.

The office is a large cinder-block room with windows looking out on the prison's main corridor. A black POW/MIA flag hangs on the back wall next to filing cabinets, and there's a bookcase filled with thick federal code books.

Ed Munis, an inmate who helps run the office, says this all started because of fellow Vietnam veteran and inmate Michael "Doc" Piper, who also runs the office.

"I got here in 2003, and right away he found out a little bit about my background and pestered me for a couple of years till we got going," Munis says.

Since the prison Veteran Service Office started more than 10 years ago, it has helped more than 1,000 incarcerated veterans get VA benefits.

It's a complicated background: Munis is serving 25 years to life for his wife's murder. Before that, he was a lobbyist in Sacramento working on veterans issues.

With the warden's approval, they started the office about 10 years ago. Now, they're not only helping veterans in this prison, they are also working with some incarcerated vets by mail at every prison in California – and in 23 other states, where word of their work has spread via newsletters. Munis says most vets didn't know they were still eligible for benefits.

"There's an awful lot of people that are in the VA, as well as general public, that are not too excited about helping out convicted felons, people that are incarcerated," Munis says. "So that's been a struggle. So far, we've prevailed."

On the two computers in their office, they've kept detailed records of their work. Their numbers show over the past decade they've helped about 1,000 incarcerated veterans get more than $15 million in benefits for themselves and their dependents.

Still, it's a tough job to do from prison. The computers don't have Internet access and their printer is locked in a cage so staff can review what they print.

They rely on help from Monterey County Veteran Service Officers, who essentially do on the outside what Munis and Piper do on the inside. The VSOs help the prison office by reviewing the inmates' claims and submitting them to the VA.

"And plus we can access and check status on appeals and help them with appeals on the outside," says Monterey County VSO George Dixon.

He says his job is not to judge these veterans for their crimes, but to help them get what they've earned.

"When you look at some of the discharges, combat experience, Vietnam, Gulf War, Persian Gulf, Grenada, Panama," says Dixon, "those are the individuals that are in there."

It's why his office is working to develop a similar program at the neighboring Salinas Valley State Prison. There they have trained seven inmates to help veterans start the VA paperwork.

Inmate Munis hopes to reach more veterans in a different way.

"I plan on paroling here. I plan on continuing to do this until they put a tag on my toe and they bury me," he says.

His first chance at parole comes up in a couple of years. If he gets out, he says he'd work to expand this program in prisons up and down the state.

This story is part of a project we're calling "Back at Base," in which NPR – along with seven public radio stations around the country – is chronicling the lives of America's troops where they live.

Reprinted from npr.com

PRISON IS BAD FOR YOUR HEALTH

Prison is a filthy, depressing, dark, disgusting, even toxic place, both physically and mentally. It's bad for your health in every way. Want some cases and solutions to the problems...read this book.

- *California Prisons Struggle with Environmental Threats from Sewage Spills, Contaminated Water, Air-borne Disease*
- *Georgia Prison Doctor Rewarded for Cutting costs as Prisoners Died Under His Care*
- *Seventh Circuit Dissent: "A Dog Would Have Deserved Better Treatment ."*
- *Major Scabies Outbreak at Core Civic Facility in Tennessee*
- *Deaths at North Carolina Jail Due to Lack of Medical, Mental Health Care*
- *Lawsuit Alleges Four Oregon Prisons Served Food "Not for Human Consumption"*
- *Tennessee: High Cost of Drugs Cited as Reason to Deny Prisoners Hep C Treatment*
- *Attica Medical Experiments Exposed*

Do I need to continue? You get it, right?

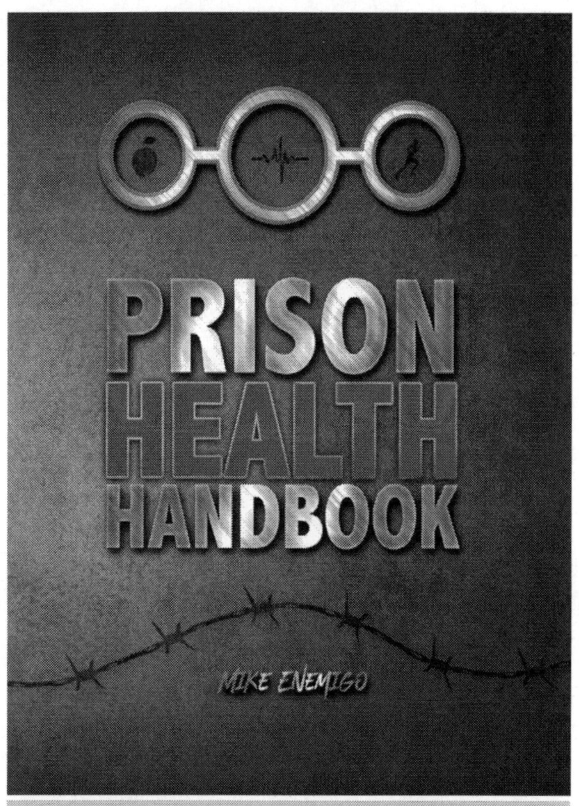

Only $19.99

plus $7 S/h with tracking

SOFTCOVER, 8" x 10", 277 pages

The Prison Health Handbook is your one-stop go-to source for information on how to maintain your best health while inside the American prison system. Filled with information, tips, and secrets from doctors, gurus, and other experts, this book will educate you on such things as proper workout and exercise regimens; yoga benefits for prisoners; how to meditate effectively; pain management tips; sensible dieting solutions; nutritional knowledge; an understanding of various cancers, diabetes, hepatitis, and other diseases all too common in prison; how to effectively deal with mental health issues such as stress, PTSD, anxiety, and depression; a list of things doctors DON'T want YOU to know; and much, much more! This book also includes your rights to adequate medical care while in prison, and how to effectively advocate for your medical needs, should you need to do so!

Don't let prison defeat you by breaking you down, little by little, mentally and physically. Protect yourself by taking your health into your own hands using this amazing collection of health knowledge, tips, secrets, and by knowing your rights!

No Order Form Needed: Clearly write on paper & send with payment of **$26.99** to:

Freebird Publishers Box 541, North Dighton, MA 02764

Diane@FreebirdPublishers.com www.FreebirdPublishers.com

Fantasy Collection: Adult Coloring Book HUGE

By Jade Summer

$ 24.99 plus $5 s/h

213 Pages Softcover

Vampires: A Vampire Coloring Book with Mythical Fantasy Women, Sexy Gothic Fashion

By Jade Summer

$10.99 plus $4 s/h

86 Pages Softcover

Balance Extreme Stress Mender Coloring Book

By Angie Grace

$15.99 plus $4 s/h

104 Pages Softcover

Vintage Classic Comic Adult Coloring Book

By Awesome Coloring Books

$12.99 plus $4 s/h

62 Pages Softcover

Color Me Beautiful, Women of the World: Adult Coloring Book

By Jason Hamilton

$11.99 plus $4 s/h

90 Pages Softcover

The Gentleman's Coloring Book

By Robert Hooper

$11.99 plus $4 s/h

24 Pages Softcover

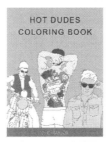

Hot Dudes Adult Coloring Book

By DC Taylor

$14.99 plus $4 s/h

64 Pages Softcover

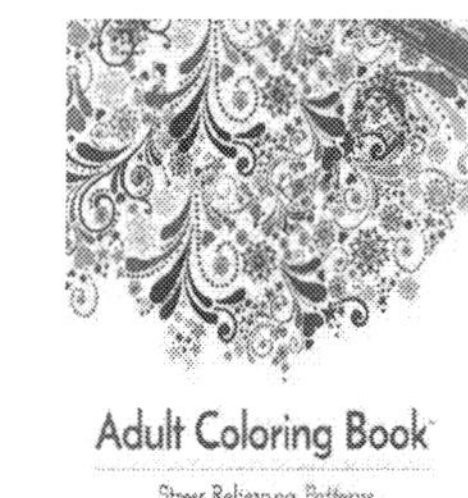

Adult Coloring Book: Stress Relieving Patterns

By Blue Start Coloring

$10.99 plus $4 s/h

106 Pages Softcover

Man Candy: An Adult Coloring Book with 30 Hot Men and Pick -up Lines to Calm and Relax

By Blue Star Coloring

$11.99 plus $4 s/h

68 Pages Softcover

Dragoon Adventure: A Kaleidoscopic Adult Coloring

By Rachael Mayo

$13.99 plus $4 s/h

110 Pages Softcover

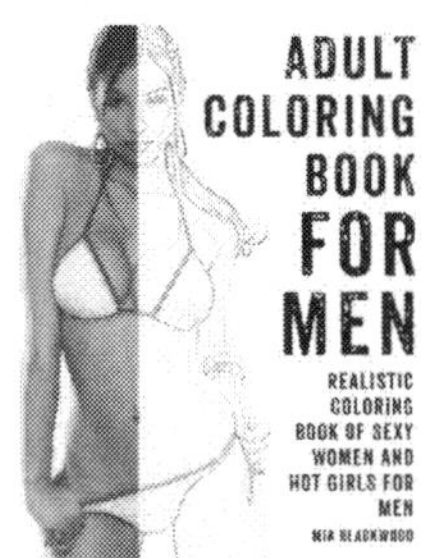

Adult Coloring Book For Men: Realistic Coloring Book of Sexy Women and Hot Girls

By Mia Blackwood

$13.99 plus $4 s/h

86 Pages Softcover

Gothic Dark Fantasy Coloring Book

By Selina Fenech

$13.99 plus $4 s/h

108 Pages Softcover

Creative Doodling & Beyond

By Stephanie Corfee

$16.99 plus $4 s/h

144 Pages Softcover

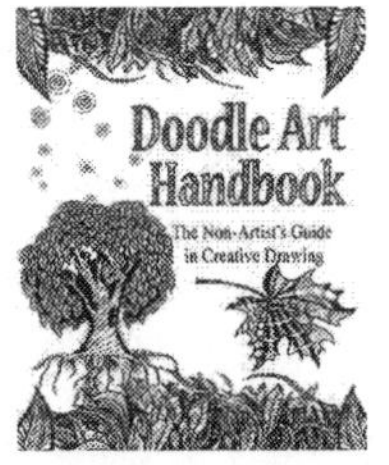

Doodle Art Handbook

By Lana Karr and Olga Dee

$18.99 plus $4 s/h

174 Pages Softcover

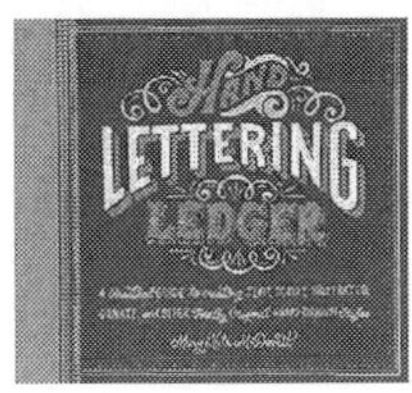

Hand Lettering Ledger: A Practical Guide to Creating Serif, Script, Illustrated, Ornate, and Other

By Parikh Publications

$15.99 plus $4 s/h

192 Pages Softcover

How to Draw What You See

By Rudy De Reyna

$14.99 plus $4 s/h

178 Pages Softcover

Drawing Dragons: Learn How to Create Fantastic Fire -Breathing Dragons

By Sandra Staple

$14.99 plus $4 s/h

160 Pages Softcover

The Lost Art of How to Draw Fantasy Females

By Frank Granados

$11.99 plus $4 s/h

80 Pages Softcover

Fantasy Art Now: The Very Best in Contemporary Fantasy Art

By Martin McKenna

$33.99 plus $4 s/h

192 Pages Hardcover

The Lost Art Vol. 2 How to Draw Fantasy Females

By Frank Granados

$14.99 plus $4 s/h

80 Pages Softcover

Pen and Ink Drawing: A Simple Guide

By Alphonso

$20.99 plus $4 s/h

166 Pages Softcover

DragonArt Fantasy Characters: How to Draw Fantastic Beings and Incredible Creatures

By Gill Barron

$23.99 plus $4 s/h

128 Pages Softcover

Origami Flowers

By Anica Oprea

$11.99 plus $4 s/h

128 Pages Softcover

Uber Origami: Every Origami Project Ever!

By Duy Nguen

$17.99 plus $5 s/h

512 Pages Softcover

Custom Tattoo 101: Over 1000 Stencils and Ideas

By Tattoo Finder

$20.99 plus $5 s/h

256 Pages Softcover

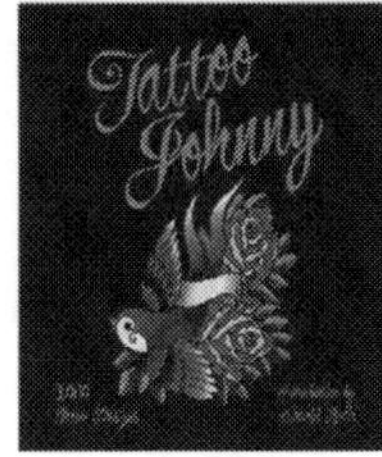

Tattoo Johnny: 3,000 Tattoo Designs

By Tattoo Johnny

$12.99 plus $7 s/h

352 Pages Softcover

2,286 Traditional Stencil Designs

By H. Roessing

$16.99 plus $4 s/h

128 Pages Softcover

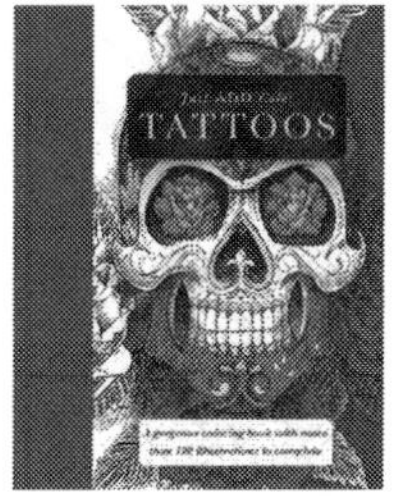

Just Add Color: Tattoos

By Carlton Publishing Group

$12.99 plus $4 s/h

128 Pages Softcover

The Mammoth Book of Tattoos

By Lal Hardy

$22.99 plus $7 s/h

512 Pages Softcover

Tattoo Lettering Bible

By Superior Tattoo

$22.99 plus $4 s/h

128 Pages Softcover

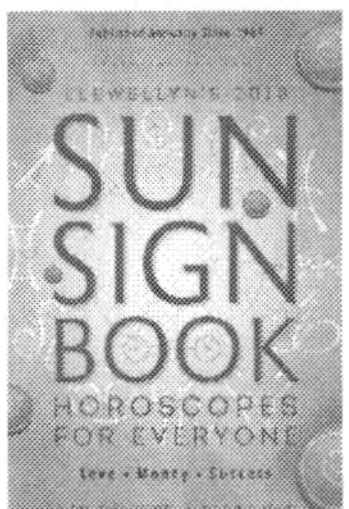

Llewellyn's 2019 <u>or</u> 2020 Sun Sign Book: Horoscopes for Everyone (Llewellyn's Sun Sign Book)

$14.99 plus $4 s/h

288 pages Softcover

Llewellyn's 2019 <u>or</u> 2020 Moon Sign Book: Plan Your Life by the Cycles of the Moon

By Llewellyn's Moon Sign Books

$14.99 plus $4 s/h

312 Pages Softcover

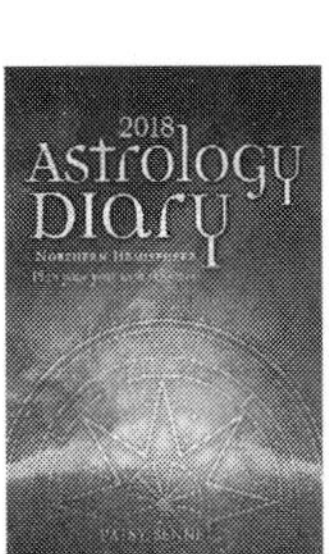

2019 <u>or</u> 2020 Astrology Diary: Plan Your Year with the Stars-Northern Hemisphere (Annual Diary)

By Patsy Bennett

$12.99 plus $4 s/h
160 Pages Softcover

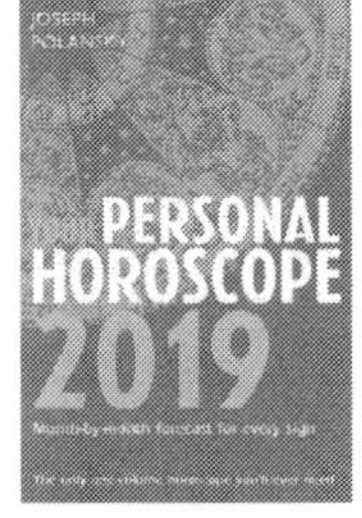

Your Personal Horoscope 2019 <u>or</u> 2020

By Joseph Polansky

$16.99 plus $4 s/h

384 Pages Softcover

2019 <u>or</u> 2020 Horoscope: Astrological Horoscope, Moon Phases, and More <u>(Books Available In EACH Zodiac Sign) Tell us what sign</u> By Crystal Sky

$15.99 plus $4 s/h
128 Pages Softcover

The Old Farmer's Almanac 2019 <u>or</u> 2020

By Old Farmers Almanac

$11.99 plus $4 s/h

304 Pages Softcover

Marvel Studio Character Encyclopedia

Marvel

$19.99 plus $7 s/h

520 pages Hardcover

Marvel Encyclopedia, New Edition

Marvel

$29.99 plus $7 s/h

176 Pages Hardcover

DC Comics Encyclopedia, All New Edition

by Matthew K. Manning

$29.99 plus $7 s/h

368 Pages Hardcover

DC Comic Ultimate Character Guide, New Edition

DC Comics

$13.99 plus $7 s/h

400 Pages Softcover

DC Comics: A Visual History

DC Comic

$36.99 plus $7 s/h

376 Pages Hardcover

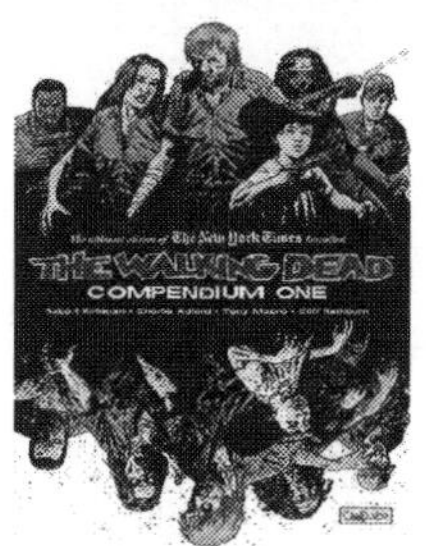

The Walking Dead: Compendium Books One, Two, Three or Four

Image Comics

$37.99 plus $7 s/h EACH (1, 2, 3)

$60.99 plus $7 s/h (book 4)

1088 Pages Softcover

The Cell Chef Cookbook

A collection of recipes by Tanner George Cummings

$13.99 plus $5 s/h

183 Pages Softcover

The Cell Chef Cookbook II

A new collection of recipes by Tanner George Cummings

$13.99 plus $5 s/h

195 Pages Softcover

High Fence Foodie: From the Big House to your House

By Celeste Johnson

$20.99 plus $4 s/h

116 Pages Softcover

The Prison Gourmet: Written by an Inmate for an Inmate

By Nicholas Terrell

$9.99 plus $4 s/h

28 Pages Softcover

Fine Dining Prison Cookbook

By Troy Traylor

$14.99 plus $5 s/h

229 Pages Softcover

The Frog Commissary Cookbook

By Steven Pose

$23.99 plus $4 s/h

272 pages Softcover

Prison Ramen: Recipes and Stories from Behind Bars

By Clifton Collins Jr., Gustavo "Goose" Alvarez, Samuel L. Jackson

$12.99 plus $4 s/h

176 Pages Softcover

Orange is the New Black Cookbook

By Jenji Kohan, Tara Hermann, Hartley Voss, Alex Regnery

$18.99 plus $4 s/h

224 Pages Softcover

Doing Time Authentic Prisoners Cookbook

By Chef J John, Batman Sanchez

$14.99 plus $4 s/h

60 Pages Softcover

Doing Time Authentic Prisoners Cookbook II Edition

By Chef J John, Batman Sanchez

$14.99 plus $4 s/h

40 Pages Softcover

Mad Dog's Favorite Prison Recipes

By Dan M. Allen

$32.99 plus $4 s/h

242 Pages Softcover

The Prison Cookbook: A Cookbook for Prison Inmates

By CJ Green

$12.99 plus $4 s/h

300 Pages Softcover

Fed Up - Prison Cookbook

By Charles Keith

$16.99 plus $4 s/h

60 Pages Softcover

Jailhouse Cookbook: The Prisoner's Recipe Bible

By Bruce Michaels

$17.99 plus $4 s/h

262 Pages Softcover

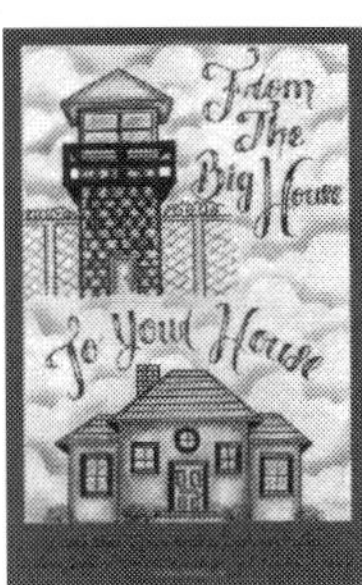

From The Big House to Your House: Cooking in Prison

Publisher: Kaplan

$15.99 plus $4 s/h

132 Pages Softcover

Creative Snacks, Meals, Beverages and Desserts

By Kevin Bullington

$6.99 plus $4 s/h

60 Pages Softcover

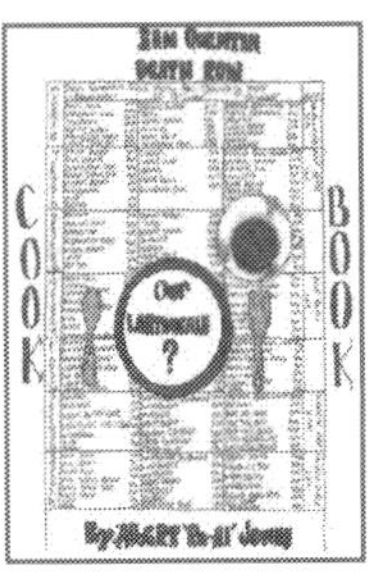

Our Last Meals: San Quentin Death Row Cook Book

By $17.99 plus $4 s/h

146 Pages Softcover

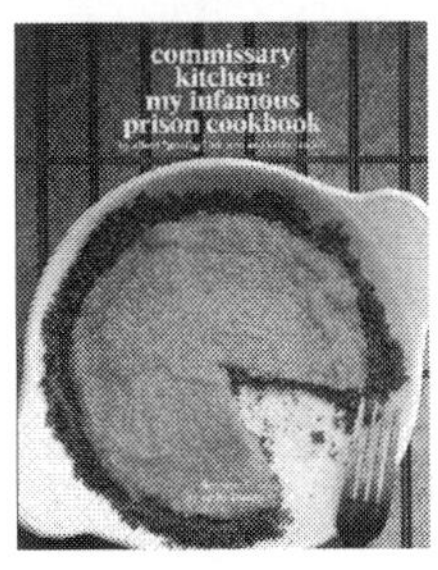

Commissary Kitchen: My Infamous Prison Cookbook

By Albert Prodigy Johnson

$17.99 plus $4 s/h

109 Pages Softcover

Woodburning Project & Pattern Treasury Create Your Own Pyrography Art with 75 Mix-and-Match Designs

$24.99 plus $4 s/h

176 Pages Softcover

A-Z of Crochet: The ultimate guide for beginners to advanced

$18.99 plus $5 s/h

160 Pages Softcover

Knitting in Plain English

By Maggies Righetti

$18.99 plus $7 s/h

304 Pages Softcover

Cozy Stash-Busting Knits - 22 Patterns for Hats, Scarves, Cowls and more

By Jen Lucas

$19.99 plus $5 s/h

96 Pages Softcover

Making Wire and Bead Jewelry-Artful Wirework Techniques

By Janice Berkebile & Tracy Stanley

$17.99 plus $5 s/h

144 Pages Softcover

750 Knitting Stitches: Guide is both stitch guide and how-to-knit primer, all in one.

$19.99 plus $7 s/h

288 Pages Softcover

A-Z Needlepoint: Over 65 stitches plus 1200 step by step photos

$19.99 plus $5 s/h

128 Pages Softcover

A-Z of Embroidery Stitches: Comprehensive Guide for Beginners to Experienced Embroiderers

$19.99 plus $5 s/h

144 Pages Softcover

A-Z Crewel Embroidery: Over flowing with hundreds stitches, designs and photos

$17.99 plus $5 s/h

144 Pages Softcover

Braids, Buns and Twist Hairstyles Over 80 classic and contemporary styles and step by step photos

$18.99 plus $5 s/h

192 Pages Softcover

Milady Standard Natural Hair Care & Braiding: A "must have" for those who are serious about developing a wide range of services.

$45.99 plus $7 s/h

320 Pages Softcover

The Ultimate Hairstyle Handbook: Everyday Hairstyles for the Everyday

$16.99 plus $4 s/h

56 Pages Softcover

Everyday Letters for Busy People, Revised Edition

By Debra Hart May

$24.99 plus $4 s/h

288 Pages Softcover

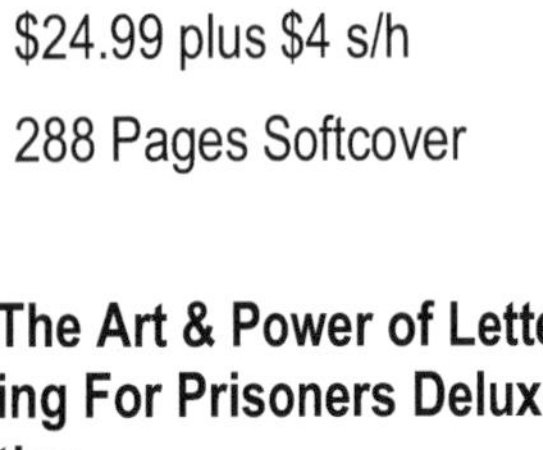

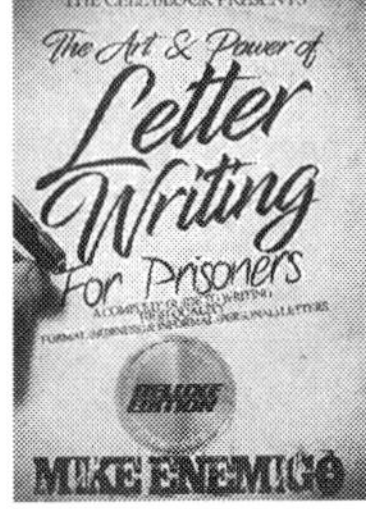

The Art & Power of Letter Writing For Prisoners Deluxe Edition

By Mike Enemigo

$24.99 plus $4 s/h

148 pages

The Bluebook of Grammar and Punctuation

By Jane Straus

$13.99 plus $4 s/h

244 Pages Softcover

How to Get Money For College 2020

Publisher: Peterson

$34.99 plus $7 s/h

960 Pages Softcover

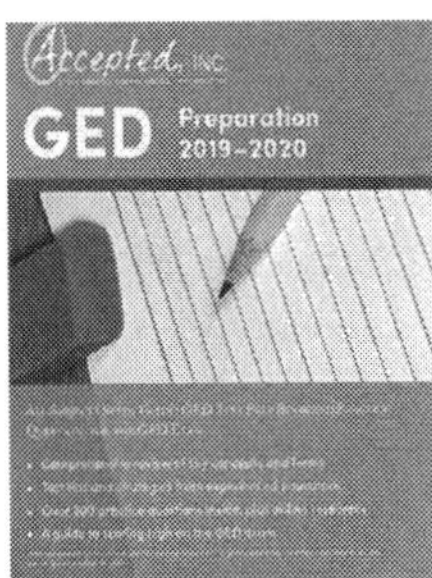

GED Test 2019-20 All Study Guide, GED Test Prep Book

By Inc. GED Exam Prep Team

$24.99 plus $7 s/h

396 Pages Softcover

Prison Grievances: when to write, how to write

By $13.99 plus $4 s/h

66 Pages Softcover

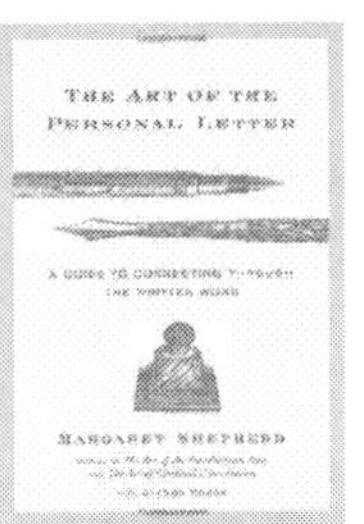

The Art of the Personal Letter: A guide to Connecting Through the Written Word

By Margaret Shepard

$12.99 plus $4 s/h

218 Pages Softcover

The Art & Power of Letter Writing for Prisoners

By Mike Enemigo

$12.99 plus $4 s/h

47 Pages Softcover

College For Convicts

By Christopher Zoukis

$35.99 plus $5 s/h

300 Pages Softcover

College in Prison

By Bruce Michaels

$16.99 plus $5 s/h

116 Pages Softcover

GED Test for Dummies, Quick Prep

Publisher: For Dummies

$9.99 plus $5 s/h

192 Pages Softcover

Merriam-Webster's Dictionary & Thesaurus Newest Edition

Publisher: Merriam-Webster

$14.99 plus $4 s/h

1260 Pages Softcover

CEO Manual: Start A Business, Be A Boss

By Mike Enemigo

$24.99 plus $4 s/h

136 Pages Softcover

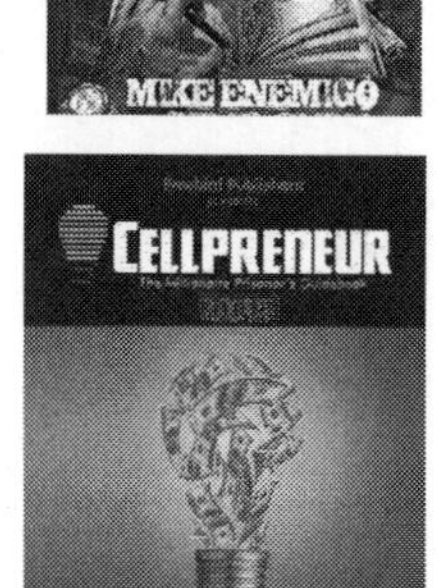

How to Write Urban Books for Money and Fame

By Mike Enemigo

$24.99 plus $4 s/h

171 Pages Softcover

Write & Get Paid REVISED 2019 Edition

By Anthony Tinsman

$22.99 plus $7 s/h

175 Pages Softcover

Cellpreneur: The Millionaire Prisoner's Guidebook REVISED 2018 Edition (Texas DCJ)

By Josh Kruger

$22.99 plus $7 s/h

288 Pages Softcover

Complete Idiots Guide to Cashing in on Your Inventions

By Richard Levy

$22.99 plus $7 s/h

400 Pages Softcover

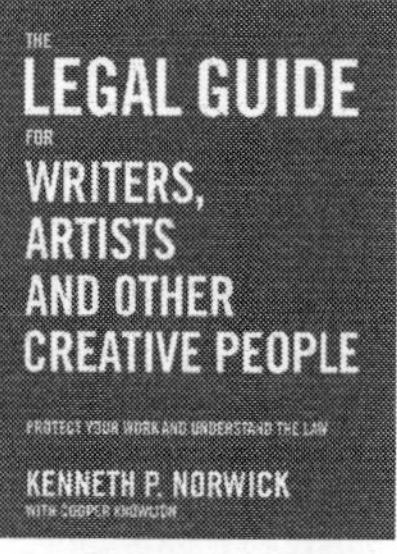

Legal Guide for Writers

By Kenneth Norwick

$22.99 plus $4 s/h

288 Pages Softcover

Start a 501c3 Nonprofit

By Audrey K. Chisholm Esq.

$28.99 plus $4 s/h

229 Pages Softcover

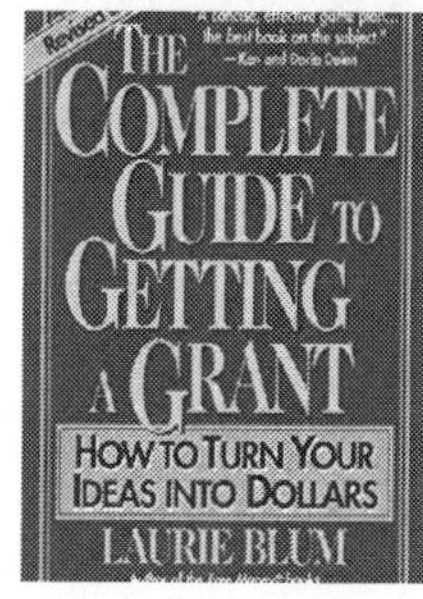

Complete Guide to Getting Grants: Turn Your Ideas into Dollars Revised Ed.

By Laurie Blum

$17.99 plus $5 s/h

368 Pages Softcover

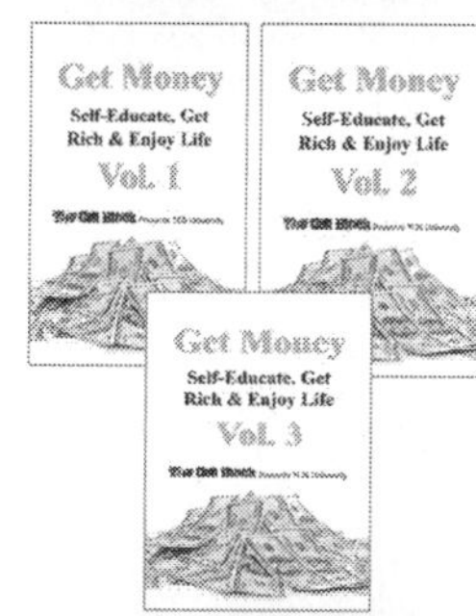

Get Money Vol. 1, By Mike Enemigo, $15.99 plus $5 s/h, 125+ Pages Softcover

Get Money Vol. 2, By Mike Enemigo, $15.99 plus $5 s/h, 125+ Pages Softcover

Get Money Vol. 3, By Mike Enemigo, $15.99 plus $5 s/h, 125+ Pages Softcover

Get Money 3 Book Set, 3 Volume Series $39.99 plus $7 s/h, 400+ Pages Softcovers

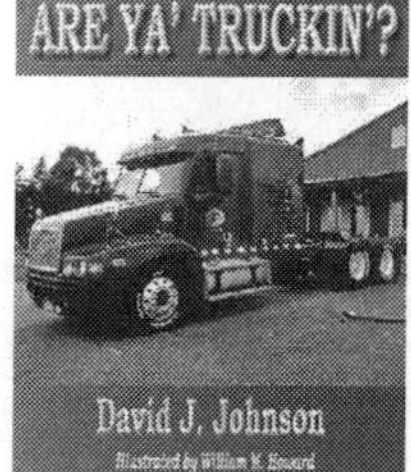

Are Ya' Trucking?

By David J Johnson

By $17.99 plus $4 s/h

246 Pages Softcover

Starting on a Shoestring

By Arnold S. Goldstein PhD

$35.99 plus $4 s/h

306 Pages Softcover

Weird O Pedia, By Alex Palmer, $9.99 plus $4 s/h, 224 Pages Softcover

Sex Weird O Pedia, By Ross Benes, $12.99 plus $4 s/h, 168 Pages Softcover

Politics Weird O Pedia, By Tim Roland, $12.99 plus $4 s/h, 240 Pages Softcover

What Did We Use Before Toilet Paper? Curious Questions

By Andrew Thompson

$14.99 plus $4 s/h

144 Pages Softcover

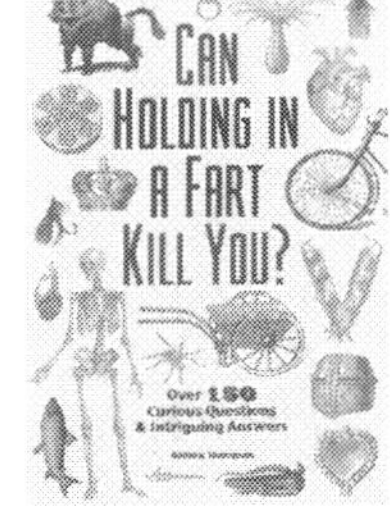

Can Holding a Fart Kill You?

By Bathroom Readers

$12.99 plus $4 s/h

280 Pages Softcover

Scared Sh*itless

By Scholastic

$16.99 plus $4 s/h

304 Pages Softcover

Ever Wonder Why?

By Douglas B Smith

$12.99 plus $4 s/h

144 Pages Softcover

Quotable Ahole** 1,200 Bitter Barbs, Cutting Comments, and Caustic Comebacks

By Eric Grzymkowski

$17.99 plus $4 s/h

256 Pages Softcover

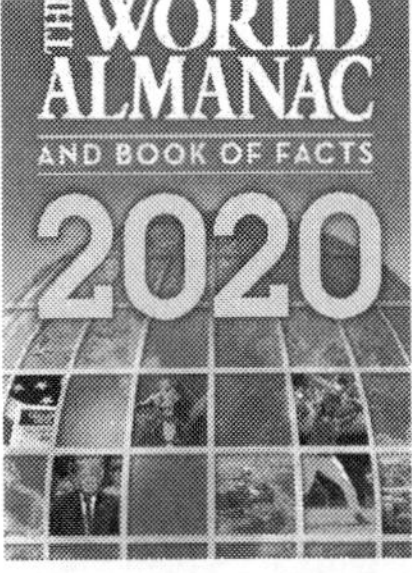

The World Almanac & Book of Facts 2019 or 2020 (preorder)

Publisher: World Almanac

$16.99 plus $5 s/h

1008 Pages Softcover

Uncle Johns Old Faithful Bathroom Reader

By Bathroom Readers Inst.

$16.99 plus $4 s/h

608 Pages Softcover

Guinness World Records Gamers Edition 2019 or 2020 (preorder)

By Guinness World Records

$16.99 plus $4 s/h

192 Pages Softcover

Uncle Johns Fully Loaded Bathroom Reader

By Bathroom Readers Inst.

$16.99 plus $4 s/h

608 Pages Softcover

Guinness World Records 2019 or 2020 (preorder)

By Guinness World Records

$19.99 plus $5 s/h 2019 ed.

$31.99 plus $5 s/h 2020 ed.

640 Pages Softcover

Sandbag Training Bible: Functional Workouts to Tone, Sculpt and Strengthen Your Entire Body

By Ben Hirshberg

$16.99 plus $4 s/h

Fitness: Bodyweight Training: Lose Weight, Build Muscle

By Chris Cole

$15.99 plus $4 s/h
122 Pages Softcover

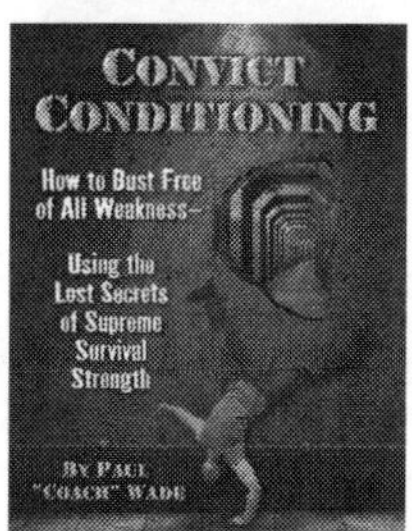

Convict Conditioning: How to Bust Free of All Weakness

By Paul Wade

$28.99 plus $7 s/h

294 Pages Softcover

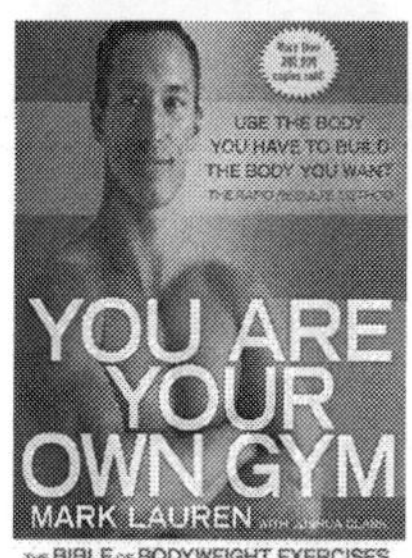

You Are Your Own Gym

By Mark Lauren and Joshua Clark

$15.99 plus $4 s/h

192 Pages Softcover

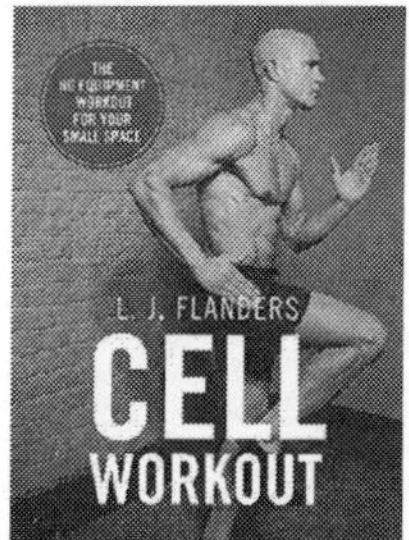

Cell Workout

By LJ Flanders

$30.99 plus $4 s/h

224 Pages Softcover

ConBody: The Revolutionary Bodyweight Prison Boot Camp

By Coss Marte

$13.99 plus $5 s/h

240 Pages Softcover

Men's Health Ultimate Dumbbell Guide: More Than 21,000 Moves Designed to Build Muscle, Increase Strength, and Burn Fat

By Michael Matthews

$18.99 plus $4 s/h

288 Pages Softcover

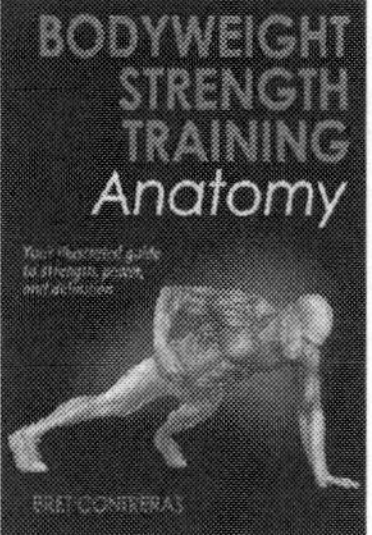

Body Weight Strength Training Anatomy

By Bret Contreras

$19.99 plus $5 s/h

224 Pages Softcover

100 No-Equipment Workouts

By Neila Rey

$17.99 plus $5 s/h

210 Pages Softcover

Your Body Is Your Barbell

By BJ Gaddour

$21.99 plus $5 s/h

224 Pages Softcover

Your Body is Your Gym: Use Your Bodyweight to Build Muscle and Lose Fat With the Ultimate Guide to Bodyweight Training

By Peter Paulson

$13.99 plus $4 s/h

172 Pages Softcover

Street Workout: Lose Weight and Gain Muscle Mass with Highly Effective Street Exercises

Publisher: Hazelton

$18.99 plus $4 s/h

64 Pages Softcover

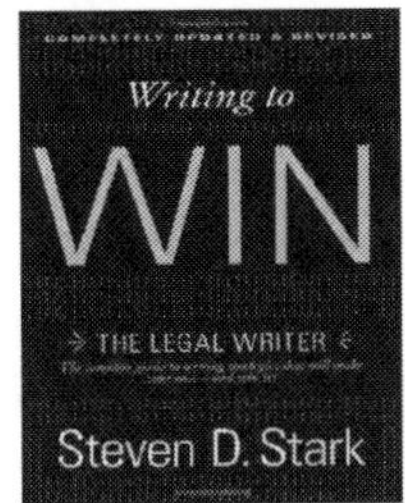

Writing to Win

By Steven D. Stark

$15.99 plus $4 s/h

320 Pages Softcover

Represent Yourself in Court

Publisher: NOLO

$35.99 plus $7 s/h

560 Pages Softcover

A Handbook of Criminal Law Terms-Black's Law

By Bryan A. Garner

$28.99 plus $7 s/h

768 Pages Softcover

Legal Research: How to Find & Understand the Law

Publisher: NOLO

$38.99 plus $5 s/h

376 Pages Softcover

Nolo's Plain-English Law Dictionary 1st Edition

Publisher: NOLO

$25.99 plus $7 s/h

477 Pages Softcover

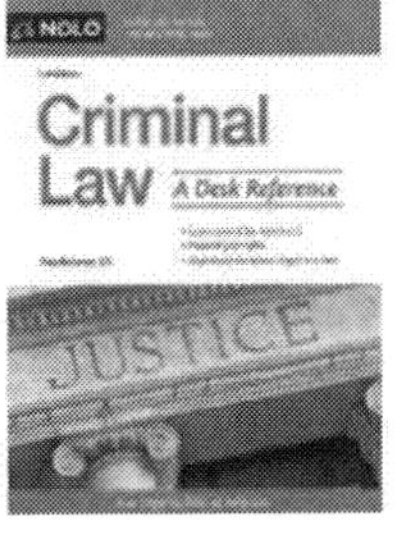

Criminal Law: A Desk Reference 2nd Edition

Publisher: NOLO

$46.99 plus $7 s/h

417 Pages Softcover

Dictionary of American Criminal Justice, Criminology and Law 2nd Edition

By David N. Falcone

$55.99 plus $5 s/h

312 Pages Softcover

Criminal Law Handbook

By Paul Burgman

$27.99 plus $7 s/h

656 Pages Softcover

Criminal Procedure/ Constitutional Limitations in a Nutshell

Publisher: West Academics

$45.99 plus $7 s/h

557 Pages Softcover

International Criminal Law in a Nutshell

Publisher: West Academic

$48.99 plus $7 s/h

445 Pages Softcover

Criminal Law in a Nutshell

Publisher: West Academic

$43.99 plus $5 s/h

387 Pages Softcover

Prisoners' Self-Help Litigation Manual

By John Boston

$38.99 plus $7 s/h

960 Pages Softcover

Post-Conviction Relief: Secrets Revealed

By Kelly Patrick Riggs

$19.99 plus $7 s/h

190 Pages Softcover

Post-Conviction Relief: The Appeal

By Kelly Patrick Riggs

$19.99 plus $7 s/h

190 Pages Softcover

Post-Conviction Relief: Advancing Your Claim

By Kelly Patrick Riggs

$19.99 plus $7 s/h

218 Pages Softcover

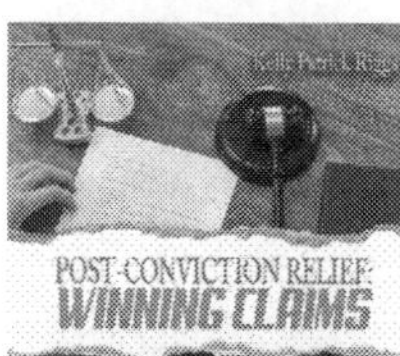

Post-Conviction Relief: Winning Claims

By Kelly Patrick Riggs

$19.99 plus $7 s/h

218 Pages Softcover

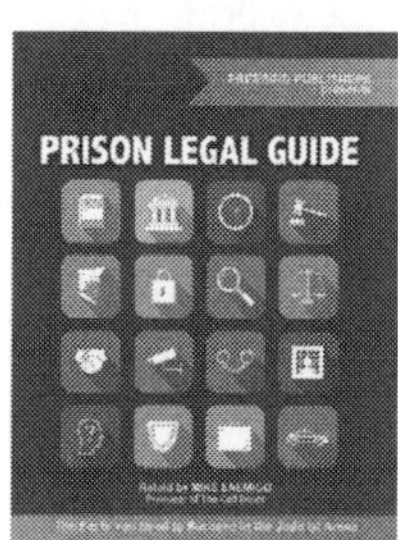

Prison Legal Guide: Know your civil rights and the procedures that can bring you the win!

Retold By Mike Enemigo

$24.99 plus $7 s/h

214 Pages Softcover

Post-Conviction Relief: C.O.A. in the Supreme Court

By Kelly Patrick Riggs

$19.99 plus $7 s/h

? Pages Softcover

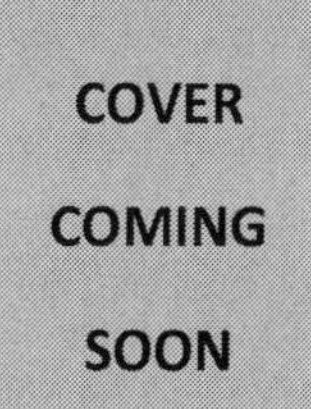

The Habeas Corpus Manual

By Raymond Lumsden

$29.99 plus $7 s/h

300+ Pages Softcover

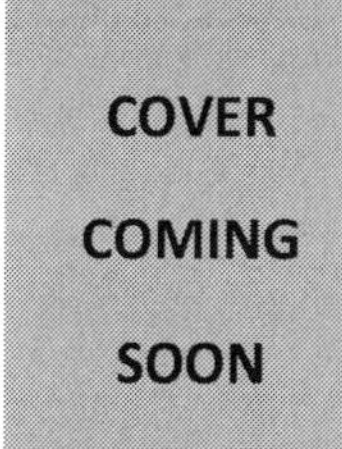

Ineffective Assistance of Counsel

By Kelly Patrick Riggs

$19.99 plus $7 s/h

350+ Pages Softcover

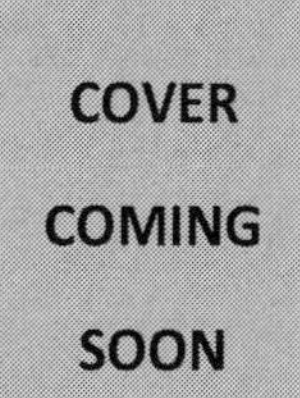

The Pro Se Section 1983 Manual

By Raymond Lumsden

$29.99 plus $7 s/h

400+ Pages Softcover

Chapter 7 Bankruptcy: Seven Steps to Financial Freedom

By William J. Patterson

$22.99 plus $7 s/h

240 Pages Softcover

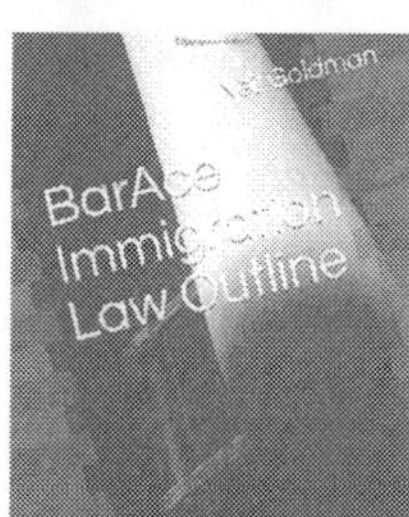

BarAce Immigration Law Outline

By Zachary A. Smith

$15.99 plus $4 s/h

29 Pages Softcover

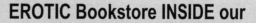

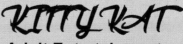

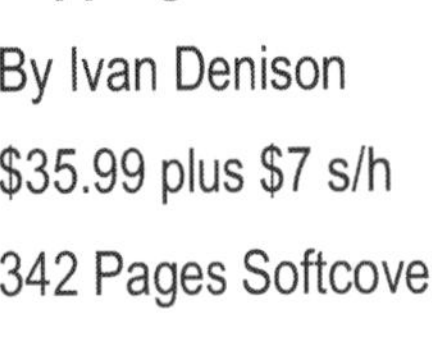

Flipping Your Habe

By Ivan Denison

$35.99 plus $7 s/h

342 Pages Softcover

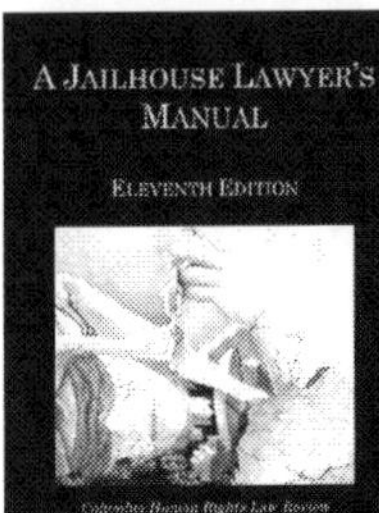

A Jailhouse Lawyers Manual

By Columbia Human Rights Law Review

$32.99 plus $7 s/h

1368 Pages Softcover

Winning Habeas Corpus and Post Conviction Relief 2019 Revised 8th Edition

By Fred Stephen

$94.99 plus $7 s/h

660 Pages Softcover

SMITH'S GUIDE to State Habeas Corpus Relief for State Prisoners

By Zachary A. Smith

38.99 plus $7 s/h

578 Pages Softcover

Smith's Guide to Second or Successive Federal Habeas Corpus Relief for State & Federal Prisoners

By Zachary A. Smith

$38.99 plus $7 s/h

352 Pages Softcover

Smith's Guide to Habeas Corpus Relief for State Prisoners

By Zachary A. Smith

$38.99 plus $7 s/h

380 Pages Softcover

The Essential Supreme Court Cases

By Ivan Denison

$22.99 plus $7 s/h

340 Pages Softcover

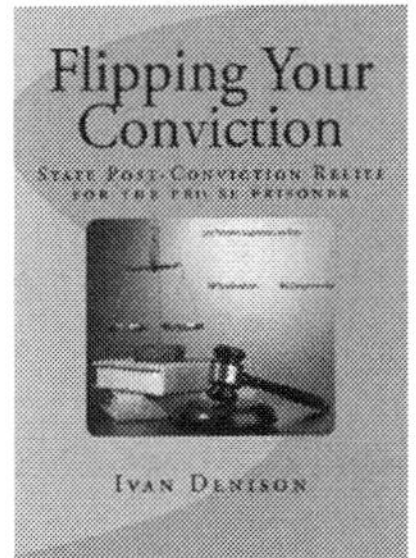

Flipping Your Conviction

By Ivan Denison

$55.99 plus $7 s/h

508 Pages Softcover

Post Conviction Relief for Washington State

By Fred Stephen

$55.99 plus $7 s/h

308 Pages Softcover

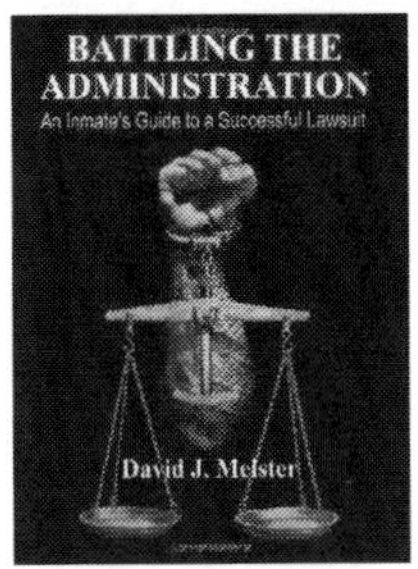

Battling the Administration–Inmate Guide

By David J. Meister

$36.99 plus $7 s/h

566 Pages Softcover

Smith's Guide to Chapter 7 Bankruptcy for Prisoners

By Zachary A. Smith

$38.99 plus $7 s/h

256 Pages Softcover

Smith's Guide to Executive Clemency for State and Federal Prisoners

By Zachary A. Smith

$38.99 plus $7 s/h

288 Pages Softcover

Amateur: A Reckoning with Gender

By Thomas Page McBee

$14.99 plus $4 s/h

244 Pages Softcover

LGBTQ: The Survival Guide for Lesbian, Gay, Bisexual, Transgender, and Questioning Teens

By Kelly Huegel Madrone

$18.99 plus $4 s/h

272 Pages Softcover

This Is a Book for Parents of Gay Kids

By Dannielle Owens

$16.99 plus $4 s/h

240 Pages Softcover

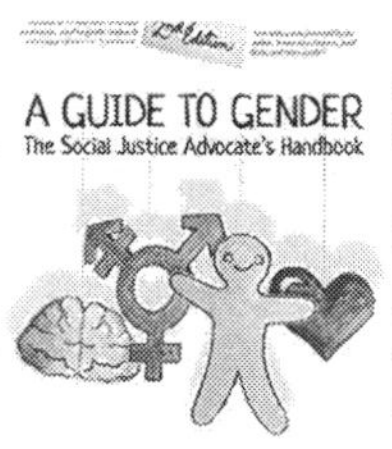

A Guide to Gender (2nd Edition): The Social Justice Advocate's Handbook

By Sam Killerman

$20.99 plus $7 s/h

312 Pages Softcover

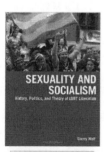

Sexuality & Socialism: History, Politics & the Theory of LGBT Liberation

By Sherry Wolf

$11.99 plus $4 s/h

240 Pages Softcover

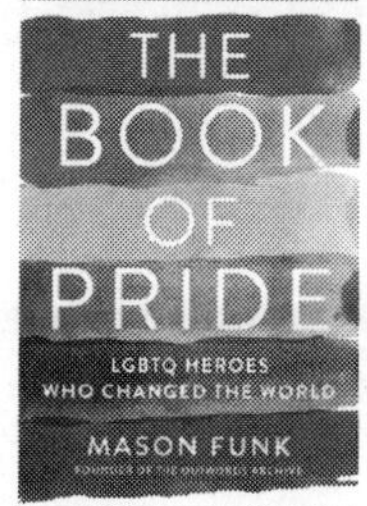

The Book of Pride: LGBTQ Heroes Who Changed the World

$21.99 plus $4 s/h

288 Pages Softcover

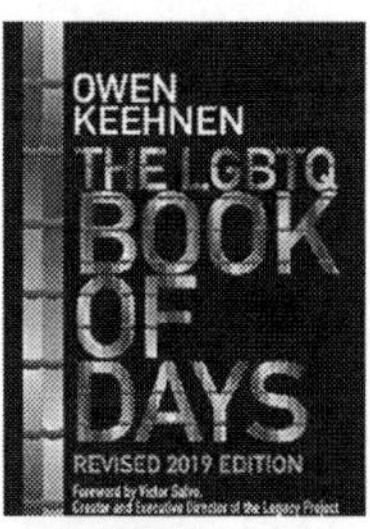

The LGBTQ Book of Days – 2019 Revised Edition

By Owen Keehan

$24.99 plus $5 s/h

440 Pages Softcover

LGBTQ Clients in Therapy: Clinical Issues and Treatment Strategies

By Joe Kort

$25.99 plus $4 s/h

480 Pages Softcover

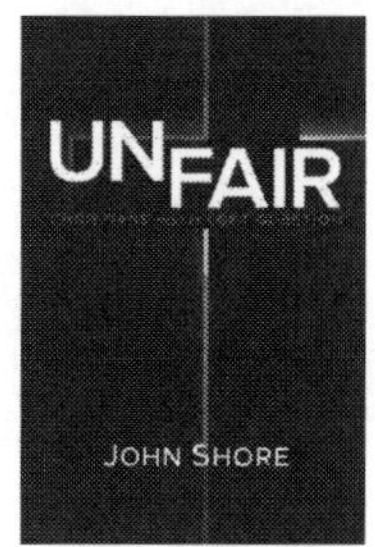

UnFair: Christians and LGBT Questions

By John Shore

$14.99 plus $4 s/h

208 Pages Softcover

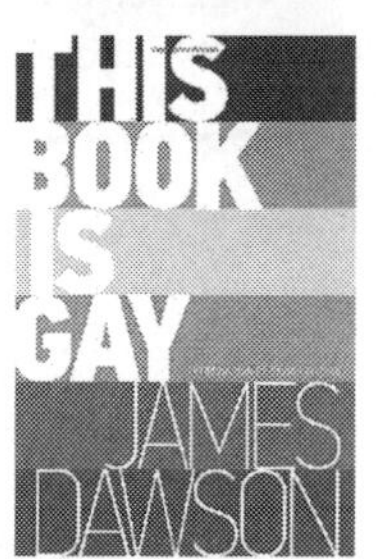

This Book is Gay

By James Dawson

$10.99 plus $4 s/h

272 Pages Softcover

Trans Bodies, Trans Selves: A Resource for the Transgender Community

By Laura Erickson-Schroth

$42.99 plus $7 s/h

672 Pages Softcover

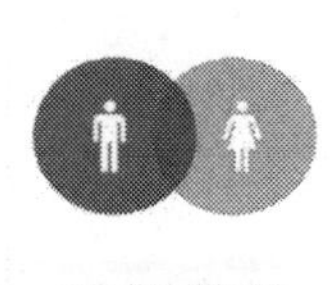

Transgender 101: A Simple Guide to a Complex Issue

By Nicholas M. Teich

$20.99 plus $4 s/h

160 Pages Softcover

Pen Pals: A Personal Guide For Prisoners

By Krista Smith

$22.99 plus $7 s/h

200 Pages Softcover

Pen Pal Success: The Ultimate Guide to Getting & Keeping Pen Pals

By Josh Kruger

$22.99 plus $7 s/h

230 Pages Softcover

Pretty Girls Love Bad Boys: A Prisoner's Guide to Getting Girls

By Mike Enemigo/King Guru

$22.99 plus $7 s/h

223 Pages Softcover

Celebrity Female Star Power

By Josh Kruger

$27.99 plus $7 s/h

216 Pages Softcover

Prison Health Handbook

By Mike Enemigo

$19.99 plus $7 s/h

277 Pages Softcover

Surviving Prison: The Secrets to Surviving the Most Treacherous and Notorious Prisons in America

By Zachary A. Smith

$24.99 plus $4 s/h

196 Pages Softcover

DIY For Prisoners

By Tanner G. Cummings

$13.99 plus $5 s/h

106 Pages Softcover

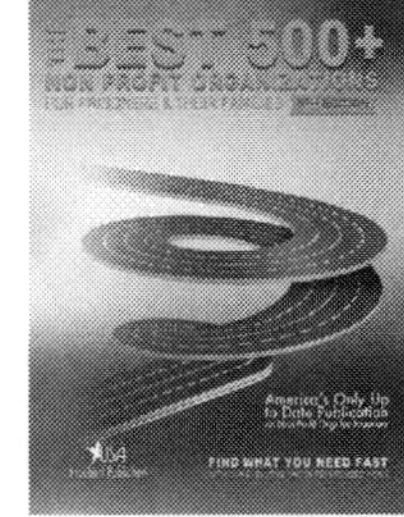

The Best 500+ Non Profit Orgs for Prisoners 5th NEW

Publisher: Freebird Publishers

$16.99 plus $5 s/h

142 Pages Softcover

Kitty Kat: Adult Entertainment Non Nude Resource Book

By Mike Enemigo

$24.99 plus $7 s/h

190 Pages Softcover

Federal Prison Handbook: The Definitive Guide to Surviving the Federal Bureau of Prisons

By Christopher Zoukis

$35.99 plus $7 s/h

522 Pages Softcover

Millionaire Prisoner Special TCB Edition

By Josh Kruger

$26.99 plus $7 s/h

290 Pages Softcover

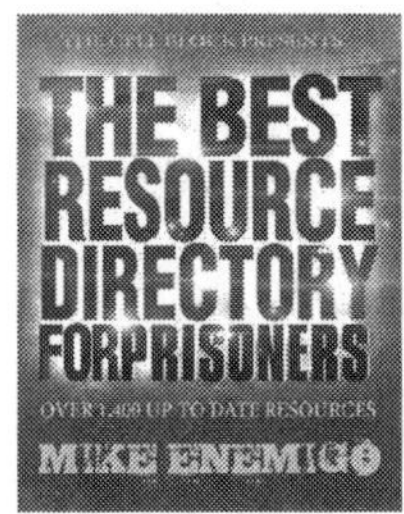

The Best Resource Directory for Prisoners

By Mike Enemigo

$22.99 plus $7 s/h

267 Pages Softcover

Inmates For Entrepreneurial Progress

By Travis E. Williams

$19.99 plus $4 s/h

120 Pages Softcover

Scared To Death... Do it anyway!

By Brian Beneduce

$22.99 plus $4 s/h

188 Pages Softcover

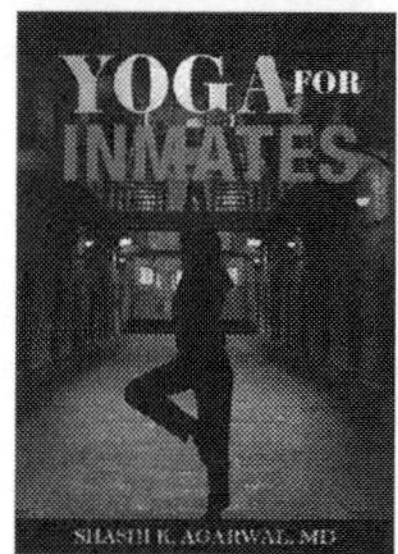

YOGA For Inmates

By Shashi k Agarwal

$18.99 plus $4 s/h

208 Pages Softcover

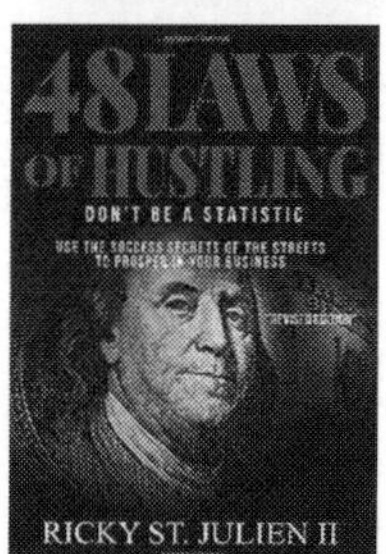

48 LAWS of Hustling

By Ricky St. Julien II

$18.99 plus $4 s/h

192 Pages Softcover

The Highway of Life

By Kiyoshi Terrell Fish

$23.99 plus $4 s/h

142 Pages Softcover

WriteAPrisoner.com's SELF-HELP GUIDE FOR INMATES: Flourishing Through Adversity

By Adam Lovell

$11.99 plus $ 4s/h

120 Pages Softcover

Illegal to Legal: Business Success For Ex-Criminals

By Mr. R. L. Pelshaw

$19.99 plus $4 s/h

258 Pages Softcover

From Inmate to Boss

By E. Fresh

$18.99 plus $4 s/h

72 Pages Softcover

Born 4 A Reason

By Anthony M Knox

$14.99 plus $4 s/h

66 Pages Softcover

Emotional Stability During Incarceration

By Shashi K Agarwal MD

$18.99 plus $4 s/h

248 Pages Softcover

Growth

By Craig A Byrnes

$16.99 plus $4 s/h

254 Pages Softcover

Prison Survival Guide: Words of Wisdom and Encouragement from an Inmate

By Russell Ferguson

$14.99 plus $4 s/h

288 Pages Softcover

The New Jim Crow: Mass Incarceration in the Age of Colorblindness

By Michelle Alexander

$17.99 plus $4 s/h

336 Pages Softcover

Felon-Attorney

By Arthur A. Duncan II Esq.

$21.99 plus $4 s/h

256 Pages Softcover

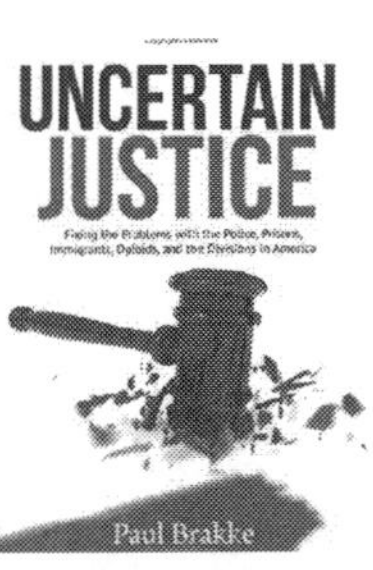

Uncertain Justice: Fixing the Problems with the Police, Prisons, Immigrants, Opioids, and the Divisions in America

By Paul Brakke

$17.99 plus $4 s/h

136 Pages Softcover

From Asylum to Prison: Deinstitutionalization and the Rise of Mass Incarceration

By Ann Parsons

$29.99 plus $4 s/h

240 Pages Hardcover

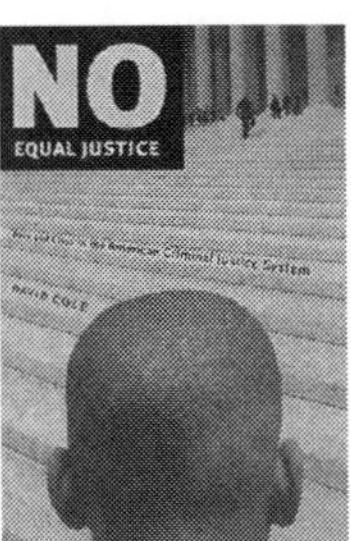

No Equal Justice: Race and Class in the American Criminal Justice System

By David Cole

$17.99 plus $4 s/h

218 Pages Softcover

Domestic Genocide: The Institutionalization of Society

By Ivan Gilmore

$26.99 plus $4 s/h

344 Pages Softcover

From Deportation to Prison: The Politics of Immigration Enforcement in Post-Civil Rights America

By Patricia Macias-Rojas

$29.99 plus $4 s/h

240 Pages Softcover

Prison Madness: The Mental Health Crisis Behind Bars

By Terry Kuper, MD

$31.99 plus $5 s/h

336 Pages Softcover

Locked In: The True Causes of Mass Incarceration

By John F. Pfaff

$23.99 plus $4 s/h

272 Pages Hardcover

American Prison: A Reporter's Undercover Journey into the Business of Punishment

By Shane Bauer

$14.99 plus $4 s/h

368 Pages Softcover

Free at Last: Daily Meditations by and for Inmates

Publisher: Hazelton

$15.99 plus $4 s/h

384 Pages Softcover

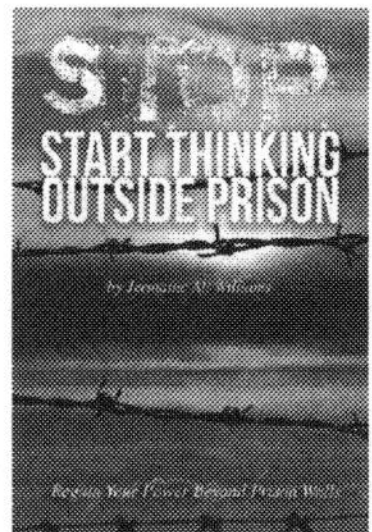

S.T.O.P: Start Thinking Outside Prison

By Jermaine Ali Williams

$13.99 plus $5 s/h

70 Pages Softcover

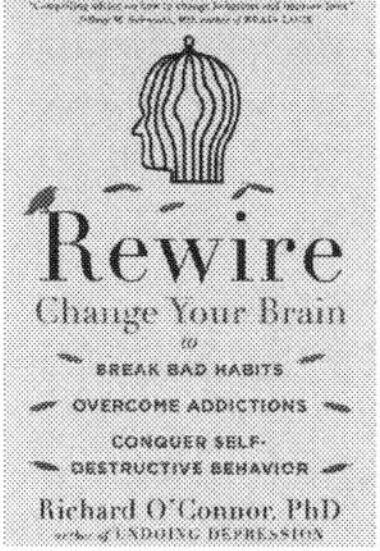

Rewire: Change Your Brain to Break Bad Habits, Overcome Addictions, Conquer Self-Destructive Behavior

By Richard O'Connor

$16.99 plus $4 s/h

304 Pages Softcover

You'll Get Through This: Hope and Help for Your Turbulent Times

By Max Lucado

$14.99 plus $4 s/h

240 Pages Softcover

Unlocked Keys to Getting Out and Staying Out

By Chance A. John Meyer

$12.99 plus $4 s/h

120 Pages Softcover

The Subtle Art of Not Giving a F*ck: A Counterintuitive Approach to Living a Good Life

By Mark Manson

$12.99 plus $4 s/h

368 Pages Softcover

Emotional Stability During Incarceration

By Shashi K Agarwal MD

$14.99 plus $4 s/h

248 Pages Softcover

Doing Time Together: Love & Family in the Shadow

By Megan Comfort

$29.99 plus $4 s/h

256 Pages Softcover

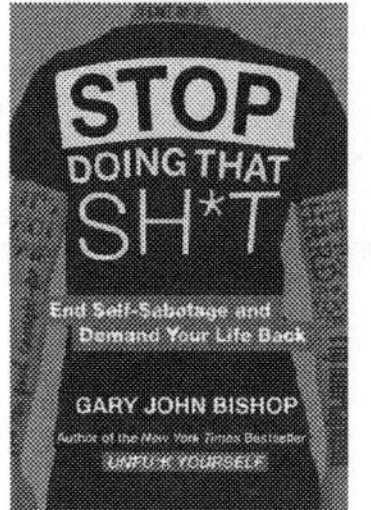

Stop Doing That Sh*t: End Self-Sabotage and Demand Your Life Back

By Gary John Bishop

$21.99 plus $4 s/h

240 Pages Softcover

Think Outside the Cell: An Entrepreneur's Guide

By Joseph Robinson

$16.99 plus $4 s/h

220 Pages Softcover

Arrested: What to Do When Your Loved One's in Jail

By Wes Denham

$16.99 plus $4 s/h

240 Pages Softcover

Serving Productive Time: Stories, Poems & Tips

Publisher: HCI

$13.99 plus $4 s/h

244 Pages Softcover

Everything Is F*cked: A Book About Hope

By Mark Manson

$21.99 plus $4 s/h

415 Pages Softcover

Funster Crossword Puzzle Book for Adults: 101 Large-Print Easy Puzzles

By Charles Timmerman

$14.99 plus $4 s/h

225 Pages Softcover

Variety Puzzle Book For Adults

By Jay Johnson

$12.99 plus $4 s/h

236 Pages Softcover

LIFE Wild & Wacky Picture Puzzle

By Editors of Life

$12.99 plus $4 s/h

112 Pages Softcover

Crossword Puzzles for Adults: Easy to Difficult

Publisher: Speedy Publishing

$8.99 plus $4 s/h

46 Pages Softcover

Jumble® Mania: A Collection for Passionate Puzzlers

By Tribune Media

$9.99 plus $4 s/h

192 Pages Softcover

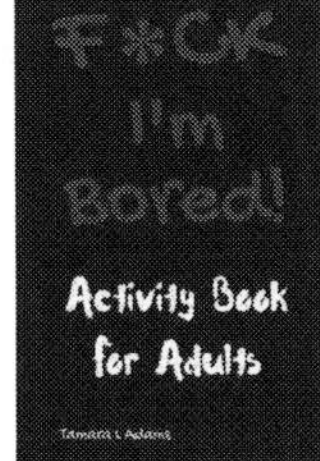

Life: The Original Picture Puzzle

Publisher: Life

$15.99 plus $4 s/h

176 Pages Softcover

USA TODAY Jumbo Puzzle Book 2: 400 Brian Games for Every Day

By Andrews McMeel Publishing

$14.99 plus $7 s/h

480 Pages Softcover

417 More Games, Puzzles & Trivia Challenges Specially Designed to Keep Your Brain Young-New Ed.

By Nancy Linde, Daniel G. Amen

$12.99 plus $6 s/h

424 Pages Softcover

Map It! Seek & Find Atlas of Brainy Challenges

Publisher: Touchstone

$10.99 plus $4 s/h

64 Pages Softcover

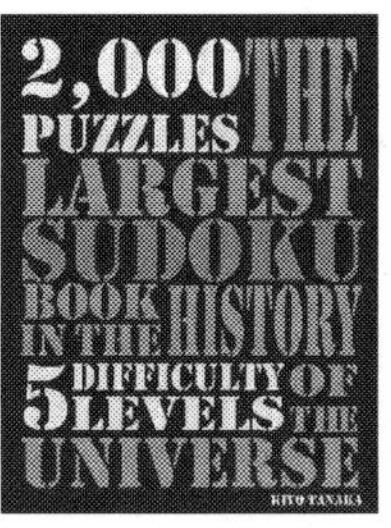

2000 Puzzles the Largest Sudoku Book in History with 5 Levels of Difficulty

By Kiyo Tanaka

$22.99 plus $7 s/h

448 Pages Softcover

The Ultimate Maze Book For Adults: Moderate To Challenging Maze Puzzles

By Puzzle Place

$14.99 plus $4 s/h

122 Pages Softcover

The Times Codeword Puzzles 1 (vol. 1-8 available)

By The Times Mind Games

$12.99 plus $4 s/h each vol.

192 Pages Softcover

Life With A Record: Reenter Society, Finish Supervision and Live Successfully

By Anthony Tinsman

$25.99 plus $7 s/h

360 Pages Softcover

Guide to Relapse Prevention for Prisoners

By Charles Howard Hottinger Jr.

$16.99 plus $4 s/h

80 Pages Softcover

No One Will Hire Me!: Avoid 17 Mistakes & Win the Job

By Ron & Caryl Krannich, Ph.D.

$13.99 plus $4 s/h

208 Pages Softcover

Earning Early Release And Reentry Planning In The United States

By Travis Williams

$12.99 plus $4 s/h

76 Pages Softcover

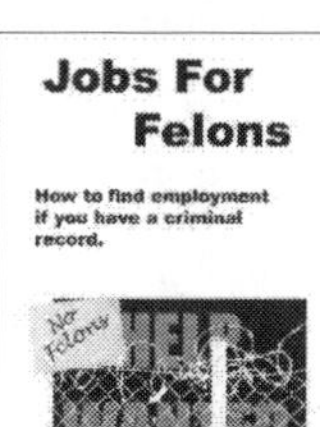

Jobs For Felons

By Michael Ford

$8.99 plus $4 s/h

60 Pages Softcover

The Ex-Offender's Quick Job Interview Guide

By Ron and Caryl Krannich Ph.D.

$11.99 plus $4 s/h

128 Pages Softcover

The Dedicated Ex-Prisoner's guide to Life & Success on the Outside

By Richard Bovan

$10.99 plus $4 s/h

80 Pages Softcover

How To Get A Job In 30 Days Or Less: Discover Insider hiring Secrets on Applying & Interviewing

By George Egbuonu

$11.99 plus $4 s/h

146 Pages Softcover

Getting Out and Staying Out: A Black Man's Guide to Success After Prison

By Demico Boothe

$12.99 plus $4 s/h

72 Pages Softcover

Beyond Bars: Rejoining Society After Prison

By Jeffrey Ian Ross Ph. D, Stephen C. Richards Ph. D.

$11.99 plus $4 s/h

240 Pages Softcover

The Ex-Offender's Quick Job Hunting Guide

By Ron and Caryl Krannich Ph.D.

$11.99 plus $4 s/h

128 Pages Softcover

Best Resumes and Letters for Ex-Offenders

By Wendy S. Enelow

$17.99 plus $4 s/h

212 Pages Softcover

Hope Reborn: How to Become a Christian and Live for Jesus

By Tope Koleoso & Adrain Warnock

$9.99 plus $4 s/h
128 Pages Softcover

Mormonism 101: Examining the Religion of the Latter-Day Saints

By Bill McKeever & Eric Johnson

$14.99 plus $4 s/h

336 Pages Softcover

Between Worlds: Dybbuks, Exorcists and Early Modern Judaism

By JH Chajes

$22.99 plus $4 s/h

228 Pages Softcover

Major Trend in Jewish Mysticism

By Gershom Scholem

$18.99 plus $7 s/h

496 Pages Softcover

The Pagan Book of Days: A guide to the Festivals, Rituals & Celebrations

By Nigel Pennick

$13.99 plus $5 s/h

160 Pages Softcover

Paganism: An Introduction to Earth-Centered Religious Movement

By Joyce & River Higginbotham

$16.99 plus $4 s/h

250 Pages Softcover

Wicca: A Guide for the Solitary Practitioner

By Scott Cunningham

$14.99 plus $4 s/h

240 Pages Softcover

Wicca for Beginners: Fundamental of Philosophy & Practice

By Thea Sabin

$14.99 plus $4 s/h

288 Pages Softcover

Wicca Candle Magic: A Beginner's Guide to Practicing Wiccan Candle Magic, with Simple Candle Spells

By Lisa Chamberlain

$ 10.99 plus $4 s/h

116 Pages Softcover

Wicca Practical Magic: The Guide to Get Started with Magical Herbs, Oils, and Crystals

By Patti Wigington

$13.99 plus $4 s/h

202 Pages Softcover

Spiritual Growth: Being Your Higher Self

By Sanaya Roman

$13.99 plus $4 s/h

252 Pages Softcover

FK It: The Ultimate Spiritual Way**

By John Parkin

$14.99 plus $4 s/h

264 Pages Softcover

The Four Agreements: A Practical Guide to Personal Freedom (Toltec Wisdom Book)

By Don Miguel Ruiz

$9.99 plus $4 s/h

160 Pages Softcover

The Fifth Agreement: A Practical Guide to Self-Mastery (Toltec Wisdom Book)

By Janet Mills

$9.99 plus $4 s/h

248 Pages Softcover

The Mastery of Self: A Toltec Guide to Personal Freedom

By Don Miguel Ruiz

$15.99 plus $4 s/h

176 Pages Softcover

Greek Mythology For Beginners

By Joe Lee

$18.99 plus $4 s/h

208 Pages Softcover

Buddha For Beginners

By Stephen T. Asma

$12.99 plus $4 s/h

160 Pages Softcover

Zen For Beginners

By Judith Blackstone

$16.99 plus $4 s/h

176 Pages Softcover

The Mastery of Love: A Practical guide to the Art of Relationship (Toltec Wisdom Book)

By Don Miguel Ruiz

$9.99 plus $4 s/h

210 Pages Softcover

Mastery of Love

By Don Miguel Ruiz

$9.99 plus $4 s/h

210 Pages Softcover

The Circle of Fire: Inspiration and Guided Meditations for Living in Love and Happiness

By Don Miguel Ruiz

$12.99 plus $4 s/h

176 Pages Softcover

-Holy Bible, King James Version
-New American Standard Bible
-Holy Bible: New Living Translation

$10.99 plus $7 s/h

Each Softcover, Number Pages Differ Per Title

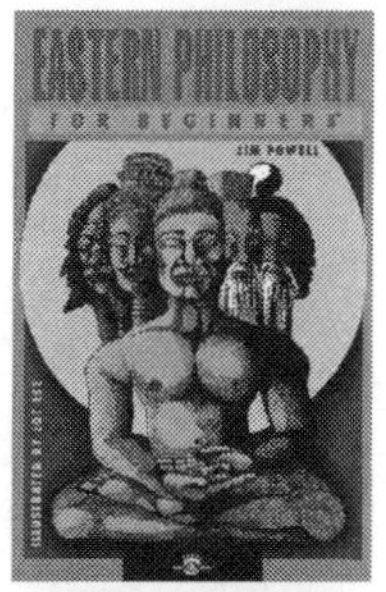

Eastern Philosophy For Beginners

By John C. Maxwell

$17.99 plus $4 s/h

192 Pages Softcover

Man's Search for Meaning

By Viktor E. Frankl

$8.99 plus $4 s/h

168 Pages Softcover

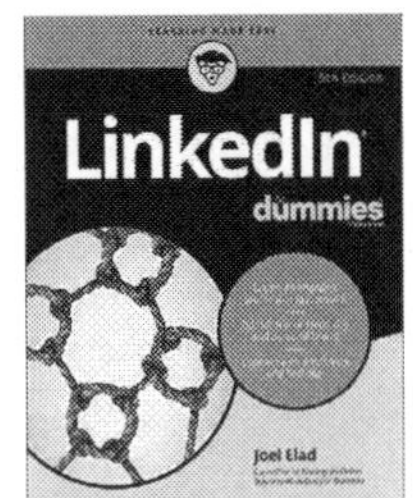

LinkedIn For Dummies

By Carolyn Abram

$23.99 plus $5 s/h

384 Pages Softcover

Facebook For Dummies

By Carolyn Abram

$24.99 plus $7 s/h

432 Pages Softcover

Social Media Marketing All-in-One For Dummies

By Jan Zimmerman

$24.99 plus $7 s/h

752 Pages Softcover

Everything You Need to Know about Social Media: Without Having to Call A Kid

By Greta Van Susteren

$16.99 plus $4 s/h

320 Pages Softcover

Instagram Black Book Everything You Need to Know For Personal and Business

By Jan Zimmerman

$17.99 plus $4 s/h

140 Pages Softcover

Facebook, Twitter, and Instagram For Seniors For Dummies

By Marsha Collier

$21.99 plus $4 s/h

352 pages Softcover

The Four: The Hidden DNA of Amazon, Apple, Facebook, and Google

By Scott Galloway

$17.99 plus $4 s/h

336 Pages Softcover

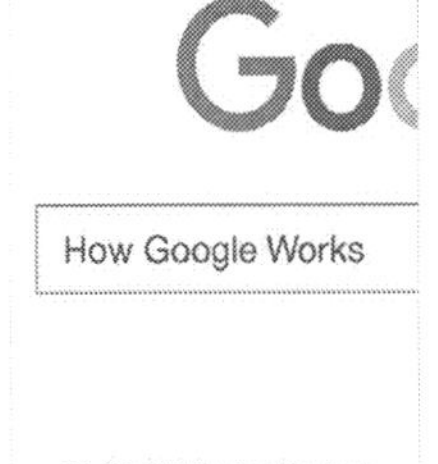

How Google Works

By Eric Schmidt

$16.99 plus $4 s/h

350 Pages Softcover

The Powerful Formula for LinkedIn Success, Completely Revised

By Wayne Breithbarth

$20.99 plus $4 s/h

248 Pages Softcover

Passive Income Ideas 2019: 10,000/ month Ultimate Guide, Amazon FBA Work Make Money

By Ronald Roberts

$19.99 plus $4 s/h

178 Pages Softcover

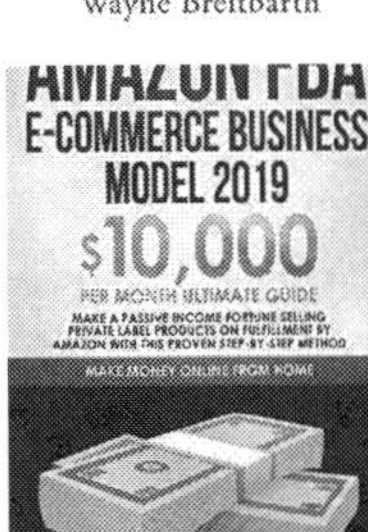

Amazon FBA E-commerce Business Model 2019

By Ronald Roberts

$19.99.99 plus $4 s/h

151 Pages Softcover

eBay Business All-in-One For Dummies (Business & Personal Finance)

By Marsha Collier

$27.99 plus $5 s/h

648 Pages Softcover

438 Days: An Extraordinary True Story Lost at Sea

By Jonathan Franklin

$12.99 plus $4 s/h

288 Pages Softcover

True Crime Stories: 12 Shocking Murder Cases (vol. 1-12 available)

By Jack Rosewood

$12.99 plus $4 s/h (each vol. 1-4)

132-177 Pages Softcover

Prison Days: True Diary Entries by a Maximum Security Prison Officer (Vol. 1-4)

By Dennis Brooks

$8.99 plus $4 s/h (each vol.)

69 Pages Softcover

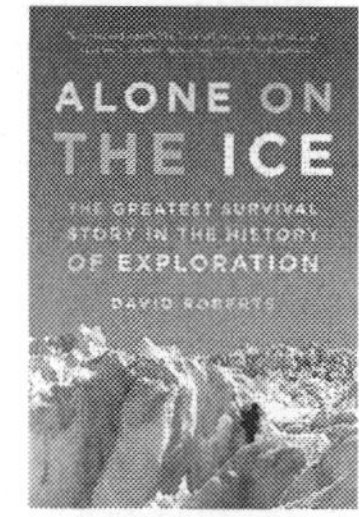

Alone on the Ice: The Greatest Survival Story in the History of Exploration

By Lauren Tarshis

$15.99 plus $5 s/h

368 Pages Softcover

Bitter Remains: A Custody Battle, A Gruesome Crime, and the Mother Who Paid the Ultimate Price

By Diane Fanning

$10.99 plus $5 s/h

416 Pages Softcover

American Prisoner: Above the Cage

By D. Razor Babb

$13.99 plus $4 s/h

164 Pages Softcover

The Illuminati in Hollywood: Celebrities, Conspiracies, and Secret Societies in Pop Culture and the Entertainment Industry

By Mark Dice

$20.99 plus $4 s/h

342 Pages Hard Cover

American Prisoner II: Still I Rise

By D. Razor Babb

$14.99 plus $5 s/h

158 Pages Softcover

Man on a Raft: Fifty Days Adrift at Sea

By Kenneth Cooke

$14.99 plus $5 s/h

172 Pages Softcover

The True Story of Fake News: How Mainstream Media Manipulates Millions

By Jonathan Jackson Jr.

$16.99 plus $4 s/h

330 Pages Softcover

HOW TO ORDER FROM THIS BOOKSTORE-Order By Mail, Online, Email or Phone

NO ORDER FORM NEEDED CLEARLY WRITE ON PAPER & SEND PAYMENT TO:

Freebird Publishers Box 541, North Dighton, MA 02764

Diane@FreebirdPublishers.com www.FreebirdPublishers.com

Toll Free: 888-712-1987 Text/Phone: 774-406-8682

We Accept All Forms of Payments

PEN PAL INDEX

Use the information in this section to help you quickly locate the business you're looking for within the following Pen Pal Directories.

PEN PAL WEBSITES

RETURN TO SENDER

Ask A Convict
Christian Prison Pen Pals
Convict Mailbag
Exclusive Prisoner
Friends With Pens
Friendships and More
Gay Prisoner USA
Hot Prison Pen Pals
Inmates For You
InmatesInWaiting.com
Jail Mail
Love By Ink Pen Pals
Lovely Friends Direct
Outlaws Online
My Jail Bird
Non-Stop Connections
PenPalsFromPrison.com
Prison Buds
Prison Inmates
Prisoner Life
TFL Services
Womeninwaiting.com

Batt Services LLC
Convict Mailbag
Friendships and More
Friends With Pens
Gay Prisoner USA
Prison Buds
Lovely Friends Direct
TFL Services

4Ever Connected, LLC
Online Inmate Dating
Rated None
Details: Send SASE
Mail: Box 471898
Tulsa, OK 74147
PH: 918-527-8290
4everconnectedllc@gmail.com
Web: 4everconnected.net
Review: Founded in 2015, they believe that everyone needs someone to connect with. We are dedicated to keeping inmates connected with the outside world. They offer not only pen pal service, but many other services too. For more information. Apr. 2018

Babes Behind Bars
Free pen pal site for women inmates
Rated 8
Details: Send SASE
Price: Use a $1.15 FCS on envelope
Mail: Admin Rodney
4246 Albert St. Ste. 403
Regina, Saskatchewan
Canada S4S 3R9
Web: babes-behind-bars.com
Review: This is website specializes in helping incarcerated women find friends as pen pals to help them through their loneliness. There are about 875 inmate ads on the site. Submit your information to produce your online profile. Your ad can be up to 100 words and one photo.

Black and Pink
LGBTQ pen pal listing plus
► **RATED 10!**
Details: Send SASE
Mail: 6223 Maple St. #4600
Omaha, NE 68104
PH:531-600-9089
Web: blackandpink.org
members@blackandpink.org
Review: Self-proclaimed radical anti-establishment, anti-capitalism, gay liberation organization started in Boston. Has monthly prisoner newspaper. Pen pal listings are created in spreadsheet format with no pictures and contain basic information. By all appearances this is first an activist site. The pen pal listing is not a primary focus. Black and Pink is an open family of LGBTQ prisoners and "free world" allies who support each other. Their work toward the abolition of the prison industrial complex is rooted in the experience of currently and formerly incarcerated people. They are outraged by the specific violence of the prison industrial complex against LGBTQ people, and respond through advocacy, education, direct service, and organizing.

BrownPride.com
Latino/Latina pen pals listing
Rated None
Details: Online only
Web: brownpride.com
Review: Strictly Latin culture and current events. The website is well done. The pen pal section is a small link located at the bottom right of the home page. The pen pal listings contain very brief bios and no pictures. Latin culture and events site.

Promotes Latin artist in music, street art and online store.

Captive Angels
Pen pal listing for women
Rated: None
Details: Send SASE
Mail: Box 13152
Las Cruces, NM 88013
Web: captiveangels.com
Info@captiveangels.com
Review: Discovered through a link from Cell Pals. It has a unique layout and shows about 75 women on the home page with links to each profile. There is an ad for Premium and economy general listings, but it does not show prices. Suggest you contact them for a brochure.

CellPals
Pen pal listing
Rated 8
Details: Send SASE
Price: Ranging from $5 to $50
Mail: Box 13278
Las Cruces, NM 88013
PH: 855-PEN-PALS (736-7257)
Web: cellpals.com
Review: New Owners, a husband and wife team, they are a nice honest couple that care. They have rebuilt the website to be easier to use and a better updated design. This is a dedicated pen pal site providing a variety of listing options, ranging from $5 listing to $50 profiles valid through your length of incarceration. Submissions can be made by the person with an institution check or through friends and family going online to Cell Pals web site. Jan. 2015

Christian Pen Pals
Christian pen pal listing
Rated None
Details: Online only
Price: Free
Web: christianpenpals.com
Review: This is a very open forum for Christian-based pen pals from all around the world. The pen pal listings are surprisingly well done considering they are free. Most profiles include pictures and personal bios of varying length and detail. The submission process is online only but very simple and can be completed in a matter of minutes. CPP is a member of a growing network of Christian web sites which they call the 'Christian Web', with ChristianWeb.com (currently under construction) being the main 'portal' to all the sites in their network as well as other fine Christian web sites they may link in the future.

CONPALS InmateConnections.com
Pen pal listing and email services
► **RATED 10!**
Details: Send SASE
Price: $45 yr.
Mail: 465 NE 181st Ave. #308
Portland, OR 97230
Web: convictpenpals.com
info@convictpenpals.com
Review: This is a dedicated pen pal site providing a variety of listing options. CONPALS begun in 2002 for the purpose of connecting prisoners with the outside world through letters and email messages. They pride themselves on offering more and better services for prisoners than any other prisoner pen pal website. They have popular category searches for your profiles, such as advanced, birthday and state. They accept facility checks, personal checks, traveler's checks, money orders, all major credit cards, debit cards, PayPal, Bill Me Later, MoneyGram, and stamps sent from prisoners. CONPALS full name written above. In addition, they offer personal email addresses. The addresses are as (yourname@conpals.com). For info on the email service, send SASE. Jun. 2019
Reader Review: Ryan D. in WI-They have competitive pricing with wide reaching profiles. Although it has been three months and my listing hasn't generated any responses yet too soon to tell. Sept. 2018
—SEE OUR AD—

Foreign Ladies
Online Dating service
► **RATED 10!**
Details: See review
Price: Free to post profile.
Phone 408-372-2100
Web: foreignladies.com
support@foreignladies.com
Review: Men, post your profile free. You will need a friend to post for you or hire one of the businesses that uploads to Facebook. First letter for new clients costs $1.95 for ten credits and additional credits for $7.50. One credit for each email. Let women write to you. Women from Russia, Philippines, China, Spain and so many more.

Forgotten Females
Free pen pal site for women inmates
Rated 8
Details: Send SASE for app.
Price: Free
Mail: C/O Mc Lloyd Services
Box 3621
Wichita, KS 67201
Web: forgottenfemales.tripod.com
forgottenfemales@yahoo.com

Review: a website designed to be a place where women of American Jails and Prisons are able to tell their stories of personal incarceration. They also include personal listings of some female inmates that wish to find pen pals. This website, which provides an opportunity for women in America, with the desire to be heard from behind bars. Women from around all parts of America featured on this site, are considered serious and hope that having the opportunity to tell their stories will alert others, in a caring concerning way.

Friends 4 Prisoners
Pen pal listing
▶ RATED 10!
Details: Send SASE
Price: $30-$50 Standard or $60-$100 Featured
Mail: 20770 Hwy 281 N. Ste. 108-178
San Antonio, TX 78258
Web: friends4prisoners.com
Review: The mission of Friends4Prisoners.com is to connect our subscribers to pen pals from all over the world. Receiving mail, making new friends and learning about other cultures is exciting and can greatly help pass the time. Featured profiles are listed before standard profiles, guaranteeing more visits to the inmate's profile. Profile comes with personal info, one photo and 250-word bio/ad. Can purchase more photos, more words and buy one- or two-year subscriptions. Accept facility checks, money orders, credit card online and stamps. For brochure send SASE. Mar. 2019
—SEE OUR AD—

Friends Beyond The Wall, Inc.
Pen pal listing
▶ RATED 10!
Details: Send SASE
Price: $39.95, 250 word ad and photo
Second Year: Add 'l $22.95
Mail: Attn: INSH 1411
55 Mansion St., #1030
Poughkeepsie, NY 12601
Web: friendsbeyondthewall.com
info@friendsbeyondthewall.com
Review: Friends Beyond the Wall is known to Inmate Shopper to be an upstanding business. Their website has an inviting, friendly flow, with custom icons making the content easy to find. Plus, visitors can search for pen pals by name, age range, state, or ethnicity. They have been in business since 1999. Featuring 2500 plus photo ads in 46 states. FBW has twelve years of experience and fantastic customer service that includes a customer assurance guarantee. Their color brochure shows an actual pen pal ad on the website, so consumers know what they're purchasing.
Reader Review: Michael R in TX-I mailed them $69 and got proof they received the funds three days after 1/19/19. Still no word from them. Mar 2019

GoodPrisoner
Pen pal listing for inmates
Rated: None
Details: See review
Mail: Box 12
Buffalo, NY 14215-0012
Web: goodprisoner.com
Review: They are free to use and available to anyone in the world who has a computer/device capable of connecting to the internet so people looking for pen pals do not have to pay to find your profile. Inmates listed on this site are required to pay a fee for a one year plus pen pal page. This site is for male inmates, but they have a sister site for female inmates www.femaleprisonerpals.com.

Inmate Classified
Pen Pal Ads
▶ RATED 10!
Details: Send SASE
Price: See review
Mail: Box 3311
Granada Hills, CA 91394
PH: 323-529-8570 (voicemail)
Web: inmate.com
Review: Founded in 1996, Inmate classified was created to address inmates needs to reconnect with friends and family as well as facilitating positive communication with pen pals around the world, Standard ad-$60 for six months (300 words, one photo) or $100 for one year (300 words, two photos). Premium ad-$120 for six months (high exposure, 300 words, one photo, five free email responses) or $200 for one year (high exposure, 300 words, two photo, ten free email responses). Additional services, send SASE for information.
Reader Review: Paul K in Wa-They are always pros. I have had most of my success through them, but I have also been catfished (not their fault). No games from the webmaster. Oct. 2017

Inmate-Connection
Pen pal listing
▶ RATED 10!

Details: Send SASE
Price: $40 for two yrs. listing
Mail: Box 83897
Los Angeles, CA 90083
Web: inmate-connection.com
info@inmate-connection.com
Review: Creating friendships from the inside out. Our mission is to attract sincere pen pals who can bring love, friendship and happiness to the lives of lonely inmates who are locked away from society and who have lost contact with the outside world. It is commonly known that most prisoners lose contact with their friends, relatives and family members after spending 3 years or more in prison. With the loss of contact with the outer world, prisoners often feel like they have lost all their independence, confidence, personality, self-esteem and pride. However, pen pals can write a letter or send a card to boost their morale in unimaginable ways. Print out an application and mail to a prisoner. Yearly fee can be processed through our secure link. It is free to outside person to mail inmates. You can have up to 100 words and one photo.
Reader Review: Paul K in WA-They are very responsive and courteous. However, I have never received one replay to my ad when placed with them. Oct. 2017
—SEE OUR AD—

Inmatelovelink.com
Pen pal service for inmates
Rated 8
Details: Send SASE
Price: See Review
Mail: 4001 Inglewood Ave. Ste.144
Redondo Beach, CA 90278
Web: inmatelovelink.com
support@inmatelovelink.com
Review: Their services offered are Pen pal, photocopying service, email service and raffles for inmates only. They offer a website launched special 5 free 4 x 6 color photocopies of your profile photo. Prices for new profile for $20 for one year (250 words, one photo), additional 75 words for $5 additional photos for $5 each. Front page ad for $20 for six months, $35 for one year. You can have a loved one sign you up for a membership and post your profile on the website.

Inmate Mingle
Pen pal site
Rated 8
Details: Send SASE for brochure
Mail: Box 23207
Columbia, SC 29224
Web: inmatemingle.com
info@inmatemingle.com
Review: New company 2017, You can have up to 250 words and one photo in your ad. You have options to add more photos, more words or a song all for $5 each. Pricing start at $30 and have three levels of membership: gallery, god and platinum. You can sign up by mail or have loved ones sigh you up online. Their brochure and Order Form are available in PDF format that can be printed by one of your loved ones and sent to you. May 2017
Reader Review: Paul K in WA-They are wonderful to deal with. Very professional and responsive. Zero hits. Oct. 2017

Inter Pals
Free pen pal site
Rated 8
Details: Online only
Price: Free
Web: interpals.net
Review: Created in April 1998, the site has become the largest and most popular free pen pal site on the web. Not only that, but it has become the go to site for language practice. Although it isn't just for prisoners, there are over 6100 pen pals on the site at this time looking for the same thing. You can have up to 100 words and one photo in your ad.

Jade Rose, The
Free pen pal site
Rated None
Details: Online only
Price: Free
Web: jaderoses.com
Review: The following information is requested but not necessarily required: name, email, address, country (where you are at now), URL (if you have one), age, gender (yours), pen pal preference, additional comments (keep it short). When someone is submitting your ad-online only-click the submit button only once and form will be mailed. Ads will be posted ASAP (sometimes 1-2 weeks). Prisoners are welcome to submit an ad to this site for free. However, prisoners must make it very clear they are incarcerated. You can have up to 100 words and one photo in your ad.

Lost Vault
Pen pal listing
Rated: None
Details: Send SASE
Price: $5 for inmates
Mail: Box 242
Mascot, TN 37806
Web: lostvault.com
Review: Lost Vault has an interesting web design. Inmate pictures are not shown on the home page or even with

their link. You have to select the listing to open the "Vault". From their homepage: Since September 2003, Lost Vault has been dedicated to maintaining a free place for inmates to find pen pals, and for people to find them. Unlike many of the other prison pen pal sites, they do not charge you or the other person for this service as long as the ad is posted via the internet by a loved one or friend. For ads posted by their staff, there is a nominal $5 fee for all inmates other than death row, who receive free ads. Oct. 2015

LoveAPrisoner.com
Pen pal site
► **RATED 10!**
Details: Send SASE
Details: See below FREE Pics
Price: Basic Ad $25
Mail: Box 192
Dequincy, LA 70633
Web: loveaprisoner.com
loveaprisoner@gmail.com
Review: LoveAPrisoner.com mission is to give inmates a sense of hopefulness by connecting them to people on the "outside world." Those from all walks of life have committed to our pen-pal service to communicate with inmates and have formed nurturing and unconditional friendships. Inmates are not only thrilled to communicate with pen-pals but have stated that it has been a "spiritually and emotionally fulfilling experience." They enable friends and family to stay in contact with their loved ones and has a 75% compatibility rating for those looking for their soul mate. So, come on and give them a try. Basic memberships start at up to 250 words and one photo in your ad, but additional options are available. Extras are additional photos at $5 each, get 50 more words for $5, or set background music for $5. LoveAPrisoner.com VIP Membership comes with 40 FREE pics, pick from either Black, White, Asian or Latin Girls. You must say what race of girls you want. TWO (2) Year VIP Membership comes with 100 FREE pics. The VIP Membership is $65 yearly. The Basic Membership is $25 yearly and comes with 20 FREE pics from choices above. For a FREE Brochure send a S.A.S.E. comes with fill-out form and instructions, mail back to them with payment. Beware if they cannot read your application then they cannot post it online. March 2018

Meet-an-Inmate.com
Photo personals of male and female inmates
► **RATED 10!**
Details: Send SASE.
Price: See review
Mail: Attn: Arlen Bischke
Box 845
Winchester, OR 97495
Web: meet-an-inmate.com
ab@bisky.com
Review: There is a downloadable application that can be printed out or send SASE. This site is designed to quickly and easily connect you with pen pals who have the same interests as you. Standard ad starts at $35 for 12 months. Featured ad starts at $70 for 12 months and they offer 24 months subscriptions too. They have special for Females Only, 12 months standard ad on Meet-An-Inmate and Jailbabes.com for $50. They make you a profile page and on their homepage, you have a thumbnail photo link. The purpose of the featured ad is to simply get more traffic to the web page. The more traffic, the better chances of acquiring pen pals. For regular ad, prices start at $35 for 6 months which include two photos and up to 250 words. Mar 2019

Men of the Pen
Pen pal listing
Rated None
Details: $15 one yr., $20 two yrs.
Mail: Customer Service
Box 864862
Plano, TX 75086
Web: menofthepen.com
Review: In business since 2003. A decent site for the cost. From their home page; "A member of our staff had an inmate friend who asked them if they could get mail for some of his inmate friends. We placed a few classified ads for them in a few magazines and were successful in getting them mail. Then a man contacted us and asked if we could get his friend in Texas some mail. It became known through word of mouth that we were very successful in getting inmates mail. With the increasing number of prisoners being incarcerated in the US we decided to start a web site dedicated to this purpose."

Paper Dolls
Pen pal site for women inmates only
Rated None
Details: Send SASE
Price: $5
Mail: Box 218
Oregon, WI 53575

Web: paperdollspenpals.com
paperdolls@mail.com
Review: For guaranteed acceptance, this site suggests a fee of $5 check or money order You MUST send a self-addressed stamped envelope for a copy of your web page and/or your photos back. Email service is available for people to write to you from your Paper Dolls web page for $5 per mon. or $50 per year for unlimited email. You can have up to 100 words and one photo in your ad.

Penacon.com
Inmate pen pal online service
► **RATED 10!**
Details: Send SASE for application
Price: offers $5 off promo
Mail: Box 533
North Dighton, MA 02764
PH: 888-712-1987
PH/Text: 774-406-8682
Web: penacon.com
pencon@freebirdpublishers.com
Corrlinks: diane@freebirdpublishers.com
Review: Penacon.com is dedicated to helping you gain connections, bringing friendship and romance to all! We have updated, upgraded and reformatted the website which encourages more people to view your profile. The site is now easier to use and has greater visibility. We make sure your profile is seen by continuously advertising and networking. One year is $35, ($5 off with promo code INSH5), profile renewals are $25 per year. Or choose for the duration of your sentence option for $95. Profiles are posted within 24 hours of receiving. Add a welcome package to your profile for $5 which includes a colored printout of your ad with welcome note and return of your mailed in photo. Penacon.com offers a Featured Member for $5 a month which gets your profiled placed on our redesigned front pages. Display your photo on the front pages of our website to be immediately seen by all web visitors entering the site. We have added new options to our site, email and text access and can tell us by which website your prison uses, if you can send and receive emails, we place that on your profile. We have upgraded the search area with more detailed choices for visitors to find you easier. We are adding more new options to display your artwork, writing and poetry, links to inmate authored published books and certificates too. We are adding more Sections for Members giving new areas to have your profile viewed like Friends Forever Member, Lookin 4 Love Member, Connected For Life Member. Penacon's big news for 2019 is that we are preparing to do a test run with an app on prisoner tablets serviced by ConnectNetwork/GTL and GettingOut.com. We will keep you all up to date as we move forward with each new improvement. Jun. 2019
Reader Review: Kyle R in PA-I believe I have accomplished what I hoped for with your company. In the light of my success could you please make my profile inactive. Thank you. Aug. 2018
Reader Review: Steven W in IL-I want to send my thanks for your services of Penacon.com (pen pal website) and express how pleased I have been. When the guys see those girls, who have been writing to me, some with pictures, they keep asking me what company I had went with. Before I kept it a secret, now that I see an incentive referral each 2-months FREE subscription and 1-month FREE featured member), I will be spreading the word. Thank you. Aug. 2018
Reader Review: Michael R in TX-I sent Penacon money 1-22-18 and received my profile, pic and thank you letter, maybe two weeks or less. Excellent customer service. They will have my business as long as I am still incarcerated. Mar 2019
Reader Review: Javann H.in NJ-I would lie f you to remove my ad off your site. Your site helped me find the woman I was looking for. Thank you for your help! Dec. 2018
Reader Review: Derrick S in NJ-I am writing to you guys for your absolute professional and wonderful service. My profile just started and already I've encountered two beautiful women, one who on all levels has surpassed my expectations. I am writing to ask that you guys delete my profile, please. I am not trying to be greedy. I am satisfied. Is and when I need a pen pal service I promise it will be Penacon. Thank you so much. Mar. 2019
Reader Review: Richard M in NC-Please terminate my profile as soon as possible. I have met someone and wish no further contacts. Thank you, guys, for everything. Mar. 2019
Reader Review: Daniel H. in OR-Can you please take my profile down. I will no longer need your services as I have found someone. Thank you for your great business. I enjoyed it and think you guys are great. Thank you! Mar. 2019
Reader Review: A few months ago, a friend of mine had his wife put me on your website. I wanted to let you know that your website was a blessing in disguise for me, I still haven't made any solid friends or pen pals, but a few

weeks ago, I received an email from my son whom I haven't seen in 15 years. He found me through your site 12 Thank you very much and God Bless. Dec. 2018

Reader Review: Jimmy S in TX-I am very satisfied with the Penacon service and have referred many of my friends to your company. Keep up the good work. PS. Send me more Penacon applications to pass around. Mar. 2019

Reader Review: Sheldon O in MS-I want to thank you all at Freebird Publishers and Penacon for your assistance in your pen pal service. I have found the most wonderful fantastic lady that I have ever had any contact with thanks to Freebird Publishers and their pen pal service and we are scheduled to get married in July 2019, We have found true love that we all are looking for as long as we are alive we are the perfect match and God brought us together through Freebird Publishers and Penacon. I would let everyone know that it is the very best website and really looked at by a lot of people. Dec. 2018

Reader Review: Darius L in NY-Dear Penacon, First, I would like to thank you for your amazing services. There's no other company that helps prisoners find friends and love as quick as you guys...I'm writing you today because I have finally found the love of my life and would like to terminate my profile at your earliest convenience. Once again, thank you for your services. Jan. 2019

Reader Review: Samantha K.in CA- Hello Penacon! I want to thank you immensely for the awesome work you guys do...and I brag about you every day. I pass out the extra applications to the ladies around me. My friend Cassandra H. just signed up with you. WE LOVE YOU PENACON. Jan. 2019

Reader Review: Steven W in IL-I want to send my thanks for your services of Penacon.com (pen pal website) and express how pleased I have been. When the guys see those girls, who have been writing to me, some with pictures, they keep asking me what company I had went with. Before I kept it a secret, now that I see an incentive referral each 2-months FREE subscription and 1-month FREE featured member), I will be spreading the word. Thank you. Aug. 2018

Letter from a Mother: Jacqueline H in CA-Hi, I was given your company name and address in regard to finding pen pals for my sons in prison. Hope your site can help me to get them each a new friend to pen pal with. I was at loss when they both asked me to find them pen pals...I think this is wonderful service. Thank you so much for being there for inmates and their loved ones. Sincerely, Jacqueline, The Mother. Mar. 2019

Reader Review: William S in MA-Dear Penacon Rep. At this time, I need my profile "TERMINATED" an taken down from your website. I have met someone very special and told her that I would do this immediately. Thank you so much for all of your help, your site is awesome I truly appreciate your time and prompt response to this request. Take care and thanks for everything. Mar. 2019

Reader Review: Rachael C in MI- I am writing because I would like to take my ad down. I have found love thanks to your site and no longer want to connect with anyone else. Thank you for your amazing service! Apr. 2019

Reader Review: Justin W in TN-I recently purchased a lifetime subscription to Penacon. Within five days of being online I already had received correspondences from 3 people! Compared to other site I have been on that cost a lot more money. This website has more traffic which gives more responses or chance of them. Definitely recommend to everyone seeking to find pen pals! A+ Great Job.

Reader Review: Jake S in WI-Thank you Penacon for your services and I appreciated all the friends that I have made because of this website. Please remove me completely from the website as your services are no longer needed. Again, thank you. Sincerely Jake.

Reader Review: Christopher R in OR-I have decided to have my profile removed from the site. I have found the one person I want to commit myself to. Please take my profile down, it will be appreciated. Thank you. June 2019

Reader Review: Armando R in NV-A friend of mine from the outside put me on your website from the internet a couple months ago. I have received five messages from five different women 12. I have not made that special connection yet, but I have no doubt that I will soon. (with your help). I tried a couple really famous websites in the past and none of them worked. Thank you for being legit. Nov. 2018

Letter from an online pen pal: Stacey O. in WA-I think the Penacon site is an awesome outlet for the guys to communicate their feelings because they really do have to be tough in prison. Just having someone to write to when you have no one is a blessing. And when you hit it off and you have some much in common....and all the stars align...that is a bonus! I am so thankful for your website because I met the love of my life ♥.

Reader Review: Frank V. in VA- I appreciate you guys and all that you do over there. I have 82 days until release and I am thankful to all the pen pals you have brought my way. I appreciate you. June 2019

Reader Review: Cayne F. in OR-Can you remove my profile from your website, all is going very well with my new pen pals. Thank you. June 2019

Reader Review: Alejandro M. in OR-I have recently formed a relationship with someone that I met from your site, Penacon.com. I appreciate you for your services and I would like to request the removal of my profile. Thank you. June 2019

—SEE OUR AD—

Pen Pal Connection

Helping friends stay connected

Rated 8

Details: Send SASE

Mail: Box 1352

Elgin, SC 29045

Web: penpalconnection.net

contact@penpalconnection.net

Review: They help people find new friends while maintaining relationships with current friendship and family. They offer pen pal plans, email plans, and social networking plans to fit everyone's needs and budgets. They offer three levels plans: Bronze, silver and gold. These profiles start at $15 per year. Corrlinks accepted

Pen Pal World

Free pen pal site

Rated None

Details: Online only

Price: Free

Web: penpalworld.com

Review: Created in 1997 and currently has over a million members. The site offers a limited free account that allows you to contact and reply to up to three members within 24 hours. They do show your age, gender, and country as a point of interest. You can message through their site without revealing an email address. You can upload 100 words and one photo.

Pen Pals NOW

Free pen pal site

Rated 8

Details: Online only

Price: Free

Web: penpalsnow.com

Review: Created in January 1998. They have over 30,000 pen pal ads from 150 countries. They do allow your snail mail address on the site. You can upload 100 words and one photo.

Pen Pal Party

Free dating site

Rated 8

Details: Online only

Price: Free

Web: penpalparty.com

Review: This site has specific rules for inmates. All is free but you have to disclose you are incarcerated as your occupation and have to have an email address on this one site and they do not allow direct posting of your snail mail address. There are almost 7500 pen pals on file that speak English as their first language. There are also about 14,000 pen pals on file from 166 countries. You can upload 100 words and one photo.

Prison Inmates Online

Online directory

Rated 6

Details: Send SASE or 2 FCS brochure

Mail: 8033 W Sunset Blvd. #7000

Los Angeles, CA 90046

Web: prisonerinmates.com

info@prisoninmates.com

Review: PrisonInmates.com and WriteToPrisoners.com is owned and operated by Prison Inmates Online LLC. They call their online service "Write To Prisoners Project". Serving inmates since 2000. They offer Corrlinks and JPay. They sort their profiles by many categories: male, female, gay, lesbian, bi-sexual, serving life, death, needs mail, and state. They also host inmates' artwork, writings, tattoos, inmates' photos, poetry, and classifies. They connect people through social networks and inmates in US prisons. It's a great place to find prison pen pals or advocate for a prisoner. It cost $50 for 300 words to list an inmate for the duration of their sentence. Inmate introduction gift cards are $50 each.

Reader Review: Allen L in NY- Recently, they created a low balance on account and emailed billed inmates outside billing contacts. Unfortunately, my people paid the bill thinking to maintain my pen pal listing. This was a fake billing and my account did not have a low balance. We have tried to contact by mail, email and phone to get a refund, all at no prevail. April 2017

Prisonpenpals.com
Pen pal service
► **RATED 10!**
Details: Send SASE, accepts FCS
Mail: Box 235
East Berlin, PA 17316
Web: prisonpenpals.com
info@prisonpenpals.com
Review: They offer five different types of ads starting at, Economy, Basic, Gold Star, Platinum, and Gallery. The prices start at $9.95 per year. You can customize your ad package to get exactly what you need with background music and additional photos for a small fee.

Prisoner Pal
Pen pal site
► **RATED 10!**
Details: Send SASE, accept FCS
Mail: TIC Interest
Box 19689
Houston, TX 77224
Web: prisonerpal.com
Advertising@prisonerpal.com
Review: They have been in business for four years and also own TradewindsPublications.com, a discount magazine service. They offer four levels of service: Basic, $9.95; Bronze, $19.95; Silver, $39.95; and Gold, $79.95.

Prison-Princess.com
Pen pal site for women inmates
Rated 8
Details: Send SASE
Price: FCS accepted
Mail: Foster-Hansen Holdings Inc.
Box 864862
Plano, TX 75086-4862
Web: prisonprincesses.com
Review: Make a lonely princess smile! There are three levels of payment; the first is the almost free ad which you need to send 2 FCS. Option two to ensure placement of your ad send in a processing fee of $7.50 (18 FCS) and your ad will receive high priority and a copy of your web page. Finally, option three is $15 (35 FCS) for a year posting of your ad on the first page with your name and address posted directly on your web page. You can have up to 100 words and one photo. Send a SASE for return of your photo.

Prison Voice
See Prison Inmates Online
Web: prisonvoice.com

Signalpenpal.net
Pen Pal Site
Rated 8
Details: Send SASE International for info packet
Price: US $10 ad, $20 with photo
Mail: Raimo Kaarna-XUA21
Purokatu 18
FI-15200 Lahti, Finland
Web: signalpenpals.net
Web: penpalclubs.net
signal@sci.sci.fi
Review: This list is published by Raimo Kaarna. There are over 50,000 pen pals on the site from all over the world. You can upload 100 words and one photo. US $10 to place pen pal ad and US $20 pen pal ad with photo. Send international stamped SASE or 3 FCS for information package. Be patient, overseas mail takes time. They also have a pen pal magazine to see more info on our Pen Pal Magazine section in this issue.

Surrogate Sisters
Pen pal services for inmates
► **RATED 10!**
Details: Send SASE
Mail: Box 95043
Las Vegas, NV 89193
Web: surrogatesisters.com
service@surrogatesisters.com
Review: There are no prices and you have to contact them for more information. This company has been around for eleven years offering other by mail services to inmates. They have expanded into the internet with the pen pal website offerings. Write or email them for more info.

The Kite Connect
Pen pal services for inmates
Rated 8
Details: Send SASE
Mail: Box 185
Springvale, ME 04083
Web: thekiteconnect.com
thekitconnect@gmail.com
Review: They provide a connection directed at the outside world to look on their site for inmates to write to. The site is a listing of inmates that people can find and write to as a pen pal. They have printable info and forms online for your loved ones to send you or you can order by mail send a SASE. New profile, 1 year, 250 words, photo $30. Accept institutional check, money order, or first class forever books ($7.50 per book of 20 / 4 books = $30). March 2017

Voice for Inmates
Pen pal service
Rated 8
Details: Send SASE
Mail: 611 Kings Rd.
Shelby, NC 28150
Web: voiceforinlates.com
signal@sci.fi
Review: They receive emails from pen pals and mail them out to you based on your level of service. Premium service for $60 per year and regular service for $15. Other options and upgrades are available. You can have up to 100 words and one photo in your ad.

Women Behind Bars
Pen pal address-pay per listing
► **RATED 10!**
Details: Send SASE
Price: Free to post
Mail: Todd Muffoletto
Box 284
Hobart, IN 46342
PH: 219-979-4629
Web: womenbehindbars.com
Review: In business since 1997, Women Behind Bars has been interviewed by hundreds of radio stations and written up in hundreds of newspapers. The listing is free for women inmates and prospective pen pals pay a small fee $4 per address. You can have up to 100 words and one photo in your ad. You will need an application.

Women In Waiting
Pen pal services
Rated None
Detail: Online only
Price: See below
Web: womeninwaiting.com
Review: This website leads you to Friend Search, an online dating site. It only has contact through online. Free service for this but online only. Not recommended.

WriteAPrisoner.com
Pen pal profiles
Rated 8
Details: Send SASE
Mail: Box 10
Edgewater, FL 32132
PH: 386-427-5857
Web: writeaprisoner.com
Review: They offer standard ad for $40 for a year (100 words and a photo). Additional words, photos, and artwork are available for a small fee. Writeaprisoner.com has an additional add-on blog starting at $15 for 250 words and you can add additional words for $5 for blocks of 50 words. They offer poetry add-on to your profile for $15 for 250 words.
Reader Review: Paul K in WA-This place is very professional but I have received few hits. A couple have been good, but all overseas and some sketchy. Oct. 2017
Reader Review: Levi L in OR-I have been on this site twice. Both times with overwhelming responses. So many great pen pals that this week I have asked to be removed from the site because my girlfriend (whom I met on the site) have moved our relationship to the next level. I could not be happier. Apr. 2018
Reader Review: Michael R in TX-I mailed them $50 and got proof they received the funds three days after 1/19/19. Still no word from them. Mar 2019

Zoosk
Online dating site
Rated 8
Details: No mailing address
Price: Free.to list profile online.
Traffic: 50 million
PH: 888-939-6675
Web: zoosk.com
Review: Zoosk's unique Behavioral Matching search engines learn as one clicks to pair you with singles who you will likely be attracted to. This means no lengthy questionnaire just great matches based on your behavior and preferences. They are on Facebook, Twitter and YouTube. They offer free access to profiles but you need to subscribe in order to read messages from other people on the site. Online only.

HAVING FUN WITH YOUR PEN PALS

See ya later, alligator...
After while, crocodile...
In an hour, sunflower...
Maybe two, kangaroo...
Gotta go, buffalo...
Adios, hippos...
Ciao Ciao, brown cow...
See ya soon, baboon...
Adieu, cockatoo...
Better swish, jellyfish...
Chop chop, lollipop...
Gotta run, skeleton...
Bye bye, butterfly...
Better shake, rattlesnake!

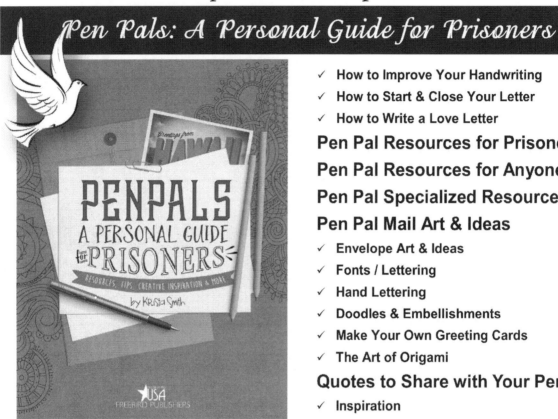

Comic Cupid (closed business)
J&J Holdings
Junk Zine
Pink
RFD Magazine
San Diego Gay & Lesbian News
Seattle Gay News
Singles Network Newspaper

3G Company
Pen pal magazine and products
Rated 7
Price: $6 per issue
Mail: Box 1022
Canfield, OH 44406
Review: They produce a 34-page pen pal listing. 3G Company includes stories, jokes, and limericks from their readers and they are Funny Stuff! There are no photos. Pen pals are 30% inmates, 70% free people. Offers a lot of ad sheets, pen pal ads, global adult ads, Big Mail, and all kinds of pen pal lists including international too.
Reader Review: Michael W in NJ- The pen pal contacts in his ad he gives you are all return to sender RTS, except for the inmates. He also advertisers, outdated pyramid schemes and Cosmic Cupid which closed years ago. Abe Andrews and Brenda's Friendship Circle advertise the same old RTS addresses. Beware. Mar 2019

Bubbles
Pen pal magazine
Rated 10
Price: Sample $5
Mail Robert A. Stewart
State Hwy 6
Coal Creek 419
Greymouth 7802
New Zealand
Review: They offer pen pal magazine called Pen Friends and take ads so you can post yourself too.
Reader Review: Manuel M in NJ- this man and his mag are good. He sent me 2 letters after I requested to have a pen pal ad in Pen Friends, we have things in common and asked me about mine. That made me feel good and he treated me respectful. I would like to give him a 10. The magazine is $5 us dollars. Oct. 2018

Fair and Dare
Pen pal, hobby and contact magazine
Rated None
Price: Sample $5
Mail Imtiaz Ahmed
195/3-A (5th floor)
Shantibagh Dhaka-1217
Bangladash
imtiaz_700@yahoo.com
Review: Published quarterly, color, 32 pages, with a circulation of 10,000 copies worldwide. Direct ads of more than 300 plus 150 photos of broadminded matrimony, travelers, offers. Phone and email friends, club ads etc. Order the latest issue for $5, they do not say if only take cash, might be best to send but western union money orders are worldwide. Place your ad for free with or without photo. Jun. 2019

Far Star Penfriend World
Pen pal magazine
Rated 10
Price: Sample $5
Mail Miss Magna-Maria (Editor in Chief)
Box 218
Freres Khezzar
Batna 05008
Algeria, NORTH AFRICA
happy_generation@hotmail.com
Review: This is a publication for pen pals, swappers, philatelists, mail-order clubs. Copy price 20 International Reply Coupon available at the post office or 20 US First Class (Forever) Stamps. Send all your ad info, better with photo, or order for just the publication. Apr. 2019

Focus Magazine (WX)
Pen pal magazine
Rated None
Price: $1 color brochure
Mail: Box 40
Minehead
TA24 5YS
England
Review: Publication is filled with pretty girls and beautiful ladies looking for your friendship. Color glossy issues, $15 per, send for the latest one today. Jun. 2019

Freebird Publishers
Pen Pal Success Book
Rated by our readers
Author: Josh Kruger
Details: $22.99 plus s/h
Mail: Box 541
North Dighton, MA 02764

Web: FreebirdPublishers.com
diane@freebirdpublishers.com
Review: PEN PAL SUCCESS: The Ultimate Guide to Getting and Keeping Pen Pals book. You've heard it said, "The game is to be sold not told." Well, now a new book is doing all the telling about the game. In 20 information-dense chapters you'll DISCOVER the secrets. Pen Pal Success contains "insiders" wisdom especially for prisoners. You owe it to yourself to invest in this book! Softcover, 8x10", B&W, 225+ pages $22.99 plus $7 s/h includes tracking. Jun. 2019
—SEE OUR AD—

Freebird Publishers
Penpals a Personal Guide for Prisoners
Rated by our readers
Author: Krista Smith
Details: $22.99 plus s/h
Mail: Box 541
North Dighton, MA 02764
Web: FreebirdPublishers.com
diane@freebirdpublishers.com
Review: PENPALS A PERSONAL GUIDE FOR PRISONERS: Resources, Tips, Creative Inspiration and more. Pen Pal Profiles & Writing Tips, Pen Pal Resources for Prisoners, Pen Pal Resources for Anyone, Pen Pal Specialized Resources

Pen Pal Mail Art & Ideas, Quotes to Share with Your Pen Pal, Pen Pal Stationary, My Pen Pal Notes and Address Book Section. Softcover, 8x10", B&W, 200 pages $22.99 plus $7 s/h includes tracking. Jun. 2019
—SEE OUR AD—

F.O.G., The
Vietnam friendship magazine
Rated 7
Details: Send SASE
Price: $18 per year, 4 issues
Mail: Box 17733
Honolulu, HI 96817
Review: They began publishing in 2006. They produce a 4.75 x 5.5 magazine.
Reader Review: Their Mingle magazine had a lot of photo copies from Hawaii newspapers. They sent me only one page with about ten addresses. Jan. 2017

Friends and Lovers
Pen pal magazine
Rated None
Details: $10 sample copy
Price: $6 per issue, $25 for a yr.
Mail: Gibmano c/o Storsteinsvn 10
N-4513 Mandal
Norway
Review: They produce a pen pal ad magazine. Filled with girls and ladies looking for friendship. Your ad with photo printed free in three issues of the magazine. Jun. 2019

Girls and Mags (GAM)
Pen Pals
Rated 10
Details: Send SASE
Mail: Box 319
Rehoboth, MA 02769
Review: No more pen pal addresses as of June 2019. For free pen pals, we still offer our newly updated list of 50 mega churches with pen pal programs for $10. Also, our revised and updated 44 Pen Pal Publications is a list of pen pal companies with magazines, pen pal list, and newsletters. Most offer free pen pal ads. We still have the largest selection of Celebrity Addresses. We offer Fan Photos of Porn Stars and Network Stars for free, you only pay printing, shipping and handling, see our listing in the main business directory for more details. May 2019
—SEE OUR AD—

Great Global Guys
Gay pen pal magazine
Rated None
Details: Send SASE
Details: Adults only 21 plus
Price: $6 per issue, $25 for a yr.
Mail: 3G Company
Box 1022
Canfield, OH 44406
Review: They produce a 20 page, 5.5 x 8.5 magazine.

Immigrant Advertiser
Pen pal magazine
Rated None
Price: $2 sample issue
Mail: Ace L
5447 Van Fleet Ave.
Richmond, CA 94804-5929
Review: Worldwide publication of friends. 10,000 worldwide circulation. To order a sample copy send $2

International Penpal Bulletin
Pen pal magazine
Rated 9
Details: Free pen pal ad
Price: US $10 issue
Mail: Miss Kiyoko Inaba
192 Shimokounushi
Kaminokawamachi
Kawachi-gun
Tochigi, 329-0529 JAPAN
Review: Worldwide friendship, pen friends and collectors. 3 issues per year February, June and October. If you would like pen pals from Japan and worldwide then this bulletin is for you. Each issue contains 300

from over 40 countries. Latest copy US$10 or Sample copy plus next issue with your ad US$20. Payments in cash only. International Reply Coupon available at the post office. Listing yourself is free, with or without photo. Send your name, full mailing address, age, sex, hobbies, interests, message, photo etc., remember to use international postage or number of stamps that add up to $1.15 for first ounce. Apr. 2019

Italian and Worldwide Penfriends
Pen pal magazine
Rated 9
Details: US$12
Mail: Guida Renato-
Via Pasini 31-/H
36033 Isola Vicentina (VI)
ITALY
Review: Pen pal magazine created for friends of both sexes, all ages, gentlemen, boys, girls, couples, diverse, wish to know all purposes of friendship, meeting, correspondence, collections, romance, marriage, intimacy, vacation etc. For a sample copy with ad for US$12. Send with all your information for your ad to be placed inside magazine or just send for copy of magazine to see what it is like first. Apr. 2019

Personal Touch Media
Adult advertising ads
Rated None
Details: Price $10 or $20 worth new stamps
Mail: Box 654
Tempe, AZ 85280
Web: personaltouchmediaHQ.com
Review: They offer hot sexy broadminded adult advertising ad, photos are required. Send you name, age, (must be 18+), address, hobbies, interests, message and photo(s). Information will be published on the internet. Latest sample issue send $10 or $20 in new stamps. Jun. 2019

Signal
Pen pal magazine
Rated 10
Details: Send SASE International for info packet
Price: US $10 issue
Mail: Raimo Kaarna-XUA21
Purokatu 18
FI-15200 Lahti, Finland
Web: signalpenpals.net
Web: penpalclubs.net
signal@sci.sci.fi
Review: One of the largest and oldest pen pal mags in the world. Published since 1960-53 years. 20 pages' full color filled with 340 ads, pen pals and photos, collectors, clubs and papers. In addition, you can place your ad and photos for pen pals too. Price is US $10 magazine, US $10 to place pen pal ad and US $20 pen pal ad with photo. Send international stamped SASE or 3 FCS for information package. Be patient, overseas mail takes time.

Starship Entertainment
Pen pal lists
Rated None
Details: Send SASE
Price: $6 per list or Book of stamps
Mail: Emanuel Beiler
2240 Robert Fulton Hwy
Peach Bottom, PA 17563
Review: They are new to the marketplace and sell pen pal lists. The lists are $6 each or book of first class stamps. Offer lists of women that will write prisoners, list of churches that offer free pen pals and information on how to get free pen pals. August 2017

Tien Shan Magazine
Pen pal magazine
Rated 9
Details: Send $2 US for info packet
Price: $7
Mail: Pyotr Mostrenki
Zhandosove 21
PO Box 39
KZ-050057 Alamty,
Republic of Kazakhstan
Review: Since 2003, yearly international color magazine for collectors, pen pals, correspondence, friends, businessmen, exchange of ideas, holidays, visits, marriage and much more. To place your ad, send your name, address, age, sex, education, occupation, languages, hobbies, photo, bio/ad with US $2. For a sample copy of the magazine send US $4. For a full magazine copy send US $7. If you want more information, send US $2. Nothing is free. If you cannot send cash, make check payable to PYOTR MOSTRENKI. Aug. 2017.

USA Friendship Magazine
Pen pal magazines
Rated 8
Details: Send 2 Int'l Stamps or $1 for info
Mail: Rinaldo Oliveira
Caiza Postal, 79376
Sao Hoao De Meriti
Cep, 25515-972-RJ
Rio De Janeiro, Brazil
Review: Rinaldo publishes a pen pal magazine that has pen pals, swaps,

info on Facebook and much more. All you need to do is send him your full information, photo and payment of $7. Make sure to include your Name, Mailing Address, Country, Age, Sex, Languages You Know, Interests and Pen Pals Wanted. He will post your profile in the magazine and send you a copy too. May 2017

Zelenkevitch Publishers
Pen pal magazines
Rated 8
Details: Send 2 Int'l Stamps or $1 for info
Mail: Box 156
Minsk – 220013
Belarus, Ex - USSR

Review: They publish Revukic, a monthly international publicity magazine (zine), that contains correspondence, collections, friendship, marriage, pen pals, ads, hobbies and more. They also offer World Wide Clubs and International Photo Bulletin. April 2017.

FUN WAYS TO GREET YOUR PEN PALS

1. WHAT'S THE CRAIC?
How they say "What's up?" in Ireland. The craic (pronounced "crack") is the news, gossip, latest goings-on, or the fun times to be planned.

2. HOW HOPS IT?
Be classically cool with this late 19th-century slang for "How's it going?"

3. AHOY
Add a little jaunty excitement by getting into pirate mode.

4. [HAT TIP]
Be the strong, silent type and forgo words entirely with an elegant tip of your hat.

5. THERE HE/SHE IS!
Make someone feel like the man or the woman of the hour.

6. CIAO
Feeling friendly and cosmopolitan? Ciao will set the mood. Add a kiss on each cheek for authenticity.

7. S.P.D.S.V.B.E.E.V.
Want to write a letter with a classical Latin feel? Open with this abbreviation for Salute plurimam dicit. Si vales, bene est, ego valeo. "Many greetings. If you're well, then that's good, and I'm well too."

8. SALUTATIONS
Show off your verbal dexterity with this gentleman's greeting.

9. GREETINGS
Or keep it simple and use the word that means just what it says.

10. HOWDY
Keep it casual, cowpoke, or get fancier with a full-on Howdydo?

11. ALOHA
Bring a little mellow sunshine to your interactions by greeting the Hawaiian way.

12. NAMASTE
Start with a show of respect. This peaceful greeting comes from the Sanskrit for "I bow to you."

13. HOW'S TRICKS?
You've got to smile when you dust off this gem from the 1920s.

14. BREAKER, BREAKER
Open the conversation like a trucker on a CB radio.

15. WELL, LOOK AT YOU!
Reminiscent of the sweet way your grandma used to express how impressed she was with you. Why not spread the love around with this opening?

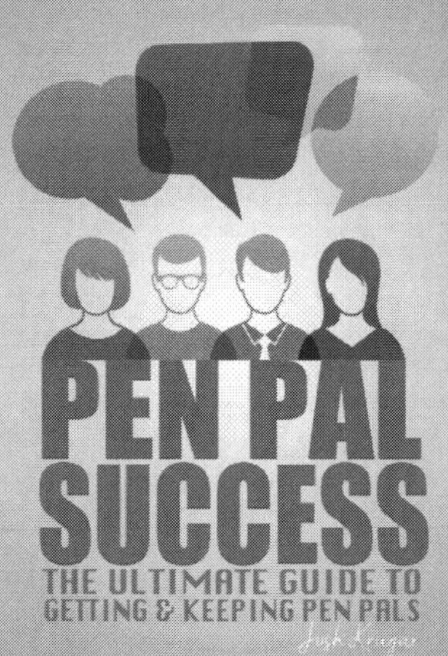

Wish You Could Get Mail From Interesting People Each and Every Day?

Tired of Wasting Money On Pen Pal Lists & Services With Too Few Results?

Then this book was written especially for you!

PEN PAL SUCCESS: The Ultimate Proven Guide to Getting & Keeping Pen Pals

You've heard it said "The game is to be sold not told." Well, now a new book is doing all the telling about the game.

In 20 information-dense chapters you'll DISCOVER the following secrets:

- How to find FREE pen pals that are willing to write prisoners.
- Make money legally in the pen pal game without running any bogus prison scams!
- *Effectively use online pen pal websites, including which ones actually work and real profiles the author used to get HITS!*
- What to do once you get your pen pal so you keep them on your team for years!
- How to write letters to pen pals that get you responses!
- One successful letter can get you multiple responses from different pen pals;
- Learn the website that the author used to get 20+ hits in the first week his profile was up!
- Find out some of the biggest myths in the prison pen pal game and how not to fall victim to them or waste your money!
- How to rekindle a lost pen pal corre-spondence and keep pen pals coming back for more;

"I'm pleased to say that your system does work, one gal has fallen madly in love with me."

- John H., Akron OH

- Get your pen pal to write you hot, freaky letters and send you sexy photos without paying!
- The act of giving gifts so you don't look like a trick-off artist;
- *What's more, this book is jam-packed with the full contact information of the people and companies that can help you succeed today!*

And There's Much, Much More!!

You have never seen a pen pal resource this detail on what it takes to succeed in the pen pal game today! Written by lifer, Josh Kruger author of *The Millionaire Prisoner.*

Pen Pal Success contains "insider's" wisdom especially for prisoners. You owe it to yourself to invest in this book!

CAUTION: This book is only of those prisoners who want to achieve their pen pal dreams and get lots of mail! ...Every word is designed so that prisoners can succeed now!

It's All Included Here In This Book!!

NO ORDER FORM NEEDED

On paper clearly write your full contact information and product info.

PEN PAL SUCCESS

Only $22.99

plus $7 s/h (priority with tracking)
Softcover, 8" x 10" over 225 pages

FREEBIRD PUBLISHERS
Box 541,
North Dighton, MA 02764
www.FreebirdPublishers.com
or Amazon.com
Diane@FreebirdPublishers.com
We accept all forms of payment

We accept all major credit cards

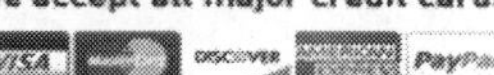

amazon.com

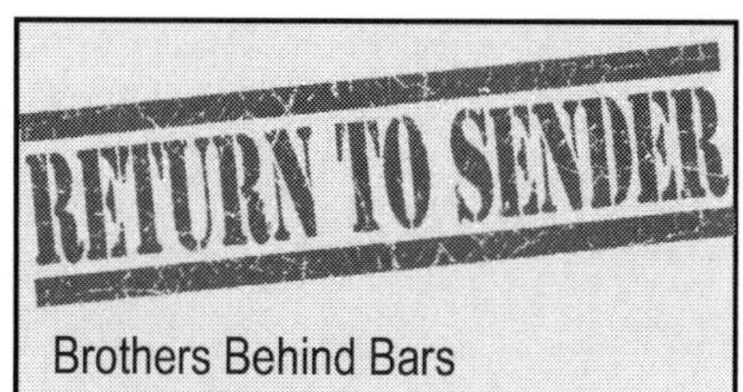

Brothers Behind Bars
Cosmic Cupid- Shut Business
Mindful Buddha Outreach Project
Texas Prisoners Network Support

3-G Company
Adult worldwide pen pals
Rated 7
Details: Send SASE, for list of all products.
Price: From $2 to $10
Mail: Box 1022
Canfield, OH 44406
Review: They produce a 34-page pen pal listing. 3G Company includes stories, jokes, and limericks from their readers and they are Funny Stuff! There are no photos. Pen pals are 30% inmates, 70% free people. Offers a lot of ad sheets, pen pal ads, global adult ads, Big Mail, and all kinds of pen pal lists including international.
Reader Review: Newer issues of the pen pal magazine was mostly inmates. I notified the publisher of some RTS and a scam. Jan. 2017
Reader Review: Paul K. in WA- Waited six weeks-zero response to query-they kept SASE. Apr. 2018

Brenda's Friendship Circle
Friendship
Rated 8
Details: Send Large SASE with $5
Mail: 379 Arcadia Drive
Lumberton, NC 28360
Review: The owner replies to all and likes to collect western paperbacks, postcards, stickers, Indian snow scenes and wolves, and coupons. Also, if you send in a note with three FCS, the owner will send an envelope out to you with a variety of items in it.
Reader Review: Never responded to my letter. In another publication, she is using the same ad but asking $5 fee. Jan. 2017

Christian Pen Pals
Offers Pen Pal Services to engage in ministry by mail
Rated 8
Details: Send SASE for info
Mail: Box 11296
Hickory, NC 28603
Web: cppministry.com
National service providing Christian pen pals to engage in ministry by mail. Request a pen pal if you're seeking a faith-focused dialogue. Include name, prison address, DOB, length of sentence and release date, religion, hobbies/interests and statement about yourself & what you want in a pen pal. Depending on region, maybe a backlog so please be patient. (free). Aug. 2016

Death Row Support Project
Offers Pen Pal Services for Death row
Rated 8
Details: Send SASE for info
Mail: Box 600, Dept. P
Liberty Mills, IN 46946
Review: They are a national org that offers pen pal services to death row inmates only. Can connect Spanish speaking pen pals on a limited basis.

Freedom through Christ Prison Ministry-FL
Compile Lists
Rated 8
Details: Free
Mail: Box 120997
Ft. Lauderdale, FL 33312
Review: They answer some questions often asked about the program, they have no charge for what they do. Donations or postage stamps are gratefully accepted to help with some of the expenses but are not required in order to be listed. They do not have lists of outsiders that they send to those in prison, but rather they send lists of prisoner names and addresses to interested citizens and/or other ministries around the country, who have expressed a desire to correspond with one or more prisoners or send them literature. They do not match up pen pals or have any control over who might pick your name and write to you. If the correspondence is not compatible, both parties are free to discontinue writing, and they hope this will be done tactfully. March 2016

Girls and Mags (GAM)
Pen Pals
Rated 10
Details: Send SASE
Mail: Box 319
Rehoboth, MA 02769
Review: No more pen pal addresses as of June 2019. For free pen pals, we still offer our newly updated list of 50 mega churches with pen pal programs for $10. Also, our revised and updated 44 Pen Pal Publications is a list of pen pal companies with magazines, pen pal list, and newsletters. Most offer free pen pal

ads. We still have the largest selection of Celebrity Addresses. We offer Fan Photos of Porn Stars and Network Stars for free, you only pay printing, shipping and handling, see our listing in the main business directory for more details. May 2019
—SEE OUR AD—

Hindustan Pen Pal Society
Free pen pal listing
Rated 7
Details: See review
Mail: Kuniayan Code
M. M. Bazar
670306 Kerala
India
Review: They offer a free pen pal ad to be listed in their pen pals. Send them your name, age, sex, address, hobbies, language, occupation etc. with photo. July 2015

Hoshia Inmate Ministry
Jewish ONLY Free pen pal program
Rated 8
Mail: Box 599
Vidor, TX 77650
Website: barunchhashem.com
Review: They offer support and a pen pal program if you are of Jewish lineage. Jan. 2017

Jewish Prisoner Services
International-Pen Pal Services
Details: Send SASE for info
Mail: Box 85840
Seattle, WA 98145
PH: (206) 985-0577
(206) 528-0363 Emergency Collect
Review: Offers support, referrals, guidance, educational, and religious programs, pen pal services, and free Jewish books. No direct financial or legal assistance.

Kaul Advarsha
Free pen pal ad
Rated 8
Sample: $1 or International SASE
Mail: 1-8536 Rehman Building
Naveen Shahdara, Delhi 110032
Country: India

Lifelines
International Pen Pals
Rated 7
International Pen Pals
Details: Send Intl SASE for info
Mail: 63 Forest Rd.
Garston, Watford
WD25 7QP, U.K.
Review: International pen pals; Airmail stamp postage; waiting list 3 to 4 months.

Marjorie Lee Publishing
Pen Pal lists and more
Rated None
Details: Send SASE.
Mail: Box 66921
Portland, OR 97290
Review: They are a mail only business. They offer American Beauties, Girls Worldwide pen pal lists, How-To Write Letters to Ladies, and Pen Pal profiles.

Meet-an-Inmate .com
Photo personals of male and female inmates
Rated 8
Details: Send SASE.
Price: See review
Mail: Attn: Arlen Bischke
Box 1342
Pendleton, OR 97801
Web: meet-an-inmate.com
ab@bisky.com
Review: There is a downloadable application that can be printed out or send SASE. This site is designed to quickly and easily connect you with pen pals who have the same interests as you. Featured ad starts at $35 for six months and they make you a web page and, on their homepage, you have a thumbnail photo link. The purpose of the featured ad is to simply get more traffic to the web page. The more traffic, the better chances of acquiring pen pals. For regular ad, prices start at $25 for six months which include two photos and up to 250 words.

Midwest Trans Prisoner Pen Pal Project
Rated 7
Details: Midwest Only
Mail: c/o Boneshaker Books
2002 23rd Ave S.
Minneapolis, MN, 55404
Web: mwtppp.wordpress.com
Review: accepts requests across LGBTQI spectrum. Not a dating service. Send name, prison address, description of yourself & what looking for in a pen pal. There is a waiting list so be patient. (free) Aug. 2016

Miss Kiyoko Inaba
Pen Pal Free Listing
Rated 7
Details: See review
Mail: 192 Shimo Kounushi
Kamino Kawa-machi
Kawachi-gun, Tochigi
329-0529 Japan
Review: They offer free pen pal ads. You send them your profile information with a photo or not and they will place you in their international pen pal ad listings. You can send them info, name, age, sex, address, hobbies, interests, message, photo etc. July 2015

Nubian Princess Entertainment
Pen Pal Services
Rated 9
Details: $3 catalog
Mail: Box 37
Timmonsville, SC 29161
Web: writesomeoneinprison.com
writesomeone@aol.com
Review: Been in business 7 plus years in the photo business, now offering a pen pal service. Erotic letters, letter correspondence and more. Jan. 2016

Pen Pal 4 Inmates
Rated None
Details: Send Intl SASE for info
Mail: Box 4234
Oakland, CA 94614
Web: inmateslittlehelper.com
Review: This company is run and owned by Inmates' Little Helpers. This is a service not a website or pen pal business. They will set you up a pen pal account and list it on four pen pal websites. They offer 18 different sites for you to pick from including their website Inmates' Little Helper website. Offer to upload two photos onto each of the four sites at no extra charge. Also, will print your profile off sites and mail to you for $6 each. But for the service of setting up your pen pal account to upload to other websites... There are no prices listed on the ad we are reading from? Send SASE for information. Nov. 2017

Pen Pal Project of Action Committee for Women in Prison
Rated 8
Details: Send Intl SASE for info
Mail: Box 9867
Marina Del Rey, CA 90295
Web: acwip.wordpress.com/positive-programs
Review: Connects incarcerated women only to a woman pen pal outside. Only for CA, NM, & TX. Matched over 500 pen pals already. SASE for application. (free) Aug. 2016

Prisoner Correspondence Project
Pen Pal Program
Rated 8
Details: Send Intl SASE for info
Mail: QPIRG Concordia
c/o Concordia University
1455 de Maisonneuve O,
Montreal, Quebec,
H3G 1M8, Canada
E-Mail: info@
prisonercorrespondenceproject.com
Review: Coordinates a direct correspondence program for LBGTTQI and gender variant prisoners in California. Coordinates a resource library of information regarding harm reduction practices, HIV and HEPC prevention, homophobia and transphobia.

Rainbow Bookstore Cooperative
LGBT Book Project
Rated None
Details: Send SASE for info
Mail: 426 W. Gilman St
Madison, WI 53703
PH: 608-257-6050
Web: rainbowbookstore.coop
Contact@rainbowbookstore.coop
Review: Third decade, they have grown since opening in 1989 with a few bookshelves of books. Run by volunteers and for this reason shipment and correspondences take average of 90 days. RBC have a project called LGBT Books to Prisoners.

South Beach Singles
Sexy Photos and pen pals
► **RATED 10!**
Details: Send SASE
for brochure
Prices: 20 pics $24 (see review)
Mail: Box 1656
Miami, FL 33238
Web: southbeachsingles.ning.com
rd@southbeachsingles.org
Review: Web page services $38, calendar $15, photos $1 each, 20 photos $24, $1 puts you on their mailing list. Send SASE for info.

Surrogate Sisters
Various products and pen pal
Rating: 8
Details: Send SASE
Mail: Box 95043
Las Vegas, NV 89193
service@surrogatesisters.com
Review: They offer many services; we recommend sending for information. They have a new pen pal website, see our pen pal website listing.
Reader Review: Paul K. in WA-I have plowed a lot of money with them over the years, some on their pen pal site. The pen pal program yielded zero results. Apr. 2018

Time Served, LLC
Voice and Video Pen Pal Service
Rated 9
Details: $25 and up
Mail: 7 Saint Clair Ave. Ste. 315
Cleveland, OH 44144
Web: timeservedllc.com
timeservedllc@gmail.com
Phone: 276-299-1199
Review: Provides Time for A Friend

Voice and Video Pen Pal service for federal and state prisoners. Packages start at $2.

Women For Sobriety
Pen Pal Program
Rated 8
Details: Send SASE for info
Mail: Box 618
Quakertown, PA 18951
Review: Information and women centered approach to drug and alcohol recovery. Pen Pal program.

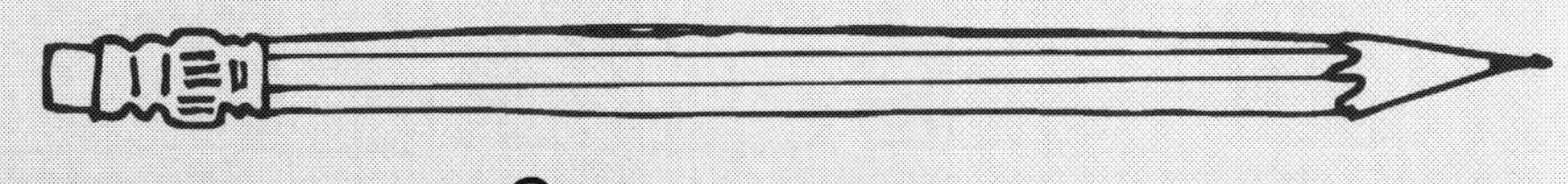

FACTS About Letter Writing

- The motion of your hand as you write calms the nervous system and forges important creative connections, engages your motor skills, and keeps your mind sharp.
- Once the mind and motor co-ordination is established properly and the motor becomes automated the student's mind is liberated to implement new ideas more creatively and effectively.
- Slow Hand writers have problems of poor mind motor co-ordination, spellings, word formation, letter creation and discrimination between upper and lower case.
- Areas of your brain light up when you write words by hand versus just studying the words closely.
- Knowing someone's handwriting can be a marker of a frienship's longevity.
- The average no. 2 pencil can draw a line 35 miles long, the average ball point pen will only get you about 5 miles.
- Handwriting identifies to the conscious and subconscious traits of an individual's personality. If anyone struggles with handwriting, they suffer from the ability of self expression.
- Handwriting is a brain's writing. One can judge an individual's state of mind and personality from his style of writing, pressure, slants, space and margin formation etc. differs every time and narrates a different story about the writer.

PHAT PUFFS MAGAZINE

CONTENT BIG BOOTY CERTIFIED

ISSUE #15

SUB 0'
PHAT PUFFS MAGAZINE
WINTER 2019 ISSUE #15
SUPER THICK MODELS STRIPPERS HOUSE WIVES PORN STARS
100 PAGES! OF THE HOTTEST LADIES AND EVENTS!
BOLD SEXUAL QUESTIONS ANSWERED!
REAL PLAYER TIPS!
INSIDE YOUR FAVORITE STRIP CLUBS EVENTS
QUEEN SHY

ISSUE #13

ISSUE #14

ISSUE #11

100 PAGES! OF THE HOTTEST LADIES AND EVENTS!

ISSUE #12

ORDER NOW!

ALL MAGAZINE ARE
$11.00 + $7.00 Shipping

$18.00 TOTAL!

Please Make all Checks and M.O Payable to:

SUB 0 ENTERTAINMENT INC.
P.O. BOX 1222
NEW YORK NY 10029
FOR FASTEST SHIPPING HAVE ORDERS PLACED ONLINE
www.PhatPuffsMagazine.com
(Shop Button)
OR CALL 646 542 4407

Name: ____________ Inmate ID# ____________

Facility Name: ____________

Address: ____________

City: ____________ State: ________ zip ________

I WANT ISSUE # ____________

SUB 0 ENTERTAINMENT INC. Are the PUBLISHERS of PHAT PUFFS MAGAZINE! These Magazines are Revised to meet All units Rules nation wide. This Order Form/ Catalog and The Actual Content in the Above Magazines Contains NO NUDITY, No inappropriate Touching, No Vaginas, No Bodily Fluids, No Nipples, Anus, etc. ALL ARE CLOTHED and are NON NUDE!

Print the puzzle then see if you can re-assemble all the pieces by filling in the letters and blocks into the correct positions in the grid. The result will be a symmetrical 15x15 crossword. One 3x3 piece has already been entered.

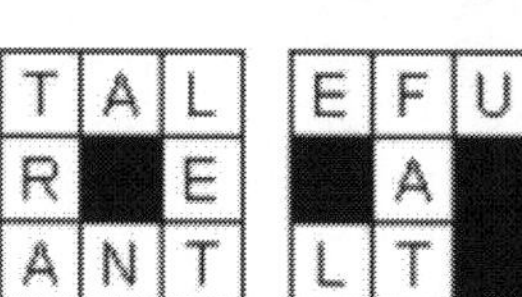
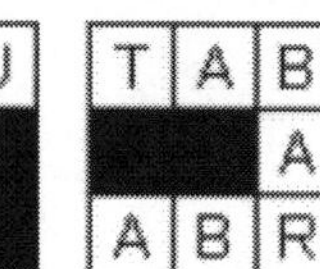

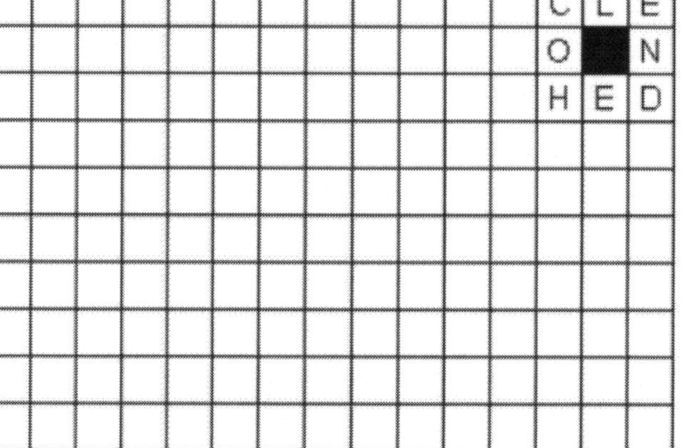

WORD LADDER 06

A word ladder is a sequence of words formed by changing just one letter each time eg CAT - COT - DOT - DOG. Can you find the missing words? Use the clues if you get stuck.

PRUNE

Clues:

Having a tendency

Communication device

Was bright

Push

Trim down

Ignominy

Pretences

Creases

Sides

Rips

PEARS

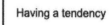

CITY SEARCH-03

Can you unscramble the letters in each word to find ten US cities?

NEARCRAB	ACATCULT	AVENGE	SERIOUSBEAN
EVINCE	PAIRS	RIPETARO	
NEWPART	NOVACURVE	HASTEN	

ANAGRAM Food and Drink

An anagram is the result of rearranging the letters of a word or phrase to produce other words, using all the original letters exactly once.
Can you find the out of this world words from the following anagrams? Word lengths are shown in brackets.

RAW INERT MEAL (7, 5)	EAT (3)
AWFUL RECOIL (11)	COOL CHEAT (9)
IN REAL EGG (6, 3)	RETGAL (5)
A MOTTO (6)	PUB TUNE TREAT (6, 6)
CRIED (5)	CAR DUST (7)
RICH EAT OKAY (9)	ORDER PIG (8)
CHANGE MAP (9)	PAST EIGHT (9)
A SUGAR SAP (9)	CRACKPOT INLAW (5, N8)
RE A JUG ON ICE (6, 5)	CHEAP (5)
EMU LEG (6)	A TROPIC (7)

ANAGRAM Sports 02

An anagram is the result of rearranging the letters of a word or phrase to produce other words, using all the original letters exactly once.
Can you work out the kind of sports from the following anagrams? Name lengths are shown in brackets.

NESTLE IN BAT (5, 6)
IS NO CHARGER (5, 6)
BAT ON MIND (9)
IN NETS (6)
KEY CHOICE (3, 6)
MYSTIC SANG (10)
TAKES ICING (3, 7)
NOW GLIB (7)
I SIGNAL (7)

ALPHA-GRIDDLE 07

Print the puzzle grid and use your compass directions to find the correct locations for the missing letters of the alphabet. When you have completed the grid, see if you can discover the hidden city, country, river or mountain. **Note**: North or south means any location along the same column. East or west means any location along the same row.

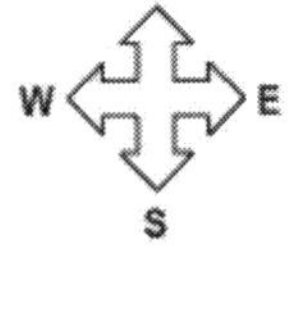

Directions:
A is east of H: C is east of F
D is east of O and south of L
E is north of W: F is west of V
G is east of W: J is north of F
M is east of Z: N is east of L
O is north of X and east of S
P is south of B: R is south of P
Q is east of Z and north of K
T is north of U and east of B
V is south of M and east of S
W is south of L: Z is south of H
X is west of K and south of H
Y is east of O and north of K

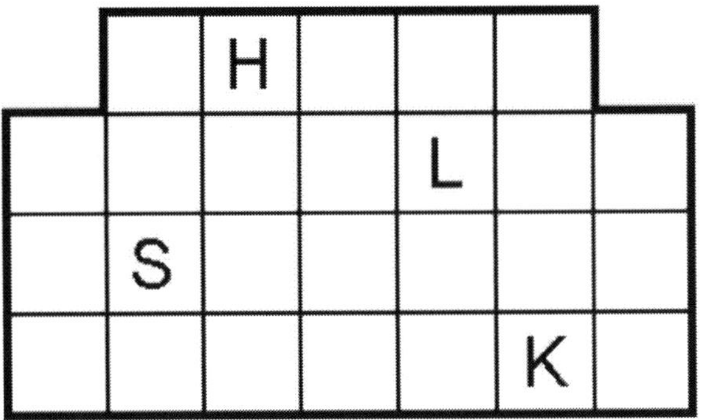

OCTA-PLUS 02

Can you work out which eight numbers correspond with the letters A-H on the Octa-Plus diagram? No two numbers are the same. Each number is a whole number and no number is less than 1 or greater than 34.

1. G minus F is either 10 or 11.
2. E is a quarter of G.
3. H is G divided by E.
4. B is F times E.
5. C is a ninth of F.
6. D is B minus G.
7. A third of F is an odd number.
8. A is 150 minus the sum o the other seven numbers.

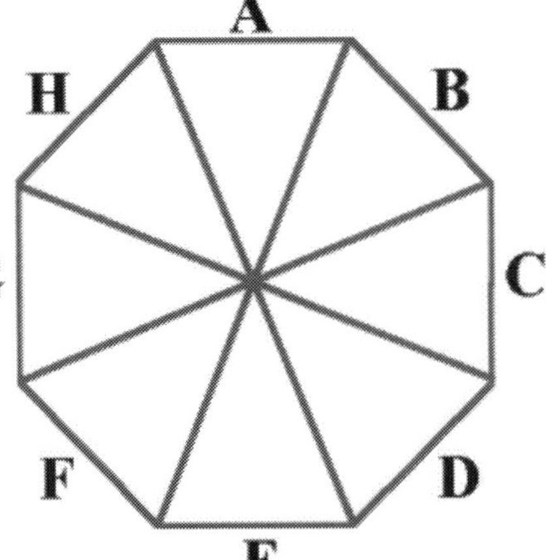

DIGI-SEARCH 05

Find the hidden numbers. They may be horizontal or vertical.

9	3	8	4	7	0	0	2	0	8	3	7	4	1	0
7	8	9	4	3	9	8	4	4	9	2	2	7	3	3
0	6	9	8	2	9	3	8	4	7	4	5	5	9	4
1	2	1	8	1	8	9	1	0	9	8	7	6	4	3
2	3	3	9	1	0	8	3	7	4	9	2	0	1	5
1	0	3	8	3	0	4	8	8	3	8	2	9	8	9
1	7	8	3	9	2	0	8	7	3	9	2	2	8	3
7	9	8	8	7	9	4	7	0	5	8	4	7	3	0
8	1	2	3	1	3	6	3	5	4	7	3	6	3	8
1	0	1	0	7	9	0	3	9	8	9	2	3	8	3
0	5	8	5	9	3	7	8	2	3	6	3	8	8	3
0	1	9	6	9	3	8	3	8	3	7	3	6	3	7
7	4	8	3	3	2	9	8	3	7	4	3	2	9	5
8	0	8	9	0	7	9	8	4	7	5	4	3	7	3
7	8	7	9	8	7	4	3	8	2	2	4	7	3	1

01211, 04883, 05847, 08374, 10790, 13388, 18833, 18910, 24813, 43593, 54373, 59283, 67452, 69829, 92763, 98879.

MIND OVER MATTER 05

Break the code to discover the missing letter. Hint: A-Z = 1-26.

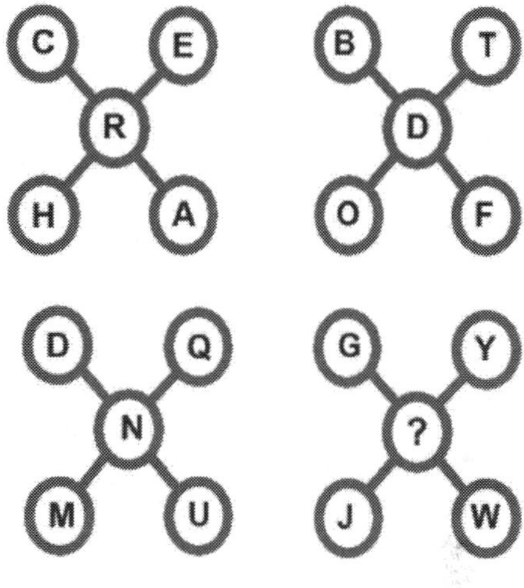

HUB-WORDS 08

How many words can you make from the letters in the wheel? Each word must contain the hub letter N. Can you find a 9-letter word and at least 25 other words of four letters or more avoiding proper nouns?

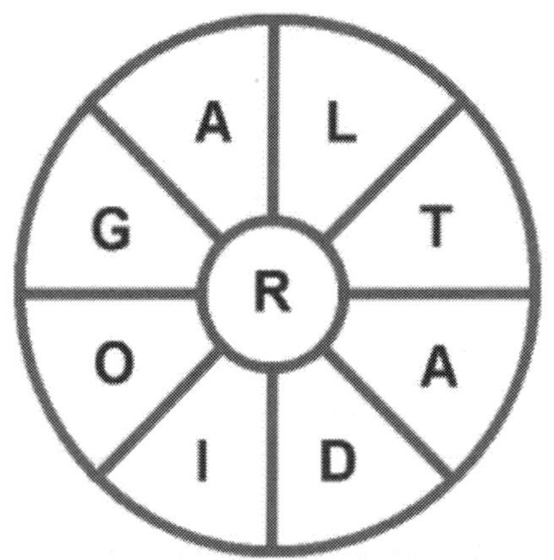

FASCINATING FACTS

- → The human brain weighs 3 pounds
- → It comprises 60% of fat and is one of the fattest organs in the human body
- → Human brain has the capacity to generate approximately 23 watts of power when awake.
- → Of the total blood and oxygen that is produced in our body, the brain gets 20% of it.
- → When the blood supply to the brain stops, it is almost after 8-10 seconds that the brain starts losing the consciousness.
- → The brain is capable of surviving for 5 to 6 minutes only if it doesn't get oxygen after which it dies.
- → The blood vessels that are present in the brain are almost 100,000 miles in length.
- → There are 100 billion neurons present in the brain.
- → In early pregnancy, the neurons develop at an alarming rate of 250,000 per minute.
- → As we grow older, we are unable to remember new things. According to the researchers in the US it is because the brain is unable to filter and remove old memories which prevent it from absorbing new ideas.

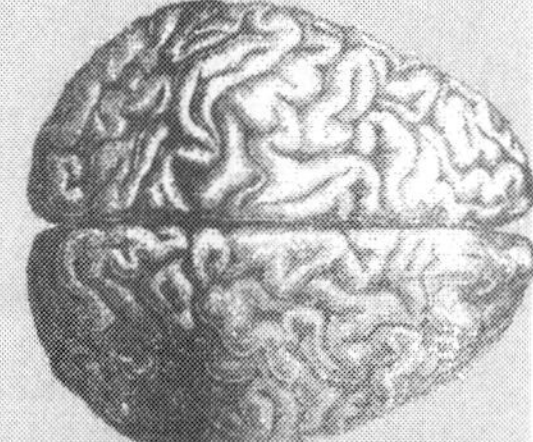

CODEWORD 08

Each letter in this puzzle is represented by a number 1-26.
Can you crack the code and solve the crossword? Every letter of the alphabet is used at least once. Three letters are already in place to get you started.

	17	23	8	8	26	13		11	5	26	24	18
26		3		5		24		26		18		21
9	23	1	11	6		12	21	25	26	1	24	12
26		22		21		10		2 V		24		22
25	21	2	21	25 R	4	21		21	3	16	21	25
		21				25		3				23
20	22	18	24	26	12		14	23	22	25	23	1
24				12		11 P				26		
11	26	12	21	25		7	26	1	4	16	21	25
12		22		22		6		26		16		24
22	1	3	24	15	23	4		24	17	5	22	22
18		17		26		24		20		21		16
21	19	26	12	16		12	7	21	25	25	6	

1	2	3	4	5	6	7	8	9	10	11	12	13
14	15	16	17	18	19	20	21	22	23	24	25	26

SUKODU MP8

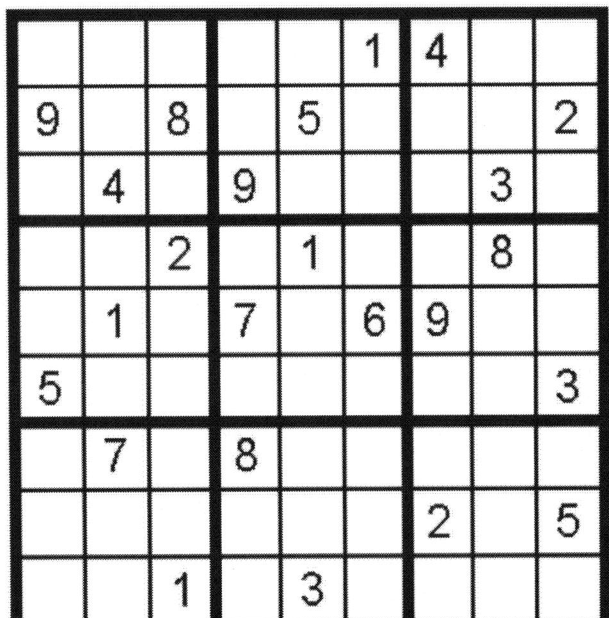

INTERESTING FACTS

- → Hot water will turn into ice faster than cold water.
- → The Mona Lisa has no eyebrows.
- → The sentence, "The quick brown fox jumps over the lazy dog" uses every letter in the English language.
- → The strongest muscle in the body is the tongue.
- → "I am" is the shortest sentence in the English language.
- → Coca-Cola was originally green.
- → The most common name in the world is Mohammed.
- → When the moon is directly overhead, you will weigh slightly less.
- → Camels have three eyelids to protect themselves from the blowing of the desert sand.
- → There are only two words in the English language that have all five vowels in order: "abstemious" and "facetious."
- → The name of all the continents end with the same letter that they start with.
- → There are two credit cards for every person in the United States.
- → TYPEWRITER is the longest word that can be made using the letters only on one row of the keyboard.
- → Minus 40 degrees Celsius is exactly the same as minus 40 degrees Fahrenheit.
- → Chocolate can kill dogs, as it contains theobromine, which affects their heart and nervous sys.
- → Women blink nearly twice as much as men!
- → You can't kill yourself by holding your breath.
- → It is impossible to lick your elbow.
- → The Guinness Book of Records holds the record for being the book most often stolen from Public Libraries.
- → People say "Bless you" when you sneeze because when you sneeze, your heart stops for a millisecond.
- → It is physically impossible for pigs to look up into the sky.
- → If you sneeze too hard, you can fracture a rib. If you try to suppress a sneeze, you can rupture a blood vessel in your head or neck and die.
- → A snail can sleep for three years.
- → On average people fear spiders more than they do death.
- → The ant always falls over on its right side when intoxicated.
- → The human heart creates enough pressure when it pumps out to the body to squirt blood 30 feet.
- → Elephants are the only animals that can't jump.
- → Butterflies taste with their feet.
- → A crocodile cannot stick its tongue out.

CATCH-WORDS 07

ACROSS

1. An ___ illusion (7)
5. Full of ___ (5)
8. The ___ of reason (5)
9. Heads or ___ (5)
10. The mighty ___ (3)
11. Fly the ___ (4)
12. Look before you ___ (4)
14. ___ of influence (6)
16. ___ for courses (6)
19. His bark is worse than his ___ (4)
20. Over the ___ (4)
21. Vanished into thin ___ (3)
23. ___ and doves (5)
24. All to no ___ (5)
25. ___ pole (5)
26. Snakes and ___ (7)

DOWN

1. Stating the ___ (7)
2. ___ and thin (5)
3. Taken to the ___ (8)
4. The ___ news (6)
5. Take the ___ (4)
6. Questions and ___ (7)
7. Counting ___ (5)
13. A ___ spiral (8)
15. Bury the ___ (7)
17. ___ to requirements (7)
18. ___ fuel (6)
19. Beauty and the ___ (5)
21. Wide ___ (5)
22. Sink or ___ (4)

THEMED CROSSWORD 15

ACROSS

1. Bucharest is the capital (7)
4. Resort in the Canadian Rockies (5)
7. Jordan's capital (5)
9. Largest city in Texas (7)
10. Island in the Persian Gulf (7)
11. Mediterranean island (5)
12. Capital of the Bahamas (6)
13. This lake sounds serene (6)
16. Asian country (5)
18. Capital of Cyprus (7)
19. Home of Disney World (7)
20. Australian town, ___ Springs (5)
21. Sea between Ireland and England (5)
22. Tirana is the capital (7)

DOWN

2. Largest city of Tennessee (7)
3. Piraeus is this city's major port (6)
5. Region of South Africa and Brazilian port (5)
6. Helsinki is the capital (7)
8. Tourist attraction ___ Falls (7)
11. Strait between Indonesia and Malaysia (7)
12. Capital of Kenya (7)
14. World's largest inland sea (7)
15. Bordered on the east by Zambia and on the west by the Atlantic Ocean (6)
17. City in 16 across (5)

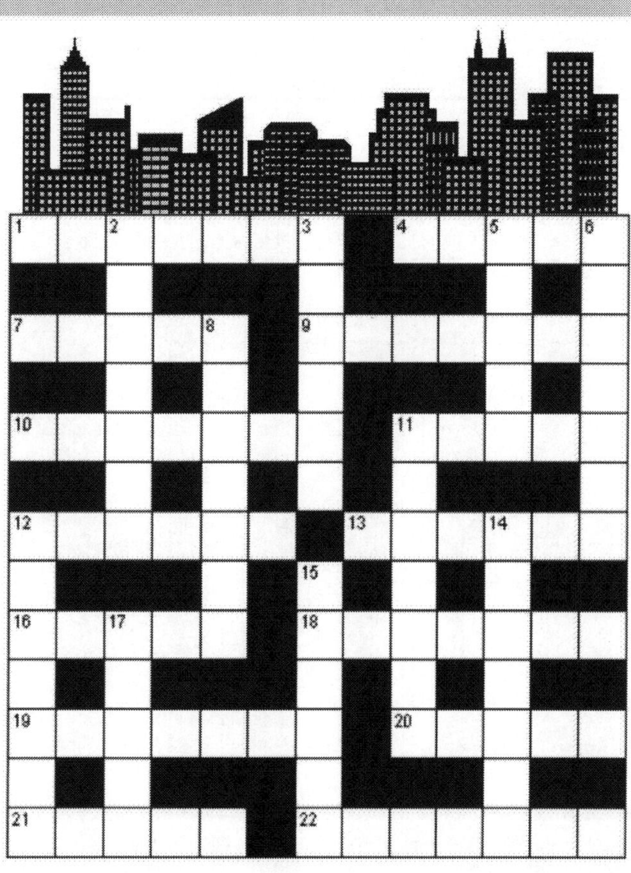

SWEET THINGS

Can you find the hidden words? They may be horizontal, vertical, diagonal, forwards or backwards.

```
C W O L L A M H S R A M I M W I E M T
M E S S U O M R A T C E N N M L O A R
N O T A G U O N M E N I L A R P H R E
O R L S U G A R T A L G B B T C T Z S
N E O A T S B M M E E C H R T E A I S
P F L C S T S B N G K R C O I S E P E
A T B P K S R O N R T N C V Y T M A D
R O F V P O E A L R R S U R H P T N G
E F V U S A M S E F R J U J O E E L Q
I F L I D C Y A P E Y P Y N N X E S E
L E A I N G C D T R I D Z M E G W T R
T E N A W L E T N V N E N M Y V S E I
L R L T E R U V S A C C H A R I N E C
W B B O N B O N C V C M B W C H C W E
L E M A R A C M U G G N I W E H C S M
E T A L O C O H C N O I T C E F N O C
V E R U T I F N O C T N A D N O F N B
P O R D M U G M A E R C E C I D V J E
N A E B Y L L E J P O P I L L O L N H
```

AMBROSIA, BLANCMANGE, BON BON, BRITTLE, BUTTER-SCOTCH, CANDY, CANDY APPLE, CANDY FLOSS, CARAMEL, CHEWING GUM, CHOCOLATE, CONFECTION, CONFITURE, CREAM, DESSERT, FONDANT, FUDGE, GUMDROP, HONEY, ICE CREAM, JELLY BEAN, JUNKET, LOLLIPOP, MARSHMALLOW, MARZIPAN, MOLASSES, MOUSSE, NECTAR, NONPAREIL, NOUGAT, PRALINE, ROCK, SACCHARINE, SUGAR, SWEETMEAT, SWEETS, SYRUP, TOFFEE,TREACLE.

CRYPTO-QUOTES 04

Each crypto-quote puzzle uses a different code to disguise a quote by someone famous. Can you break the codes to reveal the words of wisdom and their authors?

1. ZQBZTO FJ Z ILCOD-CZDJ YJCOLGS GI TGACOJQI, LSODJZP GI Z OJWGSP-CZDJ YJCOLGS GI OGXJFGPT JQOJ.
- MAPT UZCQZSP

2. WIL GDFFIS SZDGN D ADF DFWSNVFB; WIL GDF IFOW NZOH NVA PVUGIJZK VS VF NVAUZOE.
- BDOVOZI BDOVOZV

3. T KLLQ HL HGB VRHRFB SBWIRZB HGIH'Z AGBFB T'N DLTCD HL ZOBCU HGB FBZH LV NE KTVB.
- DBLFDB SRFCZ

4. SXO LCXN NZVA SXOQ RQXUIWB PE, PA'E AZVA SXO ZVJWC'A EWWC WCXOHZ BXJPWE - VII XT IPTW'E QPKKIWE VQW VCENWQWK PC AZW BXJPWE.
- EAWJW BVQAPC

COCKTAILS

The 50-50 Cocktail Bar is famous for its choice of fifty different cocktails - each named for a US state. Five friends are each having a different cocktail (one is a Nevada Knockout). The drinks are shown lined up on the bar. Can you match each cocktail with its position (1-5) and the person who ordered it?

1. The Kentucky Kick cocktail, ordered by a woman, is No 3 and is between Darlene's drink and the Washington Whammy.

2. The Alabama Slammer is pictured immediately right of Dan's cocktail.

3. Carrie's cocktail is someway right of Stella's drink (which isn't immediately next to Greg's cocktail which is immediately left of the Colorado Cliffhanger).

Pos	Cocktail	Person

QUAD-WRANGLE 02

Can you discover the sixteen numbers that match all the clues below? All the numbers are whole numbers. No two numbers are the same and no number has a value less than 1.

1. A1=B3 minus D1.
2. A2=either B4 minus D1 or B4 plus D1.
3. A3=either D1 plus A4 or a third of D1.
4. A4=either 35 or 36.
5. B1=either D2 plus C4 or A1 divided by C4.
6. B2=A4 minus C4.
7. B3=D3 minus B2.
8. B4=B1 plus D1.
9. C1=either D4 plus B2 or D4 minus B2.
10. C2=either A2 minus B1 or A2 plus B1.
11. C3=either C1 minus D1 or C1 plus D1.
12. C4=a fifth of A4.
13. D1=either B2 plus C4 or B2 minus C4.
14. D2=either C3 minus A3 or C3 minus B2.
15. D3=either A3 minus B2 or A3 plus A4.
16. D4=either A1 minus C4 or A1 plus C4.

HIDE & SEEK

Can you find the 35 hidden words? They may be horizontal, vertical, diagonal, forwards or backwards.

L	E	R	U	C	S	B	O	M	P	I	T	S	E	U	Q	V	I	N
H	C	R	A	E	S	K	E	E	S	U	J	D	L	E	I	H	S	W
S	B	S	B	W	C	T	C	O	V	E	R	I	E	D	E	G	E	R
E	T	L	U	U	R	A	V	W	J	C	N	S	W	N	N	V	N	D
X	V	R	O	R	R	A	M	N	P	G	E	R	U	H	F	R	V	G
P	V	V	I	C	F	Y	P	O	J	E	E	L	D	E	L	O	E	N
L	N	J	R	V	K	A	O	E	U	T	B	U	O	A	M	E	L	S
O	N	P	V	U	E	I	S	N	A	F	O	O	G	O	S	W	O	D
R	B	V	C	G	O	O	A	G	L	R	L	O	R	W	K	M	P	Y
E	R	F	D	M	L	C	I	T	H	I	F	A	O	P	R	P	J	E
B	R	E	U	C	S	T	S	S	S	E	E	R	G	N	S	I	M	T
V	R	H	N	S	S	A	N	V	B	T	B	V	G	E	C	T	D	A
D	Z	E	C	E	C	E	R	E	H	T	A	G	C	H	O	H	I	R
A	T	D	V	N	T	A	V	D	X	W	B	R	L	I	N	U	S	E
E	V	N	G	Q	Z	A	T	T	M	A	E	V	T	D	C	N	G	T
G	I	E	P	U	Q	G	I	E	V	T	M	K	B	E	E	T	U	I
A	D	P	B	I	S	R	J	V	E	J	D	I	Z	V	A	J	I	L
A	C	P	W	R	G	E	Y	E	G	H	E	H	N	D	L	B	S	B
M	I	H	N	E	P	H	C	Y	L	A	G	R	B	E	O	V	E	O

BEFOG, BLOCK, BROWSE, BURY, CAMOUFLAGE, CONCEAL, DISGUISE, DREDGE, ENCLOSE, ENFOLD, ENQUIRE, ENSHROUD, ENVELOP, EXAMINE, EXPLORE, GATHER, HIDE, HUNT, INVESTIGATE, LOOK, OBFUSCATE, OBLITERATE, OBSCURE, PROBE, PURSUE, QUEST, SCAN, SCOUR, SEARCH, SECRETE, SEEK, SHIELD, STRIVE, SURF, VEIL, WRAP.

LAUGHTER IS GOOD MEDICINE

→ Today at the bank, an old lady asked me to help check her balance. So I pushed her over.

→ I bought some shoes from a drug dealer. I don't know what he laced them with.

→ I told my girlfriend she drew her eyebrows too high. She seemed surprised.

→ I'm so good at sleeping. I can do it with my eyes closed.

→ My boss told me to have a good day.. so I went home.

→ Why is Peter Pan always flying? He neverlands.

→ A woman walks into a library and asked if they had any books about paranoia. The librarian says "They're right behind you!"

→ The other day, my wife asked me to pass her lipstick but I accidentally passed her a glue stick. She still isn't talking to me.

→ Why do blind people hate skydiving? It scares the hell out of their dogs.

→ When you look really closely, all mirrors look like eyeballs.

→ My friend says to me: "What rhymes with orange" I said: "No it doesn't"

→ What do you call a guy with a rubber toe? Roberto.

→ What did the pirate say when he turned 80 years old? Aye matey.

→ My wife told me I had to stop acting like a flamingo. So I had to put my foot down.

→ I couldn't figure out why the baseball kept getting larger. Then it hit me.

→ Why did the old man fall in the well? Because he couldn't see that well.

→ I ate a clock yesterday, it was very time consuming.

→ A blind man walks into a bar. And a table. And a chair.

→ I know a lot of jokes about unemployed people but none of them work.

→ Why couldn't the bicycle stand up? Because it was two tired!

→ Parallel lines have so much in common. It's a shame they'll never meet.

→ My wife accused me of being immature. I told her to get out of my fort.

→ When a deaf person sees someone yawn do they think it's a scream?

→ As I suspected, someone has been adding soil to my garden. The plot thickens.

→ I just wrote a book on reverse psychology. Do *not* read it!

FACTS YOU DIDN'T KNOW ABOUT YOUR BODY

→ If you're a female and you feel like your heart beats quicker than your male counterparts, you're not wrong. Women's hearts are proven to beat faster than men's.

→ As well as having faster heart beats, women blink twice as much as men as well.

→ Hiccups can last a very long time. The record is held by Charles Osborne – this poor man had hiccups for a total of 68 years without stopping!

→ Around 70% of people tilt their heads to the right rather than the left when kissing somebody else.

→ Can't remember your dream from last night? That's perfectly normal, since most people will forget 90% of their dreams.

→ It's not just your cheeks that turn red and expose your embarrassment when you're blushing. Your stomach also turns red, but not many people will notice this.

→ Every 3-4 seconds, around 50,000 cells in your body will die and be replaced by new ones.

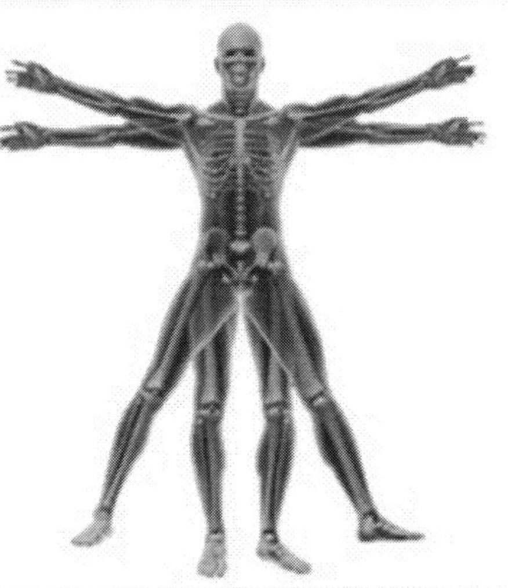

→ Fingerprints are unique to each person, making them an amazing phenomenon. Adding to this is the fact that they're developed within just three months of conception, meaning you were totally unique from the start.

→ During the average lifetime, your heart will pump a grand total of 182 million liters of blood.

→ If you're a man, the smallest cells in your body are sperm cells.

→ It's scientifically proven that children grow faster in the spring, so you're not imagining things when your little nephews and nieces seem to be suddenly older by the summer.

→ It's much less effort to be happy – you'll use 17 muscles to smile vs. 43 to frown and be miserable.

→ If you thought steel was strong and durable, your bones are five times stronger! It's difficult to break them, but that's why it hurts so much when you do.

→ No matter how many times you try, it's impossible to sneeze and keep your eyes open at the same time.

→ The average person will have sex 4,239 times during their life.

→ While you're flying in an airplane, your hair will grow at twice the rate it usually does. That's why you seem to need more regular haircuts when you've been traveling a lot.

→ Our taste buds seem to change throughout our lives, but by the age of 60, the average person has lost half their taste buds. This is why older people don't seem to care as much about bitter or unusual tastes.

→ People burn more calories being asleep than they do by watching the TV. More reason to take a nap!

→ In your mouth alone, there is more bacteria than there are people in the entire world.

→ While it's not the largest muscle, the award for the strongest muscle goes to the masseter, more commonly known as the jaw muscle.

→ The amount of bacteria in your entire body is ten times more than the amount of human cells.

→ Your fingerprints aren't the only part of your body which are completely unique to you. Your tongue also has a unique pattern and print to it.

→ Humans are constantly shedding particles of skin throughout the day. You'll mainly notice this when you get out of the bath or shower. By the time you're 70 years old, you will have shed around 100 pounds of skin.

→ You can't hear as well if you eat too much. Your hearing is affected by the amount of food you consume, so if you need to hear something well, avoid large meals.

SOLUTIONS

GRID-JIG 04

CITY SEARCH 03

CANBERRA
VENICE
ANTWERP
CALCUTTA
PARIS
VANCOUVER
GENEVA
PRETORIA
ATHENS
BUENOS AIRES

WORD LADDER 06

PRUNE, PRONE, PHONE, SHONE, SHOVE, SHAVE, SHAME, SHAMS, SEAMS, TEAMS, TEARS, PEARS

SUDOKU MP8

7	2	5	3	8	1	4	9	6
9	3	8	6	5	4	7	1	2
1	4	6	9	7	2	5	3	8
4	9	2	5	1	3	6	8	7
8	1	3	7	2	6	9	5	4
5	6	7	4	9	8	1	2	3
2	7	9	8	4	5	3	6	1
3	8	4	1	6	9	2	7	5
6	5	1	2	3	7	8	4	9

ALPHA GRIDDLE 07

	B	H	T	E	A	
J	P	Z	M	L	Q	N
F	S	O	V	D	Y	C
I	R	X	U	W	K	G

MIND OVER MATTER 05

The letters A-Z are valued 1-26. In each set, the two numbers on the left multiplied together, minus the sum of the two numbers on the right, equals the value of the middle letter, so the mystery letter is V (22).

CODEWORD 08

	G	U	F	F	A	W		P	L	A	I	D
A		N		L		I		A		D		E
J	U	M	P	Y		C	E	R	A	M	I	C
A		O		E		K		V		I		O
R	E	V	E	R	S	E		E	N	T	E	R
		E				R		N				U
Z	O	D	I	A	C		Q	U	O	R	U	M
I				C		P				A		
P	A	C	E	R		H	A	M	S	T	E	R
C		O		O		Y		A		T		I
O	M	N	I	B	U	S		I	G	L	O	O
D		G		A		I		Z		E		T
E	X	A	C	T		C	H	E	R	R	Y	

1 M	2 V	3 N	4 S	5 L	6 Y	7 H	8 F	9 J	10 K	11 P	12 C	13 W
14 Q	15 B	16 T	17 G	18 D	19 X	20 Z	21 E	22 O	23 U	24 I	25 R	26 A

ANAGRAM FOOD AND DRINK

MINERAL WATER
CAULIFLOWER
GINGER ALE
TOMATO
CIDER
ARTICHOKE
CHAMPAGNE
ASPARAGUS
ORANGE JUICE
LEGUME
TEA
CHOCOLATE
LAGER
PEANUT BUTTER
CUSTARD
PORRIDGE
SPAGTHETTI
PRAWN
COCKTAIL
PEACH
APRICOT

ANAGRAM SPORTS02

TABLE TENNIS
HORSE RACING
BADMINTON
TENNIS
ICE HOCKEY
GYMNASTICS
ICE SKATING
BOWLING
SAILING

OCTA-PLUS 02

All the numbers are whole numbers (intro), G is an even number (clue 2) and F is an odd number (clue 7), so G minus F is 11. C is a ninth of F (5).
No number is greater than 45 (intro), so C is 1 and F is 9. G is 20 (1 and above). E is 5 (2) and H is 4 (3). B is 45 (4). D is 25 (6). A is 41 (8).

CRYPTO-QUOTES 04

1. ALWAYS BE A FIRST-RATE VERSION OF YOURSELF, INSTEAD OF A SECOND-RATE VERSION OF SOMEBODY ELSE.
-JUDY GARLAND

ABCDEFGHIJKLMNOPQRSTUVWXYZ
UWRTKBOXFEPIJQSDLHNYGZCMVA

2. YOU CANNOT TEACH A MAN ANYTHING; YOU CAN ONLY HELP HIM DISCOVER IT IN HIMSELF.
-GALILEO GALILEI

ABCDEFGHIJKLMNOPQRSTUVWXYZ
MGKAFNCPOVRUBHLDJQTXSIYWZE

3. I LOOK TO THE FUTURE BECAUSE THAT'S WHERE I'M GOING TO SPEND THE REST OF MY LIFE. - GEORGE BURNS

ABCDEFGHIJKLMNOPQRSTUVWXYZ
WENGYRHTAVLOXMPZKUBIDFCQJS

4. YOU KNOW WHAT YOUR PROBLEM IS, IT'S THAT YOU HAVEN'T SEEN ENOUGH MOVIES - ALL OF LIFE'S RIDDLES ARE ANSWERED IN THE MOVIES.
-STEVE MARTIN

ABCDEFGHIJKLMNOPQRSTUVWXYZ
TMNCSZXGLVDKQWUIRPYFBAEOJH

COCKTAILS

Pos	Cocktail	Person
1	Nevada Knockout	Greg
2	Colorado Cliffhanger	Darlene
3	Kentucky Kick	Stella
4	Washington Whammy	Dan
5	Alabama Slammer	Carrie

QUAD-WRANGLE 01

All the numbers are whole numbers (intro), so A4=35 and C4=7 (clues 4 and 12). B2=28 (6). No two numbers are the same (intro), so D1=21 (13). A3=56 (3). D3=91 (15). B3=63 (7). A1=42 (1). D4=49 (16). C1=77 (9). C3=98 (11). D2=70 (14). B1=6 (5). B4=27 (8). A2=48 (2). C2=54 (2).

HUB-WORDS 08

Some other words of five letters or more containing the hub letter R: agora, altar, aorta, argal, argot, aroid, artal, atria, goral, grail, griot, groat, laird (Scot), largo, radio, raita, ratio, riata, taira, tiara, trail, triad, trial, adroit, aortal, argali, atrial, lariat, latria, radial, tailor.

CATCH-WORDS 07

O	P	T	I	C	A	L		B	E	A	N	S
B		H		L		A		A		N		H
V	O	I	C	E		T	A	I	L	S		E
I		C		A		E		T		W		E
O	A	K		N	E	S	T		L	E	A	P
U				E		T		D		R		
S	P	H	E	R	E		H	O	R	S	E	S
		A		S		F		W				U
B	I	T	E		M	O	O	N		A	I	R
E		C		S		S		W		W		P
A		H	A	W	K	S		A	V	A	I	L
S		E		I		I		R		K		U
T	O	T	E	M		L	A	D	D	E	R	S

THEMED CROSSWORD 15

Every House Has a Story

He doesn't know how it all began, only that when She calls, he cannot resist…a strange house filled with dark secrets and a century-old curse. Send $15.95 + $5.99 shipping to Winding Hall Publishers, PO Box 2689, Eugene OR 97402 or buy on Amazon.com.

Second Chance Book Catalog

General Fiction/Mystery
Horror
Fantasy
Sci-Fi
Romance
Western
Historical Fiction
Inspirational
Urban
Classics
Series
Star Trek
Star Wars
Reference
Manga
Magic: The *Gathering*
Role-Playing Game *Books*
Wicca
Adult Erotica and *more...*

Your one-stop catalog for every book that you want! If we don't have it, we will do our best to find it for you! The overwhelming majority of our main-stream books sell for $5.99-$7.99, while others may cost more. Shipping is just a flat $5 per order (up to five books per order by BOP policy).

BOP inmates add us on Tru-Lincs at
SecondChanceBooks@outlook.com

Second Chance Group LLC
14 Weaver St
Buffalo, New York 14206
(716) 969-8120

Your family/friends can now put money on your account with us quickly and easily by calling us or going to

SecondChanceCatalog.com

2019-20 SCHEDULE

NFL Schedule Grid

TEAM	1	2	3	4	5	6	7	8	9	10	11	12	13	14	15	16	17
ARI	DET	@BAL	CAR	SEA	@CIN	ATL	@NYG	@NO	SF	@TB	@SF	BYE	LAR	PIT	CLE	@SEA	@LAR
ATL	@MIN	PHI	@IND	TEN	@HOU	@ARI	LAR	SEA	BYE	@NO	@CAR	TB	NO	CAR	@SF	JAX	@TB
BAL	@MIA	ARI	@KC	CLE	@PIT	CIN	@SEA	BYE	NE	@CIN	HOU	@LAR	SF	@BUF	NYJ	@CLE	PIT
BUF	@NYJ	@NYG	CIN	NE	@TEN	BYE	MIA	PHI	WSH	@CLE	@MIA	DEN	@DAL	BAL	@PIT	@NE	NYJ
CAR	LAR	TB	@ARI	@HOU	JAX	@TB	BYE	@SF	TEN	@GB	ATL	@NO	WSH	@ATL	SEA	@IND	NO
CHI	GB	@DEN	@WSH	MIN	@OAK	BYE	NO	LAC	@PHI	DET	@LAR	NYG	@DET	DAL	@GB	KC	@MIN
CIN	@SEA	SF	@BUF	@PIT	ARI	@BAL	JAX	@LAR	BYE	BAL	@OAK	PIT	NYJ	@CLE	NE	@MIA	CLE
CLE	TEN	@NYJ	LAR	@BAL	@SF	SEA	BYE	@NE	@DEN	BUF	PIT	MIA	@PIT	CIN	@ARI	BAL	@CIN
DAL	NYG	@WSH	MIA	@NO	GB	@NYJ	PHI	BYE	@NYG	MIN	@DET	@NE	BUF	@CHI	LAR	@PHI	WSH
DEN	@OAK	CHI	@GB	JAX	@LAC	TEN	KC	@IND	CLE	BYE	@MIN	@BUF	LAC	@HOU	@KC	DET	OAK
DET	@ARI	LAC	@PHI	KC	BYE	@GB	MIN	NYG	@OAK	@CHI	DAL	@WSH	CHI	@MIN	TB	@DEN	GB
GB	@CHI	MIN	DEN	PHI	@DAL	DET	OAK	@KC	@LAC	CAR	BYE	@SF	@NYG	WSH	CHI	@MIN	@DET
HOU	@NO	JAX	@LAC	CAR	ATL	@KC	@IND	OAK	@JAX	BYE	@BAL	IND	NE	DEN	@TEN	@TB	TEN
IND	@LAC	@TEN	ATL	OAK	@KC	BYE	HOU	DEN	@PIT	MIA	JAX	@HOU	TEN	@TB	@NO	CAR	@JAX
JAX	KC	@HOU	TEN	@DEN	@CAR	NO	@CIN	NYJ	HOU	BYE	@IND	@TEN	TB	LAC	@OAK	@ATL	IND
KC	@JAX	@OAK	BAL	@DET	IND	HOU	@DEN	GB	MIN	@TEN	@LAC	BYE	OAK	@NE	DEN	@CHI	LAC
LAR	@CAR	NO	@CLE	TB	@SEA	SF	@ATL	CIN	BYE	@PIT	CHI	BAL	@ARI	SEA	@DAL	@SF	ARI
LAC	IND	@DET	HOU	@MIA	DEN	PIT	@TEN	@CHI	GB	@OAK	KC	BYE	@DEN	@JAX	MIN	OAK	@KC
MIA	BAL	NE	@DAL	LAC	BYE	WSH	@BUF	@PIT	NYJ	@IND	BUF	@CLE	PHI	@NYJ	@NYG	CIN	@NE
MIN	ATL	@GB	OAK	@CHI	@NYG	PHI	@DET	WSH	@KC	@DAL	DEN	BYE	@SEA	DET	@LAC	GB	CHI
NE	PIT	@MIA	NYJ	@BUF	@WSH	NYG	@NYJ	CLE	@BAL	BYE	@PHI	DAL	@HOU	KC	@CIN	BUF	MIA
NO	HOU	@LAR	@SEA	DAL	TB	@JAX	@CHI	ARI	BYE	ATL	@TB	CAR	@ATL	SF	IND	@TEN	@CAR
NYG	@DAL	BUF	@TB	WSH	MIN	@NE	ARI	@DET	DAL	@NYJ	BYE	@CHI	GB	@PHI	MIA	@WSH	PHI
NYJ	BUF	CLE	@NE	BYE	@PHI	DAL	NE	@JAX	@MIA	NYG	@WSH	OAK	@CIN	MIA	@BAL	PIT	@BUF
OAK	DEN	KC	@MIN	@IND	CHI	BYE	@GB	@HOU	DET	LAC	CIN	@NYJ	@KC	TEN	JAX	@LAC	@DEN
PHI	WSH	@ATL	DET	@GB	NYJ	@MIN	@DAL	@BUF	CHI	BYE	NE	SEA	@MIA	NYG	@WSH	DAL	@NYG
PIT	@NE	SEA	@SF	CIN	BAL	@LAC	BYE	MIA	IND	LAR	@CLE	@CIN	CLE	@ARI	BUF	@NYJ	@BAL
SF	@TB	@CIN	PIT	BYE	CLE	@LAR	@WSH	CAR	@ARI	SEA	ARI	GB	@BAL	@NO	ATL	LAR	@SEA
SEA	CIN	@PIT	NO	@ARI	LAR	@CLE	BAL	@ATL	TB	@SF	BYE	@PHI	MIN	@LAR	@CAR	ARI	SF
TB	SF	@CAR	NYG	@LAR	@NO	CAR	BYE	@TEN	@SEA	ARI	NO	@ATL	@JAX	IND	@DET	HOU	ATL
TEN	@CLE	IND	@JAX	@ATL	BUF	@DEN	LAC	TB	@CAR	KC	BYE	JAX	@IND	@OAK	HOU	NO	@HOU
WSH	@PHI	DAL	CHI	@NYG	NE	@MIA	SF	@MIN	@BUF	BYE	NYJ	DET	@CAR	@GB	PHI	NYG	@DAL

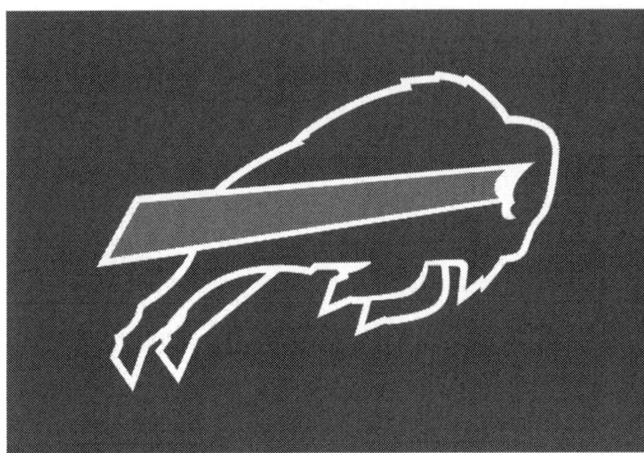

BUFFALO BILLS

BYE: WEEK 6

2019 REGULAR SEASON

Week	Date	Time		Opponent	Broadcast
1	Sep 8	1:00 PM ET	AT	JETS	TV CBS, Radio Sirius
2	Sep 15	1:00 PM ET	AT	GIANTS	TV CBS, Radio Sirius
3	Sep 22	1:00 PM ET		BENGALS	TV CBS, Radio Sirius
4	Sep 29	1:00 PM ET		PATRIOTS	TV CBS, Radio Sirius
5	Oct 6	1:00 PM ET	AT	TITANS	TV CBS, Radio Sirius
6	BYE				
7	Oct 20	1:00 PM ET		DOLPHINS	TV CBS, Radio Sirius
8	Oct 27	1:00 PM ET		EAGLES	TV FOX, Radio Sirius
9	Nov 3	1:00 PM ET		REDSKINS	TV FOX, Radio Sirius
10	Nov 10	1:00 PM ET	AT	BROWNS	TV CBS, Radio Sirius
11	Nov 17	1:00 PM ET	AT	DOLPHINS	TV CBS, Radio Sirius
12	Nov 24	1:00 PM ET		BRONCOS	TV CBS, Radio Sirius
13	Nov 28	4:30 PM ET	AT	COWBOYS	TV CBS, Radio Sirius
14	Dec 8	1:00 PM ET		RAVENS	TV CBS, Radio Sirius
15	Dec 15	1:00 PM ET	AT	STEELERS	TV CBS, Radio Sirius
16	Dec 22	1:00 PM ET	AT	PATRIOTS	TV, Radio Sirius
17	Dec 29	1:00 PM ET		JETS	TV CBS, Radio Sirius

MIAMI DOLPHINS

BYE: WEEK 5

2019 REGULAR SEASON

Week	Date	Time		Opponent	Broadcast
1	Sep 8	1:00 PM ET		RAVENS	TV CBS, Radio Sirius
2	Sep 15	1:00 PM ET		PATRIOTS	TV CBS, Radio Sirius
3	Sep 22	1:00 PM ET	AT	COWBOYS	TV FOX, Radio Sirius
4	Sep 29	1:00 PM ET		CHARGERS	TV CBS, Radio Sirius
5	BYE				
6	Oct 13	1:00 PM ET		REDSKINS	TV FOX, Radio Sirius
7	Oct 20	1:00 PM ET	AT	BILLS	TV CBS, Radio Sirius
8	Oct 28	8:15 PM ET	AT	STEELERS	TV ESPN, Radio Sirius
9	Nov 3	1:00 PM ET		JETS	TV CBS, Radio Sirius
10	Nov 10	4:05 PM ET	AT	COLTS	TV CBS, Radio Sirius
11	Nov 17	1:00 PM ET		BILLS	TV CBS, Radio Sirius
12	Nov 24	1:00 PM ET	AT	BROWNS	TV CBS, Radio Sirius
13	Dec 1	1:00 PM ET		EAGLES	TV FOX, Radio Sirius
14	Dec 8	1:00 PM ET	AT	JETS	TV CBS, Radio Sirius
15	Dec 15	1:00 PM ET	AT	GIANTS	TV CBS, Radio Sirius
16	Dec 22	1:00 PM ET		BENGALS	TV CBS, Radio Sirius
17	Dec 29	1:00 PM ET	AT	PATRIOTS	TV CBS, Radio Sirius

NEW ENGLAND PATRIOTS

BYE: WEEK 10

2019 REGULAR SEASON

Week	Date	Time		Opponent	TV / Radio
1	Sep 8	8:20 PM ET		STEELERS	TV NBC / Radio Sirius
2	Sep 15	1:00 PM ET	AT	DOLPHINS	TV CBS / Radio Sirius
3	Sep 22	1:00 PM ET		JETS	TV CBS / Radio Sirius
4	Sep 29	1:00 PM ET	AT	BILLS	TV CBS / Radio Sirius
5	Oct 6	1:00 PM ET	AT	REDSKINS	TV CBS / Radio Sirius
6	Oct 10	8:20 PM ET		GIANTS	TV FOX / Radio Sirius
7	Oct 21	8:15 PM ET	AT	JETS	TV ESPN / Radio Sirius
8	Oct 27	4:25 PM ET		BROWNS	TV CBS / Radio Sirius
9	Nov 3	8:20 PM ET	AT	RAVENS	TV NBC / Radio Sirius
10	BYE				
11	Nov 17	4:25 PM ET	AT	EAGLES	TV CBS / Radio Sirius
12	Nov 24	4:25 PM ET		COWBOYS	TV FOX / Radio Sirius
13	Dec 1	8:20 PM ET	AT	TEXANS	TV NBC / Radio Sirius
14	Dec 8	4:25 PM ET		CHIEFS	TV CBS / Radio Sirius
15	Dec 15	1:00 PM ET	AT	BENGALS	TV CBS / Radio Sirius
16	Dec 22	1:00 PM ET		BILLS	TV / Radio Sirius
17	Dec 29	1:00 PM ET		DOLPHINS	TV CBS / Radio Sirius

NEW YORK JETS JETS

BYE: WEEK 4

2019 REGULAR SEASON

Week	Date	Time		Opponent	TV / Radio
1	Sep 8	1:00 PM ET		BILLS	TV CBS / Radio Sirius
2	Sep 16	8:15 PM ET		BROWNS	TV ESPN / Radio Sirius
3	Sep 22	1:00 PM ET	AT	PATRIOTS	TV CBS / Radio Sirius
4	BYE				
5	Oct 6	1:00 PM ET	AT	EAGLES	TV CBS / Radio Sirius
6	Oct 13	4:25 PM ET		COWBOYS	TV CBS / Radio Sirius
7	Oct 21	8:15 PM ET		PATRIOTS	TV ESPN / Radio Sirius
8	Oct 27	1:00 PM ET	AT	JAGUARS	TV CBS / Radio Sirius
9	Nov 3	1:00 PM ET	AT	DOLPHINS	TV CBS / Radio Sirius
10	Nov 10	1:00 PM ET		GIANTS	TV FOX / Radio Sirius
11	Nov 17	1:00 PM ET	AT	REDSKINS	TV CBS / Radio Sirius
12	Nov 24	1:00 PM ET		RAIDERS	TV CBS / Radio Sirius
13	Dec 1	1:00 PM ET	AT	BENGALS	TV CBS / Radio Sirius
14	Dec 8	1:00 PM ET		DOLPHINS	TV CBS / Radio Sirius
15	Dec 12	8:20 PM ET	AT	RAVENS	TV FOX / Radio Sirius
16	Dec 22	1:00 PM ET		STEELERS	TV CBS / Radio Sirius
17	Dec 29	1:00 PM ET	AT	BILLS	TV CBS / Radio Sirius

BALTIMORE RAVENS

BYE: WEEK 8

2019 REGULAR SEASON

Week	Date	Time		Opponent	TV / Radio
1	Sep 8	1:00 PM ET	AT	DOLPHINS	TV CBS / Radio Sirius
2	Sep 15	1:00 PM ET		CARDINALS	TV FOX / Radio Sirius
3	Sep 22	1:00 PM ET	AT	CHIEFS	TV CBS / Radio Sirius
4	Sep 29	1:00 PM ET		BROWNS	TV CBS / Radio Sirius
5	Oct 6	1:00 PM ET	AT	STEELERS	TV CBS / Radio Sirius
6	Oct 13	1:00 PM ET		BENGALS	TV CBS / Radio Sirius
7	Oct 20	4:25 PM ET	AT	SEAHAWKS	TV FOX / Radio Sirius
8	BYE				
9	Nov 3	8:20 PM ET		PATRIOTS	TV NBC / Radio Sirius
10	Nov 10	1:00 PM ET	AT	BENGALS	TV CBS / Radio Sirius
11	Nov 17	1:00 PM ET		TEXANS	TV CBS / Radio Sirius
12	Nov 25	8:15 PM ET	AT	RAMS	TV ESPN / Radio Sirius
13	Dec 1	1:00 PM ET		49ERS	TV FOX / Radio Sirius
14	Dec 8	1:00 PM ET	AT	BILLS	TV CBS / Radio Sirius
15	Dec 12	8:20 PM ET		JETS	TV FOX / Radio Sirius
16	Dec 22	1:00 PM ET	AT	BROWNS	TV CBS / Radio Sirius
17	Dec 29	1:00 PM ET		STEELERS	TV CBS / Radio Sirius

CINCINNATI BENGALS

BYE: WEEK 9

2019 REGULAR SEASON

Week	Date	Time		Opponent	TV / Radio
1	Sep 8	4:05 PM ET	AT	SEAHAWKS	TV CBS / Radio Sirius
2	Sep 15	1:00 PM ET		49ERS	TV FOX / Radio Sirius
3	Sep 22	1:00 PM ET	AT	BILLS	TV CBS / Radio Sirius
4	Sep 30	8:15 PM ET	AT	STEELERS	TV ESPN / Radio Sirius
5	Oct 6	1:00 PM ET		CARDINALS	TV FOX / Radio Sirius
6	Oct 13	1:00 PM ET	AT	RAVENS	TV CBS / Radio Sirius
7	Oct 20	1:00 PM ET		JAGUARS	TV CBS / Radio Sirius
8	Oct 27	1:00 PM ET	AT	RAMS	TV CBS / Radio Sirius
9	BYE				
10	Nov 10	1:00 PM ET		RAVENS	TV CBS / Radio Sirius
11	Nov 17	4:25 PM ET	AT	RAIDERS	TV CBS / Radio Sirius
12	Nov 24	1:00 PM ET		STEELERS	TV CBS / Radio Sirius
13	Dec 1	1:00 PM ET		JETS	TV CBS / Radio Sirius
14	Dec 8	1:00 PM ET	AT	BROWNS	TV CBS / Radio Sirius
15	Dec 15	1:00 PM ET		PATRIOTS	TV CBS / Radio Sirius
16	Dec 22	1:00 PM ET	AT	DOLPHINS	TV CBS / Radio Sirius
17	Dec 29	1:00 PM ET		BROWNS	TV CBS / Radio Sirius

CLEVELAND BROWNS

BYE: WEEK 7

2019 REGULAR SEASON

Week	Date	Time		Opponent	TV / Radio
1	Sep 8	1:00 PM ET		TITANS	TV CBS / Radio Sirius
2	Sep 16	8:15 PM ET	AT	JETS	TV ESPN / Radio Sirius
3	Sep 22	8:20 PM ET		RAMS	TV NBC / Radio Sirius
4	Sep 29	1:00 PM ET	AT	RAVENS	TV CBS / Radio Sirius
5	Oct 7	8:15 PM ET	AT	49ERS	TV ESPN / Radio Sirius
6	Oct 13	1:00 PM ET		SEAHAWKS	TV FOX / Radio Sirius
7	BYE				
8	Oct 27	4:25 PM ET	AT	PATRIOTS	TV CBS / Radio Sirius
9	Nov 3	4:25 PM ET	AT	BRONCOS	TV CBS / Radio Sirius
10	Nov 10	1:00 PM ET		BILLS	TV CBS / Radio Sirius
11	Nov 14	8:20 PM ET		STEELERS	TV FOX / Radio Sirius
12	Nov 24	1:00 PM ET		DOLPHINS	TV CBS / Radio Sirius
13	Dec 1	4:25 PM ET	AT	STEELERS	TV CBS / Radio Sirius
14	Dec 8	1:00 PM ET		BENGALS	TV CBS / Radio Sirius
15	Dec 15	4:05 PM ET	AT	CARDINALS	TV CBS / Radio Sirius
16	Dec 22	1:00 PM ET		RAVENS	TV CBS / Radio Sirius
17	Dec 29	1:00 PM ET	AT	BENGALS	TV CBS / Radio Sirius

PITTSBURGH STEELERS

BYE: WEEK 7

2019 REGULAR SEASON

Week	Date	Time		Opponent	TV / Radio
1	Sep 8	8:20 PM ET	AT	PATRIOTS	TV NBC / Radio Sirius
2	Sep 15	1:00 PM ET		SEAHAWKS	TV FOX / Radio Sirius
3	Sep 22	4:25 PM ET	AT	49ERS	TV CBS / Radio Sirius
4	Sep 30	8:15 PM ET		BENGALS	TV ESPN / Radio Sirius
5	Oct 6	1:00 PM ET		RAVENS	TV CBS / Radio Sirius
6	Oct 13	8:20 PM ET	AT	CHARGERS	TV NBC / Radio Sirius
7	BYE				
8	Oct 28	8:15 PM ET		DOLPHINS	TV ESPN / Radio Sirius
9	Nov 3	1:00 PM ET		COLTS	TV CBS / Radio Sirius
10	Nov 10	4:25 PM ET		RAMS	TV FOX / Radio Sirius
11	Nov 14	8:20 PM ET	AT	BROWNS	TV FOX / Radio Sirius
12	Nov 24	1:00 PM ET	AT	BENGALS	TV CBS / Radio Sirius
13	Dec 1	4:25 PM ET		BROWNS	TV CBS / Radio Sirius
14	Dec 8	4:25 PM ET	AT	CARDINALS	TV CBS / Radio Sirius
15	Dec 15	1:00 PM ET		BILLS	TV CBS / Radio Sirius
16	Dec 22	1:00 PM ET	AT	JETS	TV CBS / Radio Sirius
17	Dec 29	1:00 PM ET	AT	RAVENS	TV CBS / Radio Sirius

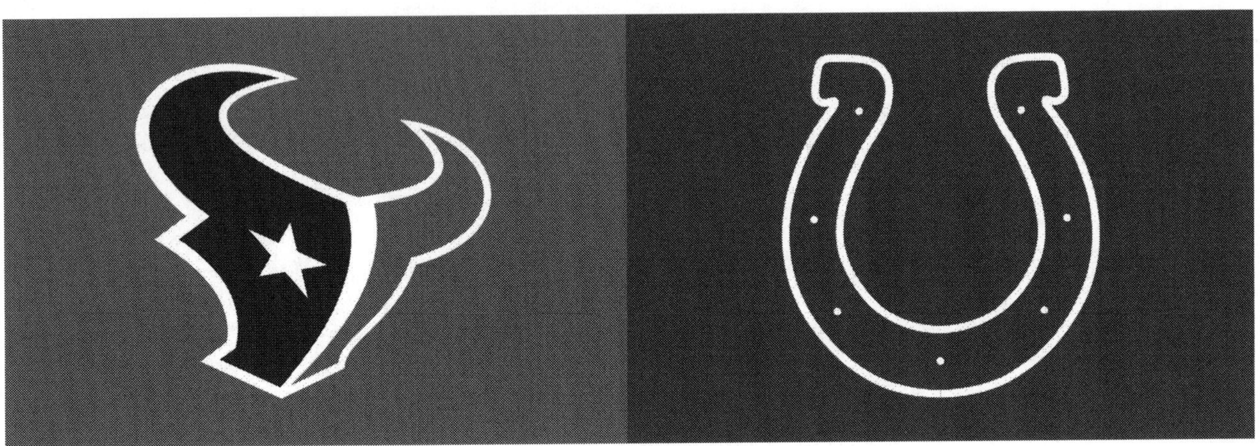

HOUSTON TEXANS

BYE: WEEK 10

2019 REGULAR SEASON

Week	Date	Time		Opponent	TV/Radio
1	Sep 9	7:10 PM ET	AT	SAINTS	TV ESPN Radio Sirius
2	Sep 15	1:00 PM ET		JAGUARS	TV CBS Radio Sirius
3	Sep 22	4:25 PM ET	AT	CHARGERS	TV CBS Radio Sirius
4	Sep 29	1:00 PM ET		PANTHERS	TV FOX Radio Sirius
5	Oct 6	1:00 PM ET		FALCONS	TV FOX Radio Sirius
6	Oct 13	1:00 PM ET	AT	CHIEFS	TV CBS Radio Sirius
7	Oct 20	1:00 PM ET	AT	COLTS	TV CBS Radio Sirius
8	Oct 27	1:00 PM ET		RAIDERS	TV CBS Radio Sirius
9	Nov 3	9:30 AM ET	AT	JAGUARS	TV NFL NETW Radio Sirius
10	BYE				
11	Nov 17	1:00 PM ET	AT	RAVENS	TV CBS Radio Sirius
12	Nov 21	8:20 PM ET		COLTS	TV FOX Radio Sirius
13	Dec 1	8:20 PM ET		PATRIOTS	TV NBC Radio Sirius
14	Dec 8	1:00 PM ET		BRONCOS	TV CBS Radio Sirius
15	Dec 15	1:00 PM ET	AT	TITANS	TV CBS Radio Sirius
16	Dec 22	1:00 PM ET	AT	BUCCANEERS	TV Radio Sirius
17	Dec 29	1:00 PM ET		TITANS	TV CBS Radio Sirius

INDIANAPOLIS COLTS

BYE: WEEK 6

2019 REGULAR SEASON

Week	Date	Time		Opponent	TV/Radio
1	Sep 8	4:05 PM ET	AT	CHARGERS	TV CBS Radio Sirius
2	Sep 15	1:00 PM ET	AT	TITANS	TV CBS Radio Sirius
3	Sep 22	1:00 PM ET		FALCONS	TV CBS Radio Sirius
4	Sep 29	1:00 PM ET		RAIDERS	TV CBS Radio Sirius
5	Oct 6	8:20 PM ET	AT	CHIEFS	TV NBC Radio Sirius
6	BYE				
7	Oct 20	1:00 PM ET		TEXANS	TV CBS Radio Sirius
8	Oct 27	4:25 PM ET		BRONCOS	TV CBS Radio Sirius
9	Nov 3	1:00 PM ET	AT	STEELERS	TV CBS Radio Sirius
10	Nov 10	4:05 PM ET		DOLPHINS	TV CBS Radio Sirius
11	Nov 17	1:00 PM ET		JAGUARS	TV CBS Radio Sirius
12	Nov 21	8:20 PM ET	AT	TEXANS	TV FOX Radio Sirius
13	Dec 1	1:00 PM ET		TITANS	TV CBS Radio Sirius
14	Dec 8	1:00 PM ET	AT	BUCCANEERS	TV CBS Radio Sirius
15	Dec 16	8:15 PM ET	AT	SAINTS	TV ESPN Radio Sirius
16	Dec 22	1:00 PM ET		PANTHERS	TV FOX Radio Sirius
17	Dec 29	1:00 PM ET	AT	JAGUARS	TV CBS Radio Sirius

JACKSONVILLE JAGUARS

BYE: WEEK 10

2019 REGULAR SEASON

Week	Date	Time		Opponent	Broadcast
1	Sep 8	1:00 PM ET		CHIEFS	TV CBS, Radio Sirius
2	Sep 15	1:00 PM ET	AT	TEXANS	TV CBS, Radio Sirius
3	Sep 19	8:20 PM ET		TITANS	TV NFL NET, Radio Sirius
4	Sep 29	4:25 PM ET	AT	BRONCOS	TV CBS, Radio Sirius
5	Oct 6	1:00 PM ET	AT	PANTHERS	TV CBS, Radio Sirius
6	Oct 13	1:00 PM ET		SAINTS	TV CBS, Radio Sirius
7	Oct 20	1:00 PM ET	AT	BENGALS	TV CBS, Radio Sirius
8	Oct 27	1:00 PM ET		JETS	TV CBS, Radio Sirius
9	Nov 3	9:30 AM ET		TEXANS	TV NFL NET, Radio Sirius
10	BYE				
11	Nov 17	1:00 PM ET	AT	COLTS	TV CBS, Radio Sirius
12	Nov 24	4:05 PM ET	AT	TITANS	TV CBS, Radio Sirius
13	Dec 1	1:00 PM ET		BUCCANEERS	TV FOX, Radio Sirius
14	Dec 8	4:05 PM ET		CHARGERS	TV FOX, Radio Sirius
15	Dec 15	4:05 PM ET	AT	RAIDERS	TV CBS, Radio Sirius
16	Dec 22	1:00 PM ET	AT	FALCONS	TV FOX, Radio Sirius
17	Dec 29	1:00 PM ET		COLTS	TV CBS, Radio Sirius

TENNESSEE TITANS

BYE: WEEK 11

2019 REGULAR SEASON

Week	Date	Time		Opponent	Broadcast
1	Sep 8	1:00 PM ET	AT	BROWNS	TV CBS, Radio Sirius
2	Sep 15	1:00 PM ET		COLTS	TV CBS, Radio Sirius
3	Sep 19	8:20 PM ET	AT	JAGUARS	TV NFL NE, Radio Sirius
4	Sep 29	1:00 PM ET	AT	FALCONS	TV CBS, Radio Sirius
5	Oct 6	1:00 PM ET		BILLS	TV CBS, Radio Sirius
6	Oct 13	4:25 PM ET	AT	BRONCOS	TV CBS, Radio Sirius
7	Oct 20	4:05 PM ET		CHARGERS	TV CBS, Radio Sirius
8	Oct 27	1:00 PM ET		BUCCANEERS	TV FOX, Radio Sirius
9	Nov 3	1:00 PM ET	AT	PANTHERS	TV CBS, Radio Sirius
10	Nov 10	1:00 PM ET		CHIEFS	TV CBS, Radio Sirius
11	BYE				
12	Nov 24	4:05 PM ET		JAGUARS	TV CBS, Radio Sirius
13	Dec 1	1:00 PM ET	AT	COLTS	TV CBS, Radio Sirius
14	Dec 8	4:25 PM ET	AT	RAIDERS	TV CBS, Radio Sirius
15	Dec 15	1:00 PM ET		TEXANS	TV CBS, Radio Sirius
16	Dec 22	1:00 PM ET		SAINTS	TV FOX, Radio Sirius
17	Dec 29	1:00 PM ET	AT	TEXANS	TV CBS, Radio Sirius

DENVER BRONCOS

BYE: WEEK 10

2019 REGULAR SEASON

Week	Date	Time		Opponent	TV/Radio
1	Sep 9	10:20 PM ET	AT	RAIDERS	TV ESPN Radio Sirius
2	Sep 15	4:25 PM ET		BEARS	TV FOX Radio Sirius
3	Sep 22	1:00 PM ET	AT	PACKERS	TV FOX Radio Sirius
4	Sep 29	4:25 PM ET		JAGUARS	TV CBS Radio Sirius
5	Oct 6	4:05 PM ET	AT	CHARGERS	TV CBS Radio Sirius
6	Oct 13	4:25 PM ET		TITANS	TV CBS Radio Sirius
7	Oct 17	8:20 PM ET		CHIEFS	TV FOX Radio Sirius
8	Oct 27	4:25 PM ET	AT	COLTS	TV CBS Radio Sirius
9	Nov 3	4:25 PM ET		BROWNS	TV CBS Radio Sirius
10	BYE				
11	Nov 17	1:00 PM ET	AT	VIKINGS	TV CBS Radio Sirius
12	Nov 24	1:00 PM ET	AT	BILLS	TV CBS Radio Sirius
13	Dec 1	4:25 PM ET		CHARGERS	TV CBS Radio Sirius
14	Dec 8	1:00 PM ET	AT	TEXANS	TV CBS Radio Sirius
15	Dec 15	1:00 PM ET	AT	CHIEFS	TV CBS Radio Sirius
16	Dec 22	1:00 PM ET		LIONS	TV Radio Sirius
17	Dec 29	4:25 PM ET		RAIDERS	TV CBS Radio Sirius

KANSAS CITY CHIEFS

BYE: WEEK 12

2019 REGULAR SEASON

Week	Date	Time		Opponent	TV/Radio
1	Sep 8	1:00 PM ET	AT	JAGUARS	TV CBS Radio Sirius
2	Sep 15	4:05 PM ET	AT	RAIDERS	TV CBS Radio Sirius
3	Sep 22	1:00 PM ET		RAVENS	TV CBS Radio Sirius
4	Sep 29	1:00 PM ET	AT	LIONS	TV FOX Radio Sirius
5	Oct 6	8:20 PM ET		COLTS	TV NBC Radio Sirius
6	Oct 13	1:00 PM ET		TEXANS	TV CBS Radio Sirius
7	Oct 17	8:20 PM ET	AT	BRONCOS	TV FOX Radio Sirius
8	Oct 27	8:20 PM ET		PACKERS	TV NBC Radio Sirius
9	Nov 3	1:00 PM ET		VIKINGS	TV FOX Radio Sirius
10	Nov 10	1:00 PM ET	AT	TITANS	TV CBS Radio Sirius
11	Nov 18	8:15 PM ET	AT	CHARGERS	TV ESPN Radio Sirius
12	BYE				
13	Dec 1	1:00 PM ET		RAIDERS	TV CBS Radio Sirius
14	Dec 8	4:25 PM ET	AT	PATRIOTS	TV CBS Radio Sirius
15	Dec 15	1:00 PM ET		BRONCOS	TV CBS Radio Sirius
16	Dec 22	8:20 PM ET	AT	BEARS	TV NBC Radio Sirius
17	Dec 29	1:00 PM ET		CHARGERS	TV CBS Radio Sirius

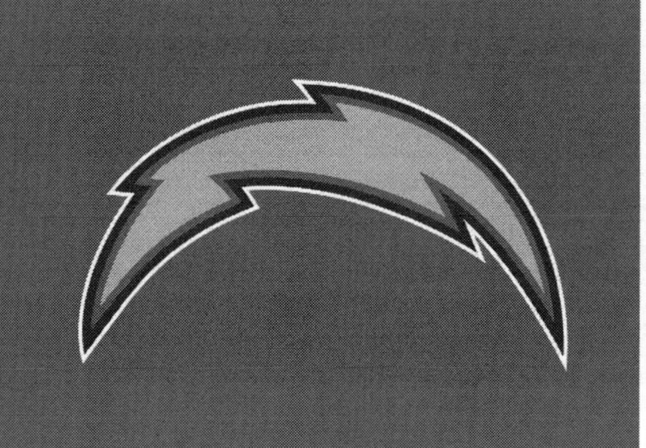

OAKLAND RAIDERS

BYE: WEEK 6

2019 REGULAR SEASON

Week	Date	Time		Opponent	TV	Radio
1	Sep 9	10:20 PM ET		BRONCOS	ESPN	Sirius
2	Sep 15	4:05 PM ET		CHIEFS	CBS	Sirius
3	Sep 22	1:00 PM ET	AT	VIKINGS	FOX	Sirius
4	Sep 29	1:00 PM ET	AT	COLTS	CBS	Sirius
5	Oct 6	1:00 PM ET		BEARS	FOX	Sirius
6	BYE					
7	Oct 20	1:00 PM ET	AT	PACKERS	CBS	Sirius
8	Oct 27	1:00 PM ET	AT	TEXANS	CBS	Sirius
9	Nov 3	4:05 PM ET		LIONS	FOX	Sirius
10	Nov 7	8:20 PM ET		CHARGERS	FOX	Sirius
11	Nov 17	4:25 PM ET		BENGALS	CBS	Sirius
12	Nov 24	1:00 PM ET	AT	JETS	CBS	Sirius
13	Dec 1	1:00 PM ET	AT	CHIEFS	CBS	Sirius
14	Dec 8	4:25 PM ET		TITANS	CBS	Sirius
15	Dec 15	4:05 PM ET		JAGUARS	CBS	Sirius
16	Dec 22	1:00 PM ET	AT	CHARGERS		Sirius
17	Dec 29	4:25 PM ET	AT	BRONCOS	CBS	Sirius

LOS ANGELES CHARGERS CHARGERS

BYE: WEEK 12

2019 REGULAR SEASON

Week	Date	Time		Opponent	TV	Radio
1	Sep 8	4:05 PM ET		COLTS	CBS	Sirius
2	Sep 15	1:00 PM ET	AT	LIONS	CBS	Sirius
3	Sep 22	4:25 PM ET		TEXANS	CBS	Sirius
4	Sep 29	1:00 PM ET	AT	DOLPHINS	CBS	Sirius
5	Oct 6	4:05 PM ET		BRONCOS	CBS	Sirius
6	Oct 13	8:20 PM ET		STEELERS	NBC	Sirius
7	Oct 20	4:05 PM ET	AT	TITANS	CBS	Sirius
8	Oct 27	1:00 PM ET	AT	BEARS	FOX	Sirius
9	Nov 3	4:25 PM ET		PACKERS	CBS	Sirius
10	Nov 7	8:20 PM ET	AT	RAIDERS	FOX	Sirius
11	Nov 18	8:15 PM ET		CHIEFS	ESPN	Sirius
12	BYE					
13	Dec 1	4:25 PM ET	AT	BRONCOS	CBS	Sirius
14	Dec 8	4:05 PM ET	AT	JAGUARS	FOX	Sirius
15	Dec 15	8:20 PM ET		VIKINGS	NBC	Sirius
16	Dec 22	1:00 PM ET		RAIDERS		Sirius
17	Dec 29	1:00 PM ET	AT	CHIEFS	CBS	Sirius

DALLAS COWBOYS

BYE: WEEK 8

2019 REGULAR SEASON

Week	Date	Time		Opponent	TV / Radio
1	Sep 8	4:25 PM ET		GIANTS	TV FOX / Radio Sirius
2	Sep 15	1:00 PM ET	AT	REDSKINS	TV FOX / Radio Sirius
3	Sep 22	1:00 PM ET		DOLPHINS	TV FOX / Radio Sirius
4	Sep 29	8:20 PM ET	AT	SAINTS	TV NBC / Radio Sirius
5	Oct 6	4:25 PM ET		PACKERS	TV FOX / Radio Sirius
6	Oct 13	4:25 PM ET	AT	JETS	TV CBS / Radio Sirius
7	Oct 20	8:20 PM ET		EAGLES	TV NBC / Radio Sirius
8	BYE				
9	Nov 4	8:15 PM ET	AT	GIANTS	TV ESPN / Radio Sirius
10	Nov 10	8:20 PM ET		VIKINGS	TV NBC / Radio Sirius
11	Nov 17	1:00 PM ET	AT	LIONS	TV FOX / Radio Sirius
12	Nov 24	4:25 PM ET	AT	PATRIOTS	TV FOX / Radio Sirius
13	Nov 28	4:30 PM ET		BILLS	TV CBS / Radio Sirius
14	Dec 5	8:20 PM ET	AT	BEARS	TV FOX / Radio Sirius
15	Dec 15	4:25 PM ET		RAMS	TV FOX / Radio Sirius
16	Dec 22	4:25 PM ET	AT	EAGLES	TV FOX / Radio Sirius
17	Dec 29	1:00 PM ET		REDSKINS	TV FOX / Radio Sirius

NEW YORK GIANTS GIANTS

BYE: WEEK 11

2019 REGULAR SEASON

Week	Date	Time		Opponent	TV / Radio
1	Sep 8	4:25 PM ET	AT	COWBOYS	TV FOX / Radio Sirius
2	Sep 15	1:00 PM ET		BILLS	TV CBS / Radio Sirius
3	Sep 22	4:05 PM ET	AT	BUCCANEERS	TV FOX / Radio Sirius
4	Sep 29	1:00 PM ET		REDSKINS	TV FOX / Radio Sirius
5	Oct 6	1:00 PM ET		VIKINGS	TV FOX / Radio Sirius
6	Oct 10	8:20 PM ET	AT	PATRIOTS	TV FOX / Radio Sirius
7	Oct 20	1:00 PM ET		CARDINALS	TV FOX / Radio Sirius
8	Oct 27	1:00 PM ET	AT	LIONS	TV FOX / Radio Sirius
9	Nov 4	8:15 PM ET		COWBOYS	TV ESPN / Radio Sirius
10	Nov 10	1:00 PM ET	AT	JETS	TV FOX / Radio Sirius
11	BYE				
12	Nov 24	1:00 PM ET	AT	BEARS	TV FOX / Radio Sirius
13	Dec 1	1:00 PM ET		PACKERS	TV FOX / Radio Sirius
14	Dec 9	8:15 PM ET	AT	EAGLES	TV ESPN / Radio Sirius
15	Dec 15	1:00 PM ET		DOLPHINS	TV CBS / Radio Sirius
16	Dec 22	1:00 PM ET	AT	REDSKINS	TV FOX / Radio Sirius
17	Dec 29	1:00 PM ET		EAGLES	TV FOX / Radio Sirius

PHILADELPHIA EAGLES

BYE: WEEK 10

2019 REGULAR SEASON

Week	Date	Time		Opponent	TV / Radio
1	Sep 8	1:00 PM ET		REDSKINS	TV FOX / Radio Sirius
2	Sep 15	8:20 PM ET	AT	FALCONS	TV NBC / Radio Sirius
3	Sep 22	1:00 PM ET		LIONS	TV FOX / Radio Sirius
4	Sep 26	8:20 PM ET	AT	PACKERS	TV FOX / Radio Sirius
5	Oct 6	1:00 PM ET		JETS	TV CBS / Radio Sirius
6	Oct 13	1:00 PM ET	AT	VIKINGS	TV FOX / Radio Sirius
7	Oct 20	8:20 PM ET	AT	COWBOYS	TV NBC / Radio Sirius
8	Oct 27	1:00 PM ET	AT	BILLS	TV FOX / Radio Sirius
9	Nov 3	1:00 PM ET		BEARS	TV FOX / Radio Sirius
10	BYE				
11	Nov 17	4:25 PM ET		PATRIOTS	TV CBS / Radio Sirius
12	Nov 24	8:20 PM ET		SEAHAWKS	TV NBC / Radio Sirius
13	Dec 1	1:00 PM ET	AT	DOLPHINS	TV FOX / Radio Sirius
14	Dec 9	8:15 PM ET		GIANTS	TV ESPN / Radio Sirius
15	Dec 15	1:00 PM ET	AT	REDSKINS	TV FOX / Radio Sirius
16	Dec 22	4:25 PM ET		COWBOYS	TV FOX / Radio Sirius
17	Dec 29	1:00 PM ET	AT	GIANTS	TV FOX / Radio Sirius

KANSAS CITY CHIEFS

BYE: WEEK 12

2019 REGULAR SEASON

Week	Date	Time		Opponent	TV / Radio
1	Sep 8	1:00 PM ET	AT	JAGUARS	TV CBS / Radio Sirius
2	Sep 15	4:05 PM ET	AT	RAIDERS	TV CBS / Radio Sirius
3	Sep 22	1:00 PM ET		RAVENS	TV CBS / Radio Sirius
4	Sep 29	1:00 PM ET	AT	LIONS	TV FOX / Radio Sirius
5	Oct 6	8:20 PM ET		COLTS	TV NBC / Radio Sirius
6	Oct 13	1:00 PM ET		TEXANS	TV CBS / Radio Sirius
7	Oct 17	8:20 PM ET	AT	BRONCOS	TV FOX / Radio Sirius
8	Oct 27	8:20 PM ET		PACKERS	TV NBC / Radio Sirius
9	Nov 3	1:00 PM ET		VIKINGS	TV FOX / Radio Sirius
10	Nov 10	1:00 PM ET	AT	TITANS	TV CBS / Radio Sirius
11	Nov 18	8:15 PM ET	AT	CHARGERS	TV ESPN / Radio Sirius
12	BYE				
13	Dec 1	1:00 PM ET		RAIDERS	TV CBS / Radio Sirius
14	Dec 8	4:25 PM ET	AT	PATRIOTS	TV CBS / Radio Sirius
15	Dec 15	1:00 PM ET		BRONCOS	TV CBS / Radio Sirius
16	Dec 22	8:20 PM ET	AT	BEARS	TV NBC / Radio Sirius
17	Dec 29	1:00 PM ET		CHARGERS	TV CBS / Radio Sirius

NFL TEAM SCHEDULES

CHICAGO BEARS

BYE: WEEK 6

2019 REGULAR SEASON

Week	Date	Time		Opponent	TV / Radio
1	Sep 5	8:20 PM ET		PACKERS	TV NBC / Radio Sirius
2	Sep 15	4:25 PM ET	AT	BRONCOS	TV FOX / Radio Sirius
3	Sep 23	8:15 PM ET	AT	REDSKINS	TV ESPN / Radio Sirius
4	Sep 29	4:25 PM ET		VIKINGS	TV CBS / Radio Sirius
5	Oct 6	1:00 PM ET	AT	RAIDERS	TV FOX / Radio Sirius
6	BYE				
7	Oct 20	4:25 PM ET		SAINTS	TV FOX / Radio Sirius
8	Oct 27	1:00 PM ET		CHARGERS	TV FOX / Radio Sirius
9	Nov 3	1:00 PM ET	AT	EAGLES	TV FOX / Radio Sirius
10	Nov 10	1:00 PM ET		LIONS	TV CBS / Radio Sirius
11	Nov 17	8:20 PM ET	AT	RAMS	TV NBC / Radio Sirius
12	Nov 24	1:00 PM ET		GIANTS	TV FOX / Radio Sirius
13	Nov 28	12:30 PM ET	AT	LIONS	TV FOX / Radio Sirius
14	Dec 5	8:20 PM ET		COWBOYS	TV FOX / Radio Sirius
15	Dec 15	1:00 PM ET	AT	PACKERS	TV FOX / Radio Sirius
16	Dec 22	8:20 PM ET		CHIEFS	TV NBC / Radio Sirius
17	Dec 29	1:00 PM ET	AT	VIKINGS	TV FOX / Radio Sirius

DETROIT LIONS

BYE: WEEK 5

2019 REGULAR SEASON

Week	Date	Time		Opponent	TV / Radio
1	Sep 8	4:25 PM ET	AT	CARDINALS	TV FOX / Radio Sirius
2	Sep 15	1:00 PM ET		CHARGERS	TV CBS / Radio Sirius
3	Sep 22	1:00 PM ET	AT	EAGLES	TV FOX / Radio Sirius
4	Sep 29	1:00 PM ET		CHIEFS	TV FOX / Radio Sirius
5	BYE				
6	Oct 14	8:15 PM ET	AT	PACKERS	TV ESPN / Radio Sirius
7	Oct 20	1:00 PM ET		VIKINGS	TV FOX / Radio Sirius
8	Oct 27	1:00 PM ET		GIANTS	TV FOX / Radio Sirius
9	Nov 3	4:05 PM ET	AT	RAIDERS	TV FOX / Radio Sirius
10	Nov 10	1:00 PM ET	AT	BEARS	TV CBS / Radio Sirius
11	Nov 17	1:00 PM ET		COWBOYS	TV FOX / Radio Sirius
12	Nov 24	1:00 PM ET	AT	REDSKINS	TV FOX / Radio Sirius
13	Nov 28	12:30 PM ET		BEARS	TV FOX / Radio Sirius
14	Dec 8	1:00 PM ET	AT	VIKINGS	TV FOX / Radio Sirius
15	Dec 15	1:00 PM ET		BUCCANEERS	TV FOX / Radio Sirius
16	Dec 22	1:00 PM ET	AT	BRONCOS	TV / Radio Sirius
17	Dec 29	1:00 PM ET		PACKERS	TV FOX / Radio Sirius

GREEN BAY PACKERS

BYE: WEEK 11

2019 REGULAR SEASON

Week	Date	Time		Opponent		
1	Sep 5	8:20 PM ET	AT	BEARS	TV NBC	Radio Sirius
2	Sep 15	1:00 PM ET		VIKINGS	TV FOX	Radio Sirius
3	Sep 22	1:00 PM ET		BRONCOS	TV FOX	Radio Sirius
4	Sep 26	8:20 PM ET		EAGLES	TV FOX	Radio Sirius
5	Oct 6	4:25 PM ET	AT	COWBOYS	TV FOX	Radio Sirius
6	Oct 14	8:15 PM ET		LIONS	TV ESPN	Radio Sirius
7	Oct 20	1:00 PM ET		RAIDERS	TV CBS	Radio Sirius
8	Oct 27	8:20 PM ET	AT	CHIEFS	TV NBC	Radio Sirius
9	Nov 3	4:25 PM ET	AT	CHARGERS	TV CBS	Radio Sirius
10	Nov 10	1:00 PM ET		PANTHERS	TV FOX	Radio Sirius
11	BYE					
12	Nov 24	4:25 PM ET	AT	49ERS	TV FOX	Radio Sirius
13	Dec 1	1:00 PM ET	AT	GIANTS	TV FOX	Radio Sirius
14	Dec 8	1:00 PM ET		REDSKINS	TV FOX	Radio Sirius
15	Dec 15	1:00 PM ET		BEARS	TV FOX	Radio Sirius
16	Dec 23	8:15 PM ET	AT	VIKINGS	TV ESPN	Radio Sirius
17	Dec 29	1:00 PM ET	AT	LIONS	TV FOX	Radio Sirius

MINNESOTA VIKINGS

BYE: WEEK 12

2019 REGULAR SEASON

Week	Date	Time		Opponent		
1	Sep 8	1:00 PM ET		FALCONS	TV FOX	Radio Sirius
2	Sep 15	1:00 PM ET	AT	PACKERS	TV FOX	Radio Sirius
3	Sep 22	1:00 PM ET		RAIDERS	TV FOX	Radio Sirius
4	Sep 29	4:25 PM ET	AT	BEARS	TV CBS	Radio Sirius
5	Oct 6	1:00 PM ET	AT	GIANTS	TV FOX	Radio Sirius
6	Oct 13	1:00 PM ET		EAGLES	TV FOX	Radio Sirius
7	Oct 20	1:00 PM ET	AT	LIONS	TV FOX	Radio Sirius
8	Oct 24	8:20 PM ET		REDSKINS	TV FOX	Radio Sirius
9	Nov 3	1:00 PM ET	AT	CHIEFS	TV FOX	Radio Sirius
10	Nov 10	8:20 PM ET	AT	COWBOYS	TV NBC	Radio Sirius
11	Nov 17	1:00 PM ET		BRONCOS	TV CBS	Radio Sirius
12	BYE					
13	Dec 2	8:15 PM ET	AT	SEAHAWKS	TV ESPN	Radio Sirius
14	Dec 8	1:00 PM ET		LIONS	TV FOX	Radio Sirius
15	Dec 15	8:20 PM ET	AT	CHARGERS	TV NBC	Radio Sirius
16	Dec 23	8:15 PM ET		PACKERS	TV ESPN	Radio Sirius
17	Dec 29	1:00 PM ET		BEARS	TV FOX	Radio Sirius

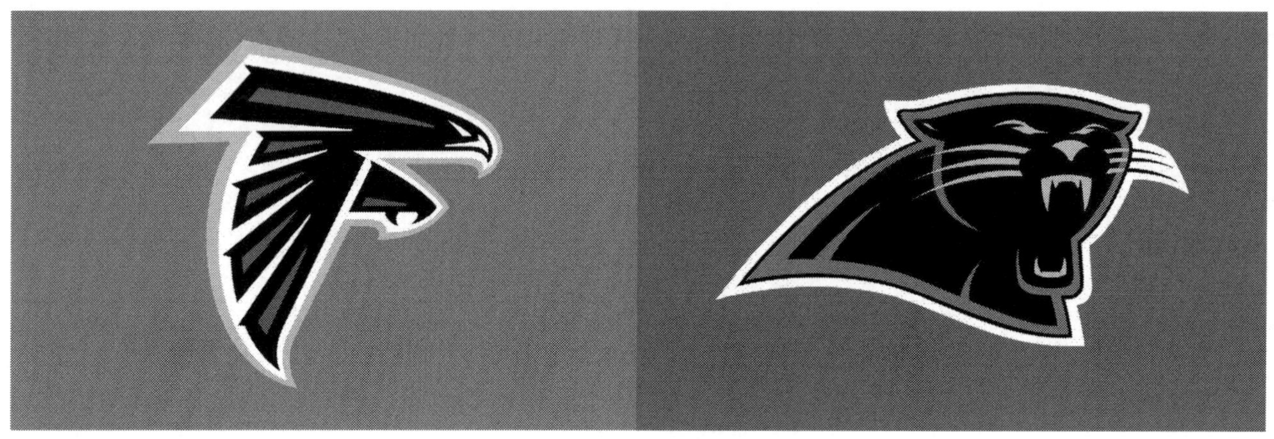

ATLANTA FALCONS

BYE: WEEK 9

2019 REGULAR SEASON

Week	Date	Time		Opponent	TV / Radio
1	Sep 8	1:00 PM ET	AT	VIKINGS	TV FOX / Radio Sirius
2	Sep 15	8:20 PM ET		EAGLES	TV NBC / Radio Sirius
3	Sep 22	1:00 PM ET	AT	COLTS	TV CBS / Radio Sirius
4	Sep 29	1:00 PM ET		TITANS	TV CBS / Radio Sirius
5	Oct 6	1:00 PM ET	AT	TEXANS	TV FOX / Radio Sirius
6	Oct 13	4:05 PM ET	AT	CARDINALS	TV FOX / Radio Sirius
7	Oct 20	1:00 PM ET		RAMS	TV FOX / Radio Sirius
8	Oct 27	1:00 PM ET		SEAHAWKS	TV FOX / Radio Sirius
9	BYE				
10	Nov 10	1:00 PM ET	AT	SAINTS	TV FOX / Radio Sirius
11	Nov 17	1:00 PM ET	AT	PANTHERS	TV FOX / Radio Sirius
12	Nov 24	1:00 PM ET		BUCCANEERS	TV FOX / Radio Sirius
13	Nov 28	8:20 PM ET		SAINTS	TV NBC / Radio Sirius
14	Dec 8	1:00 PM ET		PANTHERS	TV FOX / Radio Sirius
15	Dec 15	4:25 PM ET	AT	49ERS	TV FOX / Radio Sirius
16	Dec 22	1:00 PM ET		JAGUARS	TV FOX / Radio Sirius
17	Dec 29	1:00 PM ET	AT	BUCCANEERS	TV FOX / Radio Sirius

CAROLINA PANTHERS

BYE: WEEK 7

2019 REGULAR SEASON

Week	Date	Time		Opponent	TV / Radio
1	Sep 8	1:00 PM ET		RAMS	TV FOX / Radio Sirius
2	Sep 12	8:20 PM ET		BUCCANEERS	TV NFL NET / Radio Sirius
3	Sep 22	4:05 PM ET	AT	CARDINALS	TV FOX / Radio Sirius
4	Sep 29	1:00 PM ET	AT	TEXANS	TV FOX / Radio Sirius
5	Oct 6	1:00 PM ET		JAGUARS	TV CBS / Radio Sirius
6	Oct 13	9:30 AM ET	AT	BUCCANEERS	TV NFL NET / Radio Sirius
7	BYE				
8	Oct 27	4:05 PM ET	AT	49ERS	TV FOX / Radio Sirius
9	Nov 3	1:00 PM ET		TITANS	TV CBS / Radio Sirius
10	Nov 10	1:00 PM ET	AT	PACKERS	TV FOX / Radio Sirius
11	Nov 17	1:00 PM ET		FALCONS	TV FOX / Radio Sirius
12	Nov 24	1:00 PM ET	AT	SAINTS	TV FOX / Radio Sirius
13	Dec 1	1:00 PM ET		REDSKINS	TV CBS / Radio Sirius
14	Dec 8	1:00 PM ET	AT	FALCONS	TV FOX / Radio Sirius
15	Dec 15	1:00 PM ET		SEAHAWKS	TV FOX / Radio Sirius
16	Dec 22	1:00 PM ET	AT	COLTS	TV FOX / Radio Sirius
17	Dec 29	1:00 PM ET		SAINTS	TV FOX / Radio Sirius

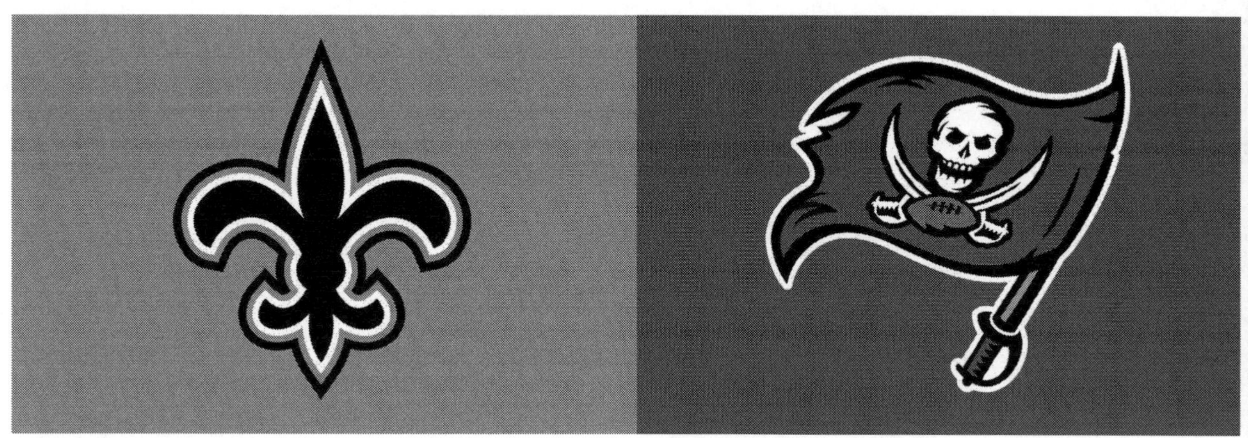

NEW ORLEANS SAINTS

BYE: WEEK 9

2019 REGULAR SEASON

Week	Date	Time		Opponent	TV	Radio
1	Sep 9	7:10 PM ET		TEXANS	ESPN	Sirius
2	Sep 15	4:25 PM ET	AT	RAMS	FOX	Sirius
3	Sep 22	4:25 PM ET	AT	SEAHAWKS	CBS	Sirius
4	Sep 29	8:20 PM ET		COWBOYS	NBC	Sirius
5	Oct 6	1:00 PM ET		BUCCANEERS	FOX	Sirius
6	Oct 13	1:00 PM ET	AT	JAGUARS	CBS	Sirius
7	Oct 20	4:25 PM ET	AT	BEARS	FOX	Sirius
8	Oct 27	1:00 PM ET		CARDINALS	CBS	Sirius
9	BYE					
10	Nov 10	1:00 PM ET		FALCONS	FOX	Sirius
11	Nov 17	1:00 PM ET	AT	BUCCANEERS	FOX	Sirius
12	Nov 24	1:00 PM ET		PANTHERS	FOX	Sirius
13	Nov 28	8:20 PM ET	AT	FALCONS	NBC	Sirius
14	Dec 8	1:00 PM ET		49ERS	FOX	Sirius
15	Dec 16	8:15 PM ET		COLTS	ESPN	Sirius
16	Dec 22	1:00 PM ET	AT	TITANS	FOX	Sirius
17	Dec 29	1:00 PM ET	AT	PANTHERS	FOX	Sirius

TAMPA BAY BUCCANEERS

BYE: WEEK 7

2019 REGULAR SEASON

Week	Date	Time		Opponent	TV	Radio
1	Sep 8	4:25 PM ET		49ERS	FOX	Sirius
2	Sep 12	8:20 PM ET	AT	PANTHERS	NFL NET	Sirius
3	Sep 22	4:05 PM ET		GIANTS	FOX	Sirius
4	Sep 29	4:05 PM ET	AT	RAMS	FOX	Sirius
5	Oct 6	1:00 PM ET	AT	SAINTS	FOX	Sirius
6	Oct 13	9:30 AM ET		PANTHERS	NFL NET	Sirius
7	BYE					
8	Oct 27	1:00 PM ET	AT	TITANS	FOX	Sirius
9	Nov 3	4:05 PM ET	AT	SEAHAWKS	FOX	Sirius
10	Nov 10	1:00 PM ET		CARDINALS	FOX	Sirius
11	Nov 17	1:00 PM ET		SAINTS	FOX	Sirius
12	Nov 24	1:00 PM ET	AT	FALCONS	FOX	Sirius
13	Dec 1	1:00 PM ET	AT	JAGUARS	FOX	Sirius
14	Dec 8	1:00 PM ET		COLTS	CBS	Sirius
15	Dec 15	1:00 PM ET	AT	LIONS	FOX	Sirius
16	Dec 22	1:00 PM ET		TEXANS		Sirius
17	Dec 29	1:00 PM ET		FALCONS	FOX	Sirius

ARIZONA CARDINALS

BYE: WEEK 12

2019 REGULAR SEASON

Week	Date	Time		Opponent	TV	Radio
1	Sep 8	4:25 PM ET		LIONS	FOX	Sirius
2	Sep 15	1:00 PM ET	AT	RAVENS	FOX	Sirius
3	Sep 22	4:05 PM ET		PANTHERS	FOX	Sirius
4	Sep 29	4:05 PM ET		SEAHAWKS	FOX	Sirius
5	Oct 6	1:00 PM ET	AT	BENGALS	FOX	Sirius
6	Oct 13	4:05 PM ET		FALCONS	FOX	Sirius
7	Oct 20	1:00 PM ET	AT	GIANTS	FOX	Sirius
8	Oct 27	1:00 PM ET	AT	SAINTS	CBS	Sirius
9	Oct 31	8:20 PM ET		49ERS	FOX	Sirius
10	Nov 10	1:00 PM ET	AT	BUCCANEERS	FOX	Sirius
11	Nov 17	4:05 PM ET	AT	49ERS	FOX	Sirius
12	BYE					
13	Dec 1	4:05 PM ET		RAMS	FOX	Sirius
14	Dec 8	4:25 PM ET		STEELERS	CBS	Sirius
15	Dec 15	4:05 PM ET		BROWNS	CBS	Sirius
16	Dec 22	4:25 PM ET	AT	SEAHAWKS	FOX	Sirius
17	Dec 29	4:25 PM ET	AT	RAMS	FOX	Sirius

LOS ANGELES RAMS RAMS

BYE: WEEK 9

2019 REGULAR SEASON

Week	Date	Time		Opponent	TV	Radio
1	Sep 8	1:00 PM ET	AT	PANTHERS	FOX	Sirius
2	Sep 15	4:25 PM ET		SAINTS	FOX	Sirius
3	Sep 22	8:20 PM ET	AT	BROWNS	NBC	Sirius
4	Sep 29	4:05 PM ET		BUCCANEERS	FOX	Sirius
5	Oct 3	8:20 PM ET	AT	SEAHAWKS	FOX	Sirius
6	Oct 13	4:05 PM ET		49ERS	FOX	Sirius
7	Oct 20	1:00 PM ET	AT	FALCONS	FOX	Sirius
8	Oct 27	1:00 PM ET		BENGALS	CBS	Sirius
9	BYE					
10	Nov 10	4:25 PM ET	AT	STEELERS	FOX	Sirius
11	Nov 17	8:20 PM ET		BEARS	NBC	Sirius
12	Nov 25	8:15 PM ET		RAVENS	ESPN	Sirius
13	Dec 1	4:05 PM ET	AT	CARDINALS	FOX	Sirius
14	Dec 8	8:20 PM ET		SEAHAWKS	NBC	Sirius
15	Dec 15	4:25 PM ET	AT	COWBOYS	FOX	Sirius
16	Dec 22	1:00 PM ET	AT	49ERS		Sirius
17	Dec 29	4:25 PM ET		CARDINALS	FOX	Sirius

SAN FRANCISCO 49ERS

BYE: WEEK 4

2019 REGULAR SEASON

Wk	Date	Time		Opponent		
1	Sep 8	4:25 PM ET	AT	BUCCANEERS	TV Radio	FOX Sirius
2	Sep 15	1:00 PM ET	AT	BENGALS	TV Radio	FOX Sirius
3	Sep 22	4:25 PM ET		STEELERS	TV Radio	CBS Sirius
4	BYE					
5	Oct 7	8:15 PM ET		BROWNS	TV Radio	ESPN Sirius
6	Oct 13	4:05 PM ET	AT	RAMS	TV Radio	FOX Sirius
7	Oct 20	1:00 PM ET	AT	REDSKINS	TV Radio	FOX Sirius
8	Oct 27	4:05 PM ET		PANTHERS	TV Radio	FOX Sirius
9	Oct 31	8:20 PM ET	AT	CARDINALS	TV Radio	FOX Sirius
10	Nov 11	8:15 PM ET		SEAHAWKS	TV Radio	ESPN Sirius
11	Nov 17	4:05 PM ET		CARDINALS	TV Radio	FOX Sirius
12	Nov 24	4:25 PM ET		PACKERS	TV Radio	FOX Sirius
13	Dec 1	1:00 PM ET	AT	RAVENS	TV Radio	FOX Sirius
14	Dec 8	1:00 PM ET	AT	SAINTS	TV Radio	FOX Sirius
15	Dec 15	4:25 PM ET		FALCONS	TV Radio	FOX Sirius
16	Dec 22	1:00 PM ET		RAMS	TV Radio	Sirius
17	Dec 29	4:25 PM ET	AT	SEAHAWKS	TV Radio	FOX Sirius

BALTIMORE RAVENS

BYE: WEEK 8

2019 REGULAR SEASON

Wk	Date	Time		Opponent		
1	Sep 8	1:00 PM ET	AT	DOLPHINS	TV Radio	CBS Sirius
2	Sep 15	1:00 PM ET		CARDINALS	TV Radio	FOX Sirius
3	Sep 22	1:00 PM ET	AT	CHIEFS	TV Radio	CBS Sirius
4	Sep 29	1:00 PM ET		BROWNS	TV Radio	CBS Sirius
5	Oct 6	1:00 PM ET	AT	STEELERS	TV Radio	CBS Sirius
6	Oct 13	1:00 PM ET		BENGALS	TV Radio	CBS Sirius
7	Oct 20	4:25 PM ET	AT	SEAHAWKS	TV Radio	FOX Sirius
8	BYE					
9	Nov 3	8:20 PM ET		PATRIOTS	TV Radio	NBC Sirius
10	Nov 10	1:00 PM ET	AT	BENGALS	TV Radio	CBS Sirius
11	Nov 17	1:00 PM ET		TEXANS	TV Radio	CBS Sirius
12	Nov 25	8:15 PM ET	AT	RAMS	TV Radio	ESPN Sirius
13	Dec 1	1:00 PM ET		49ERS	TV Radio	FOX Sirius
14	Dec 8	1:00 PM ET	AT	BILLS	TV Radio	CBS Sirius
15	Dec 12	8:20 PM ET		JETS	TV Radio	FOX Sirius
16	Dec 22	1:00 PM ET	AT	BROWNS	TV Radio	CBS Sirius
17	Dec 29	1:00 PM ET		STEELERS	TV Radio	CBS Sirius

2019 NASCAR® Schedules

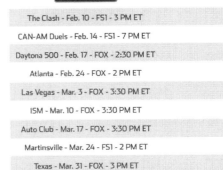

Monster Energy NASCAR Cup Series	NASCAR Xfinity Series	NASCAR Gander Outdoors Truck Series
The Clash - Feb. 10 - FS1 - 3 PM ET		
CAN-AM Duels - Feb. 14 - FS1 - 7 PM ET		
Daytona 500 - Feb. 17 - FOX - 2:30 PM ET	Daytona - Feb. 16 - FS1 - 2:30 PM	Daytona - Feb. 15 - FS1 - 7:30 PM
Atlanta - Feb. 24 - FOX - 2 PM ET	Atlanta - Feb. 23 - FS1 - 2 PM	Atlanta - Feb. 23 - FS1 - 4:30 PM
Las Vegas - Mar. 3 - FOX - 3:30 PM ET	Las Vegas - Mar 2 - FS1 - 4 PM	Las Vegas - Mar. 1 - FS1 - 9 PM
ISM - Mar. 10 - FOX - 3:30 PM ET	ISM - Mar 9 - FS1 - 4 PM	
Auto Club - Mar. 17 - FOX - 3:30 PM ET	Auto Club - Mar 16 - FS1 - 5 PM	
Martinsville - Mar. 24 - FS1 - 2 PM ET		Martinsville - Mar. 23 - FOX - 2 PM
Texas - Mar. 31 - FOX - 3 PM ET	Texas - Mar 30 - FS1 - 1 PM	Texas - Mar. 29 - FS1 - 9 PM
Bristol - Apr. 7 - FS1 - 2 PM ET	Bristol - Apr 6 - FS1 - 1 PM	
Richmond - Apr. 13 - FOX - 7:30 PM ET	Richmond - Apr. 12 - FS1 - 7 PM	
Talladega - Apr. 28 - FOX - 2 PM ET	Talladega - Apr. 27 - FS1 - 1 PM	
Dover - May 5 - FS1 - 2 PM ET	Dover - May 4 - FS1 - 1:30 PM	Dover - May 3 - FS1 - 5 PM
Kansas - May 11 - FS1 - 7:30 PM ET		Kansas - May 10 - FS1 - 8:30 PM
All-Star Race - May 18 - FS1 - 8 PM ET		Charlotte - May 17 - FS1 - 8:30 PM

Charlotte - May 26 - FOX - 6 PM ET	Charlotte - May 25 - FS1 - 1 PM	
Pocono - Jun. 2 - FS1 - 2 PM ET	Pocono - Jun. 1 - FS1 - 1 PM	
Michigan - Jun. 9 - FS1 - 2 PM ET	Michigan - Jun. 8 - FS1 - 1:30 PM	Texas - Jun. 7 - FS1 - 9 PM
	Iowa - Jun. 16 - FS1 - 5:30 PM	Iowa - Jun. 15 - FS1 - 8:30 PM
Sonoma - Jun. 23 - FS1 - 3 PM ET		Gateway - Jun. 22 - FS1 - 10 PM
Chicagoland - Jun 30 - NBCSN - 3 PM ET	Chicagoland - Jun. 29 - NBCSN - 3:30 PM	Chicagoland - Jun. 28 - FS1 - 9 PM
Daytona - Jul. 6 - NBC - 7:30 PM ET	Daytona - Jul. 5 - NBCSN - 7:30 PM	
Kentucky - Jul. 13 - NBCSN - 7:30 PM ET	Kentucky - Jul. 12 - NBCSN - 7:30 PM	Kentucky - Jul. 11 - FS1 - 7:30 PM
New Hampshire - Jul. 21 - NBCSN - 3 PM ET	New Hampshire - Jul. 20 - 4 PM	Pocono - Jul. 27 - FOX - 1 PM
Pocono - Jul. 28 - NBCSN - 3 PM ET	Iowa - Jul. 27 - NBCSN - 5 PM	Eldora - Aug. 1 - FS1 - 9 PM
Watkins Glen - Aug. 4 - NBCSN - 3 PM ET	Watkins Glen - Aug. 3 - NBC - 3 PM	
Michigan - Aug. 11 - NBCSN - 3 PM ET	Mid-Ohio - Aug. 10 - NBCSN - 3 PM	Michigan - Aug. 10 - FS1 - 1 PM
Bristol - Aug. 17 - NBCSN - 7:30 PM ET	Bristol - Aug. 16 - NBCSN - 7:30 PM	Bristol - Aug. 15 - FS1 - 8:30 PM
	Road America - Aug. 24 - NBCSN - 3 PM	Canadian Tire - Aug. 25 - FS1 - 2:30 PM
Darlington - Sep. 1 - NBCSN - 6 PM ET	Darlington - Aug. 31 - NBC - 4 PM	
Indianapolis - Sep. 8 - NBC - 2 PM ET	Indianapolis - Sep. 7 - NBCSN - 4 PM	
Las Vegas - Sep. 15 - NBCSN - 7 PM ET	Las Vegas - Sep. 14 - NBCSN - 7:30 PM	Las Vegas - Sep. 13 - FS1 - 9 PM
Richmond - Sep. 21 -NBCSN - 7:30 PM ET	Richmond - Sep. 20 - NBCSN - 7:30 PM	
Charlotte - Sep. 29 - NBC - 2:30 PM ET	Charlotte - Sep. 28 - NBCSN - 3:30 PM	
Dover - Oct. 6 - NBCSN - 2:30 PM ET	Dover - Oct. 5 - NBCSN - 3 PM	
Talladega - Oct. 13 - NBC - 2 PM ET		Talladega - Oct. 12 - FS1 - 1:30 PM
Kansas - Oct. 20 - NBC - 2:30 PM ET	Kansas - Oct. 19 - NBC - 3 PM	
Martinsville - Oct. 27 - NBCSN - 3 PM ET		Martinsville - Oct. 26 - FS1 - 1:30 PM
Texas - Nov. 3 - NBCSN - 3 PM ET	Texas - Nov. 2 - NBCSN - 8:30 PM	
ISM - Nov. 10 - NBC - 2:30 PM ET	ISM - Nov. 9 - NBC - 3:30 PM	ISM - Nov. 8 - FS1 - 8:30 PM
Homestead-Miami - Nov. 17 - NBC - 3 PM ET	Homestead-Miami - Nov. 16 - NBCSN - 3:30 PM	Homestead-Miami - Nov. 15 - FS1 -8 PM

2019 MLB SCHEDULE

Date	Ana	Bal	Bos	ChW	Cle	Det	Hou	Kan	Min	NYY	Oak	Sea	Tam	Tex	Tor
Th-3/28	@Oak	@NYY	@Sea	@Kan	@Min	@Tor	@Tam	ChW	Cle	Bal	Ana	Bos	Hou	ChC	Det
Fr-3/29	@Oak		@Sea			@Tor	@Tam				Ana	Bos	Hou		Det
Sa-3/30	@Oak	@NYY	@Sea	@Kan	@Min	@Tor	@Tam	ChW	Cle	Bal	Ana	Bos	Hou	ChC	Det
Su-3/31	@Oak	@NYY	@Sea	@Kan	@Min	@Tor	@Tam	ChW	Cle	Bal	Ana	Bos	Hou	ChC	Det
Mo-4/1	@Sea	@Tor	@Oak	@Cle	ChW	@NYY	@Tex			Det	Bos	Ana	Col	Hou	Bal
Tu-4/2	@Sea	@Tor	@Oak			@NYY	@Tex	Min	@Kan	Det	Bos	Ana	Col	Hou	Bal
We-4/3		@Tor	@Oak	@Cle	ChW	@NYY	@Tex	Min	@Kan	Det	Bos		Col	Hou	Bal
Th-4/4	Tex	NYY	@Oak	Sea	Tor	Kan		@Det		@Bal	Bos	@ChW		@Ana	@Cle
Fr-4/5	Tex		@Ari		Tor		Oak		@Phi		@Hou		@Sfo	@Ana	@Cle
Sa-4/6	Tex	NYY	@Ari	Sea	Tor	Kan	Oak	@Det	@Phi	@Bal	@Hou	@ChW	@Sfo	@Ana	@Cle
Su-4/7	Tex	NYY	@Ari	Sea	Tor	Kan	Oak	@Det	@Phi	@Bal	@Hou	@ChW	@Sfo	@Ana	@Cle
Mo-4/8	Mil	Oak		Tam			NYY	Sea		@Hou	@Bal	@Kan	@ChW		
Tu-4/9	Mil	Oak	Tor	Tam	@Det	Cle	NYY	Sea	@NYM	@Hou	@Bal	@Kan	@ChW	@Ari	@Bos
We-4/10	Mil	Oak		Tam	@Det	Cle	NYY	Sea	@NYM	@Hou	@Bal	@Kan	@ChW	@Ari	
Th-4/11		Oak	Tor		@Det	Cle		Sea			@Bal	@Kan			@Bos
Fr-4/12	@ChC	@Bos	Bal	@NYY	@Kan	@Min	@Sea	Cle	Det	ChW	@Tex	Hou	@Tor	Oak	Tam
Sa-4/13	@ChC	@Bos	Bal	@NYY	@Kan	@Min	@Sea	Cle	Det	ChW	@Tex	Hou	@Tor	Oak	Tam
Su-4/14	@ChC	@Bos	Bal	@NYY	@Kan	@Min	@Sea	Cle	Det	ChW	@Tex	Hou	@Tor	Oak	Tam
Mo-4/15	@Tex	@Bos	Bal	Kan	@Sea			@ChW	Tor			Cle		Ana	@Min
Tu-4/16	@Tex	@Tam	@NYY	Kan	@Sea	Pit	@Oak	@ChW	Tor	Bos	Hou	Cle	Bal	Ana	@Min
We-4/17	@Tex	@Tam	@NYY	Kan	@Sea	Pit	@Oak	@ChW	Tor	Bos	Hou	Cle	Bal	Ana	@Min
Th-4/18	Sea	@Tam		@Det		ChW		@NYY	Tor	Kan		@Ana	Bal		@Min
Fr-4/19	Sea	Min	@Tam	@Det	Atl	ChW	@Tex	@NYY	@Bal	Kan	Tor	@Ana	Bos	Hou	@Oak
Sa-4/20	Sea	Min	@Tam	@Det	Atl	ChW	@Tex	@NYY	@Bal	Kan	Tor	@Ana	Bos	Hou	@Oak
Su-4/21	Sea	Min	@Tam	@Det	Atl	ChW	@Tex	@NYY	@Bal	Kan	Tor	@Ana	Bos	Hou	@Oak
Mo-4/22	NYY	ChW	Det	@Bal		@Bos	Min	@Tam	@Hou	@Ana	Tex		Kan	@Oak	
Tu-4/23	NYY	ChW	Det	@Bal	Fla	@Bos	Min	@Tam	@Hou	@Ana	Tex	@Sdg	Kan	@Oak	Sfo
We-4/24	NYY	ChW	Det	@Bal	Fla	@Bos	Min	@Tam	@Hou	@Ana	Tex	@Sdg	Kan	@Oak	Sfo
Fr-4/26	@Kan	@Min	Tam	Det	@Hou	@ChW	Cle	Ana	Bal	@Sfo	@Tor	Tex	@Bos	@Sea	Oak
Sa-4/27	@Kan	@Min	Tam	Det	@Hou	@ChW	Cle	Ana	Bal	@Sfo	@Tor	Tex	@Bos	@Sea	Oak
Su-4/28	@Kan	@Min	Tam	Det	@Hou	@ChW	Cle	Ana	Bal	@Sfo	@Tor	Tex	@Bos	@Sea	Oak
Mo-4/29		@ChW	Oak	Bal			@Min	Tam	Hou		@Bos		@Kan		
Tu-4/30	Tor	@ChW	Oak	Bal	@Fla	@Phi	@Min	Tam	Hou	@Ari	@Bos	ChC	@Kan	Pit	@Ana
We-5/1	Tor	@ChW	Oak	Bal	@Fla	@Phi	@Min	Tam	Hou	@Ari	@Bos	ChC	@Kan	Pit	@Ana
Th-5/2	Tor		@ChW	Bos			@Min	Tam	Hou				@Kan		@Ana
Fr-5/3		Tam	@ChW	Bos	Sea	Kan		@Det	@NYY	Min	@Pit	@Cle	@Bal	Tor	@Tex
Sa-5/4	Hou	Tam	@ChW	Bos	Sea	Kan	@Ana	@Det	@NYY	Min	@Pit	@Cle	@Bal	Tor	@Tex
Su-5/5	Hou	Tam	@ChW	Bos	Sea	Kan	@Ana	@Det	@NYY	Min	@Pit	@Cle	@Bal	Tor	@Tex
Mo-5/6		Bos	@Bal	@Cle	ChW		Kan	@Hou	@Tor	Sea		@NYY	Ari		Min
Tu-5/7	@Det	Bos	@Bal	@Cle	ChW	Ana	Kan	@Hou	@Tor	Sea	Cin	@NYY	Ari	@Pit	Min

Date	Ari	Atl	ChC	Cin	Col	Fla	Los	Mil	NYM	Phi	Pit	Sdg	Sfo	StL	Was
Th-3/28	@Los	@Phi	@Tex	Pit	@Fla	Col	Ari	StL	@Was	Atl	@Cin	Sfo	@Sdg	@Mil	NYM
Fr-3/29	@Los				@Fla	Col	Ari	StL				Sfo	@Sdg	@Mil	
Sa-3/30	@Los	@Phi	@Tex	Pit	@Fla	Col	Ari	StL	@Was	Atl	@Cin	Sfo	@Sdg	@Mil	NYM
Su-3/31	@Los	@Phi	@Tex	Pit	@Fla	Col	Ari	StL	@Was	Atl	@Cin	Sfo	@Sdg	@Mil	NYM
Mo-4/1	@Sdg	ChC	@Atl	Mil	@Tam	NYM	Sfo	@Cin	@Fla		StL	Ari	@Los	@Pit	
Tu-4/2	@Sdg			Mil	@Tam	NYM	Sfo	@Cin	@Fla	@Was		Ari	@Los		Phi
We-4/3	@Sdg	ChC	@Atl	Mil	@Tam	NYM	Sfo	@Cin	@Fla	@Was	StL	Ari	@Los	@Pit	Phi
Th-4/4		ChC	@Atl	@Pit					Was		Cin	@StL		Sdg	@NYM
Fr-4/5	Bos	Fla	@Mil	@Pit	Los	@Atl	@Col	ChC		Min	Cin		Tam		
Sa-4/6	Bos	Fla	@Mil	@Pit	Los	@Atl	@Col	ChC	Was	Min	Cin	@StL	Tam	Sdg	@NYM
Su-4/7	Bos	Fla	@Mil	@Pit	Los	@Atl	@Col	ChC	Was	Min	Cin	@StL	Tam	Sdg	@NYM
Mo-4/8		@Col	Pit		Atl		@StL	@Ana		Was	@ChC	@Sfo	Sdg	Los	@Phi
Tu-4/9	Tex	@Col		Fla	Atl	@Cin	@StL	@Ana	Min	Was		@Sfo	Sdg	Los	@Phi
We-4/10	Tex	@Col	Pit	Fla	Atl	@Cin	@StL	@Ana	Min	Was	@ChC	@Sfo	Sdg	Los	@Phi
Th-4/11	Sdg	NYM	Pit	Fla	@Sfo	@Cin	@StL		@Atl		@ChC	@Ari	Col	Los	
Fr-4/12	Sdg	NYM	Ana		@Sfo	Phi	Mil	@Los	@Atl	@Fla	@Was	@Ari	Col		Pit
Sa-4/13	Sdg	NYM	Ana	StL	@Sfo	Phi	Mil	@Los	@Atl	@Fla	@Was	@Ari	Col	@Cin	Pit
Su-4/14	Sdg	NYM	Ana	StL	@Sfo	Phi	Mil	@Los	@Atl	@Fla	@Was	@Ari	Col	@Cin	Pit
Mo-4/15			@Fla	@Los	@Sdg	ChC	Cin	StL	@Phi	NYM		Col		@Mil	
Tu-4/16	@Atl	Ari	@Fla	@Los	@Sdg	ChC	Cin	StL	@Phi	NYM	@Det	Col	@Was	@Mil	Sfo
We-4/17	@Atl	Ari	@Fla	@Los		ChC	Cin	StL	@Phi	NYM	@Det		@Was	@Mil	Sfo
Th-4/18	@Atl	Ari		@Sdg	Phi		@Mil	Los		@Col		Cin	@Was		Sfo
Fr-4/19	@ChC	@Cle	Ari	@Sdg	Phi	Was	@Mil	Los	@StL	@Col	Sfo	Cin	@Pit	NYM	@Fla
Sa-4/20	@ChC	@Cle	Ari	@Sdg	Phi	Was	@Mil	Los	@StL	@Col	Sfo	Cin	@Pit	NYM	@Fla
Su-4/21	@ChC	@Cle	Ari	@Sdg	Phi	Was	@Mil	Los	@StL	@Col	Sfo	Cin	@Pit	NYM	@Fla
Mo-4/22	@Pit				Was			@StL	Phi	@NYM	Ari			Mil	@Col
Tu-4/23	@Pit	@Cin	Los	Atl	Was	@Cle	@ChC	@StL	Phi	@NYM	Ari	Sea	@Tor	Mil	@Col
We-4/24	@Pit	@Cin	Los	Atl	Was	@Cle	@ChC	@StL	Phi	@NYM	Ari	Sea	@Tor	Mil	@Col
Fr-4/26	ChC	Col	@Ari	@StL	@Atl	@Phi	Pit	@NYM	Mil	Fla	@Los	@Was	NYY	Cin	Sdg
Sa-4/27	ChC	Col	@Ari	@StL	@Atl	@Phi	Pit	@NYM	Mil	Fla	@Los	@Was	NYY	Cin	Sdg
Su-4/28	ChC	Col	@Ari	@StL	@Atl	@Phi	Pit	@NYM	Mil	Fla	@Los	@Was	NYY	Cin	Sdg
Mo-4/29		Sdg		@NYM	@Mil		@Sfo	Col	Cin			@Atl	Los	@Was	StL
Tu-4/30	NYY	Sdg	@Sea	@NYM	@Mil	Cle	@Sfo	Col	Cin	Det	@Tex	@Atl	Los	@Was	StL
We-5/1	NYY	Sdg	@Sea	@NYM	@Mil	Cle	@Sfo	Col	Cin	Det	@Tex	@Atl	Los	@Was	StL
Th-5/2		Sdg		@NYM	@Mil			Col	Cin			@Atl		@Was	StL
Fr-5/3	@Col	@Fla	StL	Sfo	Ari	Atl	@Sdg	NYM	@Mil	Was	Oak	Los	@Cin	@ChC	@Phi
Sa-5/4	@Col	@Fla	StL	Sfo	Ari	Atl	@Sdg	NYM	@Mil	Was	Oak	Los	@Cin	@ChC	@Phi
Su-5/5	@Col	@Fla	StL	Sfo	Ari	Atl	@Sdg	NYM	@Mil	Was	Oak	Los	@Cin	@ChC	@Phi
Mo-5/6	@Tam	@Los	Fla	Sfo		@ChC	Atl	Was	@Sdg	@StL		NYM	@Cin	Phi	@Mil
Tu-5/7	@Tam	@Los	Fla	@Oak	Sfo	@ChC	Atl	Was	@Sdg	@StL	Tex	NYM	@Col	Phi	@Mil

2019 MLB SCHEDULE

Date	Ana	Bal	Bos	ChW	Cle	Det	Hou	Kan	Min	NYY	Oak	Sea	Tam	Tex	Tor
We-5/8	@Det	Bos	@Bal	@Cle	ChW	Ana	Kan	@Hou	@Tor	Sea	Cin	@NYY	Ari	@Pit	Min
Th-5/9	@Det			@Cle	ChW	Ana	Tex			Sea	Cin	@NYY		@Hou	
Fr-5/10	@Bal	Ana	Sea	@Tor	@Oak	@Min	Tex	Phi	Det	@Tam	Cle	@Bos	NYY	@Hou	ChW
Sa-5/11	@Bal	Ana	Sea	@Tor	@Oak	@Min	Tex	Phi	Det	@Tam	Cle	@Bos	NYY	@Hou	ChW
Su-5/12	@Bal	Ana	Sea	@Tor	@Oak	@Min	Tex	Phi	Det	@Tam	Cle	@Bos	NYY	@Hou	ChW
Mo-5/13	@Min	@NYY		Cle	@ChW	Hou	@Det		Ana	Bal	@Sea	Oak			
Tu-5/14	@Min	@NYY	Col	Cle	@ChW	Hou	@Det	Tex	Ana	Bal	@Sea	Oak	@Fla	@Kan	@Sfo
We-5/15	@Min	@NYY	Col			Hou	@Det	Tex	Ana	Bal			@Fla	@Kan	@Sfo
Th-5/16		@Cle		Tor	Bal	Oak		Tex	@Sea		@Det	Min		@Kan	@ChW
Fr-5/17	Kan	@Cle	Hou	Tor	Bal	Oak	@Bos	@Ana	@Sea	Tam	@Det	Min	@NYY	StL	@ChW
Sa-5/18	Kan	@Cle	Hou	Tor	Bal	Oak	@Bos	@Ana	@Sea	Tam	@Det	Min	@NYY	StL	@ChW
Su-5/19	Kan	@Cle	Hou	Tor	Bal	Oak	@Bos	@Ana	@Sea	Tam	@Det	Min	@NYY	StL	@ChW
Mo-5/20	Min	NYY	@Tor	@Hou	Oak		ChW		@Ana	@Bal	@Cle	@Tex		Sea	Bos
Tu-5/21	Min	NYY	@Tor	@Hou	Oak	Fla	ChW	@StL	@Ana	@Bal	@Cle	@Tex	Los	Sea	Bos
We-5/22	Min	NYY	@Tor	@Hou	Oak	Fla	ChW	@StL	@Ana	@Bal	@Cle	@Tex	Los	Sea	Bos
Th-5/23		NYY	@Tor	@Hou	Tam	Fla	ChW			@Bal			@Cle		Bos
Fr-5/24	Tex	@Col	@Hou	@Min	Tam	@NYM	Bos	NYY	ChW	@Kan	Sea	@Oak	@Cle	@Ana	Sdg
Sa-5/25	Tex	@Col	@Hou	@Min	Tam	@NYM	Bos	NYY	ChW	@Kan	Sea	@Oak	@Cle	@Ana	Sdg
Su-5/26	Tex	@Col	@Hou	@Min	Tam	@NYM	Bos	NYY	ChW	@Kan	Sea	@Oak	@Cle	@Ana	Sdg
Mo-5/27	@Oak	Det	Cle	Kan	@Bos	@Bal	ChC	@ChW	Mil	Sdg	Ana	Tex	Tor	@Sea	@Tam
Tu-5/28	@Oak	Det	Cle	Kan	@Bos	@Bal	ChC	@ChW	Mil	Sdg	Ana	Tex	Tor	@Sea	@Tam
We-5/29	@Oak	Det	Cle	Kan	@Bos	@Bal	ChC	@ChW		Sdg	Ana	Tex	Tor	@Sea	@Tam
Th-5/30	@Sea		@NYY	Cle	@ChW			@Tex	@Tam	Bos		Ana	Min	Kan	
Fr-5/31	@Sea	Sfo	@NYY	Cle	@ChW	@Atl	@Oak	@Tex	@Tam	Bos	Hou	Ana	Min	Kan	@Col
Sa-6/1	@Sea	Sfo	@NYY	Cle	@ChW	@Atl	@Oak	@Tex	@Tam	Bos	Hou	Ana	Min	Kan	@Col
Su-6/2	@Sea	Sfo	@NYY	Cle	@ChW	@Atl	@Oak	@Tex	@Tam	Bos	Hou	Ana	Min	Kan	@Col
Mo-6/3							@Sea					Hou			
Tu-6/4	Oak	@Tex	@Kan	@Was	Min	Tam	@Sea	Bos	@Cle	@Tor	@Ana	Hou	@Det	Bal	NYY
We-6/5	Oak	@Tex	@Kan	@Was	Min	Tam	@Sea	Bos	@Cle	@Tor	@Ana	Hou	@Det	Bal	NYY
Th-6/6	Oak	@Tex	@Kan		Min	Tam	@Sea	Bos	@Cle	@Tor	@Ana	Hou	@Det	Bal	NYY
Fr-6/7	Sea	@Hou	Tam	@Kan	NYY	Min	Bal	ChW	@Det	@Cle	@Tex	@Ana	@Bos	Oak	Ari
Sa-6/8	Sea	@Hou	Tam	@Kan	NYY	Min	Bal	ChW	@Det	@Cle	@Tex	@Ana	@Bos	Oak	Ari
Su-6/9	Sea	@Hou	Tam	@Kan	NYY	Min	Bal	ChW	@Det	@Cle	@Tex	@Ana	@Bos	Oak	Ari
Mo-6/10	Los		Tex	Was						NYM	@Tam		Oak	@Bos	
Tu-6/11	Los	Tor	Tex	Was	Cin	@Kan	Mil	Det	Sea	NYM	@Tam	@Min	Oak	@Bos	@Bal
We-6/12		Tor	Tex		Cin	@Kan	Mil	Det	Sea		@Tam	@Min	Oak	@Bos	@Bal
Th-6/13	@Tam	Tor	Tex	NYY		@Kan		Det	Sea	@ChW		@Min	Ana	@Bos	@Bal
Fr-6/14	@Tam	Bos	@Bal	NYY	@Det	Cle	Tor	@Min	Kan	@ChW	Sea	@Oak	Ana	@Cin	@Hou
Sa-6/15	@Tam	Bos	@Bal	NYY	@Det	Cle	Tor	@Min	Kan	@ChW	Sea	@Oak	Ana	@Cin	@Hou
Su-6/16	@Tam	Bos	@Bal	NYY	@Det	Cle	Tor	@Min	Kan	@ChW	Sea	@Oak	Ana	@Cin	@Hou
Mo-6/17	@Tor	@Oak	@Min		@Tex		@Cin	@Sea	Bos	Tam	Bal	Kan	@NYY	Cle	Ana

Date	Ari	Atl	ChC	Cin	Col	Fla	Los	Mil	NYM	Phi	Pit	Sdg	Sfo	StL	Was
We-5/8	@Tam	@Los	Fla	@Oak	Sfo	@ChC	Atl	Was	@Sdg	@StL	Tex	NYM	@Col	Phi	@Mil
Th-5/9	Atl	@Ari	Fla	@Oak	Sfo	@ChC	Was				@StL		@Col	Pit	@Los
Fr-5/10	Atl	@Ari	Mil	@Sfo	Sdg	@NYM	Was	@ChC	Fla	@Kan	@StL	@Col	Cin	Pit	@Los
Sa-5/11	Atl	@Ari	Mil	@Sfo	Sdg	@NYM	Was	@ChC	Fla	@Kan	@StL	@Col	Cin	Pit	@Los
Su-5/12	Atl	@Ari	Mil	@Sfo	Sdg	@NYM	Was	@ChC	Fla	@Kan	@StL	@Col	Cin	Pit	@Los
Mo-5/13	Pit							@Phi		Mil	@Ari				
Tu-5/14	Pit	StL	@Cin	ChC	@Bos	Tam	Sdg	@Phi	@Was	Mil	@Ari	@Los	Tor	@Atl	NYM
We-5/15	Pit	StL	@Cin	ChC	@Bos	Tam	Sdg	@Phi	@Was	Mil	@Ari	@Los	Tor	@Atl	NYM
Th-5/16		StL	@Cin	ChC				@Phi	@Was	Mil	@Sdg	Pit		@Atl	NYM
Fr-5/17	Sfo	Mil	@Was	Los	@Phi	NYM	@Cin	@Atl	@Fla	Col	@Sdg	Pit	@Ari	@Tex	ChC
Sa-5/18	Sfo	Mil	@Was	Los	@Phi	NYM	@Cin	@Atl	@Fla	Col	@Sdg	Pit	@Ari	@Tex	ChC
Su-5/19	Sfo	Mil	@Was	Los	@Phi	NYM	@Cin	@Atl	@Fla	Col	@Sdg	Pit	@Ari	@Tex	ChC
Mo-5/20	@Sdg	@Sfo	Phi						Was	@ChC		Ari	Atl		@NYM
Tu-5/21	@Sdg	@Sfo	Phi	@Mil	@Pit	@Det	@Tam	Cin	Was	@ChC	Col	Ari	Atl	Kan	@NYM
We-5/22	@Sdg	@Sfo	Phi	@Mil	@Pit	@Det	@Tam	Cin	Was	@ChC	Col	Ari	Atl	Kan	@NYM
Th-5/23		@Sfo	Phi		@Pit	@Det			Was	@ChC	Col		Atl		@NYM
Fr-5/24	@Sfo	@StL	Cin	@ChC	Bal	@Was	@Pit	Phi	Det	@Mil	Los	@Tor	Ari	Atl	Fla
Sa-5/25	@Sfo	@StL	Cin	@ChC	Bal	@Was	@Pit	Phi	Det	@Mil	Los	@Tor	Ari	Atl	Fla
Su-5/26	@Sfo	@StL	Cin	@ChC	Bal	@Was	@Pit	Phi	Det	@Mil	Los	@Tor	Ari	Atl	Fla
Mo-5/27	@Col		@Hou	Pit	Ari	@Was	NYM	@Min	@Los		@Cin	@NYY			Fla
Tu-5/28	@Col	Was	@Hou	Pit	Ari	Sfo	NYM	@Min	@Los	StL	@Cin	@NYY	@Fla	@Phi	@Atl
We-5/29	@Col	Was	@Hou	Pit	Ari	Sfo	NYM		@Los	StL	@Cin	@NYY	@Fla	@Phi	@Atl
Th-5/30	@Col				Ari	Sfo	NYM	@Pit	@Los	StL	Mil		@Fla	@Phi	
Fr-5/31	NYM	Det	@StL	Was	Tor	@Sdg	Phi	@Pit	@Ari	@Los	Mil	Fla	@Bal	ChC	@Cin
Sa-6/1	NYM	Det	@StL	Was	Tor	@Sdg	Phi	@Pit	@Ari	@Los	Mil	Fla	@Bal	ChC	@Cin
Su-6/2	NYM	Det	@StL	Was	Tor	@Sdg	Phi	@Pit	@Ari	@Los	Mil	Fla	@Bal	ChC	@Cin
Mo-6/3	Los						@Ari			@Sdg		Phi			
Tu-6/4	Los	@Pit	Col	@StL	@ChC	@Mil	@Ari	Fla	Sfo	@Sdg	Atl	Phi	@NYM	Cin	ChW
We-6/5	Los	@Pit	Col	@StL	@ChC	@Mil	@Ari	Fla	Sfo	@Sdg	Atl	Phi	@NYM	Cin	ChW
Th-6/6		@Pit	Col	@StL	@ChC	@Mil		Fla	Sfo		Atl	Was	@NYM	Cin	@Sdg
Fr-6/7	@Tor	@Fla	StL	@Phi	@NYM	Atl	@Sfo	Pit	Col	Cin	@Mil	Was	Los	@ChC	@Sdg
Sa-6/8	@Tor	@Fla	StL	@Phi	@NYM	Atl	@Sfo	Pit	Col	Cin	@Mil	Was	Los	@ChC	@Sdg
Su-6/9	@Tor	@Fla	StL	@Phi	@NYM	Atl	@Sfo	Pit	Col	Cin	@Mil	Was	Los	@ChC	@Sdg
Mo-6/10	@Phi	Pit	@Col		ChC	StL	@Ana		@NYY	Ari	@Atl			@Fla	@ChW
Tu-6/11	@Phi	Pit	@Col	@Cle	ChC	StL	@Ana	@Hou	@NYY	Ari	@Atl	@Sfo	Sdg	@Fla	@ChW
We-6/12	@Phi	Pit	@Col	@Cle	ChC	StL		@Hou		Ari	@Atl	@Sfo	Sdg	@Fla	
Th-6/13	@Was	Pit	@Los		Sdg		ChC		StL		@Atl	@Col		@NYM	Ari
Fr-6/14	@Was	Phi	@Los	Tex	Sdg	Pit	ChC	@Sfo	StL	@Atl	@Fla	@Col	Mil	@NYM	Ari
Sa-6/15	@Was	Phi	@Los	Tex	Sdg	Pit	ChC	@Sfo	StL	@Atl	@Fla	@Col	Mil	@NYM	Ari
Su-6/16	@Was	Phi	@Los	Tex	Sdg	Pit	ChC	@Sfo	StL	@Atl	@Fla	@Col	Mil	@NYM	Ari
Mo-6/17		NYM		Hou		@StL	Sfo	@Sdg	@Atl	@Was		Mil	@Los	Fla	Phi

2019 MLB SCHEDULE

Date	Ana	Bal	Bos	ChW	Cle	Det	Hou	Kan	Min	NYY	Oak	Sea	Tam	Tex	Tor
Tu-6/18	@Tor	@Oak	@Min	@ChC	@Tex	@Pit	@Cin	@Sea	Bos	Tam	Bal	Kan	@NYY	Cle	Ana
We-6/19	@Tor	@Oak	@Min	@ChC	@Tex	@Pit	@Cin	@Sea	Bos	Tam	Bal	Kan	@NYY	Cle	Ana
Th-6/20	@Tor	@Sea			@Tex		@NYY	Min	@Kan	Hou	Tam	Bal	@Oak	Cle	Ana
Fr-6/21	@StL	@Sea	Tor	@Tex	Det	@Cle	@NYY	Min	@Kan	Hou	Tam	Bal	@Oak	ChW	@Bos
Sa-6/22	@StL	@Sea	Tor	@Tex	Det	@Cle	@NYY	Min	@Kan	Hou	Tam	Bal	@Oak	ChW	@Bos
Su-6/23	@StL	@Sea	Tor	@Tex	Det	@Cle	@NYY	Min	@Kan	Hou	Tam	Bal	@Oak	ChW	@Bos
Mo-6/24			ChW	@Bos	Kan			@Cle		Tor					@NYY
Tu-6/25	Cin	Sdg	ChW	@Bos	Kan	Tex	Pit	@Cle	Tam	Tor	@StL	@Mil	@Min	@Det	@NYY
We-6/26	Cin	Sdg	ChW	@Bos	Kan	Tex	Pit	@Cle	Tam	Tor	@StL	@Mil	@Min	@Det	@NYY
Th-6/27	Oak					Tex	Pit		Tam		@Ana	@Mil	@Min	@Det	
Fr-6/28	Oak	Cle		Min	@Bal	Was	Sea	@Tor	@ChW		@Ana	@Hou	Tex	@Tam	Kan
Sa-6/29	Oak	Cle	NYY	Min	@Bal	Was	Sea	@Tor	@ChW	@Bos	@Ana	@Hou	Tex	@Tam	Kan
Su-6/30	Oak	Cle	NYY	Min	@Bal	Was	Sea	@Tor	@ChW	@Bos	@Ana	@Hou	Tex	@Tam	Kan
Mo-7/1	@Tex	@Tam						@Tor					Bal	Ana	Kan
Tu-7/2	@Tex	@Tam	@Tor	Det	@Kan	@ChW	@Col	Cle	@Oak	@NYM	Min	StL	Bal	Ana	Bos
We-7/3	@Tex	@Tam	@Tor	Det	@Kan	@ChW	@Col	Cle	@Oak	@NYM	Min	StL	Bal	Ana	Bos
Th-7/4	@Tex		@Tor	Det	@Kan	@ChW		Cle	@Oak	@Tam	Min	StL	NYY	Ana	Bos
Fr-7/5	@Hou	@Tor	@Det			Bos	Ana	@Was	Tex	@Tam	@Sea	Oak	NYY	@Min	Bal
Sa-7/6	@Hou	@Tor	@Det	ChC	@Cin	Bos	Ana	@Was	Tex	@Tam	@Sea	Oak	NYY	@Min	Bal
Su-7/7	@Hou	@Tor	@Det	ChC	@Cin	Bos	Ana	@Was	Tex	@Tam	@Sea	Oak	NYY	@Min	Bal
Th-7/11							@Tex							Hou	
Fr-7/12	Sea	Tam	Los	@Oak	Min	@Kan	@Tex	Det	@Cle	Tor	ChW	@Ana	@Bal	Hou	@NYY
Sa-7/13	Sea	Tam	Los	@Oak	Min	@Kan	@Tex	Det	@Cle	Tor	ChW	@Ana	@Bal	Hou	@NYY
Su-7/14	Sea	Tam	Los	@Oak	Min	@Kan	@Tex	Det	@Cle	Tor	ChW	@Ana	@Bal	Hou	@NYY
Mo-7/15	Hou		Tor	@Kan	Det	@Cle	@Ana	ChW		Tam			@NYY		@Bos
Tu-7/16	Hou	Was	Tor	@Kan	Det	@Cle	@Ana	ChW	NYM	Tam	Sea	@Oak	@NYY	Ari	@Bos
We-7/17	Hou	Was	Tor	@Kan	Det	@Cle	@Ana	ChW	NYM	Tam	Sea	@Oak	@NYY	Ari	@Bos
Th-7/18	Hou		Tor	@Kan	Det	@Cle	@Ana	ChW	Oak	Tam	@Min		@NYY		@Bos
Fr-7/19	@Sea	Bos	@Bal	@Tam	Kan	Tor	Tex	@Cle	Oak	Col	@Min	Ana	ChW	@Hou	@Det
Sa-7/20	@Sea	Bos	@Bal	@Tam	Kan	Tor	Tex	@Cle	Oak	Col	@Min	Ana	ChW	@Hou	@Det
Su-7/21	@Sea	Bos	@Bal	@Tam	Kan	Tor	Tex	@Cle	Oak	Col	@Min	Ana	ChW	@Hou	@Det
Mo-7/22		@Ari	@Tam	Fla	@Tor		Oak		NYY	@Min	@Hou	Tex	Bos	@Sea	Cle
Tu-7/23	@Los	@Ari	@Tam	Fla	@Tor	Phi	Oak	@Atl	NYY	@Min	@Hou	Tex	Bos	@Sea	Cle
We-7/24	@Los	@Ari	@Tam	Fla	@Tor	Phi	Oak	@Atl	NYY	@Min	@Hou	Tex	Bos	@Sea	Cle
Th-7/25	Bal	@Ana	NYY	Min	@Kan	@Sea		Cle	@ChW	@Bos	Tex	Det		@Oak	
Fr-7/26	Bal	@Ana	NYY	Min	@Kan	@Sea	@StL	Cle	@ChW	@Bos	Tex	Det	@Tor	@Oak	Tam
Sa-7/27	Bal	@Ana	NYY	Min	@Kan	@Sea	@StL	Cle	@ChW	@Bos	Tex	Det	@Tor	@Oak	Tam
Su-7/28	Bal	@Ana	NYY	Min	@Kan	@Sea	@StL	Cle	@ChW	@Bos	Tex	Det	@Tor	@Oak	Tam
Mo-7/29	Det	@Sdg				@Ana		Tor							@Kan
Tu-7/30	Det	@Sdg	Tam	NYM	Hou	@Ana	@Cle	Tor	@Fla	Ari	Mil	@Tex	@Bos	Sea	@Kan
We-7/31	Det		Tam	NYM	Hou	@Ana	@Cle	Tor	@Fla	Ari	Mil	@Tex	@Bos	Sea	@Kan

Date	Ari	Atl	ChC	Cin	Col	Fla	Los	Mil	NYM	Phi	Pit	Sdg	Sfo	StL	Was
Tu-6/18	Col	NYM	ChW	Hou	@Ari	@StL	Sfo	@Sdg	@Atl	@Was	Det	Mil	@Los	Fla	Phi
We-6/19	Col	NYM	ChW	Hou	@Ari	@StL	Sfo	@Sdg	@Atl	@Was	Det	Mil	@Los	Fla	Phi
Th-6/20	Col		NYM	@Mil	@Ari	@StL	Sfo	Cin	@ChC	@Was			@Los	Fla	Phi
Fr-6/21	Sfo	@Was	NYM	@Mil	@Los	@Phi	Col	Cin	@ChC	Fla	Sdg	@Pit	@Ari	Ana	Atl
Sa-6/22	Sfo	@Was	NYM	@Mil	@Los	@Phi	Col	Cin	@ChC	Fla	Sdg	@Pit	@Ari	Ana	Atl
Su-6/23	Sfo	@Was	NYM	@Mil	@Los	@Phi	Col	Cin	@ChC	Fla	Sdg	@Pit	@Ari	Ana	Atl
Mo-6/24	Los	@ChC	Atl		@Sfo		@Ari		@Phi	NYM			Col		
Tu-6/25	Los	@ChC	Atl	@Ana	@Sfo	Was	@Ari	Sea	@Phi	NYM	@Hou	@Bal	Col	Oak	@Fla
We-6/26	Los	@ChC	Atl	@Ana	@Sfo	Was	@Ari	Sea	@Phi	NYM	@Hou	@Bal	Col	Oak	@Fla
Th-6/27	@Sfo	@ChC	Atl		Los	Was	@Col	Sea	@Phi	NYM	@Hou		Ari		@Fla
Fr-6/28	@Sfo	@NYM	@Cin	ChC	Los	Phi	@Col	Pit	Atl	@Fla	@Mil	StL	Ari	@Sdg	@Det
Sa-6/29	@Sfo	@NYM	@Cin	ChC	Los	Phi	@Col	Pit	Atl	@Fla	@Mil	StL	Ari	@Sdg	@Det
Su-6/30	@Sfo	@NYM	@Cin	ChC	Los	Phi	@Col	Pit	Atl	@Fla	@Mil	StL	Ari	@Sdg	@Det
Mo-7/1			@Pit	Mil				@Cin			ChC	Sfo	@Sdg		
Tu-7/2	@Los	Phi	@Pit	Mil	Hou	@Was	Ari	@Cin	NYY	@Atl	ChC	Sfo	@Sdg	@Sea	Fla
We-7/3	@Los	Phi	@Pit	Mil	Hou	@Was	Ari	@Cin	NYY	@Atl	ChC	Sfo	@Sdg	@Sea	Fla
Th-7/4		Phi	@Pit	Mil		@Was	Sdg	@Cin		@Atl	ChC	@Los		@Sea	Fla
Fr-7/5	Col	Fla			@Ari	@Atl	Sdg	@Pit	Phi	@NYM	Mil	@Los	StL	@Sfo	Kan
Sa-7/6	Col	Fla	@ChW	Cle	@Ari	@Atl	Sdg	@Pit	Phi	@NYM	Mil	@Los	StL	@Sfo	Kan
Su-7/7	Col	Fla	@ChW	Cle	@Ari	@Atl	Sdg	@Pit	Phi	@NYM	Mil	@Los	StL	@Sfo	Kan
Th-7/11															
Fr-7/12	@StL	@Sdg	Pit	@Col	Cin	NYM	@Bos	Sfo	@Fla	Was	@ChC	Atl	@Mil	Ari	@Phi
Sa-7/13	@StL	@Sdg	Pit	@Col	Cin	NYM	@Bos	Sfo	@Fla	Was	@ChC	Atl	@Mil	Ari	@Phi
Su-7/14	@StL	@Sdg	Pit	@Col	Cin	NYM	@Bos	Sfo	@Fla	Was	@ChC	Atl	@Mil	Ari	@Phi
Mo-7/15		@Mil	Cin	@ChC	Sfo		@Phi	Atl		Los	@StL		@Col	Pit	
Tu-7/16	@Tex	@Mil	Cin	@ChC	Sfo	Sdg	@Phi	Atl	@Min	Los	@StL	@Fla	@Col	Pit	@Bal
We-7/17	@Tex	@Mil	Cin	@ChC	Sfo	Sdg	@Phi	Atl	@Min	Los	@StL	@Fla	@Col	Pit	@Bal
Th-7/18	Mil	Was		StL		Sdg	@Phi	@Ari	@Sfo	Los		@Fla	NYM	@Cin	@Atl
Fr-7/19	Mil	Was	Sdg	StL	@NYY	@Los	Fla	@Ari	@Sfo	@Pit	Phi	@ChC	NYM	@Cin	@Atl
Sa-7/20	Mil	Was	Sdg	StL	@NYY	@Los	Fla	@Ari	@Sfo	@Pit	Phi	@ChC	NYM	@Cin	@Atl
Su-7/21	Mil	Was	Sdg	StL	@NYY	@Los	Fla	@Ari	@Sfo	@Pit	Phi	@ChC	NYM	@Cin	@Atl
Mo-7/22	Bal		@Sfo	@Mil	@Was	@ChW		Cin			StL		ChC	@Pit	Col
Tu-7/23	Bal	Kan	@Sfo	@Mil	@Was	@ChW	Ana	Cin	Sdg	@Det	StL	@NYM	ChC	@Pit	Col
We-7/24	Bal	Kan	@Sfo	@Mil	@Was	@ChW	Ana	Cin	Sdg	@Det	StL	@NYM	ChC	@Pit	Col
Th-7/25					@Was				Sdg		StL	@NYM		@Pit	Col
Fr-7/26	@Fla	@Phi	@Mil	Col	@Cin	Ari	@Was	ChC	Pit	Atl	@NYM	Sfo	@Sdg	Hou	Los
Sa-7/27	@Fla	@Phi	@Mil	Col	@Cin	Ari	@Was	ChC	Pit	Atl	@NYM	Sfo	@Sdg	Hou	Los
Su-7/28	@Fla	@Phi	@Mil	Col	@Cin	Ari	@Was	ChC	Pit	Atl	@NYM	Sfo	@Sdg	Hou	Los
Mo-7/29	@Fla	@Was		Pit	Los	Ari	@Col				@Cin	Bal			Atl
Tu-7/30	@NYY	@Was	@StL	Pit	Los	Min	@Col	@Oak	@ChW	Sfo	@Cin	Bal	@Phi	ChC	Atl
We-7/31	@NYY	@Was	@StL	Pit	Los	Min	@Col	@Oak	@ChW	Sfo	@Cin		@Phi	ChC	Atl

2019 MLB SCHEDULE

Date	Ana	Bal	Bos	ChW	Cle	Det	Hou	Kan	Min	NYY	Oak	Sea	Tam	Tex	Tor
Th-8/1		Tor	Tam	NYM	Hou		@Cle		@Fla		Mil		@Bos		@Bal
Fr-8/2	@Cle	Tor	@NYY	@Phi	Ana	@Tex	Sea	@Min	Kan	Bos		@Hou		Det	@Bal
Sa-8/3	@Cle	Tor	@NYY	@Phi	Ana	@Tex	Sea	@Min	Kan	Bos	StL	@Hou	Fla	Det	@Bal
Su-8/4	@Cle	Tor	@NYY	@Phi	Ana	@Tex	Sea	@Min	Kan	Bos	StL	@Hou	Fla	Det	@Bal
Mo-8/5	@Cin	NYY	Kan	@Det	Tex	ChW		@Bos	Atl	@Bal	@ChC		Tor	@Cle	@Tam
Tu-8/6	@Cin	NYY	Kan	@Det	Tex	ChW	Col	@Bos	Atl	@Bal	@ChC	Sdg	Tor	@Cle	@Tam
We-8/7		NYY	Kan	@Det	Tex	ChW	Col	@Bos	Atl	@Bal	@ChC	Sdg	Tor	@Cle	@Tam
Th-8/8	@Bos		Ana		@Min	Kan		@Det	Cle	@Tor					NYY
Fr-8/9	@Bos	Hou	Ana	Oak	@Min	Kan	@Bal	@Det	Cle	@Tor	@ChW	Tam	@Sea	@Mil	NYY
Sa-8/10	@Bos	Hou	Ana	Oak	@Min	Kan	@Bal	@Det	Cle	@Tor	@ChW	Tam	@Sea	@Mil	NYY
Su-8/11	@Bos	Hou	Ana	Oak	@Min	Kan	@Bal	@Det	Cle	@Tor	@ChW	Tam	@Sea	@Mil	NYY
Mo-8/12	Pit	@NYY	@Cle	Hou	Bos		@ChW			Bal			@Sdg	@Tor	Tex
Tu-8/13	Pit	@NYY	@Cle	Hou	Bos	Sea	@ChW	StL	@Mil	Bal	@Sfo	@Det	@Sdg	@Tor	Tex
We-8/14	Pit	@NYY	@Cle	Hou	Bos	Sea	@ChW	StL	@Mil	Bal	@Sfo	@Det	@Sdg	@Tor	Tex
Th-8/15	ChW			@Ana	@NYY	Sea	@Oak		@Tex	Cle	Hou	@Det		Min	
Fr-8/16	ChW	@Bos	Bal	@Ana	@NYY	@Tam	@Oak	NYM	@Tex	Cle	Hou	@Tor	Det	Min	Sea
Sa-8/17	ChW	@Bos	Bal	@Ana	@NYY	@Tam	@Oak	NYM	@Tex	Cle	Hou	@Tor	Det	Min	Sea
Su-8/18	ChW	@Bos	Bal	@Ana	@NYY	@Tam	@Oak	NYM	@Tex	Cle	Hou	@Tor	Det	Min	Sea
Mo-8/19	@Tex	Kan		@Min		@Hou	Det	@Bal	ChW			@Tam	Sea	Ana	
Tu-8/20	@Tex	Kan	Phi	@Min	@NYM	@Hou	Det	@Bal	ChW	@Oak	NYY	@Tam	Sea	Ana	@Los
We-8/21	@Tex	Kan	Phi	@Min	@NYM	@Hou	Det	@Bal	ChW	@Oak	NYY	@Tam	Sea	Ana	@Los
Th-8/22		Tam		Tex	@NYM	@Hou	Det			@Oak	NYY		@Bal	@ChW	@Los
Fr-8/23	@Hou	Tam	@Sdg	Tex	Kan	@Min	Ana	@Cle	Det	@Los		Tor	@Bal	@ChW	@Sea
Sa-8/24	@Hou	Tam	@Sdg	Tex	Kan	@Min	Ana	@Cle	Det	@Los	Sfo	Tor	@Bal	@ChW	@Sea
Su-8/25	@Hou	Tam	@Sdg	Tex	Kan	@Min	Ana	@Cle	Det	@Los	Sfo	Tor	@Bal	@ChW	@Sea
Mo-8/26								Oak		@Sea	@Kan	NYY			
Tu-8/27	Tex	@Was	@Col	Min	@Det	Cle	Tam	Oak	@ChW	@Sea	@Kan	NYY	@Hou	@Ana	Atl
We-8/28	Tex	@Was	@Col	Min	@Det	Cle	Tam	Oak	@ChW	@Sea	@Kan	NYY	@Hou	@Ana	Atl
Th-8/29				Min	@Det	Cle	Tam	Oak	@ChW		@Kan	@Tex	@Hou	Sea	
Fr-8/30	Bos	@Kan	@Ana	@Atl	@Tam	Min	@Tor	Bal	@Det	Oak	@NYY	@Tex	Cle	Sea	Hou
Sa-8/31	Bos	@Kan	@Ana	@Atl	@Tam	Min	@Tor	Bal	@Det	Oak	@NYY	@Tex	Cle	Sea	Hou
Su-9/1	Bos	@Kan	@Ana	@Atl	@Tam	Min	@Tor	Bal	@Det	Oak	@NYY	@Tex	Cle	Sea	Hou
Mo-9/2		@Tam		@Cle	ChW	Min	@Mil		@Det	Tex		@ChC	Bal	@NYY	@Atl
Tu-9/3	@Oak	@Tam	Min	@Cle	ChW	@Kan	@Mil	Det	@Bos	Tex	Ana	@ChC	Bal	@NYY	@Atl
We-9/4	@Oak	@Tam	Min	@Cle	ChW	@Kan		Det	@Bos	Tex	Ana		Bal	@NYY	
Th-9/5	@Oak	Tex	Min	@Cle	ChW	@Kan	Sea	Det	@Bos		Ana	@Hou	Tor	@Bal	@Tam
Fr-9/6	@ChW	Tex	NYY	Ana	@Min	@Oak	Sea	@Fla	Cle	@Bos	Det	@Hou	Tor	@Bal	@Tam
Sa-9/7	@ChW	Tex	NYY	Ana	@Min	@Oak	Sea	@Fla	Cle	@Bos	Det	@Hou	Tor	@Bal	@Tam
Su-9/8	@ChW	Tex	NYY	Ana	@Min	@Oak	Sea	@Fla	Cle	@Bos	Det	@Hou	Tor	@Bal	@Tam
Mo-9/9	Cle		NYY		@Ana		Oak			@Bos	@Hou				
Tu-9/10	Cle	Los	@Tor	Kan	@Ana	NYY	Oak	@ChW	Was	@Det	@Hou	Cin	@Tex	Tam	Bos

Date	Ana	Bal	Bos	ChW	Cle	Det	Hou	Kan	Min	NYY	Oak	Sea	Tam	Tex	Tor
Th-8/1		Cin	@StL	@Atl		Min	Sdg	@Oak	@ChW	Sfo		@Los	@Phi	ChC	
Fr-8/2	Was	Cin	Mil	@Atl	Sfo		Sdg	@ChC	@Pit	ChW	NYM	@Los	@Col		@Ari
Sa-8/3	Was	Cin	Mil	@Atl	Sfo	@Tam	Sdg	@ChC	@Pit	ChW	NYM	@Los	@Col	@Oak	@Ari
Su-8/4	Was	Cin	Mil	@Atl	Sfo	@Tam	Sdg	@ChC	@Pit	ChW	NYM	@Los	@Col	@Oak	@Ari
Mo-8/5	Phi	@Min	Oak	Ana		@NYM	StL	@Pit	Fla	@Ari	Mil		Was	@Los	@Sfo
Tu-8/6	Phi	@Min	Oak	Ana	@Hou	@NYM	StL	@Pit	Fla	@Ari	Mil	@Sea	Was	@Los	@Sfo
We-8/7	Phi	@Min	Oak		@Hou	@NYM	StL	@Pit	Fla	@Ari	Mil	@Sea	Was	@Los	@Sfo
Th-8/8		@Fla	@Cin	ChC	@Sdg	Atl				@Sfo		Col	Phi		
Fr-8/9	@Los	@Fla	@Cin	ChC	@Sdg	Atl	Ari	Tex	Was	@Sfo	@StL	Col	Phi	Pit	@NYM
Sa-8/10	@Los	@Fla	@Cin	ChC	@Sdg	Atl	Ari	Tex	Was	@Sfo	@StL	Col	Phi	Pit	@NYM
Su-8/11	@Los	@Fla	@Cin	ChC	@Sdg	Atl	Ari	Tex	Was	@Sfo	@StL	Col	Phi	Pit	@NYM
Mo-8/12	@Col			@Was	Ari						@Ana	Tam			Cin
Tu-8/13	@Col	NYM	@Phi	@Was	Ari	Los	@Fla	Min	@Atl	ChC	@Ana	Tam	Oak	@Kan	Cin
We-8/14	@Col	NYM	@Phi	@Was	Ari	Los	@Fla	Min	@Atl	ChC	@Ana	Tam	Oak	@Kan	Cin
Th-8/15	Sfo	NYM	@Phi	StL		Los	@Fla		@Atl	ChC			@Ari	@Cin	
Fr-8/16	Sfo	Los	@Pit	StL	Fla	@Col	@Atl	@Was	@Kan	Sdg	ChC	@Phi	@Ari	@Cin	Mil
Sa-8/17	Sfo	Los	@Pit	StL	Fla	@Col	@Atl	@Was	@Kan	Sdg	ChC	@Phi	@Ari	@Cin	Mil
Su-8/18	Sfo	Los	@Pit	StL	Fla	@Col	@Atl	@Was	@Kan	Sdg	ChC	@Phi	@Ari	@Cin	Mil
Mo-8/19	Col			Sdg	@Ari			@StL			Was	@Cin		Mil	@Pit
Tu-8/20	Col	Fla	Sfo	Sdg	@Ari	@Atl	Tor	@StL	Cle	@Bos	Was	@Cin	@ChC	Mil	@Pit
We-8/21	Col	Fla	Sfo	Sdg	@Ari	@Atl	Tor	@StL	Cle	@Bos	Was	@Cin	@ChC	Mil	@Pit
Th-8/22		Fla	Sfo		@StL	@Atl	Tor		Cle		Was		@ChC	Col	@Pit
Fr-8/23	@Mil	@NYM	Was	@Pit	@StL	Phi	NYY	Ari	Atl	@Fla	Cin	Bos		Col	@ChC
Sa-8/24	@Mil	@NYM	Was	@Pit	@StL	Phi	NYY	Ari	Atl	@Fla	Cin	Bos	@Oak	Col	@ChC
Su-8/25	@Mil	@NYM	Was	@Pit	@StL	Phi	NYY	Ari	Atl	@Fla	Cin	Bos	@Oak	Col	@ChC
Mo-8/26	@Sfo			@Fla		Cin	@Sdg	StL		Pit	@Phi	Los	Ari	@Mil	
Tu-8/27	@Sfo	@Tor	@NYM	@Fla	Bos	Cin	@Sdg	StL	ChC	Pit	@Phi	Los	Ari	@Mil	Bal
We-8/28		@Tor	@NYM	@Fla	Bos	Cin	@Sdg	StL	ChC	Pit	@Phi	Los		@Mil	Bal
Th-8/29	Los		@NYM	@Fla	Pit	Cin	@Ari		ChC		@Col	@Sfo	Sdg		
Fr-8/30	Los	ChW	Mil	@StL	Pit	@Was	@Ari	@ChC	@Phi	NYM	@Col	@Sfo	Sdg	Cin	Fla
Sa-8/31	Los	ChW	Mil	@StL	Pit	@Was	@Ari	@ChC	@Phi	NYM	@Col	@Sfo	Sdg	Cin	Fla
Su-9/1	Los	ChW	Mil	@StL	Pit	@Was	@Ari	@ChC	@Phi	NYM	@Col	@Sfo	Sdg	Cin	Fla
Mo-9/2	Sdg	Tor	Sea	Phi	@Los		Col	Hou	@Was	@Cin		@Ari	@StL	Sfo	NYM
Tu-9/3	Sdg	Tor	Sea	Phi	@Los	@Pit	Col	Hou	@Was	@Cin	Fla	@Ari	@StL	Sfo	NYM
We-9/4	Sdg			Phi	@Los	@Pit	Col		@Was	@Cin	Fla	@Ari	@StL	Sfo	NYM
Th-9/5		Was	@Mil	Phi		@Pit		ChC		@Cin	Fla		@StL	Sfo	@Atl
Fr-9/6	@Cin	Was	@Mil	Ari	@Sdg	Kan	Sfo	ChC	Phi	@NYM	StL	Col	@Los	@Pit	@Atl
Sa-9/7	@Cin	Was	@Mil	Ari	@Sdg	Kan	Sfo	ChC	Phi	@NYM	StL	Col	@Los	@Pit	@Atl
Su-9/8	@Cin	Was	@Mil	Ari	@Sdg	Kan	Sfo	ChC	Phi	@NYM	StL	Col	@Los	@Pit	@Atl
Mo-9/9	@NYM	@Phi	@Sdg			Mil		@Fla	Ari	Atl	@Sfo	ChC	Pit		
Tu-9/10	@NYM	@Phi	@Sdg	@Sea	StL	Mil	@Bal	@Fla	Ari	Atl	@Sfo	ChC	Pit	@Col	@Min

2019 MLB SCHEDULE

Date	Ana	Bal	Bos	ChW	Cle	Det	Hou	Kan	Min	NYY	Oak	Sea	Tam	Tex	Tor
We-9/11	Cle	Los	@Tor	Kan	@Ana	NYY	Oak	@ChW	Was	@Det	@Hou	Cin	@Tex	Tam	Bos
Th-9/12		Los	@Tor	Kan		NYY	Oak	@ChW	Was	@Det	@Hou	Cin	@Tex	Tam	Bos
Fr-9/13	Tam	@Det		@Sea	Min	Bal	@Kan	Hou	@Cle	@Tor	@Tex	ChW	@Ana	Oak	NYY
Sa-9/14	Tam	@Det	@Phi	@Sea	Min	Bal	@Kan	Hou	@Cle	@Tor	@Tex	ChW	@Ana	Oak	NYY
Su-9/15	Tam	@Det	@Phi	@Sea	Min	Bal	@Kan	Hou	@Cle	@Tor	@Tex	ChW	@Ana	Oak	NYY
Mo-9/16		@Det		@Min		Bal		@Oak	ChW		Kan				
Tu-9/17	@NYY	Tor	Sfo	@Min	Det	@Cle	Tex	@Oak	ChW	Ana	Kan	@Pit	@Los	@Hou	@Bal
We-9/18	@NYY	Tor	Sfo	@Min	Det	@Cle	Tex	@Oak	ChW	Ana	Kan	@Pit	@Los	@Hou	@Bal
Th-9/19	@NYY	Tor	Sfo		Det	@Cle		@Min	Kan	Ana		@Pit			@Bal
Fr-9/20	@Hou	Sea	@Tam	@Det	Phi	ChW	Ana	@Min	Kan	Tor	Tex	@Bal	Bos	@Oak	@NYY
Sa-9/21	@Hou	Sea	@Tam	@Det	Phi	ChW	Ana	@Min	Kan	Tor	Tex	@Bal	Bos	@Oak	@NYY
Su-9/22	@Hou	Sea	@Tam	@Det	Phi	ChW	Ana	@Min	Kan	Tor	Tex	@Bal	Bos	@Oak	@NYY
Mo-9/23		@Tor	@Tam										Bos		Bal
Tu-9/24	Oak	@Tor	@Tex	Cle	@ChW	Min	@Sea	Atl	@Det	@Tam	@Ana	Hou	NYY	Bos	Bal
We-9/25	Oak	@Tor	@Tex	Cle	@ChW	Min	@Sea	Atl	@Det	@Tam	@Ana	Hou	NYY	Bos	Bal
Th-9/26	Hou		@Tex	Cle	@ChW	Min	@Ana		@Det		@Sea	Oak		Bos	
Fr-9/27	Hou	@Bos	Bal	Det	@Was	@ChW	@Ana	Min	@Kan	@Tex	@Sea	Oak	@Tor	NYY	Tam
Sa-9/28	Hou	@Bos	Bal	Det	@Was	@ChW	@Ana	Min	@Kan	@Tex	@Sea	Oak	@Tor	NYY	Tam
Su-9/29	Hou	@Bos	Bal	Det	@Was	@ChW	@Ana	Min	@Kan	@Tex	@Sea	Oak	@Tor	NYY	Tam

Date	Ari	Atl	ChC	Cin	Col	Fla	Los	Mil	NYM	Phi	Pit	Sdg	Sfo	StL	Was
We-9/11	@NYM	@Phi	@Sdg	@Sea	StL	Mil	@Bal	@Fla	Ari	Atl	@Sfo	ChC	Pit	@Col	@Min
Th-9/12	@NYM	@Phi	@Sdg	@Sea	StL	Mil	@Bal	@Fla	Ari	Atl	@Sfo	ChC	Pit	@Col	@Min
Fr-9/13	Cin	@Was	Pit	@Ari	Sdg	@Sfo	@NYM	@StL	Los		@ChC	@Col	Fla	Mil	Atl
Sa-9/14	Cin	@Was	Pit	@Ari	Sdg	@Sfo	@NYM	@StL	Los	Bos	@ChC	@Col	Fla	Mil	Atl
Su-9/15	Cin	@Was	Pit	@Ari	Sdg	@Sfo	@NYM	@StL	Los	Bos	@ChC	@Col	Fla	Mil	Atl
Mo-9/16	Fla		Cin	@ChC	NYM	@Ari		Sdg	@Col			@Mil		Was	@StL
Tu-9/17	Fla	Phi	Cin	@ChC	NYM	@Ari	Tam	Sdg	@Col	@Atl	Sea	@Mil	@Bos	Was	@StL
We-9/18	Fla	Phi	Cin	@ChC	NYM	@Ari	Tam	Sdg	@Col	@Atl	Sea	@Mil	@Bos	Was	@StL
Th-9/19		Phi	StL					Sdg		@Atl	Sea	@Mil	@Bos	@ChC	
Fr-9/20	@Sdg	Sfo	StL	NYM	@Los	Was	Col	Pit	@Cin	@Cle	@Mil	Ari	@Atl	@ChC	@Fla
Sa-9/21	@Sdg	Sfo	StL	NYM	@Los	Was	Col	Pit	@Cin	@Cle	@Mil	Ari	@Atl	@ChC	@Fla
Su-9/22	@Sdg	Sfo	StL	NYM	@Los	Was	Col	Pit	@Cin	@Cle	@Mil	Ari	@Atl	@ChC	@Fla
Mo-9/23	StL					@NYM			Fla	@Was				@Ari	Phi
Tu-9/24	StL	@Kan	@Pit	Mil	@Sfo	@NYM	@Sdg	@Cin	Fla	@Was	ChC	Los	Col	@Ari	Phi
We-9/25	StL	@Kan	@Pit	Mil	@Sfo	@NYM	@Sdg	@Cin	Fla	@Was	ChC	Los	Col	@Ari	Phi
Th-9/26			@Pit	Mil	@Sfo	@NYM	@Sdg	@Cin	Fla	@Was	ChC	Los	Col		Phi
Fr-9/27	Sdg	@NYM	@StL	@Pit	Mil	@Phi	@Sfo	@Col	Atl	Fla	Cin	@Ari	Los	ChC	Cle
Sa-9/28	Sdg	@NYM	@StL	@Pit	Mil	@Phi	@Sfo	@Col	Atl	Fla	Cin	@Ari	Los	ChC	Cle
Su-9/29	Sdg	@NYM	@StL	@Pit	Mil	@Phi	@Sfo	@Col	Atl	Fla	Cin	@Ari	Los	ChC	Cle

AMERICAN HOTTIES™

Facility Friendly Non-Nude*

Here we go again! The *SEXIEST* magazine in our catalog is being followed up yet again. This time, no car shows; JUST HOTTIES! We removed all distractions and left nothing but sexy babes in an almost *TOO HOT* to print edition. Many exclusive, never before seen images from our archives. Our models wear little to *NOTHING* in this issue! It's a must have collector's item! Very limited run edition. Not available in stores.

SPECIAL INMATE SHOPPER OFFER:

Get 5 FREE 4x6 Car Show Hotties photos and a FREE photo catalog with your order of Car Show Hotties Magazine! (an $8 value-FREE!)

MUST Mention Offer Code IS-0519.

Hurry! Offer Expires May 1, 2020
(Letters must be postmarked by this date.)

*No frontal nudity. Magazine contains / displays rear nudity. Facility rules and regulations vary from state to state. Please check with your facility for rules before ordering.

Prices and availability subject to change. Not valid in combination with any other offer. Not responsible for rejected orders. $4 resend fee for rejected orders. No refunds. For free info, send a S.A.S.E. to the address on this advertisement.

To order,
Send $12.95 + $3.75 s&h to:

Villa Entertainment Co., Inc.
Offer Code IS-0518
14173 NW Freeway, Ste. 203
Houston, TX 77040

To order with a credit card by phone, call 713-465-9599

Email / Corrlinks
StreetSeen@ymail.com

Order Online at
www.PrisonMags.net

Made in the
USA
Middletown, DE